R. Gupta's®

POPULAR MASTER GUIDE

DSSSB–TEACHERS

TGT

SOCIAL SCIENCE

Recruitment Exam

by

RPH Editorial Board

2026
EDITION

RAMESH PUBLISHING HOUSE, NEW DELHI

Published by
O.P. Gupta *for* Ramesh Publishing House

Admin. Office
12-H, New Daryaganj Road, Opp. Officers' Mess,
New Delhi-110002 ✆ 23275224, 23245124

E-mail: info@rameshpublishinghouse.com
For Online Shopping: www.rameshpublishinghouse.com

Showroom
- Balaji Market, Nai Sarak, Delhi-6 ✆ 23253720, 23282525
- 4457, Nai Sarak, Delhi-6, ✆ 23918938

Book Code: R-1325

ISBN: 978-93-87604-20-9

Price: ₹ 360

Printed at: B.K. Offset Press

Contents

●●●

Previous Paper (Solved)

Delhi Subordinate Services Selection Board

DSSSB–TGT (Social Science) Recruitment Exam, 2021 *

Subject Knowledge – Social Science & Teaching Methodology

1. On the basis of period, the peasant movements in India can be divided into ____ phases.
   A. One B. Two
   C. Four D. Three

2. The Swadeshi Movement started as a reaction to the
   A. Khilafat movement
   B. Non-cooperation movement
   C. Formation of Muslim League
   D. Partition of Bengal

3. In which year, did Louis XVI flee to Paris?
   A. 1791 B. 1792
   C. 1793 D. 1794

4. Which of the following pairs of 'Rulers – Year of becoming king' is correct?
   I. Louis XVI – 1774
   II. Louis XV – 1778
   III. Louis XIV – 1779
   A. I and II B. Only II
   C. Only I D. Only III

5. In which year, was the Indian National Congress formed?
   A. 1888 B. 1886
   C. 1887 D. 1885

6. Who was not able to join the founding session of the Indian National Congress?
   A. M.G. Ranade
   B. Pherozeshah Mehta
   C. A.O. Hume
   D. Surendra Nath Banerjee

7. The industrial revolution first occurred in ______.
   A. Spain B. Germany
   C. France D. Britain

8. Who among the following formed the Indian Association in 1876?
   I. Surendra Nath Banerjee
   II. Anand Mohan Bose
   A. Only II B. Only I
   C. Both I and II D. Neither I nor II

9. Where was Louis XVI kept as a virtual prisoner?
   A. Tuileries Palace
   B. Chateau of Chantilly
   C. Palace of Versailles
   D. Luxembourg Palace

10. Who was one of the founding members of Poona Sarvajanik Sabha?
    A. Dadabhai Naoroji B. Dinshaw Petit
    C. M.G. Ranade D. Jawaharlal Nehru

11. Duma was constituted during the period of which Emperor of Russia?
    A. Nicholas III B. Nicholas II
    C. Nicholas I D. Nicholas IV

12. On 29th March, 1857 ____ opened fire on his European officers.
    A. Tantia Tope B. Wajid Ali Shah
    C. Mangal Pandey D. Nana Saheb

13. Which of the following statements is correct regarding the 'Decembrist Uprising 1825'?
    I. Participants were peasants and workers of the society.

* Online exam held on 01/10/2021

II. Participants were young men who has served as officers in the Tsar's army.

A. Both I and II B. Only II
C. Only I D. Neither I nor II

14. In which year did the Russian revolution started?

A. 1917 B. 1919
C. 1915 D. 1913

15. The policy of annexation extensively applied if the kingdom doesn't have a natural heir and if the British disapproved of the adopted heir. From the given options, select the policy discussed here.

A. Commercial Policy
B. Subsidiary Alliance
C. Paramountcy Pôlicy
D. Doctrine of Lapse

16. Before the Russian revolution, the Russian working class was largely concentrated in ______.

A. Mining industries
B. Textile industries
C. Coal industries
D. Construction industries

17. In the Soviet Union, landlordism was abolished in ______.

A. 1918 B. 1917
C. 1915 D. 1916

18. During the French revolution, when did Napoleon ascend to power?

A. 1797 B. 1799
C. 1798 D. 1800

19. Who was the last ruler before the onset of the French Revolution?

A. Louis XV B. Louis XIV
C. Louis XVI D. Louis XVII

20. Which of the following statements is correct regarding Tebhaga Movement?

I. This movement was organised by the Kisan Sabha.

II. It was against Jotedars and moneylenders

III. It was led by Swami Sadanand

A. II and III B. I and III
C. I and II D. Only I

21. The 'Sima' layer of the earth is composed of ______.

A. Selenium and Aluminium
B. Selenium and Iron
C. Silica and Manganese
D. Silica and Magnesium

22. Which of the following statements is correct regarding secondary seismic waves (S waves)?

I. They are also called longitudinal waves.

II. These waves cannot pass through liquid materials.

III. Their speed is lower than surface waves.

A. I, II and III B. Only II
C. I and II D. II and III

23. During the inter-war years, Japan left the League of nations. Which of the following is a correct reason for it?

A. Military dispute
B. Non-recognition of Manchukuo regime
C. War debt
D. Failure of disarmament

24. In context of Marxism philosophy, which of the following is correct?

I. There cannot be a peaceful transformation from capitalism to socialism.

II. The working class will seize state power by revolution.

A. Both I and II B. Only I
C. Only II D. Neither I nor II

25. Name the dictated treaty imposed on Germany after the First World War.

A. The treaty of St. Germain
B. Treaty of Versailles
C. The treaty of Neuilly
D. The treaty of Trianon

26. Which of the following rocks are formed due to the metamorphism of sandstones?

A. Quartzites B. Slates
C. Gneiss D. Marble

27. The transfer of heat through the molecules of matter in any body is called ______.
A. Conduction B. Advection
C. Radiation D. Convection

28. What is the revolution period of the Mars?
A. 4333 days B. 687 days
C. 88 days D. 365 days

29. The World War I was started in which year?
A. 1913 B. 1914
C. 1912 D. 1915

30. Which of the following was done by Germany before World War II?
I. It annexed Austria in 1938.
II. It dismembered Czechoslovakia in 1935.
A. Only I B. Both I and II
C. Neither I nor II D. Only II

31. In which year, the United States of America entered in World War II?
A. 1941 B. 1940
C. 1943 D. 1942

32. The ideas of scientific socialism are also known as ______.
A. Capitalism
B. Marxism
C. Fascism
D. Anarcho-primitivism

33. Fascism emerged in which country?
A. Greece B. France
C. Italy D. Spain

34. Which wind is known as snow eater?
A. Sirocco B. Chinook
C. Loo D. Tramontane

35. In 1796, Nebular Hypothesis about the origin of the earth was given by ______.
A. R.S. Morgan B. Laplace
C. T.C. Chamberlin D. Jean Brunhes

36. Karl Marx was a ______ thinker.
I. Mercantilist
II. Socialist
A. Only II B. Only I
C. Both I and II D. Neither I nor II

37. Prairies grassland is found in ______.
A. Africa B. North America
C. South America D. Australia

38. Which of the following statement is correct?
I. The Utopian Socialists were scientific in their outlook.
II. The Utopian Socialists were concerned about social justice.
A. Only II B. Neither I nor II
C. Both I and II D. Only I

39. Which of the following local winds is prevalent in north and south polar regions?
A. Yamo B. Zonda
C. Blizzard D. Foehn

40. Rainfall occurs in which layer of the earth's atmosphere?
A. Stratosphere B. Mesosphere
C. Thermosphere D. Troposphere

41. Which of the following is a biological disaster?
A. Soil erosion B. Nuclear explosion
C. Eutrophication D. Cold waves

42. Which of the following are the oldest folded mountain in India?
A. Vindhya Range B. Satpura Range
C. Aravalli Range D. Himalayan Range

43. Which of the following gas is NOT involved in the production of acid rains?
A. Hydrogen bromide
B. Sulphur dioxide
C. Nitrous oxide
D. Nitrogen dioxide

44. The Greater Himalaya and the Lesser Himalaya are separated by the ______.
A. Indus Suture
B. Main Central Thrust
C. Main Boundary Thrust
D. Himalayan Front Fault

45. Which of the following woods is NOT found in the Himalayan forests of India?
A. White willow B. Silver-fir
C. Blue-pine D. Ebony

46. Which of the following pair of disasters is correctly matched?

I. Slow on-set disaster – Sea level rise

II. Rapid on-set disaster – Lava flow

A. Only I B. Neither I nor II
C. Only II D. Both I and II

47. Which of the following combination of rivers is correctly sequenced according to the descending order of their area in India?

A. Indus-Ganga-Kaveri
B. Ganga-Indus-Mahanadi
C. Godavari-Indus-Narmada
D. Brahmaputra-Narmada-Ganga

48. The location of an industry is largely dependent on which of the following factors?

I. Raw material

II. Climate

A. Both I and II B. Neither I nor II
C. Only II D. Only I

49. Which of the following rivers of India drains into the Bay of Bengal?

A. Narmada B. Godavari
C. Tapi D. Sabarmati

50. The season of retreating monsoon in India starts from the month of ______.

A. August B. September
C. November D. October

51. Which country has the second largest road network in the world?

A. China B. Australia
C. India D. Russia

52. Which of the following characteristics of simple subsistence agriculture are correct?

I. The cultivated patches are usually very small.

II. It is also known as shifting cultivation.

III. A number of different crops are simultaneously grown in the same plot.

A. II and III B. I, II and III
C. I and III D. I and II

53. In 1980, which country adopted the 'One-child policy' to regulate its population?

A. Japan B. India
C. China D. Russia

54. The height of water of tsunami waves above mean sea level in the near shore zone is called ______.

A. Tsunami run-up
B. Inundation distance
C. Flow depth
D. Tsunami height

55. Which of the following pairs of 'Ocean currents–Ocean' is correct?

I. Gulf stream – Atlantic Ocean

II. Labrador current – Pacific Ocean

III. Peru current – Indian Ocean

A. I and III B. Only I
C. II and III D. I, II and III

56. Which state of India is the largest producer of rice?

A. Odisha B. Haryana
C. West Bengal D. Bihar

57. Which of the following have been identified as the problems of Iron and Steel industry in India?

I. It requires huge amount of capital.

II. The high cost of coking coal.

III. Growing competition in the International market.

A. II and III B. I and II
C. I, II and III D. I and III

58. Rabi crops are sown from ______.

A. September to October
B. October to December
C. December to February
D. April to November

59. Which of the following statements is correct regarding the methods of Environmental Impact Assessment (EIA)?

I. Ad hoc method is used in the situation where time is a constraint or there is a lack of information.

II. The matrix technique is a qualitative environmental impact assessment method.

A. Only II B. Both I and II
C. Only I D. Neither I nor II

60. Which is the only riverine major seaport of India?
A. Kolkata port B. Mumbai port
C. Paradwip D. Kochi port

61. Which of the following party systems is followed in India?
A. Multi-party system
B. Single-party system
C. Three-party system
D. Two-party system

62. Which national party of India has 'Elephant' as its symbol?
A. Bahujan Samaj Party
B. Indian National Congress
C. Bharatiya Janta Party
D. Communist Party of India

63. Which of the following cannot be considered as features of democracy?
A. Equality B. Autonomy
C. Aristocracy D. Liberty

64. The ratio of liquid assets to demand and time liabilities in India is known as the ______.
A. Marginal Standard Facility
B. Statutory Liquidity Ratio
C. Solvency Ratio
D. Minimum Support Price

65. The gross enrolment ratio (GER) is associated with which sector?
A. Industry B. Education
C. Transport D. Agriculture

66. Indian Federalism has ______ features.
A. unitarian B. authoritarian
C. majoritarian D. totalitarian

67. Which period of French revolution is known as region of Terror?
A. 1794 to 1799 B. 1789 to 1792
C. 1799 to 1815 D. 1793 to 1794

68. Which of the following is a nationalised bank in India?
A. Bandhan Bank
B. Bank of Baroda
C. Axis Bank
D. Kotak Mahindra Bank

69. Which of the following is a type of representation in a representative democracy?
I. Territorial representation
II. Functional representation
A. Neither I nor II B. Only II
C. Only I D. Both I and II

70. By which charter Act of Christian missionaries were allowed to spread Christianity in India?
A. Charter Act, 1853
B. Charter Act, 1793
C. Charter Act, 1813
D. Charter Act, 1833

71. Which of the following is a type of Public Distribution System (PDS)?
I. Universal Public Distribution System
II. Targeted Public Distribution System
A. Neither I nor II B. Both I and II
C. Only I D. Only II

72. In India, the minimum age of voting was reduced to 18 in which year?
A. 1986 B. 1985
C. 1988 D. 1987

73. Which of the following statements is correct regarding the 'Neo Classical Views of Economic Development'?
I. It considers economic development as the removal of poverty and inequality.
II. It believes that growth occurs as a result of the long-term effects of capital formation.
A. Only I B. Neither I nor II
C. Only II D. Both I and II

74. ______ duty is based on the value of the commodity imported or exported.
A. Transit B. Compound
C. Ad-Valorem D. Specific

75. Which of the following statements are correct regarding elections in India?
I. Only two major parties contest elections in India.
II. Elections to the panchayats are not held.

A. Both I and II B. Only II
C. Neither I nor II D. Only I

76. Which of the following statements is correct regarding Indian Feudalism according to K.C. Wheare?
A. a federal state with subsidiary unitary principle
B. a unitary state with subsidiary federal principle
C. a centralized government with subsidiary unitary principle
D. a centralized government with no federal principle

77. Which of the following is the issuing authority of coins in India?
A. Corporate entities
B. Commercial banks of India
C. Reserve Bank of India
D. Government of India

78. There are four alternative measures of money supply. Which among the following is correct?
A. M_2 = demand deposits of the public + savings deposits with post office
B. M_1 = currency held by the public + demand deposits of the public
C. M_4 = currency held by the public + total post office deposits
D. M_3 = time deposits of banks held by the public + savings deposits with post office

79. Superintendence, direction and control of elections in India is vested in _______.
A. National Company Law Appellate Tribunal
B. Election Commission of India
C. State Public Service Commission
D. Supreme Court of India

80. The activities of the producers in this sector are closely connected with natural resources. This sector is _______.
I. Primary sector
II. Tertiary sector
A. Only II B. Both I and II
C. Neither I nor II D. Only I

81. 'Equality before law' is envisaged in which part of the Indian Constitution?
A. Part II B. Part V
C. Part I D. Part III

82. The Royal Constitution envisaged a _______ system under a constitutional monarchy. Choose the most appropriate alternative regarding political structure in Nepal.
A. parliamentary B. socialist
C. communist D. autocratic

83. Article 76 of the Indian Constitution deals with which of the following provision?
A. Composition of the house of people
B. Special address by the President
C. Duration of Houses of Parliament
D. Attorney-General of India

84. 'Composition of Panchayats' is included in which of the following parts of the Indian Constitution?
A. Part XII B. Part X
C. Part IX D. Part XI

85. Part II of the Indian Constitution consists of which of the following features?
A. The Union Territories
B. Fundamental Duties
C. Citizenship
D. The States

86. Article 26 of the Indian Constitution deals with which of the following?
A. Protection of certain rights regarding freedom of speech, etc.
B. Freedom to manage religious affairs
C. Protection of interests of minorities
D. Freedom as to payment of taxes for promotion of any particular religion

87. Which of the following articles is NOT included in Part V of the Indian Constitution?
A. Election of Vice President
B. Attorney General for India
C. The President of India
D. Governors of States

88. 'Chaco War' was fought between which of the following two countries?
A. Peru and Chile
B. Bolivia and Paraguay

C. Argentina and Paraguay
D. Brazil and Chile

89. 'Abolition of untouchability' is included in which of the following fundamental rights?
A. Right against exploitation
B. Right to Constitutional Remedies
C. Right to freedom
D. Right to equality

90. Article ______ is associated with right to education in the Indian Constitution.
A. 21 B. 21A
C. 31A D. 22

91. In year ______ VD Savarkar organized "Abhinav Bharat".
A. 1902 B. 1904
C. 1903 D. 1905

92. Clay is a material of visual arts and crafts. What is the importance of clay?
I. It enhances creativity
II. It develops the fine motor skills
III. It helps in handling eye-hand co-ordination
IV. It improves concentration or builds interest in art activities
A. I, II and IV B. I, II and III
C. II, III and IV D. I, II, III and IV

93. Which of the following are the strategies to enhance the motivation level of the learners?
I. Build on strengths first
II. Offer choices
III. Facilitate creativity
IV. Provide a secure environment
A. I and II B. II, III and IV
C. I, II, III and IV D. II and IV

94. Which of the following combination is correct?
I. Convergent questions – More than one appropriate answer
II. Divergent questions – Only one appropriate answer
A. Only II B. Both I and II
C. Only I D. Neither I nor II

95. Which of the following is first leader of Indian community in North America to start a paper called "Free Hindustan"?
A. Kartar Singh Sarabha
B. Lala Hardyal
C. Sohan Singh Bhakna
D. Tarak Nath Das

96. If a teacher wants to use drama as a linguistic activity, then which characteristics need to be included?
I. Freedom
II. Enjoyment
A. Only II B. Only I
C. Neither I nor II D. Both I and II

97. Which of the following statement is NOT correct?
A. In formative assessment, grades do not carry much weight.
B. Summative assessment is outcome oriented.
C. Summative assessment is used to determine a student's overall performance in a certain prescribed course.
D. Formative assessment is more formal.

98. Which of the following are the causes of delayed speech?
I. Mental Retardation
II. Hearing Impairment
III. Behavioural Disorders
A. Only III B. Only I
C. II and III D. I, II and III

99. Which of the following combination of question – type of question is NOT correct?
I. What would have Gandhiji done had he lived today? – Hypothetical question
II. If you were the manager of a bank? – Provocative question
A. Only I B. Both I and II
C. Only II D. Neither I nor II

100. "Conducting election in the school for electing student's council." This above statement represents which Teaching Learning strategy used in a Social Sciences class?
A. Experiential learning
B. Story telling
C. Concept mapping
D. Problem solving

ANSWERS

1	2	3	4	5	6	7	8	9	10
D	D	A	C	D	D	D	C	A	C
11	**12**	**13**	**14**	**15**	**16**	**17**	**18**	**19**	**20**
B	C	B	A	D	B	B	B	C	C
21	**22**	**23**	**24**	**25**	**26**	**27**	**28**	**29**	**30**
D	B	B	A	B	A	A	B	B	A
31	**32**	**33**	**34**	**35**	**36**	**37**	**38**	**39**	**40**
A	B	C	B	B	A	B	A	C	D
41	**42**	**43**	**44**	**45**	**46**	**47**	**48**	**49**	**50**
C	C	A	B	D	D	B	A	B	D
51	**52**	**53**	**54**	**55**	**56**	**57**	**58**	**59**	**60**
C	B	C	A	B	C	C	B	B	A
61	**62**	**63**	**64**	**65**	**66**	**67**	**68**	**69**	**70**
A	A	C	B	B	A	D	B	D	C
71	**72**	**73**	**74**	**75**	**76**	**77**	**78**	**79**	**80**
B	C	C	C	C	B	D	B	B	D
81	**82**	**83**	**84**	**85**	**86**	**87**	**88**	**89**	**90**
D	A	D	C	C	B	D	B	D	B
91	**92**	**93**	**94**	**95**	**96**	**97**	**98**	**99**	**100**
B	D	C	D	D	D	D	D	B	A

Previous Paper (Solved)

Delhi Subordinate Services Selection Board

DSSSB–TGT (Social Science) Recruitment Exam, 2018*

Subject Knowledge – Social Science & Teaching Methodology

1. On the morning of August 6, 1945, America released Atom bomb on Japan named:
   A. Little secret
   B. Little boy
   C. Little dwarf
   D. Little girl

2. Who said this "We shall fight in the seas and oceans"?
   A. Churchill
   B. Rasewelt
   C. Hitler
   D. Mussolini

3. Which period of French revolution is known as region of Terror?
   A. 1794 to 1799
   B. 1789 to 1792
   C. 1799 to 1815
   D. 1793 to 1794

4. "The Only people who had any right in India are the British". For which government bill these lines where quoted?
   A. Cabinet mission plan
   B. Ilbert Bill
   C. Simmon Commission
   D. Pitts India Act

5. Which newspaper supported the Indigo peasant movement of Champaran?
   A. Madras Gazette
   B. Hindu Patriot
   C. Bengal Gazette
   D. The Telegraph

6. Mangal Pandey belong to which infantry?
   A. 32 native infantry
   B. 34 native infantry
   C. 33 native infantry
   D. 31 native infantry

7. By which charter Act of Christian missionaries were allowed to spread Christianity in India?
   A. Charter Act-1853
   B. Charter Act-1793
   C. Charter Act-1813
   D. Charter Act-1833

8. Which act of British government provided Diarchy at the center?
   A. Act of 1935
   B. Act of 1919
   C. Act of 1892
   D. Act of 1909

9. In which year Louis XVI was guillotine by the Republic Government?
   A. 21 March, 1792
   B. 21 March, 1793
   C. 21 January, 1793
   D. 21 February, 1793

10. Which one of these is not related to UNO as Agencies?
    A. WHO
    B. UNESCO
    C. FAO
    D. BAMCEF

11. Nana Sahib was adopted son of which Peshwa?

* Online exam held on 15/10/2018

A. Shivaji
B. Balaji Vishavnath
C. Peshwa Baji Rao I
D. Peshwa Baji Rao II

12. Who among the following did not sign the Nehru Committee report?
A. Subash Chandra Bose
B. GR Pardhan
C. Jawaharlal Nehru
D. Sardar Mangal Singh

13. In 1945, how many countries signed the charter of UNO?
A. 52 Countries
B. 53 Countries
C. 50 Countries
D. 51 Countries

14. In year ____ VD Savarkar organized "Abhinav Bharat".
A. 1902 B. 1904
C. 1903 D. 1905

15. Who was the political Guru of Mahatma Gandhi?
A. Gopal Krishna Gokhale
B. Justice Ranade
C. Dada Bhai Naroji
D. Firoz Shah Mehta

16. France went to war in 1792 with which country?
A. Austria
B. Spain
C. England
D. Germany

17. Bal Gangadhar Tilak started the newspaper "Maharatta" in which language?
A. Marathi B. English
C. Hindi D. Urdu

18. Which of the following is first leader of Indian community in North America to start a paper called "Free Hindustan"?
A. Kartar Singh Sarabha
B. Lala Hardyal
C. Sohan Singh Bhakna
D. Tarak Nath Das

19. Which pair is not correct?
A. Laxmi Bai — Jhansi
B. Kunwar Singh — Lucknow
C. Tantia Tope — Gwalior
D. Nana Sahib — Kanpur

20. Which of the following battles Hitler lost to USSR?
A. War of Stalingrad
B. War of Narmandy
C. War on Poland
D. War of Dunkrik

21. Who wrote these lines "All our palaces, all our theatres, all these riches of ours, we owe to the effort of these same hungry People, who make these things"?
A. Anton Chekhov
B. Leo Tolstoy
C. Maxim Gorkey
D. Lenin

22. Arch Duke Franz Ferdinand was killed on which date?
A. 28 June 1914
B. 27 July 1914
C. 27 June 1914
D. 28 July 1914

23. How many members were in cabinet mission plan?
A. 5 member B. 2 member
C. 4 member D. 3 member

24. Industrial Society "May truly be said to be a miserly, selfish system" which socialist thinker wrote these words in 1857?
A. Robertowen
B. Pierre Joseph Proudhan
C. Friedrich Engles
D. Karlmarx

25. What was the position of the "Mensheviks" in 1903?
A. Majority B. Minority
C. Popular D. Moderate

26. "Workers of the world unite! You have nothing to lose but your chains" who wrote these lines?

A. Lenin
B. Voltare
C. Maximgorkey
D. Karl Marx

27. In First round table conference which of these members participated as Hindu Maha sabha members?
A. Jaikar and BS Munje
B. Dr. B.R. Ambedkar
C. K.T. Paul and Sampurn Singh
D. C.Y. Chintamani and T.V. Sapru

28. When was Rome Berlin Axis signed?
A. November 1935
B. October 1935
C. October 1936
D. November 1936

29. Lord Canning was the Governor General of India from:
A. 1857 to 1863
B. 1858 to 1862
C. 1856 to 1862
D. 1855 to 1861

30. USA entered in First World War in which year?
A. March, 1916
B. March, 1917
C. April, 1916
D. April, 1917

31. Civil disobedience moment was taken back in which year?
A. 7 April, 1932
B. 7 April, 1934
C. 6 April, 1932
D. 6 April, 1934

32. Who gave the slogan "Peace, Land and Bread"?
A. Karl Max B. Lenin
C. Trotasky D. Stalin

33. Who declared "Either they will give us the government or we shall take it by descending on Rome"?
A. F.D. Rarewelt
B. Mussolini
C. General Franko
D. Adolf Hitler

34. By which law Nazi deprived Jews of German Citizenship?
A. Treaty of Versailles
B. Nuremberg Laws
C. Enabling Act
D. Mein Kamph

35. Karl Marx used which word for factory owning middle class?
A. Surfs
B. Proletariat
C. Lores
D. Bourgeoisie

36. When did Germany invade Poland?
A. September 1939
B. December 1939
C. October 1939
D. November 1939

37. "Quit India" resolution was moved by which leader?
A. Mahatma Gandhi
B. Jawaharlal Nehru
C. Maulana Abul Kalam Azad
D. Subhas Chandra Bose

38. Who gave "Father of the Nation title" to Mahatma Gandhi?
A. Subhas Chandra Bose
B. G.K. Gokhale
C. Rabindra Nath Tagore
D. Jawaharlal Nehru

39. Kanpur conspiracy case was framed against whom in 1924?
A. Congress
B. Hindu Maha Sabha
C. Muslim League
D. Newbie Communist

40. Who was the King of Russia during Russian Revolution of 1917?
A. Nicholas II
B. Stalin
C. Lenin
D. Alexander III

41. Which of the following countries have two party system?

A. Pakistan B. India

C. USA D. China

42. Right to Constitutional Remedies is mentioned in which article of constitution?

A. Article 30

B. Article 14

C. Article 32

D. Article 23

43. In Indian Council Act 1909 (Minto-Morley act) seats of legislative council was increased to:

A. 70 B. 60

C. 50 D. 40

44. Among the following which country suffered disintegration due to political fights on the basis of religious and ethnic identities?

A. Yugoslavia

B. Netherland

C. Germany

D. Belgium

45. Which provision of Constitution provide power to parliament to establish a ne.. state?

A. Article 2 & 3

B. Article 5 & 6

C. Article 3 & 4

D. Article 4 & 5

46. Lord Pethick-Lawrence, Sir Stafford Cripps, A.V. Alexander are related to which of the following?

A. Wavell plan

B. Mount Beaton plan

C. Cabinet mission plan

D. Cripps mission

47. "Separate Electorate system" was introduced in which Act?

A. Pitt's India Act

B. Act 1909

C. Act 1861

D. Regulating Act

48. Different arguments are usually put forth in favour of and against power sharing. Identify those which are in favour of power sharing:

(*a*) Reduced conflict among different communities.

(*b*) Decrease the possibility of arbitrariness.

(*c*) Delay decision making process.

(*d*) Accommodates diversities.

(*e*) Increases inability and divisiveness.

(*f*) Strengthen the unity of the country.

(*g*) Divided the people.

A. (*a*), (*b*), (*d*), (*g*)

B. (*a*), (*b*), (*d*), (*f*)

C. (*a*), (*c*), (*e*), (*f*)

D. (*b*), (*c*), (*d*), (*g*)

49. By which Act Federal structure was introduced by British?

A. Ramsay Macdonald Award

B. Act of 1909

C. Act of 1919

D. Act of 1935

50. By which Article of constitution untouchability was removed by constitution?

A. Article–14 B. Article–17

C. Article–19 D. Article–21

51. Which one is not the power of Parliament?

A. Parliament can increase or decrease area of any state.

B. Can change the name of any state.

C. Can impose any language in the state.

D. It can change the boundaries of any state.

52. In ________ year an act was passed to recognize Sinhala as the only official language in Sri Lanka.

A. 1962 AB B. 1956 AD

C. 1948 AD D. 1965 AD

53. Communist Party of India Marxist was founded in which year?

A. 1964 B. 1984

C. 1980 D. 1925

54. On ______ Pt. Jawaharlal Nehru introduced the "Objectives Resolution" in Constituent Assembly.

A. 15th January 1946
B. 13th December 1946
C. 12th November 1946
D. 11th October 1946

55. Which of the following states has the highest Lok Sabha seats?
A. West Bengal
B. Maharashtra
C. Bihar
D. Andhra Pradesh

56. According to which Amendment, words "socialist and secular" were added on preamble of Indian constitution.
A. 78 Amendment
B. 42 Amendment
C. 44 Amendment
D. None of these

57. What is the duration of Question hour in Lok Sabha and Rajya Sabha?
A. 30 minute before session
B. 1 hour 30 minute before session
C. 1 hour before session
D. 2 hour before session

58. By which amendment of constitution the Panchayati Raj system's sub-article was added?
A. Article 71 & 72
B. Article 70 & 71
C. None of these
D. Article 73 & 74

59. Who has the power to implement fundamental right?
A. Supreme and High Court
B. All courts of India
C. Parliament
D. President

60. Below is the list of Rajya Sabha Seats for different states which one of these is correct?
A. Andhra Pradesh–16
Gujarat–18
Tamil Nadu–10
Rajasthan–19
B. Andhra Pradesh–11
Gujarat–11
Tamil Nadu–18
Rajasthan–10
C. Andhra Pradesh–18
Gujarat–18
Tamil Nadu–12
Rajasthan–31
D. Andhra Pradesh–11
Gujarat–16
Tamil Nadu–18
Rajasthan–19

61. According to B.R. Ambedkar which of the following provisions is a part of one of the criticisms of Indian Constitutions?
A. Directive Principles of State Policy
B. Fundamental Duties
C. Fundamental Rights
D. Federal System

62. Considering the following statements, which of the following statements is/are correct?
1. Natural gas occurs in the Gondwana beds.
2. Mica occurs in abundance in Kodarma.
3. Dharwars are famous for petroleum.

Which of the statement given above is/are correct?
A. I & II B. II & III
C. II only D. III only

63. Match the Columns:

(*a*) Horizon A	(*i*) Sub-soil
(*b*) Horizon B	(*ii*) Bedrock
(*c*) Horizon C	(*iii*) True soil
(*d*) Horizon D	(*iv*) Weathered soil

	(*a*)	(*b*)	(*c*)	(*d*)
A.	(*ii*)	(*iv*)	(*iii*)	(*i*)
B.	(*iii*)	(*i*)	(*iv*)	(*ii*)
C.	(*iv*)	(*ii*)	(*iii*)	(*i*)
D.	(*iii*)	(*iv*)	(*i*)	(*ii*)

64. In which of the following Articles of Indian constitution the Election Provision are mentioned?
A. 329-334 B. 324-329
C. 339-334 D. 334-329

65. Narmada Bachao Andolan is a good example of ________ .
A. Pressure group

B. Interest group
C. Political party
D. Movement

66. In which year Nagarjunasagar project was launched?
A. 1956 B. 1975
C. 1967 D. 1965

67. 73rd and 74th amendment for Panchayti Raj was not mandatory for which below mention states and Union territories?
A. Goa
Daman
Pondicherry
Andaman
B. Lakshadweep
Diu
Chandigarh
Delhi
C. Meghalaya
Mizoram
Nagaland
Manipur
D. Goa
Chandigarh
Diu
Delhi

68. What is the total area of Andaman and Nicobar Islands?
A. 8249 sqkm B. 8532 sqkm
C. 8921 sqkm D. 8191 sqkm

69. Which one of these is not a Pressure group?
A. INTUC B. AITUC
C. INC D. ABVP

70. Which of the following is correct statement related to Biomass?
A. Comprised of plants and animals.
B. Quantity or weight of living matter per unit area and per unit time.
C. Both quantity or weight of living matter per unit area and per unit time, and Comprised of plants and animals are correct.
D. Both quantity or weight of living matter per unit area and per unit time, and Comprised of plants and animals are incorrect.

71. Which of these is not correctly matched?
A. Bolivia – FEDECOR
B. BAMCEF – USA
C. None of these
D. Nepal – SPA

72. Which of the following is the first corporatized port of India?
A. Ennore Port
B. Paradeep Port
C. Kandla Port
D. Tutikorin Port

73. The Green belt movement of Kenya was led by __________ .
A. Wangari Maathai
B. Baba Amte
C. Nelson Mandela
D. Thambu Mabiki

74. Seiche is the type of __________.
A. A glacier
B. Natural vegetation
C. A current
D. A wave

75. Identify what kind of democratic challenge is this Iraq wide spread sectarian violence as the new government fails to establish its authority.
A. Foundational challenge of democracy
B. Challenge of expansion
C. Deepening of democracy
D. None of these

76. What is the Position of Moon in Perigee?
A. Farthest to earth
B. Nearest to earth
C. Nearest to poles
D. Nearest to quarter

77. What is the full form of NRSA?
A. The Non-Religious and Secular Association.
B. The National Remote Sensing Agency.
C. The National Remote Sensing Association.
D. The National Research and Science Agency.

78. When was popular movement started in Nepal?
A. March 1990
B. February 2006
C. March 2005
D. April 2006

79. "I am in favour of strong center" who said these words?
A. Jawaharlal Nehru
B. Sardar Vallabh Bhai Patel
C. Dr. Rajendra Prasad
D. B.R. Ambedkar

80. What is Khamsin?
A. Stable air mass
B. Local winds
C. Precipitation
D. Tropical monsoon climate

81. Which of the following latitudes are known as "Horse latitudes"?
A. 75–90 degrees north and south of the equator
B. 25–35 degrees north and south of the equator
C. 45–65 degrees north and south of the equator
D. 0–25 degrees north and south of the equator

82. What is the surface temperature of sun?
A. 3550 k B. 4290 k
C. 9940 k D. 5778 k

83. Prasar Bharati came into existence in:
A. 1994 B. 1999
C. 1997 D. 1991

84. Expand TPDS:
A. Total Population Distributed in States
B. Total Public Diverse Society
C. Target People Development System
D. Targeted Public Distribution System

85. Who said, "Give me detailed map of country and I shall conquer it"?
A. Wegner
B. Hitler
C. Mackinder
D. Humbolt

86. When was the Survey of India established?
A. 1864 B. 1764
C. 1767 D. 1867

87. Which of the following mountain range is in Maharashtra?
A. Abor range
B. Barail range
C. Dalma range
D. Bamnoli range

88. What is the relative humidity of Griffith Tailor's climograph?
A 10% to 60% B. 20% to 70%
C. 20% to 80% D. 10% to 70%

89. National urban livelihoods mission was launched in which of the following five-year plan?
A. 11th five year plan
B. 13th five year plan
C. 10th five year plan
D. 12th five year plan

90. What is Moose?
A. Type of wind
B. Type of glacier
C. Type of animals
D. Type of natural vegetation

91. How many school aged girls currently in our society are not enrolled in school?
A. 60 million B. 50 million
C. 80 million D. 10 million

92. The Standard of denying inclusive education to a student is:
A. Low B. Average
C. Very low D. very high

93. All children who come to school are born with:
A. A desire of knowledge
B. A desire of entertainment
C. A desire of studies
D. A desire of living

94. What is the collaboration that teacher need to build among students?
A. Meaningful collaboration
B. Education collaboration
C. Collaboration about public services
D. Art of collaboration

95. Which type of education should be included in teachers?
A. Secondary education
B. Nursery education
C. Tertiary education
D. Primary education

96. For how many years that primes had attracted students and mathematicians?
A. 1000 years B. 2000 years
C. 10,000 years D. 5000 years

97. Who is influenced by educational debates in colonial period?
A. Lal Bahadur Shastri
B. Mahatma Gandhi
C. Bhagat Singh
D. Jawaharlal Nehru

98. In which year the general assembly has adopted the UN convention on the Rights of the Child?
A. 2000 B. 1930
C. 1999 D. 1989

99. In which age a student can be able to expand into simple dramatic scripts?
A. 8 B. 11
C. 10 D. 15

100. What are filled with facts that students are expected to memorize?
A. Note books
B. Text books
C. Running notes
D. Rough books

ANSWERS

1	2	3	4	5	6	7	8	9	10
B	A	D	B	B	B	C	A	C	D
11	**12**	**13**	**14**	**15**	**16**	**17**	**18**	**19**	**20**
D	C	D	B	A	A	B	D	B	A
21	**22**	**23**	**24**	**25**	**26**	**27**	**28**	**29**	**30**
B	A	D	A	B	D	A	C	C	D
31	**32**	**33**	**34**	**35**	**36**	**37**	**38**	**39**	**40**
B	B	B	B	D	A	B	A	D	A
41	**42**	**43**	**44**	**45**	**46**	**47**	**48**	**49**	**50**
C	C	B	A	A	C	B	B	D	B
51	**52**	**53**	**54**	**55**	**56**	**57**	**58**	**59**	**60**
C	B	A	B	B	B	C	D	A	B
61	**62**	**63**	**64**	**65**	**66**	**67**	**68**	**69**	**70**
C	C	B	B	D	A	C	A	C	C
71	**72**	**73**	**74**	**75**	**76**	**77**	**78**	**79**	**80**
B	A	A	D	A	B	B	D	D	B
81	**82**	**83**	**84**	**85**	**86**	**87**	**88**	**89**	**90**
B	D	C	D	B	C	D	C	D	C
91	**92**	**93**	**94**	**95**	**96**	**97**	**98**	**99**	**100**
A	D	A	A	C	C	D	D	B	B

Previous Paper (Solved)

DSSSB—TGT (SOCIAL SCIENCE) TEACHER Recruitment Exam, 2015

POST SPECIFIC SUBJECT-RELATED QUESTIONS

1. The Law of Diminishing Returns to Scale holds true in the:
A. Market – Period
B. Short – Period
C. Long – Period
D. Secular – Period

2. The first stage in the Demographic Transition Theory of population was characterised by:
A. High BR and high DR
B. High BR and low DR
C. Low BR and low DR
D. Low BR and high DR

3. The Phillips Curve shows the relation between:
A. Income and consumption
B. Income and price level
C. Income and investment
D. Inflation and unemployment

4. The doctrine of unbalanced growth has not been advocated by:
A. H.W. Singer
B. W.A. Lewis
C. A.O. Hirschman
D. C.P. Kindleberger

5. Purchasing power parity theory was given by:
A. Haberler
B. J.S. Mill
C. J.E. Meade
D. Gustav Cassell

6. The price elasticity of demand is equal to one for a demand curve, which is:
A. Horizontal line
B. Vertical line
C. Rectangular hyperbola
D. Downward moving line

7. Which one of the following is not an instrument of fiscal policy?
A. Public Revenue
B. Public Expenditure
C. Public Borrowing
D. Cash Reserve Ratio

8. The concept of single factoral and double factoral terms of trade have been given by:
A. Haberler
B. Jacob Viner
C. Snider
D. Scammel

9. Which report used the term, "sustainable development" for the first time?
A. Brundtland Report
B. Vienna Report
C. Bretton Wood Report
D. World H.D. Report

10. The concept of 'Reserve Army of Labour' is given by:
A. Karl Marx
B. David Ricardo
C. Adam Smith
D. J.S. Mill

11. The earliest duopoly model was developed by:

A. Bertrand
B. Cournot
C. J.B. Clark
D. Edgeworth

12. Human Development Index was formulated by:
A. World Bank
B. International Monetary Fund
C. UNTAD
D. UNDP

13. AFC equals the vertical distance between the:
A. AC curve and MC curve
B. AVC curve and MC curve
C. AC curve and AVC curve
D. TC curve and TVC curve

14. In the Hekscher-Ohlin theory, the most important cause of the difference in relative commodity prices and trade between nations is a difference in:
A. Factor endowments
B. Technology
C. Tastes
D. Comparative cost

15. Who led the Narmada Bachavo Andolan?
A. Medha Patkar
B. Sundarlal Bahuguna
C. Rajiv Dixith
D. Chandi Prasad Bhatt

16. Critical Minimum Effort theory is given by:
A. Leibenstein
B. Rosenstein Rodan
C. Arther Lewis
D. Marx

17. Which of the following is least liquid asset?
A. Money
B. Machines
C. Shares
D. Bonds

18. Which of the following are leakages from the circular flow?
A. Consumption and savings
B. Imports and exports
C. Exports and savings
D. Savings and imports

19. Lorenz curve is used to measure:
A. Inequality
B. Poverty
C. Inefficiency
D. Production possibility

20. Which country is the largest producer of mica?
A. India
B. USA
C. China
D. Australia

21. Wagner's law is based on:
A. Rising prices
B. Rising public expenditure
C. Rising public receipts
D. Rising public debts

22. Incidence of tax is:
A. First point of contact
B. Final resting place
C. Both A and B
D. None of the above

23. 'Free Rider' problem arises in the case of:
A. Private goods
B. Consumer goods
C. Public goods
D. Capital goods

24. Specific tax is:
A. Fixed amount
B. Irrespective of output
C. Per value of output
D. Per unit of output

25. Bretton Woods twins are:
A. UK and USA
B. WTO and ITO
C. IMF and World Bank
D. Britain and Woodland

26. Price Rigidity is the feature of:
A. Monopoly
B. Oligopoly
C. Duopoly
D. Duopsony

27. In which year the Forest Rights Act was passed?
A. 1969 B. 1970
C. 1975 D. 1965

28. Price discrimination is followed by:
A. Monopoly producer
B. Oligopoly producer
C. Duopoly producer
D. Duopsony producer

29. Kinked demand curve is related to:
A. Monopoly
B. Oligopoly
C. Duopoly
D. Duopsony

30. Firm attains equilibrium under perfect competition when:
A. MR = AR B. MC = AC
C. MC = MR D. TR = TC

31. According to Say's law of market:
A. Supply is greater than demand
B. Supply is less than demand
C. Demand creates its own supply
D. Supply creates its own demand

32. Kalinga war of Ashoka is evidenced by:
A. Brahmagiri edict
B. Bhabru edict
C. Maski edict
D. Rock edict XIII

33. Allahabad inscription was issued by:
A. Chandragupta I
B. Samudragupta
C. Ramagupta
D. Chandragupta II

34. 'Rajatarangini' was composed by:
A. Kalhana
B. Mahendravarman I
C. Parameshwaravarman
D. Bilhana

35. In which year Food Corporation of India was established?
A. 1965 B. 1969
C. 1970 D. 1960

36. The Kailasa temple at Ellora was built by:
A. Krishna I
B. Govinda III
C. Dhruva
D. Krishna III

37. 'Lakh Baksh' was the title of:
A. Qutubuddin Aibak
B. Iltutmish
C. Alauddin Khilji
D. Firoz Shah

38. Muhammad Bin Tughlaq transferred the capital from:
A. Delhi to Ujjaini
B. Delhi to Devagiri
C. Delhi to Mathura
D. Delhi to Allahabad

39. Talikote battle was fought between:
A. Vijayanagara and Bahamani
B. Chalukyas and Kadambas
C. Keladi and Vijayanagara
D. Vijayanagara and Wodeyars

40. I[st] Battle of Panipat was fought between:
A. Babur and Sher Shah
B. Babur and Rana Pratap
C. Akbar and Hemu
D. Babur and Ibrahim Lodi

41. The famous Madarasa at Bidar was built by:
A. Muhammad Gawan
B. Muhammad Shah
C. Ibrahim II
D. Muhammad Adil Shah

42. In which year the Tata Iron and Steel Company was set up?
A. 1907 B. 1910
C. 1900 D. 1903

43. The battle of Plassey was fought in the year:
A. 1761 B. 1756
C. 1764 D. 1757

44. Treaty of Mangalore ended:
A. I Anglo Mysore war
B. II Anglo Mysore war

C. III Anglo Mysore war
D. IV Anglo Mysore war

45. Permanent settlement was introduced by:
A. Lord Wellesley
B. Lord Cornwallis
C. Lord Hastings
D. Lord William Bentinck

46. Doctrine of Lapse was introduced by:
A. Lord Dalhousie
B. Lord Cornwallis
C. Lord Wellesley
D. Sir John Shore

47. Indian National Congress was founded by:
A. A.O. Hume
B. Mahatma Gandhi
C. Annie Besant
D. Bal Gangadhar Tilak

48. In which year the Telecom Regulatory Authority of India was set up?
A. 1997 B. 1985
C. 1990 D. 1995

49. 'Lion of Karnataka' was the title given to:
A. R.R. Diwakar
B. Gangadhar Rao Deshpande
C. K.C. Reddy
D. S. Nijalingappa

50. Decision made directly by the people without guidance or moral suasion is called:
A. Direct democracy
B. Representative democracy
C. Aristocracy
D. Federalism

51. Government led by religious beliefs or culture is called:
A. Aristocracy
B. Technocracy
C. Theocracy
D. Totalitarian

52. Distribution of power between central government and state government is:
A. Unitary feature
B. Federal feature
C. Dyarchy
D. Autonomy

53. State list consisted which one of the following item?
A. Post and Telegraph
B. Insurance
C. Land policies
D. Shipping and Navigation

54. Which of the following has launched Sagar Samruddhi Project near Mumbai?
A. ONGC B. IOCL
C. BPCL D. HPCL

55. Susan B. Anthony was a leader of the movement of:
A. Guaranteed former slaves the right to vote
B. Guaranteed women the right to vote in national elections
C. Ensure that the harsher laws against criminals
D. Reduce the authority of the Constitution of United States

56. What was the source of the following phrase, 'Government of the people, by the people, for the people'?
A. US Constitution
B. Declaration of Independence
C. Geltysburg address
D. The speech "I have a dream"

57. The phase that in America there should be a "Wall of separation between church and state" appears in:
A. Thomas Jefferson's letter
B. George Washington's farewell address
C. May Flower Compact
D. The US Constitution

58. In "I have a Dream" Speech Dr. Martin Luther King:
A. Expressed his hopes for social justice and brotherhood
B. Advocate black separatism
C. Argued for the abolition of slavery
D. Morally defended affirmative action

59. Which group of countries are termed as "Third World" countries?

A. Panchasheela B. NAM
C. NATO D. SEATO

60. 'Gujral Doctrine' gives more importance to have good relations with:

A. NATO countries
B. ASEAN
C. SAARC
D. SEATO

61. Which of the following statements is true about abortion?

A. It was legal in most states
B. The Supreme Court struck down most legal restrictions
C. Supreme Court rules that underage women must notify their parents of an unpending abortion
D. The National Organization for Women has lobbied for legal restriction on it

62. Which "Designation" or "Position" is the head of all civil services in India?

A. HRD Commissioner
B. Cabinet Secretary
C. President
D. Speaker

63. Who was the first Chief Election Commissioner of India?

A. T.N. Sheshan
B. Sukumar Sen
C. I.K. Gujral
D. V.K. Menon

64. One of the official retreats of the President of India is "Rastrapathi Bhavan" in Secunderabad. Which is the other?

A. The retreat building of Bhagalpur, Bihar
B. The retreat building of Mashobra, Shimla
C. The retreat building of Sambhalpur, Odisha
D. The retreat building of Khandwa, Madhya Pradesh

65. How many members are nominated to the Rajya Sabha by the President of India?

A. 15 B. 14
C. 13 D. 12

66. The International Data Line is approximately equal to:

A. The Equator
B. 100th Meridian
C. 180th Meridian
D. None of these

67. Which of the following types of paper money is presently in circulation?

A. Inconvertible
B. Flat
C. Convertible
D. Representative

68. Which is the only state that touches Sikkim?

A. Assam
B. West Bengal
C. Arunachal Pradesh
D. Meghalaya

69. The Bhakra Dam is built across the river:

A. Ravi
B. Chenab
C. Sutlej
D. Jhelum

70. Over 90% of the world's biomass is in:

A. Fresh water wet lands
B. Tropical rain forest
C. Oceans
D. Topsoils

71. What is a 'cloudburst'?

A. It refers to sudden and copious rainfall over a small area which often lasts only a few minutes
B. It refers to 50 mm rain over a period of time
C. It is caused by rapid condensation of very high clouds
D. It refers to a thunderstorm with little rain

72. One purpose of education is to help students to acquire the skills they need to be successful in society. This is an example of a:

A. Manifest function

B. Constructed reality
C. Latent function
D. Entrenched function

73. When conducting social research, what is the next step in the scientific method after a review of literature?
A. Collecting data
B. Choosing a research design
C. Selecting a researchable problem
D. Formulating a hypothesis

74. What did education development see as major focus of education?
A. The reproduction of labour power
B. The transmission of society's goals and values
C. Providing capitalists with workers most useful to them
D. The development of strong sense of individualists

75. Which of the following is part of the critique of education by the Australian Democrats?
A. Spending more money on education would not increase the efficiency of the workforce
B. State interventions in education promote inequalities
C. Poverty is an insurmountable barrier to the full realization of intelligence and talent for pupils of lower socio-economic causes
D. The Australian education system created equality of opportunities but not equality of outcome

76. A .... style is the pattern of behaviour an individual develops in response to conflict with others, such as difference of opinion.
A. Conflict management
B. Consultative management
C. Laissez-faire management
D. Autocratic management

77. For which of the following country-of-origin is important in customer's eyes?
A. Airline B. Electronics
C. Cars D. All the above

78. The first Factories Act was enacted in:
A. 1881 B. 1895
C. 1897 D. 1885

79. How many nationalised banks are operating in India at present?
A. 19 B. 18
C. 17 D. 20

80. Disasters frequently result in all of the following except:
A. Damage to the ecological environment
B. Displacement of population
C. Destruction of a population's homeland
D. Sustained public attention during the recovery phase

81. The decision to offer humanitarian aid is determined by:
A. Theories of social justice
B. Teleological reasoning
C. Socio-cultural factors
D. All of the above

82. Social workers skilled in crisis management where:
A. Flood
B. Violent events such as child abuse, domestic abuse
C. Car accident, life threatening illness
D. With all the above

83. The population pyramid of a population that has had a slightly larger birth rate than death rate for several generations will most likely to have which of the following shapes?
A. Wider at the top than in the middle
B. Wider at the bottom than at the top
C. Bulging in the middle
D. Having parallel sides

84. Which of the following aspect of social life is used in the text to illustrate insights provided by all three theoretical paradigms?
A. Sports B. War
C. Family D. Education

85. Years of productive life are calculated based on the age of death being:

A. 60 B. 65
C. 70 D. 75

86. Fertility can be best brought under rational control by:
A. Legal enactments
B. Coercion
C. Education
D. Schemes of incentives

87. What is the Target Growth Rate of 12th five year plan?
A. 9% B. 8%
C. 10% D. 7%

88. The study of factors that influence the frequency distribution and causes of injury, disease and other health related events in a population is called:
A. Sociology
B. Anthropology
C. Epidemiology
D. Pathology

89. Who inaugurated 'Sansad Bhavan' building where the Lok Sabha and Rajya Sabha are given separate chambers to meet?
A. Linlith Gow
B. Lord Irwin
C. Wavell
D. Lord Mountbatten

90. The first woman President of UN General Assembly:
A. Sarojini Naidu
B. Annie Besant
C. Vijayalaxmi Pundit
D. Subbalaxmi

91. The real executive power under the Constitution of India rests with:
A. President
B. The Prime Minister
C. The Parliament
D. The Prime Minister and his council

92. What was the former name of SBI?
A. Imperial Bank of India
B. National Bank of India
C. Residential Bank of India
D. Federal Bank of India

93. Where is the headquarter of the International Court of Justice?
A. Paris
B. Rome
C. The Hague
D. Washington

94. In the election of the President which of the following do not take part?
A. Members of Legislative Council
B. Elected members of Lok Sabha
C. Elected members of Rajya Sabha
D. None of the above

95. Where is the HQ of IMF located?
A. Washington DC
B. New York
C. Geneva
D. London

96. 'Servants of India Society' was founded by:
A. Srinivasa Shastri
B. Pundit Hirdaya Nath Kunzru
C. Gopala Krishna Gokhale
D. Bal Gangadhar Tilak

97. Which five year plan is called Mahalanobis plan?
A. II FYP B. I FYP
C. III FYP D. IV FYP

98. Who called Britain a nation of shopkeepers?
A. Hitler
B. Garibaldi
C. Napoleon
D. Mussolini

99. Asiatic Society was founded by:
A. Max Muller
B. Cunningham
C. Sir John Marshal
D. William Jones

100. Who said "I Came, I saw, I conquered"?
A. Napoleon
B. Shakespeare in Julius Caesar
C. Admiral Nelson
D. Hitler

ANSWERS

1	2	3	4	5	6	7	8	9	10
D	A	D	B	D	C	D	B	A	A
11	**12**	**13**	**14**	**15**	**16**	**17**	**18**	**19**	**20**
B	D	C	A	A	A	B	D	A	A
21	**22**	**23**	**24**	**25**	**26**	**27**	**28**	**29**	**30**
B	B	C	D	C	B	A	A	B	C
31	**32**	**33**	**34**	**35**	**36**	**37**	**38**	**39**	**40**
D	D	B	A	A	A	A	B	A	D
41	**42**	**43**	**44**	**45**	**46**	**47**	**48**	**49**	**50**
A	A	D	B	B	A	A	A	B	A
51	**52**	**53**	**54**	**55**	**56**	**57**	**58**	**59**	**60**
C	B	C	A	B	C	A	A	B	C
61	**62**	**63**	**64**	**65**	**66**	**67**	**68**	**69**	**70**
B	B	B	B	D	C	A	B	C	B
71	**72**	**73**	**74**	**75**	**76**	**77**	**78**	**79**	**80**
A	A	D	B	C	A	D	A	A	D
81	**82**	**83**	**84**	**85**	**86**	**87**	**88**	**89**	**90**
D	D	A	A	B	C	A	C	D	C
91	**92**	**93**	**94**	**95**	**96**	**97**	**98**	**99**	**100**
D	A	C	A	A	C	A	C	D	B

SOCIAL SCIENCE

HISTORY

INDIAN HISTORY

The history of India is not the history of area carved out after partition on 15th August, 1947. It is the history of the subcontinent, whose vast territory had the Great Ocean in the south, west and east and mountain ranges stretching in the north like the string of a bow. Patkai, Lushai and Chittagong hills in the east, Suleiman and Kirttar ranges in the west and Himalayas in the centre give India a separate identity. India is known to the Hindus as Bharatavarsha or the land of Bharata, a King famous in Puranic traditions. The name India was applied to the country by the Greeks, deriving it from the river Indus or the Sindhu, which was the cradle of its earliest known civilization.

The course of Indian history, like in other countries, is in large measure determined by its geography. India has been primarily divided into four identifiable units — hilly terrain in the north; plains in the centre, peninsula in the south and the long and narrow plains in the east and west lying between the sea and ghats. High mountains, deep rivers, sandy deserts and impenetrable forests gave rise to a spirit of isolation and divergences but in the plains and peninsular area, a large exchanges took place. The fencing provided by mountains in the north favoured a distinct type of civilisation. However, the ambitious Kings and wandering nomads from other areas came several times and left their influence and sometimes, stayed back and got assimilated.

Besides enormity of the geographical dimensions, the population of India has been large. People here differ in religion, language, caste or creed besides living at great distances. Despite this, there lies a deep underlying unity. It got cemented in the 19th century due to the uniform system of administration, easy means of communication and spread of education. This spirit of unity existed even in the ancient times as suggested in epics and Puranas.

In India, the men might have existed several thousand years back, but since history is based on facts and records, the earliest proof we have is of Paleolithic age. In this age, men used chipped stones which were fitted with handles of sticks or bones. The men, at that time, was a wanderer, and had no idea of agriculture, pottery and probably, fire. Negrito race with short stature, dark skin and flat noses are supposed to be descendents of Paleolithic men.

After several hundred or thousand years, men acquired knowledge and skill to master the forces of nature. In this Neolithic or New stone age, a distinctly higher type of civilization evolved in India. The stones were not only chipped but also ground and polished, ready for use for various purposes. They cultivated land and grew fruits. They knew the art of producing fire by friction and domesticated animals. They lived in caves and decorated their walls by painting scenes of hunting and dancing. They knew the art of pottery making and weaving cloth. The records of neolithic men, in forms of painted caves, tombs for the dead and a stone tool factory have been found in several parts of India. The age of paleolithic and neolithic men is called pre-historic because there is no definite knowledge or written records of this age.

As the man developed, he learnt about metals. In northern India, copper started replacing stone in tools and weapons and for sometime, both co-existed. In the next hundreds of year, use of iron developed. However, in southern India, Iron age came immediately after the stone age. Bronze was developed as a metal stronger than copper and more suitable for manufacturing tools and weapons. Since the development of metals, ample records are available with the historians to know the lifestyle and other details of the men. In India, the Indus Valley civilization grew during the copper age.

Indus Valley Civilization

About 2.5 thousand years back, a highly civilised community flourished in the banks of Indus river and adjoining areas. A number of seals discovered during excavations have a few letters engraved on them, but deciphering has not been successful. Due to absence of written records accurate details of the history of the civilisation and its culture and lifestyle is not available.

The excavation of the sites have led to the belief that cities and towns were well planned and nicely built. Burnt bricks were used for buildings. Some of the houses were multi-storeyed and furnished with paved floors and courtyards, doors, windows and narrow stairways. Every house had wells, drains and bathrooms. A few spacious buildings have also been found which contained large pillared halls and were probably used as palaces, temples or municipal halls. Great baths are important examples of the civilisation's architectural skills.

People of Indus Valley enjoyed relatively free life, compared to other civilisations. Wheat was their staple diet but barley, date, mutton, pork and eggs were also used. Cotton and wool were used by them. Men and women were fond of ornaments, with necklaces, rings, bangles and armlets being worn by both. Gold, silver, ivory, copper and precious stones were used for making ornaments.

Vessels made of metals, porcelain and clay were used with the earthenware being the most common one. They were sometimes painted or glazed also. People were fun-loving and enjoyed to play the game of dice. Several toys for the children have also been found. Bull, buffalo, sheep, elephant and camel were domesticated. People used axes, spears, daggers and slings as weapons but did not know about sword. All these were made of copper and bronze. Discovery of terra-cotta seals, containing fine representation of animals, exhibit their high degree of excellence. People of Indus Valley used to trade not only with other parts of India but also other Asian countries. The trade also led to cultural exchanges. The people worshipped trees, animals and stones in the belief that these are abodes of spirits. Mother Goddess and a Male God, prototype of God type, seem to be their favourite deities.

Reasons of Indus Valley Civilisation's decline are not confirmed but it is clear that it contributed immensely in the growth and development of subsequent civilisation in the country.

Vedic Age

With the arrival of Aryans, a new era began in India. Vedas were their early literature but period to which they belonged has not been exactly defined. Aryans did not live in cities. In their religion, the images played no part. Indra, Varuna, Surya and fire were among their prominent deities. Aryans lived in the area, stretching from eastern Afghanistan to the upper valley of the Ganges. The major part of this area came to be known as Sapta Sindhu, the land of seven rivers. In the remaining area, Dasyus, a dark-skinned, flat-nosed race lived.

Politically and socially, the society that time was based on patriarchal system. Village was the smallest unit of administration and the king was the lord of the land, with unlimited powers. Kingship was usually hereditary though there has been explicit references in the Vedas to the elective monarchies. The King lived a luxurious life and in return he was expected to protect his natives and their territory. He also made arrangements for the administration and maintaining law and order.

For the counsel of the king, bodies like Sabha and Samiti existed. Samiti was a assembly of common people while Sabha was a gathering of selected people.

Since the families were patrilineal, people desired for son. Girls were often neglected. Polygamy was practised by some but polyandry was not allowed. Widows were permitted to remarry. Women were respected but had to look to the male relations for aid and support.

People in this age were fun and adventure loving. Exhilarating drinks such as Soma or Sura was consumed. Racing, hunting and the war-dance were favourite pastimes. Dancing, music and playing dice were also very popular.

There were no rigid restrictions with regard to occupations. The three higher castes were expected to pass through the rigorous discipline of the four stages of life, called Ashramas — Brahamcharya, Grihastha, Vanaprastha and Sannyas.

Rearing of cattle and other domestic animals also quite common cow, ox, horse, dog, goat and sheep were the domesticated animals. Trade and commerce was insignificant though currency was unknown and exchanging goods or the barter was used. Chariots were used for the transportation.

During the early Vedic age, art of poetry flourished. Early literature of the Aryans were transmitted orally, indicating their lack of knowledge of a script. People made advances in the fields of architecture, sculpture, science and astronomy.

As the time passed by, Aryans occupied more territories and their kingdom's boundaries moved towards the east and the south. Kings claimed to be absolute masters of all their subjects, monopolizing political, economic and judicial powers. Brahamans played an important role in the society. The caste structure became rigid and an important factor. Prominent dynasties and kingdoms came into being, by the end of the vedic age. Agriculture, during the period, became main occupation of the people. Agriculture and cattle rearing made progress. New grains like wheat and rice were produced. The agricultural implements like ploughs were much improved. Trade and Industry made progress, a new class of merchants called Vanika came into existence and a large number of professions grew.

The religious books of the Aryans show their culture at their highest perfection. The most important of these books are four Vedas — Rig Veda, Yajur Veda, Sama Veda and Atharva Veda, the Upanishads containing philosophical treatises, the Epics — Ramayana and Mahabharata, 18 Puranas, 6 Shastras and the Manusmriti. The Rig Veda consists of hymns most of which are invocations addressed to various gods, praising and imploring them for worldly comforts. The Sama Veda has very little independent value as it chiefly consists of hymns taken from the Rig Veda and arranged with reference to their place in the sacrifice. It is rendered musically. The Yajur Veda, in prose form, contains sacrificial prayers. The Atharva Veda is the repository of magic and spells and efficacy of plants to cure diseases. It came into vogue much later than other Vedas. The Puranas deal with primary creation, secondary creation, genealogies of gods, reign of' Manu and history of various dynasties.

India Before Alexander

As the Kings became powerful, they made attempts to expand their kingdoms. This phenomenon began in the 6th century BC, with the establishment of following kingdoms — Anga in East Bihar, Magadha in South Bihar, Kosala in Oudh, Chedi between Yamuna and Narmada rivers, Kuru in Delhi, Meerut and Thanesar, Vatsa in Allahabad region, Panchala in Bareilly, Badaun and Farrukhabad, Avanti in Malwa region, Gandhar in Peshawar and Ravalpindi and Kamboj in parts of Kashmir. In between these kingdoms, there surfaced a nation, called Vidhehas or Vrijis which had no monarch but a popular assembly to carry out the business of the state. Its capital was Vaisali. There were smaller republics also, like Sakyas and Bhargas but all of them were taken over by their formidable neighbouring kings.

Chanda Pradyota Mahesena of Avanti, Udayan of Vatsa, Prasenajit of Mahakosala and Bimbisara and Ajatsatru in Magadha were prominent kings of that time. Among them, Magadha kingdom occupied a prominent status as it was compact, protected on all sides by mountains and rivers. The country was prosperous due to fertile land and booming trade. Bimbisara used war-elephants to great effect to score victories. He also entered into matrimonial alliances with other kingdoms which helped Magadha. It attracted the most enlightened men of the age, including Gautama Buddha and Vardhamana Mahavira. His son, Ajatsatru, continued the expansionist policies and developed tshe stately city of Pataliputra which continued to be the axis of India for their four centuries.

After a few generations of Bimbisara, the reins of Magadha were passed on to the Nanda dynasty who were ultimately overthrown by Chandragupta Maurya. A brahamin from Takshila, Kautilya or Chanakya played an important role in the dethroning of Nandas. While struggle for the Magadha throne was going on, a foreign invader was marching into India through western borders.

Alexander's Invasion

Alexander, a prince of remarkable energy and ability occupied the throne of Macedonia in 336 BC. After defeating the Persian king, he moved towards India. In 327 BC, he crossed the Hindukush mountains and by the next year he had forced his way through dense jungles and crossed the Indus river by a bridge of boats. He conquered several small kingdoms in the North-West but was strongly opposed on the banks of Jhelum by a huge army, led by King Porus. In the battle of Hydaspes (Jhelum), Porus fought valiantly but was defeated. Alexander, acting generously, gave back the kingdom to Porus and advanced further upto river Beas. He wished to press forward to the Ganges Valley but his war-worn troops requested him not to go further. Alexander on his way back, died at Babylon in 323 BC.

Mauryan Empire

Chandragupta established the Maurya empire in around 321 BC, after overthrowing the Nanda King in Magadh. He solicited the support of Indian Kings in overthrowing the Greek Generals who were ruling after Alexander's departure; He spread his empire upto Saurashtra in the West and Punjab in the North. Selucus surrendered areas of Kabul and Gandhar in the north-west to Chandragupta, making him one of the greatest kings in Indian history.

The successor of Chandragupta was his son Bindusara who took over in around 293 BC. He retained the empire of his father and continued to follow his policies. He, however, could not conquer new areas.

Bindusara was followed by Ashoka, the Great in around 273 BC. He had slain several of his brothers on his way to the throne. He fought a war to win Kalinga. Thus, his empire included almost the whole of non-Tamil India and a considerable portion of Afghanistan. However, the Kalinga war proved to be a turning point in Ashoka's life and produced results of far-reaching consequences. The sight of misery and bloodshed awakened Ashoka's conscience and he became devoted to Buddhism. He eschewed military campaigns, hunting and slaughtering animals. He worked for spreading the message of Buddhism to the nook and comer of India and other countries. Due to his tireless zeal in improving the condition of humanity, Ashoka has been called the Great by historians.

During Ashoka's regime, the army remained inactive and even the thoughts of military conquests were shunned. Military preparedness declined. There were rebellions in the frontier areas which could not be suppressed. Other Kings became stronger and within few years of Ashoka's death in 232 BC, Mauryan empire finally disintegrated.

Satavahanas

King Simuka established Satavahana dynasty in the Andhra region. Their empire, at one time, was expanded in a large Deccan area. Paithan, Vaijayanti and Amaravati were famous towns of that time.

Tamil Kings

In the far South of India, three major kingdoms flourished at different times. The Cholas occupied the present Tanjore and Trichirrapally districts and showed great military activity in the second century BC. Rajendra and Rajaraja were some of the famous kings of Chola dynasty. The Pandyas occupied Madurai and Tirunelveli districts. They excelled in trade and learning. Another important kingdom in the area belonged to the Cheras who ruled in Malabar, Cochin and Travancore.

The Pallavas also ruled in the region from 600 AD to 750 AD. Their territories included the modern districts of North and South Arcot, Chengulputt, Tanjore and Trichirapally.

The Hoysalas Kings, who ruled in the present day Karnataka, built elegant statues (Gomateswara at Sravenbelagola) and temples (at Belur and Halebid).

Dynasties Having Foreign Roots

As the Mauryan empire declined, foreign invaders from the west attacked India. Most of them were from Greece, Syria and Bactria. As the kings departed, some of their warriors stayed back and occupied various areas. Three groups — Saka, Parthian and Kushan were the prominent ones. The Sakas originally belonged to Central Asia and settled in Afghanistan and the Indus Valley in the 1st and 2nd Centuries AD. Parthians coexisted, alongside Saka. In the latter half of 1st Century AD, Yue-chi nomads of Central Asia, called Kushans attacked the Parthians and took control of Indian borders. Kodphises I founded Kushan dynasty in India and Kanishka was their greatest ruler. His empire expanded from U.P. in the east, Vindhyas in the south and Ujjain in the west to remote regions beyond the Pamir passes. The Kushan dynasty survived till about 225 AD.

Gupta Empire

In the fourth century AD, the Gupta dynasty set up a powerful empire in Magadha. Chandragupta-I ascended the throne in 320 AD. Samudragupta, the successor, was the greatest king of the dynasty. He expanded his territory in the south and the west. Besides military laurels, personal accomplishments of Samudragupta were not less remarkable. He was intellectual, with knowledge of scriptures, literature and proficiency in music. He not only worked for the political unification of India but also for enrichment and spread of Indian culture in all its varied aspects. Samudragupta was succeeded by Chandragupta II who assumed the title of Vikramaditya. He came to the throne in 380 AD and ruled for 33 years. He carried on the policy of military campaigns, pursued by his predecessor. He also continued peaceful initiatives to spread his empire, which included matrimonial alliances with other rulers. He was a great patron of arts, literature, science, architecture etc. with nine gems or Navaratna, adorning his court. Kalidas and Varahamihira were two of them. A Chinese pilgrim Fa-Hien came to India during Vikramaditya's rule and spoke highly of the administrative system and general well-being of people of that time.

Kumaragupta I and Skandagupta were other prominent kings of Gupta dynasty. Gupta era is called the golden era of India because of all round development of the country.

The Huns

The Huns were a race of fierce barbarians who originally belonged to Central Asia. In the 5th Century AD they took over western areas of the Gupta empire. Their expansion was however checked by Guptas and their allied kings. Finally they were confined to a small area in North-West India and Malwa and were finally absorbed into the Rajput population.

Harshavardhana

Harshavardhana took over as the King of Kannauj in 606 AD and went on to occupy whole of northern India. He was the last great Hindu king of northern India who was not only a great warrior but also a liberal patron of art and literature. He was a great philanthropist and tolerant towards all religions. He gathered around himself some of the intellectuals and holiest sages — men like Banabhatta, Divakara and Chinese pilgrim Hiuen Tsang. Harshavardhana died in 647 AD.

Rajputs

Harshavardhana was the last emperor of a large India. However, after his death, the rulers of various provinces declared themselves independent and fought wars to prove their supremacy. In Rajputana, several Rajput Kings established themselves —

Kannauj was ruled by Jaichand; Ajmer and Delhi by Chauhans; Bundelkhand by Chandelas and Gujarat by Solankis. These small Rajput Kingdoms continued for about 500 years till Muslim invaders finished them one by one. The most illustrious Rajput rulers were Prithviraj Chauhan, Rana Sanga and Rana Pratap. Rajputs' origin is a matter of controversy and are considered descendents of' various tribes of foreign settlers and ancient Kshatriyas. They were known for their bravery, hospitality, loyalty and clanfeeling but also had customs of Jauhar and Sati which showed too much ego and individualism.

The Pala And The Pratihar

During Mauryan and Gupta empire, Bengal formed part of the empire of Magadh. In the eighth century, Gopala began the Pala dynasty and ended anarchy in the region. Under the Pala kings, Bengal enjoyed an era of prosperity. Some Pala kings ventured in the north and the south but their successors were short-lived. The Pala dynasty lasted till 11th century.

The Pratihar dynasty came to rule in Kannauj in the 9th century and soon expanded their kingdom to Punjab, Deogarh, Kathiawar and North Bengal. Their well-known ruler was Bhoja who was strong and maintained peace and order in the kingdom. By the end of the 10th century, Pratihar's grip over their kingdom declined. Their former feudal chiefs took over the areas under their occupation. The Chalukyas made themselves independent in Maharashtra, Andhra and Gujarat, the Parmaras in Malwa, the Chandellas and Chedis in the country between the Yamuna and the Narmada rivers.

The Pallavas of Kanchi, Rashtrakutas in Andhra, and Senas in Bengal were other prominent dynasties that came up before the 12th century in India.

Muslim Rule In India

The Arabs, roused to energy and enthusiasm by the new found unity inspired by Islam, won Sindh in 8th century itself but for the next 300 years, they could not move further. In the 11th century, Sultan of Ghazni, Mahmud launched massive attacks on India. Though he was patron of arts and letters, his main object of Indian expedition seems to be to plunder the wealth of India and destroy the morale of the rulers. His victory over Punjab and entry upto Gujarat had grave political implications. The attacks opened floodgates for foreign invaders from the west and since no great empire existed in India, the country went into their grips and continued under foreign rule for several centuries.

The next important attack on India came from Muiz-ud-din Muhammed bin Sam or Muhammed of Ghori. He began first Indian expedition in 1175 with a victory over Multan. After forging strategic alliances, he marched towards Delhi which was ruled by Prithviraj Chauhan that time. In the first battle of Tarain near Thanesar, Chauhan scored an outright victory but a year later, Muhammed returned, with adequate preparations and this time, the Rajput king was defeated and slain afterwards. It laid the foundation of Muslim domination in northern India.

Slave Dynasty

As Muhammed Ghori had no male heir his provincial viceroys established their own authority in their respective jurisdictions after his death. Qutb-ud-din became the ruler of Indian territory and established the Slave Dynasty in the early 13th century. He was originally a slave of Turkestan and grew up to become a king. So, the dynasty founded by him in India is known as the Slave Dynasty. He was a great warrior, a capable ruler and even-handed monarch. His devotion to Islam was remarkable, famous for his charity, he started the construction of Qutub Minar. He died in 1210. As Qutb-ud-din's successor was not competent, Iltutmish, the Governor of Badaun took over the Delhi throne. His rule was even recognised by Calipha of Baghdad. He consolidated the conquests of Qutb-ub-din into a strong and compact monarchy. His kingdom included whole of India, except a few outlying provinces. Besides a great warrior, he was a patron of arts and letters. He completed the Qutub Minar. Iltutmish, overruling the claim of his surviving sons, named daughter Razia as his heiress. She took over in 1236 but was met with resistance from nobles who could not reconcile themselves to the rule of a woman and organized opposition against her. Raziyya, using diplomacy, overcame her enemies and became first woman Muslim ruler in India. However, her rule did not last long as undue favours shown by her to Abyssinian slave offended the nobles, while trying to suppress the rebellion. She was killed in 1240, thus ending her reign of three and a half years. The removal of Raziyya was followed by a period of disorder and confusion. In 1265, Ghiyas-ud-din Balban, got the Delhi crown. By that time, the treasury was almost bankrupt. Mongols were attacking and the authority of the crown went, down in the eyes of people. Balban organised a strong army, restored order in the area, putting robbers and other troublemakers to the sword. He took steps to check the advance of Mongols. He did his best to regain the prestige and majesty of the Delhi Sultanate. Balban's career as, a Sultan was one of struggle against internal troubles and external dangers. He could rule for 20 long years because of his personal strength. But after his death in 1286, slave dynasty came to an end.

Khilji Dynasty

Jalal-ud-din Firoz set up the Khilji dynasty in the end of 13th century. But the first well known Khilji ruler was Ala-ud-din, who took over the Delhi throne in 1296. During his reign, the muslim dominion rapidly expanded over different parts of India, including Mysore in the south and Gujarat in the west. He attacked southern states' and looted their wealth. In a pathbreaking style, he acted on political matters, without the guidance of clergy. He established a strong government at the centre, strictly prohibited consumption of liquor, drugs and dicing and set up an efficient body of spying. He introduced military, revenue and economic reforms. Ala-ud-din was, however, harsh on Hindus. The ambitious and self-willed ruler died in 1316 but since he did not allow any of his general or son to establish firm roots or grip over political or military matters, the successors of Ala-ud-din could not continue his legacy and Khilji dynasty ended a few years later.

Tughlaq Dynasty

Ghazi Malik, with the support of nobles assumed the throne of Delhi, under the title of Ghiyas-ud-din Tughlaq in 1320 and established Tughlaq dynasty. Though possessing mild and liberal disposition, he introduced reforms in administration and checked wasteful expenditure. He continued the policy of military domination and imperialism but died in 1325. Muhammed bin Tughlaq, the successor of Ghiyas-ud-din, was an extraordinary personality. Some have described him as a genius, visionary and a benevolent King while others have branded him as a lunatic, idealist and tyrant. He had a vast knowledge of literature, arts, philosophy and medicine but he lacked practical knowledge and commonsense. He transferred his capital Delhi to Daulatabad (Devagiri) and introduced token currency. His schemes proved to be impracticable in actual operation and ultimately brought disorder to his kingdom. Despite his stern policies, he could not succeed much and died in 1351. Firoz Tughlaq became his successor. He was a religious bigot and persecuted the Hindus. He was great builder and founded the town of Jaunpur, Fatehabad, Firozepur and Firozabad. He conformed to the principle of Quranic law in the administration of justice. He also possessed excellent qualities of heart, such as affection and benevolence and his 38 year reign was marked by peace and prosperity.

Lodhi Dynasty

Bahlol Khan, belonging to the Lodhi tribe of Afghans, came to power in Delhi in 1451 and established Lodhi dynasty after overthrowing the Sayyed dynasty. Sayyed dynasty, during its 37 years of rule, produced four rulers but none was great enough to stay firmly in the seat. He restored the prestige of muslim power in India by his courage, energy and tactfulness. He forced several feudal chiefs and rulers of small areas to accept his authority. After his death in 1489, Nizam Khan, under the title of Sikander Shah took over the Delhi throne. He strengthened his kingdom, and curbed the powers of chieftains. He was the ablest of the

Lodhi rulers. Besides being firm, upright, brave ruler, Sikander had excellent qualities of head and heart, sympathising with the poor, patronising learned men and dispensing justice even handedly. However, he was not free from religious intolerance. Sikander's successor, Ibrahim was a man of irritable temper and was tactless. Despite being skillful in warfare, he alienated most of the nobles.

Those nobles and other provincial chiefs then invited Babur, the ruler of Kabul to invade which brought about the final collapse of Delhi Sultanate and paved the way for the establishment of a new Turkish rule in India.

As the rulers of Delhi got weakened, several provincial governors declared themselves independent. In North India, Jaunpur, Bengal, Malwa, Gujarat, Mewar, Assam, Orissa and Kashmir got new rulers and dynasties which continued for varying periods.

In Central India, several small kingdoms sprang up. In South India, Vijayanagar and Bahmani empires were the prominent ones, while Hindu rulers became kings in Vijayanagar. Muslims ruled the Bahmani kingdom. Bahmani Kingdom gave way to different dynasties in Berar, Ahmednagar, Bijapur, Golkunda and Bidar.

The Sufi Movement

The movement grew among the Muslims around 10th century. However, some of their practices such as penance, fasting and breath control are sometimes attributed to Hindu and Buddhist yogic influence. Some of the early Sufis laid great emphasis on love as the bond between God and the individual soul.

The Sufis, in 12th century, were divided into 12 orders, broadly divided into the followers of Islamic law — Shara and those not bound by it Be-Shara. The latter were more of a wondering saints. The prominent Sufi saints were Khwaja Moinuddin Chishti, Bakhtiyar Kaki, Nizamuddin Auliya and Nasir-ud-din Chiragh-i-Delhi.

The saints, belongs to Suhrawardi did not believe in leading a life of poverty and some of them even held ecclesiastical posts.

The Bhakti Movement

The followers of this movement stress the mystical union of the individual with the God. The real development of Bhakti took place in South India between the Seventh and the Twelfth Century and became more popular in fifteenth and sixteenth centuries. Namadeva, Ramananda, Ravidas, Kabir, Sadhana, Sena, Nanak and Meera Bai were prominent followers of the Bhakti movement.

Mughal Dynasty

Babur, a Chaghatai Turk, was connected with the families of Chengaiz Khan and Timur. At the age of 11 years, he inherited a small principality of Farghana. His ambition to expand the kingdom in the north-west was thwarted by Uzbek rulers. So, on the invitation of nobles in India, he began the south-east campaign. After conquering Punjab, his forces met Ibrahim Lodhi's forces in Panipat in 1526. Though far less in number, Babur led forces to a decisive victory. He occupied Agra and Delhi but he was opposed by Afghan military chiefs and Rajputs under Rana Sanga. But Babur defeated most of them and won over rest of them by threatening them or by offering gifts and fiefdoms. He won the battles of Khanwah, Chenneri and Ghagra, and established Mughal dynasty in the northern India. He died in 1530.

Humayun sat on the throne of Agra as Babur's successor. Since Babur was too busy fighting his adversaries he did not have time to establish good administration or coherent army and his son had to pay for this. In 1540, Afghan nobles, under the leadership of Sher Shah defeated Humayun in 1540. A brave warrior and a successful conqueror Sher Shah set up Suri dynasty. He was the architect of a brilliant administrative system. He introduced reforms in the fields of land revenue, currency and tariff. To improve communication, he connected important places of the kingdom by a chain of excellent roads. The police system was reorganised. Sher Shah had a strong army. His military character was accompanied by religious tolerance, even handedness and interest in architecture. Sher Shah, however, died in 1545, and his successors could not keep control over the regime. Humayun rejuvenated and reinforced captured the Agra throne once again. Humayun, a thorough gentleman, highly cultured but a weak administrator, died in 1556.

Akbar, who was 13 years old at the time of his father's death, was proclaimed Humayun's successor. His empire was, however, unsafe from all sides. A year after his coming to power, Akbar's forces defeated Afghan forces, led by Hemu in the Battle of Panipat. The victory was decisive, helping him in taking control over India. Akbar's empire was spread over whole of India, except Southern peninsula and Assam. He introduced many social, political, religious and administrative reforms. Liberal and tolerant of all religions, Akbar founded a new religion, Din-i-Ilahi. He planned a new synthesis of the conflicting religions in India with a view to find a common basis acceptable to all. Din-i-Ilahi borrowed good points of all religions and recognised no gods and prophets. The Emperor was its chief exponent. Since Akbar did not promulgate the religion in the spirit of a missionary it did not attract many followers. He was a great patron of arts. Akbar was the greatest ruler of medieval India. He died in 1605.

Akbar was succeeded by his son, Salim or Jahangir who had even rebelled against his father earlier. His wife Nurjahan played important role in the state administration. Jahangir had military ambitions, and his notable victories were against Afghans and Rajputs of Mewar and capture of Kangra fortress. Jahangir was a mixture of opposites — an autocrat, lover of justice, generous, kindhearted, lover of flowers and poetry but was less tolerant towards other religions and addicted to worldly pleasures. His reign saw the beginning of new interaction between India and Europe.

Shahjahan, third son of Jahangir ascended the throne in 1628. He ventured in the North-west and Deccan to expand the kingdom. He checked the growing influence of Portuguese in Bengal. He was a conqueror and unsparing to his political rivals. He was a good administrator, helping in alleviating the sufferings of the people. He was a zealous champion of Islam and imposed pilgrimage tax and took steps to spread Islam. He had an intense love for wife Mumtaz Mahal, who died in 1631 during child-birth and to immortalise her name, Shahjahan built Taj Mahal on her grave. Besides this, Shahjahah built several grand buildings, including Red Fort and Jama Masjid in Delhi. Shahjahan's regime is considered to be the golden period of the Mughal rule in India. There was no serious challenge to the Emperor's authority until the last period of his life when war of succession broke out. After Shahjahan's illness in 1657, terrible war of succession among his four sons began. Dara Shikoh, the eldest son had declared himself king but Aurangzeb and Murad joined hands to dethrone him, through successive wars. Victorious Aurangzeb placed even his father under strict confinement, denying him even the common convenience. Shahjahan died in 1666, still in captivity.

Aurangzeb crowned himself as Emperor in 1658. He possessed uncommon industry and profound diplomatic and military skill and an admirable quality for administration. He was a zealous Sunni Muslim, but intolerant of other religions. Initially, he concentrated on the north-west India, consolidating his grip. But subsequently he went to south India to take total control of Deccan. He fought wars with Jats, Bundelas, Sikhs, Rajputs and Marathas. However, he initiated diplomatic relations with the Muslim world outside India. Aurangzeb lived a simple, pious and austere life, abstaining from indulgences. He did not encourage arts and letters. His sternness with non-Muslims made large population hostile to his rule. Owing to Aurangzeb's lack of political foresight, disintegration of Mughal empire seemed imminent. He died in 1707, and his weak successors only hastened the process of decay.

Origin And Growth of Sikh Power

The first Sikh Guru, Nanak Dev was born in Talwandi on October 14, 1469. Nine more Gurus succeeded him before the last one declared a religious book — Adi Granth to be their master and guide (guru). The word Sikh means follower in Sanskrit. Other gurus to follow Guru Nanak were — Angad, Amardas, Ramdas, Arjundev, Hargovindsingh, Har Rai, Harkishan, Teg Bahadur and Gobind Singh.

Guru Gobind Singh was a warrior. He constituted Khalsa Panth, asked his followers to grow hair and fought several ways. His followers continued his policies and opposed the Mughal empire. As the rulers in Delhi got weakened, the influence of Sikhs in Punjab and adjoining areas increased. When Ahmed Shah Abdali attacked India in 1760s, the Sikhs fought valiantly but suffered major setbacks. Their religious places were also damaged. When Ranjit Singh became king in 1802, the powers of Sikhs expanded. However, after his death in 1839, the British rulers took over the area and the separate identity of Sikhs was lost.

Growth of Marathas

During Aurangazeb's reign, Marathas grew in Deccan and became a power to reckon with, particularly in the second half of the seventeenth century. Shivaji was the hero of the Maratha national unity which helped them grow. The self-reliance, courage, preservence, simplicity, social equality and other virtues propagated by several religious reformers helped sow the seeds of self-awakening, followed by political strengthening. Shivaji's kingdom extended roughly along the entire coast from Ramnagar in the North to Karwar in the South, including parts of Mysore kingdom. After Shivaji's death, Mughal army caused considerable damage to Maratha empire and weakened it. However, in early 18th century, Marathas again started capturing areas and attacking Mughal army. Peshwas or the Prime Ministers got the leadership of Marathas. They obtained important concessions from the Delhi rulers. Important Peshwas were Balaji Vishwanath, Baji Rao and Nana Saheb. They followed their policy of expansion towards the north. In 1757, they even attacked Delhi and compelled Ahmad Shah Abdali's representative who was then ruling Delhi, to surrender. They even marched upto Lahore and appointed their viceroy. But in 1759-60, Abdali started his march towards Delhi and the next year, defeated Marathas in Panipat. It produced disastrous consequences for the Marathas and seriously deflected their imperialistic ambition. They could not return to the position they had established before 1761.

Fall of Mughal Dynasty

The Mughal dynasty became extinct with Bahadur Shah II or Zafar who ascended the throne in 1837 and was deported to Rangoon by Britishers on suspicion of assisting the 1857 mutiny. He was a great poet but failed to lead the Indian sepoys in a unique opportunity. He died in 1862.

As the Mughal dynasty declined gradually, several new powers grew up to fill the vacuum. India, famous for its riches, became exposed to the menace of foreign invasion. Ruler of Persia, Nadir Shah marched towards India in 1738 and next year, after defeating the Mughal emperor entered Delhi. His troops killed Delhites enmasse. After taking all crown jewels, including Kohinoor diamond and making Mughal king to surrender several north-west provinces Nadir left India. Ahmad Shah Abdali, officer in Nadir's army and later independent ruler of Afghanistan, attacked India several times between 1748 and 1767. Mughal emperors transferred Multan and Punjab to Abdali. In 1757, he captured Delhi and was involved in carnage and arson for about a month. He defeated Maratha army in the Battle of Panipat within the country, chiefs in provinces declared themselves independent of the Mughal emperor in Delhi, merely paying theoretical allegiance to him. Bengal, Avadh, Hyderabad, Mysore, Carnatic, Malwa, Rohilkhand, Gujarat, Jats, the Rajput states and the Sikhs in Punjab were prominent ones.

Arrival of Europeans

India had commercial relations with the Europe, since times immemorial. In 1498, discovery of sea route by Vasco-da-gama opened new vistas of trade and cooperation. Portuguese were the first to come and establish trading centres at Cochin, Calicut and Cannanore. Several important Portuguese settlements were made at Goa, Daman, Diu, Hugli and Bombay. But their powers declined by the 18th century because their religious intolerance provoked the Indian powers and back home Portuguese could not compete successfully with other European powers.

The Netherlands, with their main interest in spice trade, came in 16th century, under the umbrella of the Dutch East India Company. They established factories in Gujarat, Bengal, Bihar, Orissa and into the interior of lower Ganges valley. However, the Dutch concentrated more on far east Asia and their interest in India remained insignificant.

Denmark also tried to have a foothold in India but after a few unsuccessful attempts, completely washed hands off India in 19th century.

Englishmen came to India in early 17th century. East India Company was set up in 1600 and granted charter to trade by the Queen. It obtained concessions from the Mughal emperors to set up factories and trade in India. In the second half of 17th century, it got British government's approval to raise armed forces, appoint Governors, build forts and declare war or make peace. The English used political, economic and military means to consolidate their position. They were emboldened by their country's superior position in Europe. After Battle of Plassey and Buxur, the British East India Company became a territorial power in India. Later, British Crown took over the administration of Company's possessions in India for direct rule.

France was a little late in starting organised trading activities with India. The first French factory was set up in Surat in 1667. Pondicherry became their headquarter. They went onto occupy Mahe and Karaikal. Initially, French had only trade motives on their minds and even their troops were used for defence. Later, in the second half of 18th century, they developed political ambitions which led to conflict with Britishers.

Anglo-French Struggle

The French and the English companies fought three Carnatic wars in the Deccan and those wars sealed the fate of France in India. Carnatic was ruled by a Nawab, with headquarters at Arcot. Nawab behaved, more or less, independent of the Nizam of Hyderabad. The 1st Carnatic war was merely an echo of the War of Austrian Succession in which France and England were on the opposite side. The war had repercussions in India also and both the companies tried to harm each other and capture their protected areas and factories. The Nawab of Carnatic tried to discipline French troops but was defeated. When war ended in Europe, peace returned in India also. But then dispute arose between French and English companies over the candidate for the Nawabship of Carnatic. In the second war in 1751, French were defeated; but they continued to have influence in Hyderabad. When the Seven Year War broke out in Europe in 1756, third and final phase of Anglo-French conflict started. French were overwhelmingly defeated, ending their political ambitions for ever and confining them to trade activity only.

British Success in Bengal

The Nawab of Bengal, during the middle of 18th century, was, for all practical purposes, an independent ruler though he nominally acknowledged the supremacy of Mughal king. However, Bengal lacked any political strength cr stability. Utilising the opportunity, the English Company not only strengthened themselves but also interfered in Bengal politics. Nawab Siraj-ud-dullah, realising the danger of English power, captured their Calcutta Fort. English got reinforcement from Madras and regained Calcutta Fort. In the Battle of Plassey in 1757, Englishmen, getting the support from Siraj-ud-dullah's commander-in-chief Mir Jafar, defeated Bengal's army. This battle marked the beginning of the establishment of British power in India. Subsequently, the English Company became all powerful, with Nawab Mir Jafar being a puppet only. The Company made unreasonable demands, leaving Nawab's treasury empty. Mir Qasim, the successor of Mir Jafar, realised the desperate position and took steps to strengthen his position. English angered at it, defeated him in a battle, forcing him to take refuge in Awadh. The combined forces of Nawabs of Awadh and Bengal and Mughal Emperor Shah Alam fought war against British forces in Buxar but were defeated. The Battle of Buxar in 1764 proved to be a turning point in Indian history as Britishers got right to collect revenue in Bengal, Bihar and Orissa and were left with no potential enemy in the Gangetic plains of India.

Growth of British Influence

By 1765, the British had become the virtual rulers of Bengal, Bihar and Orissa. The Nawabs of Awadh and Carnatic were dependent on them. At the same time, Marathas, in the western India, were on the rise despite defeat in the Battle of Panipat. In 1772, there was a problem of succession and the British tried to interfere. From 1775 to 1782, the Maratha and British armies fought a war which remained indecisive.

Britishers fought wars with Mysore during that period. Mysore was led by Hyder Ali and later by his son Tipu Sultan. France initially helped the Nawab of Mysore but later withdrew their support. Three Anglo-Mysore wars were fought and by the end of it in 1792, Tipu had surrendered half of his dominions, paid indemnity and even sent his two sons as hostages to the British.

So, during this period, British could not move towards south but they were able to extend their influence in the plains of India. Moreover, after the American War of Independence, there was a lot of criticism of East India Company's policies back home and it was decided not to interfere in the internal affairs of the local rulers. This policy was, however, continued selectively and for a very small period from 1785 to 1797.

After French Revolution, England and France were constantly engaged in war in Europe which had repercussions in India also. Moreover, Napoleon Bonaparte had undertaken an expedition into Egypt with a view to threatening the British position in India. Back home, Nizam and Tipu Sultan had allied with France. To safeguard and further the influence of British empire, Governor General Wellesley followed the policy of subsidiary alliances. Under it, the Indian rulers were made to keep a British force within his territory and pay its maintenance. The whole exercise was meant to keep the Indian ruler dependent on British forces. Several weak rulers accepted the arrangement while others were forced to do so. Marathas, who had become a great power in Western Indian in the late 18th century, became weak in early 19th century, due to disessions and death of their leaders — Nana Phadanvis and Mahadoji Sindhia. Young Peshwa, in a bid to protect his crown from the enemies, consented to accept subsidiary alliance and signed Treaty of Bassein. By the time Peshwa realised his mistake and declared war against British forces it was too late. British forces won at most of the places, including Ahmednagar in the south and Delhi and Agra in the north. Subsequently, the Marathas tried to regain their territories and lost power but British had taken a firm grip of the situation.

The British tried to extend their influence in Afghanistan, Iran and in the north-western region of India. Afghan leaders, also aimed at supremacy in India following decline of Mughal empire. Moreover, Afghanistan was important from the British point of view of checking Russian ambition in Asia. But they could establish their influence in Sindh only and could not go further militarily, British forces could not get better of Afghan forces. Punjab was the only independent state in India in the first quarter of 18th century.

Maharaja Ranjit Singh, who was brave, well-organised and a good administrator, had extended upto Peshawar, Multan, Kashmir and hill states. However, his kingdom's expansion was restricted by the British who had Sikh states to the east of Sutluj under their influence. After Ranjit Singh's death, two Anglo-Sikh wars were fought and Punjab was annexed by the British. The British also fought wars with Burma, who were increasing their influence in Assam.

After the defeat of Burmese army, Assam came under British control and Burma was forced to accept several conditions. By the year 1856, the British became the paramount power in India. A large part of India had come directly under British rule while in some areas, there were nominal Indian rulers who were completely dependent on the British.

The main reasons for the British ascendancy were — unity of command among the East India Company officials; internal weaknesses of Indian rulers; incapacity of Indian rulers to devise a stable political order and an efficient administrative system; military superiority of the British; and the economic and technological backwardness of India.

The Revolt of 1857

The rapid expansion of the British dominion was accompanied by changes in political and social order and administrative system in India. It brought about changes in the lifestyles of Indians who could not assimilate them, easily and naturally. The British regularly faced revolts in one part of the country or the other. The Indian rulers, angry at being denied the powers, their sepoys, courtiers, officials and other nobles simmering at denial of their livelihood and other disgruntled elements combined with the exploited peasants and native people, tried to stop the British conquest several times but failed. The volcano of discontent erupted massively in 1857 in the form of revolt. The revolt, which at one time looked like developing into a real war of Independence, shook the foundations of the British empire in India.

The revolt of 1857 was the most widespread challenge to the British rule, at that time. It brought together people of various sections, regions, religions and occupations with one objective of overthrowing the British empire. The reasons were different — political, economic, social, religious and military but there was a common ground.

As regards the political cause, policy of conquest pursued by the British had created unrest among many Indian rulers and the chiefs. Subsidiary alliance arrangements, doctrine of lapse and annexation of territories, threat to derecognise Mughal emperor's successors as kings gave rise to considerable uneasiness and suspicion in the minds of the old ruling princes, Hindu and Muslims both. The annexation of native states also limited the scope of Indians to get higher administrative jobs. New land revenue system displaced the landowning class, creating bitterness among them and leaving them without means of sustenance. In addition, the English officers quite often insulted the native gentry. Moreover, application of rule of law to all Indians, irrespective of caste, creed and clan but keeping Europeans out of the ambit of law, were not approved by the people.

On the economic front, the condition of peasants became worse, following introduction of new land systems. The old handicrafts were ruined, following absence of patronage. The growing unemployment among the followers and retainers of the dispossessed rulers gave rise to acute economic grievances and social unrest.

One of the causes of the revolt was the fear among Indians that their religion will be destroyed by the British. Some European missionaries openly decried the practices of Islam and Hinduism and went about converting people to Christianity. Some of the social reforms processes like abolition of Sati, widow remarriage, abolition of caste system in recruitment, opening of educational institutions by the British government added to the fears. The fear of loss of religion ultimately proved to be the immediate cause of the outbreak of the revolt.

As regards the military cause, there was lot of discontentment among the Indian soldiers. They could not hope to rise in the hierarchy of the army as promotional avenues were closed for them. There was a wide disparity between salaries of Indian and English soldiers. Moreover, despite constituting seveneighth of the British army, Indian soldiers were treated with contempt. The general decline of the Indian people also affected the soldier.

The growing resentment against the foreign rule came out in the open in the 1857 revolt. The immediate reason was the British government's decision to introduce a new, type of rifle in the army. To load the cartridge, its paper covering smeared with grease had to be bitten off. The soldiers believed that the grease was made from the fat of a cow or a pig. The use of cartridges offended the religious sentiments of both Hindu and Muslim soldiers. They refused to touch these cartridges but their British officers insisted on its use. The Mutiny sparked off on May 10, 1857 in Meerut when Indian soldiers were convicted and imprisoned for their refusal to use these cartridges. About two months earlier, Mangal Paridey had rebelled in Barrackpore on the same issue and had wounded two Englishmen. The colleagues of the convicted soldiers in Meerut attacked the jail and set them free. The Meerut soldiers, on arrival in Delhi, were joined by local infantry. They proclaimed Bahadur Shah as Emperor of India, who became the rallying point of the opponents of British rule. Uprisings were there in

Assam, Orissa, Uttar Pradesh, Bihar, Sindh, Rajasthan, Punjab, Maharashtra, Hyderabad, and Bengal. At many places, the people revolted even before the soldiers did or even when army regiments were present. Even where the people did not revolt, they showed strong sympathy for rebels.

Uprising was widespread in Awadh, Rohilkhand, Bundelkhand, Kanpur, Meerut and Westem Bihar, Tantia Tope, Kunwar Singh in Bihar, Bakht Khan in Delhi, Nana Sahib in Kanpur, Rani Lakshmi Bai in Jhansi and Maulvi Ahmadullah in Lucknow were prominent leaders of the 1857 revolt.

The revolt could not be sustained and within six months, the British had regained the lost ground. In September 1857, Delhi was recaptured and Bahadur Shah arrested. Most of the rebels fought valiantly but were either killed or weakened beyond repair. The revolt failed tiecause it could not spread throughout the country and remained localised. The rebels lacked leadership, with Delhi emperor refusing to lead from the front. The rebels did not have any common plan or coordination among various units. Various rebel leaders were suspicious and jealous of each other. The leaders of the revolt were deposed rulers or Zamindars who did not inspire confidence among the people. Moreover, the educated Indians and people getting benefit from the British rule, did not join the revolt. The rebel soldiers were ill-equipped, failing to utilise contemporary scientific, improvements in communication, transportation and planning.

The suppression of the revolt was accompanied and followed by inhuman atrocities by the British troops on rebel leaders and the common civilian population. The revolt was neither a war of independence nor a mere military uprising. It proved to be a turning point in Indian history, the Company's rule coming to an end and British govemment taking the reins of administration directly in its hands. The army was thoroughly reorganised, with increase in European soldiers. In the administration, all essential services were placed under the charge of Europeans. Indian states lost their independence, recognising the paramountcy of the British crown. The indirect effects of the revolt were growth of extremism in Indian politics and the use of "divide and rule" policy on religious ground by the British government.

National Movement

After the suppression of the 1857 revolt, the East India Company's rule in the administration of India came to an end and the country came under the direct control of the British Government. After 1858, the British used the political power in India to make political gains. To preserve their rule, the British tried to maintain old social order, showing no interest in reforms. They encouraged division on religious grounds.

They used India for making the British prosperous. Indian peasants, artisans and the workers suffered the most and the emerging middle class realised the drawbacks of the British rule. All this led to the nationalist movement which was basically a challenge to the foreign domination. Improvements in the means of transport and communication, social and religious reforms movements, influence of the press and literature, spread of education, and new ideas added to the nationalistic spirit in the country.

For many years after the suppression of the 1857 revolt, armed uprisings against the British rule continued to break out in different parts of the country. The Wahabis in Uttar Pradesh, the Kukas in Punjab, rose against the British. The peasants in Bengal, Bihar and Maharashtra and tribals in several parts revolted, against their oppression and exploitation. Syed Ahmed Barlevi, Guru Ram Singh, Birsa Munda and Vasudeo Balwant Phadke were some of the prominent rebel leaders during the second half of the 19th century. However, their actions were localised and did not pose any serious threat to the British government.

In the middle of the 19th Century, the political associations had begun to be formed, especially in the presidency towns of Madras, Bombay and Calcutta. Their initial demands were more representation of Indians in the administration and promoting welfare of the people. These organisations adopted the means of peaceful protest meetings and petitioning the government for their cause. These organisations were confined to their respective regions only and due to lack of leadership and popular support, they did not prove effective.

Birth of Congress

In December 1885, the Indian National Congress was formed with 72 delegates from all over India meeting in Bombay. A retired British official, A.O. Hume played a leading role in the formation of the Congress, thinking it will act as a safety valve for the nationalist leaders. The first President of the Congress was W.C. Bannerjee. The British government helped in the setting up of the Congress whose initial aim was — to bring together leaders from different parts of the country; to eradicate social, religious or provincial prejudices; to promote national unity; to present the popular demands before the government; and to educate and form public opinion in the country.

The Congress proved to be the embodiment of the national awakening in the country. It started holding annual sessions, usually at a different place each time. Its membership grew, with several new leaders joining the organisation. Its roots spread upto the village level and in course of time, it became the representative organisation of the people of the country. Dadabhai Naoroji in 1886 at Calcutta session, Badruddin Tyabji in 1887 at Madras session, and George Yule in 1888 at Allahabad session were the Presidents of the Congress during its infancy.

List of Congress Presidents Till Independence

Year	Venue	President
1885	Bombay	W.C. Bannerjee
1886	Calcutta	Dadabhai Naoroji
1887	Madras	Badruddin Tyabji
1888	Allahabad	George Yule
1889	Bombay	Willam Wedderburn
1890	Calcutta	Pherozeshah Mehta
1891	Nagpur	P. Anand Charlu
1892	Allahabad	W.C. Bannerjee
1893	Lahore	Dadabhai Naoroji
1894	Madras	Alfred Webb
1895	Poona	S.N. Bannerjee
1896	Calcutta	Rahimatulla M. Sayani
1897	Amraoti	C. Sankaran Nair
1898	Madras	Anand Mohan Bose
1899	Lucknow	R.C. Dutt

Year	Venue	President
1900	Lahore	N.C. Chandravarkar
1901	Calcutta	Dinshaw E. Wacha
1902	Ahmedabad	Surendra Banerjee
1903	Madras	Lal Mohan Ghose
1904	Bombay	Henry Cotton
1905	Benaras	G.K. Gokhale
1907	Surat	Arvind Ghose
1908	Madras	Rash Behari Ghosh
1909	Lahore	Madan Mohan Malviya
1910	Allahabad	William Wedderburn
1911	Calcutta	Bishan Dhar
1912	Bankipur	R.N. Mudholkar
1913	Karachi	Nawab Mohammad
1914	Madras	Bhupendranath Basu
1915	Bombay	S.P. Sinha
1916	Lucknow	A.C. Mazumdar
1917	Calcutta	Annie Besant
1918	Bombay	Imam Hasan
1919	Amritsar	Moti Lal Nehru
1920	Nagpur	C. Vijayaragavachariar
1921	Ahmedabad	C.R. Das
1922	Gaya	C.R. Das
1923	Kakinada	Moulana Mohammed
1924	Belgaum	M.K. Gandhi
1925	Kanpur	Sarojini Naidu
1926	Gauhati	S. Srinivas Aiyengar
1927	Madras	M.A. Ansari
1928	Calcutta	M.L. Nehru
1929	Lahore	J.L. Nehru
1930	Lahore	J.L. Nehru
1931	Karachi	Vallabhbhai Patel
1932	Delhi	Amrit Ranchhoddas Seth
1933	Calcutta	Nellie Sengupta
1934	Bombay	Rajendra Prasad
1935	Luknow	J.L. Nehru
1936	Faizpur	J.L. Nehru
1937	Faizpur	J.L. Nehru
1938	Haripura	S.C. Bose
1939	Tripura	S.C. Bose
1940 to 1945	Ramgarh	Maulana Azad
1946	Meerut	Acharya Kriplani
1947	Jaipur	Pattabhi Sitaramaiyya

Moderate Phase

During the initial 20 years, the Congress was dominated by liberal politicians. They asked for gradual introduction of reforms and increased say of the Indians in the government and administration of the country. In this era of moderate phase, the Congress demanded larger share of Indians in public services, reform and expansion in the powers of legislatures. It also demanded reduction in land revenue and change in government's economic policies to facilitate the growth of Indian industries. It asked for freedom of speech and expression, spread of education, expansion of welfare programmes and an end to the exploitation of India.

The leaders of the Congress in this era looked forward to a self-governing India, on western ideas. They were well-educated and usually belonged to upper strata of the Indian society. They believed that the British government could be persuaded to see the justness of their demands and would concede them. To do so, they passed resolutions, prepared petitions and tried to influence the British government, which, in turn, paid no heed to their demands. Initially, the British government supported the Congress leaders but soon their attitude became one of open hostility. As the Congress grew in strength and popularity, the British government became suspicious of the movement and started speaking ill of it. The government employees were debarred from attending the Congress sessions. The government tried to divide the Indian people on the basis of religion and encouraged pro-British individuals. Though the moderates did not achieve much success and failed to keep pace with the yearnings and aspirations of the people, yet their efforts need to be appreciated. They succeeded in creating a wide political awakening, arousing the nationalist feeling among the people, exposing the true character of British imperialism and most importantly; on laying the strong foundations for the national movement to grow upon.

Growth of Extremism

The younger generation in the Congress grew impatient with the moderate leaders policies. Bipin Chandra Pal in Bengal, Lokmanya Tilak in Maharashtra and Lala Lajpat Rai in Punjab emerged as the leaders who propagated the militant form of nationalism. They came to be known as extremists. Some international events like Japanese victory over mighty Russia and national events like Partition of Bengal encouraged the growth of extremism in the country. It led to the confrontation within the Congress and in 1907, at the Surat session, the split finally came. The extremist leaders described the British rule a curse and were totally opposed to it. Against the policy of conciliation and compromise of the moderates, the extremists wanted total Swaraj. To achieve their objective, they believed in a policy of passive resistance like Swadeshi movement, so that the governance of India by the British becomes impossible. The extremists tried to bring in more people in their support and were even ready for sacrifices and sufferings. The 1907 split virtually destroyed the effectiveness of the Congress for the next eight years when in the Lucknow Session in 1916, the moderates and the extremists agreed to join hands once again.

Partition of Bengal

In the early 20th century, Bengal was the largest province of British Empire, comprising Bengal, Bihar and parts of Orissa. The government decided to divide it into two provinces, pleading that it was difficult to administer such a big province. However, instead of separating non-Bengali areas from the province, the government in 1905 proposed the separation of East Bengal. The real aim was to weaken the forces of nationalism as the nationalist movement in Bengal was very strong. Another aim was to sow seeds of disunity among the Hindus and Muslims, with the latter being in majority in the new province. The national leaders and the people realised the gameplan and protested against the partition scheme. Both the moderate and extremist leaders launched movements against the partition. The day of partition was observed as a day of mourning as well as a day of unity and brotherhood. Swadeshi and boycott of foreign goods was carried out. People were asked not to cooperate with the government. The British government's move to divide the people backfired and the partition of Bengal became an important factor in the growth of nationalism. Finally, bowing to the popular pressure, the British government in 1911 announced the cancellation of the partition.

Morley-Minto Reforms

To pacify the aggrieved moderates, the British Government in 1909 announced Morley-Minto reforms, providing of association of qualified Indians with government to a greater extent in deciding public questions. So, the representation of Indians in executive and legislative councils increased. The Act introduced the principle of communal representation. The Act was seen as a positive step towards participation of the people but was rejected by one and all due to its "divide and rule" policies.

Militant Movement

Besides the moderates and the extremists, there were some other revolutionary groups who believed in the overthrow of the British rule by force. They were organized into secret societies, and were more active in Bengal and Maharashtra. They sometimes restored to attacking unpopular British officials, Indian employees and others working for the government. They also had international connections. Khudiram Bose, Profulla Chaki, Aurobindo Ghosh in his early life, Madam Bhikaji Cama, Lala Hardyal, V. D. Savarkar, Rashbehari Bose, V.V.S. lyer and M.N. Rao were some of the revolutionaries in the early 20th century. Bhagat Singh, Chandra Shekhar Azad, Ram Prasad Bismil, Ashfaquallah Khan, Roshan Singh, B.K. Dutt, Rajguru, Surya Sen and Sukhdev also used revolutionary means.

Muslim League

When the British came to India, the Muslims were the ruling class. So, the British treated them as their main enemies and discriminated against them. However, as the nationalist movement gained momentum, the British changed track. They tried to win over the Muslims, by persuading them to be loyal to the government. The use of religious beliefs and symbols by some national leaders also kept some Muslims away from the National movement. In 1906, pro-British Muslim leaders set up All-India Muslim league. They proposed the introduction of communal electorates. The Muslim league declared at birth that its aims were to promote loyalty to the government, and to protect and advance the interests of Muslims. However, later in 1913, it declared self government as its aim.

Home Rule Movement

When Britain was involved in the first world war, Indian leaders like Tilak and Annie Besant decided to put new life in the national movement. Home rule leagues were set up all over the country with the aim of attaining self-government within the British empire by all constitutional means and to educate and organise public opinion for the purpose. The leaders of the movement toured all over the country. The British government, in order to curb the activities of the leaders, took stern action. Tilak was prosecuted and prohibited from entering Punjab and Delhi. Annie Besant and her colleagues were interned.

Lucknow Pact

In 1916, the Congress and the Muslim League signed a pact in Lucknow to work together to attain self-government or Swaraj. The Congress accepted separate representation of Muslims in the Councils, thereby removing the Muslims apprehension of not getting proper representation. In 1916, the extremist and the moderate sections of the Congress were also reunited.

Arrival of Gandhiji

The Indian National Movement got a major turn by the end of the First World War, with the return of Mahatma Gandhi from South Africa in 1915. Influenced by Tolstoy, Ruskin and Thereau, Gandhiji gave shape to a new philosophy and method of struggle based on truth and non-violence. The concept of passive resistance or Satyagraha became the main weapon of the people's fight for freedom. He identified himself with the common people as no other national leader had done before. In 1917, Gandhiji arrived at Champaran in North Bihar to take up the cause of peasants suffering under an oppressive system of Indigo plantation. In 1918, his support of the workers's legitimate demands against textile mills owners in Ahmedabad led to arbitration and acceptance of the involvement of the common people in local issues. Gandhiji eventually emerged as the greatest leader in India's freedom struggle.

Jallianwala Bagh Tragedy

On April 13, 1919, a public meeting was held in the Jallianwala Bagh of Amritsar to protest against the arrest of two nationalist leaders, Satya Pal and Dr. Saifuddin Kitchlew. The Bagh or Park is surrounded by high walls on three sides and the entrance is through only a narrow tane. The meeting was peaceful, with young and old, men and women, taking part in it. However, a British military officer, General Dyer came there with his platoon. Without giving a warning, he ordered his troops to fire on the unarmed assembly. About a thousand people were killed and several thousand injured. The massacre aroused the fury of the Indian people which was replied with further brutalities by the government. In December 1919, the Congress session was held in Amritsar, to pay homage to the martyrs. Poet Rabindranath Tagore renounced his Knighthood in protest against the massacre.

Khilafat Movement

Turkey was among the defeated countries in the First World War while Britain was among the winners. Turkey and its ruler the Caliph or Khalifa were subjected to injustices by the British. Since Khalifa were the religious head of Muslims, a movement, was launched by Ali brothers Mohammad Ali and Shaukat Ali in 1920 to force the British government to undo the injustices. The Khilafat movement soon merged with the movement against the repression in Punjab and for Swaraj.

Non-Cooperation Movement

Under the leadership of Mahatma Gandhi, the Congress decided in 1920 to start the Non-Cooperation Movement. It was for the first time that the Congress decided to follow a policy of direct action. It involved the surrender of titles and honorary offices and resignation from nominated posts in local bodies. People were called upon not to attend government functions and withdraw their children from government schools and colleges. They were asked to boycott government jobs, courts and services. They were asked to use home-made clothes. Non-violence was to be strictly observed by the non-cooperators, and follow truth. Mahatma Gandhi promised Swaraj within one year if people followed his programme sincerely and whole-heartedly. The non-cooperation movement captured the imagination of the people, with Hindus and Muslims joining hands. In the next stage of the movement, a call was issued to the people to refuse to pay taxes. It was started in Bardoli in Gujarat.

The British government was totally shaken by the response to the noncooperation movement. However, some of the overzealous people on February 22, 1922 in Chauri Chaura in Uttar Pradesh, attacked a police station after being beaten up. 22 policemen, inside the Station were killed. Gandhiji, greatly disturbed at the incident, called off the movement. Gandhiji's move was criticised by several national leaders and the thankless British government sentenced Gandhiji to 6 years imprisonment. The Non-cooperation movement was a popular, spontaneous move, based on non-violence and religious amity.

Moplah Rebellion

The Moplahs of Malabar had been restless since middle of nineteenth century. The greatest of their rebellion took place in 1921 by an attack on the police who had arrested the Moplah criminals. The Moplahs were influenced in this attack by the Khilafat agitation in India. The rebels in two Taluks established their authority. The Hindus and the British were killed. However, the authorities imposed martial-law and used force to thwart the rebellion.

The Swarajist Party

Serious differences erupted among the Congress leaders following the termination of Non-cooperation movement. While C.R. Das, Moti Lal Nehru and Hakim Ajmal Khan were in favour of entry into legislative councils and obstruct their working, from within. Some others like Sardar Patel, C. Rajagopalachari and Rajendra Prasad opposed this.

The supporters of C.R. Das formed the Swarajist party in 1923 who were allowed by the Congress to contest the elections. The Swarajist party did well in central and provincial legislature. They played a significant role in keeping the anti-British spirit alive, passing several resolutions and forcing the British Government to be people sensitive. However, after the death of C.R. Das in 1925, the Swarajists found it difficult to do much in the legislature politics and in 1926, they walked out of the legislatures.

Simon Commission

In 1927, the British government appointed a Commission to enquire- into the working of the Government of India Act of 1919 and to suggest further reforms in the Constitution. It consisted of seven members of the British Parliament and chaired by Sir John Simon. The Congress and other Indian parties decided to boycott the Commission as it did not have representative from India. On its arrival; the Commission was greeted with a countrywide hartal: Wherever it went, the Commission faced strikes, demonstration and black flags. Lala Lajpat Rai, leading a massive demonstration against the Commission received several lathi blows from the police and finally succumbed to his injuries, a few weeks later. Govind Ballabh Pant was crippled for life, following lathi charge on him in Lucknow. The Commission visited India twice and its report was published in May 1930.

Demand for Complete Independence

In 1928, the Congress passed a resolution, demanding dominion status which was less than complete independence. It was also declared that if the dominion status was not granted by the end of 1929, the Congress would demand complete independence and would launch a mass movement to achieve the goal. The British government did not pay any heed to the Congress demand. So, in the Lahore session in December, 1929, a resolution was passed that the word Swaraj in the Congress Constitution would mean complete independence. At midnight of December, 1929, the tricolour flag of Independence was hoisted on the banks of river Ravi by the Congress President Jawaharlal Nehru. All Congressmen taking part in the national movement were asked not to participate in future elections and the sitting members were asked to resign their seats. It was decided to launch a programme of Civil disobedience, including the non-payment of taxes. January 26, 1930 was declared Independence Day and a pledge was taken by the people of India on that date and the same was repeated year after year.

Civil Disobedience Movement

The Civil Disobedience Movement began with the famous Dandi March of Gandhiji. The march began on March 12, 1930, when Gandhiji and his followers reached Dandi after covering 200 miles from Sabarmati Ashram. Gandhiji violated the Salt law which signalled the beginning of countrywide agitation. All over the country, liquor shops, opium dens and foreign cloth dealers shop were picketed. Hundreds of government servants left their jobs. Peasants refused to pay taxes and debts. Thousands of women came out to offer Civil disobedience in response to Gandhiji's stirring appeal. The country appeared to be in open revolt. The Government followed a policy of repression to suppress the movement. Thousands of Congress workers, including top leaders were sent to jail. Restrictions were put on the press, civilian property was destroyed, innocent men and women were beaten up and hundreds were killed in police firing. The movement had spread to every corner of the country.

Meanwhile, the British government convened the First Round Table Conference in London to consider the reforms proposed by the Simon Commission. Not much was achieved at the conference on account of the absence of any representative of Congress. Realising the importance of Congress, British government made efforts to persuade it to join the Second Round Table Conference. An agreement was signed on March 5, 1931 between Gandhiji and Viceroy Irwin, according to which the government agreed to release all political prisoners against whom there were no charges of violence. The Congress agreed to suspend the Civil Disobedience movement. Despite the Government's violation of its commitment, Gandhiji fulfilled his promise and went to London to attend the Conference.

The Second Round Table Conference was held in London in September, 1931. Gandhiji attended the Conference as sole representative of the Congress. He demanded control over defence and foreign affairs. There was a complete deadlock on the question of representation of minorities. M.A. Jinnah, Aga Khan and Dr. Ambedkar were not willing to corpe to a settlement with Mahatma Gandhi. The Indian princes were also not interested in India's independence. No agreement could be reached and the talks ended in a failure. Gandhiji returned to India and the Civil Disobedience movement was revived. The government again resorted to repressive measures, arresting lakhs of people, including Mahatma Gandhi. The Congress was declared illegal. In spite of the pressure, the Civil Disobedience movement continued. The boycott programme, no-tax campaign and picketing of liquor and foreign-made goods shops continued. The movement was suspended in May 1933 and a year later, completely withdrawn. Gandhiji also withdrew himself from active politics.

Communal Award

In August, 1932, the British government announced Communal Award, providing for separate electorates for Muslim, Sikh, European voters, depressed classes besides reservation for women. Gandhiji strongly opposed the scheme of separate electorates for the untouchables and undertook a fast unto death as a protest. An agreement was arrived at Poona, called Poona Pact, which considerably amended the award on the issue.

The Third Round Table Conference was held in November 1932 in London in which the Congress did not send any representative. A small number of Indian leaders and Princes attended the conference. The agreements reached at the round table conference and subsequent discussions led to the promulgation of Government of India Act, 1935. The Act sought to form All India federation, dyarchy at the centre, the federal legislature, the federal court and gave autonomy to the provincial legislatures. The Act did not make any reference even to granting dominion status, much less independence to India. The voting right was given only to 14 per cent of the population.

The Congress rejected the Act but decided to participate in the provincial legislative assemblies elections in 1937. Despite tacit support of the British to the communal and pro-government groups, the Congress swept the polls. It won absolute majority in six provinces and emerged as single largest party in three others. Muslim League, claiming to represent all the seats, could win less than a quarter of seats reserved for Muslims. The Congress formed ministries in 9 out of 11 provinces. These ministries did some useful work in the field of education, economic reforms and removing restrictions on the press and political activities.

Second World War and India

The Second World War began on September 1, 1939. Two days later, the Viceroy of India declared war against Germany without consulting or taking into confidence the Indian leaders. Indian troops were sent to battle fields to defend the British empire. The Indian leaders realised that fascist forces could not be trusted either. The Congress demanded that a national government should be immediately formed and Britain should promise to make India independent, immediately after the war. The British government refused to meet the demand and in November, 1939, the Congress ministries in the provinces resigned. In August, 1940, the Viceroy issued a statement saying that the new Constitution would be primarily a responsibility of Indians themselves. It however added that the representative Indian Constitution-making body would be setup after the war. It also refused to recognise the Congress as the sole representative of the Indians. The Congress wholly disappointed with the August offer, decided to launch individual Satyagraha movement.

In the World War, the British suffered severe reverses in the initial phases. Both in Asia and Europe, Japan and Germany respectively were gaining upper hand. In March 1942, Sir Stafford Cripps led mission came to India, with certain proposals with a view to seek the cooperation of the Congress. It seems the British were more keen to buy time, rather than agree to the formation of a truly national government. So, the talks with the Cripps mission failed.

Quit India Movement

On August 8, 1942, the Congress passed the 'Quit India' resolution, which declared that the immediate ending of the British rule was an urgent necessity, both for the sake of India and for the success of the cause of freedom and democracy, for which the countries of the United Nations were fighting. The resolution said that free India would join the forces who were against fascism and imperialist aggression. Mahatma Gandhi gave a mantra "Do or Die" to the people but cautioned that the movement should be non-violent. The next day itself, the government arrested senior leaders like Mahatma Gandhi, Jawahar Lal Nehru, Sardar Patel, Rajendra Prasad, Maulana Azad and others. The people, stunned and leaderless, carried on the movement in any way they could. All over the country, there were strikes in factories, schools, offices and public demonstrations. Angered by repeated firing and lathi-charges, the people took to violence at many places. Public property was damaged, with rail, postal and telegraph services badly affected. At some places, parallel governments were setup. The Quit India Movement was a grand popular revolt against the British empire. However, it failed due to lack of planning, arrest of top leaders, high handedness of the government, aloofness of the Muslim league and consolidation of Allied forces in the World War.

Wavell's Plan

After the failure of Cripps Mission and arrest of most of the congress leaders, political deadlock remained for around three years. Due to imprisonment of moderate leadership in the country, workers got demoralised and Muslim League, with the British cooperation, succeeded in expanding its area of influence. Meanwhile, Gandhiji, who was in jail, initiated communication with Jinnah to solve the problems but no agreement emerged. In May 1944 Gandhiji was released on medical grounds. Viceroy Wavell, in 1945 declared a plan which offered nothing to India except an opportunity to take part in the Central Government with the position of Viceroy and Commander-in-chief intact. The plan would have given several portfolios like Home, Finance and External Affairs to Indian members but the veto power would have been with the Viceroy. Wavell's plan had given six of the fourteen proposed seats in Executive Council to Muslims. However, both the Congress and the Muslim League rejected the plan though for different reasons. Wavell dropped the plan subsequently.

Azad Hind Fauj

The Azad Hind Fauj or the Indian National Army was setup by an Indian revolutionary Rash Behari Bose. He used the services of thousands of Indian soldiers of the British army who had been arrested by Japan while conquering South East Asia. Subhash Chandra Bose, who had gone to Germany to have talks with Hitler, came to Singapore in 1943 to lead the Indian Independence League and rebuild Azad Hind Fauj. Subhash Chandra Bose, or Netaji, proclaimed the formation of the provisional government of independent India on October 21, 1943. He led his INA in attacking the British government from the north-eastern India. He gave the slogans "Delhi Chalo" and "Jai Hind. The INA made some advances but suffered setbacks as the Japanese forces, the world over were being beaten by Allied forces. Moreover, the INA did not get the support of Indian nationalists who did not view the Japanese government as a friend of India. Netaji was reported killed in an air crash in 1945.

Cabinet Mission

After the end of second world war, Labour party won the general elections in Britain. In 1946, the British government announced its willingness to end their rule over India. They said India himself must decide her future Constitution and no minority in India would be allowed to place a veto on the advance of the majority. A Cabinet Mission was sent to India to hold negotiations with Indian leaders on the transfer of power. It proposed the formation of an interim government and the convening of a constituent assembly, composed of members elected by provincial legislatures and the nominee of the rulers of Indian states. Jawahar Lal Nehru formed the interim government on September 2, 1946. The constituent assembly met on December 9, 1946 but was boycotted by the Muslim League. They demanded a separate state of Pakistan. The British government had declared that it would transfer power into the Indian hands by a date not later than June 1948. Lord Mountbatten was sent to India as the Viceroy in March 1947 to oversee the handover of the charge. He presented a plan for the division of India into two Independent States — India and Pakistan. His plan came in the wake of increasing communal riots in several parts of India. However, the announcement of partition was followed by more riots, particularly in Punjab. Thousands were killed and lakhs became homeless.

The Congress, which had stood for a united India, agreed to the partition plan because it felt that there was no other way to achieve freedom and prevent further worsening of the situation. The Indian Independence Act was passed in July 1947 and India became independent on August 15, 1947. A separate country of Pakistan comprising West punjab, East Bengal, Sindh and North-West frontier province was created. According to the Independence Act, the boundaries of the provinces of Bengal, Assam and Punjab would be determined by a Commission. The legislatures of dominion would have full power to pass laws for dominions and no Act of British Parliament would extend to them. Till the framing of new constitutions, each dominion would be governed in accordance with the Government of India Act, 1935 and constituent assemblies would function, in the first instance, as the legislatures. The Indian Armed forces would be divided between India and Pakistan.

India After Partition

During the initial years of freedom, India had to face many problems. The partition was disastrous, involving lives and fortunes of millions of people. The division bred animosity between India and Pakistan which got reflected in their disputes concerning Kashmir, sharing of river waters, restoration of evacuee property and final settlement of boundaries. The partition and dislocation of millions of people adversely affected the economy. The problem of settlement of refugees was a big one. Moreover, the foundations of administration had been undermined by large scale defections and transfers to Pakistan. The British policy of ignoring the infrastructure sector, the problem of uniting Princely States and early deaths of formidable leaders like Mahatma Gandhi and Sardar Patel made the task of Indian Government a difficult one. However, patience, patriotism and determination helped the Indians triumph over their tribulations.

Religious and Social Reforms

In the second half of the 19th century, reform activities in religion and society gained momentum, taking India from medievalism to the modern age. The Indian mind gained new ideas, following contact with the foreigners, especially Europeans. The advent of modern and universal education also helped the reforms movement. Raja Ram Mohan Roy was the pioneer in the field. He first established Atmiya Sabha and later Brahmo Samaj in 1828. Brahmo Samaj advocated the worship of one God and the brotherhood of man, with respect for all religions and their scriptures. Ram Mohan Roy was a well read man. He published a journal and made contribution to literature also. He stood for the abolition of Sati, the inhuman practice of burning the wife alive with the dead body of the husband. His efforts bore fruit in 1829 when the government banned Sati.

After the premature death of Raja Ram Mohan Roy, the Brahmo Samaj had a doctrine till Devendra Nath Tagore took over the leadership. Tagore had earlier founded a cultural organisation, Tattvabodhini Sabha. He converted the Brahmo Samaj into a spiritual fraternity. Keshav Chandra Sen was also an important leader of the Samaj, but his stress on. Christian and Vaishnav teachings and support to inter-cast and widow remarriage led to the division of the Brahmo Samaj.

The supporters of Brahmo Samaj spread to several places in the country. In Maharashtra, under their, influence, Prarthna Samaj was established by Dr. Atma Ram Pandurang. The objective was rational worship and social reforms. They started night schools for the working class, formed association for educating girls and ran orphanages. They stressed in intermarriage among different castes, remarriage of widows and improvement of the lot of women and depressed classes. One of the member of the Samaj, Justice M.G. Ranade also founded Deccan Education Society. R.G. Bhandarkar was another important leader of the Samaj. G.K. Gokhale founded the Servants of India Society and N.M. Joshi started the Social Service League.

The Arya Samaj took inspiration from India's past and derived its basic principles from its ancient scriptures. It was founded by Swami Dayananda Saraswati. His motto was "Go to the Vedas". He believed in one God and decried polytheism and the use of images. He opposed casteism, child-marriage and prohibition of sea-voyage. He encouraged female education and widow remarriage. He began the Shuddhi movement to convert non-Hindus to Hinduism. Mahatma Hans Raj, Guru Dutt Vidyarthi and Lala Lajpat Rai were the leaders of the Arya Samaj.

The Theosophical Society was started by two Americans, Col. Alcott and Madam Blavatsky who made Adyar, near Madras the headquarter of the Society. The Society had great faith in the ancient religions and worked for the revival, strengthening and uplifting of Hinduism, Buddhism and Zoroastrianism. This brought in a new self-respect, a pride in the past, a belief in the future and as a result, a great wave of patriotic life and the beginning of the rebuilding of a nation.

Pandit Ishwar Chandra Vidyasagar and Malabari worked for the uplifting of women.

The Ramakrishna Mission was setup by Swami Vivekananda in the memory of his guru, Ramakrishna Paramhansa. The followers of the mission are free thinkers, synthesising the thinking of Oriental as well as Western. The Mission aimed at the spiritual development of the man, along with idol worship and modern developments in natural sciences and technology. It undertook social service, opening several schools and dispensaries and helping people at the time of distress. Swami Vivekananda promoted patriotism, besides advocating superiority of Hindu culture and civilisation. He insisted on character-building, discipline and strength of mind.

Among the Muslims, the urge of change began quite later. Sir Syed Ahmed Khan took the initiative to bring about a change in the outlook of the Muslims. He started a college in Aligarh. He advocated abolition of Purdah and education of women. He helped in the establishment of several Anjumans or societies to serve the Muslim community.

Among the Sikhs, Shiromani Gurudwara Prabhandak Committee was setup to get rid of the corrupt Mahants or priests, and reform the Gurudwaras. Several schools and colleges were also started. Nirankari, Namdhari and Akali movements were part of reforms in the Sikh religion.

Governor-Generals and Viceroys of India

Year	Name
1772	Warren Hastings
1786	Earl Cornwallis
1793	Sir John Shore
1798	Earl Wellesley
1807	Baron Minto I
1813	Earl of Moira
1823	Earl Amherst
1828	Lord William Bentinck
1836	Earl of Auckland
1842	Earl of Ellenborough
1844	Sir-Henry Hardinge
1848	Earl of Dalhousie
1856	Earl Canning
1862	Earl of Elgin (I)
1864	Sir John Lawrence
1869	Earl of Mayo
1872	Earl of Northbrook
1876	Earl Lytton I
1884	Earl of Duffrein
1888	Marquess of Lansdowne

Year	Name
1894	Earl of Elgin II
1905	Earl Minto II
1910	Baron Hardinge
1916	Baron Chelmsford.
1921	Earl of Reading
1926	Lord Irwin
1931	Earl of Willingdon
1936	Lord of Linlithgow
1943	Earl Wavell
1947	Earl Mountbatten (First Govemor-General of Free India)
1948	Chakravarthi Rajagopalachari (First Indian to be the Governor-General)

Important dates in Indian History

BC	
2400	Indus Valley seals, dating back to this age, found
563	Birth of Gautama Buddha
540	Birth of Mahavira
483	Nirvana of Gautama Buddha
468	Nirvana of Mahavira
327-326	Alexander's invasion of India
321	Rise of Maurya dynasty
273-232	Reign of Ashoka
187	Rise of dynasty of Pushyamitra
58	Vikrama Era begins

AD	
78	Saka Era begins
320	Gupta dynasty comes to power
399-414	Chinese traveller Fa-hien comes to India
606	Accession of Harshavardhana
609	Chalukya King Pulakesin II ascends the throne
622	Hijra era begins
636	First recorded Arab expedition comes to Indian Coast, the main objective being loot
713	Capture of Multan by Muslims
753	Rise of Rashtrakuta empire
788	Birth of Adi Sankaracharya
836	Bhoja I becomes King of Kannary
893	Pratihara King Mahendrapala I ascends
1014	Mahmud of Ghazni defeats Hindu Kings in the Battle of Thanesar
1026	Mahmud of Ghazni plunders and ransacks Somnath Temple
1191	In the first battle of Tarain (Taraori),. Prithviraj Chauhan defeats Muhammad Ghori
1192	In the second battle of Tarain, Muhammed Ghori defeats Prithviraj Chauhan
1206	Muhammed Ghori dies; Qutb-ud-din establishes Slave Dynasty
1210	Death of Qutb-ud-din
1211	Accession of Iltutmish
1221	Mongols under Chengiz Khan invade India
1236	Razia Sultan crowned queen of Delhi
1265	Accession of Balban
1290	Khilji dynasty takes over in Delhi
1320	Ghiyas-ud-din Tughlaq establishes Tughlaq dynasty
1333	Ibn Batutah arrives in India
1398	Timur Lang invades India
1469	Birth of Guru Nanak, founder of Sikhism
1498	Vasco-da-Gama, a portuguese sailor, discovers sea route to India
1510	The Portuguese settle in Goa
1526	In the first battle of Panipat, Babur defeats Ibrahim Lodhi and established Mughal dynasty
1527	Battle of Khanwah
1529	Battle of Ghagra
1530	Death of Babur and accession of Humayun
1538	Death of Guru Nanak
1539	Sher Shah defeats Humayun at Chunar

1545 Death of Sher Shah
1555 Humayun regains the throne of Delhi
1556 Akbar ascends the throne following death of Humayun; In the second battle of Panipat Akbar defeats Hemu
1565 Battle of Talikota in which the Vijayanagar King is defeated by combined forces of Ahmednagar, Golkunda and Bidar
1576 In the battle of Haldighati, Mughal forces defeat the forces of Mewar's ruler Rana Pratap
1581 Din-i-Elahi—Divine faith promulgated
1597 Death of Rana Pratap
1600 Mughal forces defeat Chand Bibi of Ahmednagar and annex it. East India Company given charter by Queen Elizabeth to trade with East Indies
1605 Death of Akbar and accession of Jahangir
1606 Fifth Sikh guru Arjun executed
1612 First English factory set up at Surat
1627 Death of Jahangir; Birth of Shivaji
1628 Shahjahan becomes Mughal emperor
1646 Shivaji captures Torna
1657 War of succession begins following Shahjahan's illness; Shivaji raids Ahmednagar and Junnar
1658 Aurangzeb coronated after victories in battles of Dharmat and Samugarh.
1666 Shahjahan dies; Shivaji visits the Mughal court at Agra and escapes after being imprisoned
1675 Ninth Sikh Guru Tegh Bahadur executed
1680 Death of Shivaji
1707 Death of Aurangzeb
1739 Persian King Nadir Shah invades India
1747 Ahmad Shah Abdali invades India
1757 Nawab of Bengal, Siraj-ud-daulah defeated by English forces in battle of Plassay; Abadali enters Delhi and plunders
1760 Battle of Wandiwash, leading to French forces defeat at the hands of English. forces, ending French political ambition in India
1761 Ahmed Shah Abdali-defeats the Marathas in the third battle of Panipat
1764 English forces defeat combined forces of Nawab of Bengal and Awadh
1765 The British get Diwani rights of Bengal, Bihar and Orissa
1767-69 First Mysore war
1770 Great Bengal famine
1775-82 First Anglo-Maratha war
1780-84 Second Mysore war
1784 Pitt's India Act
1789-92 Third Mysore War
1793 Permanent Settlement of Bengal, Bihar and Orissa
1799 Fourth Mysore war; Death of Tipu Sultan
1803-05 Second Anglo-Maratha war
1817-19 Last Anglo-Maratha war
1824-26 First Burmese war
1829 Prohibition of Sati
1839 Death of Maharaja Ranjit Singh; First Anglo-Afghan war begins
1845-46 First Anglo-Sikh war
1848-49 Second Anglo-Sikh war
1852 Second Anglo-Burmese war
1853 First Railway line in India between Bombay and Thane
1857 The Sepoy Mutiny
1858 East India Company abolished; British government takes over the Administration of India
1861 Indian Councils Act passed; Indian High Courts Act for a High Court in each Presidency passed
1869 Birth of Mahatma Gandhi
1878-80 Second Anglo-Afghan war
1883 Ilbert Bill
1885 First session of Indian National Congress

1892	Indian Councils Act
1905	Partition of Bengal; Launch of Swadeshi movement
1906	Formation of Muslim League; Congress declaration of Swaraj as its aim
1909	Morley-Minto reforms; Separate electorates for the Muslims provided
1911	King George V visits India; Delhi Darbar held; Transfer of Capital of India from Calcutta to Delhi; Partition of Bengal annulled
1916	Lucknow Pact of the Congress and the Muslim League; Moderates and Extremists in the Congress come together; Home Rule League founded
1919	Montagu-Chelmsford reforms; Third Anglo-Afghan war; Jallianwala Bagh massacre; Rowlatt Act passed
1920	Khilafat Movement and Non-Co-operation Movement started
1921	Moplah rebellion among the Muslims of Malabar; Chauri-Chaura incident
1923	Swarajists enter legislative councils
1927	Appointment of Simon Commission
1929	Resolution of complete independence passed at the Lahore session of the Congress
1930	Civil Disobedience movement launched; Dandi March by Gandhiji; First Round Table Conference in London
1931	Irwin-Gandhi Pact; Second Round Table Conference; Civil Disobedience Movement suspended
1932	Communal award; Gandhiji goes on fast; Pune Pact; Third Round Table Conference
1935	New Government of India Act; Burma separated from India
1939	British government declares India to be party in the second world war; Congress ministries in provinces resign in protest
1942	Cripps Mission comes to India; The Congress rejects its offers; Quit India movement launched; Most of the prominent leaders arrested
1943	Bengal famine; Indian National Army organised by Subhash Chandra Bose
1944	Gandhi-Jinnah talks in Bombay to break the constitutional deadlock
1945	Simla Conference; Wavell plan fails;Trial of INA men opens
1946	Mutiny in Indian Navy; Cabinet Mission visits India; Interim government formed; Constituent assembly holds its first meeting; Muslim League withdraws from the interim government and decides on a policy of direct action
1947	British government announces its intention to transfer power to the Indian representatives not later than June 1948; Lord Mountbatten appointed Viceroy of India; Plan for partition of India announced; Indian Independence Act passed; Country divided into two nations; Communal riots break out; Jawaharlal Nehru sworn-in as the first Prime Minister of free India; Kashmir signs instrument of accession; Indian troops reach Kashmir
1948	Mahatma Gandhi assassinated; C. Rajagopalachari becomes the Governor-General

Battles and Wars in India

- **Battle of Hydaspes (326 BC):** Alexander's forces defeated the Indian King Porus on the banks of Jhelum.
- **War against Selukas (305 BC):** Selukas Nikator, the ruler appointed by Alexander was defeated by Chandragupta Maurya in 305 BC and he had to relinquish territory.
- **Battle of Kalinga (261 BC):** The Mauryan King Ashoka defeated the King of Kalinga after a bloody war. The bloodshed moved Ashoka to embrace Buddhism and preach peace.

- **Battle of Thanesar (1014 AD):** Mahmud of Ghazni defeated the ruler of Thanesar, Anandpal.
- **First Battle of Tarain (1191 AD):** Rajput ruler of Delhi, Prithviraj Chauhan defeated Sultan of Ghazni, Muhammad Ghori.
- **Second Battle of Tarain (1192 AD):** Muhammad Ghori took revenge against Prithviraj Chauhan.
- **First Battle of Panipat (1526 AD):** Babar defeated Ibrahim Lodhi, laying the foundation stone of Mughal empire.
- **Battie of Khanwah (1527 AD):** Babar defeated Rajput ruler of Mewar, Rana Sanga.
- **Battle of Chausa (1539 AD):** Sher Shah Suri defeated Humayun and became the Ruler of Delhi.
- **Second Battle of Panipat (1556 AD):** Akbar's General Bairam Khan defeated Hemu, the General of Muhammad Shah Adil.
- **Battle of Talikota (1565 AD):** Allied forces of Bijapur, Bidar; Ahmednagar and Golkonda defeated the King of Vijayanagar.
- **Battle of Haldighati (1576 AD):** The Battle of Haldighati was fought between Rana Pratap of Mewar and Mughal army led by Man Singh and Asif Khan.
- **Invasion by Nadir Shah (1739 AD):** Nadir Shah, Ruler of Iran, attacked India and defeated Mughal forces. He plundered Delhi and massacred the citizens.
- **Battle of Plassey (1757 AD):** British forces defeated Nawabs of Bengal, Sirajud-daula and laid the foundation stone of their empire.
- **Battle of Wandiwash (1760 AD):** British forces defeated their French counterpart, sealing their fate in India.
- **Third Battle of Panipat (1761 AD):** Marathas were defeated by Ahmed Shah Abdali.
- **Battle of Buxar (1764 AD):** British forces defeated the combined forces of Mir Qasim of Bengal and Shah Alam of Oudh.
- **First Anglo-Maratha War (1775-82 AD):** British troops defeated Marathas.
- **Second Anglo-Maratha War (1803-05 AD):** Inconclusive.
- **Third Anglo-Maratha War (1817-1818 AD):** Marathas were conclusively defeated.
- **First Anglo-Mysore War (1766-69 AD):** Alliance of British, Nizam of Hyderabad and Marathas fought against Hyder Ali.
- **Second Anglo-Mysore War (1780-84):** British forces and Hyder Ali faught the inconclusive war.
- **Third Anglo-Mysore War (1789-92):** British forces defeated Tipu Sultan.
- **Fourth Anglo-Mysore War (1799):** Tipu Sultan died fighting the British forces.
- **First Sikh War (1846):** British forces defeated Sikh armies.
- **Second Sikh War (1849):** British forces annexed Punjab from Sikh rulers.
- **Indian Revolt (1857):** The revolt by severa! leaders and armies of certain areas was suppressed brutally by the British forces.
- **Indo-China War (1962):** China attacked India unilaterally and annexed some areas. India repulsed and by the time the international agencies intervened, China had already taken over some Indian land.
- **Indo-Pakistan War (1965):** Pakistan attacked India but had to suffer severe setbacks. India had an upper hand.
- **Indo-Pak War (1971):** Pakistan declared war against India. India retaliated strongly; got East Bengal liberated from Pakistan and went deep inside Pakistani territory. After ceasefire, the territory was returned.
- **Kargil War (1999):** Pakistani infiltrators crossed the LoC; Indian army launched 'Operation Vijay'. Infiltrators pulled back and captured all territory. Indian causualty were 407 dead, 584 wounded and six missing.

Indian National Leaders

Mahatma Gandhi

Mohandas Karamchand Gandhi, the Father of the Nation was born on October 2, 1869 at Porbander in Kathiawar. At the age of 79, on January 30, 1948, he was shot dead at Delhi. He was a barristor, by profession. During his stay in South Africa in connection with a professional work, he was initiated into politics. He learnt the lessons of non-violence, truth and grew up resisting the evil, the wrong and the injustice. He came to India in 1915, after gaining name and stature. During his early political years in India, Gandhiji had faith in the love of justice of the Englishmen. So, he asked Indians to cooperate with the British government. But soon, the sympathy evaporated as he saw the ruthlessness and insincerity of the British. He took over the Congress, and believing in the ideal of Hindu-Muslim unity, combined his non-cooperation movement with the Khilafat movement. He withdrew the movement following upsurge of violence, which he said was mandatory.

Gandhiji dominated not only the Congress but also the entire politics of the country. Though several leaders differed with him on issues and principles, yet respected him. He went on fast on many occasions for various causes. He made the nationalist movement a mass movement, involving people irrespective of caste, religion, sex or region. Gandhiji was very firm in his beliefs. He defied the might of the British empire, to get the country liberated and the people emancipated. Gandhiji was a great social reformer, taking up the cause of the depressed classes in India and asking the upper caste Hindus to give up their prejudices. He advocated the policy of prohibition. He advocated the rights of women and stood for giving them equal status with men. Gandhiji advocated a system of education which was more suited to Indian needs and had utilitarian value. Gandhiji stood for Swadeshi, with special emphasis on Khadi.

He advocated the establishment of cottage industries and making villages self-dependent. Gandhiji was a religious man, always reading 'Gita' and worshipping. But he was not a bigot. He put great emphasis on communal unity. During the partition, there were communal riots at several places. It was the fast of Gandhiji for 72 hours that brought about change of atmosphere in Calcutta. He had to pay through his life for bringing peace and communal harmony in the country.

Jawahar Lal Nehru

Popularly known as Pt. Nehru or Chacha Nehru, he was born in a rich family on November 14, 1889 in Allahabad. He died on May 27, 1964. He studied for the bar in England. After his retum, he came in contact with Gandhiji and was deeply influenced. He plunged into active politics, going to jail several times. He was instrumental in the passing of the Congress resolution in Lahore, demanding complete independence. He was a true follower of Gandhiji and fully subscribed to the doctrine of non-violence. Pt. Nehru was a humanist, socialist and internationalist. When the British decided to make India independent, Pt. Nehru was the automatic choice. He followed a policy of non-alignment which was liked by several other countries. He worked for the end of colonialism, and apartheid and the strengthening of the UNO. In the field of development he believed in planning and socialism. As Chairman of the Planning Commission, he drafted schemes for the rapid industrialisation and progress of the country. He encouraged scientific temperament. His firm belief in the democracy and secularism is reflected in the Constitution. He was a great author, having written three famous books during stay in the prison—"The Discovery of India, “Glimpses of World History” and “An Autobiography”.

Rabindranath Tagore

The youngest son of Maharshi Debendranath, was born on May 7, 1861. Born in a talented, and scholarly family, he had most of his education at home. Full of creativity, he started composing verses and proses which had a distinct note of originality in theme and technique. His genius expressed itself through every form of literature besides music, dance and painting. He was awarded the Nobel Prize for literature for his work GITANJALI in 1913. Tagore was an educationist, involved in designing policy for the country. He was, however, against the nationalists demand to boycott government schools and foreign goods. He started a school at Santiniketan and a university named Vishwa Bharati. Tagore was a humanist, who rose above the narrow divisions to give people the vision of peace and love. Tagore wanted the spiritual freedom of the human spirit. He spoke against the social evils in the country, asserting that the Indians will have to put their own house in order before their demands could be heard by the foreign masters. Tagore had a broad outlook and he was the cultural messenger of India. He opposed the British government at the time of partition of Bengal and even gave up his Knighthood after Jallianwala Bagh tragedy. But, he felt that the British rule also brought in some positive features and these should be accepted. Rabindranath was a critic as well as admirer of Mahatma Gandhi. He died in 1941.

Vallabh Bhai Patel

Born in 1875, he was known as the Iron man of India. Popularly called Sardar, he did to India what Bismark did for Germany unification or Garibaldi did for Italy. The name 'Sardar' was given by Gandhiji after he became the hero of famous Bardoli Satyagraha by the peasants against the unjust increase in land revenue. He had his education in law in England and then started a flourishing practice at Ahmedabad. But he soon gave it up after coming under the irresistible spell of Mahatma Gandhi. He became an important leader of Congress and was known for his strong actions and determination. He played a crucial role in negotiations with the Britishers. In Nehru's Cabinet, he was the Deputy Prime Minister besides holding the portfolios of Home and Information and Broadcasting. His most important contribution was the unification of princely states into a unified country. He used tact and even threat, wherever it was needed to make the states fall in line. He abolished the ICS and brought in new IAS to administer the country. He contributed significantly to the Constitution of India. He ably solved the huge problem of refugee influx and communal violence. He was a successful administrator and even a frontrunner for the post of Prime Minister of free India. His untimely death in 1950 left a big vacuum which could never be filled.

Subhash Chandra Bose

Born in 1897, he was popularly called Netaji. He was a doughty champion of freedom, and intrepid fighter. His political mentor was Chittaranjan Das. He worked with the terrorists for a while and was jailed for 3 years. Later, he joined Congress and became its President twice. But he was forced to resign because of ideological fight with the old guard led by Gandhiji. He then started Forward Block. He was totally opposed to the idea of India contributing to the British efforts in the world war. He was kept under house arrest but he escaped mysteriously. He went to Germany and met Hitler. Then he went to Japan and reorganised Indian National Army with the help of Japanese army. He brought INA to the Burmese front to fight the British government. He established a provisional government of free India and gave a famous battle cry *'Delhi Chalo'*. But due to unfamiliar terrain, lack of training and setbacks of Japan, INA could not march further. He left Rangoon in a Japanese plane for an unknown destination: The plane was reported to have crashed over Formosa and he is reported to have died in the crash. The death remain shrouded in mystery. He was posthumously awarded Bharat Ratna but his family members did not accept it.

Swami Vivekananda

Swami Vivekananda was born in Calcutta in 1865 and his original name was Narendra Nath Dutta. At the young age itself, he became a Sanyasi and travelled all over in search of truth. He was the disciple of Ramakrishna Paramhansa, who was a priest in a Kali temple. He preachad and practised the highest ideals of Hindu religion and philosophy, besides serving the poor and the lowly. He called upon his countrymen to shake off the age-old lethargy, remove the abuses that had crept into their society and work for the freedom of their motherland. He insisted on character-building, on discipline and on strength of mind, physical and spiritual. He contributed towards the social and cultural regeneration of the nation. He stood for social reforms and was concerned about the position of woman in the society. His speech in the Parliament of Religions at Chicago on September 11, 1893 stirred the West. He established Ramakrishna Mission to train workers, entirely devoted to the social and national service. He died at a young age of 37 years in 1902.

Swami Dayanand Saraswati

He was a great Hindu Social reformer and the founder of Arya Samaj. He was born in 1824 and was called 'Mool Shanker'. A few experiences in his daily life during the childhood made him an opponent of idol worship. He fought for the removal of untouchability, widow remarriage and the abolition of social evils. He introduced the 'Sudhi Movement' for conversion of other religionists to Hinduism. He had great influence on the masses of North India. He regarded the Vedas as infallible, as the inspired word of God and the fountain of all knowledge. He called for 'Back to Vedas'. He was opposed to idolatry, rituals and priesthood, and prevalent caste practices. He died in 1883.

Bal Gangadhar Tilak

Born in 1856, he was affectionately called Lokmanya Tilak by millions of his countrymen. He was one of the chief architects of freedom movement in India. He was uncompromisingly opposed to British imperialism and used his two newspapers *'Kesari'* and 'Maratha' to propagate his staunch nationalistic ideals. He was arrested on several occasions. He opposed the partition of Bengal. Alongwith Annie Besant, he launched the Home Rule Movement. He belonged to the famous 'Lal-Bal-Pal' triumvirate who were considered of having extreme views. He was not a communalist but thought it was not improper to arouse religious feelings of the people to fight the foreign rule. He revived the Ganesh Puja in his home state, Maharashtra and brought back the memories of Chhatrapati Shivaji. He had his differences with Mahatma Gandhi and this led to split in the Congress. He died in 1920.

Bhim Rao Ramji Ambedkar

Born in 1891 in a Scheduled Caste family, he became a well known jurist, statesman, social reformer and leader of the depressed class. He had to struggle a lot in his childhood and that made him determined to fight the caste tyranny. He organised All India Depressed Classes Federation for this purpose. In 1927, he organized a Satyagraha movement to establish the civic rights of the untouchables. He was a powerful writer and used the media to propagate his message. He was elected to the legislative assembly from 1926 to 1934. He demanded a separate electorate for depressed classes but gave it up after a pact with Gandhiji. He became a member of the Viceroy's Executive Council in 1942. He was the chairman of the drafting body of the Constitution and the Constitution bears the imprint of his farsightedness. He was the first law minister of free India and was responsible for the Hindu Code Bill. He died in 1956.

Maulana Abul Kalam Azad

Born in 1888, he stood tallest among nationalist Muslims and was one of the chief policy makers of the Indian National Congress. He was an editor of a journal, espousing the cause of the nationalist. In 1920, he came under the spell of Gandhiji and participated in Khilafat and Non-Cooperation movements. He presided over the Delhi Congress session in 1923 and advocated the entry to the council and to carry the fight into the Legislatures. He was elected Congress President in 1939 and remained in the position till 1946. He was against partition and appealed to Gandhiji to use his influence in preventing it. He was called 'Showboy of Congress' by Jinnah and Muslim League. After Independence, he became the education minister and was instrumental in establishing the University Grants Commission. His autobiography 'India Wins Freedom' created a controversy when he withheld its last thirty pages and were published 30 years after his death in 1958.

Sarojini Naidu

Born in 1879, she was a poetess besides a full time participant in the national movement. She was a follower of Gandhiji and went on to become the first woman president of the Congress. She was affectionately called the nightingale of India. She was the Governor of Uttar Pradesh from 1947 to 48. She died in 1948.

Mohammad Ali Jinnah

Born in 1876, he is known as Qaid-e-Azam by the people of Pakistan for creating a country on the basis of religion. He was highly westernised in his outlook. He began his political career at the Calcutta Session of Congress in 1906 and became a member of the Central Legislative Council representing the Muslims of Bombay. He resigned his membership following the promulgation of Rowlatt Act. He was never an ardent follower of Muslim religion and once Gokhale even praised him as a symbol of Hindu-Muslim unity. In 1920, he resigned from the Congress and became a member of Muslim League which championed the cause of Muslims only. In the 1937 provincial elections, the congress won most of the seats. Jinnah suggested a coalition with his party. The rejection of his proposal embittered him and made him a fanatical protagonist of 2 nation theory. When Congress formed an interim government at the Centre from which the League stood out by choice, he called for a direct action day which led to violence at several places and deaths to innocent persons. Pakistan came into being on 14 August, 1947 and he became its first Governor General. It is believed that he died in 1948, completely disillusioned with the state of affairs in Pakistan and wished that he had not been instrumental in creating it.

Rajendra Prasad

Popularly known as Rajen Babu, he was born in the Saran district of Bihar in 1884. He was a lawyer by profession. Starting with the Champaran Satyagraha of 1917, he went on to become a trusted lieutenant of Gandhiji. He took part in several national movements and went to prison also. He was an educationist also, setting up National College at Patna. He joined the interim government in 1946 and later became President of the Constituent Assembly. He was sworn in as the first President when the Constitution came into effect. He stayed in office for two terms. He died in 1963.

Lala Lajpat Rai

Born in 1865, he was affectionately called the lion of Punjab. He advocated aggressive nationalism. He instilled self-confidence in the minds of people and made them look definitely at the foreign rulers through his fiery speeches and actions. He was an active member of the Arya Samaj. He joined the Congress in 1888 but soon became disheartened with it and called it a party of holiday patriots who merely mouthed meaningless platitudes. He turned his attention to social and educational reforms. He was deported to Burma for sometimes by the British rulers. He joined Congress once more and became its President in 1920 but did not see eye to eye with Gandhiji on the question of non-violence. He was responsible for founding All India Trade Union Congress. In 1925, he joined Swaraj Party but soon parted. In 1928, while leading a demonstration against the Simon Commission, he was brutally beaten up by a policeman. He died a few days later. He constituted a triumvirate with Tilak and Bipin Chandra Pal.

Sri Aurobindo

He was born in 1872 to a rich family. He was thoroughly westernised in his outlook in his early years. He passed I.C.S. examination in London but could not join the service because he refused to take the compulsory horse riding test. He returned to India and worked as administrator and Professor. In 1906, he became deeply involved in the freedom movement. He wrote for newspapers and started his own Bengali daily 'Yugantar'. He was arrested as an accused in Alipore Conspiracy case but was acquitted for the want of evidence. The case brought about a change in him. He retired from active politics and settled down in Pondicherry in 1910, devoting all his time to spiritual pursuits. He represented the amazing phenomenon of a revolutionary in politics taking to a spiritual life and becoming a saintly soul universally adored. He died in 1950.

Bhagat Singh

He was born in 1907 in Punjab. At a young age of 18, he joined the revolutionary organisation—Hindustan Socialist Republican Army. He organised Naujawan Bharat Sabha in Punjab. To avenge the fatal lathi attack on Lala Lajpat Rai, he killed the police officer Saunders responsible for the attack. On April 8, 1929, he and B.K. Dutta exploded bombs in the Central Legislative Assembly to protest against the British's anti-people attitude. He was arrested.

In the Saunders' murder case, he was sentenced to death and along with Sukhdev and Rajguru was hanged in 1931. His act of bravery and slogan of "Inquilab Zindabad" inspired several youths for the national cause.

Chakravarthi Rajgopalachari

He was born in a village in Salem district in 1878. He was a successful practising lawyer when he decided to join the national movement. He took part in all the main movements launched by the Congress. He led the Congress to victory in the 1937 provincial elections in Tamil Nadu and became the premier. He came up with a formula to solve the constitutional tangle in 1944, popularly called Rajaji formula. He was a minister in the interim cabinet and then joined as Bengal Governor. In 1948, he took over as the first Indian Governor-General of India till the Constitution came into effect. He then joined the Nehru cabinet and later became the Chief Minister of Madras. Due to differences with the Congress on social and economic issues, Rajaji founded the Swatantra Party in 1959. He advocated prohibition, and Khadi and criticised the nuclear weapons. He died in 1972.

Syed Ahmed Khan

Born in 1817, Sir Syed Ahmed Khan was responsible for bringing about a change in the outlook of the Muslims. He asked the Muslims to change their social, political, religious and educational ideas and bring about a working harmony between the East and the West. He went to England and on his return, started Muslim Anglo-Oriental College at Aligarh in 1875 which ultimately grew into a University. He was also in favour of the abolition of Purdah and education of women. His life-work stirred several prominent muslims who came forward to work for their community. He was given knighthood by the British government. He died in 1898.

Gopal Krishna Gokhale

Born in 1866, he was a typical representative of the moderate school in Congress. He also enjoyed the confidence of British rulers. He joined Congress at the young age of 23 and was soon selected to given evidence before the Welby Commission on Indian expenditure. He was elected to the Imperial Legislative Council for successive terms from 1901 to 1915. He presided over Benaras session of Congress in 1905. He participated in the formulation of Minto-Morley reforms of 1909. He laid the foundation of Servants of India Society to train the national missionaries for the service of India and to promote true Interests of Indians through constitutional means. He denounced the caste system and untouchability. He worked for emancipation of women and spread of education. Gokhle has often been described as India's Gladstone for his brilliance in parliamentary debates. When Gandhiji came to India, he treated Gokhale as his political Guru. Gokhle died in 1915.

Annie Besant

She was born in 1847 in Ireland. After an unsuccessful marriage and separation from her husband, she plunged into the public life, campaigning for a free thought. She joined the Fabian Society initially but came to India subsequently to become the President of Theosophical society. Though new to the country, she was deeply interested in Hindu and other ancient religions. She made Madras her Headquarter. She edited a newspaper called 'New India' which furthered the cause of Indian nationalism. She started Home Rule Movement in the country. She presided over the Calcutta session of the Congress in 1917. She established many educational institutions. She died in 1933.

Jaya Prakash Narayan

Born in 1902, he was educated in the United States. He became a follower of Marxism but later joined Congress. Along with Lohia, Achyut Patwardhan, Acharya Narender Dev, he founded the Congress Socialist Party—a splinter group within the Congress itself. He played an important role in the Quit India Movement. After independence, the socialists broke away from the parent organization. But in 50s, he was attracted by Vinobaji's Bhoodan movement and he gave up active politics. He continued to work for the socio-economic changes brought about by

Gandhi philosophy. However, in 1974, he came out of his retirement and took part in the agitation launched by students against the Bihar government. People then called him Lok Nayak. He then led people against the Indira government at the Centre which he thought was corrupt and anti people. He was instrumental in bringing together various opposition groups into Janta Party which won 1977 general elections. But the endless squabbling left him a frustrated, disappointed man. He died in 1979.

Rafi Ahmed Kidwai

Born in 1894, he was a staunch nationalist Muslim. He came under the influence of Gandhiji and jumped into the national struggle. He led an agrarian movement and no-tax campaign in his home state, Uttar Pradesh. In 1946, he became Home Minister of U.P. Later, he became Union Minister of Communication and then, Minister of Food and Agriculture. He was an orthodox muslim but held liberal views in regard to the emancipation of women. He died in 1954.

Jamna Lal Bajaj

Born in 1889 he belonged to a very rich family in Wardha. He renounced his wealth at an early age and became a disciple of Gandhi. He surrendered the title of Raj Bahadur in protest against British atrocities. He took part in the freedom movement and suffered imprisonments. He worked for the uplift of Harijans, women's education and promotion of basic education. He was the treasurer of Congress from 1920 till his death in 1942. He gave Sevagram to Gandhiji in 1936. An award was instituted in his name for promoting contribution in the field of constructive work.

Pandit Madan Mohan Malaviya

He was born in 1861 into a poor family and educated himself with great difficulty. He started, his career as a teacher but soon changed over to journalism and launched a Hindi weekly and an English daily. He attacked the unpopular measures of the British government with his pen. He joined Congress and became its President on four occasions. He started Hindu Mahasabha to counter Muslim Communalism. He founded Benaras Hindu Assembly for six years and resigned from the membership to participate in Gandhiji's salt satyagraha. He was invited by the British govemment to participate in the 1st Round Table Conference. He had courage of conviction and did not hesitate to openly disagree with Gandhiji on several occasions. He died in 1946.

Chittaranjan Das

Born in 1870, he was affectionately called Deshbandhu by his compatriots. He was a legal luminary and a brilliant intellectual. In 1908, he defended Sri Aurobindo successfully in the famous Alipore Conspiracy Case. After 1917, he began his brief but meteoric career in politics. In 1920, when Gandhiji started his Non-Cooperation Movement, he vehemently opposed the boycott of Councils. But then convinced by Gandhiji's arguments, he gave up his lucrative legal practice and began to lead an austere life. He was elected President of the Gaya Congress. He died in 1925. He was a leader of Swaraj Party that advocated opposition from within to the British government.

Vasudeo Balvant Phadke

Born in 1845, he is regarded as the first revolutionary of modern India to have taken up arms to drive away the British. He is called the father of the armed struggle for India's freedom and is said to have inspired Bankim Chandra to write the patriotic novel 'Anand Math'. He joined the public agitation for redressing people's grievances at Pune in 1870 and took a vow to use only homespun cloth and Swadeshi articles. He established the first school of national education in Pune in 1874. He established a secret organisation to work for overthrowing the British power in India. His efforts met with limited success. He was captured in 1879 and sentenced to life imprisonment and died in 1883.

Motilal Nehru

Born in 1861, he had a very successful career as a lawyer at Allahabad. He left the princely life for participating in the freedom movement. He started as a moderate and joined Home Rule League. He was elected President of Congress in 1918. In 1920, he took part in Gandhiji's Non-Cooperation Movement. He also presided over 1928 session of Congress at Calcutta. Under his direction, a report on the future Constitution of India was prepared. He defined the attainment of Dominion status as the goal while his son, Jawahar Lal Nehru and Subhash Bose pleaded for complete independence. He favoured talks with the Britishers and felt that the freedom movement should not adopt the path of conflict. He led Swaraj Party which was keen to participate in the council elections.

Bhula Bhai Desai

Born in 1877, he was an outstanding lawyer and went on to become Advocate-General of Bombay. He joined Home Rule League for some time. He joined Congress in 1930 and suffered imprisonment several times. He was leader of the opposition in the central legislative assembly. His brilliant defence of the officers of the INA army captured by the British during the war and tried for waging war against the government gave him his moment of glory. The officers were first given harsh sentences but later acquitted. The brilliant lawyer died in 1946.

Maulana Mohammad Ali

Born in 1878, he was educated at Oxford. He served in the states of Rampur and Baroda for sometime. He was a powerful writer and he soon graduated from a political journalist to a staunch nationalist. He took part in the Khilafat movement. The movement was to protest against the mistreatment given to Calipha of Turkey by the Britishers. He was supported by Gandhiji in this movement and it became a common endeavour of Hindus and muslims to liberate the country. He started a national muslim university called the Jamia Milia Islamia. He attended the round table conference in 1930 at London. He was sick that time and could not return. He died at London that year.

Dinshaw Wacha

Born in 1844, Wacha worked for the progress of his country towards the goal of freedom. He was the founder member of Indian National Congress. He worked with such stalwarts as Dadabhai Naoroji and Pherozeshah Mehta, He also became a member of Bombay Municipal Corporation. He appeared before the Welby Commission in 1897 and gave masterly expositions of the finances of the country. He was for rigid control over military and wasteful civil expenditure. He died in 1936.

Bankim Chandra Chatterjee

Born in 1838 in Bengal, he acquired proficiency in English and Sanskrit. He had the distinction of being the first graduate of the Calcutta University. He entered the government service and retired as Deputy Collector in 1891. He wielded a powerful pen and wrote about nationalism, religion, society and the ideals of life. He attacked polygamy and championed the cause of widow remarriage. He was a seer and a nation builder. He wrote the national Song 'Vande Matram' which inspired thousands of countrymen during freedom struggle. He died in 1894.

Fherozeshah Mehta

Born in 1845, he was the founder member of Indian National Congress. He studied for the Bar in England but after return, he plunged into the political life of the country. He became the Commissioner of Bombay. During the Congress split in the Surat Session in 1907, he played a conciliatory role. He was a known moderate in politics and disapproved of the extremists and their policies. He also disapproved the communal politics of Sir Syed Ahmed Khan. He presided over the Calcutta session of the Congress in 1890 and took a leading part in the framing of the Congress Constitution. He died in 1915.

Surendra Nath Banerjee

Born in 1848, he was once a member of coveted Indian Civil Service. But later he dedicated himself fully to the cause of national emancipation and political freedom of the country. He undertook extensive tours and organised meetings all over the country. He built up a National Fund with the objective of espousing the cause of political freedom of the country, through constitutional means. Subsequent endeavours made in this regard resulted in a national conference held in Calcutta with representatives of the people from all corners of the country. This ultimately paved the way towards the setting up of Indian National Congress in the year 1885. He presided over the Congress session in 1895 and 1902. He died in 1925.

Badruddin Tyabji

Born in 1844, he belonged to a rich Arab family, settled in Bombay. He became bar-at-law and started practising in England. But soon he returned to become a judge of the Bombay High Court. He become the first Indian Chief Justice of that High Court.

He, along with Telang and Ferozeshah Mehta, came to be known as the triumvirate of Bombay. He presided over the 1887 Congress session. He organized the Anjuman-i-Islam school in Bombay for the uplift of Muslims. He campaigned against the Purdah system. He provided Congress a respectability as it came to be representing both the Hindus and Muslims. He died in 1906.

Rash Behari Ghosh

Born in 1845, he had a very distinguished academic career. He was a member of the Calcutta University Syndicate. He presided over the Congress Surat Session in 1907 and Madras Session in 1908. He was known as a moderate in politics. He gave credit to Britishers for many benefits that accrued from their rule. He advocated autonomy under the overall control of the British. He died in 1908.

Madame Cama

Bhikaji Cama was born in 1861 to an affluent family. Inspired by Dada Bhai Naoroji, she became a revolutionary. She acted as the moving spirit behind the secret society 'Abhinav Bharat', which trained young men to make bombs. She exhorted her countrymen to fight against the British. She was jailed in France, on request of the Britain. She unfurled her version of Indian flag in the Socialist Congress in Europe.

Charles F. Andrews

He was bom in 1871 in Britain. He was a Christian missionary belonging to the society of quakers who worked in India. When he came to India he became a great admirer of Tagore and life long friend of Gandhiji. He advocated the cause of India's independence and pleaded the cause of freedom fighters with the British authorities. He was well known for his concern for the poor and the workers. He worked with Ambedkar for the welfare of Harijans. He was known as Deenbandhu. He died in 1940.

Kasturba Gandhi

Born in 1869, she was popularly called 'Ba'. She participated in the freedom movement along with her husband, Mahatma Gandhi. She adapted herself to the rigorous of Ashram life. She was intensely religious. She strongly supported her husband's work and went to jail for several times. She led the women satyagrahis both in Africa and India. She was kept along with Gandhi in the Aga Khan Palace in Pune where she died in 1944.

Prominent Persons of Ancient India

- **Alexander:** King of Macedonia who invaded India in fourth century BC.
- **Aryabhatta:** Famous mathematician and astronomer.
- **Ashoka:** Great Mauryan King who won wars but later propagated Buddhism.
- **Ashvaghosha:** Famous Buddhist philosopher and author.
- **Banabhatta:** Court poet of Harsha who wrote "Kadambri" and "Harsh Charitra".
- **Bhaskara I:** A noted astronormer of 9th century.
- **Bhaskara II:** One of the distinguished astro-nomer and mathematicians of 12th century.
- **Bimbisara:** Famous King of Magadh.
- **Bindusara:** Mauryan King and father of Ashoka.

- **Chandragupta I:** First important ruler of the Gupta dynasty.
- **Chandragupta II:** Gupta ruler who came to be known as Vikramaditya.
- **Chandragupta Maurya:** Ruler of Magadha and founder of Magadha dynasty.
- **Charaka:** Famous Indian practitioner of medicine.
- **Fa-Hien:** Chinese traveller who came to India during the Gupta period to study Buddhist scriptures.
- **Gautam Buddha:** Founder of Buddhism.
- **Gautamiputra Satkarni:** Famous Satavahana ruler.
- **Harshavardhan:** Famous ruler of Thaneswar and last of the great Indian Kings to reign large area.
- **Hieun Tsang:** Chinese pilgrim who visited India during the reign of Harsha.
- **Kalidasa:** Famous Sanskrit poet and playwright. His works include "Abhijnana Shakuntalam", "Raghuvansha", "Meghdoot", "Kumarsambhava", "Vikramorvashiya".
- **Kanishka:** Great Kushan ruler of North-West India.
- **Kautilya**: Commonly known as Chanakya. He planned to overthrow Nanda dynasty in Magadh and install Maurya dynasty. His policies as Prime Minister of Maurya Kings were well known. He also wrote "Arthashastra".
- **Kumarila Bhatt:** A well-known preacher of Hinduism during 8th century.
- **Mahavira:** 24th Tirathankar of Jain religion who is the most known one.
- **Megasthenes:** Greek ambassador to Mauryan empire and known for account of India in book "Indica".
- **Menender:** Indo-Greek ruler of North-West India who later practised Buddhism.
- **Panini:** A great Sanskrit grammarian of ancient India.
- **Pulakesin II:** Well known Chalukya ruler who defeated Harshavardhan.
- **Seleucus Nicator:** Greek ruler who was made in-charge of Indian areas won by Alexander. He was later defeated by Chandragupta Maurya.
- **Samudragupta:** Gupta ruler who besides being a great warrior possessed good taste for art and music.
- **Shankaracharya:** Great Hindu philosopher who established four dhams (monasteries) in four parts of the country to propagate the religion. They are at Sringeri in South, Dwarka in West, Puri in East and Badrinath in North.
- **Susruta:** Well known practitioner of Indian medicine.
- **Varahamihira:** Well known astronomer and astrologer.

Prominent Persons of Medieval India

- **Abul Fazal:** Great scholar in the court of Akbar - one of the Navratnas. He wrote "Akbarnama".
- **Akbar:** Great Mughal King who ruled a large area of India for a long time. He respected other religious and promoted arts and culture.
- **Ala-ud-din Khilji:** Most well-known Khilji king who spread his empire. He also built several structures like Sirifort, Alai Darwaza. He was killed and Tughlaqs took over the Delhi throne.
- **Alberuni:** Great Persian scholar who visited India.
- **Amir Khusrau:** Great poet, musician and writer.
- **Aurangzeb:** He was the last great Mughal emperor. He strictly preached and practised Islam and thereby offended the majority Hindus. His successors proved weak.
- **Babur:** First Mughal King in India. He defeated Ibrahim Lodhi in a battle in Panipat to establish his Kingdom.

- **Balban:** Belonged to Slave Dynasty who rose to become Delhi Sultan due to his bravary and intelligence. Amir Khusrau was in his court.
- **Bairam Khan:** Turkish Commander of armies of Akbar and Humayun. He acted as guardian of Akbar and won the second battle of Panipat for him.
- **Bahadur Shah II:** Last Mughal emperor to sit on Delhi throne. He took part in 1857 revolt and was sent to Rangoon after imprisonment.
- **Birbal:** Minister of Akbar known for his wits and intelligence.
- **Chaitanya:** Famous Vaishnava Saint.
- **Firdausi:** Famous Persian poet-writer who wrote "Shahnama".
- **Guru Nanak:** Founder and first guru of Sikh religion.
- **Guru Gobind Singh:** Tenth and last Guru of Sikhs who gave his followers a distinct identity.
- **Harihar and Bukka:** Two brothers who founded the Vijaynagar Kingdom.
- **Hassan Gangu:** Founder of the Bahmani Kingdom.
- **Humayun:** Son of Babar who ruled over Delhi. However, he could not rule for a long period and had to surrender to Sher Shah Suri.
- **Hyder Ali:** Great Mysore King who opposed the Britishers.
- **Ibn Batutah:** African traveller who wrote his Indian experiences.
- **Jahangir:** Mughal King who is known for his sense of Justice.
- **Jayadeva:** Author of "Geet Govinda".
- **Kabir:** Famous Bhakti saint known for his couplets or dohas.
- **Kalhana:** Kashmiri poet who is known for writing "Rajtarangani".
- **Krishnadeva Rai:** He was the most famous Raja of Vijaynagar kingdom and last great Hindu ruler of Southern India.
- **Moin-ud-din Chisti:** Well-known Sufi Saint.
- **Mirabai:** Princess from Rajasthan who devoted herself to devotion.
- **Muhammad Tughlaq:** Most well known Tughlaq ruler. He was a master of politics, Science and Medicine. However, due to improper policies, he proved to be a failure.
- **Mahmud of Ghazni:** He attacked India several times and plundered the wealth of India.
- **Muhammad Ghori:** He defeated Prithvi Raj Chauhan and put his slave Qutub ud-din Aibak incharge of the victorious land.
- **Namdev:** Bhakti saint belonging to Maharashtra.
- **Nadir Shah:** He came from North-West, plundered India and massacred a large number of Delhites.
- **Qutab-ud-dln Aibak:** He was a slave of Muhammed Ghori. However, he was given charge of the victorious areas and he established slave dynasty.
- **Ramanuja:** Vaishava philosopher and a follower of Bhakti Movement.
- **Razia Begum:** She was the first woman ruler to sit on the throne of Delhi. However, the nobles protested against her and dethroned her.
- **Shahjahan:** A great Mughal King who is known for various structures built by him like Taj Mahal, Red Fort in Delhi.
- **Sher Shah Suri:** He defeated Humayun and became the ruler of India. He was a good administrator and planner.
- **Shlvaji:** Great Maratha King who proved a match for Aurangazeb.
- **Thomas Roe:** British ambassador to the Court of Jehangir.
- **Tukaram:** Bhakti Saint of Maharashtra.
- **Tulsidas:** Well known poet and author. His most famous book is Ramacharitamanas.
- **Vasco-da-Gama:** First European to reach India via sea route.

WORLD HISTORY

Man has lived on the earth for several hundred thousand years but it is only a few thousand years back, man learned the art of writing. The story of man's progress for which written records are available is called history while the long, distant past prior to that time for which man kept no written records is called prehistoric era. The main sources of information about pre-historic man have been their tools and weapons, their paintings, artifacts and fossils of men and animals.

Palaeolithic age

The early period in man's development is known as the old Stone age or Palaeolithic age. This was a very long period, extending from 5 lakh years ago to about 15,000 years ago. The man made small but significant improvements during the period. During the period, there were very major geographical changes on earth. During this time, man had learnt to move in groups in search of food and shelter. He learnt to make tools of stone, build shelters and use animal skins to cover himself. The major achievement was the knowledge of using fire and convey messages through a language. This was the first stage of development and lasted several thousand years.

Mesolithic age

During the mesolithic or middle stone age, the speed of development was rather fast. Man learnt to make a variety of fine tools. It was from about 10,000 B.C. to 8,000 B.C. People took to fishing, in several parts, to supplement their diet. In some areas, people started to harvest crops, domesticate animals and breed goats and sheep. In this age, men used to move to a new fertile land, after some time.

Neolithic age

The era from 6000 B.C. to 4000 B.C. is called new stone age. The man changed from getting food to producing food. The weapons and tools became more sophisticated yet the basic material remained stone. Domestication of animal, weaving and pottery were learnt by the man. He started making permanent house which were made of wood, mud and had thatched roofs. The settlements were generally near the fields which the people cultivated. These dwellings gradually took the shape of villages and thus organized social life developed. During this period religious beliefs also grew. The dead were buried with weapons, pottery, food and drink in their graves. Each tribe had its own totem, the image of an animal or a plant as a symbol for a clan, or group of families living together. Small clay figures of women have been found, indicating, the worship of mother goddess. The invention of wheel also dates back to this age.

Important Ancient Civilizations

As the man progressed in his life and acquired knowledge, different cultures and civilizations grew. The growth of civilization was not uniform, it began to emerge in some parts of the world in about 4000 B.C. However, at several other places, it came up several thousand years later.

Most of the early civilizations arose in certain river valleys as conditions there were favourable. Fertile soil was available on the banks of the rivers. Water required for drinking and irrigation was in abundance. Man found important use of river, as a means of transportation. This led to the transportation of merchandize—excess foodstuff or animals and thus developed the trade and commerce. Since men did not have to spend all his time in gathering food or protecting himself from wild animals, he found enough time to observe and think. This led to the development of science, engineering, mathematics, architecture, sculpture, music, dance and painting.

The discovery and the use of Copper and Bronze metals marked an important milestone in men's development. The metals are more durable than stones and can be given any shape to form tools, weapons or other implements. Copper was the metal to be discovered and for a long time, both stone and copper coexisted. This period was called Chalcolithic age, with chalkes meaning Copper, and lithos meaning stone. In course of time, man learned to mix Copper with Tin or zinc to produce Bronze alloy which is harder and more useful in making tools, weapons and implements. Due to the importance of Bronze in the growth of first civilizations, these are called Bronze Age Civilizations.

By about 4,500 years back, the Indus Valley in India, the Hwang-Ho Valley in China, the Valley of the Tigris and the Euphrates in Mesopotamia (presently Iraq), the Nile Valley in Egypt and the areas around the Mediterranean and Aegean Sea had become centres of civilization. Each civilization developed its own political and social system, trade and commerce, religious beliefs, art and science.

All these civilizations, though spread out over a large geographical area, had some common characteristics. All of them had large areas under cultivation. They had set up elaborate system of migration canals. All of them had central authority whose will could be enforced. Since food-producing effort did not require everyone's involvement, several other occupations developed. It led to division of work and specialisation. Villages grew up into towns and cities. The life became complex and to manage and maintain law and order, a highly developed organization called Government came up. All the civilizations were involved in trading activities. They also had scripts of their own.

Indus Valley Civilization

It existed in north-western regions of the present Indian sub-continent between 2700-2350. Some of its towns were located in the valley of Indus river. Though it was not the oldest of the Bronze age civilization, it extended over a bigger area than any other. The excavations in Baluchistan, Sind, Punjab, Haryana, Gujarat, Rajasthan and Western Uttar Pradesh have led to the evidence of this civilization. The land of the valley was very fertile and farmers from further west moved there and settled there. They dug canals to control and distribute floodwater, making farming more productive. The prominent cities were Harappa, Mohan-jo-daro, Lothal, Banavali and Chanudero: Among these, the first two cities were the major ones, well planned and thickly populated. They were well over 2 sq km in area.

All the cities of the Indus Valley Civilization were well planned. The roads were wide and straight. Houses were made of burnt bricks and some had more than one storey. The drainage system in those cities was very good. The cities had well planned tanks and ponds for community bathing. Granaries were used to store extra crops. Indus Valley cities were built according to a grid system— each of the main street was parallel. Streets were lined with terraced houses.

The common crops of the Indus Valley Civilization were wheat, barley, peas and cotton. Wheel was used to make pottery. People used to keep domestic animals. The metallurgy, sculpture and painting were quite famous. Indus Valley traders used to exchangc things with other civilizations, particularly Mesopotamia.

Not much is known about the government in the Indus Valley Civilization because the script has not been fully understood yet. But it is felt that absence of palaces indicate rule by a body of important men rather than by a King. However, similarity in planning and layout of various towns indicate a central administration.

The people worshipped an early form of Siva and Goddess. They used to participate in religious bathing. The dead were either cremated or buried. The civilization at the banks of Indus Valley flourished for nearly 1,000 years but around 1,700 BC, the cities were probably devastated by earthquakes and floods. Aryans, people of the northwest later invaded and allowed the cities to decay further.

Mesopotamian Civilization

Bound by Armenia plateau in the North and Persian Gulf in the South, this civilization existed on the land between Tigris and Euphrates rivers. Presently, Syria and Iraq countries exist in the area. Its northern part was called Assyria while Southern part was called Babylonia. The northern portion of Babylon was called Akkad while southern portion was Sumer. In ancient times, great civilizations existed in these areas.

All the Mesopotamian civilizations are known by their cities. These cities were named by the citizens on the basis of their gods. These cities used to fight among themselves for the territorial or water-irrigation rights. With the changing times, the authority and prominence of these cities also kept on changing.

The Mesopotamians devised ways and means of a perennial irrigation system to keep flood in check. The river-bed was high and the canals were made wide so that while the water rushed from the river to the canal, the banks would not be destroyed. The canals were navigable channels and thus helped in transport as well as in irrigation.

The earliest civilization grew up in Sumer. They built their temples and prayer-places, even in 4000 B.C. Since the area was fertile, people used to get good harvest. Some of them had time to devote to other things and several art forms and skills developed.

The most important contribution of Sumerians was the discovery of Script. The wedge shaped script is called Cuneiform. They used to write on clay tablets using sharp stylus made of reed. Some of the tablets recovered from excavation, show business documents, letters, royal inscriptions, religious texts and stories.

Another major contribution of Sumerians was the Sexagesimal system. In this system, they wrote the numbers 1 to 9 by making the sign for 1 and repeating as many times as necessary. Similarly they repeated the sign for 10 to represent multiples of 10. They had the same symbol for 60 as 1, though it was written much bigger. There was no sign higher than 60. The sexagesimal system is not of much use but is used in the division of time into minutes and seconds and circle into 360 degrees.

People of Babylon were also interested in astronomy and geometry. In geometry, Mesopotamians had discovered what was later called the Pythagoras' theorem. By observing Stars, Sun and Moon, they divided the sky into twelve parts. They also developed lunar calendar. Babylon was known for its hanging gardens besides having several roads, bridges and canals. They manufactured coins, weights and measures. Observatories were built to observe the motion of stars and planets.

Assyrian civilization flourished around 1,600 BC. Since the Assyrians were warriors they stressed manufacturing of arms and weapons, maintaining a big army and giving soldiers a special status in the society. People worshipped idols, particularly Assyr (Sun). They built magnificent palaces and statues of lions, bulls and other hunting scenes.

The Mesopotamian cities were well planned and divided into three main divisions—the Sacred area, the walled city on the mound and the outer town. The king was regarded as the God's representative on earth while the slaves, mostly prisoners of war, were lowest in the social level.

Agriculture was the main occupation of Mesopotamians. They used cattle to draw the plough. They wore clothes made of sheepskin. They used the potter's wheel for making pottery and later used it for making chariots. By 2500 B.C., Mesopotamians had developed high technical knowledge and skill about metals. The prosperity of the Mesopotamians depended largely on foreign trade. They exported foodgrains to buy stone, timber, gold, silver and other metals. Mesopotamians were the, first to use coloured tiles in buildings. They had the knowledge of columns, arches and minarets.

Egyptian Civilization

Egypt is called the "Gift of the Nile river" because Nile river, for centuries, has been spreading layers of fertile black soil in the area. Between 5000 and 4000 B.C., the skill of agriculture was developed by the farmers in the area. With this, grew the concept of permanent house which led to the coming up of villages and kingdoms.

The history of Egypt is divided into three periods. The old age is also called the age of Pyramids. Memphis was the capital during the period in which advancements in art, religion and sciences were made. This age lasted from 3000 to 2000 B.C. During the middle age, early period saw speedy development but in the 18th century B.C., Egypt was overrun by a nomadic tribe, Hyksos. However, the Egyptian Kings regained the land and established new kingdom. This period became the golden period of Egyptian civilization till about 1000 BC when rulers became weak and were overrun by enemies.

Ancient Egyptian Kings—Pharaohs, were great architects. They made several huge buildings. Though their palaces and other public buildings do not exist anymore, but the Pyramids stand testimony of their knowledge and skill. These 30 large and several small Pyramids are among the wonders of the ancient world. These pyramids were tombs of Pharaohs containing their mummies and precious things, they contained. Egyptians believed in life after death. So, they used to preserve the bodies of their kings, using chemicals. These preserved bodies are called Mummies..

Another specimen of Egyptian architecture is Sphinx, which is a mythological animal with the body of a lion and the head of a man. Each Sphinx was carved out of a single solid stone. Egyptian temples are also remarkable buildings.

Sun was the most important God of Egyptians. They also had other gods like king of the other world, god of the flood, moon and several local gods, which were represented with symbols like Jackal, Cow etc. Pharaohs were initially priests of the God but subsequently they were prayed and temples in their names made. The kings were mostly despotic who acted as chief administrator as well as religious head. Ministers were appointed for consultation. The country was divided into units and disputes were settled on the basis of written laws. Women were given a high place in the society.

Agriculture was the most important occupation of the people. They built canals to grow crops throughout the year. They were perhaps using ox to draw the plough as early as 3000 B.C. They domesticated animals like goats, dogs, pigs etc. They used horse to draw chariots. They used to wear linen clothes. Egyptians made beautiful furniture and stone vessels. They also developed the art of making glass. Egyptians used to live lavishly and were involved in importing luxury items.

Egyptians developed a script, called Hieroglyphic. They developed a decimal system of numeration. They were good in geometry and arithmetic. The Egyptians developed solar calendar, based on 365 days. They also developed papyrus or technique of making paper. Egyptian civilization ended by 1000 B.C. They used decimal system in mathematics.

Chinese Civilization

The first centre of civilization in China developed in the region of the Hwang-Ho river valley around 2000 B.C. Hwang-Ho Was called "the Sorrow of China" because the river often changed its course, damaging homes, fields and canals. Around 1600 B.C., the Shong dynasty was established. By 14th Century B.C., these rulers had developed a high level of culture comparable to the Centres of other early civilizations.

The prosperity of Chinese civilization depended mainly on agriculture. They had developed an elaborate system of irrigation to reduce the distress caused by floods. Chinese wore linen and silk clothes. The sericulture was started by Chinese and they used to weave clothes out of silk yarn.

Chinese learnt the use of iron, besides brass. This helped them increase the farm production and make various tools, and weapons. Chinese were very skillful in making arts and handicrafts items. They used to export them to India and other places. They made very fine pottery which they learned to glaze. The wares of porcelain are still called Chinaware.

During this period, Chinese rulers made the Great Wall of China to protect their empire from Huns attack from the north-west. Chinese were first to develop explosives and used it in firearms. Another major achievement of Chinese civilization was the development of paper. They developed an ideographic script in which a sign represents an idea. The Chinese calendar was a combination of solar and lunar calculations. They had made advances in astronomy. Their buildings, which may have included temples, were made with earth, timber and mud bricks. They manufactured inks and printing press. They introduced the notes and taking of tea.

The Buddhism spread from India to China. Earlier, ancestor worship was the most popular practice. They believed in spirits and used to place furniture, pottery, vessels and other objects besides the dead body in grave. Lao-Tse and Confucious were the main philosophers of China. They worshipped their Kings ancestors as gods, and built several Pagoda temples.

Greek Civilization

Greeks came to the region of the Aegean Sea and by 600 B.C. spread their common culture from the south of France to the Black Sea. They had many Gods whom they imagined to be like human beings though more powerful and immortal. They had no knowledge of writing until around 800 B.C. but passed the stories of their life through folk-songs and ballads. However, the discovery of script helped them in growing their knowledge in several fields. Homer was a famous poet who wrote Iliad and Odyssey.

The Greek world was a mosaic of city states, each one ruling the land around it and frequently at loggerheads with its neighbours. Sparta, Athens, Macedonia and other City-States had many common features, but each had its own character. Spartans lived under the strictest discipline, leaving no scope for family life or for learning. On the other hand, Athenians experienced democracy and built a prosperous trade and rich culture. Macedonia came into limelight when its ruler Alexander setout to conquer the world and brought large area upto the Indian border, under his control. Alexander founded the City of Alexandria which became a seat of Greek culture and education for a long time after the fall of Greece.

Greek civilization had a large number of slaves who did most of the work, leaving time to think and create and live the good life. The life was easy, simple and enjoyable. They had music, wine and festivities. There was good development of literature, drama, theatre and philosophy. Socrates, Plato and Aristotle were great philosophers. Euclid and Pythagoras were great mathematician while Hippocrates was father of medicine. In the fields of science, astronomy, architecture and sculpture. Greeks went on sea voyages and had a full fledged Navy which helped in its expansion. Greeks were good architects and artists, and built several magnificent temples. Greeks introduced the Olympic Games which became forerunner for the present day games. Greeks made new discoveries. The infighting among the city-state led to the fall of Greek civilization and it was won over by Romans in 2nd AD and for the first time introduced rule of law and democracy in the world.

Roman Civilization

The city of Rome was founded about 1000 B.C. and its principal language was Latin. The Roman Civilization started developing around 6th century B.C. as groups of Indo-Europeans and Greeks began settling there. Initially, Romans had a King, an assembly and a senate but towards the end of the 6th century, a republic was established. As a republic, Romans expanded and controlled all of Italy, parts of South and West Europe, North Africa and West Asia.

In Rome, slavery was quite prominent. Slaves were employed for hard and dirty jobs while other Romans enjoyed luxurious life. Since large army was required to suppress rebellion from slaves and fight wars, army leaders gained importance in the society.

Rome acted as a link between the eastern civilizations and Europe. They also made some contributions of their own, with law and principles of govemance being the greatest one. Laws encouraged travel and boosted trade. The roads, built primarily for the movement of armies, were used for carrying goods.

Latin language, developed by Romans, became the language of all educated people in Europe. The Roman Civilization developed its literature, philosophy, science, art and architecture. The names of month — July, August, September, October, November and December — as used presently, are the gifts of Roman Civilization. The rule of Romans was organised and united. The main occupation of people was agriculture but traders and artisans also flourished. Religious tolerance was there, with Jupiter, Mars, Minerva etc. being their deities. Romans are known for the laws made by them. Roads and bridges of Rome were world famous. They were good architects also. The arts and literature were well developed in Rome. Julius Ceasar and Augustus were prominent rulers of Rome.

Roman empire decayed as imperialism destroyed democracy, encouraged slavery and created political conflicts. Since agriculture and industry were left to slaves, the productivity remained low. The coming of Christians to Rome also weakened the empire as the oppressed people of Rome were attracted by it. Rome, however, continued to be centre of Christianism with the present of Pope there.

Maya Civilization

The Maya Civilization extended over a large area of Central America, covering parts of present Guatemala, Mexico and Honduras. It began around 1500 B.C. and reached its peak between 300 A.D. and 900 A.D. Mayans grew Maize, Beans, Potato, Papaya and Chilli. Their most important achievements were their perfect calendar, knowledge of mathematics, hierographic writing and use of paper.

Byzantine Civilization

Constantine became the King of the whole Roman empire in 324 AD. That year he moved the capital from Rome to the town of Byzantium in the eastern empire, founding Byzantine empire which remained for over one thousand years. A new city was built at Byzantine, called Constantinopole. During the reign of Constantine, Christianity got firm roots. A few years after Constantine's death, the empire was divided into east and west, with the former surviving for a long period.

The Arab Empire

The Prophet of Islam encouraged his followers to convert as much of the world as possible to new faith. When he died in 632 AD, his father-in-law Abu Bakr took the title of Calipha and became chief defender of Islam. Later, new Islamic dynasties were set up which tried to change the world in earnest. Damescus in Syria became the centre of an Islamic empire stretching from Morocco to India of Omayyad dynasty. Later, the descendants of Mohammad's family, belonging to Abbasid dynasty made Baghdad the Islamic centre. Baghdad, besides being a prosperous centre of a huge trading empire, also became a centre of learning.

Crusades

In the late 11th century, Turks overran Palestine, the holy place for Christians. Moreover, they began attacking Christians on pilgrimage to holy places. This angered the churches and the Christian kings also sought the help in resisting the aggression. In 1095, the Pope called for a Crusade, or Holy War against Muslim Turks. Thousands of ordinary people responded. In 1096, an official European force joined with a Byzantine army attacked Turks and in 1099, they took Jerusalem. Muslims also got rearranged and made a bid to recapture Palestine. These efforts led to Second (1144), Third (1189) and Fourth (1202) Crusades. The crusades continued till 1291. Thousands of children were used in these wars. At the end of the war, the Palestine remained with the Muslims. The crusades provided Europeans with an opportunity to learn several new things which led to increase in trade, decline of feudalism, intellectual development, decline in Church's powers and urge to explore new areas.

Inca Empire

The Inca empire grew in the Andes Mountain region in South America in the 14th and 15th centuries. It stretched from Ecuador, Peru and Chile. The Incas were famous for their engineering skill, building palaces, temples, official storehouses and fortresses. There was a wide network of roads. Medicine and surgery were highly developed. Arts and crafts were also highly developed, particularly pottery-making, cotton-weaving and wool.

Important Events

Magna Carta

The barons, the clergy and the people combined to compel the King of England, John II to redress their grievances by signing the great charter in 1215. It contained 63 clauses guaranteeing the freedom of barons, the church and the people. The charter was intended to put a check upon the arbitrary powers of the king by securing the rights of all orders and classes. It laid down the important principle that Englishmen should be governed by definite laws and not by whims or uncontrolled will of a despotic ruler Magna Carta is said to be the foundation stone of the rights and liberties of the English people.

BLack Death

The black death, an infection of bubonic plague, struck Europe in 1347. The disease was spread by fleas that lived on rats. The fleas got transferred to humans when the rats died. By 1351, the disease, which affected rich and poor alike had spread over most of Europe. The plague killed about one-third of the total European population.

Feudalism

A system developed in the middle age in Europe whereby peasants had to give a part of their produce to the lords in the form of rent or taxes or had to work for the lords without any payment. This system developed as there was no central authority. The society was hierarchial with every person allotted a position. There was a king at the top who bestowed estates on a number of lords, known as dukes or earls. The earls, in turn, distributed a part of their estate among barons and in return, secured their military support. The knights formed the lowest category of feudal lords. The relationship from top to bottom was one of allegiance. While these lords levied taxes, acted as judges and owned armies, peasants at the lowest stand suffered. Some of them were forced to work for their lords for no wages. They suffered several restrictions and some of them were tied to the land and could not leave the place.

Feudalism served its purpose of bringing a measure of orderliness, safety and security in Medieval Europe. Social and economic activity appeared normal though there were several aberrations. It was based on a rigid class system and promoted political disunity. The ruling class did not care for the common men. There was wasteful consumption. The lords indulged in wars, in order to gain new lands.

As Lords needed luxury items, trade grew and with this towns developed as centres of manufacture and trade. Towns, gradually freed themselves from feudal control and established own government, police and court. Towns provided freedom to peasantry. With the growth of trade, money's use increased and thus Capitalism grew to kill Feudalism. Other factors that led to the decline of feudalism were emergence of powerful kings, decline in powers of lords due to mutual fighting, strengthening of the feeling of nationalism, growth of middle classes, inventions of gunpowder and printing press, influence of church and development of democracy in several areas.

Renaissance

Renaissance means rebirth. It was initially used to describe revival of interest in the learning of older civilizations of Greece and Rome. Knowledge of their achievements led to a series of new developments in the field of art, literature, religion, science and politics. Renaissance began in Italy in the 16th century. Its main emphasis was on freedom of the individual, inalienable rights of the individual and respecting the dignity of man. It stressed on the limitless potentialities of man rejected religious asceticism and withdrawal from the world. It aimed at providing happiness to man. The emphasis shifted from divinity to humanity, i.e., human being. The Renaissance era gave rise to quest for knowledge, especially history and literature. The effects of Renaissance were development of humanism, nationalism, spread of education, growth in trade and commerce, exposure of myths and establishment of reasoning. Some of the greatest achievements were made in painting, sculpture and architecture. Leonardo da Vinci, Michael Angelo and Raphael were famous artists of that time. Dante was a great poet of that time while Machiavelli, a diplomat, historian and political philosopher wrote about statecraft. As the Renaissance spread throughout Europe, it took on a more religious character, paving the way for Reformation. Moreover, during the period, Europeans began to look for sea route to Asia, with Columbus reaching Central America in 1492 and Vasco-da-Gama in India in 1498.

Reformation

The key event of the 16th century in Europe was the Reformation, a movement to reform the Catholic church. It began in Germany and then spread throughout northern Europe. Martin Luther, a German theologian and religious transformer set alight widespread discontent against the Church. New Protestant Church belonging to reformers sprang up, with the aim of following only the teachings of the Bible, and getting rid of church traditions. Several powerful kings and princes supported the reformers like John Calvin, Olrich Zwingli and others. Although the Catholic church responded by introducing reforms from within, violent conflicts between Catholics and Protestants erupted. In 1534, King Henry VIII took the help of the English church because the Pope would not let him divorce his first wife. Though Queen Mary tried to restore Church's authority in England, getting the nickname "Bloody Mary" due to execution of Protestants, the Catholics were reduced to minority in England.

The Slave Trade

The practice of slavery, the buying and selling of people against their will, goes back to ancient times. Slaves had no rights or freedoms and were owned entirely by their masters. Selling African people as slaves was begun on a large scale by Arabs about 1,000 years ago. However, mass demand for slaves arose when Europeans needed workers for plantations in America. The slaves were later taken to other places by Europeans for hard work. The slaves lived a miserable life, living in cramped quarters, unable to move for days and getting whipped at slightest pretext. The slavery continued till about 150 years ago.

English Revolution of 1688

England was ruled by despotic rulers in the first half of 17th century — James I and Charles I. They believed that they were appointed by God, not answerable to Parliament or people. The dispute between the King and Parliament led to civil war in England in 1642. James I was defeated and executed. In 1660, Charles II was appointed king on the condition that he will not interfere in religious affairs of the people and rule with consultation with Parliament. However, James II followed his father's footsteps and tried to breakaway from Parliament's supervision and gave more powers to Catholics in the Protestant dominated country. This led to revolt by the people who invited the Dutch Protestant King William to come to England. James II fled to France. Williams and daughters of James II, Mary were declared joint Monarchs. The revolution has been described as Glorious due to lack of bloodshed. The revolution led to end of divine rights of Kings, acceptance of the authority of the Parliament, independent judiciary, freedom of Press and supremacy of Protestants in England.

American War of Independence

With the rise of Capitalism and industrial revolution in Europe, the demand for raw materials, cheap labour and markets grew. European kings encouraged exploration of new areas which were subsequently colonized. In 1492, Columbus had discovered West Indies and later America was found. By the middle of 18th century, a large part of North America had come under England's occupation. Landless peasants, Protestants and others started living in this area. English Parliament put severe restrictions on the American colonies, politically as well as economically. Colonies were forbidden to start certain industries and heavy duties were imposed. The imposition of stamp duty in 1765 aroused violent resentment among Americans and there were uprisings, besides boycott of English goods. Though English Parliament agreed to revoke stamp duty, it later imposed tax on tea to assert their right to levy taxes. Several colonies refused to unload the tea and in 1773, a group of people boarded a ship in Boston and threw tea into water. The incident is called "Boston Tea Party". Subsequently, in 1775, English troops fought with local troops. On July 4, 1776, the Declaration of Independence was adopted by American leaders. It said all men are created equal; People have a right to set up their own government and the colonies have right to be free and independent states. The war between English and American forces intensified with other European countries favouring the colonial forces. The English forces surrendered in 1781 and in 1783, England recognized the independence of its 13 former colonies.

England, despite being a powerful nation, lost against the local troops due to distance constraints, help by other European nations to American leaders, good leadership of the war of Americans and lack of coordination among English Generals.

The independence of America was an important event in the world history. For the first time, a federal Government, democratic in character, was sworn in under the written constitution. The event was a great setback to England. It served as an example to other revolutionaries of the world and the French Revolution followed a few years later.

French Revolution

France was a strong and powerful state in the 18th century. However, internally there were problems. A small section of people owned most of the land and occupied all senior administrative and army positions. There was a large number of peasants who lived under miserable conditions. In between was the middle class, which was educated and sometimes rich, yet did not have social status or political rights. There were a large number of thinkers in France who advocated rationalism, democracy and attacked clergy. Moreover, the wars abroad and large patronage brought the King to the point of bankruptcy. A stand off between the royal forces and protestors led to the fall of Bastille prison on July 14, 1789. A new constitution was adopted, declaring equality, liberty and fraternity for everyone. The privileged class people tied to other countries to sought their help and France was involved in wars with its neighbouring countries. However, a new order had been established in France and it reached new heights under the leadership of Napolean Bonaparte.

Industrial Revolution

In middle ages, the occupation of majority of the population in Europe was Agriculture and whatever trade was undertaken, was done on barter system: However, discoveries and new inventions, spread of education and new ideas led to development of methods and machineries that could produce faster, better and cheaper goods. The industrial revolution began in England because of availability of coal and iron, availability of labour, peaceful atmosphere and availability of good Navy to carry new methods to England and finished goods to the markets. However, it spread to other European nations as well because colonies were being established in Asia and Africa and cheap raw material and labour was easily available. These were good markets for ready material and the businessmen supported the scientists and engineers to do more research. The profits made from selling goods were ploughed back into the industry, leading to more development. The development of mechanical and electrical energy and establishment of big industries also helped the revolution. It led to large scale changes in textiles, iron extraction, mining, transportation, communication, agriculture and energy. The industrial revolution also had some adverse impacts as small farmers and industries were wiped off. It led to exploitation of poor, ladies, children and people of colonies; unemployment, wars for colonies, urbanization and increase in crimes. The positive impact was improvement in life-styles, increase in national income, increase in agricultural output and enactment of legislations for workers' welfare.

Colonialism

To sustain the growth of their industries, European nations needed raw material, cheep labour and ready markets. Asian and African nations were their easy targets. Moreover, for strategic, religious and military reasons, it was found useful by Europeans to have as many colonies as possible. However, these European nations fought among themselves several times to take control over colonies. The colonies were economically exploited by the Europeans and their social and political setup demolished. Their cultures were spoiled -and their inhabitants were tortured. The positive aspect of colonialism was spread of education, scientific temperament, nationalism, good administration and development of infrastructure in these colonies. Some of the colonies and colonisers were as follows:

- ❖ **Colonies of Belgium:** Congo
- ❖ **Colonies of England:** Cape Colony, Bechuanaland, Rhodesia, Natal, Transvaal, Orange Free State, Gold Coast, Nigeria, Egypt, Sudan, India, Canada, New Zealand, Australia
- ❖ **Colonies of France:** Algeria, Tunisia, Senegal, Moracco, Somaliland, Madagascar, Cambodia, Parts of India, Laos
- ❖ **Colonies of Holland:** Malaya Islands, Indonesia
- ❖ **Colonies of Germany:** Tanganika, Cameroon
- ❖ **Colonies of Portugal:** Angola, Goa in India
- ❖ **Colonies of Italy:** Eritrea, Syria, parts of Somaliland, Libya
- ❖ **Colonies of Russia:** Afghanistan, Persia, Manchuria, Korea

Nationalism

The spirit of love for the nation got prominent in the 18th century. It began in Europe and then spread to Asia and Africa. Several countries became independent consequently:

(*a*) **Spain:** Democratic government established in 1870

(*b*) **Greece:** Got independence from Turkey in 1829

(*c*) **Belgium:** Got independence from Holland in 1930

(*d*) **Poland:** People of Warsaw revolted against Russian rule in 1848

(*e*) **Australia:** Democratic Constitution accepted in 1867

(*f*) **Balkon States:** Serbia, Romania and Montanegro got liberated from Turkey in 1855

(*g*) **Italy:** Unification of Italy completed in 1871 with the efforts of Mazzini and Garibaldi

(*h*) **Germany:** Unification of Germany completed in 1870 with the efforts of Bismarck

(*i*) **China:** Dr Sun-Yat-Sen led a successful movement in establishing a democracy in 1911 but in 1949, a Communist government was set up under Mao-Tse-Tung

(*j*) **Turkey:** Mustafa Kamal Pasha established democracy in 1923, after ousting the forces of Italy, France and Greece

(*k*) **Iran:** Feudalism ended in 1925 and Sardar Raza Khan became King

(*i*) **Syria:** Syrians opposed French forces and became independent in 1936

(*m*) **Palestine:** After England's departure, Jews declared an independent nation by name 'Israel'

(*n*) **Afghanistan:** Rebellion in 1926 forced the British to free it

(*o*) **Egypt:** Movement under the leadership of Jagalul Pasha led to independence in 1936; Suez Canal nationalised in 1956 leading to end of European interference

(*p*) **Indonesia:** It was a colony of Holland but went under Japan's control during Second World War. However, after the end of war, Indonesia became independent in 1949

(*q*) **Malaysia:** People there opposed the British rule and it got independence in 1957

(*r*) **Ghana:** Got independence in 1957

(*s*) **Algeria:** National Movement got momentum during Second World War and independence came in 1963

(*t*) **Kenya:** "Mao-Mao" movement led to its independence in 1965

In 1960, Congo and Mali became independent while in 1961, Sierre Lone, Somalia, in 1962 Jamaica, Rwanda, Trinidad, Tobago, Uganda and in 1965, Zanzibar became independent. East Timor(2002) is the latest country to join the independent nations.

Russian Revolution

In 1917, the monarchs of Russia Czars were overthrown and the world's first communist state was set up by Bolsheviks under the leadership of Lenin. The revolution was sparked by Russia's crippling defeat in the first world war, the resultant hardship at home and the inability of the king to cope up with this. Riots and strikes spread throughout the country. The removal of the Czar was an easy job but Bolsheviks were opposed by nationalists, non-Russians, democrats and military dictators but by 1920, the Communist government was firmly in the seat.

First-World War

Rivalry between European nations over the issue of colonies and political dominations led to tension that had been building up since late 19th century. Germany was a late entrant into the race for colonies and hence resented the expansion of French and British empire. France had been defeated completely by Germans in 1870. In Balkan area, Russia and Austria-Hungary had deep suspicion about each other. Britain had been traditional rival of France but fearing the might of German navy, both countries agreed to cooperate in case of an attack. Moreover, German economy had made tremendous progress, leaving Britain and France far behind. The Ottoman Empire, comprising Turkey had occupied areas in Balkan but in 1912 they became independent after fighting a war. The precipitating matter for the first world war was the assassination of Archduke Francis Ferdinand, heir to the throne of Austria-Hungary in Sarajevo. Austria, suspecting Serb hand, declared war on Serbia. Russia declared support for Serbia. Germany declared war on Russia and France while Britain declared war on Germany. A large number of new weapons, like aircrafts, tanks, submarines and poison gas were used in the war. America entered into the war in 1917, siding with France and Britain. Russia withdrew from the war in 1918, after the revolution at home. All the colonies in the world took part in the war as per their ruler's intention. The war ended in 1918 with Bulgaria, Germany, Turkey and Austria-Hungary surrendering.

Second World War

The Second World War, like the first, started in Europe and assumed the character of a world war. In Germany, the Nazi forces under the leadership of Adolf Hitler, had come into power, exploiting Germany's humiliation at defeat in the first world war and signing of an unjust treaty after the war. The League of Nations set up after the first world war did not prove effective in dealing with the problems of that period. Fascist forces had taken over Italy while Japan was pursuing policies of expansion and militarism. Britain, France, USA initially overlooked the German invasion and avoided Russia's call to form alliance to check the aggression, but finally they had to come under an umbrella of Allied Power to check the advance of Axis powers which included Germany, Italy, Japan and their satellites. Allied powers included Britain, France, Russia, USA, China, Australia, Belgium, etc. The war started on September 1, 1939 when Germany attacked Poland. This was followed by attacks on Norway, Denmark, Belgium and Holland. France surrendered in June, 1940. A year later, Germany attacked Soviet Union, Japan attacked American naval base of Pearl Harbour in Hawai in December, 1941 bringing USA into war. By the middle of 1942, Axis forces had reached their peak but then their decline began. In all fronts, Germany and Italy suffered setbacks and they surrendered in May 1945. But Japan had to be attacked by nuclear bombs twice before being subjected to surrender.

World War II Main Events

- **September 1, 1939:** German forces invade Poland.
- **September 3, 1939:** Britain and France declare war on Germany.
- **September 17, 1939:** Soviet forces invade Poland; Warsaw captured after two weeks of intensive bombing.
- **April 9, 1940:** Germans invade Denmark and Norway.
- **May 10, 1940:** Germans invade Belgium and Holland; Churchill becomes British Prime Minister.
- **May 12, 1940:** German army enters France.
- **June 10, 1940:** Italy declares war against France and Britain.

- **June 22, 1940:** France surrenders.
- **August, 1940:** German air force bombards airfields and towns of Britain.
- **September 13, 1940:** Italy attacks British-controlled Egypt.
- **October 28, 1940:** Italy attacks Greece.
- **March 1941:** USA grants land-lease arrangements to help Britain fight Germany.
- **April 6, 1941:** Germany invades Yugoslavia.
- **June 22, 1941:** Massive German army invades Soviet Union.
- **September 4, 1941:** Germany begins the 900 day seige of Leningrad.
- **December 7, 1941:** Japan attacks the US fleet in Pearl Harbour; United States declares war on Japan.
- **December 25, 1941:** Hong Kong, a British colony fells to Japan paving its entry into South East Asia.
- **June 3, 1942**: US warplanes defeat Japanese naval force.
- **January 23, 1943:** German troops trapped in Stalingrad surrender.
- **July 10-11, 1943:** Allies invade Sicily leading to its fall a month later.
- **July 25, 1943:** Mussolini the Italian dictator resigns.
- **September 2, 1943:** Allied forces invade Italy mainland.
- **June 6, 1944:** Allies invade Normandy.
- **August 1944:** Soviet forces break into east Persia and Poland.
- **August 1944:** Citizens of Paris drive out German forces.
- **March 7, 1945:** US troops cross into Germany.
- **April 30, 1945:** Hitler commits suicide.
- **May 8, 1945:** Formal declaration of the end of war in Europe.
- **August 6, 1945:** First atomic bomb dropped on Hiroshima.
- **August 14, 1945:** Japan surrenders; World War II over.

Reunification of Germany

Mikhail Gorbachev's tenure as the President of Soviet Union was a period of weakening of Communist forces all over the world. The East Germany Communist regime collapsed in late 1989, as waves of East Germans took advantage of ending of travel restrictions between Hungary and Austria to leave their country. About 2 lakh East Germans left for the West and on November 9, 1989, the Berlin Wall was breached and within a weak, 3 million East Germans crossed over. The Politburo and Central Committee of Communist Party resigned within weeks. In 1990, the action of reunification got unprecedented momentum and on October 3, 1990, the two states became one country. Two months later, a united Germany voted in the first nationwide elections since 1932.

Important Wars and Battles in World

- **Battle of Marathon (490 BC):** United Greek army defeated the invading Persian army. A messenger, Pheidippides ran 30 km to Athens to give the good news and died after delivering the news. The marathon race commemorates the brave feat.
- **Battle of Saloms (480 BC):** Greece again repulses the Persian attack.
- **Paloponnesian Wars (459-404 BC):** Two Greek City-States Athens and Sparta struggled for supremacy in those wars. The first war was 459 to 446 BC while the second war lasted from 431 to 404 BC.
- **Alexander's Invasion (336 to 323 BC):** Alexander of Macedonia went on to capture Greece, Achalmend empire and upto Indian borders.
- **Punic Wars (264 to 146 BC):** Romans attacked Carthage, set the city on fire and enslaved people of the losing side.
- **Battle of Actium (31 BC):** Roman king Octavien's naval force defeated the combined strength of Mark Antony and Cleopatra.

- **Battle of the Yarmuk (636 AD):** In the early days of Islam, Muslim leader Abu Bakr defeated Christian empire of Byzantium in a clash near the Yarmuk river. It resulted into expulsion of Byzentium and spread of Islam in Syria and Palestine.
- **Battle of Hastings (1066 AD):** The Duke of Normandy, William invaded England and defeated Harold. The English Crown was passed from Saxons to the Normans who brought England in contact with the rest of Europe.
- **Crusades (1095-1444 AD):** Christians, encouraged by Popes, attacked Muslims to recover the holy city of Jerusalem. In the first war, 1095-99, they succeeded in defeating Muslims in Asia minor and Palestine and captured Jerusalem. However, they lost it back to Muslims in 1187. The Christians attempted several times to regain but failed. In the earlier attempts, serious efforts were made and even children were recruited in the name of God. But subsequently, crusades became ineffective. In the name of Crusade, several Kings in Europe killed people of non-Christian sects. But the end of 13th century, the impact and popularity of Crusades diminished. The positive aspect of these wars was that Europeans came in contact with Arab civilization and gained knowledge and experience.
- **Battle of the Neva (1240 AD):** Russian forces, under the leadership of Alexander Nevsky defeated Swedes on the banks of the Neva river.
- **Hundred Years War (1338-1453 AD):** England and France fought over to claims of the English Kings to the French throne. War of the Roses—Two rival royal houses of Lancaster (Red rose as symbol) and York (White rose) struggled for the throne of England.

  The wars began when Richard, Duke of York rebelled against Henry VI but was killed in the battle of Wakefield. The throne kept on passing from one hand to another but finally Henry VII of Lancashire won and established Tudor dynasty with a victory in battle of Bostworth.
- **Italian Wars (1494-1559 AD):** Valois dynasty of France and Hapsbugs fought for the control of Italy. The result was inconclusive but French army was forced to retreat.
- **Malta Siege (1565 AD):** Turkish navy laid siege of Malta for about four months but could not enter. The siege was the beginning of the decline of Ottoman empire.
- **English Civil War (1642-49 AD):** King Charles I forces (called Caveliers) and Parliament forces (Roundheads) fought due to policy differences on religious and political matters. Foremost part, it consisted of skirmishes, marches and sieges. Parliament forces joined hands with Scotland and this scored victory in 1646. There was a brief second civil war but the result was the same.
- **War of Spanish Succession (1702-13 AD):** In this war of succession in Spain, one claimant to the throne was supported by France while the other was supported by Britain, Austria and the Netherlands. During the battle of Blenheim, the British-Austrian army, defeated the French army and Bavarian forces. It lowered the prestige of France which was considered invincible before.
- **Battle of Banker Hill (1775 AD):** First major clash in the American War of Independence. Though the number of American forces was less, the British army suffered heavy casualties and with great difficulty captured Bunker hill.
- **Battle of Yorktown (1781 AD):** British troops under Charles Cornwallis surrendered to an American force led by George Washington, ending the American War of independence.
- **Battle of the Nile (1798 AD):** The British navy under Lord Nelson defeated France in Aboukir bay, near Alexandria. It established British supremacy over the Mediterranean Sea and halted Napolean's expedition towards east.
- **Battle of Trafalgar (1805 AD):** It was fought between the British navy and a combined Franco-Spanish fleet. The British commander Nelson used daring tactics to break enemy's formation and secure overwhelming victory for his country. Nelson was killed but Napolean's hopes of invading England ended forever.

- **Battle of Austerlitz (1805 AD):** Emperor Napolean of France led his troops of victory over Austro-Russian forces commandered by their Emperors. This is also called the battle of three Emperors.
- **Battle of Borodino (1812 AD):** Napolean's forces attacked Russia. They faced stiff resistance but went on to capture Moscow.
- **Battle of Leipzig (1813 AD):** Combined armies of Austria, Prussia and Russia defeated Napolean's troops. It resulted in ending the domination of Napolean over Europe and liberation of Germany from French rule.
- **Battle of Waterloo (1815 AD):** Napolean was finally defeated by the combined armies of Britain, Holland, Belgium and Prussia led by the Duke of Wellington. Napoleon was arrested.
- **Crimean War (1854-56 AD):** Russia fought against the combined force of Britain, France and Turkey. The main issue was Russia's increasing influence in Turkey and its possession of the holy places in Palestine. The war ended with Russia offering peace.
- **Battle of Gettysburg (1863 AD):** In this crucial battle of American Civil war, the union troops of President Abraham Lincoln halted the march of confederate army, supported by Southern states. The defeat at Gettysburg was a big blow to the rebels.
- **Franco-Prussian War (1870-71):** North German Confederation states led Prussia defeated France. As a result, a unified Germany emerged and the balance of power in Europe changed. France, after loss, founded the third republic.
- **Sino-Japanese Wars (1894 and 1931-45 AD):** Japan and China first fought in 1891 for domination in Korean peninsula. Japan, despite being a small nation won an easy victory. The Japanese aim of waging war the second time was to capture whole of mainland China. It gained several military successes but after Japanese collapse in the second world war, China ultimately won.
- **Spanish-American War (1898 AD):** Spain and America fought a war, following mysterious destruction of a US battleship in Havana harbour. USA, aiming to help Cuba in gaining independence and suspecting Spain's hand in the ship destruction, attacked Spanish army as well as navy. It won easily, with Spain giving up all claims to Cuba, and ceding Puerto Rico, Guam and the Philippines.
- **Russo-Japanese War (1904-05 AD):** Japan and Russia fought for domination in Korea and Manchuria. Russia suffered heavy losses and defeats; forcing the Czar Nicholas II to make peace.
- **Balkan Wars (1912-13 AD):** Serbia, Greece, Bulgaria and Montnegro joined hands to strip Turkey of most of its European territory. But a year later, these forces fought among themselves, bringing in other great powers in the area.
- **First World War (1914-18 AD):** The allied Powers (Britain, France, USA, Belgium), etc., defeated Germany and her associates.
- **Battle of Jutland (1916 AD):** It was the greatest naval battle of the First World War. It was fought in the North Sea between Britain and German navies. Both sides suffered heavy losses.
- **Battle of Passchendacle (1917 AD):** Allied forces made a bloody attempt to attack German positions in heavy rain and through thick mud, gaining only a small area but losing over 4 lakh men.
- **Spanish Civil War (1936-39 AD):** The supporters of the republican socialist government of Spain and the conservative, fascist backed forces of General Franco fought a war which soon became an ideological battleground between left and right all over Europe and America. Republican army lost the war.
- **Second World War (1939-45 AD):** The Allies (Britain, France, USA and Russia and Benelux countries, etc. defeated the Axis Powers (Germany, Italy and Japan).
- **Battle of Britain (1940-41 AD):** German air force launched heavy offensive against Britain, with the help of 2,500 aircrafts. However, British

royal air force, despite being smaller in number, put up stiff resistance and forced Germany to abandon plans of landing on British islands.

- **Korean War (1950-53 AD):** The Communist North Korea, backed by China attacked South Korea which was supported by America. United Nations intervened with force, driving North Koreans back. At one point, China and the USA had come face to face but fortunately, the situation stabilised. As per the agreement, the 38th parallel line divided the two countries.
- **Suez Invasion (1956 AD):** Egyptian President Naseer's move to nationalize the Suez Canal, angered France and Britain and they tried to secure control of it. International criticism and pressure forced the Anglo-French forces to agree to ceasefire within a few days and eventually withdraw.
- **Arab-Israel War:** A Jewish state of Israel came into being in Palestine in 1948, displacing Arabs who were staying there. Arabs resisted it and fought a war in 1948-49 but had to settle for co-existence. The tension, due to displaced Palestinian, led to wars in 1967 and 1973. Arab states, Egypt, Jordan, Syria and Lebanon's joint forces were repulsed by Israeli forces and Israel went on to occupy large Arab areas.
- **Iran-Iraq War (1980-88 AD):** Iran and Iraq were interested in becoming the leader of Arabs. After the installation of Islamic regime in Iran, an attempt was made to obstruct entry of ships to Iraq through a waterway. In retaliation, Iraq claimed 3 small but strategic islands, which were in Iran's possession. The war continued for eight years with both sides suffering heavy casualties and economic ruin. The war ended with the UN intervention but no side could claim victory.
- **Gulf War (1991 AD):** Iraq, three years after war with Iran, sent its forces to Kuwait, in August, 1990 and annexed it. The whole world opposed the move and the UN sanctioned a strike by 28 forces, led by America. The war lasted just 40 days, with Iraq suffering humiliating defeat. The war witnessed use of hi-tech weapons. Kuwait became an independent nation again.

Important Religions of The World

Baha'i

This is one of the new religions of the world, founded in 19th century in Persia by prophet Baha-u-llah. It is based on the principle of progressive revelation. There are no priests and leaders. Baha'i is based on the idea that all religion reveal different aspects of the same one truth. Divine revelation never ceases and one day the world will unite and there will be one language in the world. Different religions have grown with various stages of human progress but ultimately the singular truth will prevail.

Buddhism

Gautama Buddha founded Buddhism in the 6th century BC. He was born in a royal family but sorrows and sufferings of the world bothered him so much that he left earthly world for forests. He got enlightenment at Bodh Gaya and gave his first sermon at Sarnath. He dedicated the rest of his life to teaching. He did not claim to be God but after his death, his followers formed a new religion to worship him and to spread his ideas.

Buddha taught four noble truths — there is suffering in the world; this suffering has a cause; the cause is desire; and it is possible to put an end to suffering if desire is removed. To attain freedom from birth and rebirth or nirvana, eight fold path should be adopted which includes Right view, Right resolution, Right words, Right action, Right living, Right effort, Right thinking and Right concentration. The religion stresses the importance of the middle path, avoiding the extremes of strict asceticism or too much indulgence in worldly pleasures. Buddha also preached non-violence. He rejected the authority of the Vedas and caste-system. The Buddhist monks lived a strict disciplined life. They had to renounce most of their possessions, keeping only a ribe, a needle, water strainer and a begging bowl.

A few centuries later, Buddhism divided into two sects—the Hinayana and the Mahayana. The Hinayana (Lesser Vehicle) sect lays emphasis on the salvation of the individual by directly observing the eight fold path, i.e., teachings of Buddha is original form. It is prevalent in Myanmar, Sri Lanka, Cambodia and Vietnam. The followers of Mahayana (Greater Vehicle) worshipped the Buddha as a god and stressed that salvation is open to all. This sect is popular in China, Tibet, Korea and Mongolia.

Christianity

Jesus founded the Christianity religion. He was born as a Jew at Bethlehem near Jerusalem in 4 BC. He went about preaching his message in simple words and come to be known as a great leader. His simple life, magnetic personality and outstanding love and compassion for all made large followers of him. His fearlessness in criticizing the evil made Jewish priests and noble men his enemy. He was crucified but according to legends he rose on the third day after crucifixion. All the years in history are compared in Christian era with the birth of Jesus. BC means Before Christ, and AD means Anno Domini or "in the year of the lord".

Jesus said the authority of God was the Supreme power on earth. He referred to God as father and called himself son of the God. He loved his followers and taught people to love their neighbours. Christians believe that Jesus came to earth and died to redeem from sin and restore him to communion with God. After worldwide preaching of the gospel by his followers, he would reveal himself at the last judgement and reign as universal king. The holy book of Christianity is the Bible, containing two parts—Old Testament has religious beliefs of the Jews while New Testament contains the biography and teachings of Jesus Christ. Jerusalem is the most sacred place for Christians,.

Christianity has three major sects: (1) Roman Catholics are the followers of Roman Church, with Pope as the representative of God; (2) Protestants are the followers of Martin Luther and have separate churches; (3) Orthodox are a Catholics but authority of the Pope and recognise the authority of a Patriarchate of Constantinople.

Confucianism

It was founded by Confucius or King Futse, as the Chinese called him, in the sixth century BC. He did not say much about God or other mystical things but placed more emphasis on the proper management of the society. He was primarily concerned with governance and administration. He advocated discipline in life, temperance in eating and drinking habits, respect to elders, justice for all and trustfulness. He asked people to revere the customs of the past. Confucius was more of a moralist and expected all to be true to their duties and responsibilities.

Hinduism

Unlike many other religions, Hinduism does not have any founder. Its sacred writings, 'beliefs and practices came from widely different places and era. It is more of a way of life. Despite several attempts at forced and organised conversions, Hinduism is one of the few surviving religion with a large following in South Asia. The Hindus have multiple Gods and Goddesses, with Vishnu, Brahma, Mahesh and Shakti being prominent ones. They are prayed by different names. and picturised differently all over. The scriptures of Hinduism are many in number, with the important ones being from Vedas, Gita and Ramayana.

Hinduism teaches the existence of one supreme universal spirit but allows the followers to worship him in any form. It believes in the doctrines of Karma and re-births. Soul within the body is believed to be immortal. It considers Dharma, or virtue, Artha or material well-being and Karma or gratification of the senses as three main aims of human life. Moksha or salvation is the ultimate aim of life, according to Hinduism. Another characteristic of Hinduism is Varnashrama. According to it, there are four Varnas as per the occupation and four ashramas as per different stages of life. The religion has never been static or uniform and has adopted itself to the changing circumstances and conditions of life. Different sects of Hinduism have various doctrines, principles, philosophies and rituals but all of them have co-existed, respecting each other. Since Hinduism did not have any central authority and permitted individuals to think and act on their own, it never developed as an organised religion like others.

Islam

Prophet Muhammad founded in sixth century AD, the religion of Islam, literally meaning submission to God. A muslim is one who submits. Muhammad was born in Mecca in 571 AD. At the age of 40, he had visions of truth and became a prophet. Due to opposition to his preachings, Prophet fled to Medina in 622 AD (Hejira or Mohammedan calendar begins from this date). He came back to capture Mecca with the help of his supporters. Prophet died in 632 AD.

Islam believes in a single God as supreme lord of the universe, arbiter of man's fate, all-powerful, all-knowing and all-pervading. Man is powerless before Allah and must, therefore, submit to his will. Muslims pray and bow before the God only. They recognize earlier prophets before Muhammad as well but believe that he was the last and the greatest. Islam speaks of a life after death and of a last judgement when all men shall receive the reward for their actions on earth. Muslims all over the world regard themselves as brothers and equals. A muslim must (1) proclaim the unity of God and the prophethood of Muhammad, (2) pray five times in a day; (3) give alms to the poor; (4) keep fast during the days of Ramazan month and (5) make pilgrimage to Mecca. Islam lays down some observation and forbids some practices. Muslims are forbidden from worshipping an Idol, eating pork and lending money on interest. Islam's emphasis on a life of virtue and benevolence made it one of the great humanitarian religions. Quran is their holy book which is believed to have the word of God, received by Muhammad. Islam's followers got divided into Shias and Sunnis, but both believe in Quran and Prophet Muhammad.

Jainism

Jainism derives its name from Jaina (the conqueror), the surname of Vardhamana Mahavira who lived in the 6th century BC. Mahavira was the last of the 24 Tirthankaras or great religious leaders. The Jains believe that every object, living or non-living, has a soul. So, they lay great emphasis on ahimsa or non-injury. Mahavira denied the authority of the Vedas. He laid emphasis on food conduct and taught right belief, right knowledge and right conduct for attaining salvation. Jainism believes in the doctrine of Karma and rebirth but shunned rituals. Jainism later on split in two sects—the Digambaras (who wear no clothes) and the Shvetambaras (who wear white clothes).

Judaism

It is the religion of the Jews or the Hebrew people who had settled in Mesopotamia under the leadership of Abraham. Later, Moses united different tribes who worshipped Yahweh or Jehovah. Judaism is the world's most ancient religion, honouring a single God and from which Islam and Christianity grew. It is a blend of religious doctrine, prophecy and social laws. The ten commandments, believed to have been revealed by God to Moses, lay down laws to guide the life of the followers. Some prophets of Jews proclaimed that God loves man and is ready to forgive a sinner who repents, Judaism preaches justice, mercy and humanity. Jews believe that the Messiah will one day appear on earth, purify the Hebrew and cleanse the world of sin and wickedness. Judaism does not believe Jesus Christ to be the Messiah. Old Testament is the sacred book of Judaism while Jerusalem is their holy place.

Zionism developed on the longing of Jews to return to their holy land of Zion (Jerusalem). It began to become an international force in the late 19th century and by 1948, Israel had been established. Presently, it is a nationalist movement, seeking to bring back the dispersed Jews to Israel.

Shintoism

It is the combination of traditional religious beliefs and practices of the Japanese. It is one of the oldest surviving religion, having its origin into nature worship and allowing followers to pray different gods and spirits. The religion does not have any sacred book or moral code. It is a largely a set of traditional rituals.

Sikhism

The founder of Sikhism, Guru Nanak stressed unity of God and condemned idolatory, ritualism and caste system. He emphasised the necessity of worshipping God through love. He assimilated good features of Hinduism and Islam. His teachings were compiled in a book called Adi-Granth. The tenth Guru of Sikhism Govind Singh instituted the institution of "Panj Piaras" and five customs—Kesh (hairs of head and beard to be grown), Kaccha (underwear), Kara (bracelet), Kangha (comb) and Kirpan (sword). Guru

Govind Singh was the last Guru of Sikhs. Sikhs pray in Gurudwara and their sacred places are Amritsar, Nanakana Sahib and Anandpur Sahib.

Taoism

Leo-tse, meaning older master, was born in China in 604 BC. A short book "Tao te King" was written by him containing the essence of Taoism. It asked men to follow the natural way and to live a simple life. It stressed on meditation which would help man achieve inner power and confidence. Taoism which had originally preached enlightenment and inner joy for individual, got lost in magical practices.

Zoroastrianism

It was founded by prophet Zoroaster in 6th century BC in Persia. He said life was a struggle between the forces of good, the Ahura Mazda and evil the Angra Mainyu and man cannot be neutral in the struggle. He said those who lived in a righteous life went to heaven while the impious were condemned to hell eternally. After spread of Islam, followers fled to other places and called themselves Parsis. Their place of worship is called fire temple and holy book is Avesta.

Eminent Personalities of The World

- **Alexander, the Great (356-323 BC):** King of Macedonia, he led the Greek states against Persia, captured Egypt and penetrated upto India. He founded the City of Alexandria.
- **Antonius Marcus (Mark Antony) (83-30 BC):** He was in the Court of Julius Ceasar, along with Brutus and Cassius. After Ceasar's death, he was defeated by Octavian. His association with Egyptian Queen Cleopatra is the subject of Shakespeare's play.
- **Antony, St. (251-356):** He was early promoter of monastic life.
- **Arafat, Yasser (1929-2004):** He was President of the Palestine. He led the Palestinian Liberation Organisation that opposed the Israeli occupation of Muslim-majority areas. He shared the Nobel Peace Prize for solving the West Asia problem in non-violent method.
- **Archimedes (287-212 BC):** He was a Greek mathematician who is known for his contributions to pure mathematics, mechanics and hydrostatics.
- **Aristotle (384-322 BC):** The pupil of Plato, he was a greek philosopher. He taught the young prince Alexander and established a school in Athens.
- **Armstrong, Neil (1930-2012):** He was the US astronaut who became the first man to set foot on moon.
- **Ataturk, Kamal (1881-1938):** He was the builder of modern Turkey, being its President from 1923 to 1938. He defended against the British and drove the Greeks out of Turkey.
- **Augustus, C. Octavianus (63 BC-14AD):** He was nephew of Julius Ceasar. He became Roman emperor whose reign was notable for peace and creative activities.
- **Ayub Khan, Mohammed (1907-74):** He was the army chief of Pakistan who took over the reigns of the country after military coup. He was the longest serving President of Pakistan from 1958 to 1969.
- **Bhandarnaike, Sirimavo:** She was the world's first woman Prime Minister. She took reigns of Ceylon (Sri Lanka) after the assassination of her husband in 1960. She again became Prime Minister in 1970 and 1994.
- **Bernard, Christian N. (1922-2001):** South African surgeon who pioneered heart transplant surgery in 1967.
- **Beatles, The:** Famous English music group whose highly original melodic songs took the youth of the world by storm in 1960s. The original group comprised Paul McCartney, John Lennon, George Harrison and Ringo Starr. They parted ways in 1971.
- **Beethoven, Ludwig Van (1770-1827):** One of the greatest musician who became deaf later in his life. His composition of nine symphonies is ranked the greatest one.
- **Bismarck (1815-98):** Prusso-German diplomat and statesman who became chief architect of the German unification.

- **Bolivar, Simon (1783-1830):** South America revolutionary leader who led independence movements in the north-west of South America against Spanish rule and became a Latin American hero.
- **Bradman, Donald (1909-2001):** Australian captain and cricketer who scored 29 centuries in test matches and is known as one of the greatest batsman of all time. He died in Adelaide (Australia) on February 25, 2001.
- **Brezhnev, Leonid Ilyich (1906-82):** He took over the reigns of Soviet Union in 1964 which was also the period of cold war. During his leadership, Soviet Union achieved strategic parity with US as his country tried to spread communism worldwide.
- **Ceasar, Julius (101-44 BC):** He was Roman General who paved the way for glorious years for his country. He was murdered by his friends and ministers.
- **Castro, Fidel (b. -1927):** Cuban revolutionary who overthrew the Government in 1959 and took over the country's reigns. He had good relations with Soviet Union and has steered his country for over 3 decades despite stiff resistance from neighbouring America.
- **Chaplin, Charles Spencer (1889-1977):** A comic character who became the first international screen star. He worked and directed hundreds of films.
- **Chenghis Khan (1162-1227):** Mongol conqueror who overran and devastated a large portion of Asia.
- **Chou-en-Lai (1898-1976):** He was the revolutionary leader of China who, along with Mao-Tse-Tung brought communism. He became Prime Minister of the Communist China in 1949.
- **Churchill, Winston (1874-1967):** British statesman who led the country during the World War II as its Prime Minister. He again became the Prime Minister from 1950 to 1955.
- **Columbus, Christopher (1451-1506):** Italian navigator who, with spanish support, discovered Cuba, Bahamas and Islands of West Indies.
- **Constantine (247-338):** He was the first Christian Roman emperor. He founded a new capital at Constantinopole.
- **Copernicus, Nicolas (1478-1543):** Polish astronomer and scientist who put forward the theory of Earth being of moving around the Sun.
- **Dante (1265-1321):** He was an Italian poet whose book "Divina Commedia" is world famous.
- **Darwin, Charles (1809-82):** English biologist who gave theory of evolution of species.
- **Deng Xiaoping (1904-97):** Chinese politician who steered his country in 1980s and 90s by introducing economic reforms without political freedoms.
- **Disraeli Benjamin (1804-81):** British statesman and novelist who became its Prime Minister twice.
- **Einstein, Albert (1879-1955):** German scientist who later migrated to America. He gave Theory of Relativity and won Noble Prize.
- **Franklin Benjamin (1706-90):** American statesman who helped in framing of American Constitution and getting French support for their war against the British. He also explained lightening and invented lightening conductor.
- **Gagrin, Yuri (1934-68):** Soviet cosmonaut who became the first man to go into space and come back safely.
- **Galileo (1564-1642):** Italian scientist who laid the foundations of modern science. He discovered telescope, thermometer and supported Sun-Centre Theory.
- **Gama, Vasco da (1460-1524):** Portuguese navigator who discovered the sea route to India through Cape of Good Hope.
- **Garibaldi, Giuseppe (1807-82):** Italian statesman who with Mazzini and Cavour created a united Italy.
- **Gaulle, Charles de (1890-1970):** French general and statesman who became the first President of the fifth republic in 1958.
- **Gorbachev, Mikhail (1931-2022):** Soviet politician who became the General Secretary of

Communist Party and President of Nation. He practiced the policies of Glasnost (Openness) and Perestroika (Restructuring) which led to revolutionary changes in Eastern Europe and Soviet Union. His country disintegrated, economy backfired and political crisis grew, forcing him to resign in 1991. He won Nobel Peace Prize in 1990.

- **Harun-al-Rashid (763-809):** Caliph of baghdad whose court became a centre for art and learning.
- **Herodotus (485.425 BC):** Greek historian, often called the father of history.
- **Hippocrates:** Greek physician who contributed towards separation of medicine from superstition. Medical students are supposed to take a oath after his name.
- **Hitler, Adolf (1889-1945):** Dictator of Germany who founded Nazi Party. He destroyed working class movement, prosecuted opponents, particularly Jews and communists and took aggressive postures against the neighbours. This led to Second World War in which his troops were defeated. He committed suicide as the Russian troops closed in on Berlin.
- **Ho Chi-Minh (1892-1969):** The Communist leader of Vietnam who struggled for his country's independence and later as President of North Vietnam, fought to control South Vietnam, even defying United States.
- **Homer:** Greek poet who wrote Iliad and Odyssey.
- **Jinnah, Mohammed Ali (1876-1948):** Pakistani statesman, who forced two nation theory on the British by going on direct action. India was divided into two dominions and he became first Governor-General of Independent Pakistan.
- **Khomeini, Ayatollah (1900-89):** Iranian religious leader who after 16 years in exile returned home to overthrow the King and set up Islamic republic. He was, totally anti-west and fought war with Iraq for about a decade.
- **Kublai Khan (1216-94):** Grandson of Chengis Khan who become the first Mongol emperor of China. He won several new areas and merged them into his empire.
- **Lee Kuon Yew (b. 1923):** First Prime Minister of Singapore who continued from 1959 to 1990. He is the architect of Singapore's economic prosperity. However, he did not permit any political activity or opposition.
- **Lenin (1870-1924):** His original name was Vladimir Ilyich Vlyanov. He was revolutionary leader and statesman of Russia. He led the Bolsheviks in the 1917 revolution and headed the new government.
- **Leonardo da Vinci (1452-1519):** He was Italian artist as well as scientist. His painting "Monalisa" and "The Last Supper" are world famous. He studied anatomy, waves, currents and motions.
- **Lincoln, Abraham (1809-65):** He was the President of America who had to fight civil war to end slavery in the country. He coined the phrase "for the people, of the people, by the people". He was assassinated.
- **Luther, Martin (1483-1546):** He was German protestant and reformer who preached against the indulgences and luxurious life style of the church.
- **Mandela, Nelson (1918-2013):** He was the former President of South Africa. He was imprisoned for 27 years for opposing the racist rule. His release paved the way for end of apartheism. He won the Nobel Peace Prize in 1993.
- **Mao-Tse-Tung (1893-1976):** He was communist leader of China who founded communist government in 1949 in the mainland. He promoted cultural revolution which led to China's isolation from the world.
- **Marx, Karl (1818-83):** He was the founder of modern international communism and wrote 'Das Kapital', a book on economics. Along with Engels, he wrote the Communist Manifesto. He helped in founding of the first international. He is treated as the guru by all the left-thinking people.
- **Michel Angelo (1475-1564):** World famous Italian painter, sculptor and poet.
- **Mussolini Benito (1883-1945):** Fascist dictator of Italy who sided with Germany during Second World War. He was shot dead while trying to flee Italy.

- **Napolean Bonaparte (1769-1821):** He was emperor of France who made attempts to expand its boundaries. He succeeded initially but was defeated in Waterloo in 1815.
- **Nasser, Gamal Abdul (1918-70):** He was leader of modern Egypt and Arab world. He introduced democracy, nationalised Suez Canal despite opposition from France and Britain, and led Arabs against Israel in 1967 war.
- **Nightingale Florence (1820-1910):** English nurse and pioneer of hospital reforms who came to be known as "the lady with the lamp".
- **Omar Khayyam (1050-1123):** Persian poet and mathematician whose Rubbaiyat became world famous.
- **Picasso, Pablo (1881-1973):** Spanish painter who was brilliant in sculpture, ceremonies and graphic arts also.
- **Polo, Marco (1256-1323):** Traveller from Italy who went to China and India and left an account of his travels.
- **Rousseau, Jean-Jacques (1712-78):** French political philosopher and educationist whose views stimulated the people and led to French revolution.
- **Shakespeare, William (1564-1616):** Greatest poet and playwright of English whose mastery of language, understanding of character and their dramatic perception has been unsurpassed. His major contributions were Romeo and Juliet, The Merchant of Venice, Much Ado About Nothing, Julius Ceasar, Hemlet, Macbeth, Othello, Anatony and Cleopatra, Measure for Measure.
- **Shaw, G.B. (1856-1950):** Dramatist who used wit in his plays to highlight hypocrisy and rational weaknesses. His important writings are Mali and Superman, The Apple Cart and Heartbreak House.
- **Socrates (470-399 BC):** Greek philosopher and intellectual leader.
- **Stalin (1879-1953):** Joseph Vissarionovich Djugashvili was his original name. After the death of Lenin, he took the reigns of Soviet Union. He used ruthless means to bring about economic prosperity and political discipline. He was the architect of five-year plans.
- **Tito, Joseph Broz (1892-1980):** He was the leader of Yugoslavia who secured its independence and later on became a pillar of Non-Aligned Movement in the world.
- **Washington, George (1732-99):** He became the first President of America. He led his forces to defeat Cornwallis. He presided over the Philadelphia Convention that formulated the Constitution.

Nicknames of World Personalities

- **Bard of Avon:** Shakespeare
- **Duce:** Mussolini
- **Desert Fox:** General Rommel
- **Father of English Poetry:** Chaucer
- **G.B.S.:** George Bernard Shaw
- **Grand Old Man of Britain:** Gladstone
- **G.I.:** American Soldier
- **Great Commoner:** Pitt the Young
- **Iron Duke:** Duke of Wellington
- **Iron Butterfly:** Margaret Thatcher
- **Ike:** Eisenhower
- **John Bull:** England and English people
- **K of K:** Kitchner of Khartoum
- **King maker:** Earl of Warwick
- **Little Corporal:** Napolean
- **Lady with the Lamp:** Florence Nightingale
- **Mark Twain:** Samuel Clemens
- **Mandarin:** Chinese official
- **Man of Destiny:** Napolean
- **Maiden Queen:** Elizabeth
- **Maid of Orleans:** Joan of the Arc
- **Man of Blood and Iron:** Bismarck
- **Negus:** Kings of Ethiopia
- **Poolu:** French Soldier
- **Tom Atkins:** British Soldier
- **Uncle Sam:** Americans
- **Yankee:** Americans

Multiple Choice Questions

1. Harappan people had a common burial system which is proved by:

A. The earth burials with head of the dead normally laid towards the north.

B. The burial of commonly used items with the dead.

C. Both A and B above.

D. The burial of the dead body in the sitting posture.

2. Pair the Harappan settlements with the banks of rivers on which they were located:

Sites	*Banks of Rivers*
(*a*) Lothal	I. Indus
(*b*) Kalibangan	II. Sutlej
(*c*) Ropar	III. Ravi
(*d*) Harappa	IV. Ghaggar
(*e*) Mohenjo-daro	V. Bhogava

	(*a*)	(*b*)	(*c*)	(*d*)	(*e*)
A.	V	IV	II	III	I
B.	II	V	I	IV	III
C.	IV	V	II	III	I
D.	V	IV	III	II	I

3. Four largest Harappan settlements in the Indo-Pak subcontinent are

(*i*) Harappa (*ii*) Mohenjo-daro

(*iii*) Ganeriwala (*iv*) Dholavira

(*v*) Kalibangan

A. (*i*), (*ii*), (*iv*) and (*v*)

B. (*i*), (*ii*), (*iii*) and (*iv*)

C. (*ii*), (*iii*), (*iv*) and (*v*)

D. (*i*), (*iii*), (*iv*) and (*v*)

4. Which of the following birds was worshipped by the Harappan people?

A. Crow B. Peacock

C. Pigeon D. Eagle

5. Match the following ancient sites with their respective archaeological findings:

Sites	*Findings*
(*a*) Lothal	1. Ploughed field
(*b*) Kalibangan	2. Dockyard
(*c*) Dholavira	3. Terracotta replica of a plough
(*d*) Banwali	4. An inscription comprising ten large sized signs of the Harappan script.

	(*a*)	(*b*)	(*c*)	(*d*)
A.	1	2	3	4
B.	2	1	4	3
C.	1	2	4	3
D.	2	1	3	4

6. The Indus Valley Civilisation is:

A. About ten thousand years old

B. Seven thousand years old

C. Five thousand years old

D. Three thousand years old

7. The biggest building at Mohenjo-daro was the:

A. Assembly Hall

B. Great Bath

C. Rectangular Building

D. Great Granary

8. Name the city which had houses with entrances on the main street.

A. Kalibangan B. Lothal

C. Mohenjo-daro D. Chanhu-daro

9. Find out the most acceptable cause that made the Harappans move away from their urban settlements.

A. Ecological changes

B. Foreign invasion

C. Demographic changes

D. Hydrological changes

10. (A): In comparison to the Egyptians and Sumerians, Indus people made limited use of their script and languages.

(R): The 'pictographic' script of the Indus people is derived partly from the 'Cuneiform' writing of the Sumerians and partly from the 'Hieroglyphics' of the Egyptians.

A. Both (A) and (R) are correct and (R) explains (A).

B. Both (A) and (R) are correct but (R) does not explain (A).

C. (A) is correct but (R) is not.
D. (A) is wrong but (R) is not.

11. Which of the following was the most important industry of the Harappans at Lothal and Chanhudaro?
A. Ship building B. Bead making
C. Weaving D. Metallurgy

12. The Indus Valley people used lime and expensive burnt bricks instead of sun dried bricks, because of
A. Advanced technology
B. Better planning
C. A moist climate on account of the close proximity of the civilisation to the river valleys.
D. Their knowledge of the manufacture of lime.

13. The Indus Valley Civilisation specialised in
A. Town Planning B. Architecture
C. Craftsmanship D. All of these

14. The Indus religion did not include the worship of
A. Forces of Nature.
B. Mother Goddess.
C. Certain animal chimeras and their anthropic figures.
D. Trees and their spirits.

15. How many granaries are there in Harappa?
A. Six B. Four
C. Eight D. Seven

16. The largest number of Harappan sites in post-independence India have been discovered in
A. Rajasthan
B. Punjab and Haryana
C. N.W. Uttar Pradesh
D. Gujarat

17. Which of the following was not the likely purpose of the Great Bath in the citadel at Mohenjo-daro?
A. Swimming exercises and water sports.
B. Some elaborate ritual of vital importance, including a corporate social life.
C. Storage of water to be used during drought or emergency.
D. Community bathing.

18. In most of the Indus seals, there is representation of:
A. Tiger
B. Elephant
C. Humped bull
D. Humpless bull or unicorn bull

19. No trace of .... has been found in the Indus Valley Civilisation.
A. Sugarcane B. Mustard
C. Sesamum D. Barley

20. The number of seals which constitute the primary source of knowing the Civilisation of the Indus Valley people is about:
A. 1,000 B. 2,000
C. 3,000 D. 4,000

21. Match the following Vedic gods with their actual status or functions:

(*a*) Pushan	I. God of heaven and father of Surya
(*b*) Savitri	II. Mother of Surya
(*c*) Aditi	III. God of light
(*d*) Dyaus	IV. God of marriages

	(*a*)	(*b*)	(*c*)	(*d*)
A.	IV	III	II	I
B.	IV	II	III	I
C.	II	III	IV	I
D.	I	II	III	IV

22. The famous Vedic saying, "War begins in the minds of men", is stated in the
A. Rigveda
B. Samaveda
C. Atharvaveda
D. Mundaka Upanishad

23. Which of the following was not one of the reasons for the gradual weakening of the tribal assemblies in the later Vedic period?
A. Increase in the royal power.
B. In large territorial states ordinary people could not travel long distances to attend their meetings.
C. The assemblies acquired an aristocratic character which took away most of their effectiveness.
D. They also surrendered some of their activities to the new officials called *ratnins*.

24. Among the various units of the tribal kingdom (rashtra) of the Vedic society, which one of the following was the basic unit?
A. *Vish* B. *Jana*
C. *Kula* D. *Grama*

25. Which of the following statements about the system of taxation and revenue administration in the Later Vedic period is *NOT* correct?
A. Settled life and stable agriculture led to the production of surplus which could be collected by the king in the form of taxes.
B. The king received regular contributions from the people in the shape of *bali* and *shulka*
C. One-sixth of the produce of the land was payable to the king
D. An official called *bhagadugha* collected the royal share of the produce.

26. In the Vedic Age
A. polygamy was unknown
B. child marriage became prominent
C. widows could remarry
D. hypergamy was allowed

27. Which of the following is/are matched correctly?
I. *Samaveda*—melody.
II. *Atharvaveda*—mainly magical spells.
III. *Aranyakas*—forest books.
IV. *Srauta Sutra*—ceremonies of domestic life.
A. I and III B. II and III
C. I, II and III D. I, III and IV

28. Name the Rig Vedic god who is believed to be the upholder of the "*Rita*" or Cosmic order.
A. Agni B. Soma
C. Indra D. Varuna

29. 'Sruti' literature does not include the
A. *Vedangas* B. *Brahmanas*
C. *Upanishads* D. *Aranyakas*

30. Where do we find the mention of the Eastern and the Western Seas for the first time?
A. *Aithareya Brahmana*
B. *Kausitaki Brahmana*
C. *Taittiriya Brahmana*
D. *Satapatha Brahmana*

31. Buddhist literary texts attach importance to a Buddhist overseas mission. To which place was the mission sent?
A. Java B. Sumatra
C. Malaysia D. Sri Lanka

32. Vardhamana was said to have attained Nirvana under the
A. Sal tree B. Pipal tree
C. Neem tree D. Banyan tree

33. There is evidence to show that Vishnu cult spread overseas in the early centuries of the Christian era. Which was the place that this cult spread to?
A. Greece B. Cambodia
C. Thailand D. China

34. Identify the place which is said to be the birth place of Buddhism.
A. Rajagriha B. Kusinagara
C. Lumbini D. Sarnath

35. Which of the following is not a biography of Lord Buddha?
A. *Lalitavistara* B. *Mahavastu*
C. *Nidankatha* D. *Mahavamsa*

36. During the reign of which of the following kings did Mahayanism formally come into existence?
A. Ajatshatru B. Dharmpala
C. Ashoka D. Kanishka

37. Find out the number of stories included in the Jatakas?
A. 750 B. 320
C. 860 D. 500

38. Which of the following was NOT one of the "Three Jewels" of Buddhism?
A. Buddha B. Ahimsa
C. Dhamma D. Sangha

39. The first Buddhist nun was
A. Gautami B. Mahamaya
C. Yasodhara D. Sujata

40. The first *Tirthankara,* according to Jaina tradition, was
A. Hemchandra B. Rishabha
C. Sthulabahu D. Augisara

41. Which of the following is NOT among the 'three ratnas' or gems of Jainism?
A. Full knowledge B. Action
C. Liberation D. Belief in God

42. What was the name of the Jaina monk under whose leadership a large Jain community migrated from Magadha to Shravanabelagola in Karnataka in the fourth century BC?
A. Nagarjuna B. Sanghadasa
C. Haribhadra D. Bhadrabahu

43. Which of the following were NOT one of the royal patrons of Jainism?
A. Satvahanas
B. Gangas
C. Chalukyas of Gujarat
D. Rashtrakutas

44. At which of the following places did Mahavira's death take place?
A. Kusinagara B. Vaishali
C. Rajagriha D. Pava Puri

45. The real founder of Jainism was:
A. Vardhaman Mahavira
B. Neminath
C. Parsvanath
D. Rishabhanath

46. Name the earliest known follower of Bhagavatism.
A. Demetrius B. Antialkidas
C. Megasthenese D. Heliodorus

47. The traces of the Bhagavata cult is not found in the:
A. *Upanishads* B. *Brahmanas*
C. *Puranas* D. *Epics*

48. Arrange the Avatars in the chronological order.
(*i*) Rama (*ii*) Kelkin
(*iii*) Krishna (*iv*) Buddha
(*v*) Parasurama
A. (*v*), (*i*), (*iii*), (*iv*), (*ii*)
B. (*ii*), (*iv*), (*i*), (*iii*), (*v*)
C. (*v*), (*iv*), (*ii*), (*iii*), (*i*)
D. (*i*), (*ii*), (*iii*), (*v*), (*iv*)

49. What was the other name for "Tevaram"?
A. Dravida Veda B. Pattapattu
C. Prabhandhas D. Ettatogai

50. Where did Buddha attain enlightenment?
A. Lumbini B. Sarnath
C. Bodh Gaya D. Kusinagara

51. The sacred books of Jains are called:
A. *Agama-Sidhanta* B. *Angas*
C. *Parvas* D. *Upangas*

52. Who wrote *Milanda-panho*?
A. Buddhadutta B. Nagasena
C. Buddaghosha D. Kautilya

53. Among the 12 *Angas*, which was the most important?
A. Second B. Fifth
C. Sixth D. First

54. Who was responsible for the revival of Brahmanical Hinduism?
A. Kautilya B. Harshavardhana
C. Bijjala D. Shankaracharya

55. Identify correctly the following terms:

List I	List II
(*a*) Upasaka	I. Monk
(*b*) Bhikshu	II. Lay disciple
(*c*) Sangha	III. Eight-fold Path
(*d*) Ashtangika-marga	IV. Community of Buddhist monks

	(*a*)	(*b*)	(*c*)	(*d*)
A.	I	II	III	IV
B.	II	I	IV	III
C.	IV	III	II	I
D.	III	IV	II	I

56. 'The torch that would dispel the gloom of misery and ignorance was lighted at Gaya under the Holy tree'. Whom is the author referring to?
A. Buddha B. Mahavira
C. Ashoka D. Krishna

57. *Tripitakas* are the sacred books of the:
A. Jains B. Hindus
C. Buddhist D. Muslims

58. The first human statues worshipped in India were those of:
A. Brahma B. Vishnu
C. Buddha D. Shiva

59. What metal was first used by the Vedic people?
A. Silver B. Gold
C. Iron D. Copper

60. The Sarvastivadin school of Buddhism mainly flourished in:
A. Bengal
B. Magadha
C. The Punjab and NW Front
D. Maharashtra

61. The chief centre of the Chola power was at:
A. Uraiyur B. Madurai
C. Puhar D. Vanji

62. Who founded the port city of Puhar?
A. Elara B. Karikala
C. Senguttuan D. Nedunjeral

63. The Sangams were:
A. the Buddhist religious texts
B. the Hindu-religious texts written in Tamil
C. titles of a south Indian dynasty
D. societies of learned men

64. The Sangams flourished in:
A. the Pandya kingdom
B. the Chola kingdom
C. the Chera kingdom
D. the Pallava kingdom

65. The Sangam age was between:
A. 1500 BC - 1000 AD
B. 1000 BC - 1000 AD
C. 500 BC - 500 AD
D. 250 BC - 250 AD

66. Which of the following is not a great epic of the Sangam literature?
A. Silappadikaram B. Manimekalai
C. Paltupattu D. Ettutoggai

67. The centre of Sangam literature and its patrons were:
A. the Chers of Vanji
B. the Cholas of Uraiyur
C. the Pandyas of Madurai
D. All of above

68. The spies during the Sangam age were known as:
A. Spasas B. Dutas
C. Orrars D. Sanjayans

69. Small village assemblies during the Sangam Age were known as:
A. Manaram B. Ambalan
C. Avai D. Podiyil

70. Which of the following institutions did not exist during the Sangam Age?
A. Slavery
B. Sati
C. Ritualistic marriage
D. Courtesans

71. The most favourite God of the Tamils during the Sangam age was:
A. Indra B. Murugan
C. Tirumal D. Varuna

72. The latest inscriptions of Ashoka were discovered from:
A. Kandhar
B. Sannatai inscriptions
C. Maski
D. Bhabru edict

73. The Kandhar inscriptions were written in .... script.
A. Kharosthi B. Greek
C. Aramaic D. Both B and C

74. For the early life of Chandragupta Maurya, we have to depend on the:
A. Puranas B. Buddhist sources
C. Jain sources D. Greek accounts

75. In which of the following sects was Bindusara interested?
A. Buddhism B. Jainism
C. Ajivikas D. Lokayats

76. The key note of Ashoka policy of dhamma was:
A. self-control B. kindness
C. charity D. moderation

77. In which year of Ashoka coronation did the Kalinga war take place?
A. First B. Fifth
C. Eighth D. Thirteenth

78. Indica was written by:
A. Megasthnese B. Strabo
C. Pliny D. Justin

79. During the rule of the Mauryans, normally the revenue was:
A. 1/2 of the produce
B. 1/4 of the produce
C. 1/6 of the produce
D. 1/8 of the produce

80. During the Mauryan age, land was accepted as the property of:
A. The State
B. The Village-Panchayat
C. The Individual
D. The Zamindars

81. Which of the following Chinese pilgrims to India gives us some informations about the first Gupta ruler?
A. Huen-Tsang B. Fa-Hien
C. It-sing D. Wang-Hien-Tse

82. Which of the following cities lost its prominence during the post-Gupta period?
A. Mathura B. Pataliputra
C. Varanasi D. Kannauj

83. The Hunas occupied large parts of central India and the first Huna king was:
A. Varahamihira B. Mihirkula
C. Toramana D. Rudravarman

84. Which of the following titles was not adopted by Chandragupta-II?
A. Vikramaditya B. Narendrachandra
C. Simhachandra D. Devagupta

85. Who among the following rulers was called Kaviraja?
A. Kumar Gupta-I
B. Chandragupta Vikramaditya
C. Chandragupta-I
D. Samudragupta

86. Twelve kings of Dakshinapath were captured and liberated by:
A. Kumara Gupta B. Skanda Gupta
C. Samudragupta D. Chandragupta

87. Harisena prashasti refers to the exploits of:
A. Rama Gupta
B. Chandragupta Vikramaditya
C. Samudragupta
D. Sri Gupta

88. Which was the main market of the Kushana period?
A. Begram B. Broach
C. Karkai D. None of the above

89. Which term does not have any connotation with guilds?
A. Gana B. Sresthi
C. Nigama D. Vithi

90. Which of the following was not among the main water ways of the Gupta era?
A. Ganges B. Yamuna
C. Krishna D. None of the above

91. Which of the later Guptas assumed the imperial title of Maharajadhiraj and performed the horse sacrifice?
A. Kumara Gupta B. Mahasena Gupta
C. Ram Gupta D. Adityasena

92. Which of the following refers to unpaid labour?
A. Bali B. Sulka
C. Udranga D. Visti

93. The term brahmadeya occurs for the first time in :
A. early Vedic texts
B. early Buddhists texts
C. pre-Gupta inscriptions.
D. post-Gupta inscriptions

94. Ghatiyantra was used in early India for:
A. manufacture of vessels of metal
B. pouring of water in sacrificial rituals
C. conducting tantric rituals
D. irrigation from wells

95. The power of the Hunas was consolidated in India by their leader:
A. Toramana B. Mihirkula
C. Sala D. Dantidurga

96. From whose accounts do we get an idea of the important Indian ports of the Gupta era?
A. Fa-Hein B. Narada
C. Periplus D. None of the above

97. The beginning of Gupta era was marked with:
A. Accession of Chandragupta-I
B. Samudragupta's accession
C. Samudragupta's military exploits
D. Chandragupta-II's accession

98. Which ruler built the royal highway for Pataliputra to Taxila?
A. Satavahanas B. Mauryas
C. Alexander D. None of the above

99. South India is known for giving numerous land grants to secular as well as religious bodies and temples. Which of the following were the recipients of such land grants?
A. Brahmanical temples
B. Converts to Christianity
C. Buddhist establishments
D. None of the above

100. Consider the following kings:
1. Bhanugupta 2. Budhagupta
3. Kacha 4. Purugupta

The correct chronological sequence of their rulers is:
A. 4, 3 1, 2 B. 4, 3, 2, 1
C. 3, 4, 2, 1 D. 3, 4, 1, 2

101. The credit for completing the conquest of South India goes to:
A. Muhammad Jauna Khan
B. Nusarat Khan
C. Jalaludin Khan
D. Malik Khan

102. The conquest of South India was completed during the reign of:
A. Mubarak Shah Khalji
B. Alauddin Khalji
C. Muhammed Bin Tughlaq
D. Ghiyasuddin Tughlaq

103. The state-promoted canal irrigation system was initiated by:
A. Ghiyasuddin Tughlaq
B. Firoz Tughlaq
C. Muhammad Bin Tughlaq
D. Alauddin Tughlaq

104. Ghiyasuddin Tughlaq attempted to improve agricultural production by:
A. Giving up the oppressive methods for the collection of land revenue
B. Encouraging the cultivation to bring the unreclaimed land under the plough
C. Discarding the system of measurement of land for the assessment of land revenue
D. All of the above

105. The land revenue-yielding territories of the Sultanate were divided into Khalisa or Crown lands and lands ——.
A. Waqf B. Barren
C. Inam D. Iqta

106. The term used for measurement of land in the Sultanate period was:
A. Ghazi B. Masahat
C. Ghola-bakshi D. Kismat-i-ghalla

107. Which of the following was not one of the popular methods of land revenue assessment?
A. Kankut
B. Sharing
C. Qabuliat or Contract
D. Measurement

108. For the collection of the land revenue, the farming system was prevalent. Which of the following did not usually act as a tax farmer?
A. Patwari B. Governor
C. Tributary chief D. Village headman

109. The Sultan who is said to have raised the land revenue to one-half of the produce, was:
A. Muhammad Bin Tughlaq
B. Alauddin Khalji
C. Ghiyasuddin Balban
D. Ghiyasuddin Khalji

110. The administrative set-up to look after and regulate the market control system introduced by Alauddin Khalji was under the purview of:
A. Diwan-i-arz
B. Diwan-i-insha
C. Diwan-i-risalat
D. Diwan-i-riyasat

111. The first Sultan to adopt the principle of measurement of cultivable land for determinating land revenue was:
A. Alauddin Khalji
B. Ghiyasuddin Tughlaq
C. Balban
D. Iltutmish

112. One of the following officers who was the chief revenue collector and was also empowered to settle revenue disputes at pargana level was:
A. Sahib-i-diwan B. Munsif
C. Wali D. Amil

113. The maximum number of Mongol invasions took place during the reign of:
A. Firoz Tughlaq
B. Muhammad Bin Tughlaq
C. Alauddin Khalji
D. Balban

114. The administrative officer whose functions and duties are not matched properly is:
A. Naib-i-mulk – Deputy Prime Minister
B. Akhurbek – Superintendent of royal horses
C. Hamir-i-hajib – Master of ceremonies at the Court
D. Walk-i-dar – Controller of the royal household

115. The provincial governors during the Sultanate period were designated as:
A. Naib B. Muqti or Muqtai
C. Wali D. All of the above

116. Which of the following classes had to pay the maximum amount of Jaziyah?
A. Brahmins, scholarsand Hindu writer
B. Women, children and slaves
C. Money–changers, cloth dealers, land owners, merchants and physicians
D. Tailors, dyers, artisans and shoe-makers

117. The largest standing army of the Sultanate directly paid by the State was created by:
A. Sikander Lodi
B. Muhammad Bin Tughlaq
C. Alauddin Khalji
D. Iltutmish

118. Which of the following Sultans tried to organise the army on the decimal system on the Mongol pattern?
A. Muhammad Bin Tughlaq
B. Firoz Tughlaq
C. Alauddin Khalji
D. Ghiyasuddin Balban

119. The military officer of the Sultanate who was the highest in the military gradation was:
A. Wali B. Amir
C. Malik D. Khan

120. The most important branch of the army of the Sultanate was:
A. Artillery B. Elephants
C. Cavalry D. Infantry

121. Which of the following were not one of the main constituents of the corps of ahadis?
A. Clerks of the imperial offices
B. Officers of the harem
C. Painters of the court
D. Foremen in the royal karkhanas

122. In which of the following wings of the Mughal army were foreingners like Ottomans and Portuguese employed?
A. Navy B. Artillery
C. Matchlockmen D. War-boat-operators

123. A Mughal queen whose name was written to all the Mughal farmans and inscribed on the coins, was:
A. Maham Anaga B. Nur Jahan
C. Mumtaz Mahal D. Mariam Makari

124. Which of the following was in charge of law and order in the villages?
A. Muqaddam B. Patwari
C. Karkun D. Qanungo

125. The Hindu doctrines which greatly impressed Akbar were the doctrines of:
A. karma
B. transmigration of the soul
C. both (A) and (B)
D. predetermination

126. Which of the following was responsible for expounding Muslim law?
A. Qazi-ul-quzat B. Qazi
C. Mufti D. Miradil

127. Which of the following was not a function which the qazi performed in addition to his Judicial responsibilities?
A. Collection of Jeziya
B. Collection of Khams
C. Amin of the Public Treasury
D. Registration of the sale deeds etc.

128. Akbar conferred the title of Jagatguru on:
A. Brahmin philosopher Purushottam
B. Jain Saint Harivijaya Suri
C. Parseee priest Dastur Mahyarji Rana
D. Father Jerome Xavier

129. Which of the following contemporary sources of the Mughal period is especially useful for obtaining information on the agrarian conditions?
A. Akbarnama
B. Ain-i-Akbari
C. Muntakhab-ul-Lubab
D. Tarikh-i-Firishta

130. For which of the following products of Bengal during the Mughal period, was that province especially famous?
A. Rice B. Indigo
C. Sugar D. Cotton

131. Introduction of which of the following crops during the Mughal period brought about a most remarkable change in the cropping pattern?
A. Tea B. Tobacco
C. Indigo D. Potato

132. The first Mughal emperor to organise some sort of distress relief during the famines was:
A. Akbar B. Jahangir
C. Shah Jahan D. Aurangzeb

133. Under the zabti system the most fertile land was classified as:
A. Polaj B. Parauti
C. Chachar D. Banjar

134. What portion of actual produce was fixed as the demand of the state under the zabti system?
A. One-half
B. One-third
C. One-fourth
D. One-fifth

135. In the Mughal period the zamindars served the state as:
A. village administrators
B. village chiefs
C. an agency for collection of land revenue
D. feudatory chiefs

136. Under which system of land revenue assessment was the provision for relief in case of a bad harvest?
A. Batai B. Kankut
C. Zabti D. All of the above

137. The Amalguzar or revenue collector was in charge of:
A. subah B. sarkar
C. pargana D. village

138. Which of the following was not one of the names by which the zamindars were known in different parts of India?
A. Maharaja B. Deshmukh
C. Patil D. Nayak

139. To which of the following categories of persons were Jagirs not normally assigned?
A. Royal princes B. Queens
C. Nobles D. Religious divines

140. Which of the following was not one of the leaders of the Jat uprising during Aurangzeb's time?
A. Gokla, zamindar of Tilpat
B. Champat Rai
C. Rajaram
D. Churaman

141. The credit for founding Calcutta in 1690 goes to:
A. Captain William Heath
B. William Hedges
C. Job Charnock
D. Robert Clive

142. Aurangzeb's policy towards the European merchants was to:
A. suppress piracy
B. keep the sea-route open for the Indian Muslim pilgrims going to the holy cities of Arabia
C. realise the prescribed custom duties
D. all of the above

143. The French Company for the trade of the East India was founded in India by:
A. Colbert B. Francois Martin
C. Francois Caron D. De la Haye

144. The most important French settlement in Bengal was:
A. Hughli B. Murshidabad
C. Chandranagar D. Decca

145. The English governor in India who was expelled by Aurangzeb was:
A. Aungier B. Sir John Child
C. Sir John Gayer D. Sir Nicholas Waite

146. From Bengal the English largely exported:
A. sugar B. saltpetre
C. silks D. all of the above

147. The founder of Madras was:
A. Robert Clive B. Francis Day
C. Gabriel Boughton D. Streynsham Master

148. Who called the English in Bengal "a Company of base, quarrelling people and foul dealers"?
A. Aurangzeb
B. Shayista Khan, Mughal governor of Bengal
C. Mir Jumla
D. Murshid Quli Khan

149. The French got the site of Pondicherry from:
A. the Adilshahi Sultan of Bijapur
B. the ruler of Chandranagar
C. Shaysta Khan, the Mughal viceroy in the Deccan
D. the Qutbshahi Sultan of Golcunda

150. Job Charnock founded Calcutta at the site of:
A. Sutanauti B. Kalikata
C. Govindpur D. All of the above

151. The commodity structure and direction of India's foreign trade was changed by:
A. Portuguese B. Dutch
C. English D. French

152. Indian economy was transformed from a self-sufficient and surplus economy to colonial economy after:
A. Battle of Plassey
B. Battle of Buxer
C. Annexation of Bengal
D. Permanent Settlement

153. The worst sufferers of the British economic policies in India were:
A. peasants
B. artisans
C. both (A) and (B) above
D. merchants and bankers

154. The English greatly enriched themselves by forcing the Indians to produce:
A. cotton B. indigo
C. opium D. (B) and (C) above

155. The growth of modern industries in India was greatly hampered on account of the lack of:
A. Indian capital
B. technical education
C. both (A) and (B) above
D. spirit of enterprise

156. In course of time, the dadni merchants in India were found to be too independent and disinclined to comply with their contracts. In 1753, the dadni merchants were replaced by:
A. Banians B. Gomashtas
C. Dubashes D. Paikars

157. The Lancashire Cotton textiles were first introduced in India, in:
A. 1786 B. 1815
C. 1831 D. 1852

158. In which of the following industries did Indians have a large share from the beginning?
A. Cotton textile B. Jute
C. Coal mining D. Sugar

159. Which of the following was not one of the important European-owned plantation industries of the nineteenth century?
A. Indigo B. Tea
C. Coffee D. Rubber

160. The Ryotwari Settlement was first introduced by
A. Thomas Munro
B. Captain Read
C. Both (A) and (B) above
D. Lord Hastings

161. Which of the following factors caused the greatest racial cleavage in India before the foundation of the National Congress?
A. The Ilbert Bill controversy
B. The reduction of age for entry to the Civil Services
C. The Arms Act of 1878
D. The Vernacular Press Act

162. The Indian Association and National Conference were both founded by:
A. Surendra Nath Banerjee
B. Anand Mohan Bose
C. Both (A) and (B)
D. Sisir Kumar Ghosh

163. During the first twenty years of the Congress, which of the following acted as President of the INC thrice?
A. Surendra Nath Banerjee
B. Dadabhai Naoroji
C. Gopal Krishna Gokhale
D. Sankaran Nair

164. Which of the following founded a National Society, a National Paper, a National School and National Gymnasium and made the word "National" popular in the later half of the 19th century?
A. Jyotindranath Tagore
B. Rajanarayan Bose
C. Nabagopal Mitra
D. Satyendra Tagore

165. Which of the following organisations "anticipated the Congress by two years and in large measure prepared the ground for the Congress"?
A. Indian Association
B. All-India National Conference
C. Indian National Union
D. India League

166. Aurobindo Ghosh was brilliantly defended in the Alipur Conspiracy case by:
A. Chitta Ranjan Das B. W. C. Bonnerjee
C. Motilal Nehru D. Tej Bahadur Sapru

167. Which of the books is not correctly matched with the Author:

	Author	*Book*
A.	Dadabhai Naoroji	Poverty and un-British rule in India
B.	R. C. Dutt	Economic History of India
C.	William Digby	Prosperous British India
D.	D. R. Gadgil	Indian Industry, Today and Tomorrow

168. Ridiculing the idea of Swarajya in 1903 who said: "Only mad men outside lunatic asylums could think or talk of independence"?
A. Lord Curzon
B. Lord Hardinge
C. Gopal Krishna Gokhale
D. Pherozshah Mehta

169. During the British rule the only British King to visit India and hold his magnificent Durbar, was:
A. Edward-VII B. George-V
C. James-II D. Edward-VI

170. A Muslim organisation, which proposed during the First World War that Muslims should participate and try to reach an accord with the Congress, was:
A. Muslim League
B. Ahmadiya movement
C. Ehrar League
D. Deoband movement

171. Bal Gangadhar Tilak was given the epithet of Lokmanya (Universally Respected) during:
A. Swadeshi movement
B. Revolutionary movement
C. Home Rule movement
D. His imprisonment in 1908

172. The only Indian prince, who actively participated in the revolutionary movement within and outside India, was:
A. Raja Mahendra Pratap
B. Kunwar Singh
C. Chhatrapati Sahu
D. Raju Ripudaman Singh

173. Dadabhai Naoroji was elected to the British house of Commons as a member of the ...... Party.
A. Conservative
B. Liberal
C. Labour
D. Labour-Liberal combine

174. Which of the following was not a leader of the All-India Hindu Mahasabha?
A. V. D. Savarkar
B. Bhai Parmanand

C. Dr. Syama Prasad Mookerji
D. M. R. Jayakar

175. Who founded a social organisation, the 'Jatpat Torak Mandal' in 1922, for breaking the caste barriers among the Hindus?
A. Bhai Parmanand
B. Dr. B. R. Ambedkar
C. M. G. Ranade
D. Keshav Chandra Sen

176. Who gave the title of Rani to the Naga woman leader Gaidinliu?
A. Subhas Bose
B. Jawaharlal Nehru
C. Thakkar Bapa
D. Mahatma Gandhi

177. Who was the first to unfurl the first Indian National Flag, the parent and precursor of the flag of independent India?
A. Madam Bhikaiji Cama
B. Dadabhai Naoroji
C. Raja Mahendra Pratap
D. Taraknath Das

178. The Nehru Committee Report got a decent burial at the hands of the Congress at the .... session of the INC.
A. Calcutta B. Madras
C. Lahore D. Bombay

179. Which of the following revolutionary and terrorist organisations had a large number of young women revolutionaries?
A. Yugantar
B. Anushilan Samiti
C. Bharat Mata Society
D. Indian Republican Army

180. Who was instrumental in founding the National Planning Committee (the forerunner of the Planning Commission) in 1938, for drawing up a plan of economic development on the basis of industrialisation?
A. Subhas Chandra Bose
B. Jawaharlal Nehru
C. Mahatma Gandhi
D. Maulana Abul Kalam Azad

181. Which of the following acted as President of the Indian National Congress for six consecutive years?
A. Jawaharlal Nehru
B. Dadabhai Naoroji
C. Abul Kalam Azad
D. Gopal Krishna Gokhale

182. The Vaikkom Satyagraha was launched in 1924 for
A. opening the temples to the low caste Hindus
B. fighting against the exploitation by the landlords
C. removal of Press restrictions
D. democratisation of the administration of Travancore State

183. Gopal Hari Deshmukh is popularly known as Lokhitwadi, because:
A. he was a great philanthropist and social worker
B. he distributed money and medicines to the poor and the needy
C. he edited a monthly magazine the Lokhitwadi
D. All the above

184. Madan Lal Dhingra murdered Curzon Wyllie in London, who was a/an ....
A. Adviser to the Secretary of State for India
B. Secretary of State for India
C. Former Governor of the Punjab
D. Law Member of the Viceroy's Executive Council

185. This great revolutionary summed up the great ideal of his life: "The only lesson required in India at present is to learn how to die and the only way teach is by dying ourselves. Therefore, I die and glory in my martyrdom". He was
A. Bhagat Singh
B. Ram Prasad Bismil
C. Madan Lal Dhingra
D. Surya Sen

186. Who edited a Bengali weekly the Jugantar and the Basumati, the oldest Bengali daily paper?
A. Barindra Ghosh B. Aurobindo Ghosh
C. Ganesh Ghosh D. Anand Mohan Bose

187. He was a great Indian revolutionary who was a Professor of Sanskrit and Philosophy in the Universities of Berkeley and Stanford and died as a Sanyasi in Philadelphia. He was:
A. Shyamji Krishna Varme
B. Lala Hardyal
C. Bhai Parmanand
D. Ram Chandra Bhardwaj

188. The European organisation in India which launched agitation against the Ilbert Bill was:
A. European Defence Association
B. Indo-British Association
C. Anti-Ilbert Bill League
D. European Rights Front

189. After the Surat Split in 1907, the second split in the Congress took place in 1918 on the issue of:
A. Lucknow pact
B. Montagu Declaration
C. Election of Mrs. Annie Besant as President of the INC (1917)
D. Both (B) and (C) above

190. A public Service Commission was established in India for the first time by:
A. The Indian Council Act, 1892
B. The Act of 1909
C. The Government of India Act, 1919
D. The Government of India Act, 1935

191. The day Mahatma Gandhi launched the Non-Cooperation movement, a great national leader died. He was:
A. Gopal Krishna Gokhale
B. Bal Gangadhar Tilak
C. Pherozshah Mehta
D. C. R. Das

192. The founder President of the Harijan Sevak Sangha, founded by Mahatma Gandhi, was:
A. Mahadev Desai B. G. D. Birla
C. Amrit Lal Thakkar D. B. R. Ambedkar

193. Who killed Michael O' Dwyer, the Governor of Punjab, who had ordered the brutal firing on the innocent people at Jallianwala Bagh, Amritsar?
A. Madan Lal Dhingra
B. Sardar Udham Singh
C. Sohan Singh Bhakna
D. Kanhai Lal Dutt

194. After the partition of Bengal, the two new provinces which came into existence, were:
A. East Bengal and Bengal
B. East Bengal and West Bengal
C. East Bengal and Assam
D. East Bengal and North Bengal

195. The brain behind the bomb attack on Viceroy Lord Hardinge at Chandni Chowk, Delhi in December 1912, was:
A. Rasbehari Bose
B. Bhai Parmanand
C. Sachindranath Sanyal
D. Shohan Lal Pathak

196. The historic Lucknow Session of the Congress in 1916 was presided over by ....
A. Mrs. Annie Besant
B. R. N. Mudhokar
C. Ambika Charan Mazumdar
D. Madan Mohan Malaviya

197. The Congress decided to raise a Swaraj Fund of one crore rupees for:
A. organising the Non-Cooperation movement
B. memorial of Bal Gangadhar Tilak
C. building the headquarters of the Congress
D. supporting the families of the political workers

198. The leader of the Ghadar Party in Bengal and Orissa was:
A. Jatindranath Mukherjee
B. Jatindranath Das
C. Barindra Ghosh
D. M. N. Roy

199. The earliest Indian politico-economist and a great champion of Swadeshi was:
A. Dadabhai Naoroji B. Dr. R.C. Dutt
C. Aurobindo Ghosh D. M.G. Ranade

200. Who made the greatest contribution in organising the Kisan Sabha movement?
A. Swami Sahajanand Saraswati
B. Vallabhbhai Patal
C. Jawaharlal Nehru
D. Indulal Yajnik

ANSWERS

1	2	3	4	5	6	7	8	9	10
C	A	A	C	B	C	D	B	D	A
11	**12**	**13**	**14**	**15**	**16**	**17**	**18**	**19**	**20**
B	C	D	A	A	D	C	D	A	B
21	**22**	**23**	**24**	**25**	**26**	**27**	**28**	**29**	**30**
A	C	A	C	C	C	C	D	A	D
31	**32**	**33**	**34**	**35**	**36**	**37**	**38**	**39**	**40**
D	A	B	D	B	D	D	B	A	B
41	**42**	**43**	**44**	**45**	**46**	**47**	**48**	**49**	**50**
D	D	A	D	A	D	B	A	A	C
51	**52**	**53**	**54**	**55**	**56**	**57**	**58**	**59**	**60**
A	B	B	D	B	A	C	C	D	C
61	**62**	**63**	**64**	**65**	**66**	**67**	**68**	**69**	**70**
A	B	D	C	C	C	C	C	A	B
71	**72**	**73**	**74**	**75**	**76**	**77**	**78**	**79**	**80**
B	B	D	B	C	D	C	A	C	A
81	**82**	**83**	**84**	**85**	**86**	**87**	**88**	**89**	**90**
B	B	A	C	D	C	C	A	D	C
91	**92**	**93**	**94**	**95**	**96**	**97**	**98**	**99**	**100**
A	D	C	D	B	C	A	B	A	C
101	**102**	**103**	**104**	**105**	**106**	**107**	**108**	**109**	**110**
A	D	A	D	D	B	C	A	B	D
111	**112**	**113**	**114**	**115**	**116**	**117**	**118**	**119**	**120**
A	B	C	A	D	C	C	A	D	A
121	**122**	**123**	**124**	**125**	**126**	**127**	**128**	**129**	**130**
B	B	B	B	C	C	B	B	B	C
131	**132**	**133**	**134**	**135**	**136**	**137**	**138**	**139**	**140**
B	A	B	B	C	D	B	A	D	B
141	**142**	**143**	**144**	**145**	**146**	**147**	**148**	**149**	**150**
C	D	A	C	B	D	B	B	A	D
151	**152**	**153**	**154**	**155**	**156**	**157**	**158**	**159**	**160**
B	C	C	C	C	B	A	B	D	C
161	**162**	**163**	**164**	**165**	**166**	**167**	**168**	**169**	**170**
A	C	B	C	B	A	D	C	B	C
171	**172**	**173**	**174**	**175**	**176**	**177**	**178**	**179**	**180**
C	A	B	D	A	B	A	C	D	A
181	**182**	**183**	**184**	**185**	**186**	**187**	**188**	**189**	**190**
C	A	D	A	C	A	B	A	B	C
191	**192**	**193**	**194**	**195**	**196**	**197**	**198**	**199**	**200**
B	B	B	A	A	C	B	A	A	A

●●●

Unit 2

GEOGRAPHY

WORLD GEOGRAPHY

The Solar System

The solar system is a group of celestial bodies comprising the sun and the large number of bodies that are bound gravitationally to the sun and revolve around it.

The Sun

The sun is the star at the centre of the solar system. It is the nearest star to the earth. The next nearest star, Alpha Centauri, is more than 4.0×10^{13} km away. The general statistics of the sun is as:

Diameter : 1.392×10^6 km

Volume : 1.304×10^6 times the volume of earth

Temperature : 6000°C at surface and 15000°C at the centre

Relative density : 1.4

Gravitational Pull : 28 times the gravitational pull of the earth

The outermost part of sun's atmosphere is called corona. The visible surface of the sun and source of the absorption spectrum is called *Photosphere* which is characteristic of the most stars. The stratum of sun's atmosphere immediately above the photosphere and below is *Chromosphere*. The whole body of the sun is gaseous in form. The gas is mostly hydrogen, which accounts 70% of its mass. The remainder is made up of 28% helium and 2% all other heavier elements from lithium to uranium. The generation of solar energy comes from thermo-nuclear reactions.

The dark spot in the Sun is called sunspot which appears dark by contrast with the solar surface, because they have a somewhat lower temperature of about 4500° K. The number of sunspot are found to vary from year to year with a period of about 11 years. This periodicity is known as Sunspot-cycle.

The Earth

The earth is a member of a group of celestial bodies which comprises the sun and Eight planets, Mercury, Venus, Earth, Mars, Jupiter, Saturn, Uranus and Neptune. Planets have no light of their own and all of them, except Venus and Uranus rotate upon their axis from west to east. Venus and Uranus rotate upon their axis from east to west. Many satellites are revolving around their respective planets. Thousands of comets and billions of meteoroids are there in the space. The Earth has only one satellite the moon, while Mercury and Venus have none. The average distance of the earth from the sun is 1.496×10^8 km. The earth is the third nearest planet to the sun and is the fifth largest planet.

The Earth: Facts and Figures

Mass of Earth : 5.880×10^{21} tons

Density of Earth : 5.517 times that of water

Volume of Earth : 1.083×10^{11} cubic km

Equatorial circumference : 4.007×10^4 km

Polar Diameter : 12, 714 km

Equatorial Diameter : 12,756 km

Polar or Meridional circumference : 4.0×10^4 km

Estimated Age : At least 4600 million years

Land Surface : 148,951,000 sq km

Water Surface : 361,150,000 sq km (71 per cent of total area)

Highest Point of the land surface : Mt. Everest (8,848 metres)

Lowest point of the land surface : Shores of the Dead Sea (396 metres below the sea level)

Greatest Ocean depth : Mariana Trench, East of Philippines (11,033 metres below the sea level)

Shape of the Earth

The earth is an oblate spheroid and not a true sphere because it is flattened at the poles and bulges out at the equator. The polar diameter of the earth is 42 km shorter than the equatorial diameter, therefore the earth oblate.

Motion of the Earth

The earth spins like a top on its axis completing one rotation every 24 hours and revolves around the sun once in 365.25 days. While the daily rotation, i.e., spin of the earth causes day and night, the revolution is responsible for the change of the seasons. The earth is a non-luminous sphere, emitting no light of its own. The part of the earth's surface which is towards the sun at any time is lit, while the remaining past, on the other side of the earth, is dark. The earth rotates from west to east. That is why the sun, the moon and the stars appears to us to be moving in the opposite direction.

Effect of Rotation

The daily axial rotation of the earth causes:

(*i*) Formation of day and night
(*ii*) Difference in Longitude and Time
(*iii*) Change in direction of winds and currents
(*iv*) Tides occur twice a day

Effect of Revolution

The earth revolves around the sun in a vast elliptical orbit. One such revolution takes about 365.25 days. One ordinary year contains 365 days, and to make up for the difference, every fourth year which is called a Leap Year, is calculated as 366 days. The change of seasons is mainly due to the revolution.

21st June: At this time it is summer in the Northern Hemisphere and winter in the Southern Hemisphere. The midday sun shines vertically over the Tropic of Cancer.

22nd December: At this time it is winter in the Northern Hemisphere and summer in the Southern Hemisphere. The midday sun shines vertically over the Tropic of Capricorn.

Equinoxes

On 21st March and 23rd September the season is either spring or Autumn. These days, days and nights are equal everywhere. Sun's rays fall vertically on the equator. These two position of the earth are called Equinoxes due to the equal length of the days and nights.

Inclination of the Earth's Axis

The earth's polar axis is not vertical but inclined and it make an angle of 66½° with the plane of the elliptic and is tilted 33½° from a line perpendicular to the plane in which the earth's orbit and the sun lie. The plane is imagined to be horizontal and to pass through the centre of globe. As a result of the inclination of the axis of the earth and its elliptical orbit around the sun, the earth attains four critical position in respect of the sun. On 21st June, the earth is so located in its orbit that the north polar end of its axis leans at the maximum angle of 23½° towards the sun, *i.e.*, the Tropic of Cancer receives the vertical rays of the sun. This condition is known as summer solstice, the longest day in the northern hemisphere. On 22nd December the earth is in an equivalent but opposite position in its orbit, *i.e.*, the Tropic of Capricorn receives the vertical rays of the sun. This condition is the winter solstice, the longest day in the southern hemisphere. Equinoxes occur when the earth's axis makes 90° angle with a line drawn to the sun, *i.e.*, the equator receives the vertical rays of the sun and day and night are equal. The vernal equinox occurs on 21st March and autumnal equinox on 23rd September. At the time of winter solstice the sun is not visible to a person on the north pole and during the summer solstice, the sun is not visible to a person on the south pole.

Latitude and Longitude

Lines of latitude and longitude are drawn on a map to locate position of the place on the surface of the earth. The latitude of place is defined as its distance north or south of the equator, measured as an angle. Latitudes are thus lines drawn parallel to the equator which is at 0° and they are counted up to 90° north and south, the two poles. The longitudes show the distance of a point east or west of the Prime Meridian which is at 0° and passes through Greenwich village near London in U.K. There are 360° Longitude and all the longitudinal lines join the poles. The longitude of a place can be defined as its distance east or west the meridian of Greenwich, measured as an angle.

Tropics

Tropics are literally the turning points. They refer to those parallels where the sun is imagined to stop its movement and turn about northward or southward, as the case may be. They are the 23° North parallel or Tropic of Cancer and 23½° South parallel or Tropic of Capricorn. Both are imaginary lines.

- **Local Time:** The system in which we measure time is based on the concept of the solar day. The time when the sun's altitude is the highest at that place, the shadow of a vertical rod fixed in the ground is the shortest. If at this time we set our watch at 12 O'clock. It will indicate local time.
- **Standard Time:** If every place were to are its own local time that would cause confusion in administration and other activities. So the local time of a place generally in the middle of the country, is used everywhere in that country as the Standard Time of that country and is taken in to be uniform throughout. Standard Time of India is the local time of a place near Allahabad situated at 82½° E longitude.

However, in bigger countries like Russia, America etc, it is not possible to have a single standard time for the whole country. Therefore, a number of standard times are chosen which are applicable for a limited region.

The Moon

Moon is the only natural satellite of the earth. It has diameter of about 3,480 km and has a mass of 1/81 that of the earth. The moon's period of revolution with reference to the sun is about 29.53 days. This period is called a synodic month. Moon also rotates on its own axis. The time taken by the moon to complete one rotation on its axis is 27.32 days. This fact has an important bearing upon the earth-moon relationship. Consequent to this relationship, we always see the same face of the moon from the earth. Only 59% of the moon's surface is directly visible from earth.

- **Eclipses:** Eclipses are caused by the fact that light travels in a straight line, producing clearly well defined shadows of objects in its path. When the earth comes between the moon and the sun, and it shuts off the light of the sun from falling upon the moon and this is called *Lunar Eclipse*. When the moon comes directly between the sun and the earth it obstructs light of the sun from falling upon the earth and this is called Solar Eclipse. Solar and Lunar eclipses do not occur every month because the moon's path around the earth is at an angle to the path of the earth around the sun. Sometimes only, the bodies fall in a line, producing an eclipse.
- **Tides:** Tides are the periodical rise and fall of sea water twice in about 24 hours and 56 minutes. Tides are primarily a result of the attraction of the moon. This force is more potent upon water since the mass involved is liquid and can easily rise under the pull force exerted by the moon.
- **Neap Tide:** It is that tide when the rise and fall of water are the lowest. It occurs when the moon and the sun make a right angle with the earth, *i.e.,* on the half Moon.
- **Spring Tide:** It is that tide when the rise and the fall of water are the highest. It is caused when the sun and the moon are in a straight line and their attraction force acts in unison on New Moon and Full Moon days.

The tides can be between 15% and 20% greater or less than the average depending upon whether the moon is in perigee or apogee. These are known as Perigean and Apogean tides. Tides affect the water level of rivers and estuaries etc. Also, sometimes the rising water may advance upstream as a nearly vertical wall several feet high. This is known as a tidal bore. The mouth of the river Hoogly in West Bengal is well known for this phenomenon.

Atmosphere

Atmosphere is the thin gaseous envelope surrounding and protecting the earth. It contains about 5.0×10^2 tonnes of gases a small amount of water vapour and some dust particle. The dry air of the atmosphere comprises of nitrogen 78.09%, oxygen 20.95%, and argon 0.93%. Besides, there are minute proportions of other gases, including carbon dioxide, helium, methane, hydrogen, ozone, neon, xenon, etc. The amount of carbon dioxide varies from place to place being greatest around the cities and smallest in the countryside.

The atmosphere is essential for life on earth. Oxygen and carbon dioxide in the atmosphere are necessary for animal and plant life. The ozone layer in the stratosphere protects life on earth by absorbing most of the sun's harmful radiation.

Atmospheric Layers

The atmosphere has been divided into subspheres according to the general characteristics of temperature variations. The different atmospheric layers are:

(*i*) **Troposphere:** It is the nearest to the earth's surface and extends to a distance of about 13 km. In Troposphere, generally, the temperature decreases as height increases. It is the densest of all layers and contains water vapours, moistures and dust. It also profoundly influences earth's climate since 80% of the mass of air comprising the entire atmosphere is concentrated in this zone.

(*ii*) **Tropopause:** It refers to the boundary region which separates troposphere from the adjoining atmospheric layer known as stratosphere.

(*iii*) **Stratosphere:** It is a region of uniform temperature extending from an altitude of about 11 km above the earth to a height of nearly 30 km. It is free from water vapour, clouds and dust. The upper part of stratosphere has plenty of ozone which affords protection to human beings on the earth against the fatal effects of solar ultraviolet radiations.

(*iv*) **Mesosphere:** It is a very cold region above the ozone rich layer of stratosphere.

(*v*) **Ionosphere:** It comes immediately above mesosphere, extends from about 50 km to 500 km above the earth. It includes the thermosphere and exosphere. The region contains ionised or electrically charged air and reflects radio waves facilitating wireless communication between distant places. The ionised air also protect those on earth from the falling meteorites, most of which are made to burn out at this region.

(*vi*) **Thermosphere:** It constitutes the middle layer of ionosphere and has a temperature of 100° C.

(*vii*) **Exosphere:** It is the uppermost region of the atmosphere, where the air density is so low that an air molecule moving rapidly straight upward is more than 50% likely to escape from the atmosphere instead of hitting other molecules.

Weather: It refers to conditions of temperature wind, humidity, rainfall at a given time and place.

Climate: It refers to the average weather conditions of a region as a whole over a comparatively long period of time.

Insolation and Temperature

Insolation is the energy received from the sun in form of heat. It is the most important single source of atmospheric heat. The amount of insolation over the globe varies a great deal depending upon factors like latitude, altitude and duration of sunlight.

Factors affecting Temperature

(*i*) **Latitude:** The temperature decreases as we go further away from the Equator towards the Poles.

(*ii*) **Distance from the Sea:** Places near the sea enjoy the moderating influence of the water moisture which keeps the day and night temperature almost the same.

(*iii*) **Wind:** The effect of prevailing winds in determining the temperature of a place depends upon the nature of region from which the wind blows. A wind coming from the sea lowers the summer temperature and raises the winter temperature. On the other hand, a wind coming from the land will lower the winter temperature and raise the summer temperature.

Dew Point and Condensation

The term Condensation is applied to the process of the change of state of water from vapour to liquid. This is the basis of all kinds of precipitation. The term dew point is applied to that critical temperature at which air is fully saturated. Condensation usually follows if the temperature is further lowered.

Precipitation

The term precipitation refers to falling of water snow or hail from the clouds and results when condensation is occurring rapidly within a cloud. The most common form of precipitation is rain and is formed when many cloud droplets coalesce into drops too large to remain suspended in the air. Sometimes the raindrops freeze before reaching the ground, then the precipitation occurs in form of pellets, called sleet. Precipitation can be orographic, conventional or cyclonic in nature. When the air is caused to rise upwards due to cyclonic circulation, the resulting precipitation is said to be of the cyclonic type.

Clouds

Clouds are huge collection of water-vapours. They are formed by very minute suspended water particles present in the air. When there is very low temperature, they are formed by huge collection of very small crystal like structure of snow.

Clouds are of different type and they can be classified on the basis of their form and altitude. On the basis of form clouds are known as stratiform or layered types, and cumuliform or massive type. According to the altitudes, clouds are called cirrus and the combination of these two lead to the cirrocumulus, cirrostratus.

Fog

When moist air meets cold surface of earth, some of the water vapours condense on the particles of dust in air. This cloud of condensed vapour is called fog.

Mist

Like fog, it is also formed on account of the fall of temperature of air. Here the droplet of water formed on account of condensation are heavier than those of the fog, therefore, mist is always seen close to the earth and does not rise up so high as the fog.

Dew

At night, the earth may frequently become cooler than the air above it. This causes water vapour contained in the air to get condensed and deposited on the cooled surface. This is known as dew. Dew is more likely to occur on clear and calm nights.

Rainfall

When the rain-laden clouds rise up, they expand and become cooler. They also become cooler because they are moving away from hotter region. The cooling of the air resulting in the precipitation of rain etc. It may be due to relief, convention and cyclone.

As we ascend a hill or a mountain temperature decreases. If, then, a wind blowing from the sea and saturated with water vapour comes to a mountain, it is forced to rise. On rising the clouds reach thinner layers of air and consequently it expands. Expansion produces cooling. The moisture in the clouds is then condensed and falls as rain. Such rains are called the relief rains.

When air is heated, it tends to rise up. As it rises, it is cooled and rain falls even though there are no mountains nearby. The air at the Equator is intensely heated almost each day and hence it rises each day, causing rain each afternoon. This rising of the wind when heated is called convection, and the rain that is so caused is called the convectional rain.

A cyclone has a low pressure at the centre, and it brings rainy or stormy weather. The rain brought about by a cyclone is called the cyclonic rain.

Winds

Air moving from one direction to another horizontally is known as winds. It is air in motion and is caused by difference in pressure. Wind blows from region of high pressure to a region of low pressure. Due to earth's rotation on its axis from west to east, all winds are deflected to the right in the northern hemisphere and to the left in the southern hemisphere. There are certain identifiable wind systems in the world:

1. **Doldrum:** The low pressure region round the equator, is calm usually and is called doldrum. Although there are no regular winds there, violent squalls and thunderstorms are frequent which come from high pressure areas north and south of the equator.
2. **Trade Winds:** As the temperature at equators is high, the air becomes hot and rises up. The air moves northwards and southwards and descends near 30ºN and 30ºS, causing high pressure. The wind then blows from here towards the equator and this is called trade wind. They are named so because trading ships take advantage of the direction of these winds.
3. **Westerlies:** These are also called anti-trade winds as they blow from about 40ºN to the Arctic circle and from about 35ºS to the Antarctic circle throughout the year. They derive their name from the direction in which they blow. In the northern hemisphere, they blow in the south-westerly direction and in the north-westerly direction in the southern hemisphere.
4. **Polar winds:** They blow from the high pressure area around the poles towards the temperate regions. Since they rise from the colder regions, they are extremely cold.
5. **Periodical Winds:** They blow in one direction at a particular time or during a particular season. Monsoons and land and sea breezes belong to this category. In India, South-west monsoon blow in summer and North-east in winter.
6. **Variable winds:** They are irregular winds like cyclones and anti-cyclones which originate due to local factors.

Cyclones and Anticyclones

Cyclones is wind rotating round the centre of minimum of low barometric pressure. The wind rush inwards from all direction. Due to the inclination of earth's axis and the rotation of the earth, in northern hemisphere the winds circulates in an anticlockwise direction and in the southern hemisphere in clockwise direction.

Anticyclone refers to the region in which the atmospheric pressure is high, with the highest point at the centre. In this situation the winds blow spirally outwards from the centre, clockwise in northern hemisphere and anticlockwise in southern hemisphere. In summer anti-cyclones are associated with warm and sunny conditions, in winter they imply frost and fog as well as sunshine.

Humidity

Air is made up of a number of different gases such as oxygen, nitrogen, carbondioxide etc. One of the important component is the evaporated water or water vapour. The amount of water vapour that air can hold at any time is determined by the temperature. Higher the temperature, more water vapour the air can hold. When air cannot take any more water vapour, the saturation point is reached. And if any more water vapour is added condensation takes place which result in rain, hail, mist, dew or snow.

Humidity, simply means the amount of water vapour in the air at any given point of time. Absolute humidity refers to the weight of water vapour per cubic cm. of air. Relative humidity refers to the percentage of water vapour in the air with respect to the total amount of vapour that the air can hold at any given time at given temperature. Thus when we say that temperature is 32° and relative humidity is 78% what we mean is that air has 78% of water vapour that it can hold the temperature of 32°C. Since our body needs some water vapour, very dry air may cause us discomfort. But excessive humidity along with high temperature is also a source of discomfort. We are most comfortable when humidity is neither too high nor too low.

Hydrosphere

Hydrosphere is the name given to the masses of water that cover about 70.8% of the surface of the earth. The great stretches of salt water called oceans and seas. Pacific ocean, which is the largest among the ocean sprawls over an area of about 1.65×10^8 sq. km an area which is more than total combined area of all the continents. The average depth of oceans is about 4 km.

The water in the oceans totals over 1,300 million cubic km which is more than 97% of world's total water. The balance of water resources are contributed by glaciers, ice and snow, fresh water lakes, rivers and the underground water.

The oceans occupy the deep hollows of the earth's crust. The floor of the ocean beds are covered with ridges and valleys. The raised parts of the ocean floor are called ridges. The valley are called deeps or trenches. The most famous ridge is the Mid Atlantic Ridge and the most famous trenches include the Tuscarora Deep and Mariana Trench.

All the oceans of the world are interconnected. Antarctica is entirely surrounded by a great stretch of water called the southern ocean. From there stretch northwards, the three most oceans — the Indian, Pacific and Atlantic Oceans. The fifth ocean is the Arctic ocean which surrounds the North pole.

Life in the Sea

The life began in the sea and it contains representatives of almost all the main groups of animals including mammals, the order to which man belongs. About 1,60,000 species of marine animals are known to exist. The plants in the sea occupy a large area and there is a large variety of them. Free-floating microscopic plants are known as phytoplankton. These are food for minute animals called zooplankton, which are then preyed upon by larger animal species. They are consumed by bigger creatures and thus a never-ending cycle continues.

Lakes

They are water reservoirs, surrounded by land. They differ in size from small ones to very large ones covering thousands of square kilometres, and in depth from a few metres to more than 1000 metres. Most of the lakes contain fresh water reserves. However, lakes with no river outlet to carry away dissolved minerals are salty. Lakes are formed in many ways:

1. Debris transported by ice may block valleys and stop the water from flowing downwards.
2. Certain volcanoes, when become extinct, form lakes in the craters.
3. Landslides may form depressions in which water deposits to form lake.
4. Earth movements such as folds and faults can give rise to lakes.
5. Violent movement of earth like earthquakes.
6. Chemical action, e.g., in limestone rocks, water may dissolve the limestone producing underground caverns which sometime collapse to form depressions.
7. Man-made reservoirs act as lakes.

The Ocean Floor

The bottom of oceans is not as smooth as it is presented to be. It can categorised into four parts:

1. **Continental Shelf:** It is the seaward extension of the continent and is a shallows platform with a variable width of a few miles in the north-west pacific coast to over 100 miles near north-west Europe. They are of great significance because shallow water enables sunlight to penetrate and help growth of planktons. This helps in large growth of fishes in the area near the banks.

2. **Continental Slope:** The continental shelf abruptly starts declining and showing large slopes.
3. **Ocean Trough:** They are deep sea plains which are undulating with an average depth of 3000 organic deposits. They have extensive submerged plateaus, ridges, trenches, basins and oceanic islands.
4. **Ocean Deeps:** They are long, narrow and deep trenches, often plunging upto 30,000 feet.

Salinity

A number of minerals which are held in solution in the sea water have great importance. As a result of large concentration of minerals, like sodium sulphate, sodium chloride, magnesium chloride and calcium chloride etc., sea water is salty to taste. The proportion of dissolved salts to pure water is called Salinity. It varies from place to place in the oceans. The average figure being 35 gm per 1000 cc. Usually salinity is higher where the addition of fresh water is less and evaporation is high and vice-versa. Chlorine is the most abundant element causing salinity in sea water.

Waves and Current

Wave is a disturbance on the surface of a liquid body e.g. a sea or a lake. Wave is mainly caused by the wind which heaps up the water. Along coasts, waves are destructive agents of erosion.

Currents are those powerful movements of the ocean that proceed regularly, constantly and in definite direction. The movement of these current is clearly visible on the surface of the water and may be called gushing streams of water over the otherwise calm surface of the ocean. Hence streams of water move with a greater velocity than their counterparts do on the surface of the earth. They modify the climate of a coastal region. The warm Gulf stream brings in ice-free winter conditions along the south eastern coast of USA. Winds passing over warm current pick up moisture and bring rain. Japan, British Isles etc. receive rainfall in this manner. Kalahari and Atacama deserts are drier than they would be because of cold Peruvian current. The meeting of cold and warm current causes dense fog which is dangerous for navigation. However, at the meeting place, growth of the fishes gets enhanced due to abundance of nutrients.

Lithosphere

The Lithosphere refers to the top crust of the earth on which our continents countries and the ocean basins rest. The lithosphere has a thickness between 38 to 52 km in the continental regions, but becomes thin between 7 to 13 km under the ocean beds. In the high mountain regions, its thickness is estimated at about 65 km. It includes both the land mass as well as the ocean floors, generally it is used to denote only the land surface which occupies a little less than 30% of total area of the earth.

Interior Structure of the Earth

The interior structure of the earth is based on the seismic waves, as they travel through the earth. The centre of the earth is occupied by the core, about 3500 km in radius. The outer part of the core is believed to have the properties of a liquid and the innermost part of the core may be called solid. The core is the densest part of the earth and is known as nife. Outside the core lies the mantle, a layer about 2925 km thick, composed of minerals in a solid state. The rocks in this layer may be in glassy state. The topmost portion of earth, the crust is the land mass comprising soil, sand and rock. In fact all the sand and much of the soil that we have has come to us from ancient rocks that crumbled down under the impact of heat of the sun and the cool of the rain, a process that has gone on for thousands years.

Plain

A plain is defined as an area with gently sloping land and very low local relief. It can be classified as peneplain, flood plain, delta plain, alluvial plain, coastal plain, lacustrine plain, karst plain and glacial plain etc.

The combined action of weathering and streams on land makes peneplain. The deposition of material by rivers makes flood plains, delta plains and alluvial plains. Coastal plains are those parts of the continental shelf which have been uplifted. Lacustrine plains are old lake beds and are made up of sediments deposited by rivers. Karst plains are formed in limestone areas mainly by the agency of underground water. Glacial plains are formed through glacial erosion and deposition.

Plateaus

It can be classified as intermontane, piedmont and continental. Intermontane plateaus are formed in association with mountains and are enclosed by them e.g. the Tibetan plateau. Piedmont plateaus lie between mountains on one side and the sea on the other e.g. the Patagonian plateau in South America. Continental plateau rise abruptly from the seas or low lands and are extensive e.g. the Indian plateau and Greenland.

Mountains

Mountains are masses of land considerably higher than the surrounding areas, higher than a hill, and with fairly steep slopes. They are classified as fold mountain, block mountains, volcanic mountains, and residual mountains.

As the molten centrosphere cooled and contracted, the crust at several places became crumpled, *i.e.*, full of wrinkles or folds. The elevated parts became mountains termed as fold mountains and the intervening depressions are known as valleys. The great mountain chains of the world like, the Himalayas, the Alps, Andes and the Rockies have been formed by this process.

If there are two parallel vertical faults in the earth's crust, the contraction of the inner molten rock to matter causes the parts on either side of the middle block of the rock to subside. This process causes the formation of a Block Mountain.

Volcanic mountains results from volcanic eruptions and the outflow of lava. The Fujiyama of Japan is an example of volcanic mountains. Sometimes, the mountains are carved out as a result of erosion of plateaus and high plains by various agents of erosion. These are known as residual mountains e.g. the Highlands of Scotland and the Sieroas of Central Spain.

The sinking down of the part of the earth's crust between two parallel vertical faults forms a Rift Valley. It is U-shaped, whereas a Fold Valley is V-shaped. The Red Sea, Dead Sea and Narmada Valley in India are example of rift valleys.

Rocks

Rocks are the main materials composing the earth's crust. Rocks are composed of minerals. Minerals are natural inorganic substance each with a fairly definite chemical composition and recognisable crystal form, colour, hardness, lustre, texture and other physical characteristics. Rocks of the earth are grouped in three principal classes — Igneous, Sedimentary and Metamorphic.

Rocks which are solidified directly from molten materials are called igneous rocks. These rocks are crystalline in nature and make up nearly 85 per cent of the earth's crust. Granites, Basalt are examples of Igneous rocks. Sedimentary rocks are formed in layers on beds of rivers, lakes and seas. They are formed over a long period of time and natural factors like Streams, Rivers, Glaciers or Wind etc. play an important role in their formation. They often contain fossils of plants, animals and other micro-organisms. Sandstone, Shale, Clay, Rock salts, Gypsum, Potash and Nitrates are examples of Sedimentary rocks. Metamorphic rocks are literally rocks which have changed their form. In course of time, the original form of these rock is changed owing to excessive heat and great pressure, like clay changing into slate. Granite changes into gneiss, limestone into marble, sandstone into quartzite and coal into graphite.

Volcano

It is an opening in the earth's crust through which lava is ejected. The thrown up lava forms a conical hill with a funnel-shaped hollow called Crater at its top. Crater is the mouth of a volcano. It is usually cup-shaped and serves as the vent for the lava to erupt. Volcanoes which are no longer active are called extinct volcanoes. A volcano which is only sleeping and may become active is called a dormat volcano. The volcanoes which erupt frequently are called active volcanoes. Mt Etna in Italy is an example of active volcano while Fujiyama in Japan and Chimborazo in Andes are examples of dormant and extinct volcanoes respectively. The eruption of lava from a volcano can be of explosive type or quiet type.

There are several thousands volcanoes in the world. They are distributed in several belts across the continents. The most important belt runs right round the Pacific ocean. Another, rather less important, runs from Iceland just touching the British Isles, through the Azones across the Atlantic to the West-Indies with a branch running through the Mediterranean sea.

Earthquakes

It is the shaking of the earth's crust sometimes accompanied by a permanent elevation or depression, but often no lasting effect is visible on the surface except the damage done by shaking. The main cause of earthquakes are due to sudden cooling and contraction of the earth's surface, coming into activity of some dormant volcanos, and due to internal heat, sometimes water changes into steam, expands and this causes an earthquake. Earthquakes occur in almost every part of the world. They are very common in volcanic districts, and where the earth's crust is weak. The most active region is a belt surrounding the Pacific ocean which includes western coasts of North and South America, the eastern coast of Asia, New Zealand and the islands of the South-east Pacific. In India, the North-East region and Shivalik range of Himalayas are more susceptible of earthquakes though Plateau has also experienced it sometimes. The intensity of an earthquake is measured on Richter-Scale by an instrument seismograph. An earthquake that originates in or near the sea, causing gigantic waves, is called Tsunami.

Weathering

It is well known fact that external forces work slowly but continuously to level down all irregularities. This natural process of decay and decomposition of rocks under the action of heat, cold, wind, rain water and frost is termed as weathering. External factors caused mechanical weathering whereas atmospheric gases dissolved in rain water carry out chemical weathering. Carbon dioxide in water forms carbonic acid which acts on rocks containing limestone. Weathering is followed by scraping, scratching and grinding processes, collectively called erosion. The chief agents of erosion are running water, moving ice, wind, waves and underground water. The weathered material is then picked up and transported to other places. These agents can carry the eroded material, either by sheer physical force or in the form of a solution or suspension.

The water running over the surface, gives rise to various shapes of the surface, depending on the type of surface. When water moves over mountainous on the type of surface. When water moves over mountainous course, it causes down cutting or vertical erosion. Thus Gorges, Canyons V-shaped Valley and waterfalls are formed. However, over the plains, the water's main task is transportation. Water takes a winding course due to gravity and irregularities of the ground force it to move in the loop form. When a narrow neck of the land is cut off, a lake is left behind and river starts flowing straight. Silt is deposited at the entrance to this back water. This shape is called ox-bow lake which gradually dries up. When river enters the lower end, it faces obstruction due to alluviam deposited earlier. Due to lack of height gradient, the flow is slow and the river divides into a number of channels called distributaries to discharge its water. Thus triangular shaped alluvial tract is formed by deposits of the river near the mouth and it is called delta. However, some rivers have a gradually widening bay cutting deep inland called 'estuary' near its mouth.

In the colder regions, water exists in the form of ice and the moving body or river of ice is called a glacier which moves down due to gravity. Greenland and Antarctica are continental glaciers. When Glaciers move down, they form U-shaped valleys and hanging valley.

The work of wind is most marked in an arid region. The wind lifts and blows the loose particles (deflation) and rubs them against the rocks (abrasion) to carry out its erosional task. In the process, the particles collide against each other forming finer grains (attrition). Due to erosion, Mushroom rocks, Zeugen, Yardang or Inselberg are formed while Dunes, Barkhans, Seiffs and Loess are formed by the depositional action of the wind.

Waves are the most powerful agent of marine erosion among the three agents — waves, tides and currents. Swash is the wave that rushes up the coast and backwash is the water that recedes back. The waves form bays, cliffs, caves, arch, stack and stump.

Work of Underground Water

Water gets collected in the earth when it is porous or keeps flowing if the earth is pervious. A rock which is both porous and pervious is called an equilier and hold great quantities of water within them. The surface below which all opening in soils and rocks are filled with water is known as the water table. This level fluctuates with increase or decrease of rainfall. Water starts moving laterally after reaching impervious rock layer and gushes out after reaching the surface or opening. This is called a spring. Water trapped in permeable rock layer between two impermeable rock layer comes out with force when wells are dug to this level. Such wells are known as Artesian wells. A geyser is a special type of thermal spring that throws hot water and steam at regular intervals.

Main Natural Regions of the World

A natural region is a geographical unit which contains countries or parts of countries, where the condition of temperature, rainfall and cultivated vegetation and consequently human activity are almost uniform.

(*i*) **Hot Deserts:** They are situated near the tropics between 20° and 30° in the West of the land masses. These occupy about one-fourth of the land surface of the earth. The climate of the region is mostly hot and dry. The Sahara, Arabia, West Rajasthan and Sindh deserts are included in this region. Gold, silver, copper and diamonds are available in these deserts.

(*ii*) **Tropical Grasslands:** Agriculture and cattle-rearing are the chief occupations, and wool, skins and hides the chief commercial products of this region.

(*iii*) **Monsoon Region:** It lies mostly in the south-east of Asia and includes portions of Australia, Africa and America. Hence the climate is hot and moist in summer and warm and dry in winter. Natural vegetation is forests.

(*iv*) **Equatorial Region:** These regions have dense forests of evergreen trees but they are not suitable for human habitation. Some medicinal forest products are gathered.

(*v*) **Mediterranean Region:** This region lies around the Mediterranean sea and on both sides of the equator, in the west of the land masses and between 30° and 45° north and south of equator. The climate is hot in summer and wet in winter. It is famous for fruit trees like olive, vine, lemon, almonds, etc.

(*vi*) **Cool Temperate Region:** On the western margins of continents. In these regions cereals are grown, cattle are raised for dairy product and fishing is also important. In the eastern margins coniferous forests provide soft wood. Lumbering, fishing and farming are important.

(*vii*) **Polar Tundra Regions:** Too cold for most human activity. Only mineral extraction can attract a large concentration of people in the future. Gold and oil are found in Alaska, and nickel in Siberia.

(*viii*) **Siberian Type Region:** It includes Siberia, north Europe, specially north Russia, Finland, Scandinavian countries, etc. Here winters are very severe. Natural vegetation is coniferous forests. Wheat, potatoes, etc. are grown in summer.

(*ix*) **China Type Region:** It lies in the east of land masses between 30° and 45° degree. Here summers are warm and moist and winters are very cold. Natural vegetation is forests.

(x) **British Type:** It includes the area of British Columbia, North-West Europe including British Isles, South Chile, Tasmania and South Islands of New Zealand. The countries in this region are industrially advanced, and agriculture is carried on by scientific method. People on the whole are engaged in different industries.

Pattern of Climate

Different regions of the world have different climates and the factor for this variation is presence of different temperature, winds, precipitation and their interaction with the surface of the earth. The hottest and wettest regions of the world are found along the equators. The areas located near Tropic of Capricorn usually have dry climates, except for small area of Australia, Africa and South America. There is more climate variation along the Tropic of Cancer. The climate of a region is an important factor in the lifestyle of people, crop pattern, housing pattern and economic pattern. The main types of climates are as follows:

(a) **Equatorial Climate:** This type of climate is found in the area lying in a belt stretching about 5° on both sides of the equator. The temperature is high all round the year and does not vary much. Rainfall is large and continues for the whole year, making the climate sultry. The Amazon and Congo basins, East and West Indies, the Malay Peninsula and Andaman and Nicobar show this type of climate.

(b) **Desert Climate:** As the sand heats up quickly and losses heat also fast, the highest temperatures in the world are found in the regions affected by desert climate. The nights are very cold. The hot deserts, occupy lowlands along the Tropics of Cancer and Capricorn. Sahara, Thar and deserts of Arabia, Australia, South Africa (Kalahari) and South America (Atacama) are examples of such deserts. However, cold deserts are also found in plateaus outside the tropics. They show very low temperatures, particularly during winter. Gobi (Central Asia), Colorado (North America) and deserts of Iran belong to this climate.

(c) **Mediterranean Climate:** The climate in areas around the Mediterranean sea is known by the sea. The region lies between latitudes 30° and 45°. The area is hot and dry in summer but moist and mild weather is observed during winter. This type of climate is also prevalent on western sides of North and South America, South Africa and South of Australia.

(d) **Temperature Maritime Climate:** This type of climate is prevalent in North-West Europe, West Canada, South Chile and New Zealand. The area gets rain throughout the year but compared to tropical regions, the quantum is usually less.

(e) **Continental Climate:** This type of climate is found in regions far away from the oceans. Due to lack of moderating influence of seas, the summers are very hot and winters are very cold. Rains fall mostly in spring and early summer but quantity is not much. The grasslands where this climate occurs are the Prairies of Canada and USA, the Steppes of Russia, Pampas of South America, Downs of Australia and Veldt of South Africa.

(f) **Monsoon Climate:** The areas which receives rain in summer due to monsoon, show this type of climate. It is characterised by three seasons — the cold season with a little rain from November to February, the summer from March to June and finally rainy season from late June to October. The summers are hot. The climate is prevalent in northern hemisphere around the Indian ocean area like India, Myanmar etc. North-West Australia and parts of the Africa also show the climate.

(g) **Cold Forest Climate:** The summers are cool and winter are colder with moisture coming down as snow and not as rain. The area is known for coniferous trees, and occurs in Northern parts of America, Europe and Asia.

(*h*) **Tropical Climate:** This climate is found on either side of the equatorial belt and is well developed in Africa. Rainfall is heavier during summer and winter remains dry.

(*i*) **Alpine Climate:** The climate has been named after the mountain chain of Europe, the Alps. The climate changes as the height of mountain increases and becomes colder. Due to low density of air, the climate is different from other snow bound areas of Arctic or Antarctica.

(*j*) **Arctic Climate:** The winters here are very long and very cold. The summers are very short. The climate is prevalent in the Arctic and Antarctica circles.

On the South and North poles, permanent ice and snow exists and these are called Polar Caps. They receive very little sunlight. During winter, no sunlight touches either pole while in summer, much of the light reaching the poles is reflected into space by the glare of the snow. The North Pole lies on a frozen sea, the Arctic Ocean while the South Pole sits upon the continent of Antarctica, covered by a layer of ice and snow at least a mile deep.

Terms Used for Climatic Definition

- **Isopleth:** It is a line on the map connecting places of equal incidence of a meteorological or geographical features.
- **Isohyet:** It is a line on the map connecting places receiving same amount of rainfall.
- **Isobath:** It is a line on the map connecting places of equal depth in sea.
- **Isobront:** It is a line on the map connecting places experiencing thunderstorm at the same time.
- **Isobar:** It is a line on the map connecting places with the same atmospheric pressure.
- **Isotherm:** It is a line drawn on map connecting places having similar temperature.
- **Isochromes:** It is a line on the map connecting places located at equal travel time from a common point.
- **Isohel:** It is a line on the map connecting places with the same duration of sunshine.

Agricultural Products

The cultivation of crops depends on a number of physical and economic factors. The physical factors are temperature, rainfall, soil and topography. Irrigation, addition of fertilizers and pesticides, using better crop harvesting techniques, use of high yielding varieties and practising crop rotation can improvise the crop yield. Among the economic factors determining the type of farming are market demands, labour supply, transportation, capital availability and economic policies of the state.

The crops cultivated are grouped as either food crops or cash crops. All grains and pulses fall under the category of food crops. Crops that are cultivated for sale and not for the consumption of a farmers are known as cash crops. Plantation crops, commercial crops and fibre crops belong to the category of cash crops.

Rice

It is the staple diet of the oriental countries, grown in tropical and sub-tropical regions. Most of the thickly populated countries are major rice producers as well as consumers and only a small fraction of output enters the world trade. The rice production needs hot moist climate with a temperature of about 24°C and rainfall between 150 to 200 cms. It can even be cultivated at higher altitudes and mountains if temperature requirement is fulfilled. Alluvial soil is ideal for rice production while clayey loam capable of retaining moisture is also good. Abundant cheap labour is required for various processes of sowing, transplanting, harvesting, winnowing etc. China is the largest producer of rice while India, Bangladesh, Indonesia, Thailand and Philippines are other major producers.

Wheat

It is a crop of temperate region, grown in almost every continent. The development of hybrid varieties has made it possible to cultivate it in even arctic or equatorial climate. Usually, the crop requires cool and moist climate during the growing period and warm and dry conditions at the time of harvesting. A temperature of 10-15°C and a rainfall of 75 cm is sufficient. A well drained loam or clay loam is considered ideal for the production of wheat. China is the largest producer of wheat with Russia, USA, India, France, Canada, Australia and Argentina being major producers. West European countries usually import wheat.

Maize

It is the one of the most easily grown crop, ranking second to wheat in the order of world grain production. It is used as a food crop, for animal fattening and even for alcohol distillation. It grows best in sub-tropical regions, needing 20-30°C temperature and a moderate rainfall between 75 to 150 cm. The soil best suited is deep, well drained loams, rich in nitrate. USA, China, Argentina, Brazil, France, India and Russia are major producers.

Millets

They are inferior quality hard cereals. Sorghum, Bajra, Ragi etc belong to this group. These crops are grown in regions where climatic conditions are not preferable for other crops. They are cultivated on inferior sandy soils where the climate is hot semi-arid. China, India, Russia and USA are major producers of millets.

Pulses

They are leguminous crops which are usually rotated with other crops to maintain or restore soil fertility as they fix nitrogen. They include gram, tur, black-gram, green gram, lentil, peas etc. They are grown on variety of soils ranging from loams to light and medium soils. They require a low to moderate rainfall and temperature varies on variety of pulses. China, India, Russia, Brazil and USA are major producers of pulses.

Groundnut

It is grown in light sandy soils, where temperature varies from 22°C to 28°C and rainfall is between 40 to 70 cm. China, India, USA, Sudan and Nigeria are major producers.

Sugarcane

It is grown in hot and humid climate, where temperature ranges between 24°C to 27°C and rainfall is between 100 to 170 cm. Alluvial or lava soil rich in lime or potash is most suited and regular supply of fertilizers is needed. Abundant labour is required. India, Brazil and Cuba are major producers.

Tobacco

It is grown in well drained sandy loams or sandy clays rich in potash and lime. Temperature should range from 20 to 25°C and rainfall from 75 cm to 100 cm. A large labour supply is needed. China, USA, India, Japan, Brazil and Russia are major producers.

Tea

It is a tropical and sub-tropical crop. Two main types of tea are green tea (no fermentation) and black tea (fermented after curing). High humidity and heavy dew favours rapid growth of the plant. Temperature can be within the range of 13 to 35°C but high rainfall between 150 to 250 cm is required. Sandy loams rich in iron is ideal. It grows best on highlands and well drained slopes. China, India, Sri Lanka, Japan, East Africa and Bangladesh are major producers.

Rubber

It is a tropical plantation crop. It needs high uniform temperature of about 30°C throughout the year and rainfall of at least 200 cm well distributed throughout the year. Malaysia, Indonesia, Thailand, Sri Lanka, India and China are major producers of natural rubber. Synthetic rubber is now giving competition to the natural one.

Cotton

It is the oldest and most common fibre plant. It requires warm and moderately moist climate but dry sunny conditions at the time of harvesting. Temperature ranging between 16 to 25°C, well distributed rainfall of 80 to 120 cm and 200 days of frost free are required for proper growth. Light sandy/ medium loams and black soil are good for cotton. China, USA, India, Brazil, Ukraine, Egypt and Pakistan are major producers.

Jute

This fibre is most commonly used for packing as it is rough in nature. It grows in hot moist climate. Temperature of around 25ºC and rainfall of 200 cm spread across the growing season is essential. The soil required is well drained rich loans or alluvial soil. Ample water supply is needed. India, Bangladesh and China are major producers.

Animal Products

Wool

It is obtained from sheep, cashmere goat, angora goat, llamas, alpacas, vicunas camels and other hairy creatures. These animal are available mostly in temperate region, particularly in grasslands. Australia, Russia, New Zealand, China, Argentina and USA are major producers of wool.

Meat

The cattle are first reared on large areas of pastures and then sent to centres for fattening. At most of the places, mixed farming are resorted to whereby the leavings of agricultural produce are fed to the cattle. However, some countries have ranches for rearing of the cattle. USA, Russia and Argentina are chief producers of meat. Mutton is produced in Australia and New Zealand.

Dairy products

Cool temperate regions of the world are suitable for commercial dairying. Wet climates aid the growth of grass and low temperature helps in preservation of milk and other dairy products. France, Netherlands, Denmark, Switzerland, Australia, New Zealand and USA are major producers of dairy products like milk, butter and cheese.

Types of Agriculture

Intensive and Extensive Farming

Cultivation can be extensive or intensive, depending on the availability of arable land and population pressure. In intensive farming, capital, labour and skill are intensively applied to a limited land to obtain high yields. On the other hand, when the cultivation is carried out on a large scale with the help of modern machinery and implements, it is known as extensive farming.

Shifting Agriculture

In some places, it is the practice of the people to clear and cultivate a patch of forest, till the fertility of soil is exhausted. Then they move on to a new patch of land. This type of farming is practised by tribals in South and South East Asia. The practice causes massive deforestation and is being discouraged.

Sedentary Agriculture

Cultivating the same piece of land year after year is termed Sedentary agriculture. Since the soil gradually loses fertility due to frequent usage, manures or fertilizers or crop rotation has to be used to improve the productivity. The modern day farming is of sedentary type.

Subsistence Agriculture

When the produce of the farm is consumed locally or in-house and is not used for trading, it is called subsistence agriculture. When the farm size is small or productivity is low, the type of agriculture is used. Mainly foodgrains are grown for the consumption.

Mixed Farming

When both farming and animal husbandry are practised on the same farm, it is known as mixed farming. Cereals, root crops, vegetables and fruits are raised along with pig, poultry, cattle and sheep. Modern machinery, selected seeds and chemical fertilizers are used. This form of agriculture is used in developed countries where large farms are available.

Plantation Agriculture

It is the form of agriculture where a single crop is raised on a scale, resembling factory production. The crop is mainly cultivated for the market and hence crops are also called cash crops. Rubber, coffee, tea, sugarcane and cocoa are some of the crops, grown under the system.

Dairy Farming

When cattle rearing is done for obtaining milk on a large scale, it is called dairy farming. Mild climate in the temperate regions favour this activity. In this type of farming, high-tech transportation and refrigeration techniques are used.

Market Gardening

The cultivation of vegetables, fruits and flowers for market is termed as market gardening. The farms are usually small with labour, manure and capital applied intensively in order to get high yields and maximum cash return. Due to easy perishability of the crops, efficient transportation is a must.

Collective Farming

In Communist countries, the farms are administered by elected representatives and income and produce of the farm is distributed among the farmers who are real owners. Since the farms size are large, a large number of machines are used. The produce of the farm is sold to the State procurement organisation. The peasants have no option, but to abide by rules of the government.

Cooperative Farming

When farmers opt to pool their sources and take advantage of large scale financial and technical organisations, it is called cooperative farming. Seeds, fertilizers, implements can be procured at a lesser rate and product sold at higher rate due to bulk orders.

The Continents

Asia

Asia, the largest continent, extends over nearly one-third of the land surface of the earth. **Chief Mountain Ranges:** Himalayas, Kunlun, Tien shah, Altai, Tibetan Plateau. **Chief Rivers:** Ganges, Yantze, Yamuna, Yenisei, Amur, Hwang-ho, Mekong. **Deserts:** Arabia, Thar. **Climate:** Very varies, extreme in north, monsoonal in the south and east. **Minerals:** Gold, coal, oil, iron, manganese. **Principal countries in Asia:** India, Iran, Iraq, Israel, Jordan, Pakistan, Sri Lanka, Myanmar, China, Vietnam, Indonesia, Malaysia, Japan, Bangladesh. **Important Cities:** New Delhi, Mumbai, Tokyo, Dhaka, Beijing, Yangon, Bangkok, Colombo, Hanoi, Tashkent, **Area:** 30,757,714 sq. km.

Africa

Africa, the second largest continent, is bounded by Mediterranean sea on the north, by Red Sea and Indian Ocean in east, by Atlantic Ocean in the west, adjoins Asia and isthmus of Suez. It exhibits diverse physical and cultural conditions. **Principal Countries:** Egypt, Sudan, Ethiopia, Kenya, Somalia, Congo, Zambia, South Africa, Nigeria, Angola. Desert in north, forest in centre and lofty plateaus in the south. **Highest Mountain:** Kilimanjaro, 5,895 metres. **Chief Rivers:** Nile, Congo, Niger, Zambezi. **Largest Lake:** Victoria, Great Rift Valley in East Africa. **Rainfall:** Heavy near equator almost rainless in Sahara and Kalahari, elsewhere moderate. **Agriculture:** Wine olives, wheat, esparto grass in north, cocoa, oil palm, ground nut, coffee, cotton in centre; wheat, maize, wool in south. **Minerals:** Gold, diamonds, copper. **Important Cities:** Cairo, Lusaka, Cape-town, Mombasa, Nairobi, Adis Ababa, Harare, Pretoria. **Area:** (approx. 29,807,200) sq. km. (22.6 per cent of world's land).

Europe

It is the western peninsula of European land mass but with no well defined boundary with Asia but line normally accepted runs along Ural mountains to Caspian Sea and Caucasus to Black sea. After Australia, it is the smallest continent in area but is the nerve centre of world's political and economic activity. **Area:** (approx) 9,938,000 sq. km (6.7%) greatest length north to south 3,860 km; breadth east to west 5,300 km. **Chief Mountains:** Alps, Pyrenees, Carpathians, Balkans, Apennines, Sierra Nevada, Urals, Caucasus. **Chief Rivers:** Volga, Danube, Rhine, Dnieper, Ural, Don. **Chief Lakes:** Ladoga, Onega, Peipus, Vanern Vaitern. **Climate:** Arctic border, long cold winter; short cool summer; snow. **Agriculture:** Cereals, fruits, sugarbeet, potato, wax, hemp, pastoral—cattle-rearing, dairying, fishing, forestry, wood, pulp, paper, iron, coal, petroleum, hydroelectric power, etc. **Principal Countries:** U.K., France, Germany, Poland, Czech Republic, Hungary, Norway, Sweden, Portugal, Italy, Serbia, Spain, Switzerland, Russia, Austria, Romania. **Important Cities:** Berne, Paris, Berlin, London, Bonn, Viena, Munich, Prague, Warsaw, Rome, Budapest, Stockholm, Moscow, Belgrade, Madrid, Oslo.

North America

It is northern continent of Western Hemisphere, Comprising Mexico, U.S.A., Canada, Greenland, Central America and the West Indies on west high chain of mountains, lower range of latitude and altitude. **Agriculture:** Temperate and tropical products, cereals, tobacco, sugarbeet, potatoes, etc., lumbering, rich in minerals, coal, petroleum, iron, manganese, etc. **General Industries:** Ship building. Occupied formerly by Red Indians; now mainly by white races with many Negroes in south. **Important Cities:** New York, Washington D.C., San Francisco, Chicago, Mexico, Montreal, Ottawa. **Area:** 27,261,439 sq. km.

South America

It is southern continent of Western Hemisphere including Argentina, Bolivia, Brazil, Chile, Columbia, Ecuador, Paraguay, Peru, Uruguay, Venezuela and Guyana. **Climate:** Diverse, varying with latitude and altitude, equatorial, hot and wet. Atacama, a rainless desert on middle west coast in south temperate. **Chief Industries:** Tropical agriculture: Cocoa, coffee, sugarcane, rubber, cereals. **Minerals:** Gold, silver, copper, tin, diamonds, nitrates, factory industries developing gradually. Portuguese descent, Indian's negroes, Mulattoes and Mestizos (mixed races). **Important Cities:** Rio de Janeiro, Salvador, Trinidad, Buenos Aires, La Paz, Bogota. **Area:** 17,522,371 sq. km.

Australia

Australia, with a population of 41.66 million (2021), is an island continent of 8,426,638 sq. km and is the smallest continent. In the continent, besides Australia, New Zealand, New Guinea and neighbouring archipelagos are other members. The commonwealth of Australia, including the islands of Tasmania, is nearly as large as Europe but has only 19.7 million inhabitants, most of whom are of British origin but there are about 50,000 native aborigines. Australia country is made up of the following states: New South Wales (Cap. Sydney); Queensland (Cap. Brisbane); South Australia (Cap. Adelaide); Western Australia (Cap. Perth); Victoria (Cap. Melbourne); Tasmania (Cap. Hobart). All these capital cities are ports though Perth is served by the port of Fremantle. An area largely uninhabited, is the Northern Territory. Its capital is Darwain and another famous town is Alice Springs. The Territory does not yet govern itself in the way other states do. The federal capital is Canberra. Australia produces more wool than any other country in the world. The country also has rich supplies of gold, iron ore, lead and zinc and has a new growing steel industry. One of the most important rivers is the Snowy in New South Wales and Victoria. A big new irrigation scheme is being carried out on this river and the Murray which involves taking the river waters through the mountains. The first free immigrants arrived from Britain in 1793, the east coast of Australia having been discovered by Captain Cook about twenty years before. These settlers came to New South Wales which is thus the oldest state in Australia. In 1910 the six states were all united in a Federation called the Common wealth of Australia.

Antarctica

It is 16 million sq km uninhabited land, located at South Pole. It is covered with snow and has extensive ice sheets, glaciers, volcanoes and islands. The area south of 60° latitude is reserved for peaceful international research.

Continent	Highest Elevation
Africa	Mt Kilimanjaro (Tanzania) (5895 m)
Antarctica	Vinson Massif (5140 m)
Asia	Mt Everest (Nepal) (8848 m)
Australia	Mt Kosciusko (2229 m)
Europe	Mt Elbrus (5642 m)
North America	Mt McKinley (6194 m)
South America	Aconcagua (6959 m)

Important Boundary Lines

- **Durand Line:** Represents the boundary line between Pakistan and Afghanistan. It was demarcated by Sir Mortimer Durand.
- **Hindenberg Line:** The line to which the Germans retreated during the First World War, representing the boundary between Poland and Germany.
- **MacMohan Line:** The boundary between India and China as demarcated by Sir MacMohan.
- **Maginot Line:** Boundary between France and Germany.
- **Oder Neisse Line:** Boundary between Germany and Poland.
- **Radcliffe Line:** Boundary between India and Pakistan as demarcated by Sir Cyril Radcliffe.
- **38th Parallel:** Boundary between North and South Korea.
- **49th Parallel:** Boundary between USA and Canada.

Important Places of the World

- **Abu Dhabi:** This emirate is part of the United Arab Emirates. It is located in 2,07,200 sq km area in the South-East of Arabian peninsula. It is known for its rich oil reserves.
- **Abu Simbal:** This place in the Nile river valley of Egypt is known for its ancient temples carved out of solid sandstone. It was relocated as such to save from drowning due to construction of a dam on Nile.
- **Adam's bridge:** It is a 35 km long stretch of sandbanks in Palk strait between India and Sri Lanka.
- **Alaska:** It is arctic state of the United States of America, separated from the mainland. The state has major oil and gas reserves but exploitation is difficult due to inclement weather.
- **Alexandria:** It is chief port of Egypt, used for export of cotton, wheat, rice etc.
- **Antwerp:** It is the seaport in Belgium on river Scheldt and is major transit point for European Community. It is known for diamond industry and historic and artistic interest.
- **Asia Minor:** It is peninsula, approximately coextensive with Turkey. Also known as Anatolia, it is bounded by black sea, Mediterranean sea and Aegean.
- **Babylon:** It is ancient capital of Babylonian empire. It is located in European valley about 90 km south of Baghdad. Its hanging gardens are world famous.
- **Bahamas:** It consists of over 700 coral atolls, located in Atlantic Ocean and is part of West Indies. The climate is tropical and tourists are plenty.
- **Bali:** This island of Indonesia is known as tourist resort.
- **Balkan peninsula:** It is located in Europe, covered by Black sea, Adriatic sea, lonian seas, and Aegean seas. It includes Turkey, Yugoslavia, Croatia, Slovenia, Bosnia, Bulgaria, Albania and Greece.
- **Bermuda:** These are 360 British group of coral islands out of which only a few are inhabited. They are located in North Atlantic and known for winter tourism and as tax-heaven.
- **Bethlehm:** This town of Israel is supposed to be the birthplace of Jesus Christ.
- **Borneo:** It is an island in Malay archipelago. The island is divided among Malaysia, Indonesia and Brunei.
- **Canary islands:** They are group of 7 volcanic islands located in North Atlantic Ocean. They belong to Spain and are tourist attractions.
- **Cape of Good Hope:** It is the southern most tip of Africa, belonging to South Africa. It is known as Cape Province.
- **Champagne:** This province of France is know for its wine production.
- **Chechnya:** This was part of Russia but undertook massive war in an attempt to gain independence.
- **Diego Garcia:** This islands are in Indian Ocean. Under British possession, they are being used as naval bases by USA.

❖ **East Indies:** Islands lying between South East Asia and Northern Australia are called East Indies. These belong to Malaysia and Indonesia.

❖ **Falkland:** These islands exist off the coast of Argentine in Atlantic Ocean but come under British control. In 1982, Argentina and Britain fought war over them.

❖ **French Polynesia:** It is overseas territory of France in South Pacific Ocean and comprises several archipelagoes. It came into prominence as France carried out its nuclear tests in the area.

❖ **Gaza Strip:** It is coastal area in West Asia which was occupied by Israel from Egypt. Now, Palestine has been given some autonomy in the area.

❖ **Greenwich:** It is located in London, Britain. The longitudes are conventionally calculated from Greenwich meridian.

❖ **Hawaii:** It is an island, located in Pacific ocean and was admitted as 50th state of the USA in 1959.

❖ **Hiroshima:** It is a city of Japan and was first city to be destroyed by atomic bomb on August 6, 1945.

❖ **Hollywood:** This is a suburb of Los Angles, USA and is centre of film industry.

❖ **Hong Kong:** It is located in South East Asia and was formerly a part of British empire. But in 1997, its status got changed and it returned to Chinese sovereignty. It has deep water harbour and became a major trading centre of the world despite a few natural resources. The existing capitalist system will continue for another 50 years.

❖ **Indo-China:** The area in South-East Asia, comprising Vietnam, Cambodia and Laos is collectively called Indo-China. The area was under French control till 1954.

❖ **Jerusalem:** It is a town of Israel, which is sacred to Muslims, Christians and Jews. There have been several battles for occupying this town.

❖ **Latin America:** The Spanish, Portuguese and French speaking countries of both American continents are collectively called Latin America. The important countries covered are Argentina, Brazil, Chile, Colombia, Cuba, Ecuador, Haiti, Mexico, Nicaragua, Panama, Paraguay, Peru, Uruguay and Venezuela.

❖ **Macao:** It is Portuguese colony in South East China and will return to China in 1999. It has deep water port and is known centre for trade, tourism and gambling.

❖ **Mecca:** This Saudi Arabian city is a holy place for Muslims as it is the birthplace of Mohammed.

❖ **Palestine:** This 'holy land' is located in West Asia, bounded by Syria, Lebanon, Jordan, Egypt and Mediterranean Sea. It was under Israeli occupation but after 1993, self-rule has been granted in limited amount.

❖ **Pearl Harbour:** It is a landlocked harbour on Hawaii island of the USA. It is a naval base of the US and attack by Japan in December 1941 without warning precipitated the US entry into the Second World War.

❖ **Polynesia:** Islands in Pacific Ocean lying between 30oN and 30oS are called Polynesia. These islands lie between 135oE and 135oW.

❖ **St. Petersburg:** It is a city of Russia, formerly called Leningrad. It is the major cultural centre, industrial centre and major port. It was scene of very long seizure by German forces during Second World War.

❖ **Scandinavia:** It is the name given to large peninsula in North-West Europe. It comprises Sweden, Finland and Norway and sometimes include Denmark, Finland and Iceland. The climate in the area is very cold and the area is rich in timber and mineral ores.

❖ **Siberia:** This territory is in Russia, extending from Ural mountains to sea of Okhotsk and bounded by Arctic on north and Mongolia and Turkmenistan on south. The climate is very severe and the area is rich in minerals and oil.

❖ **Spartley Islands:** They are cluster of islands in South China Sea. They are supposed to be containing Petroleum reserves and so ownership is disputed by China, Taiwan, Philippines and Vietnam.

❖ **Tibet:** It is autonomous region in the South West of China. The plateau is called "roof of the world". The area is semi-desert and people follow Buddhist religion. The people of the area have been demanding independence from China.

❖ **West Indies:** These are group of islands in Atlantic Ocean, south east of the USA. It includes Cuba, Haiti, Dominican Republic, Bahamas, Barbados, Jamaica, Leeward Islands, Trinidad and Tobago, Puerto Rico, Virgin Island, Windward Island, Marginique Curacaro and Guadeloupe. They are mostly volcanic and coral islands.

National Emblems of Different Countries

Country	Emblem
Australia	Kangaroo
Canada	White lily
Denmark	Beach
France	Lily
Germany	Corn Flower
India	Lioned Capital
Iran	Rose
Ireland	Shamrock
Italy	White lily
Japan	Chrysanthemum
Pakistan	Crescent
Spain	Eagle
United Kingdom	Rose
U.S.A.	Golden Rod

Flower Emblems

Country	Flower Emblem
Canada	Maple
France	Lily
Germany	Corn flower
India	Lotus
Ireland	Shamrock
Japan	Chrysanthemum
Scotland	Thistle
Spain	Pomegranate
United Kingdom	Rose

World Time

Local Time of any place is 12 noon when the sun is exactly overhead. It will vary from the Greenwich time at the rate of four minutes for each degree of longitude.

Standard Time is the uniform time fixed by each country. It is fixed in relation to mean time of a certain meridian which generally passes through it.

Greenwich Mean Time (GMT) is the U.K. Standard time. It is based on local time of the meridian passing through Greenwich near London.

Indian Standard Time is fixed on the mean time of 82½° meridian which passed through Varanasi and Kakinada. It is 5½ hours ahead of the Greenwich Mean Time.

International Date Line roughly corresponds to 180° E or W meridian of longitude which falls on the opposite side of the Greenwich meridian and the date changes by one day (*i.e.*, 24 hours) as this line is crossed. On crossing this line from east to west a day is added, and a day is subtracted on crossing it from west to east.

Shipping Canals of the World

Kiel

This canal shortens the mileage between London and the Baltic ports by about 250 miles. This was opened in 1895, and is 61 miles long with a depth of 40 ft. It is an international canal that links North Sea with the Baltic Sea. Germany, which is cut off from the main sea, depends for navigation on this canal.

Panama

This canal constructed above sea-level with locks has linked the Atlantic and Pacific Oceans with Colon and Panama (ports) on the coastal ends respectively. The credit for this engineering feat goes to the U.S. Government.

This has shortened the distance by 6000 miles between London and San Francisco; 9000 miles between New York and San Francisco; and 4000 miles between New York and Japan. This canal is of prime importance because it passes through a region which is tremendously rich in petroleum. Hence it meets trade, defence and strategic purpose.

It is 50.72 miles long, 500 ft. wide and about 45 ft. deep and was opened in 1914. The Panama Canal has been transferred to Panama by Ist January, 2000. An agreement to this effect had been signed by Panama and USA in 1979.

White Baltic Sea Canal

The Soviet Union has constructed this canal which joins Baltic Sea and Arctic Ocean. It connects Leningrad with the White Sea. It is the longest shipping canal, 140 miles long.

Suez Canal

The important link between the Mediterranean Sea and the Red Sea has shortened the distance between London and Mumbai by about 4000 miles. On the Mediterranean side we have Port Said, and the Suez Port is on the Red Sea. This canal is 175 km long and about 380 ft. wide with a depth of 35 ft., it was constructed in 1869 by a French engineer, Ferdinand de Lesseps.

It was first administered by a limited company in which Britain held a major portion of the shares. Egypt demanded the evacuation of the British troops from the Suez Canal Zone and they were withdrawn in June 1956. The Canal was nationalised by Col. Nasser on 26th July, 1956.

In June 1967 Israel occupied the eastern bank of Suez Canal and it was closed to traffic till 1975. It was opened to traffic after 8 years on June 8, 1975. The Suez Canal has now been widened in order to enable some of the larger ships and oil tankers to pass through the canal.

Ocean Routes

The sea lanes constitute the largest binding links of the world's economy. The oceans are natural waterways and prove to be the cheapest mode of transport. The major ocean trade routes are as follows:

(*a*) **North Atlantic:** It links the most densely populated and industrially and economically most advanced regions of the world. It is the busiest and most important route. London, Southampton, Hamburg, Liverpool, Glasglow, Rotterdam, Antwerp, Bremen are important ports on the European side and New York, Boston, Philadelphia, Baltimore, New Orleans, Montreal, Quebec are major ports on the American side. The east-bound traffic includes foodgrains, meat, cotton, tobacco, petroleum and metallic ores while goods going towards American side include manufactured goods.

(*b*) **Mediterranean: Red sea Route:** This route came into existence after the completion of Suez Canal and links Asia with Europe. The new route has brought about large reduction in the distance between the countries of the two continents. It touches more lands and serves more people than any route. Some important ports of cell are London, Lisbon, Marseilles, Naples, Aden, Mumbai, Colombo, Calcutta, Singapore, Malacca, Manila, Hong Kong, Adelaide, Melbourne and Sydney. Raw materials like wheat, minerals, petroleum etc are carried towards the west and manufactured goods and machineries from the west.

(*c*) **Cape Route:** It is one of the oldest sea route and was used by Europeans to come to Asia and eastern Africa. However, after the opening of Suez Canal, its importance has gone down. Despite this, large vessels prefer this route. More-over, the ships using this route do not have to pay the heavy toll of Suez Canal.

(*d*) **South Atlantic Route:** It links the countries of South America with West Europeans. The movement is limited. The items from America include wheat, meat, coffee and dairy products and from Europe come machines, chemicals and manufactured goods.

(e) **Pacific Route:** This is the longest route and is gaining importance with the development of east. Asian countries and western North America. The important ports of the cell are Yokohama, Manila, Sydney and Auckland on the Western Pacific Coast and Vancouver, San Francisco and Panama on the east coast. Wheat, meat, dairy products, wool, manufactured goods etc move along the route.

Important Towns and Rivers of India and World

Town	River
Karachi (Pakistan)	Indus
Chittagong (Bangladesh)	Maiyani
Ludhiana (India)	Sutlej
Lucknow (India)	Gomti
Prayagraj (India)	At the confluence of Ganges, Yamuna and Saraswati (invisible)
Jamshedpur (India)	Subarnarekha
Vijayawada (India)	Krishna
Srinagar (India)	Jhelum
Surat (India)	Tapti
Lahore (Pakistan)	Ravi
Ferozepur (India)	Sutlej
Delhi (India)	Yamuna
Kanpur (India)	Ganges
Hardwar (India)	Ganges
Patna (India)	Ganges
Cuttack (India)	Mahanadi
Kolkata (India)	Hooghly
Nasik (India)	Godavari
Varanasi (India)	Ganges
Yangoon (Myanmar)	Irrawady
Akyab (Myanmar)	Irrawady
Shanghai (China)	Yang-tse-kiang
Canton (China)	Si-kiang
Nanking (China)	Yang-tse-kiang
Chungking (China)	Yang-tse-kiang
Kabul (Afghanistan)	Kabul
Cairo (Egypt)	Nile
Basra (Iraq)	Euphrates and Tigris
Ankara (Turkiye)	Kizil
Baghdad (Iraq)	Tigris
Khartoum (Sudan)	At the Confluence of Blue and White Nile
Lisbon (Portugal)	Tagus
Cologne (Germany)	Rhine
Berlin (Germany)	Spree
Vienna (Austria)	Danube
Belgrade (Serbia)	Danube
Warsaw (Poland)	Vistula
Paris (France)	Seine
Humburg (Germany)	Elbe
Danzig (Germany)	Vistula
Dresden (Germany)	Elbe
Budapest (Hungary)	Danube
Rome (Italy)	Tiber
London (England)	Thames
Glassgow (England)	Clyde
New Castle (England)	Tyne
Bristol (England)	Avon
Liverpool (England)	Mersey
Dundee (Scotland)	Tay
Quebec	St. Lawrence
Ottawa	Ottawa
Montreal	St. Lawrence
New York	Hudson
Philadelphia	Delaware
Washington	Potomac
New Orleans	Mississippi
Moscow	Moskva
Leningrad	Neva
Stalingrad	Volga
Kiev	Dneiper

Geographical Surnames

Bengal's Sorrow	Damodar River
Blue Mountains	Nilgiri Hills
City of Palaces	Kolkata
China's Sorrow	Hwang Ho
City of Eternal Springs	Quito (South America)
City of Seven Hills	Rome
City of Skyscrapers	New York
Cockpit of Europe	Belgium
Dark Continent	Africa
Emerald Isle	Ireland
Eternal City	Rome
Empire State	New York
Forbidden City	Lhasa
Gift of the Nile	Egypt
Gateway of India	Mumbai
Gateway of Tears	Strait of Beb-el-Mandeb (Jerusalem, Palestine)
George Cross Island	Malta
Granite City	Aberdeen
Holy Land	Jerusalem
Hermit Kingdom	Korea
Island of Cloves	Zanzibar
Key to Mediterranean	Gibraltar
Land of the Thousand Lakes	Finland
Land of the Midnight Sun	Norway
Land of the Golden Fleece	Australia
Land of Rising Sun	Japan
Land of Morning Calm	Korea
Land of Maple Leaf	Canada
Land of White Elephants	Siam (Thailand)
Land of Thousand Elephants	Laos
Land of Thunderbolt	Bhutan
Land of Five Rivers	Punjab
Manchester of the Orient	Osaka (Japan)
Pillars of Hercules	Straits of Gibraltar
Playground of Europe	Switzerland
Queen of the Adriatic	Venice
Rose-pink City	Jaipur
Roof of the World	The Pamirs in Central Asia
Sickman of Europe	Turkiye
Venice of the North	Stockholm
Windy City	Chicago
Whiteman's Grace	Guinea (West Coast of Africa)
World's Loneliest Island	Tristan De Cunha (Mid Atlantic)

Major Rivers of the World

River	Origin	Falls in	Length (Km.)
Nile	Victoria lake	Mediterranean Sea	6,650
Amazon	Andes (Peru)	Atlantic Ocean	6,428
Yangtze	Tibetan Kiang Plateau	China Sea	6,300
Mississippi Missouri	Itaska lake (USA)	Gulf of Mexico (USA)	6,275
Yenisei	Tannu-Ola Mts.	Arctic Ocean	5,539
Hoang Ho	Kunlun Mts.	Gulf of Chibli	5,464
Ob	Altai Mts., Russia	Gulf of Ob	5,410
Congo	Lualaba & Luapula rivers	Atlantic Ocean	4,700
Amur	Northeast China	Sea of Okhotsk	4,444
Lena	Baikal Mts	Laptev Sea	4,400
Mekong	Tibetan Highlands	South China Sea	4,350
Mackenzie	Great Slave Lake	Beaufort Sea	4,241
Niger	Guinea	Gulf of Guinea	4,200

Important Straits of the World

Straits	Water Bodies joined	Area
Bab-al-Mandeb	Red Sea & Arabian Sea	Arabia & Africa
Bering	Arctic Ocean & Bering Sea	Alaska & Asia
Bosphorus	Black Sea & Marmara Sea	Turkey
Dover	North Sea & Atlantic Ocean	England & Europe
Florida	Gulf of Mexico & Atlantic Ocean	Florida & Bahamas Islands
Gibralter	Mediterranean Sea & Atlantic Ocean	Spain & Africa
Malacca	Java Sea & Bay of Bengal	India & Indonesia
Palk	Bay of Bengal & Indian Ocean	India & Sri Lanka
Magellan	South Pacific & South Atlantic Ocean	Chile
Sunda	Java Sea & Indian Ocean	Indonesia

Major Gulfs of the World

Names	Area (Sq. Km.)
Gulf of Mexico	15,44,000
Gulf of Hudson	12,33,000
Arabian Gulf	2,38,000
Gulf of St. Lawrence	2,37,000
Gulf of California	1,62,000
English Channel	89,900

Oceans of the World

Names	Area (Sq. Km.)	Greatest Depth
Pacific	166,240000	Mariana Trench
Atlantic	86,560000	Puerto Rico Trench
Indian	73430000	Java Trench
Arctic	13230000	—

Important Lakes of the World

Lake	Location	Area (Sq. Km.)
Caspian	Russia and CIS	371000
Superior	Canada and USA	82414
Victoria	Tanzania (Africa)	69485
Huron	Canada and USA	59596
Michigan	USA	58016
Tanganyika	Africa	32892
Baikal	Russia (CIS)	31502
Great Bear	Canada	31080
Malawi	Malawi (Tanzania)	30044
Great Slave	Canada	28438

Highest Waterfalls of the World

Name(s) (Foreign)	Location
Angel (Salto Angel)	Canaima National Park, Venezuela
Tugela	Natal National Park, South Africa
Utigord (Utigordsfoss)	Norway
Monge (Mongefoss)	Marstein, Norway
Gocta Cataracts	Chachapoyas, Peru
Mutarazi (Mtarazi)	Nyanga National Park, Zimbabwe
Yosemite	Yosemite National Park, California, U.S.
Espelands (Espelandsfoss)	Hardanger Fjord, Norway
Lower Mar Valley (Ostra Mardolafoss)	Eikesdal, Norway
Tyssestrengene	Odda, Norway

International Airports

INDIA	Lokpriya Gopinath Bardoloi	Chennai
	Chaudhary Charan Singh	Lucknow
	Chatrapati Shivaji	Mumbai
	Indira Gandhi	Delhi
	TIA	Thiruvanantapuram
	Shri Guru Ram Das Jee	Amritsar
U.S.A.	J.F.K. (J.F. Kennedy) La Guardia	New York
RUSSIA	Sherematevo Vnukovo	Moscow
FRANCE	Orly and Charles de Gaulle	Paris
BRITAIN	Heathrow and Gatwick	London
JAPAN	Narita, Haneda	Tokyo
SWEDEN	Arlanda	Stockholm
DENMARK	Kastrup	Copenhagen

Highest Mountain Peaks of the World

	Mountains	Height in Metres
1.	Mount Everest	8,848
2.	K-2 (Godwin Austen)	8,611
3.	Kanchenjunga	8,597
4.	Lhotse	8,511
5.	Makalu I	8,481
6.	Dhaulagiri I	8,167
7.	Mansalu I	8,156
8.	Chollyo	8,153
9.	Nanga Parbat	8,124
10.	Annapurna I	8,091
11.	Gasherbrum I	8,068
12.	Broad Peak I	8,047
13.	Gasherbrum II	8,034
14.	Shisha Pangma (Gosainthan)	8,014
15.	Gasherbrum III	7,952

Important Boundaries

Durand Line	Pakistan & Afghanistan
MacMohan Line	India & China
Radcliff Line	India & Pakistan
Maginot Line	France & Germany
Oder Niesse Line	Germany & Poland
Hindenberg Line	Poland & Germany (at the time of First World War)
38th Parallel	North & South Korea
49th Parallel	USA & Canada

Different Minerals and their Primary Producers

Aluminium	China, Peru, Australia, Russia, Canada
Asbestos	Russia, China
Bauxite	Australia, Gini, China
Chromium	South Africa, Kazakhstan, Turkiye, India
Coal	China, India, Indonesia, USA., Russia
Copper Ore	Chile, Peru, China
Crude Oil	U.S.A., Saudi Arabia, Russia
Diamonds	Russia, Botswana, Canada
Gold	China, South Africa, Australia, Canada, Russia
Graphite Ore	China, India, Brazil
Iron Ore	China, Brazil, Australia, U.K., U.S.A.
Lignite	Germany, Russia
Manganese Ore	S. Africa, Australia, China, Russia, India
Mercury	China, Mexico
Mica	China, U.S.A., Madagascar, India, South Africa
Natural gas	U.S.A., Russia, Iran
Nickel ore	Indonesia, Philippines, South Africa, Russia
Platinum	South Africa, Russia, Zimbabwe
Petroleum	U.S.A., Saudi Arabia, Venezuela
Phosphate	U.S.A., Russia
Salt	U.S.A., China
Silver	Mexico, Peru, China, Russia
Sulphur	U.S., Canada
Tin	China, Indonesia
Uranium	Kazakhstan, Canada, Australia
Zinc ore	Canada, Australia

Principal Languages of the World

Rank	Language	Speakers (million)
1.	Chinese	1,322.8
2.	Spanish	471.4
3.	English	369.9
4.	Arabic	349.3
5.	Hindi	342.2
6.	Bengali	228.7
7.	Portuguese	232.4
8.	Russian	153.7
9.	Japanese	126.3
10.	Lahnda	99.6
11.	Marathi	83.1
12.	Telugu	82.6
13.	Turkish	82.2
14.	Malay	81.6
15.	Korean	81.5
16.	French	79.6
17.	Tamil	77.5
18.	German, Standard	76.5
19.	Vietnamese	76.1
20.	Urdu	69.0
21.	Javanese	68.3
22.	Persian	65.7
23.	Italian	64.8
24.	Gujarati	56.9
25.	Pushto	53.1
26.	Bhojpuri	52.3
27.	Hausa	48.6
28.	Kannada	43.6
29.	Yoruba	41.0
30.	Polish	40.0

Facts about Planets

Closest to Sun	Mercury
Farthest from Sun	Neptune
Heaviest	Jupiter
Hottest	Venus
Inner	Mercury, Venus, Earth, Mars
Largest	Jupiter
Smallest	Mercury
Moons, None	Mercury, Venus
Moon; Largest	Ganymede (Jupiter), larger than Mercury
Nearest to Earth	Venus
Orbits; Order	Mercury (closest to Sun), Venus, Earth, Mars, Jupiter, Saturn, Uranus, Neptune.
Rings/largest number	Saturn
Spin; Backwards	Venus (East to West)

Geographical Discoverers

- **Marco Polo:** Italian traveller who explored China, India and South East Asian countries in twelfth century and published records of his journeys.
- **Columbus:** Spanish explorer who discovered West Indies in 1492 and South America in 1498.
- **Cabot:** Italian sailor discovered New Foundland in 1494.
- **Vasco-da-Gama:** Portuguese sailor went around the Cape of Good Hope to discover sea route to India in 1498.
- **Magellan:** He was the commander of the first expedition that sailed around the world in 1519. He discovered passage to the Pacific from the Atlantic through straits.
- **Pedro Alvares Cabral:** Portuguese sailor who reached Brazil in 1500.
- **Tasman:** Dutch navigator who discovered Tasman island and New Zealand in 1642.
- **Captain Cook:** English sailor who discovered Hawaii Island in 1776.
- **Francis Younghusberg:** He explored the frontier regions of India, China and Tibet.
- **Robert Peary:** He was the first man to reach North Pole in 1909.
- **Amundsen:** Norwegian explorer discovered South Pole in 1912.
- **Nansen:** Norwegian explorer to discover Greenland.
- **Byrd:** American aviator who flew over the North Pole in 1926 and made the first flight over the South Pole in 1929.
- **Edmund Hillary:** New Zealander who was the first person to conquer the highest peak Mt. Everest along with Tenzing Sherpa.
- **Yuri Gagarin:** Russian who was the first man to go in space.
- **Neil Armstrong:** American was the first man to set foot on moon.

INDIAN GEOGRAPHY

Physiographic Division of India

Size and Location

India, the seventh largest country in the world, is well-marked off from the rest of Asia by the mountains and the seas, which give the country a distinct geographical entity. Bounded by the great Himalayas in the North, it stretches Southwards and at the Tropic of Cancer, tapers off into the Indian Ocean between the Bay of Bengal on the East and the Arabian Sea on the West, it covers an area of 32,87,263 sq. km.

Lying entirely in the northern hemisphere, the Mainland extends between latitudes 8°4′ and 37°6′ North and longitudes 68°7′ and 97°25′ East and measures about 3,214 km. from North to South between the extreme latitudes and about 2,933 km. from East to West between the extreme longitudes, it has a land frontier of about 15,200 km. The total length of the coastline of the Mainland, Lakshadweep group of Islands and Andaman and Nicobar group of Islands is 7,516.5 km.

Physical Boundaries

The Himalayas and the other lofty mountains, viz., Muztagh Ata, Aghil Kunlun mountains to the North of Kashmir and Zaskar mountains to the East of Himachal Pradesh—from India's Northern boundary, except in the Nepal region. The Himalayas are adjoined in the North by China, Nepal and Bhutan. A series of mountain ranges in the East separates India from Myanmar. Also, in the East, lies Bangladesh bounded by the Indian states of West Bengal, Assam, Meghalaya, Tripura and Mizoram in the North-West.

Afghanistan and Pakistan border on India. The Gulf of Mannar and the Palk Straits separate India from Sri Lanka. The Andaman and Nicobar Islands in the Bay of Bengal and Lakshadweep in the Arabian Sea are parts of the territory of India. Indira point (earlier called Pugmallion point) in Great Nicobar in the Andaman and Nicobar Islands is the Southern most territory of India.

Geological History

The Indian Sub-Continent is characterised by a great diversity in its physical features. It may be divided into three broadly defined physiographic units:

(*i*) The Himalayas and the associated mountain chains;

(*ii*) The Indus-Ganga–Brahmaputra plain; and

(*iii*) The peninsular plateau.

The Himalayas were formed by Earth movements which affected the relief of the earth in the last phase of its physical history. It is generally helps to have been formed in the Tertiary era. Because of their sharp and striking contrasts in altitude the Himalayan relief features are described as youthful. The peninsular plateau, on the other hand, is an old mass of the Earth's Crust worn down by continual erosion. As a consequence the plateau has acquired the look of old age.

It has a characteristically senile topography and has existed since the pre-Cambrian era, 600 million years ago. In between the two main physiographic units lies the Northern plain which marks an initial marine depression filled by deposits brought down by the rivers over the ages. The filling has been done so uniformly that the plain gives an impression of a flat surface, though it is not so.

The senile and the youthful features in the peninsular block and the young-folded mountains of the north are not mutually exclusive. Their physical history reveals that there have been deep-rooted interactions, between the two units. Their structural characteristics, and their mode of building, as brought out by the tectonic details, furnish evidence of their mutual interdependence and borrowing. The outlying fragments of the peninsular block, such as noticed in the Shillong plateau, the Aravallis and the Kirana Hills near the Chenab in the Punjab, played a very important role in defining the trendines of the Himalayan ranges. The

Sediments embedded in the rocks of the Himalayan ranges have similarities to the rock Strata found on the peninuslar block, the huge accumulations of the sediments forming the surface of the great plain, lying between the two main physiographic divisions, have been contributed by both of them.

Physiography

Major divisions

On account of the differences in geological structure and history and the involved denudational processes, India's relief is marked by a great variety.

It is divided into three Major physiographic units; the Himalayan mountain complex, the great plains and the peninsular plateau, including the coasts and islands.

Himalayan Mountain Complex

The Himalayas and the associated mountain arcs girding the sub-continent on the North stretch in a consistent North West-South East direction for about 2,400 kilometres between the gorges of the Indus and the Tsangpo-Brahmaputra. The section between the Indus and the Sutlej is referred to as the Punjab Himalayas; the section between the Sutlej and the Kali is termed as Kumaon Himalayas.

The other two sections between the Kail and the Tista and between the latter river and the Dihang (Tsangpo Brahmaputra) are described as the Nepal and the Assam Himalayas.

The Himalayan mountain chain, all along its longitudinal axis, is arranged into three main series of parallel ranges sometimes referred to as the Greater Himalayas (the Himadri), the Lesser Himalayas (the Himachal) and the sub-Himalayas (the Siwaliks) and at others as the inner, the middle and the outer Himalayas.

The altitude as well as physiographic complexity increases from the outer to the innermost Himalayan ranges.

The Greater Himalayas have an average altitude of 6,000 metres and all the prominent Himalayan peaks such as Everest (8,848 m) Kanchenjunga (8,598 m), Nanga Parbat (8,126 m), Nanda Devi (7,817), and Namcha Barwa (7,756 m). In the northwest the Himalayan ranges coalesce with the diversely arranged mountain chains of the Karakoram, the Hindu Kush, Kun Lun, Tien Shah, Pamir, Alay and the Trans Alay Ranges which converge on the central promontary of Pamir.

The Eastern Himalayas rise rather abruptly from the plains of Bihar and Bengal with the highest peaks of Everest and Kanchenjunga located quite close together.

In contrast, the Western Himalayas attain height through a graded series of low ranges. Here the first stage is set by the sub-Himalayan hills of Jammu and Kashmir, the second by the lesser Himalayan ranges of Pir Panjal and the Dhauladhar and the third by the Great Himalayan, North Kashmir and the Zaskar ranges. Further Northward they are replaced by the Ladakhkailash and the Karakoram ranges.

The four-fold geological divison of the Himalayas based on the age of rock formations and their type are

(*i*) The Tibetan Zone, composed of fossil-bearing sedimentary rocks ranging from palaeozoic to Eocene of the pleistocene era, lies to the North of the Great Himalayas.

(*ii*) The central or the Himalayan zone is mainly composed of crystalline and metamorphic rocks.

(*iii*) The Himalayan Nappe Zone consists of overfolds and thrust faults of a more complex type where large bodies of older rocks have been physically displaced and thrust on the newer ones along the recumbent folds over large areas.

(*iv*) The outer or the Sub-Himalayan zone, corresponding to the Siwaliks, is composed to the Sedimentary deposits belonging to upper Tertiary and believed to have been derived from the eroded materials of the main Himalayan ranges themselves.

Some of the high peaks in the Kumaon Himalayas are Nanda Devi (7817 metres), Badrinath (7040 m), Kedarnath (6841 m), Trisul, Mana, Gangotri and Jamnotri. In the Nepal Himalayas the highest peaks are Mount Everest (8848 metres), Kanchenjunga (8598 m), Makaly (8481 m), Dhaulagiri (8172 m), Annapurna (8050 m) and Gosainthan (8018 m).

The Indus-Ganga-Brahmaputra Plain

The Great plain of India is formed by the Indus, Ganga and the Brahmaputra rivers. The plain extends for 3,200 kilometres between the mouths of the Ganga and the Indus, all along the foot of the mountain rim, with a width varying from 150 to 300 kilometres.

The longitudinal extent from the banks of the Ravi and the Sutlej to the Ganga delta alone is of 2,400 kilometres, the plain is the narrowest in Assam (90 to 100 kilometre) and broadens towards the west. It is 160 kilometres wide near the Rajmahal Hills and 280 kilometres near Allahabad. The plains are alluvial in nature.

Peninsular Plateau

Rising from the alluvial plains of Uttar Pradesh and Bihar, South of the Yamuna Ganga line, the great Indian plateau extends towards the south to encompass the whole of the peninsula. With a general elevation of 600–900 metres, the plateau makes an irregular triangle with its concave base lying between the Delhi Ridge and the Rajmahal hills and the apex formed by Kanya Kumari.

The outlying projections of the Peninsular plateau presented by the Aravallis, Rajmahal and Shillong hills, convey some idea of its original northerly limits.

As suggested by the Chambal, Sone and the Damodar, the plateau first slopes to the North and the East and thence, after the Vindhyan-Kaimur Range, to the West South of the Satpura-Maikal line, the general grain of the land is to the East and the South-East. On its extreme Western edge the plateau, however, slopes with a steep gradient on to the narrow coastal plain facing the Arabian Sea.

The Western and the North–Western flank of the plateau are occupied by the Aravallis. Having a North-East-South West axis the Arvallis form discontinuous ridges between Gujarat and Delhi. The main hills lie in Rajasthan. On the periphery of the Vindhayan upland to the West of the Aravallis Range lies the sandy waste of the Desert. The upper Chambal and the Betwa together drain the relatively open Malwa Plateau.

The relief of the plateau in the middle Sector is dominated by the great escarpment formed by the Vindhyan-Kaimur range between the valleys of the Narmada and the Sone. East of the Sone, the Chota Nagpur plateau rises to culminate in the Hazaribagh range.

The location of another fragment of the peninsular block in the Shillong plateau gives the indication of a possible connection. The Shillong plateau, a highly dissected and Jungly tract, descends in a steep slope towards the Surma Valley. The Northern outliers are represented by the Mikir and the Rangma hills.

The Deccan lava plateau has a generally homogeneous relief. The plateau surface made up of flat lava floors generally slopes to the East and the South East. To the south the Deccan lava formations give way to the gneisses and the granites of the Karnataka plateau. The Karnataka plateau has its two main sub divisions in the Malnad and the Maidan.

Western Ghats

The topography of the Deccan and the Karnataka plateaux is dominated by the Western Ghats, which stretch uninterruptedly to the Southern tip of the peninsula. They have a general altitude of 900–1100 metres but occasionally rise upto 1600 metres or even more.

Near Goa the lava rocks are replaced by the smoothly rounded hills of granites and gneisses. In this stretch the Ghats dip but rise once again in the Nilgiris, further south, the continuity of the Ghats is disturbed by the Palghat Gap and the Shencottah Gap.

East of Nagpur, the Deccan lava region is flanked by the plateau surface containing the Wainganga valley and the upper Mahanadi Basin in Chhatisgarh, a region interposed between the Mikir and the Odisha Hills.

Eastern Ghats

The Eastern Ghats are generally less impressive than the Western Ghats and form a discontinuous crest on the eastern periphery of the plateau. They are represented by an irregular line of hills. Such as the Nallamalais, Velikondas, Palkondas and the Pachaimalais. These hills are often referred to as the Northern hills in the Northern sector, Cuddapah Ranges in the Middle and the Tamil Nadu hills in the South.

The Coastal plains and the Islands

The plateau is flanked by a coastal plain of varied width extending from Kutch to Odisha. There are striking differences between the Eastern and the Western coastal plains, with the notable exception of Gujarat, the West coast has a narrow alluvial margin interspersed by hilly terrain. It has little indentations except in the south where the beautiful lagoons introduce an element of diversity.

The Eastern coast has a wide plain with well developed deltas of the major rivers. The climatic transition between the South-West monsoon regime of the North and North-East monsoon regime of the South has given rise to interesting differences in the alluvial features in the two different stretches of the East coastal plain.

The Indian islands in the Bay of Bengal consist of the Andamans and the Nicobar group, some of which are of volcanic origin. There are as many as 200 islands in the Andaman group alone, extending for 350 kilometres. There are 19 islands in the Nicobar group.

The Arabian Sea islands consist of the Lakshadweep group. They are formed on a coral deposit off the Kerala coast. The Southern-most of these lies just to the North of the Maldive islands which is an independent territory.

Climate, Vegetation and Soil

India has 'Monsoon' type of climate. The word 'monsoon' has been derived from the Arabic word ***'Mausim'*** which means seasonal reversal of the winds during the course of the year.

Factors Affecting The Climate Of India

Latitude

India lies between 8°N and 37°N latitudes. The Tropic of Cancer passes through the middle of India, thus making the southern half of India in the **Torrid Zone** and the northern half in the **Temperate Zone.**

Himalaya Mountains

The Himalayas play an important role in lending a sub-tropical touch to the climate of India. The lofty Himalaya Mountains form a barrier which affects the climate of India. It prevents the cold winds of north Asia from blowing into India, thus protecting it from severely cold winters.

It also traps the Monsoon winds, forcing them to shed their moisture within the sub-continent.

Altitude

Temperature decreases with height. Places in the mountains are cooler than places on the plains. Places on the Deccan Plateau are not very hot in spite of being near the Equator.

Distance from the Sea

With a long coastline, large coastal areas have an equable climate. Areas in the interior of India are far away from the moderating influence of the sea. Such areas have extremes of climate.

Geographical Limits

(*a*) **Western Disturbances :** The low pressure systems that originate over the eastern Mediterranean region in winter and move eastwards towards India passing over Iran, Afghanistan and Pakistan are responsible for the winter rain in northern India.

(*b*) **Conditions in the Regions Surrounding India:** Temperature and pressure conditions in East Africa, Iran, Central Asia and Tibet determine the strength of the monsoons and the occasional dry spells.

For example, high temperatures in East Africa may draw the monsoon winds from the Indian Ocean into that region thus, causing a dry spell.

(*c*) **Conditions Over the Ocean :** The weather conditions over the Indian Ocean and the China Sea may be responsible for typhoons which often affect the east coast of India.

(*d*) **Jet Streams :** Air currents in the upper layers of the atmosphere known as jet streams could determine the arrival and the departure of the monsoons. The scientists are studying the jet streams and how it may affect the climate of India but much remains to be learned about this phenomenon.

Climate of India

1. The whole of India has a tropical monsoonal climate, since
   - the greater part of the country lies within the tropics, and
   - the climate is influenced by the S.W. and N.E. monsoons.
2. The position of the mountain ranges and direction of the rainbearing winds are the two main factors that determine the climate of India.
3. Alternating season is the chief characteristic of India's climate.

Climatic Regions of India

A climatic region is a homogeneous climatic condition which is the result of combined effects of climatic factors. The two important factors of climatic classification are ***temperature*** and ***rainfall***.

Koppen's Climatic Classification

The following five climatic regions have been identified in India according to Koppen's climatic classification : He used letters A, B, C, D and E to denote these climatic types:

A - Tropical climate (with mean monthly temperature over 18°C).

B - Dry climate (If dryness is less, semi desert (S); if it is more, desert (W).

C - Warm climate (with mean temperature between 18°C and 3°C).

D - Snow climate (with mean temperature under -3°C).

E - Ice climate (mean temperature under -10°C).

Köppen further sub-divided these types on the basis of seasonal variations, *e.g.*, f (sufficient precipitation), m (rain forest despite a dry monsoon season), w (dry winter), h (dry and hot), c (less than 4 months with mean temperature over 10°C) and g (Gangetic plain).

Climatic Regions of India According to Koppen's Scheme

Type of Climate	*Areas*
Amw - Monsoon with short dry winter	• West Coast of India, South of Goa
As - Monsoon with dry Summer	• Coromondal coast of Tamil Nadu
Aw - Tropical Savannah	• Most of the Peninsular Plateaus, south of the Tropic of Cancer
BShw - Semi arid steppe climate	• North western Gujarat, Same parts of West Rajasthan and Punjab
BWhw - Hot Desert	• Extreme Western Rajasthan
Cwg - Monsoon with dry winter	• Ganga plain, eastern Rajasthan, northern M.P., most of NE India.
Dfc - Cold humid winter with short summer	• Arunachal Pradesh
E - Polar type	• Jammu and Kashmir, H.P. and Uttaranchal

Moisture Index of Thornthwaite

Thornthwaite index is based on the concept of water balance. He found out the water balance for each month for all the places.

If the water balance has a water surplus solution, it is called *humid* and if it is water deficient it is called *arid*.

He also used English letters to classify different types of climate

1. Prehumid (A)
2. Humid (B)
3. Moist sub-humid (C_2)
4. Dry sub-humid (C_1)
5. Semi-arid (D)
6. Arid (E)

Climatic Regions of India as per Thornthwaite's Scheme

Types of Climate	*Areas*
A - Pre-humid	Mizoram, Tripura, Meghalaya, Lower Assam, Arunachal Pradesh in NE India and Western Coast of India, south of Goa.
B - Humid	Nagaland, Upper Assam, Manipur, North Bengal, Sikkim and West Coast.
C_2 - Moist sub-humid	West Bengal, Odisha and Eastern Bihar, Panchmari, eastern slopes of Western Ghats
C_1 - Dry sub-humid	Ganga plain, M.P., Chhattisgarh Jharkhand, Telangana, Northern Punjab and Haryana, north-eastern Tamil Nadu, Uttaranchal, Himachal Pradesh and J & K.
D - Semi Arid	Tamil Nadu, Andhra Pradesh, Karnataka, E. Maharashtra, N.E. Gujarat, Rajasthan and most of Punjab and Haryana
E - Arid	West Gujarat, West Rajasthan and Southern Punjab.

Dr. Trewartha's Classification

As per Dr. Trewartha's modified form of Koppen's classification, India can be divided into following climatic regions.

(i) Tropical Rain Forest

(*a*) This type of climate is found on the west coastal plain and Sahyadris and in parts of Assam.

(*b*) The temperatures are high, not falling below 18.2°C even during winter and rising to 29°C in April and May, the hottest months.

(*c*) Dense forests and plantation agriculture with crops like tea, coffee and spices are the characteristic vegetation in the area.

(ii) Tropical Savannah

(*a*) Most of the peninsula, except the semi-arid zone in the leeside of the Sahyadris experience this type of climate.

(*b*) A long dry weather lasting through winter and early summer and high temperatures remaining above 18.2°C even during the winter season and rising as high as 32°C in summer are the chief characteristics of this climate.

(*c*) Nagpur has a mean temperature of 35.4°C for May which is the hottest month and 20.7°C for December the coldest month in the year.

(*d*) The natural vegetation all over the area is savannah.

(iii) Tropical Semi-arid Steppe Climate

(*a*) The rain-shadow belt, running southward from central Maharashtra to Tamil Nadu, in the leeside of the Sahyadris and Cardamom Hills come under this type of climate of low and uncertain rainfall.

(*b*) Temperatures varying from 20° to 23.8°C for December and 32.8°C for May. Agriculturally, the climate is suitable only for dry farming and livestock rearing.

(iv) Tropical and Sub-Tropical Steppe

(*a*) This type of climate occurs over a broad crescent from Punjab to Kachchh between the Thar Desert to its west and the more humid climates of the Ganga Plain and the Peninsula to its east and south respectively.

(*b*) The climate, therefore, is transitional between these two areas. The annual rainfall is not only low but it is also highly erratic.

(v) Tropical Desert

(*a*) The western parts of Barmer, Jaisalmer and Bikaner districts of Rajasthan and most of the part of Kachchh form the sandy wastes of the Thar which experiences a typical desert climate.

(*b*) Ganganagar has recorded a maximum temperature of 50°C, the highest record.

(*vi*) *Humid Sub-tropical With Winter*

(*a*) A large area to the south of the Himalayas, east of the tropical and sub-tropical steppe and north of the tropical savannah running in a long belt from Punjab to Assam with a south-westward extension into Rajasthan east of the Aravalli Range, has this type of climate.

(*b*) Winters are dry except for a little rain received from the westerly depressions.

(*vii*) *Mountain Climate*

(*a*) The Himalayan and the Karakoram ranges experience this type of climate with sharp contrasts between the temperatures of the sunny and shady slopes, high diurnal range of temperatures and high variability of rainfall.

(*b*) The trans-Himalayan region, Ladakh, where the south-west monsoon fails to reach, has a dry and cold climate and a sparse and stunted vegetation.

(*viii*) *Drought and Floods in India*

(*a*) The dry areas of Rajasthan and the adjoining parts of Haryana and Gujarat are liable to frequent drought conditions.

(*b*) Another area liable to frequent drought lies on the leeward side of the Western Ghats.

El Nino and The Indian Monsoon

El Nino is a cold gean current that flows along the western coast of South America. The system involves oceanic and atmospheric phenomena with the appearance of warm currents off the coast of Peru in the Eastern Pacific and affects weather in many places including India. It is merely an extension of the warm equatorial current which gets replaced temporarily by cold Peruvian current or Humbolt current.

This results in :

(*i*) the distortion of equatorial atmosphere circulation;

(*ii*) irregularities in the evaporation of sea water;

(*iii*) reduction in the amount of planktons which further reduce the number of fish in the sea.

It is also called the Peru or Humboldt. It is a complex weather system that appears once every three to seven years, bringing drought, floods and other weather extremes to different parts of the world.

Effect of El Nino over India

1. Whenever, El Nino appears there is bound to be arid condition in India.
2. In a total of 27 El Nino years since 1875 India experienced at least 10 per cent less than normal rainfall 11 times.
3. On 15 other occasions when the Peruvian coast had experienced the appearance of El Nino, rainfall has been normal in India.
4. The interesting thing is that it never rained 10 per cent of what is normal for India even once during an El Nino year.
5. In 1979, the monsoon experiment (MONEX), the largest of its kind involving nations, saw the discovery of the dramatic bursts of energy over Indian west coast just before rains. But eight years later they are still to find a satisfactory explanation. They now believe that Tibet holds the clue for many of the unexplained phenomena.

Seasons in India

Seasons Based on Monsoon

The climate of India may be described as tropical monsoon. Even northern India, lying beyond the tropical zone, acquires a tropical touch marked by the relatively high temperatures and dry winters. The large size of the country and its varied relief play a crucial role in determining the climatic variations in different parts of India. But the seasonal rhythm of the monsoon is apparent throughout India. It may conveniently form the basis for dividing the year into different seasons. The most characteristic feature of the monsoons is the complete reversal of winds. It eventually leads to the alternation of seasons. Therefore, India is known as the '*land of the endless growing season*'. On the basis of the monsoon variations the year is divided into four seasons:

(I) The Cold Weather Season (N.E. Monsoons)

The cold weather season starts in early December, and at the beginning of January the north-east monsoon is fully established over India. The mean January day temperature in Madras and Calicut is about 24°-25°C while in the northern plains it is about 10°-15°C. In December, the sun shines directly over the Tropic of Capricorn. The landmass of Asia, including the sub-continent, cools down very rapidly. There is a high pressure over the continent. The Indian Ocean, being warmer, has a relatively low pressure.

Three Reasons for Excessive Cold in North India:

1. States like Punjab, Haryana and Rajasthan being far away from the moderating influence of sea experience continental climate.
2. The snowfall in the nearby Himalayan ranges creates cold wave situation.
3. Around February, the cold winds coming from Caspean Sea and Turkmenistan bring cold wave along with frost and fog over N. Western parts of India.

N.E. Trade Winds (prevailing winds in the tropical Latitudes), blow, land to sea.

These winds, being offshore do not give rain. They are dry except for the branch that blows over the Bay of Bengal and gives rainfall to the east coast of India.

These winds are also known as the N.E. Monsoons or the Winter Monsoons in India.

The Peninsular region of India, however does not have any well-defined cold weather season. There is hardly any seasonal change in the distribution pattern of the temperature in coastal areas because of moderating influence of sea and the proximity to equator. These western disturbances bring light rainfall, most beneficial to the rabi crop. This rainfall decreases towards the east and the south. The Tamil Nadu coast also receives rainfall during this season. The north-eastern winds absorb fresh moisture while blowing over the Bay of Bengal before crossing the coasts south of Chennai.

(ii) The Hot Weather Season

From March to May the sun moves from over the Equator towards the Tropic of Cancer. By June 21, it is directly overhead the Tropic of Cancer. In March, the highest day temperatures of about 38°C occur in the Deccan Plateau. Therefore :

(*a*) **Peninsular India,** places south of the Satpuras experience temperatures between 26°C-32°C. Coastal areas, due to the moderating influence of the sea, have lower temperatures (27°-32°).

(*b*) **Central India,** comprising Delhi and Madhya Pradesh experiences temperatures between 40°-45°C.

(*c*) **North-west India,** comprising mainly Rajasthan has very high temperatures (45°C), due also to features like sandy soil, direct insolation and lack of cloud cover.

Storms during the Hot Weather Season

(*a*) **Mango Showers** (since the rain showers are good for the mango trees) occur along the coast of Kerala.

(*b*) **Norwester/Kalbaisakhi** (meaning the calamity of the month of baisakh) occurs in Assam and West Bengal. These are thunderstorms, accompanied by strong winds and heavy rainfall. This is good for the tea crop in Assam and the jute and rice in West Bengal. In Assam these storms are called **Bardoli Chherha**.

(*c*) **Loo** is the name given to the hot, dry winds that blow in the Northern Plains. It is very common in Punjab, Haryana, Western Uttar Pradesh (called **"aandhi"**) and Bihar.

(*d*) **Blossom Shower** with this shower, coffee flowers blossom in Kerala and its nearby areas.

(iii) The South-West Monsoon Season

This season begins in June and lasts until September. The low pressure which existed over the Northern Plain is further intensified. It is strong enough to attract the moisture bearing winds from the Indian Ocean.

Facts about S.W. Monsoon

1. The bulk of the rainfall is received during this season in almost every part of India except Tamil Nadu.
2. The amount of rainfall received depends on the relief of the region.
3. The rain is unreliable and there are dry intervals.

The S.E. Trade Winds from the Southern Hemisphere are drawn into India as the S.W. Monsoon Winds after they cross the Equator. Due to the triangular shape of India, the S.W. Monsoon Winds are divided into two branches—the Arabian Sea Branch and the Bay of Bengal Branch.

The Arabian Sea Branch : It gives very heavy rainfall, more than 200 cm, to the windward side of the Western Ghats. The Deccan Plateau, which lies on the leeward side of the Western Ghat, receives less than 150 cm of rainfall.

Further east, rainfall decreases, *e.g.,* Hyderabad gets less than 100 cm while Chennai gets even less than 40 cm of rainfall. It does not give much rain to Rajasthan because the Aravali ranges lie parallel to the direction of winds and hence condensation does not occur. Therefore, Rajasthan gets less than 25 cm of rainfall.

These winds advance northwards, attracted to the low pressure in India. Punjab, at the foothills of the Shiwalik, gets Relief Rainfall.

Bay of Bengal Branch : The Bay of Bengal Branch which also blows from the southwest direction, is deflected by the Arakan Mountains of Myanmar and the N.E. Hills of India (Garo, Khasi and Jaintia). They blow into India as the S.E. Monsoons.

The delta of the Ganga-Brahmaputra and the wind-ward side of the N.E. Hills of India get heavy rain. For example, Cherrapunji on the windward side gets 2500 cm of rainfall, while Shillong on the leeward slope gets about 250 cm. The rainfall decreases as the winds reach the eastern Himalayas and blow westward into the Ganga Plain, attracted by the low pressure in Punjab and Rajasthan. Bikaner, lying in the rainshadow of the Aravali, gets little or no rain.

They give the lower Ganga Valley 200 cm of rainfall, the middle 150 cm and the upper 100 cm. Thus, Kolkata (lower Ganga), gets more than 200 cm of rainfall, Patna (middle Ganga) 150 cm and Amritsar (upper Ganga) 100 cm.

(iv) *The Retreating S.W. Monsoon Season*

This season lasts through October and November. The temperature in the Northern Plain begins to decrease as the sun's rays no longer fall directly at the Tropic of Cancer. In September, the sun shines directly at the Equator.

The low pressure over the Northern Plain is no longer strong enough to attract the Monsoon Winds into the heart of India.

By the end of September, the Monsoon Winds are drawn only upto Punjab, by mid-October upto the Central India and by early November upto Southern India.

Thus, the S.W. Monsoon Winds seem to withdraw in stages during this season. That is why this season is known as the Retreating S.W. Monsoon Season.

This season is marked by cyclones in the Bay of Bengal. They hit the east coast of India and Bangladesh causing widespread damage to life, property and crops.

Traditional Indian Seasons

Seasons	*Indian Calender*	*Gregarian Calender*
Vasanta	Chaitra-Vaisakha	March-April
Grishma	Jyaistha-Asadha	May-June
Varsha	Sravana-Bhadra	July-August
Sharada	Asvina-Kartika	Sept.-Oct.
Hemanta	Margashirsa-Pausa	Nov.-Dec.
Shishira	Magha-Phalguna	Jan.-Feb.

Difference between The Retreating S.W. Monsoons and North East Monsoons

Retreating South West Monsoons	*North-east Monsoons*
1. They blow during the months of October and November.	1. They blow during the months of December, January, February.
2. This is a season of transition between the hot, rainy season and the cold, dry season.	2. This is the cold weather season.
3. Characterised by oppressive heat and humidity known as **'October Heat'**.	3. This is a very pleasant season with low temperatures, low humidity and clear sky.
4. They blow in the S.W. direction but are not strong enough to blow right into the Northern Plain.	4. These winds blow in the N.E. direction from the land to the sea.
5. They withdraw in stages which results in decreasing rain.	5. They do not give rain to any part of India. Only the Bay of Bengal branch gives rain to the east coast.

Distribution of Rainfall in India

Rainfall is the important element of Indian economy. Although the monsoons affect most part of India, the amount of rainfall varies from very heavy to scanty on different parts. There is a great regional and temporal variation in the distribution of rainfall. Over 80% of the annual rainfall is received in the four rainy months of June to September. The average annual rainfall is about 125 cm. but it has great spatial variations.

(*a*) **Areas of Heavy Rainfall (over 200 cm) :** The highest rainfall occurs in west coasts, on the Western Ghats as well as the Sub-Himalayan areas in N. East and Meghalaya Hills, Assam, West Bengal, West Coast and Southern slopes of eastern Himalayas.

(*b*) **Areas of Moderately Heavy Rainfall (100-200 cm) :** This rainfall occurs in Southern Parts of Gujarat, East Tamil Nadu, North-eastern Peninsular, Western Ghats, eastern Maharashtra, Madhya Pradesh, Odisha and the middle Ganga valley.

(*c*) **Areas of Less Rainfall (50-100 cm) :** Upper Ganga valley, eastern Rajasthan, Punjab, Southern Plateau of Karnataka, Andhra Pradesh and Tamil Nadu.

(*d*) **Areas of Scanty Rainfall (less than 50 cm):** Northern part of Kashmir, Western Rajasthan, Punjab and Deccan Plateau.

The two significant features of India's rainfall are, (*a*) in the north India, rainfall decreases westwards and (*b*) in Peninsular India, except Tamil Nadu, it decreases eastward.

Soil of India

Classification

Climate and nature of the parent rock are the two most important factors that determine the types of soils found in India.

Soils may also be categorized according to their formatting:

(*a*) **Residual Soil :** These are found where they are formed hence called "In Situ". The red, laterite, black, podzolic soils of forests, saline and alkaline and peaty and other organic soils are residual soils. Of these, the red and the laterite soils are zonal soils developed under hot and humid conditions through the laterisation process on a variety of rocks including the archaean granite. The black soil is an intrazonal soil developed on Deccan lavas.

(*b*) **Transported Soil :** These are the soils which are carried down by agents of gradations such as rivers and wind.

The Indian Council of Agricultural Research (ICAR) divides the soil found in the country into 8 major groups which are

(*i*) ***Alluvial soils*** including the coastal and deltaic alluvium,

(*ii*) ***Black soils***, of varying types

(*iii*) ***Red soils,*** including red loams, yellow earths, etc.

(*iv*) ***Laterite*** and ***lateritic soils***

(*v*) ***Forest soils***

(*vi*) ***Arid*** and ***Desert soil***

(*vii*) ***Saline*** and ***Alkali soils*** and

(*viii*) ***Peaty*** and ***Organic soils***.

(i) Alluvial Soils

It is by far the largest and the most important soil group of India contributing to the largest share of the country's agricultural production. Alluvial soils cover about 22.1 per cent of the country's total land surface. Composed of sediments deposited by rivers in the interior and sea waves along the coasts, these soils constitute the surface of the Great Plains from Punjab to Assam. They also occur in the valleys of the Narmada and Tapti in Madhya Pradesh and Gujarat, Mahanadi in Madhya Pradesh and Odisha, Godavari in Andhra Pradesh, and Cauvery in Tamil Nadu. Along the coast of Kerala, they are referred to as coastal alluvium and in the deltas of the Mahanadi, Godavari, Krishna and Cauvery as deltaic alluvium. Alluvial soils are generally deficient in Nitrogen and humus; this necessitates heavy fertilisation particularly with nitrogenous fertilisers. Phosphorus is also deficient in some areas. These soils are suitable for the cultivation of almost all kinds of cereals, pulses, oil seeds, cotton, sugarcane and vegetables. Jute can be grown in the eastern areas. In the upper and middle Ganga plain two different types of alluvial soils have developed, viz., ***Khadar*** and ***Bhangar***. ***Khadar*** is a newer alluvium developed behind the levees of the numerous streams flowing in this section of the Ganga plain. ***Bhangar*** represents a system of older alluvium developed on the upper reaches of the streams where floods generally do not reach.

(ii) Black Cotton Soils

These soils are black in colour and they are eminently suitable for the cultivation of cotton. In some areas they are also called ***regur***. These soils have developed over deccan lavas, gneisses and granites under semi-arid conditions and they occupy many areas of Maharashtra, Gujarat, Madhya Pradesh, Karnataka, Andhra Pradesh, Tamil Nadu, Uttar Pradesh, and Rajasthan. The black colour is variously attributed to the presence of titaniferous magnetite, compounds of iron and aluminium, accumulated humus and colloidal hydrated double iron and aluminium silicate. They are usually deficient in nitrogen, phosphoric acid and organic matter, but rich in potash, lime, aluminium, calcium and magnesium carbonates.

They are sticky when wet and develop deep wide cracks on drying which helps in the process of self-aeration and absorption of nitrogen from the atmosphere. An extreme degree of moisture retentiveness is another characteristic of these soils. Black soils are well-known for their fertility. Cotton, cereals and oilseeds, like linseed and safflower, many kinds of vegetables and citrus are some of the crops well suited to black soils. Very good results have also been obtained in crops like sugarcane and tobacco. On account of their moisture-retentive qualities, the black soils are ideally suited to dry farming.

(iii) Red Soils

These soils comprising red loams and yellow earths and derived from crystalline and metamorphic rocks rich in ferromagnesium minerals occupy much of the Peninsula reaching up to Rajmahal Hills in the East, Jhansi in the North and Kachchh in the west. These soils are generally characterised by light texture with porous and friable structure, absence of lime and free carbonates and presence of soluble salts in a small quantity. They are neutral to acid reaction and deficient in nitrogen, humus, phosphoric acid and lime. These soils occupy over two-thirds of the total area of Tamil Nadu. Almost all kinds of crops are grown on red soils, though they seem to be more suitable for the cultivation of rice, ragi, tobacco and vegetables. Groundnut and potato can be grown on coarse soils at higher level and sugarcane on heavy clays at lower level. Red soils are airy and need irrigation support for cultivation.

(iv) Laterite and Lateritic Soils

Lateritic soils are formed under conditions of high rainfall and temperature with alternate wet and dry periods. The soil consists of a honeycombed mass of iron oxides which turn black after exposure to rain. Usually laterite soils are poor in nitrogen, phosphoric acid, potash, lime and Magnesia. When they are of low fertility generally, they readily respond to manuring and valley soils are found to be suitable for a variety of crops particularly rice, ragi and sugarcane. Lateritic soils occur especially on the summits of the Sahyadric, Eastern Ghats, Rajmahal Hills and many other hills in the eastern parts of the peninsula, East Godavari districts in Andhra Pradesh, some districts in Odisha and West Bengal also have laterite soils.

(v) Forest Soils

The forest soils are characterized by the deposition of organic matter derived from forest growth. Humus predominates in all forest soils and it is more raw at higher levels leading to acidic conditions. The Himalayas and the other ranges in the north and the high hill summits in the Sahyadris, Eastern Ghats and the Peninsula have forest soils. Forest soils are deficient in potash, phosphorus and lime and need fertilisation for good yields. Plantations of tea, coffee, spices and tropical fruits are laid out on these soils in Karnataka, Tamil Nadu, Kerala and Manipur. Temperate fruits, maize, wheat and barley are raised on them in Jammu and Kashmir and Himachal Pradesh.

(vi) Arid and Desert Soils

These soils are formed under arid and semi-arid conditions in the north-western parts of the country. The entire area west of the Aravalli range in Rajasthan has desert soils. The soils extend to the southern districts of Haryana and Punjab in the north and the Rann of Kachchh in the south. These soils often have a high soluble salt content and a low to very low humus content. They are quite rich in phosphate but poor in nitrogen. Generally, desert soils improve in fertility towards east.

(vii) Saline and Alkali Soils

Soils of many parts of the arid and semi-arid areas of Rajasthan, Punjab, Haryana, Uttar Pradesh and Bihar have saline and alkaline effervescences mainly of sodium, calcium and magnesium. These soils called ***reh, kallar*** and ***usar*** variously, are infertile. Saline soils contain free sodium and other salts whereas alkali soils contain large quantities of sodium chloride. These salt-impregnated soils can be reclaimed by providing good drainage.

(viii) Peaty and other Organic Soils

Peaty soils have developed under humid conditions as a result of an accumulation of large amounts of organic matter. In addition, they contain considerable amount of soluble salts. These soils are highly saline, rich in organic matter but deficient in phosphate and potash. Marshy soils with a high quantity of vegetable matter frequently occur in the coastal areas of Odisha, West Bengal and Tamil Nadu, in central and northern Bihar and Almora district of Uttarakhand.

Pattern of Soil erosion

In India, soil erosion is the wearing away of the topsoil cover by natural agencies such as water and wind and also as a result of human and animal interference. ***Sheet erosion*** is common on relatively steep slopes of the heavy rainfall areas in the Himalayan Foothills, over the north-eastern parts of the Peninsula, in Assam and in the Sahyadris and the Eastern Ghats. ***Rill erosion*** is active over a wide area in Bihar, Uttar Pradesh, Madhya Pradesh, and in the semi-arid parts of the Peninsula in Maharashtra, Karnataka, Telangana, Andhra Pradesh and Tamil Nadu. The ***chhos*** of northern Haryana and Punjab and the badlands of Madhya Pradesh, Rajasthan and Uttar Pradesh, have resulted due to gully erosion on an extensive scale. ***Gully erosion*** is the most spectacular type of erosion. It has already degraded about 40 lakh hectares of land in the country. This problem affects mainly the states of

Uttar Pradesh, Madhya Pradesh, Bihar, Rajasthan and Gujarat. ***Wind erosion*** is active in dry areas devoid of vegetation cover. This type of soil erosion is common all over Rajasthan and Gujarat.

Human and animal interference in a variety of ways leads to soil erosion. Deforestation, overgrazing and shifting cultivation are responsible for soil erosion in large areas. ***The chhos*** of Punjab and Haryana and the ***ravines*** of Madhya Pradesh, Rajasthan and Uttar Pradesh have resulted, to a certain extent, due to reckless cutting of forests in these areas. Erosion due to overgrazing by sheep and goats is very common over the hilly areas of Madhya Pradesh, Rajasthan and the low rainfall areas of Maharashtra, Karnataka, Telangana and Andhra Pradesh. It is also common in Jammu and Himachal Pradesh. ***Shifting cultivation*** is responsible for soil erosion in many tropical forest areas in the country. This mode of cultivation is a serious menace in Assam, Meghalaya, Tripura, Nagaland, Mizoram, Kerala, Andhra Pradesh, Odisha and parts of Madhya Pradesh. It is estimated that over 80,000 hectares of cultivated land of India have already been lost.

Soil Conservation

Soil conservation includes all such measures which help in protecting the soil from erosion. Contour terracing and bunding, construction of bunds across gullies, levelling of uneven land and raising grass and other vegetation on land are the small measures which are usually taken by farmers to protect soil from erosion. Such methods are quite effective in areas where the degree of erosion is not serious as in the semi-arid tracts of the peninsula and part of Gujarat, Madhya Pradesh, Uttar Pradesh, Haryana and Punjab. Extensive reclamation schemes are under implementation in these states. Construction of bunds across gullies and levelling of surface, control of overgrazing by animals, and afforestation are some of the steps taken under these schemes. In the tropical forest areas, shifting cultivation known as ***jhoom*** in Assam, ***ponam*** in Kerala, ***podu*** in Andhra Pradesh and Odisha, and ***bewar, masham, penda*** and ***beera*** in different parts of Madhya Pradesh is a serious problem. It is necessary to educate the *adivasis,* who practise it, in better farming techniques. The Central Government created the Central Conservation Board in 1953 to co-ordinate the soil conservation schemes on an all India basis.

Soil conservation is a method, especially used by man to prevent the soil erosion which can be done by the following methods :

Contour Ploughing

If ploughing is done at right angles to the hill slope, following the natural contour of the hill, the ridges and furrows break the flow of the water down the hill. This prevents excessive soil loss, as gullies are less likely to develop and also reduce run-off so that plants receive more water. Row crops and small grains are often planted in contour pattern so that the plants can absorb much of the rain, and erosion is minimized.

Terracing

Slopes may be cut into a series of terraces with sufficient level ground on each terrace for cultivation, and an outer wall at the edge to retain the soil and to slow down the flow of rain-water down the slope. Terracing is widely used in Monsoon Asia for wet paddy cultivation, as the excess water and silt can be retained at each terrace to form flooded paddy-fields. Many tree crops such as rubber are also planted on terraces to combat soil erosion. Terraces are also used in temperate and semi-arid regions where slopes are steep. Terracing enables farmers in mountainous regions to utilize the steep ground on the favoured 'sunny slopes' of valleys for vines or other crops.

Strip Cropping

Crops may be cultivated in alternate strips, parallel to one another. Some strips may be allowed to lie fallow while others are sown to different kinds of crops, *e.g.,* grains, legumes, small tree crops. The various crops ripen at different times of the year and are harvested at intervals. This ensures that at no time will the entire area be left bare or exposed. The tall-growing crops act as wind-breaks and the strips, which are often parallel to the contours, help to increase water absorption by the soil by slowing down run-off.

Fallowing

Sometimes it is important to allow much used land to rest or lie fallow, so that the natural forces can act on the soil. The decayed natural vegetative matter helps to increase the plant nutrients in the soil. Fallowing also increases the sub-soil moisture and improves the general structure of the soil. Winter fallow is commonly practised in temperate regions after the harvest, but cultivation is resumed in the spring after the snow and frost have weathered the top soil. Long periods of fallow cannot be allowed, however, in intensively run farms as farmers cannot afford it. In semi-arid areas fields may be allowed to lie fallow for several years, though they are often ploughed or mulched, *i.e.,* spread with straw or the stubble of the previous year's harvests. This enables them to build up a sufficient supply of moisture by reducing evaporation, and a crop can be grown every few years. This system of dry farming is practised in the western U.S.A. and in parts of Mediterranean Europe.

Cover Cropping

In some cases, as in plantations, where the gestation period of tree crops is long, cover crops may be interplanted between the young trees. Creepers are preferred because they spread around and form a useful cover that protects the top soil from the full force of the tropical downpours. Care must be taken that the cover crop does not compete with the young trees for the essential plant nutrients, and leguminous crops are often used because they add nitrogen to the soil. Cover crops may be grown simply to protect the soil or may consist of other valuable plants such as vegetables which provide an income while the plantation crop matures. Some such catch crops, *e.g.,* cotton, maize or tobacco, should be avoided because they exhaust the soil or promote soil erosion instead of preventing it.

Crop Rotation

It is not advisable to grow the same crop in the same field for more than two years in succession as the crop will tend to exhaust one particular kind of mineral nutrient. For example potatoes require much potash, but wheat requires nitrates. Thus it is best to alternate crops in the fields. Legumes such as peas, beans, clover, vetch and many other plants, add nitrates to the soil by converting free nitrogen in the air into nitrogenous nodules on their roots. Thus if they are included in the crop rotation nitrogenous fertilizers can be dispensed with. By rotating different types of crops in successive years, soil fertility can be naturally maintained. The best known crop rotation is the Norfolk Rotation which involves the growing of four crops in a given field over a period of four years. These crops are wheat (cereal); clover or beans (legume); barley (another cereal); and turnips or sugar-beet (root crops).

Crop Diversification

This practice is often like crop rotation in the sense that it helps to maintain soil fertility. Where annually-harvested crops are grown they can be alternated in the field. Where perennial crops like tree crops are grown, however, the chief importance of crop diversification to the farmer is economic. In particular it reduces the danger of depending on a single crop (monoculture) when world commodity prices are falling. All the primary commodities, *e.g.,* rubber, oil palm, cocoa, cotton, are subject to great fluctuation in prices, much depending on the demand of the western world. Overdependence on one crop can be disastrous to the national economy as well as to the individual farmer, as in the case of Brazil's coffee, Ghana's cocoa, or Malaysia's rubber, when prevailing prices for the major money-earning crop are low. Crop diversification overcomes this difficulty as when one crop is only fetching low prices another may be in good demand. Another great advantage of crop diversification is that all types of land can be used, *e.g.,* rubber can be grown on hill slopes, oil palm on flat plains, coconuts on sandy soils. Thorough crop diversification on a national and local level can lead to the most economic use of land.

Use Of Fertilizers

Farmers all over the world have found that soils vary in their fertility and crop-bearing capability, because of the different proportions of mineral nutrients they contain. Continuous cultivation will exhaust some or most of the nutrients and soil fertility has to be maintained by the application of manures or fertilizers. Organic manures such as animal dung, compost or decomposed vegetation usually provide a balanced supply of the major soil minerals. Nowadays, however, manufactured chemicals are more commonly used partly because they are easier to apply and partly because of the enormous world demand for fertilizers.

Water Management

One of the major ways in which land can be improved for farming is by water management. By regulating the amount of water in the soil aeration can be improved, activity by useful bacteria can be stimulated and crop yields can be improved.

The Drainage Systems of India

Of the total land surface of India, 90 per cent drains into the Bay of Bengal and the remaining drains into the Arabian Sea. Only a very small percentage of the area has an inland drainage system.

The Bay of Bengal and the Arabian Sea drainage systems are separated along a distinct divide which lies approximately along the Sahyadris, Amarkantak, Aravallis and the Satluj-Yamuna divide.

The drainage of the Indian subcontinent has adjusted itself with the evolution of three main geomorphological entities, viz., the Northern Mountains, the Northern Plains and the Peninsular Plateau. On the basis of their origin, the river systems of the subcontinent can be divided into two classes-the Himalayan rivers and the Peninsular rivers. The Indus, Ganga and Brahmaputra river systems comprise the Himalayan group while the major rivers in the peninsular systems are the Narmada, Tapti, Mahanadi, Godavari, Krishna and Cauveri.

Evolution of River System

Himalayan Rivers

These rivers originate on the southern slopes of the Tibetan highlands and after following the main Himalayan axis for some length (the Indus, Satluj towards the west and the Brahmaputra towards the east), they bend southwards along the syntaxian bend cutting through Himalayan ridges, forming deep gorges and descend on to the Northern Plains.

Deep gorges formed by the Indus, Satluj, Alaknanda, Gandak, Brahmaputra and Kosi indicate that these rivers are older than the mountains themselves and have continued to flow all through the building phase of the Himalayas, their banks rising steeply while the beds went lower and lower, thus defining the profile of a deep gorge. This type of drainage, which is not consequent to a topography but exists prior to its origin, is called antecedent drainage.

Indo-Brahm Theory

One school of geologists attributes the evolution of the present-day north Indian drainage to changes produced in the drainage pattern of an original mighty stream called the Indo-Brahm.

According to some geologists, initially, the region of the Ganga plains was drained by a mighty stream flowing from Assam towards Punjab and incorporating the present courses of the Brahmaputra, Ganga, Indus and finally emptying itself into a gulf situated at the present location of Sind.

The dismemberment gave birth to the rivers of the present with a reversed flow pattern and the Ganga annexing the Yamuna as its tributary (the Yamuna must have been a south-west flowing tributary of the Indus). This exchange of tributaries between the Ganga and the Indus has continued till recent times. Thus, according to this theory, the Indo-Brahm was the parent stream from which the present river systems of northern India have evolved.

Peninsular Rivers

These rivers have acquired maturity as suggested by broad, largely graded and shallow valleys and the fact that they have existed for a longer period than the Himalayan rivers, with the exception of limited reaches of some of the rivers where recent faulting has occurred. The beds generally have a subdued gradient, as the erosional forces do not act laterally.

Most of the peninsular rivers flow eastwards, as the main watershed runs through the Western Ghats close to the west coast. The notable exceptions are the Narmada and the Tapti which flow westwards in troughs, which are not of their own making. These facts are explained by assuming that the Western Ghats were the original watershed and their subsidence below sea has disturbed the generally symmetrical plan of the rivers on either side of the original watershed.

A second major distortion was introduced during the Himalayan upheaval when the northern flank of the peninsular block was subjected to subsidence and consequent trough-faulting. The Narmada and the Tapti rivers flow in such trough-faults and have courses consequent to their general trend. During the course of their alluvial activity, they seem to have filled the original cracks with their detritus. This largely explains the lack of alluvial and deltaic deposits in their valleys.

The Indian river system can be studied under the Himalayan and the peninsular categories.

Himalayan Rivers

The Himalayan mountain complex is the source of the following three drainage systems:

1. The Indus system
2. The Ganga system
3. The Brahmaputra system

The Indus System

The Indus rises in Tibet at an altitude of 5,180 metres near the Mansarovar Lake. With a total length of 2,880 km, the Indus is one of the world's largest rivers. It has a catchment area of 1,165,000 square kilometres, of which 3,21,290 square kilometres lie within India. It flows through a spectacular gorge cutting through the Kailash ranges and enters Jammu and Kashmir.

The Jhelum rises in Verinag at the foothills of Pir Panjal and its drainage area in India is 28,490 square kilometres. It flows through the Kashmir valley and Lake Wular before entering Pakistan through a narrow gorge. The Chenab is the largest of all the Indus tributaries and is formed by two streams Chandra and Bhaga which rise in the snow-covered Himachal Mountains near Kulu. Its drainage area in India is 26,755 square kilometres.

The Ravi also rises in Kulu hills, near Rohtang Pass, of Himachal Pradesh and drains 5,957 square kilometres in India. The Beas originates at a place called Beas Kund near Rohtang Pass in the Himachal hills. In its early stages, its valley is called the Kulu valley. Since some of its tributaries originating from the southern side of the Great Himạlayas are snowfed, it has a relatively large volume of water even during the long dry season. It joins the Satluj near Harike after flowing for a distance of 615 km. It drains an area of 25,900 square kilometres in India.

The Satluj originates from the Rakas Lake situated at an altitude of 4,555 metres in Tibet. The Rakas Lake is connected with the Mansarovar Lake by a stream. The Satluj enters India through Shipki La. Before entering the Punjab plains, it cuts a deep gorge through Nainadevi Dhar ranges. A dam has been constructed across this gorge near village Bhakra.

This dam is called the Bhakra Dam and the reservoir which it forms is called the Gobind Sagar Lake. The Satluj drains 24,087 square kilometres in India and is of immense economic value for the Punjab plains.

The Ganga System

The Ganga river basin, with an area within India of 8,61,404 square kilometres, is the largest in the country. This river basin drains the middle part of the Himalayas in the north, the northern part of the Indian plateau (roughly, north of the line running along the Vindhya Range, the Amarkantak Plateau and the watershed lying to the east of Subarnarekha) in the south and the Ganga plain in between. The Ram Ganga, Gomati, Ghaghra, Gandak and the Kosi are the Ganga's major left-bank, tributaries and the Yamuna and the Son, its major right-bank tributaries.

The Ganga rises in the Gangotri glacier in Uttarakhand. Its two main headstreams—Bhagirathi and Alaknanda—meet at Devaprayag, from where onwards it is called the Ganga. Its total length is

2,525 km, and it drains 9,51,600 sq. km. Of its length in the plains, the longest stretch lies in Uttar Pradesh, and the rest of it lies mostly in Bihar and West Bengal. Beyond Farakka, the mainstream of the Ganga flows southeast into Bangladesh and is known as the Padma.

The Yamuna is the most important tributary of the Ganga. It rises at the Yamnotri glacier in Uttarakhand. From its source upto Allahabad, where it meets the Ganga, the Yamuna's length is 1,376 km and it drains an area of 3,59,000 square kilometres. Important towns such as Delhi, Mathura and Agra are situated on the Yamuna's banks. The Chambal, Betwa and Ken are the major tributaries of the Yamuna.

The headwater of the Ghaghra, the Karnali, is of trans-Himalayan origin and crosses the western part of the Nepal Himalayas through deep and narrow gorges. It joins the Ganga near Chapra. It is a large river choked with silt which keeps shifting its course.

The Ram Ganga rises in the Kumaon Himalayas and enters the Ganga Plains near Kalagarh. It joins the Ganga near Kannauj.

The Gandak rises near the Sino-Nepal border and joins the Ganga at Sonpur. It drains an area of 9,540 square kilometres. The Gandak also keeps shifting its course and is notorious for its floods.

The Kosi has its sources in the Himalayan heights of Sikkim, Nepal and Tibet. It drains 21,500 square kilometres in India and joins the Ganga below Bhagalpur. The river has shifted its course westwards by 112 km during the last 200 years converting 7,000-8,000 sq. km of cultivable land into wasteland.

The Son is a right-bank tributary of the Ganga which, after rising from the Amarkantak Plateau, joins the Ganga near Patna. It drains an area of 71,900 square kilometres.

The Damodar which actually meets the Bhagirathi-Hooghly in West Bengal, rises in the hills of Chhotanagpur Plateau. It drains an area of 22,000 square kilometres. Formerly referred to as the 'Sorrow of Bengal' on account of its floods, the Damodar has transformed itself into a boon to West Bengal after the completion of the Damodar valley multi-purpose project.

The Brahmaputra System

The Brahmaputra rises in a glacier, about 100 km south-east of the Mansarovar lake in Tibet. Before entering India, it is called the Tsang-Po in Tibet. Chinese maps show it as Yarlung Zangbo Jiang. It crosses the Assam Himalayas under the name of Dihang. The total length of the Brahmaputra in India is 2,900 km, and it drains an area of 2, 40,000 square kilometres in India. The Subarnasiri, Bhareli and Manas are its main right-bank tributaries and the Dibang, Luhit, Buri Dihang, Dhansiri and Kapili are its left-bank tributaries.

The catchment areas of these streams receive heavy rainfall during the monsoons, as a result of which the Brahmaputra becomes slow-moving and silt-laden. Its channel is braided and it is notorious for floods and erosion of its banks. Recurrent floods hamper not only navigation through the river but also the establishment of large towns on its bank. The Brahmaputra enters Bangladesh near Dhubri. The stretch from Sadiya to Dhubri has been declared as the National Inland Waterway No. 2.

Peninsular Rivers

The Western Ghats are the main watershed in the peninsula and the major rivers are the east-flowing ones. These rivers are characterised by huge deltas at their mouths, while the west-flowing ones are small with no deltas at their mouths. The Narmada and the Tapti are unusually large west-flowing rivers, flowing through troughs which have been formed due to faulting.

East-Flowing Peninsular Rivers

The Mahanadi rises in the Sihawa range in Chhattisgarh. It is 857 km long and drains an area of 1,41,600 square kilometres in Chhattisgarh, Odisha, Bihar and Maharashtra. The left-bank tributaries of the Mahanadi include the Seonath, Hasdo, Mand and lb, while the Jonk, Ung, Tel are among the right-bank tributaries.

After crossing the Eastern Ghats through a gorge, it divides itself into distributaries at Cuttack. The smaller basins of Subarnarekha, Brahmani and

Baitarni are interposed between the Ganga and the Mahanadi basins. The Brahmani is known as South Koel in its upper reaches in Jharkhand. These rivers draining the eastern parts of the peninsula have drainage and discharge patterns similar to the Mahanadi. The Brahmani is 800 km long with a drainage area of 39,000 square kilometres. The Subarnarekha is 395 km long with a catchment area of 19.500 square kilometres. The Baitarni has its source region in the Keonjhar Plateau in Odisha.

The Godavari basin is the largest river system in the peninsula and second only to the Ganga system in India. It rises in the Nasik district of Maharashtra, and drains an area of 3,12,812 square kilometres, half of which lies in Maharashtra. Besides Maharashtra, the basin is shared by Madhya Pradesh, Karnataka, Odisha, Telangana and Andhra Pradesh. The Godavari flows for a length of 1,465 km and is often referred to as Vridha Ganga or Dakshina Ganga because of its large size and extent. The major tributaries of the Godavari are the Pravara, Purna, Manjra, Penganga, Wainganga, Wardha, Pranhita, Indravati, Maner and Sabari.

The Krishna is the second largest east-flowing river. It rises from a spring near Mahabaleshwar in Maharashtra. Its total length of 1,400 km is shared by Maharashtra, Karnataka and Andhra Pradesh. The Krishna drains an area of 2, 58,948 square kilometres. The Bhima and the Tungabhadra are the two most important tributaries of the Krishna, besides the Koyna, Ghataprabha, Malaprabha, Musi (Hyderabad is situated on its bank), Muneru, Yerla, Panchganga and Dudhganga.

The Pennar basin lies between the Krishna basin and the Cauveri basin, and drains an area of 55,213 square kilometres, most of which lie in Karnataka. Its principal tributaries are the Jayamangali, Kunderu, Sagileru, Chitravati, Papagin, and Cheyyeru.

The Cauveri rises in the Brahmagir range of the Western Ghats. It flows for a length of 800 km before falling into the Bay of Bengal near Kaveripattinam. It drains an area of 87,900 square kilometres, which is shared by Kerala, Karnataka and Tamil Nadu. The Cauveri basin is one of the most developed regions of India from the point of view of power and irrigation. Ninety to ninety-five per cent of the total potential in these two spheres have already been exploited.

The left-bank tributaries of the Cauveri include the Herangi, Hemavati, Shimsha and Arkavati, and the right-bank tributaries include the Lakshamantirtha, Kabini, Suvarnavati, Bhawani and Amravati.

West-Flowing Rivers

The Narmada rises near Amarkantak in Madhya Pradesh and flows for 1,300 km, while draining an area of 98,796 square kilometres, most of it lying in Madhya Pradesh. The Narmada basin is characterised by the lack of development of the tributary streams. The Narmada valley is gorge-like and full of rapids and waterfalls between Handia and Mandhata.

The Kapildhara and the Dhvandhar are the most important waterfalls. The Orisan is the major tributary and others include the Burhner, Banjar, Shar, Shakkar, Dudhi and the Tawa on the south and the Hiran, Barna and the Kolar on the north.

The Tapti is the second largest west-flowing peninsular river. It rises in the Betul district of Madhya Pradesh and while flowing for a length of 724 kilometres, it drains an area of 65,145 square kilometres in Madhya Pradesh, Maharashtra and Gujarat. The left-bank tributaries of the Tapti are Purna, Veghar, Girna, Bori and the Panjhra and those joining it on the right bank are the Aner, Betul, Ganjal, Arunavati and Gomai.

The north-western flank of the plateau is drained by the Sabarmati and the Mahi. The Sabarmati rises in the Aravalli hills and flows for a length of 300 km. It drains an area of 21,674 square kilometres in Gujarat and Rajasthan. The Mahi rises in the east of Udaipur and drains an area of 34,842 square kilometres while flowing for a length of 533 km in Madhya Pradesh, Rajasthan and Gujarat.

There are also a large number of coastal streams draining the narrow coastal plains on the western edge of the peninsula. There are as many as 600 tiny streams which drain the western face of the Western Ghats alone. The most important among these are the Mandovi, Zuari and Rachol in Goa; Kalinadi, Gangavalli-Bedti, Sharavati, Tadri and

Netravati in Karnataka; Beypore, Ponnam, Bharatapuzha, Periyar and Pamba in Kerala.

All these streams have carved out narrow valleys with steep gradients and often descend to the plains in the form of cascades and waterfalls. The famous Jog Falls (271 metres) is on the Sharavati river.

Ethnic Diversities

The species known as *Ramapithecus* was found in the Siwalik foothills of the northwestern Himalayas. This species believed to be the first in the line of hominids lived some 14 million years ago. Researches have found that a species resembling the Australopithecus lived in India some 2 million years ago. Scientists have so far not been able to account for an evolutionary gap of as much as 12 million years since the appearance of Ramapithecus.

The people of India belong to different anthropological stocks. According to Dr. B. S. Guha, the population of India is derived from six main ethnic groups:

1. Negritos

The Negritos or the brachycephalic (broad headed) from Africa were the earliest people to inhabit India. They are survived in their original habitat in the Andaman and Nicobar Islands. The Jarewas, Onges, Sentelenese and Great Andamanis tribes are the examples. Studies have indicated that the Onges tribes have been living in the Andamans for the last 60,000 years. Some hill tribes like Irulas, Kodars, Paniyans and Kurumbas are found only in patches among the hills of south India on the mainland.

2. Pro-Australoids or Austrics

This group was the next to come to India after the Negritos. They represent a race of people, with wavy hair plentifully distributed over their brown bodies, long heads with low foreheads and prominent eye ridges, noses with low and broad roots, thick jaws, large palates and teeth and small chins. Austrics tribes, which are spread over the whole of India, Myanmar and the islands of South East Asia, are said to "form the bedrock of the people". The Austrics were the main builders of the Indus Valley Civilisation. They cultivated rice and vegetables and made sugar from sugarcane. Their language has survived in the Kol or Munda (Mundari) in Eastern and Central India.

3. Mongoloids

These people have features that are common to those of the people of Mongolia, China and Tibet. These tribal groups are located in the Northeastern part of India in states like Assam, Nagaland and Meghalaya and also in Ladakh and Sikkim. Generally, they are people of yellow complexion, oblique eyes, high cheekbones, sparse hair and medium height.

4. Mediterranean or Dravidian

This group came to India from the Southwest Asia and appear to be people of the same stock as the people of Asia Minor and Crete and the pre-Hellenic Aegeans of Greece. They are reputed to have built up the city civilization of the Indus Valley, whose remains have been found at Mohenjodaro and Harappa and other Indus cities. The Dravidians must have spread to the whole of India, supplanting Austrics and Negritos alike. Dravidians comprise all the three sub-types, Paleo-Mediterranean, the true Mediterranean and Oriental Mediterranean. This group constitutes the bulk of the scheduled castes in the North India. This group has a sub-type called Oriental group.

5. Western Brachycephals

These include the Alpinoids, Dinaries and Armenois. The Coorgis and Parsis fall into this category.

6. Nordics

Nordics or Indo-Aryans are the last immigrants into India. Nordic Aryans were a branch of Indo-Iranians, who had originally left their homes in Central Asia, some 5000 years ago, and had settled in Mesopotamia for some centuries. The Aryans must have come in India between 2000 and 1500 B.C. Their first home in India was western and northern Punjab, from where they spread to the Valley of the Ganga and beyond. These tribes are now mainly found in the Northwest and the Northwest Frontier Province (NWFP). Many of these tribes belong to the "upper castes".

Indian Tribal People

Indian tribal people play a key part in constructing the cultural heritage of India. They occupy a major part in the history of India as they are considered as the true habitants of India. The tribal people are scattered in different parts of India and they form a considerable number of the population of India. The traditional and cultural distinction of each tribal community has made them distinguishable from each other and their cultural and traditional heritage add colour and variation to the Indian culture as a whole and form a compact culture. Indian tribal people reside in approximately fifteen per cent of the country's area. They primarily live in various ecological and geo-climatic conditions ranging from plains, forests, hills and inaccessible areas that perhaps lie dotted in the panoramic Indian terrain.

According to Article 342 of the Indian Constitution, at present, there exist six hundred and ninety seven tribes as notified by the Central Government. These Indian tribal groups of people have been notified to reside in more than one State. More than half of the Indian tribal population is concentrated in the States of Madhya Pradesh, Chhattisgarh, Maharashtra, Odisha, Jharkhand and Gujarat, whereas in Haryana, Punjab, Delhi, Puducherry and Chandigarh no community has been notified as a specific tribal group. Though the tribal people in the earlier eras were not much forward but in recent times they are seen in some sectors of economical, educational and social development. The history says that India was the abode of various tribal groups since the commencement period of Indian history.

Tribes of North East India

In the north eastern part of India, there is a concentration of a number of tribes. Meghalaya is the abode of a number of tribal communities who have settled down in large numbers. The tribal people of Meghalaya are categorised into two major groups, viz., Garos and Hynniewtreps. The Garo tribal community occupies a major part of tribal communities of Meghalaya. Some of the Mizoram tribes are Chakma tribes which is one of the important tribes of Mizoram. The Pawi Tribes of Mizoram are named not after the name of the clan but after the name of the place where they are residing. Another important tribe of Mizoram is Ralte tribe. Manipur houses quite a number of tribes. The tribes of Manipur are as follows: Aimol, Anal, Angami, Chiru, Chothe, Gangte, Hmar, Kabui, Kacha Naga, Koirao, Koireng, Kom, Lamgang, Mao, Maram, Maring, Lushai tribes, Monsang, Moyon, Paite, Purum, Ralte, Sema, Simte, Sukte, Tangkhul, Thadou, Vaiphei and Zou. The largest population in Assam is that of the Tibeto Burmese descent known as the Bodo tribe and Mishing tribe. Major tribes of Assam make out their livelihood through agriculture and by selling their handicrafts.

Tribes of North India

North India also encompasses many tribes. Tribes of Jammu and Kashmir have strictly descended from the Indo-Aryan group of people, which can be credited for the sublime beauty of this exceptional north Indian tribe. With normal Indian food being their staple diet, these north Indian tribes believe in both Hinduism and Islam. Tribes of Uttar Pradesh and Uttarakhand comprise a colossal portion under the north Indian tribal section, with a variety speaking out from every section and every sphere of daily life.

Tribes in Haryana basically are consisted of nomadic and semi-nomadic individuals, with a somewhat decaying condition of their social and economic condition. There are approximately twenty-five nomadic tribes, with their total count exceeding fifteen lakh. Tribes of Himachal Pradesh can be singled out for their looks, good conduct and religious behaviour towards all kinds of situations and places.

Tribes of East India

East Indian tribes come to a significant numbering count under the vast section of Indian tribes. Tribes of West Bengal with their incredible talents and improvisations have elevated Bengali tribes into a prestigious hold. Just like customary Bengal tradition, festivals and ceremonies are an integral part of this East Indian tribe. Tribes of Odisha reflect an unusualness right from the infantry stage. Known to have deep-rooted faith in their aboriginal God and animism, tribal people of Odisha have their own set of faiths when it comes to marriage and holy union. Classified into four primary groups of hunter gatherers, shifting agriculture, basic artisans and settled agriculturists, tribes of Jharkhand are diversified through their handiwork and religious customs. East Indian tribes mostly make themselves noticeable in every sphere of day-to-day life, commencing from level-headed past times in culture and entertainment, coupled with rugged outlook in cultivation.

Tribes of West India

West India, comprising the states of Rajasthan, Gujarat, Maharashtra and Goa house sufficient section of Indian tribes. West Indian tribes have been pocketed in several far-away areas, living a life of their own. Tribals of Gujarat today have divided themselves into several places of dwelling by the sea, amidst the Western Ghats and the plains. Agriculture and harvesting seem to be Gujarat tribals' basic occupations since olden times. Tribes of Rajasthan have been involved with rest of the Rajasthani population since ancient times, with their unique customs and culture spreading each other day. The touch of modernisation has wholly caught up with the tribes of this West Indian bunch, paving way for novel ways of occupation and popularity. Tribes of Maharashtra are primarily classified in the groups of nomadic tribes and scheduled tribes. West Indian tribes are truly elevated to escalading heights when Maharashtrian aboriginal men and women are concerned.

Tribes of Central India

Tribal life in Central India is an excellent instance of the blending of rural and urbanity. Central Indian tribes can bravely be designated with their exquisite stretch of flora and fauna, which is always coupled with ancient richness in cultural heritage. Tribes of Madhya Pradesh is basically classified under the group of scheduled tribes, with other sub-groups of tribes also making their presence felt. Cultivating and farming being a basic tribal occupation the men and women from Madhya Pradesh like to concentrate wholly upon their festivities and celebrations. Tribes of Chhattisgarh primarily consist of a significant number that even surpasses the urban population. Central Indian tribes amount to an overwhelming number, with prestigious lineage and are trying to govern themselves in a strict aboriginal manner.

Tribes of South India

The numbers of South Indian tribes are perhaps unlimited with their miscellaneous existence, which has now gained popularity throughout the country. The tribes of Tamil Nadu comprise significant number of population ranging from dwindling to massive. These Tribes are engaged in intellectual activity like tea or coffee cultivation, or mass milk producing. Tribes in Karnataka are astoundingly enormous in number, with the count exceeding a bare minimum. With Hinduism being the most prevalent religion, other religions are also seen to have their existence. Kannada being the most spoken language, Malayalam and Hindi also find place in this south-Indian tribe. Tribes of Kerala are perhaps the most unique among all the south Indian tribes discussed. Residing basically in the mountainous terrains of the state, they have been striving to uphold their indigenous traditions and customs from any foreign influence.

The interesting and novel mode of lifestyle that such Indian tribal people lead, accounts for a vast section of Indian travelogue. Be it in the sphere of much-retold Indian tribes or yet-to-be-known tribes, various styles of eating, drinking, working, singing, dancing, clothing, accessorising, or religious customs, Indian tribal people lead a life of their own. This distinctness is as if encased and enveloped within a protective covering, that at times receives massive public coverage.

Mineral and Power Resources in India

The social and economic development of a nation depends on its capacity to utilise its natural resources, avoiding its wasteful use to the extent possible. Mineral and power resources are important natural resources which help in the industrial development of a nation and ultimately in improving the standard of living of the people.

Minerals in India

India's mineral resources are sufficiently rich and varied to provide the country with a strong industrial base. The country is particularly rich in the metallic minerals of the ferrous group such as iron ores, manganese, chromite and titanium. It has the world's largest reserves in mica and bauxite. The situation is also satisfactory in coal, felspar, fluorides, limestone, dolomite and gypsum. But the reserves of petroleum and some non-ferrous metallic minerals especially copper, lead, zinc, tin and graphite are inadequate. Country fulfils internal demands for these metallic minerals by importing them from other countries. India is rich in the metalic minerals of the ferrous groups such as iron ores, manganese, chromite and titanium. But the reserves of petroleum and some non-ferrous metalic minerals especially copper, lead, zinc, tin, graphite are inadequate.

Coal

Coal has been used as a source of energy since very long time. If formed the foundation of the industrial revolution. In India, coal is the primary source of commercial energy. It is used as fuel in industries, thermal power stations and also for domestic purposes in some parts of the country. It is also used as a raw material in chemical and fertiliser industries and in the production of thousands of items of daily use.

The total known geological reserves of all types of coal in Gondwana and tertiary coal-fields stands estimated at 378.21 billion tonnes as on April 1, 2023. The reserves of lignite has been estimated at around 47.37 billion tonnes as on March 31, 2023 out of which the major contributor is the lignite basins of Tamil Nadu. Total production of coal during 2023-24 have been estimated at 997.828 million tonnes.

Distribution : Coal in India occurs in two important types of coal fields. They are Gondwana coal fields and Tertiary coal fields. Out of the total coal reserves and production in India, Gondwana coal fields contribute 98% and the rest 2% is production by tertiary coal fields. Jharkhand ranks highest in production as well as reserves of coal in India.

In comparison to India's coal reserves, lignite reserves are relatively modest. The bulk of lignite reserves are located in and around Neyveli in Tamil Nadu. Significant lignite reserves are found in Rajasthan, Gujarat, Pondicherry and Jammu & Kashmir.

- Coal is used as raw material in chemical and fertiliser industries and in the production of thousands of items of daily use.
- Coal is mainly found in Gondwana and Tertiary coal fields.
- The states of Jharkhand, West Bengal, Chhattisgarh, Andhra Pradesh and Odisha are the leading producers of coal.
- The bulk of lignite reserves are found in and around Neyveli in Tamil Nadu.

Petroleum

Petroleum has often been called liquid gold because of its value in our modern civilization. Our agriculture, industry and transport system depend on petroleum in several ways.

The crude petroleum is a mixture of combustible hydrocarbons in solid, liquid and gaseous forms. Petroleum-products used as fuel, lubricants, material for manufacturing synthetic derivatives and chemicals required in industries. Petrol, kerosene, diesel, detergents, synthetic fibres, plastics, cosmetics, etc., are important products derived from petroleum.

Distribution : Petroleum occurs in anticlines and fault traps. In India, it is found in the sedimentary rock formation. Most of such areas lie in Assam, Gujarat and the offshore areas along the western coast.

The entire production of India till today comes from the Assam belt, Gujarat-Cambay belt and Bombay High. The Assam belt extends from Dehang basin in the extreme north-east of Assam along the outer flanks of hill ranges forming the eastern border of Bhitra and Surma Valley.

The Gujarat-Cambay belt extends from Mehsana (Gujarat) in the north to the continental shelf off the coast right up to Ratnagiri (Maharashtra) in the south. It covers Bombay High which is the largest producer of petroleum in the country.

- Petroleum occurs in anticlines and fault traps. In India it is found in sedimentary rocks. Most of such areas lie in Assam, Gujarat and the offshore areas along the western coast.
- Petrol, kerosene, diesel, detergents, synthetic fibres plastics, cosmetics, etc., are important products derived from petroleum.
- Petroleum products are used as fuel, lubricant material for manufacturing synthetic derivatives and chemicals required in industries.

Important Minerals

Iron Ore

China is the largest producer in the world, India ranks fourth in production. India produces four types of iron ores—Haematite, Magnetite, Limonite and Siderite. Karnataka has the largest reserve of Magnetite ore followed by Odisha, Jharkhand, Chhattisgarh and Andhra Pradesh. Odisha has the largest reserve (33%) of haematite followed by Jharkhand, Chhattisgarh and Karnataka.

Odisha : In Odisha main producing areas are Mayurbhanj, Keonjhar and Sundargarh.

Karnataka : Important areas are—Bellary, Chitradurga (Bababudan Hills) Chikmaglur, Bijapur, Dharwad, Tumkur and Shimoga districts.

Chhattisgarh: Dantewada, Bastar, Durg, Rajnadgaon, Raigarh, and Bilaspur districts are main producers.

Jharkhand : Major producers are Noamundi and Gua in Singhbhum, Daltonganj in Palamau.

Andhra Pradesh and Telangana : Anantpur, Khammam, Krishna, Kurnool, Cuddapha and Nellore.

Goa: Pirna adol, Tolsia, Borgadogar, and Rivora are important regions, minings are open and mechanised, mainly exported to Japan.

Manganese

Occurs mainly in the Dharwar system of rocks. Odisha has the highest reserve (34%) followed by Karnataka, Madhya Pradesh, Maharashtra, and Goa. Odisha is the leading producer followed by Maharashtra, Madhya Pradesh and Karnataka.

Odisha : Keonjhar, Sundargarh, Koraput, Kalahandi and Bolangir.

Maharashtra : Main regions are—Nagpur-Bhandara Belt, and Ratnagiri.

Madhya Pradesh : Balaghat, Chhindwara, Jabalpur and Jhabua.

Karnataka : Bellary, Uttar Kannad, Shimoga, Tumkur and Belgaum.

Jharkhand : Birmitrapur in Chaibasa, Singhbhum, Hazaribagh and Dhanbad districts.

Copper

Important non-ferrous metal, earliest metal used by man. Highest reserve in Rajasthan (52%) followed by Madhya Pradesh, Jharkhand, Andhra Pradesh and Gujarat. Madhya Pradesh is the largest producer followed by Rajasthan.

Madhya Pradesh : Malajkhand in Balaghat district, Sidhi and Jabalpur.

Rajasthan: Khetri Belt in Aravalli range, Kho Dariba near Alwar, Delwara and Debari in Udaipur districts are important mining centres.

Jharkhand : Mosabani, Rakha and Ghatshila

Andhra Pradesh & Telangana : Agnigumdala belt near Guntur.

Bauxite

Mainly spread over the Eastern Ghats. Scattered in Laterite rocks. Odisha ranks first in reserve (52%) followed by Chhattisgarh, Andhra Pradesh, Gujarat, Jharkhand and Maharashtra. Odisha is the largest producer followed by Gujarat, Jharkhand and Maharashtra.

Odisha : 41% of country's production comes from this state alone. Kalahandi-Koraput belt is famous for its production.

Gujarat : Another important producer in the country. Bhavnagar-Junagarh–Amreli Belt is the main region.

Jharkhand : Ranchi, Palamau, Lohardaga and Muri.

Maharashtra : Production comes mainly from Kolhapur, Ratnagiri, Thane, Satara and Kolaba.

Zinc

Sphalerite is the chief ore. Largely used for galvanising or coating iron and steel. **Rajasthan** has a monopoly in zinc production. Main areas are– Zawar in Udaipur district. This area has two main zones of mineralisation.

(*i*) Pipli mine to Barla mine

(*ii*) Mochia Magra, Balaria.

Other producing areas are Bhilwara, Ajmer, Alwar and Sawai Madhopur. Bhotang of Sikkim, Riasi of Jammu and Kashmir, Almora and Tehri Garhwal of Uttarakhand are other producing areas of the country.

Gold

Karnataka is the largest producer of gold in the country. It has a monopoly in production of gold. Kolar, Hutti in Rachur and Gulbarga are main gold fields. Ramagiri in Andhra Pradesh. Nilgiri and Coimbatore in Tamil Nadu. Singhbhom in Jharkhand. Kojhikod in Kerala.

Largest resources of gold ore (primamy) are located in Bihar, followed by Karnataka, Rajasthan, West Bengal, Andhra Pradesh and Madhya Pradesh. In terms of metal content Karnataka remained on the top followed by Rajasthan, West Bengal, Bihar and Andhra Pradesh.

Silver

Silver is found in the galena ores that may have up to one per cent of the metalic mineral. **Andhra Pradesh including Telangana** is the main producer of silver in the country. More than 40 per cent of its production comes from this state. Guntur, Cuddapah, and Kurnool districts are important producers. **Jharkhand** including Bihar is the second largest producer of silver. Singhbhum, Dhanbad and Dumka districts are important producers. Zawar mines in Udaipur, Rajasthan. Vadodara in Gujarat, and Baramula in Jammu and Kashmir.

Atomic Minerals

Atomic energy can be produced by fission or fusion of the atoms or rather the nuclear parts of radio-active minerals like uranium, thorium and radium. India possesses the world's largest reserves of monazite, the principal source of thorium and some reserves of uranium.

Uranium

In India, uranium is embedded in the igneous and metamorphic rocks in Jharkhand, Rajasthan, Andhra Pradesh and some parts of as Himalayas. A substantial source of uranium deposits is also found in the monazite sands along the Kerala coasts. The pro-duction of uranium at present is confined to the mines at Jaduguda in Singhbhum district of Jharkhand.

Thorium

Thorium is principally obtained from monazite. The beach sands of Kerala in Palghat and Quilon districts contain the world's richest monazite deposits. It also occurs on the sands of Visakhapatnam in Andhra Pradesh.

- The production of Uranium is presently confined to the mines of Jaduguda in Singhbhum district of Jharkhand.
- India possesses the world's largest monazite reserves, the principal source of thorium.
- The beach sand of Kerala in Palghat and Quilon districts contain world's richest monazite deposits.
- In India Uranium is found in the igneous and metamorphic rocks in Jharkhand, Rajasthan, Andhra Pradesh and some parts of the Himalayas.

AGRICULTURE IN INDIA

About 54.6% of total work force in India is engaged in agriculture and allied activities. It still provides livelihood to the people in our country. It fulfils the basic need of human beings and animals. It is an important source of raw material for many agrobased industries. India's geographical condition is unique for agriculture because it provides many favourable conditions.

There are plain areas, fertile soil, long growing season and wide variation in climatic condition, etc. Apart from unique geographical conditions, India has been consistently making innovative efforts using science and technology to increase production.

Types of Farming in India

The country has Himalayan mountain ranges extending from Jammu and Kashmir in the west to Arunachal Pradesh in the North-East. They have hill ranges in the form of Eastern Ghats and Western Ghats. India has one of the largest plain areas of the world in the form of Indo-Ganga plain. Central part of India is dominated by plateau area. Apart from variation in landform, the country has varieties of climatic conditions, and soil types. These physical variations along with other factors like availability of irrigation, use of machinery, modern agricultural inputs like High Yielding Varieties (HYV) of seeds, insecticides and pesticides have played their respective roles in the evolution of different farming practices in India. Some of the major types of farming are discussed below.

1. Subsistence and commercial farming

Majority of farmers in India practise subsistence farming. This means farming for own consumption. In other words, the entire production is largely consumed by the farmers and their family and they do not have any surplus to sell in the market. In this type of farming, landholdings are small and fragmented. Cultivation techniques are primitive and simple. In this farming, farmers mostly cultivate cereals along with oil seeds, pulses, vegetables and sugarcane.

Commercial farming is just the opposite to subsistence farming. In this case, most of the produce is sold in the market for earning money. In this system, farmers use inputs like irrigation, chemical fertilizers, insecticides, pesticides and High Yielding Varieties of seeds, etc.

Some of the major commercial crops grown in different parts of India are cotton, jute, sugarcane, groundnut, etc. Rice farming in Haryana is mainly for commercial purpose as people of this area are predominantly wheat eaters. However, in East and North-Eastern states of India, rice cultivation would be largely of subsistence type.

2. Intensive and Extensive Farming

The basic difference between these two types of farming is the amount of production per unit of land. In comparison with temperate areas of USA, Canada, and former USSR, India does not practise extensive cultivation.

When we use large patch of land for cultivation, we call it extensive farming. Here, total production may be high due to larger area but per unit production is low. **Intensive Farming** records high production per unit of land. Best example of intensive cultivation is in Japan where availability of land for cultivation is very limited. Similar kind of situation can be observed in the state of Kerala in India.

3. Plantation Farming

It is an estate where a single cash crop is grown for sale. This type of agriculture involves growing and processing of a single cash crop purely meant for sale.

Tea, coffee, rubber, banana and spices are all examples of plantation crops. Most of these crops were introduced in India by the Britishers in the 19th Century.

4. Mixed Farming

It is a situation in which both raising crops and rearing animals are carried on simultaneously. All classifications are based on nature and purpose of farming. It may overlap.

Major Revolution

Green Revolution

It stands for a major technological breakthrough in India based on

(*i*) improved seeds of high yielding varieties,

(*ii*) adequate and assured supply of water for irrigation, and (*iii*) increased and appropriate application of chemical fertilizers for increasing agricultural production.

White Revolution

It stands for remarkable increase in milk production and establishment of a national milk grid, removing regional and seasonal imbalances. Among the technological inputs there are:

(*i*) crossbreeding of indigenous cows with high milk yielding European breed;

(*ii*) pasteurization of milk for keeping it for a longer duration;

(*iii*) collection of quality milk from members in rural areas; and

(*iv*) refrigerated transport system which helps sending milk to far off metropolitan centres both by road and rail.

Blue Revolution

It refers to big rise in catching of fresh water and marine fish.

Yellow Revolution

It refers to remarkably steady and assured supply of poultry products.

Pink Revolution

It refers to a considerable rise in the production of quantity of apples particularly in the states of Himachal Pradesh and J&K.

Measured to Raise Cropping Intensity

1. **Irrigation :** Irrigation has played an important role in raising the cropping intensity in northern states where it has raisen considerably.
2. **Fertilisers :** The need to leave the land fallow for some period to regain the lost nutrients can be dispensed with using fertilisers and following some other suitable cropping practices like crop rotation, mixed cropping and relay cropping.

Crop Rotation : It is the suitable arrangement of successive crops in such a way that different crops draw nutrients in different proportions or from different strata.

Mixed Cropping : This works on similar principles.

Relay Cropping : This means simultaneous sowing of different crops with different nurturing periods in the same field and harvesting them one after the other.

Selective Mechanisation : Use of tractors, tillers, threshers, etc., can save critical time between raising two crops, thus enabling the showing of more than one crop.

Use of Fast Maturing Varieties : These varieties can enable growing of more than one crop within one growing season.

Appropriate Plant Protection : These measures include the use of pesticides and insecticides, seal treatment, weed control, rodent control measures etc.

The role of modern inputs in raising cropping intensity can be illustrated by comparing the extent of these inputs used in an agriculturally developed state like Punjab and an agriculturally moderately developed state Gujarat.

Crop Combinations in Different Regions of India

Using the method of 'least square' given by J.T. Coppock in 1964, 'Eleven crop zones' or the regions of first order and thirty-eight 'crop combination regions' can be delimited. These regions are based on eleven 'first ranking crops'–rice, jowar, wheat, maize, bajra, pulses, ragi, barley, cotton, groundnut and tea. Other crops are grown in combination with the major crops. The absolute percentage under the major crop may vary from 100% to 40%.

Rice

There are seven regions in India where rice is the 'first ranking crop'—(i) Rice Monoculture Zone—This region includes eastern Madhya Pradesh, Chhotanagpur Plateau, Coastal Odisha, West Bengal, Brahmaputra valley, Tripura, Manipur, Nagaland, Andaman and Nicobar Islands and the deltas of Krishna, Godawari and Cauveri.

Western Coast : This zone includes Kerala and the Konkan coasts. Other crops of this region are betelnut, ragi, fodder, coconut, vegetables and rubber.

Eastern Coast : This region includes the non-delta regions of Tamil Nadu, groundnut, bajra, Jowar, cotton, millets and pulses are other crops grown in this region.

Ganga Plains of Eastern Uttar Pradesh and Bihar : In these regions, pulses, wheat, barley, sugarcane and maize are the other crops grown.

Southern Karnataka Plateau : The other crops of this region include coffee, ragi, pulses, cardamom, citrus fruits and coconut.

Northern Hill Districts of West Bengal : Tea and maize are other crops, while jute is grown in Jalpaigudi.

Meghalaya Plateau : Potato, maize and cotton are other crops in the combination.

Condition of Growth : Rice cultivation is conditioned by temperature parameters at the different phases of growth. The critical mean temperature for flowering and fertilisation ranges from 16°C to 20°C whereas during ripening the range is from 18°C to 32°C. Temperatures beyond 35°C affect not only pollen shedding but also grain-filling. High temperatures and high light intensity adversely affect grain-filling. A seasonal rainfall of 112 cm to 150 cm is required. Rice needs much water both in and upon the soil. As such the monsoonal lands are best suited for rice production or heavy irrigation is required. Alluvial soil suits cultivation. Deltas, estuaries, flood plains and vallies of rivers and coastal plains with heavy soils make excellent rice fields or lands.

Rice is sown in India in three ways—by broadcast, drill and transplantation from a seedbed. The first method is practised where labour is scarce and soil is infertile. The second method is mostly confined to Penninsular India. The third method is common in river deltas and plains.

Wheat

Wheat is the second most important foodcrop after rice. There is no wheat monoculture zone, because it is not double cropped. Wheat crop occupies 40% of the cropped area in the wheat zone. There are four regions where is the first ranking crop.

(*i*) **Ganga-Yamuna Doab :** Pulses, rice, maize bajra, fodder and sugarcane are other crops entering this region.

(*ii*) **Eastern Haryana :** In this region, pulses, jowar, bajra, fodder and sugarcane are other crops.

(*iii*) **Himachal Pradesh and parts of Punjab :** These districts of Punjab are Gurdaspur and Hoshiarpur. Maize, rice and pulses are other crops of the region.

Rest of Punjab : Fodder, maize, pulses, rice, cotton and groundnut are other crops entering the region.

Condition of Growth : The cool winters and the hot summers are conducive to a good crop of wheat. Wheat does not grow well in areas of high heat and high humidity. 15°C during summer is the lower limit of temperature.

In India the Indo-Gangatic Plains form the most important wheat area. It is grown in the Rabi season when the tempe-ratures are 10-15°C and the rainfall 5-15 cm. An annual precipitation of 50-100 cm is best suited for wheat plant requires a fair amount of moisture with cool weather followed by warm and sunny weather.

Pulses

It includes a number of crops which are mostly leguminous and provide invaluable proteins to the vegetarian population of India.

As they have fewer sources of proteins in comparison to those who consume meat and fish. They also serve as excellent forage and grain concentrates in the cattle feed.

Gram

It is the most important of all the pulses. It accounts for about 37% of the production and about 30% of the total area of pulses in India. It is a rabi crop which is sown between September and November and is harvested between February and April. It is either cultivated as a single crop or mixed with wheat, barley, linseed or mustard.

Some of the geographical conditions are as follows:

(*a*) **Temperature:** It is grown in a wide range of climatic condition. Mild cool and comparatively dry climate with 20°C-25°C temperature.

(*b*) **Rainfall:** 40-45 cm rainfall is favourable for gram cultivation.

(*c*) **Soil:** It grows well on loamy soils.

(*d*) **Distribution:** Although gram is cultivated in several parts of the country, however, 90% of the total production comes from five states. These states are Madhya Pradesh, Uttar Pradesh, Rajasthan, Haryana and Maharashtra.

Commercial Crops

Commercial crops are those crops which are grown for sale either in raw form or semi-processed form.

Sugarcane

It also provides raw material for the manufacturing of alcohol. Bagasse, the crushed cane residue, has also multiple uses. It is used for manufacturing of paper. It is also an efficient substitute for petroleum products and a host of other chemical products. A part of it is also used as fodder.

Some of the geographical conditions for the growth of sugarcane are as follows:

(*a*) **Temperature:** It requires hot and humid climate with an average temperature of 21°C to 27°C.

(*b*) **Rainfall:** 75-150 cm rainfall is favourable for sugarcane cultivation. Irrigation is required in those areas where rainfall is less than the prescribed limit.

(*c*) **Soil:** It can grow in a variety of soils. In fact sugarcane can tolerate any kind of soil that can retain moisture. But deep rich loamy soil is ideal for its growth. The soil should be rich in nitrogen, calcium and phosphorous but neither it should be too acidic nor alkaline. Flat, plain and level plateau is an advantage for sugarcane cultivation because it facilitates irrigation and transportation of cane to the sugar mills. Sugarcane cultivation requires heavy manures and fertilizers because it exhausts the fertility of soils quickly and extensively.

(*d*) **Distribution:** India has the largest area under sugarcane cultivation in the world and the second largest producer next to Brazil. As far as distribution of sugarcane cultivation in India is concerned, there are three distinct geographical regions in the country. These regions are:

(*i*) The Satluj-Ganga plain from Punjab to Bihar containing 51% of the total area and 60% of the country's total production.

(*ii*) The black soil belt from Maharashtra to Tamil Nadu along the eastern slopes of the Western Gahats.

(*iii*) Coastal Andhra Pradesh and Krishna river valley.

Cotton

Cotton is the most important fibre crop not only of India but also of the entire world. It not only provides a raw material for cotton textile industry but also its seed is used in Vanaspati oil industry. The cotton seed is also used as part of fodder for milch cattle for better milk production. Cotton is basically a kharif crop. It grows in tropical and sub-tropical areas.

Some of the geographical conditions are as follows:

(*a*) **Temperature:** Cotton is the crop of tropical and sub-tropical areas and requires uniformly high temperature varying between 21°C and 30°C.

(*b*) **Rainfall:** It grows mostly in the areas having at least 210 frost free days in a year. It requires modest amount of rainfall of 50 to 100 cm. However, cotton is successfully grown with the help of irrigation in the areas where rainfall is less than 50 cm. High amount of rainfall in the beginning and sunny and dry weather at the time of ripening are very useful for a good crop.

(*c*) **Soil:** Cotton cultivation is very closely related to Black soils of Deccan and Malwa plateau. However, it also grows well in alluvial soils of thc Satluj-Ganga plain and red and laterite soils of the peninsular region.

(*d*) **Distribution:** India has the largest area under cultivation and third largest producer of cotton next only to China and the USA. Within the country two third of total area and production is shared by four states. The main states for cotton production are Punjab, Maharashtra, Gujarat and Haryana.

Oilseeds

It is one of the important groups of commercial crops in India. In fact, India has the largest area and production of oilseeds in the world. Oil extracted from oilseeds not only forms an important item of our diet but also serves as a raw material for the manufacturing of hydrogenated oils, paints, varnishes, soaps, lubricants, etc. Oil-cake (the residue after the oil is extracted from the oilseeds) forms an important cattle feed and manure.

Groundnut

It is the most important oilseed of India. Groundnut is grown both as kharif and rabi crop but 90-95% of the total area is devoted to kharif crop.

Some of the geographical conditions are as follows:

(*a*) **Temperature:** It thrives best in the tropical climate and requires 20°C to 30°C temperature.

(*b*) **Rainfall:** 50-75 cm rainfall is favourable for groundnut cultivation. It is highly susceptible to frost, prolonged drought, continuous rain and stagnant water. Therefore, dry winter is needed at the time of ripening.

(*c*) **Soil:** Well drained light sandy loams, red, yellow and black soils are well suited for its cultivation.

(*d*) **Distribution:** It is the most important oilseed of India and accounts for about half of the major oilseeds produced in the country. India is the largest producer of groundnut in the world and accounts for about one third of the world's production. Gujarat, Rajasthan and Tamil Nadu are three main producers of groundnut in India and account for about 60% of the total production. Another 30% of the total production comes from Maharashtra, Karnataka, Andhra Pradesh and Odisha.

Plantation Crops

Tea

Tea is made from tender sprouts of tea plants by drying them. At present, China is the leading tea producing country in the world. India and Sri Lanka are respectively second and third largest producers of tea.

Some of the geographical conditions for the growth of tea are as follows:

(*a*) **Temperature:** It requires hot and wet climate. The ideal temperature for the growth of tea bushes and leaf varies between 20°C and 30°C. If temperature either rises above 35°C or goes below 10°C, it would be harmful for the growth of tea bushes and leaves.

(*b*) **Rainfall:** As mentioned above tea requires a good amount of rainfall ranging between 150-300 cm and the annual rainfall should be well distributed throughout the year. Long dry spell is harmful for tea.

(*c*) **Soil:** Tea bush grows well in well drained, deep, friable loamy soil. However, virgin forest soils rich in humus and iron content are considered to be the best soils for the tea plantation. Tea is a shade loving plant and grows better when planted along with shady trees.

(*d*) **Distribution:** Assam is the leading producer that accounts for more than 50% of tea production of India. Tea producing areas of Assam are the hill slopes bordering the Brahmaputra and Surma valleys. West Bengal is the second largest producer of tea where tea is mostly grown in the districts of Darjeeling, Siliguri, Jalpaiguri and Cooch Bihar. Tamil Nadu is the third largest producer where tea growing areas are mostly restricted to Nilgiri hills.

Coffee

Some of the geographical conditions for the growth of coffee are as follows:

(*a*) **Temperature :** It requires hot and humid climate with temperature varying between 15°C and 28°C. It is generally grown under shady trees. Therefore, strong sun light, high temperature above 30°C, frost and snowfall are harmful for coffee cultivation. Dry weather is necessary at the time of ripening of berries.

(*b*) **Rainfall:** Rainfall between 150 to 250 cm is favourable for coffee cultivation.

(*c*) **Soil:** Well drained, rich friable loamy soil containing a good deal of humus and minerals like iron and calcium are ideal for coffee cultivation. The soil must be properly manured to retain and replenish fertility and to increase productivity.

(*d*) **Distribution:** Karnataka, Kerala and Tamil Nadu are the main states of coffee production in India.

INDUSTRIAL DEVELOPMENT

A large number of industries have been established in the post-independence India in Private, Public and Joint sectors. There are a lot of industrial resources and raw materials available in India.

In India, the modern industries sector on an organised pattern started with the establishment of cotton textile in Mumbai in 1854 with predominantly Indian capital and enterprise. Large-scale industries started in the first fifteen years of planning in India. Rate of industrial growth was fluctuating between 2 and 12 per cent.

The process of industrialisation started with the launching of the first five year plan and continued through successive plan periods.

First and Second Fiver Year Plans (1952-1961)

Emphasis was laid on growth as well as diversification on industries. While three new steel plants at Bhilai, Rourkela and Durgapur were set up in the public sector, the private sector plants were also encouraged to increase their capacity.

Third and Fourth Five Year Plans (1961-1974)

There were setbacks to the pace of industrial development during the third and the fourth plan periods due to the wars of 1962 (with China) and 1965 (with Pakistan) and severe drought conditions in 1965-66 and 1966-67.

New capacity was created in iron and steel, mining and power generation. The country became self-sufficient in rail and road transport. During the third plan there was substantial shortfall in the production of iron and steel.

Fifth Plan (1974-78)

The emphasis during the fifth plan period was on production of export-oriented goods, goods of mass consumption and on the growth of core sector industries.

Sixth Plan (1979-80–84-85)

The industrial policy during the sixth plan period emphasised the optimum utilisation of existing capacities, quantitative increase in the output of consumer and capital goods and improvement in productivity.

Seventh Plan (1985-86 to 1990-91)

The policy thrust aimed at achieving growth with social justice and improved productivity, ensuring adequate supply of consumer goods of mass consumption of acceptable quality of reasonable prices and introducing technological upgradation.

Eighth Plan (1992-97)

This plan period began in an era of liberalisation and globalisation. The new economic policy and the accompanying industrial policy in 1991 marked a radical departure from the planned approach.

Ninth Plan (1997-2002)

In the Ninth plan, several areas were identified for urgent government action to realise a target of 8.2 per cent annual growth rate of industry.

Tenth Plan and Industry

In 10th Plan, there was an acceleration in the industrial growth rate. The tenth plan targets a gross domestic product (GDP) growth rate of 8 per cent per annum. The corresponding growth target for the industrial sector is 10 per cent. The tenth plan target of 10% industrial growth has not been met, but there was an acceleration in the industrial growth rate during the plan period and the target exceeded in the terminal year.

Eleventh Five Year Plan

During eleventh five year plan targeted growth of industrial production is set at 10% per annum and manufacturing sector growth target is set at 12% per annum. However, in the wake of global recession, the government is contemplating a moderation in these rates.

Twelfth Five Year Plan (2012-2017)

India has become one of the fastest growing economies in the world over the last two decades, undoubtedly aided in this performance by economic reforms. The Government of India needs a strategy to accelerate the growth of the country's manufacturing and industrial sectors to meet the goals and obtain the outcomes mentioned. The concept of 'Industrial Policy' has varied across countries and also over time. In India, industrial policy becomes assaulted under a stifling system of bureaucratic controls through licenses and quotas for industrial production.

In planning a strategy for rapid growth of industry in India we need to learn from these success stories and apply them suitably to our circumstances.

Automobile Industry

The Indian Automobile Industry is one of the largest in the world. The Industry accounts for 7.1 per cent of the country's Gross Domestic Product (GDP). The two wheelers segment with 81 per cent market share is the leader of the Indian Automobile market owing to a growing middle class and a young population.

Moreover, the growing interest of companies in exploring the rural markets further aided the growth of the sector. The overall passenger vehicle segment has 13 per cent market share.

At present the Indian automobile industry, a significant global player, directly employs around 37 million people. The industry offers a wide range of job opportunities, including roles in manufacturing, sales, engineering and more. With the additional investment and increase in production, it is expected that the direct employment in the sector will double in the next five years.

Information Technology

India is the world's largest sourcing destination for the Information Technology (IT) industry, accounting for approximately 67 per cent of the US$ 124-130 billion market. The industry employs about 5.4 million workforces. More importantly, the industry has led the economic transformation of the country and altered the perception of India in the global economy. However, India is also gaining prominence in terms of intellectual capital with several global IT films setting up their innovation centres in India.

The IT industry has also created significant demand in the Indian education sector, especially for engineering and computer science. Information technology industry caters to both the domestic and the foreign market, But it is the software and services sector which has made impressive growth in the foreign as well as domestic market.

India has exported its information technology services to more than hundred countries around the world, but there is a heavy reliance on the USA market, which accounts for 62 per cent of the total software exports.

Indian information technology industry, which was started by small group of enterpreneurs, without any government intervention, has grown into a large and growing industry providing all types of services and high end products.

REGIONALISATION OF INDIA

Physiographic

Planning concerns itself with decision about the general direction order and progress in economic development relating to human welfare. In India our planning process has mostly been centralized and a single level sectoral planning has been going on for a long time.

On the other hand in the multilevel planning process, the national territory is divided into small territorial units, their number depending upon the size of a country.

It integrates the physical, economic and social goals within each such region and between different sets of regions from local to national level.

For regionalizing such a complex country as India, the criteria have to be multifactorial and even divergent at the same level of hierarchy. This is because all the distinguishing factors could not be of equal importance, and much less for all regions, also the homogeneity of a region, distinctiveness from other regions, will be determined by only certain of the factors or a particular group associated factors.

While some other set or association from amongst the same factors will be offering the key for other neighbouring regions.

Thus, the physical factors, which do offer same broad regions because of their relatively static and bold character, could not take us further in our task—after all the natural areas they offer form the medium or the material and it is the culture of man-in group which plays the agent to work out the region.

Geology, structure, relief and physiographic together with the positional factor provide a fairly clear-cut division of India into four units—the Himalayan mountain region, the great plains, the peninsular uplands and the India coasts and islands. These are simple but effective macro divisions of the country and go well with the various patterns of the land in general. They are mutually distinct from each other, each having distinctive regional personality, and providing distinctive 'living space' with different set of factors. Each of these contrasts with the other in structure, landforms, climate, soils, natural vegetation, population and settlement distribution patterns, cultural aspects, economic development and above all in the range of possibilities and challenge.

The scope of regional planning in India (dividing the country into planning regions and preparing regional plans) is limited, because the states act as independent political entities and have their own planning machinery.

Intra-State Planning

Some states such as Andhra Pradesh, Tamil Nadu and Uttar Pradesh identified sub-regions for planning. The plan by Andhra Pradesh for the Rayalseema region aimed at development of surface and groundwater potential for irrigation, industrial development, dairy farming and utilisation of forest and mineral resources.

Inter-State Schemes

Damodar Valley Project : This is a multi-purpose project and includes irrigation, drinking water, electricity, flood control, afforestation and optimum use of forest, mineral and other resources as its objectives.

Dandakaranya Project : This project includes, the tribal areas of Odisha and neighbouring states. Its objective was to resettle the refugees from East Pakistan (now Bangladesh) through integrated planning with special reference to tribal interests.

South-East Resource Region : The town and country planning organisation (which had drafted the plans for Damodar Valley and Dandakaranya) realised the importance of linking these two regions through the intervening region which has strong resource linkages and faces similar development problems.

Bundelkhand : This region includes six districts from Madhya Pradesh and five from Uttar Pradesh. The region faces the problems of scarcity of water, low levels of agricultural activity, lack of industries and poor communication network.

Western Ghats : This region includes six states—Gujarat, Maharashtra, Goa, Karnataka, Tamil Nadu and Kerala. An integrated plan is to consider the issues of afforestation, soil conservation, hydel power development, plantation agriculture, mineral resources development and wildlife protection.

North-Eastern Region : This region includes the 'Seven Sisters'—Assam, Meghalaya, Arunachal Pradesh, Nagaland, Manipur, Mizoram and Tripura. The problems faced by this region include inaccessibility due to difficult terrain and poor physical infrastructure, soil erosion, floods, low agricultural yield and low level of industrialisation.

Regional Disparities in Development in India

Spectacular growth attained by some regions and in some sectors in India, after independence, is in contrast to low levels of development still prevailing in many parts. The reasons for these regional imbalances are roofed in historical processes and in varied levels of natural resource endowment in various regions of the country.

Multi-Level Planning–State, District and Block Level Planning

The Case for Decentralised Planning

1. In order to bridge the potential–performances utilisation gap in different areas within the state. It is essential to have a local level assessment of the problems, resources and of the potential or productive capacities. The local level assessment gives a more realistic picture.
2. Monitoring of the ongoing projects is more effective at the local level with participation of beneficiaries and the implementing officials.
3. In order to ensure proper phasing to achieve synchronisation with other projects, detailed working out of plans at the local levels is necessary.
4. Only a systematic study and planning of infrastructure at the local level can enable the state super structure to be established.
5. To create dynamic clusters and local growth centres to stimulate economic growth, in the hinterland, local level planning and assessment is required.
6. A district is large enough a unit to serve as a viable planning unit and is characteristed by its closeness to the people.

Objectives of Local Level Planning

Some of the major objectives of local level planning are as follows:

1. Optimum utilisation of resources and capacities.
2. Proportionate accruing of the development benefits to the poor, and progressively ushering in a more egalitarian ownership structure.

The Regional Approach

India is a vast and humanly too complex a country for any facile generalization or comprehension to be meaningful, and it is difficult to grasp it and to understand it in its entirety; hence the need and scope for its regionalization, and yet the problem remains whether the dictum that the whole can be understood through its parts, holds good for India.

Moreover, the task of regional division is a difficult and challenging one and yet it is vastly rewarding because it is the surer way of investigating into and finding out the really significant aspects of the geography of the country.

Tribal Areas

Tribal is expected to possess some, if not all of the following characteristics:

1. Their roots in the soil date back to a very early period.
2. They line in relative isolation of hills and forests.
3. Their sense of history is shallow, in the sense that after some generations the remembered history tends to fade out into mythology.
4. They have a low level of techno-economic development.

Integrated planning of regions inhabited by tribal populations is necessary to ensure popular interest and participation in the planning process and an equitable distribution of the fruits of economic growth.

Tribal Development Through Plans

The basic strategy has been aimed at providing protection to the tribes and bringing about their economic development.

Tribal Sub-plan Approach

The tribal sub-plan approach marked an important change of emphasis from disjointed efforts to comprehensive, well knit and integrated programmes for special development of special areas.

The tribal sub-plan approach strategy involves in a single programme of development—the financial aspects, physical planning, administrative considerations of the government, semi-government and voluntary agencies.

Social-Cultural and Economic Regionalisation of India

Culture has been increasingly viewed as influencing the daily life and behaviour of the individuals. It is a man-made part of environment and it largly determines the course of our lives.

Culture operates various levels of society, nation, industry occupation, corporate and organisation. India is home to several thousand ethnic groups, tribes, castes and religions.

The castes and sub-castes in each region relate to each other through a permanent hierarchical structure, with each caste having its own name, traditional occupation, rank and distinctive subculture.

Tribes do not have a cast hierarchy but often have their own internal hierarchical organization. The Indian society is 'regionally diverse (north/south/east/west), communally differentiated (Hindu/Muslim/Sikh/Christian/Buddhist, etc.) socially stratified and culturally discrete.

India is a multicultural country with multitudinous groups and subgroups. The total geographical area is 329 million acres, which is roughly the size of western Europe and is inhabited by one million people.

India is a vast country with diverse regional and sub-regional variations. The country abounds with economic, caste, ethnic, religion and linguistic diversities.

Types of Regions on the Basis of Stages of Economic Development

Developed/Development Regions

Developed regions are naturally those which are having a high rate of accretion in goods and services, their share in the GDP of the country is relatively high. This may be with or without rich natural resources by most certainly because of use of upgraded technology by highly skilled and motivated persons.

A developed region is the counterpart of the backward region, the 'positive' side is emphasized in case of the developed region while the 'negative' aspects are emphasized in case of the backward region.

Backward Regions

There can be 'backward or depressed' regions in the developing as well as the developed economies. Backward economies are throughly depressed regions.

Regions, in which the economy is largely subsistence one, have in the most co-existed with the modern sector regions since long. There is development even in these regions but these regions have not come out of the low level equilibrium trap.

Depressed regions have rudimentary type of industrial activity; major centres of industrial and economic activity are not in the region and/or are at a distance from the region.

Compared to developed regions, wide chasms exist in most of the economic activities leading to wide differentials in the per capita income and intensity of productive and well paying employment.

Multiple Choice Questions

1. Geology defines to:
A. Fauna B. The Earth surface
C. Interior of the sun D. Flora

2. Geomorphology is the interpretative description of the relief features. This definition was given by:
A. Thornburi, W.D. B. Lobeck, A.K
C. Strathler A.N D. Worcester, P.G.

3. Who was the founder of Plutonist school?
A. Carl Ritter B. Grifit Taylor
C. Werner D. James Hutton

4. What is the name of the first geomorphologist who said that rivers make their own valley?
A. Buffen B. Leonardo da vinci
C. Guettard D. Targioni tozefti

5. Second order relief features refer to:
(1) Plains (2) Plateaus
(3) Continents (4) Mountains
A. 1 and 2 B. 2 only
C. 3 only D. 1, 2 and 3 only

6. The concept of ice age was propounded by:
A. Albrecht B. Penck
C. Lui Agasees D. James Hutton

7. Who first propounded the study of geomorphology in the modern age?
A. W.M. Devis B. Walter penk
C. Ritchthopen D. James Hutton

8. Catastrophism defines:
A. The flood
B. The sudden construction and destruction of the landforms on the earth.
C. The drought
D. Earthquakes and volcanoes.

9. No vestige of a beginning, no proposed of an end. Who said this statement?
A. Alexander von Humboldt
B. Carl Ritter
C. Alfred Hetner
D. James Hutton

10. 'Principles of Geology' was written by:
A. Charles Lyell B. Play Fair
C. Cvijic D. Brukner

11. Submarine form is studied in:
A. Oceanography B. Coral reefs
C. Geomorphology D. Geology

12. 'The Physical Basic of Geography: An outline of Geomorphology' was written by:
A. King, L.C. B. Malott, C.A
C. Ulrij and Morgon D. Stress, J.A.

13. The advance ideas of pleistocene ice age were given by:
A. Asian School
B. American School of Thoughts
C. African School
D. European School of Thoughts

14. 'Morphology of the Earth' was written by:
A. Penk B. L.C. king
C. Brown E.H. D. Wooldride

15. Deep weathering theory was propounded by:
A. Schumn B. Marie Morisawa
C. Linton D. None of these

16. Complexity of geomorphic evolution is more common than simplicity was defined by:
A. Strahler B. Streets
C. Thonbury D. Monkhouse

17. Geodesy is a science which studies of:
A. The space
B. Interior of the earth
C. Earth measurement
D. The Earth's surface

18. Historical geology was founded by:
A. Jovan Cvijic B. Charles Lyell
C. A.F. Bernhardi D. Walter Penk

19. The concept of geographical cycle of erosion was propounded by:
A. W.M. Devis B. Cvijik
C. L.C. King D. Walter Penk

20. The concept 'cyclic nature of the earth history' was propounded by:
A. Demarest B. James Hutton
C. Leonardo da Vinci D. W.M. Davis

21. Submergence of the land refers to:
A. Decline of sea level in relation to the land
B. Land beneath the water
C. Upliftment of the land
D. Rise of sea level in relation to the land

22. Diastrophic forces are:
A. The forces that were generated due to widening of valley
B. Endogenetic forces
C. The forces that were generated due to deepening of the valley.
D. Exogenetic forces

23. Transgression of the land defines:
A. The area where there was the sea during the past
B. A narrow trip of land between the seas.
C. Area occupied by the sea
D. A narrow water body between the two land masses

24. Deepening of river valley is:
A. Epeirogenetic force B. Endogenetic force
C. Exogenetic force D. None of these

25. What is anticline?
A. A valley which follows an anticlinal axis
B. A rock structure in which the bed rock is folded into an arc
C. A downfold in the strata of the earth crust
D. None of these

26. Endogenetic forces are:
A. The forces which are very active on the interior of earth.
B. The forces which are very active in the earth surface
C. The forces which are very active in the earth surface and the interior of the earth.
D. None of these

27. Which of the following is not the endogenetic force?
A. Faulting B. Erosion
C. Compression D. All of these

28. Landslides occur due to:
A. Earth movement
B. Endogenetic forces
C. Exogenetic forces
D. None of these

29. Fold in which the limbs dip away symmetrically from the axis of fold is :
A. Monoclinal fold B. Asymmetrical fold
C. Isoclinal fold D. Symmetrical fold

30. The parallel and horizontal limbs of a recumbent fold are:
A. Thrust B. Recumber folds
C. Nappes D. None of these

31. What is orgogenesis?
A. Crustal bending
B. The deformation and movement of rock in the earth crust
C. UP wraping
D. Crustal fracture

32. The deepest rift valley in the world is:
A. Dead sea B. Jorden valley
C. Death valley D. Narmada valley

33. The force generated by the earth rotation which causes the deflection of winds to the right in the northern hemisphere and to the left in the southern hemisphere is called:
A. Radio waves B. Gravitation
C. Magnetic force D. Coriolis force

34. What is drip?
A. An embankment
B. The angle of maximum slope of an inclined surface
C. The direction of the horizontal line on an inclined rock stratum
D. None of these

35. A limb of the recumbent folds slides forward and ovrrides the other fold is called:
A. Recumbent folds B. Nuppes
C. Thrust D. None of these

36. The process of disintegration and decomposition of rocks in situ is called:
A. Landslips B. Landslides
C. Erosion D. Weathering

37. Which of the following is not the biotic weathering?
A. Animal weathering
B. Plant weathering
C. Bio-chemical weathering
D. None of these

38. The repetition of expansion and contraction weakens the outer of rock which eventually peels away is known:
A. Oxidation B. Carbonation
C. Exfoliation D. Leaching process

39. Which is not the agent of chemical weathering?
A. Hydrogen B. Oxygen
C. Carbon dioxide D. None of these

40. Which is not the agent of physical or mechanical weathering?
A. Frost B. Wind
C. Insolation D. None of these

41. *Problems de Geographie Humaine* is written by:
A. Jean Brunhes B. Ratzel
C. Martonne D. Albert Demangeon

42. *Geographie Humaine* is authored by:
A. La Blache B. Ratzel
C. Miss Semple D. Jean Brunhes

43. *Principles de Geographie Humaine* is written by:
A. Martonne B. Jean Brunhes
C. La Blache D. Albert Demangeon

44. Most universally accepted criterion to define a town is:
A. population density
B. population size
C. municipally administered
D. function

45. Which of the following are not pastoral nomads?
A. Pygmies B. Kazaks
C. Masai D. Lapps

46. Hunting and gathering is the main occupation of which tribe?
A. Turks B. Bushmen
C. Negroes D. None of these

47. Urban growth is now taking place at a faster rate in the:
A. tropics than in the North America
B. western world than in the tropics
C. western world
D. None of these

48. The villages of Lorraine (France) are notable for their:
A. linear pattern B. star shaped pattern
C. square and compact D. rectangular pattern

49. Which of the following settlements is of relatively recent date?
A. Star type B. Dispersed type
C. Linear type D. Nucleated type

50. Zone of contact settlement occurs:
A. between village and towns
B. between hill tops and low lands
C. between forests and cultivated lands
D. Only B and C

51. Hyper markets are shopping centres located:
A. near the C.B.D.
B. near rail-road junction
C. out of town
D. none of these

52. Christaller's K = 4 represents:
A. Marketing principle
B. Traffic principle
C. Administrative principle
D. All of these

53. The rank size rule of the spacing of cities was given by:
A. C. D. Harris B. Ulman
C. G. K. Zip D. G. Sjoberg

54. The sector theory of urban structure was given by:
A. H. Hoyt B. M. R. Davie
C. Both A and B D. None of these

55. The Radiant city idea of city planning was propounded by:
A. Clarence Perry (American)
B. Le Corbusier. (French)
C. A. S. Mata. (Spanish)
D. F. L. Wright (American)

56. The concentric or zonal theory was porpounded by:
A. Burgess B. Vance
C. Murphy D. Ullman

57. The multiple nuclei theory of town planning was given by:
A. C. D. Harris B. Ullman
C. Burges D. Both A and B

58. The term 'megalopolis' was coined by:
A. J. Gottman B. Burgess
C. H. Hoyt D. C.D. Harris

59. Hinter Land is frequently applied to:
A. the area in the middle of the plateau
B. the area commanding a central position
C. the areas served by a port
D. None of the above

60. The central place theory of town planning was given by:
A. M. Jafferson B. Christaller
C. Burgess D. None of these

61. Shanty town refers to:
A. extreme poverty, backing in menities and exceptionally high morality rate
B. a district of temporary, squatter dwellings
C. Generally overcrowded
D. All of the above

62. Christaller's $k = 7$ represents:
A. marketing principle
B. administrative principle
C. traffic principle
D. None of these

63. Wet point settlement occurs near the:
A. source of water B. coastal plains
C. deltas D. passes

64. The dispersed city has idea of city planning was given by:
A. Ullman B. F. L. Wright
C. Harris D. None of the above

65. The pioneer study of the CBD was done by:
A. Burges
B. Murphy and Vane
C. C. D. Harris and Ullman
D. None of the above

66. The book 'Pre Industrial City' was written by:
A. G. S. Joberg B. J. Gottman
C. G. K. Zipf D. Ullman

67. The law of primate city was propounded by:
A. M. Jafferson B. G. K. Zipf.
C. Burgess D. Christaller

68. The idea of Garden Cities was given by:
A. G. T. Ranner B. Semple
C. Howard D. P. Hall

69. All the urban settlements in an area are ranked in descending order of population. The population of then town will be $^1/_4$th that of the largest.
A. Central place theory
B. Hierarchy of towns
C. Rank-size rule
D. Law of primate city

70. The tone of discard is the:
A. CBD of present B. CBD of past
C. CBD of future D. None of these

71. The prairie settlement of N. America is of:
A. Linear type
B. Dispersed type
C. Sometimes both nucleated and dispersed
D. Always nucleated type

72. Permating is:
A. a dry point settlement in Malaysia
B. a wet point settlement in the Netherlands
C. a dry point settlement in Indonesia
D. none of these

73. Dry point settlements are:
A. always nucleated type
B. always dispersed type
C. sometimes both nucleated and dispersed
D. neither nucleated nor dispersed type

74. Terpen is:
A. a rural settlement built on a man made mounds in the Netherlands
B. a rural settlement in Malaysia
C. a rural settlement in Indonesia
D. none of these

75. Who divided any urban area into three zones?
A. A. E. Smailes B. Dickinson
C. J. H. Johnson D. Harris

76. Who presented an important modification of Christallers's central place theory?
A. Ullman B. Murphy
C. Losch D. J. Watson

77. Jengka triangle is located in:
A. Malaysia B. Indonesia
C. the Netherlands D. none of these

78. The peasant Chalets are a type of settlement common in:
A. Germany B. Hungary
C. the Netherlands D. Switzerland

79. Who divided an urban area into three zones, *viz.*, a core area, outer area and a fringe area:
A. J.H. Johnson B. Dickinson
C. A.E. Smailes D. Harris

80. The major theme in human geography in the 1960s was:
A. the study of behaviour
B. the study of Spatial environmental determinism
C. the study of Spatial Organization of Society
D. None of these

81. The highest temperature 58°C is found in:
A. Azizia (insolation desert)
B. the equator
C. Jakowabad (In Thar desert)
D. None of these

82. Why is the length of days and nights equal in the equator?
A. Because sun rays fall vertically over the equator throughout the year
B. The equator is very nearer to the sun
C. There is a large proportion of the ocean near the equator.
D. None of these

83. Why is the temperature variation highest in continental areas than in the coastal areas?
A. Because oceans become slowly cool and slowly hot than the land
B. The proportion of the sun rays is less in the ocean than in the land
C. None of these
D. Both A and B

84. Meridional is:
A. The poleward flow of heat
B. The equatorward flow of heat
C. Heat caused by solar rays
D. None of these

85. Sensible temperature means:
A. The sense of temperature that human body feels
B. The sensation of the temperature that does not affect the human body at all.
C. None of these
D. Both A and B

86. Daily range of temperature is greater in:
A. Coastal areas
B. Small areas
C. Interior regions
D. Highly elevated mountains submits

87. The basic control for the earth temperature pattern is:
A. Distribution of insolation
B. Land water contrasts
C. Oceanic currents
D. Surface elevation

88. The atmosphere gets heated by:
A. Direct rays of the sun
B. Radiation from the earth
C. Heat from the interior of the earth
D. Volcanic activity

89. Temperature generally decreases towards the poles because:
A. Air movement is towards the equator
B. Cold polar air masses prevent surface heating of the land
C. Cold surface does not absorb solar energy as readily as warm
D. None of these

90. Radiation is a process that:
A. transfers all solar energy to the earth surface
B. transfers all lunar energy to the earth surface
C. generates the heat in the atmosphere
D. None of these

91. Condensation is a process that:
A. conducts the heat from warmer to colder regions
B. conducts the heat from cooler to warmer regions
C. does not conduct heat to any of the two objects
D. None of these

92. Convention is a process:
A. non-existent in any region of temperature
B. of transferring solar energy
C. that involves transfer of energy through the movement of air and water masses
D. That puts hazard in the transfer of energy

93. Latent energy is:
A. hidden energy or invisible energy
B. found in the form of stored energy
C. motional energy
D. caused by general circulation

94. Seasonal temperature variation is caused by:
A. Low angle of the sun
B. Horizontal rays of the sun
C. Vertical rays of the sun
D. None of these

95. The maximum atmospheric pressure is found at the:
A. sea level B. middle of atmosphere
C. upper atmosphere D. None of these

96. What is the relationship between atmospheric pressure and temperature?
A. When temperature increases, pressure decreases and vice-versa.
B. When temperature increases, pressure also increases
C. There is no relationship between the two
D. None of these

97. The lines joining the places of equal pressure at sea level are called:
A. Isobars B. Isohyets
C. Isotherms D. None of these

98. The controlling factor of distribution of atmospheric pressure is:
A. Altitude B. Air circulation
C. Temperature D. None of these

99. Doldrum is:
A. Equatorial low pressure belt
B. Sub-tropical high pressure belt
C. Sub-polar low pressure belt
D. None of these

100. The winds blowing in almost the same direction throughout year are called:
A. Chinook B. Monsoon
C. Planetary winds D. Local winds

101. The 'horse latitude' is:
A. Equatorial low pressure belt
B. Sub-tropical high pressure belt
C. Sub-polar low pressure belt
D. None of these

102. The difference of pressure between any two places is called:
A. Pressure gradient
B. Pressure difference
C. Barometric slope
D. None of these

103. Coriolis forces are caused by:
A. rotation of earth
B. rotation of the moon
C. due to volcanic eruption
D. None of these

104. Winds blow from:
A. Low pressure belt to high pressure belt
B. High pressure belt to low pressure belt
C. Poles to equator
D. Equator to poles

105. The hill slope or ground slope facing the winds is called:
A. Leeward slope B. Windward slope
C. Composite slope D. None of these

106. The unit of Beaufort scale which measures velocity of wind is:
A. Heartz B. Horse power
C. Knot D. None of these

107. Trade wind blows:
A. Near the equator
B. Near the tropic of cancer
C. Near the arctic
D. None of these

108. NICT stands for:
A. North Inter Tropical Convergence
B. North Indian Tropical Convergence
C. None of these
D. Both A and B

109. Which wind is known as doctor wind?
A. Bora B. Foehn
C. Harmattan D. Chinook

110. Wind wave is an instrument that determines the:
A. direction of the winds
B. speed of the winds
C. force of the winds
D. None of these

111. Foehn and Chinook winds are caused by:
A. strong regional winds while passing over the mountain region
B. strong local wind
C. westerlies
D. None of these

112. Rain shadow is a belt of:
A. humid climate
B. dry climate
C. higher precipitation
D. None of these

113. Local winds are caused due to:
A. Gravitation
B. Variable nature of heating in land and water
C. Friction
D. None of these

114. Winds are:
A. Horizontal air movement
B. Vertical air movement
C. Sluggish air movement
D. Movements of velocity

115. Whirlwinds occur commonly in:
A. Summer
B. Winter
C. Rainy season
D. Throughout the year

116. Winds blowing from the hilltops to the valley are called:
A. Valley breezes B. Mountain breezes
C. Land breezes D. None of these

117. Winds blowing from the land to the sea are called:
A. Land breezes B. Valley breezes
C. Sea breezes D. None of these

118. Low pressure is also called:
A. anticyclone B. monsoon
C. cyclone D. None of these

119. Humans suffer from nose and ear bleed at higher altitude on mountains because:
A. the atmospheric pressure decreases with increasing altitude
B. the atmospheric pressure increases with increasing altitude
C. None of these
D. Both A and B

120. When the velocity of winds increases to such an extent that they attain gate force, the atmospheric disturbance is called:
A. Cyclonic storm B. Cyclonic pressure
C. Cyclonic winds D. None of these

121. The maximum rainfall area of India, *i.e.*, Meghalaya has average rainfall of:
A. 795 cm B. 1150 cm
C. 1000 cm D. 1050 cm

122. The Eastern Ghats and the Western Ghats meet at the:
A. Nilgiri hills B. Cardamon hills
C. Palani hills D. Annamalai hills

123. Some of the rivers of peninsular India are non-perennial mainly because:
A. Rainfall is low
B. Rainfall is seasonal
C. Water is diverted to tanks
D. Rainfall varies from year to year.

124. Assertion (A): Himalayan rivers are perennial
Reason (R) : The region gets rainfall from the South West monsoon season only
A. A and R are correct and R explains A
B. A and R are correct and R does not explain A
C. A is false but R is true.
D. A is correct but R is false:

125. The highest peak Mount Everest is:
A. 7,760 metres B. 9,740 metres
C. 8,848 metres D. 4,390 metres

126. Of which river system does the Koyna river form a part?
A. The Mahanadi B. The Godavari
C. The Krishna D. The Cauvery

127. Area of Western Himalayan sub-region is:
A. 85,190,000 acres B. 85,180,000 acres
C. 67,200,000 acres D. 67,300,000 acres

128. The distance between the Northern most point of Kashmir and Kanyakumari covers about:
A. 20° Latitude B. 35° Latitude
C. 25° Latitude D. 30° Latitude

129. How much per cent land area of India is coverd by plains?
A. 40.3 B. 44.3
C. 42.3 D. 43.3

130. The west flowing rivers of the Deccan plateau have not created deltas on the Arabian sea coast mainly because:
A. they are too short
B. they have a steep gradient
C. they do not carry much silt
D. they do not have large volume of water.

131. How much percentage of land area of India is covered by mountains?
A. 11.7 B. 10.8
C. 10.7 D. 9.7

132. Assertion (A): Narmada river has few tributaries
Reason (R) : It flows through an arid region.
A. A and R are correct and R does not explain A.
B. A and R are correct and R explains A.
C. A is false but R is true
D. A is correct but R is false.

133. Driest areas of India which lie in Rajasthan have an average annual rainfall of:
A. less than 1 cm B. 10 cm
C. 20 cm D. 100 cm

134. The Southernmost point of India lies in:
A. Lakshadweep B. Nicobar Island
C. Kerala D. Kanyakumari

135. Western coastal plains of India are:
A. Flat B. Level
C. Round D. None of these

136. Divisions of India designated as: Himalayan Region, Northern plains Region, Western Ghats and Coastal Region and Eastern Ghats and Coastal Region represent
A. agronomic regions
B. natural regions
C. administrative regions
D. meteorological regions

137. Assertion (A): Rajasthan is mainly a region of interior drainage
Reason (R) : It is mainly a structural basin surrounded by hill ranges.
A. (A) is false but (R) is true.
B. (A) is correct but (R) is false.
C. (A) and (R) are correct and (R) does not explain (A).
D. (A) and (R) are correct and (R) explains (A).

138. The Himalayas are approximately .... kilometres long.
A. 3000 B. 1500
C. 3500 D. 2500

139. The Jog waterfalls are on the river:
A. Sharavathi B. Koyna
C. Netravathi D. Tungabhadra

140. The Himalayas are approximately .... kilometres broad.
A. 150 to 300 B. 150 to 200
C. 150 to 400 D. 200 to 400

141. Lahul and Spiti are located in:
A. The Punjab Himalaya
B. The Kashmir Himalaya
C. The Assam Himalaya
D. The Naga Hills.

142. Number of consecutive months of different amount of monthly rainfall during a season or year in an area constitutes:
A. Rainfall frequency B. Rainfall events
C. Rainfall sequence D. Rainfall pattern

143. Jojila pass is in:
A. Uttar Pradesh B. Ladakh
C. Himachal Pradesh D. Andhra Pradesh

144. The Narmada and Tapti rivers of the peninsular India flow westwards:
A. along joints
B. along troughs bounded by faults
C. along old river courses.
D. along valleys carved by erosion.

145. Which is the largest of the peninsular rivers?
A. Krishna B. Cauvery
C. Godavari D. Mahanadi

146. The average height of Sivaliks is:
A. 1500 to 2000 metres
B. 700 to 1000 metres
C. 1000 to 1500 metres
D. None of these

147. Assertion (A): The Himalayas do not form a watershed for the major rivers.
Reason (R) : Rivers like the Indus, Sutlej and the Brahmaputra originate beyond the Himalayas
A. (A) is correct but (R) is false
B. (A) is false but (R) is true
C. (A) and (R) are correct and (R) does not explain (A)
D. (A) and (R) are correct and (R) explains (A)

148. Luni river is in:
A. Gujarat B. Himachal Pradesh
C. Punjab D. Rajasthan

149. The average height of inner Himalaya is:
A. 6100 B. 8100
C. 5100 D. 7100

150. Pir Panjal range is in:
A. Sivaliks
B. Sikkim Himalaya
C. The greater Himalaya
D. The middle Himalaya

151. On the basis of rainfall patterns, India has been divided into the following number of rainfall regions:
A. 121 B. 62
C. 174 D. 69

152. The Himalayas consist of ...... main parallel ranges from North to South.
A. four B. five
C. six D. seven

153. Nanga Parbat has a height of metre:
A. 8125 B. 8137
C. 8136 D. 8126

154. Nanda Devi lies in:
A. Naga Hills B. Himachal Himalaya
C. Kumaon Himalaya D. Kashmir Himalaya

155. The driest areas of India which fall in Rajasthan, Punjab, Haryana, Himachal Pradesh and Kashmir have a monthly rainfall of:
A. 15 cm B. 18 cm
C. more than 10 cm D. less than 10 cm

156. Kashmir Himalaya is famous for its:
A. Dal lake B. Glaciers
C. Poverty D. Scenic beauty

157. Nathula pass is in:
A. Arunachal Pradesh B. Jammu and Kashmir
C. Sikkim D. Bhutan

158. Sahyadri ranges refer to:
A. Western Ghats B. Eastern Ghats
C. Satpura Range D. Siwaliks

159. Kanchanjunga has a height of — metre:
A. 8,597 B. 6,700
C. 8,800 D. 8,930

160. Which of the following regions has the oldest rocks?
A. Indo-gangetic plain B. Himalayas
C. Siwaliks D. Aravallis

161. Match the following:
(*a*) Primary sector I. Service
(*b*) Secondary Sector II. Agriculture
(*c*) Tertiary Sector III. Industrial
(*d*) Quaternary Sector IV. Business

	(*a*)	(*b*)	(*c*)	(*d*)
A.	II	III	I	IV
B.	I	II	III	IV
C.	III	II	IV	I
D.	IV	III	II	I

162. Which activities comes under secondary sector?
A. Manufacturing of goods
B. Rearing animals
C. Trade and Transport
D. Govt. services

163. Teaching comes under:
A. Primary Sector B. Secondary Sector
C. Tertiary Sector D. Quaternary Sector

164. Export of goods is a:
A. primary activity B. secondary activity
C. tertiary activity D. quaternary activity

165. Which activities comes under agricultural sector?
A. Establishment of industry
B. Production of wheat crop
C. Working in army force
D. Cloth's shop

166. Developed countries of the world are mostly engaged in:
A. primary activities
B. secondary activities
C. tertiary activities
D. quaternary activities

167. Developing countries of the world are:
A. primary activities
B. secondary activities
C. tertiary activities
D. quaternary activities

168. Singapore is engaged with:
A. primary activities
B. secondary activities
C. tertiary activities
D. quaternary activities

169. The percentage of world population engaged in agriculture is:
A. 60% B. 80%
C. 70% D. None of these

170. What is monoculture?
A. In it is a single crop is produced.
B. In it two crops a year are produced.
C. In it at least four crops per year are produced.
D. None of these

171. Humid farming depends on:
A. rainfall that exceeds twenty inches.
B. rainfall that exceeds thirty inches.
C. rainfall that exceeds fifteen inches.
D. none of these

172. What is done in dry farming?
A. In dry farming deep ploughing is done to make water sink and thus to conserve the moisture.
B. In dry farming deep ploughing is done in order to remove the content of humidity from the soil.
C. None of these
D. Both A and B

173. Mixed farming has:
A. two types of production.
B. only one type of production.
C. three types of production including cereal crops, pasturing for animals and cash crops.
D. none of these

174. Plantation comes in the category of:
A. horticulture B. animal husbandry
C. monoculture D. None of these

175. Subsistence farming means:
A. farming for commercial purposes
B. farming for export purposes
C. farming for fulfilling the needs of commoners
D. None of these

176. Market gardening comes in the category of:
A. horticulture B. monoculture
C. subsistence farming D. None of these

177. What is the main food staple of eastern area?
A. Rice B. Rye
C. Wheat D. Maize

178. Posturing or livestock farming is done for:
A. fattening the animals
B. just domesticating the animals
C. the healthy growth of animals
D. None of these.

179. Posture land provides:
A. fifty per cent food
B. forty per cent food
C. sixty per cent food to the animals of the world
D. None of these

180. Bio gas is:
A. renewable B. non-Renewable
C. metallic D. non-metallic

181. Which of the following is renewable?
A. Petroleum B. Coal
C. Iron ore D. Solar energy

182. How much of the land surface in the world is under cultivation?
A. 28% B. 23%
C. 14% D. None of these

183. Rubber plantation are found in:
A. temperate forest region
B. steppe forests
C. pampas
D. equatorial forest regions

184. Which country uses much synthetic rubber as natural rubber?
A. Malaysia B. India
C. USA D. None of these

185. Which food stuff is supposed to be the aristocrat among all cereals?
A. Rice B. Rye
C. Wheat D. maize

186. Soil suitable for wheat production should be:
A. deep drained B. light
C. fine texture D. None of these

187. Which country is the main supplier of camphor?
A. Hawaii B. Taiwan
C. Hongkong D. Thailand

188. Chinar a tall tree of platanaceae family is largely found in:
A. Madhya Pradesh
B. Jammu and Kashmir
C. Kerala
D. Tamil Nadu

189. Talcher Thermal Power plant is located in:
A. Karnataka B. Odisha
C. Kerala D. Tamil Nadu

190. The biggest producer of wheat in the world is:
A. USA B. China
C. Canada D. None of these

191. Russia produces:
A. one quarter of the total production of wheat in the world.
B. one half of the total production of the wheat in the world.
C. thirty per cent of the total production of wheat in the world.
D. None of these

192. Nagarjuna Sagar Project is situated on the river:
A. Tungabhadra B. Krishna
C. Cauvery D. None of these

193. Victoria lake is located in the continent:
A. Asia B. Europe
C. Africa D. None of these

194. Barley can be grown only in:
A. wet regions
B. drier regions
C. regions of scanty rainfall
D. None of the above

195. The grassland of Argentina is known as:
A. Campas B. Pampas
C. Savanna D. None of these

196. The main element in beer is:
A. wheat B. maize
C. barley D. None of these

197. Maize is grown in:
A. temperate regions
B. tropical and subtropical regions
C. in marine climatic zone
D. None of these

198. The growing period of maize is:
A. 140 days B. 150 days
C. 100 days D. None of these

199. The biggest maize producing country in the world is:
A. Russia B. China
C. USA D. Iran

200. The Girnar Hills are situated in which of the following states?
A. Gujarat
B. Karnataka
C. Madhya Pradesh
D. Maharashtra

ANSWERS

1	2	3	4	5	6	7	8	9	10
C	D	D	B	C	C	D	B	D	A
11	**12**	**13**	**14**	**15**	**16**	**17**	**18**	**19**	**20**
A	C	D	B	C	A	C	B	A	B
21	**22**	**23**	**24**	**25**	**26**	**27**	**28**	**29**	**30**
D	B	C	C	C	A	B	C	D	C
31	**32**	**33**	**34**	**35**	**36**	**37**	**38**	**39**	**40**
B	A	D	B	B	D	D	C	D	D
41	**42**	**43**	**44**	**45**	**46**	**47**	**48**	**49**	**50**
D	D	A	D	A	B	A	A	B	D
51	**52**	**53**	**54**	**55**	**56**	**57**	**58**	**59**	**60**
C	B	C	A	B	A	D	A	C	B
61	**62**	**63**	**64**	**65**	**66**	**67**	**68**	**69**	**70**
D	B	A	B	B	A	A	C	A	B
71	**72**	**73**	**74**	**75**	**76**	**77**	**78**	**79**	**80**
B	A	A	A	A	A	A	D	C	C
81	**82**	**83**	**84**	**85**	**86**	**87**	**88**	**89**	**90**
A	A	A	A	A	C	A	B	C	A
91	**92**	**93**	**94**	**95**	**96**	**97**	**98**	**99**	**100**
A	C	A	C	A	A	A	D	A	C
101	**102**	**103**	**104**	**105**	**106**	**107**	**108**	**109**	**110**
B	A	B	B	B	A	A	A	C	A
111	**112**	**113**	**114**	**115**	**116**	**117**	**118**	**119**	**120**
A	B	B	A	A	B	A	C	A	A
121	**122**	**123**	**124**	**125**	**126**	**127**	**128**	**129**	**130**
D	A	B	B	C	C	A	D	D	B
131	**132**	**133**	**134**	**135**	**136**	**137**	**138**	**139**	**140**
C	D	A	B	A	B	B	D	A	C
141	**142**	**143**	**144**	**145**	**146**	**147**	**148**	**149**	**150**
A	D	B	B	C	A	D	D	A	C
151	**152**	**153**	**154**	**155**	**156**	**157**	**158**	**159**	**160**
B	A	D	D	D	B	C	A	A	D
161	**162**	**163**	**164**	**165**	**166**	**167**	**168**	**169**	**170**
A	A	C	D	B	B	A	D	D	A
171	**172**	**173**	**174**	**175**	**176**	**177**	**178**	**179**	**180**
A	A	C	C	C	A	D	A	A	A
181	**182**	**183**	**184**	**185**	**186**	**187**	**188**	**189**	**190**
D	D	D	C	C	C	B	B	B	B
191	**192**	**193**	**194**	**195**	**196**	**197**	**198**	**199**	**200**
A	B	C	B	B	C	B	A	C	A

●●●

ECONOMICS

INTRODUCTION OF ECONOMY

Central Problems of An Economy

Production, exchange and consumption of goods and services are among the basic economic activities of life. In the course of these basic economic activities, every society has to face **scarcity** of resources and it is the scarcity of resources that gives rise to the problem of **choice**. The scarce resources of an economy have competing usages. In other words, every society has to decide on how to use its scarce resources. The problems of an economy are very often summarised as follows:

What is produced and in what quantities?

Every society must decide on how much of each of the many possible goods and services it will produce. Whether to produce more of food, clothing, housing or to have more of luxury goods. Whether to have more agricultural goods or to have industrial products and services. Whether to use more resources in education and health or to use more resources in building military services. Whether to have more of basic education or more of higher education. Whether to have more of consumption goods or to have investment goods (like machine) which will boost production and consumption tomorrow.

How are these goods produced?

Every society has to decide on how much of which of the resources to use in the production of each of the different goods and services. Whether to use more labour or more machines. Which of the available technologies to adopt in the production of each of the goods?

For whom are these goods produced?

Who gets how much of the goods that are produced in the economy? How should the produce of the economy be distributed among the individuals in the economy?

Who gets more and who gets less? Whether or not to ensure a minimum amount of consumption for everyone in the economy. Whether or not elementary education and basic health services should be available freely for everyone in the economy.

Thus, every economy faces the problem of allocating the scarce resources to the production of different possible goods and services and of distributing the produced goods and services among the individuals within the economy. *The allocation of scarce resources and the distribution of the final goods and services are the central problems of any economy.*

Production Possibility Curve

We explained above the behaviour of the firm in choosing the factor combination for producing a product. We have assumed so far that the firm is a single product firm, that is, it produces only one product or good. But the majority of firms produce more than one product. For convenience, we take a firm producing two products X and Y. To produce two products the firm has to decide the proportion in which to produce them. For this, the concept of **production possibility curve,** or the **transformation curve** is used.

The concept of production possibility curve is based on the following assumptions :

1. The firm has given quantities of an input with which it produces the two products.

2. There is no change in the production technique.
3. It can produce the two goods X and Y in different proportions.

The concept of production possibility curve can be understood from the following table. The table given below displays various production possibilities of products X and Y.

Alternative Production Possibilities

Production Possibilities	*Product X (Hundreds)*	*Product Y (Hundreds)*
A	0	15
B	1	14
C	2	12
D	3	9
E	4	5
F	5	0

If all the given resources are employed by the firm for the production of product Y and none for X, 15 hundred units of product Y are produced. On the other hand, if the firm devotes all the resources for the production of X and none for Y, then 5 hundered units of product X are produced. But these are only two extreme production possibilities. In between these two there will be many other production possibilities, such as B, C, D and E. As the firm moves from production possibility A towards F it withdraws some resources from the production of product Y and devotes them to the production of product X.

In other words, the firm gives up some of product Y in order to produce some more of product X. It is thus clear that with a given amount of one product only by cutting down the production of the other product. As it moves for alternative A to B, it sacrifices one hundred units of product Y for the sake of one hundred units of product X. Again, as the form moves further from alternative B to C, it sacrifices two hundred units of product for one hundred units of product X.

The alternative production possibilities of the table have been graphically illustrated in figure 1. The curve AF has been obtained when the data of the table are plotted. This curve AF is called the **production possibility curve** which represents the various combinations of two products that the firm can produce with a given amount of resources. The production possibility curve shows that, with given resources, an increase in the production of one good necessitates the reduction in the output of the other good.

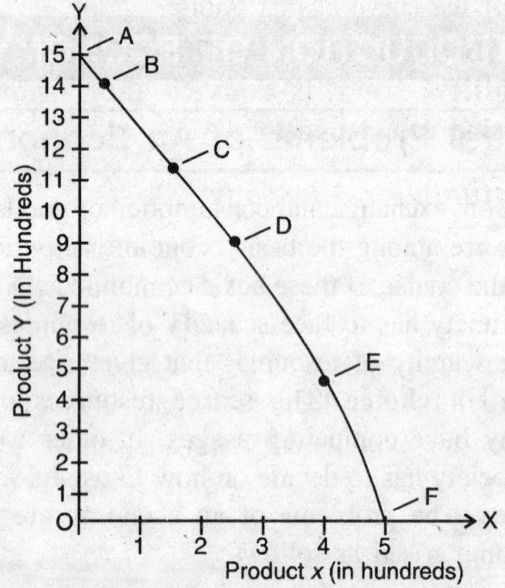

Fig. 1 : *Production Possibility Curve*

The production possibility curve is also called the **Product Transformation Curve** or simply the **Transformation Curve** because in moving from one point to another on it, one product is transformed into another, not physically but by transferring resources from one line of production to the other. With given resources being fully employed and utilized by the firm, the combination of two products produced must lie anywhere on the production possibility curve AF and not inside or outside it. The greater the amount of resources available with the firm for production, the higher the level of production possibility curve.

The rate at which one product is transformed into another, resources remaining unchanged, is called the marginal rate of transformation. In other words, the marginal rate of transformation between X and Y is the amount of transformation between X and Y is the amount of Y which is sacrificed for the production of an additional unit of X. As shown above, the sacrifice of product Y for an additional unit of X goes on increasing as the firm produces more of X and less of Y. Thus, **the marginal rate of transformation increases as the firm produces more of X and less of Y.** The increasing marginal rate of transformation makes the production possibility curves **concave to the origin.** The marginal rate of transformation (MRT) at a point on the production possibility curve is given by the slope of the curve at that point.

It should be noted here that the production possibility curve is convex only when the increasing returns occur.

Opportunity or Alternative Cost

The concept of opportunity cost occupies a very important place in modern economic analysis. The opportunity cost of any good is the next best alternative good that is sacrificed. The factors which are used for the manufacture of a car may also be used for the production of an equipment for the military. Therefore, the opportunity cost of production of a car is the output of the military equipment foregone or sacrificed, which could have been produced with the same amount of factors that have gone into the making of a car.

Two points must be noted in the above definition of opportunity cost. **Firstly,** the opportunity cost of anything is only the **next-best alternative** foregone. That is to say, the opportunities cost of producing a good is not any other alternative good that could be produced with the same factors, it is only the most valuable other good which the same factors could produce. Second point worth nothing in the above definition is the addition of the qualification or "by an equivalent group of factors, costing the same amount of money." The need for the addition of this qualification arises because all the factors used in the production of one good may not be the same as are required for the production of the next best alternative good.

In the words of **Benham,** "The opportunity cost of anything is the next best alternative that could be produced instead by the same factors or by an equivalent group of factors, costing the same amount of money''.

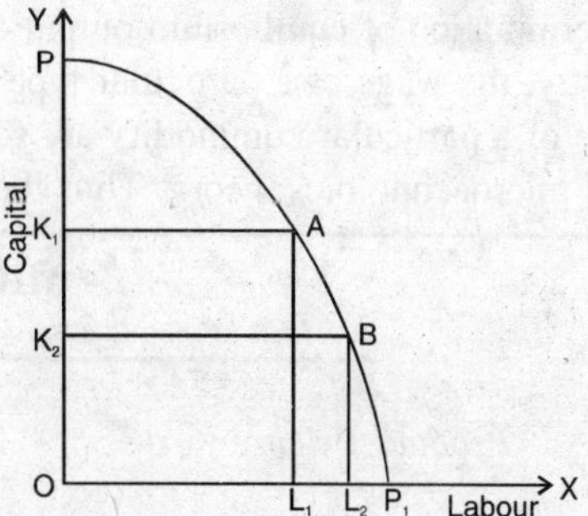

Fig. 2 : *Opportunity Cost*

The concept of opportunity cost is explained diagrammatically in figure 2 with the help of production possibility curve PP_1. At combination A on this curve, the producer uses OL_1 of labour and OK_1 of capital. If he wants to use L_1L_2 more labour, he will have to forgo K_1K_2 of capital. Thus the opportunity cost of L_1L_2 labour is K_1K_2 of capital.

The concept of opportunity cost has a wide application to economic problems. It is applicable to the determination of factor prices and in international trade. It can also be applied to consumption and public expenditure.

CONSUMER BEHAVIOUR AND DEMAND

Demand Analysis

The Subject-matter of economics has been divided into two Parts—**Microeconomics** and **Macro-economics. Ragner Frisch** was the first to use the terms "micro" and "macro" in economics in **1933.** The term microeconomics is derived from the Greek word **mikros,** meaning **"small"** and the term macroeconomics is derived from the Greek word **makros,** meaning **"large"**. Thus micro economics related to the study of individual economic units while the latter is a study of the economy as a whole.

Micro Economics

Microeconomics is the study of economic actions and behaviour of individual units and small groups. In the other words, in microeconomics we make a microscopic study of the economy.

The determination of equilibrium output of the firm or industry, the wage of a particular type of labour, the price of a particular commodity are some of the fields of microeconomics theory. Thus the theory of product pricing and the theory of factor pricing (or the theory of distribution) fall within the domain of microeconomics. The whole content of micro-economic theory is presented in the following chart:

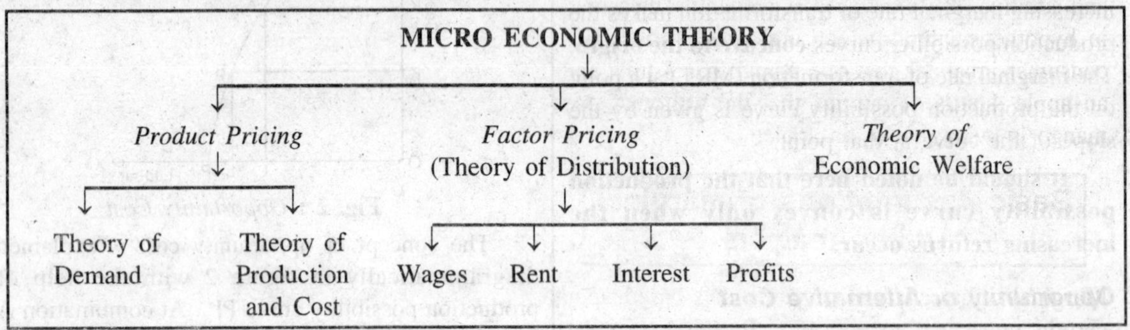

Macro Economics

Macroeconomics is the study of aggregates or averages covering the entire economy, such as total employment, the national product or income, the general price level of the economy. Therefore, macroeconomics is also known as **aggregative economics.** Macroeconomics analyses and establishes the functional relationship between these large aggregates. Thus **Professor Boulding** says, "Macroeconomics deals not with individuals quantities as such but with the aggregates of these quantities; not with individual incomes but with the national income; not with individual prices but with the price level; not with individual outputs but with the national output." Macroeconomics is also known as the theory of income and employment, or simply income analysis. It is concerned with the problems of unemployment, economic fluctuations, inflation or deflation, international trade and economic growth. We have now stated, in brief, all aspects of macro-economic theory. These various aspects of macro-economic theory are shown, in the following chart:

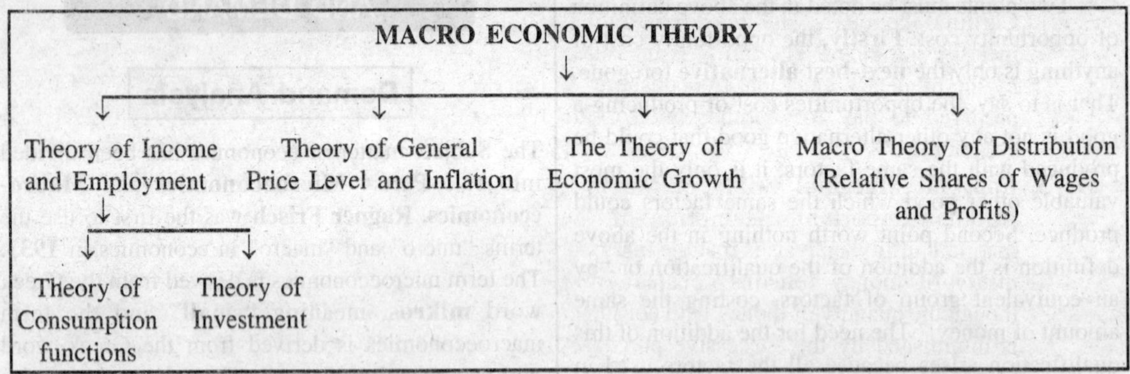

Consumer Demand Theory

There are two basic approaches to the study of consumer demand theory. The first, or **classical approach,** involves the use of measurable marginal utility (satisfaction). It is generally called the **Cardinal utility approach.** The second, or indifference curve approach, is generally called the **ordinal approach.**

Marginal Utility Analysis

Marginal utility analysis is the oldest theory of demand which provides an explanation of Consumer's demand for a product and it derives the law of demand which establishes an inverse relationship between price and quantity demanded of the product. Though marginal utility approach to the theory of demand is very old, its final shape emerged at the hands of **Marshall.** Marginal utility analysis is based on the concept of **Cardinal approach** which assumes that utility is measurable and additive. It is expressed as a quantity measured in hypothetical units which are called **'utils'.** If a consumer imagines that one mango has 8 utils and an apple 4 utils, it implies that the utility of one mango is twice that of an apple.

Basic Assumptions of Marginal Utility Analysis

Marginal utility analysis of demand is based upon certain important assumptions. Before explaining how utility analysis explains consumer's equilibrium in regard to the demand for goods, it is essential to describe those basic assumptions on which the whole utility analysis rests. The following are the main assumptions.

1. **Rationality :** The consumer is rational. He aims at the maximisation of his utility subject to the constraint imposed by his given income.
2. **Cardinal Utility :** The utility of each commodity is measurable. Utility is a Cardinal concept. The most convenient measure is money. The utility is measured by the monetary units that the consumer is prepared to pay for another unit of the commodity.
3. **Constant Marginal Utility of Money :** Another important assumption of the marginal utility analysis is that the marginal utility of money remains constant even though the quantity of money with consumer is diminished by the successive purchases made by him. It is assumed that while marginal utility of a commodity varies with the quantity of the commodity purchased, the marginal utility of money remains throughout the same as the quantity of the good purchased varies. This assumption becomes necessary because the marginal utility of a commodity is measured in terms of money.
4. **Diminishing Marginal Utility :** The utility gained from successive units of a commodity diminishes. In other words, the marginal utility of a commodity diminishes as the consumer acquires large quantities of it. This is the axion of **diminishing marginal utility.**
5. **Utilities are Independent :** Marginal utility analysis assumes that the utilities of different commodities are independent of one another. That is, the utility of one commodity does not in any way affect that of another. In other words, the satisfaction derived from the consumption of one good is the function of that good alone and is not affected by the consumption of another. On this assumption, the total utility of all goods consumed by a consumer is simply the sum of total of the separate utilities of all the goods consumed by a consumer. If there are *'n'* commodities in the bundle with quantities $x_1, x_2, ..., x_n$, the total utility is

   $$U = f(x_1, x_2, ... x_n)$$

   Thus, according to this assumption, the utilities of various goods are **additive.**
6. **Introspective Method :** Another important hypothesis of the marginal utility analysis is the use of introspective method in judging the behaviour of marginal utility. "Introspection is the ability of the observer to reconstruct events which go on in the mind of another person with the help of self-observation. This form of comprehension may be just guess work or intuition or the result of long-lasting experience."

Total Utility and Marginal Utility

When a consumer purchases a good, he obtains satisfaction from the possession of that good. That is, he derives utility from the possession of the good. When the consumer buys apples he receives them in units, 1, 2, 3, 4, etc. 2 apples have more utility than 1, 3 more utility than 2, and 4 more than 3. The units of apples which the consumer chooses are in a descending order of their utilities. In his estimation, the first apple is the best out of the lot available to him and thus gives him the highest satisfaction, measured as 20 utils. The second apple will naturally be the second best with lesser amount of utility than the first, and has 15 utils.

The third apple has 10 utils and the fourth 5 utils. In our illustration, the total utility of two apples is 35 = 20 + 15 utils, of three apples is 45 = 20 + 15 + 10 utils, and of four apples is 50 = 20 + 15 + 10 + 5. **Marginal utility is the addition made to total utility by having an additional unit of the commodity.** The total utility of the two apples is 35 utils. When the consumer consumes the third apple, the total utility becomes 45 utils. Thus, marginal utility of the third apple is 10 utils (45 – 35). In other words, marginal utility is defined as the change in total utility resulting from a unit change in the consumption of the good in question per unit of time.

Algebraically, the marginal utility (MU) of n units of a commodity is the total utility (TU) of n units minus the total utility of (*n* – 1). Thus,

$$MU_n = TU_n - TU_{n-1}$$

The relation between the total and marginal utility is explained with the help of Table 1.1.

TABLE 1.1

Units of Apple	*TU in Utils*	*MU in Utils*
0	0	0
1	20	20
2	35	15
3	45	10
4	50	5
5	50	0
6	45	– 5
7	35	– 10

So long as total utility is increasing, marginal utility is decreasing upto the 4th unit. When total utility is maximum (at the fifth unit), marginal utility is zero. It is the point of **Satiety (Saturation)** for the consumer. When total utility is decreasing, marginal utility is negative.

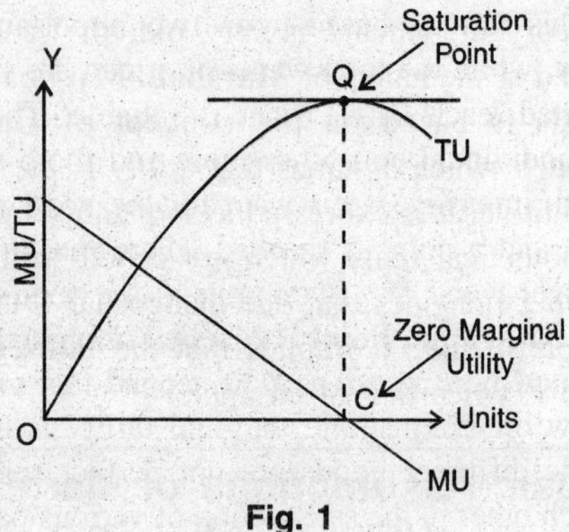

Fig. 1

In Figure 1, TU is the total utility curve and MU is the marginal utility curve. Geometrically the marginal utility curve is the slope of the total utility curve. So long as the TU curve is rising, the MU curve is falling. When the former reaches the highest point Q, the latter touches the X-axis at C where MU is zero and when the TU starts falling from Q and the MU becomes negative from C onwards.

Law of Diminishing Marginal Utility

Satisfaction of human wants follows some very importants laws and one of them is the Law of Diminishing Marginal utility. **Hermann Heinrich Gossen** was the first to formulate this law in 1854 though the name was given by Marshall. **Javons** called it **Gossen's First Law.** Gossen stated it thus. "The magnitude of one and the same satisfaction, when we continue to enjoy it without interruption, continually decreases until satisfaction is reached." According to this law the marginal utility of a good diminishes as an individual consumes more units of a good. In other words, as a consumer takes more units of a good, the extra utility or satisfaction that he derives from an extra unit of the good goes on falling. It should be carefully noted that it is the marginal utility and not the total utility that declines with the increase in the consumption of a good. The law of diminishing marginal utility means that the total utility increases but at a decreasing rate.

Marshall states the Law thus : "The additional benefits which a person derives from a given increase of his stock of a thing diminishes with every increase in the stock that he already has."

This Law is based upon two important facts. **Firstly,** while the total wants of a man are virtually unlimited, each single want is satiable. Therefore, as an individual consumes more and more units of a good, intensity of his want for the good goes on falling and a point is reached where the individual no longer wants any more units of the good. That is **when Saturation Point is reached marginal utility of a good becomes zero.** The second fact on which the law of diminishing marginal utility is based is that the different goods are not perfect substitutes for each other in the satisfaction of various particular wants. When an individual consumes more and more units of a good, the intensity of his particular want for the good diminishes but if the units of that good could be devoted to the satisfaction of other wants and yielded as much satisfaction as they did initially in the satisfaction of the first want, marginal utility of the good would not have diminished.

The significance of the diminishing marginal utility of a good for the theory of demand is that the quantity demanded of a good rises as the price falls and **vice-versa.** Thus it is because of the diminishing marginal utility that the demand curve slopes downward.

Law of diminishing marginal utility is a universal law and applies to all objects of desire including money. But, it is worth mentioning that marginal utility of money is generally never zero or negative. Money represents purchasing power over all other goods, that is, a man can satisfy all his material wants if he possesses enough money. Since man's total wants are practically unlimited, therefore the marginal utility of money to him never falls to zero.

Its Limitations

Law of diminishing marginal utility holds only under certain conditions —

(*a*) There should be continuity in the consumption of the commodity. Units of the commodity should be consumed in succession at one particular time.

(*b*) There should be no change in the taste, habit, custom, fashion and income of the consumer.

(*c*) All units of a commodity should be of the same weight and quality.

(*d*) Units of the commodity should be of a suitable size. Giving water to a thirsty person by spoons will increase utility of the subsequent spoons of water.

(*e*) Prices of the different units and of the substitutes of the commodity should remain the same.

Law of Equi-Marginal Utility

The Law of equi-marginal utility is known by various names. It is termed as the Law of substitution, the Law of Maximum Satisfaction and **Gossen's Second Law.**

Law of equi-marginal utility occupies an important place in marginal utility analysis. It is through the principle that **Consumer's equilibrium is explained.** A consumer has a given income which he has to spend on various goods he wants. Now the question is how he would allocate his money income between various goods, that is to say, what would be his equilibrium position in respect of the purchases of the various goods.

Suppose there are only two goods A and B on which consumer has to spend a given income. The consumer's behaviour will be governed by two factors: **Firstly,** by the marginal utilities of the goods and **secondly,** by the prices of two goods. Suppose the prices of the goods are given for the consumer. The Law of equi-marginal utility states that the consumer will distribute his money income between the goods in such a way that the utility derived from the last rupee spent on each good is equal. In other words, the consumer will spend his money income on different goods in such a way that marginal utility of each good is proportional to its price. That is, consumer is in equilibrium in respect of the purchases of two goods A and B when

$$\frac{MU_A}{P_A} = \frac{MU_B}{P_B}$$

where MU_A is the marginal utility of A, MU_B is the marginal utility of B and P_A is the price of A, P_B is the price of B.

Now, if $\frac{MU_A}{P_A}$ and $\frac{MU_B}{P_B}$ are not equal and $\frac{MU_A}{P_A}$ is greater than the $\frac{MU_B}{P_B}$, then the consumer will substitute good A for good B. As a result of this substitution, the marginal utility of good A will fall and marginal utility of good B will rise. The consumer will continue substituting good A for good B till $\frac{MU_A}{P_A}$ becomes equal to $\frac{MU_B}{P_B}$. When $\frac{MU_A}{P_A}$ becomes equal to $\frac{MU_B}{P_B}$, the consumer will be in equilibrium.

But the equality of $\frac{MU_A}{P_A}$ with $\frac{MU_B}{P_B}$ can be achieved not only at one level but at different levels of expenditure. The question is how far does a consumer go in purchasing the goods he wants. This is determined by the size of his money income.

If there are more than two goods on which the consumer is spending his income, the above equation must hold good for all of them. Thus

$$\frac{MU_A}{P_A} = \frac{MU_B}{P_B} = ... = \frac{MU_n}{P_n}$$

Law of equi-marginal utility is explained with the help of table given below –

TABLE 1.2

Number of units	MU_A	MU_B
1	20	24
2	18	21
3	16	18
4	14	15
5	12	9
6	10	3

Let the prices of goods A and B are Rs. 2 and Rs. 3 respectively. Reconstructing the above table by dividing marginal utilities of A (MU_A) by Rs. 2 and marginal utilities of B (MU_B) by Rs. 3 We get:

TABLE 1.3

Number of units	$\frac{MU_A}{P_A}$	$\frac{MU_B}{P_B}$
1	10	8
2	9	7
3	8	6
4	7	5
5	6	3
6	5	1

By looking at the table it is clear that $\frac{MU_A}{P_A}$ is equal to 6 utils when the consumer purchases 5 units of good A and 3 units of good B and will be spending (Rs. 2 × 5 + Rs. 3 × 3) = Rs. 19 on them.

Demand

Demand is a function of price, income, price of related goods and tastes and is expressed as

$$D = f(p, y, pr, t).$$

When income, prices of related goods and tastes are given, the demand function is

$$D = f(p).$$

It shows quantities of a commodity purchased at given prices. Demand is also related to a period of time. In the **Marshallian analysis,** the other determinants of demand are taken as given and constant.

Types of Demand

Three kinds of demands may be distinguished :

(*a*) Price Demand

(*b*) Income Demand

(*c*) Cross Demand

Price Demand : Price demand refers to the various quantities of a commodity or service that a consumer or service that a consumer would purchase at a given time in a market at various hypothetical prices. It is assumed that other things, such as consumer's income, his tastes and prices of inter-related goods, remain unchanged.

The demand of the individual consumer is called **Individual Demand** and the total demand of all the consumers combined for the commodity or service is called **Industry Demand.** The total demand for the product of an individual firm at various prices is known as firm's demand or **Individual Seller's Demand.**

Income Demand : The income demand refers to the various qualities of goods and services which would be purchased by the consumers at various levels of incomes. Here we assume that the price of the commodity or service as well as the prices of inter-related goods and the tastes and desires of consumers do not change.

Cross Demand : The cross demand means the quantities of a good or service which will be purchase with reference to change in price not of this good but of other inter-related goods. These goods are either substitutes or complementary goods. A change in the price of tea, for instance, will affect the demand for coffee.

Law of Demand

This law expresses a relationship between the quantity demanded and its price. It may be defined in Marshall's words as "the amount demanded increase with a fall in price, and diminishes with a rise in price." Thus it expresses an inverse relation between price and demand. The inverse price-demand relationship is based on **other things remaining equal.** This phrase points towards certain important assumption on which this law is based.

These assumptions are :

(*i*) There is no change in the tastes and preferences of the consumer;

(*ii*) The income of the consumer remains constant;

(*iii*) There is no change in customs;

(*iv*) There should not be any change in the prices of other products;

(*v*) There should not be any change in the quality of the product;

(*vi*) The habits of the consumers should remain unchanged.

Given these conditions, the law of demand operates. If there is change even in one of these conditions, it will stop operating.

Why Demand Curve Slopes Downwards?

Generally, a demand curve slope downward from left to right. The following are the main reasons for the downward sloping demand curve.

1. The law of demand is based on the law of diminishing marginal utility. According to this law, when a consumer buys more units of a commodity, the marginal utility of that commodity continues to decline. Therefore, the consumer will but more units of that commodity only when its price falls. When less units are available, utility will be high and the consumer will be prepared to pay more for the commodity. This proves that the demand will be more at a lower price and it will be less at a higher price. That is why the demand curve is downward sloping.
2. Every commodity has certain consumers but when its price falls, new consumers start consuming it, as a result demand increases. On the contrary, with the increase in the price of the product, many consumers will either reduce or stop its consumptions and the demand will be reduced. Thus due to the **price effect** when consumers consume more or less of the commodity, the demand curve slopes downward.
3. When the price of a commodity falls, the real income of the consumer increases because he has to spend less in order to buy the same quantity. On the contrary, with the rise in the price of the commodity, the real income of the consumer falls. This is called the **income effect.** Under the influence of this effect with the fall in the price of the commodity the consumer buys more of it and also spends a portion of the increased income in buying other commodities. Thus, due to the income effect the demand curve slopes downward.
4. The other effect of change in the price of the commodity is the **substitution effect.** With the fall in the price of a commodity, the price of its substitutes remaining the same, consumes will buy more of this

commodity rather than the substitutes. As a result, its demand will increase. On the contrary, with the rise in the price of the commodity its demand will fall.

5. There are different uses of certain commodities and services that are responsible for the negative slope of the demand curve. With the increase in the price of such products, they will be used only for more important uses and their demand will fall. On the contrary with the fall in price, they will be put to various uses and their demand will rise.

Exceptions to the Law of Demand

As we have said above, generally the demand curve slopes downward to the left. But some times, the demand curve, instead of sloping downward, will rise upwards. In other words, some time people will buy more when the price rises. This can be represented only by a rising demand curve. These were first investigated by **Sir Robert Giffen.** The **Giffen Paradox** holds that the demand is strengthened with a rise or weakened with a fall in price.

Many causes are attributed to an upward sloping demand curve :

1. War
2. Depression
3. Giffen Paradox
4. Demonstration Effect
5. Speculation

Increase and Decrease Vs. Extensive and Contraction of Demand

When the demand changes merely because the price has changed, it is a case of **extension** or **contraction.** If the change in demand is due to a factor other than the price, it is known as **increase** or **decrease** in demand.

A **movement along a demand curve** indicates that a different quantity is being demanded because the price has changed. A shift of a demand curve indicates that different quantity will be demanded at each possible price because something else, either incomes, tastes or the price of some other good, has changed.

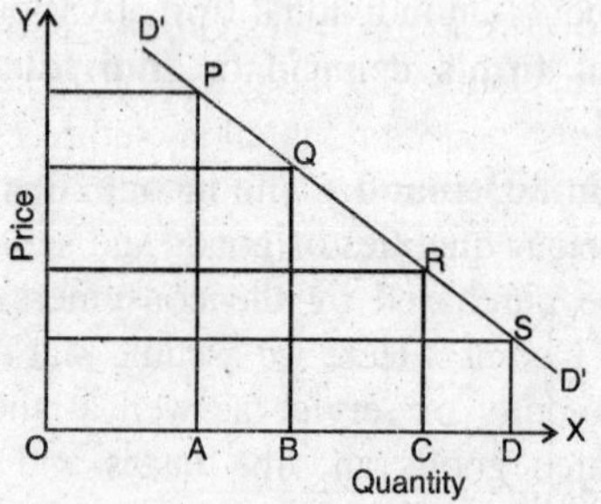

Fig. 2: *Extension and Contraction of Demand*

When we refer to a movement along a curve, to a change in the quantity demanded because price has changed, we shall refer to a change in the **quantity demanded,** specifically, to an increase in the quantity demanded, indicating a movement down the curve because of a fall in price, or a decrease in the quantity demanded, indicating a movement up the curve because of a rise in price.

When the economist speaks of an **increase** or a **decrease** of demand, he is usually referring to a **shift of the whole curve.**

In the Figure 2, when price rises from QB to PA, demand **contracts** from OB to OA. The movement on the demand curve is to the left from Q to P. On the other hand, a fall in the price from RC to SD brings an **extension** in demand from OC to OD. It is a movement to the right on the same demand curve from R to S.

Figure 3 illustrates an increase and decrease in demand. Let D be the original demand curve where at price OP, quantity OB is demanded. D_1 shows an increase in demand. An increase in demand can be either of the two ways : larger quantity at the same price or the same quantity at a higher price. When the demand increases to D_1, larger quantity OC is bought at the original Price OP, or the same quantity OB is bought at the higher price OP_1. On the contrary, a decrease in demand implies same quantity at a lower price or smaller quantity at the same price, D_2 shows decrease in demand, the same quantity OB is bought at the lower price OP_2 or the smaller quantity PT is purchased at the same price OP. Demand curves are thus not stationary, rather they shift to the right or left due to a number of causes. They are changes in tastes, habits and customs of the consumers; changes in income expenditure; changes in the prices of substitutes and complements; expectations about future changes in prices and incomes; and changes in the age and composition of the population.

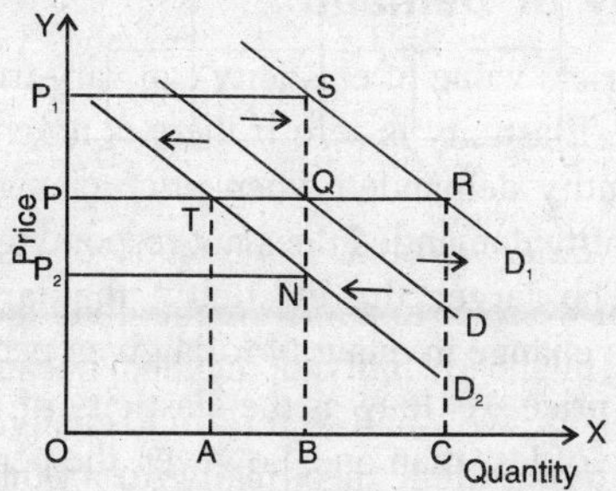

Fig. 3: *Increase and Decrease of Demand*

***A Rise (Increase) in Demand :** The demand curve shifts to the right indicating that more is demanded at each price.

This can be caused by : (1) a rise in income; (2) a rise in the price of a substitute; (3) a fall in the price of a complement; (4) a change in tastes in favour of this commodity.

***A Fall (Decrease) in Demand :** The demand curve shifts to the left indicating that less is demanded at each price.

This can be causes by : (1) a fall in income; (2) a fall in the price of a substitute; (3) a rise in the price of a complement; (4) a change in taste against this commodity.

Elasticity

In this section we shall consider the degree to which the quantity demanded and the quantity supplied respond to changes in price. The concept of elasticity has a very great importance in economic theory as well as in applied economics.

Various Concepts of Demand Elasticity

It is price elasticity of demand which is usually referred to as elasticity of demand. But, besides price elasticity of demand, there are various other concepts of demand elasticity. Demand for a good is determined by its price, incomes of the people, prices of related goods etc. Quantity demanded of a good will change as a result of a change in the size of any of these determinants of demand. The concept of elasticity of demand therefore refers to the **degree of responsiveness** of quantity demanded of a good to a change in its price, income or prices of related goods. Accordingly, there are three kinds of demand elasticity–

1. Price Elasticity
2. Income Elasticity
3. Cross Elasticity

Price Elasticity of Demand

Price elasticity means the degree of **responsive-ness** or **sensitiveness** of quantity demanded of a good to a changes in its prices. In other words, Price elasticity of demand is a measure of the relative change in quantity purchased of a good in response to a relative change in its Price. Price elasticity can be precisely defined as "the proportional change in the quantity purchased divided by the proportional change in price." Thus

$$\text{Price Elasticity} = -\frac{\text{Percentage change in quantity}}{\text{Percentage change in price}}$$

$$= -\frac{\text{Change in quantity demanded / Quantity demanded}}{\text{Change in price / Price}}$$

or, in symbolic terms

$$e_P = -\frac{\Delta q / q}{\Delta P / P} = -\frac{\Delta q}{q} \times \frac{P}{\Delta P}$$

where,

e_P stands for price elasticity

q stands for quantity

P stands for price

Δ stands for change

Mathematically speaking, Price elasticity of demand is negative. Since demand curves slope down wards, the change in quantity will always have the opposite sign to the change in price. The minus sign in the definition of elasticity is simply designed to **'neutralize'** this negative relation between price and quantity changes and thus to make elasticity of demand a positive number. This is a matter of convenience only; it has no more profound Justification than that.

Marshall who Introduced the Concept of Elasticity into Economic Theory remarks that the elasticity or responsiveness of demand in a market is great or small accordingly as the amount demanded increases much or little for a given fall in Price, and diminishes much or little for a given rise in price. This will be clear from figures. Figures A and B represent two demanded curves.

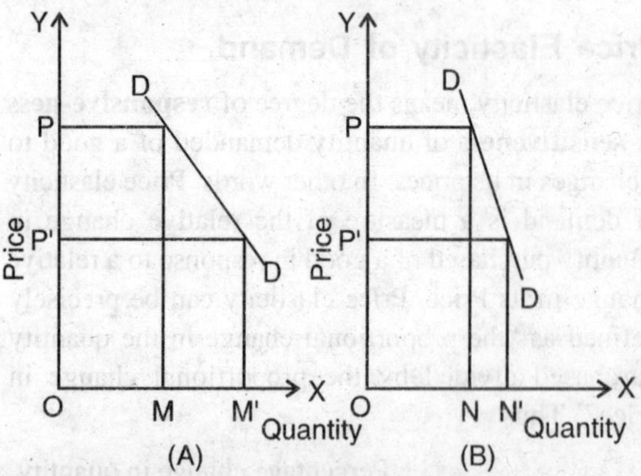

Fig.: *More Elastic Demand* **Fig. :** *Less Elastic Demand*

For a given fall in price, from OP to OP′, increase in quantity demanded is much greater in Fig. A than in Fig. B. Therefore, demand curve in Figure A is more elastic than the demand curve of Fig. B, for a given fall in price. Demand for the good represented in Fig. A is generally said to be elastic and the demand for good in Fig. B to be inelastic.

Interpreting Numerical Values of Elasticity of Demand

The numerical value of elasticity can vary from zero to infinity. Elasticity is zero if there is no change at all in quantity demanded when price changes, *i.e.*, when quantity demanded does not respond to a price change. The larger the elasticity, the larger the percentage change in quantity for a given percentage change in price. As long as the elasticity of demand has a value of less than one, however, the percentage change in quantity is less than the percentage change in price. When elasticity is equal to one, then the two percentage changes are equal to each other. While, when the percentage change in quantity exceeds the percentage change in price, then the value for the elasticity of demand will be greater than one.

When the percentage change in quantity is less than percentage change in price (elasticity less than one), the demand in said to be **INELASTIC.** When the percentage change in quantity is greater than the percentage change in price (elasticity greater than one), the demand is said to be **ELASTIC.**

Price Elasticity : Measures, Meaning and Nomeclature

Numerical measure of elasticity	*Verbal description*	*Terminology*
Zero	Quantity demanded does not change as price changes	Perfectly inelastic
Greater than Zero, but less than one	Quantity demanded changes by a smaller percentage than does price.	Inelastic
One	Quantity demanded changes by exactly the same percentage as does price.	Unit elasticity
Greater than one, but less than infinity	Quantity demanded changes by a larger percentage than does price	Elastic
Infinity	Purchasers are prepared to buy all they can obtain at some price and none at all at an even slightly higher price	Perfectly elastic

We may now consider briefly the graphical representation of demand curves of various elasticity. These are summarized in Figure 4. Zero elasticity occurs when the quantity demanded does not change as the price changes. The graph of a demand curve of zero elasticity will thus be a vertical straight line indicating that the same quantity is demanded whatever the price. Unit elasticity occurs when a given percentage change in quantity at all points on the curve. The graph of a curve of unit elasticity over its whole range is shown in Figure 4 *(ii)*. A demand curve of infinite elasticity means that there exists some small price reduction which raises the demand from zero to infinity. This case occurs when, at some price, consumers will but all that they can obtain of the commodity (an infinite amount if they could get it), while at an even slightly higher price they would but nothing at all. In Figure 4 *(iii)*, demand is zero for all prices above OP but at price OP demand is infinite.

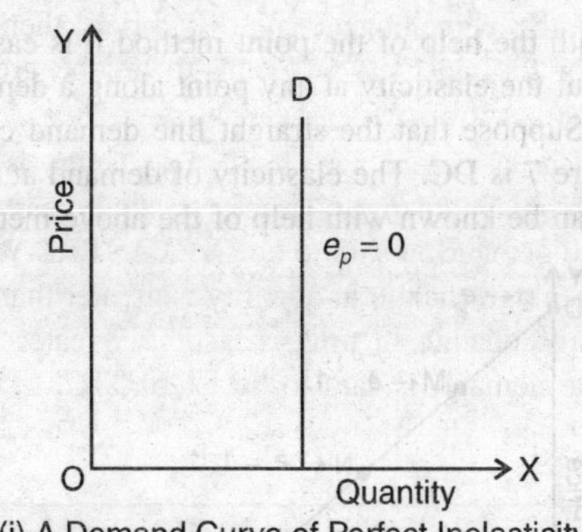

(i) A Demand Curve of Perfect Inelasticity

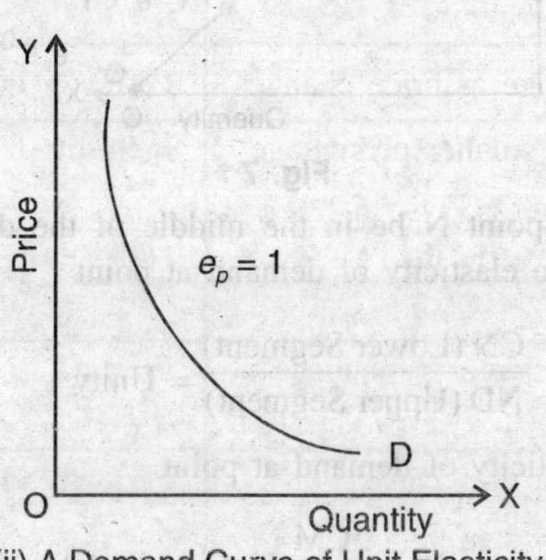

(ii) A Demand Curve of Unit Elasticity

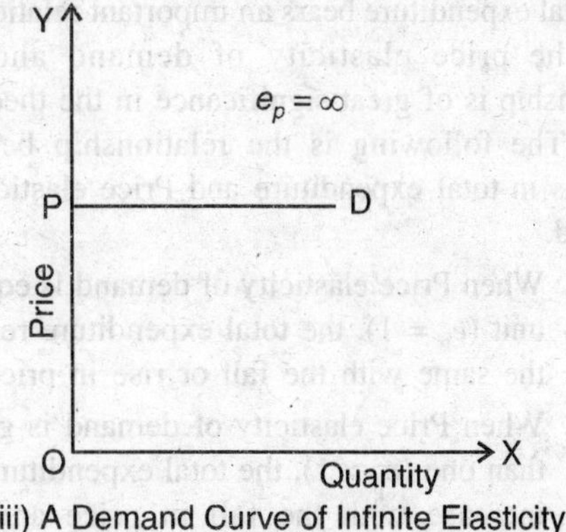

(iii) A Demand Curve of Infinite Elasticity

Fig. 4

Price Elasticity and Changes in Total Expenditure

It is often useful to known what happens to total expenditure made by the consumers on a good when its price changes. In Figure 5, a demand curve DD of a good is shown. When the price of the good is OP, its quantity demanded is OQ. Since the total expenditure is price multiplied by the quantity of the good purchased, therefore

Consumer's Total Expenditure = OP × OQ

= area OQRP

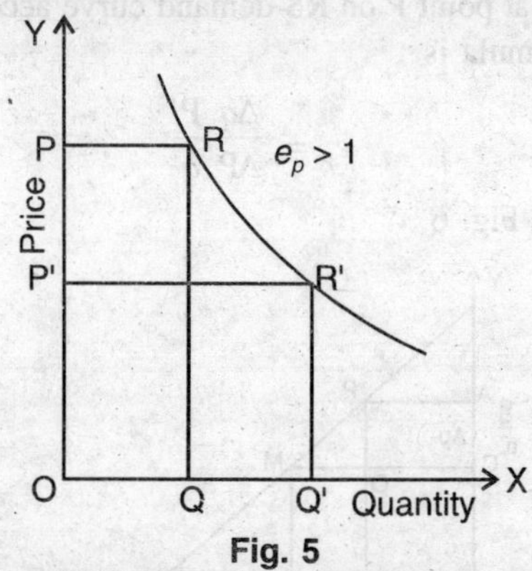

Fig. 5

Now, if the price of the good falls from OP to OP′ the quantity demanded rises from OQ to OQ′. At new Price OP′, therefore

Total Expenditure = OP′ × OQ′ = area OQ′R′P′

Now, whether the total expenditure rises or falls or remains the same with the change in the price of the good depends upon the price elasticity of demand.

The total expenditure bears an important relationship with the price elasticity of demand and this relationship is of great significance in the theory of price. The following is the relationship between changes in total expenditure and Price elasticity of demand.

1. When Price elasticity of demand is equal to unit ($e_P = 1$), the total expenditure remains the same with the fall or rise in price.
2. When Price elasticity of demand is greater than one ($e_p > 1$), the total expenditure will increase with the fall in price and will decrease with the rise in price.
3. When Price elasticity of demand is less than one ($e_P < 1$), the total expenditure will decrease with the fall in price and will increase with the rise in price.

Measurement of Elasticity At A Point On The Demand Curve

Prof. Marshall devised a geometrical method for measuring elasticity at a point on the demand curve.

Let RS be a straight line demand curve. If the Price falls from PB (= OA) to MD (= OC), the quantity demanded increases from OB to OD. Elasticity at point P on RS demand curve according to the formula is

$$e_P = \frac{\Delta q}{\Delta P} \cdot \frac{P}{q}$$

From Fig. 6

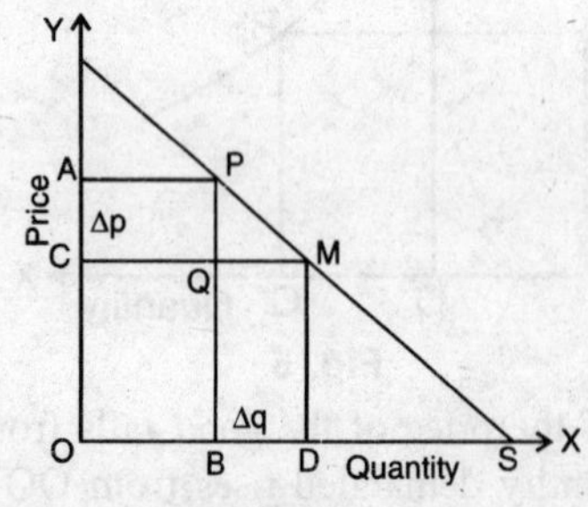

Fig. 6

$$\Delta q = BD = QM$$
$$\Delta p = PQ$$
$$p = PB$$
$$q = OB$$

Substituting these values in the elasticity formula:

$$e_P = \frac{QM}{PQ} \times \frac{PB}{OB}$$

Moreover,

$$\frac{QM}{PQ} = \frac{BS}{PB}$$

[$\angle PQM = \angle PBS$ being right angles and ΔPQM and ΔPBS are similar]

$$\therefore \quad \frac{BS}{PB} \times \frac{PB}{OB} = \frac{BS}{OB}$$

Since ΔPBS and ΔROS are similar, price elasticity of demand at point

$$P = \frac{BS}{OB} = \frac{OA}{AR}$$

$$= \frac{PS}{PR} = \frac{\text{Lower Segment}}{\text{Upper Segment}}$$

With the help of the point method it is easy to point out the elasticity at any point along a demand curve. Suppose that the straight line demand curve in Figure 7 is DC. The elasticity of demand at each point can be known with help of the above method.

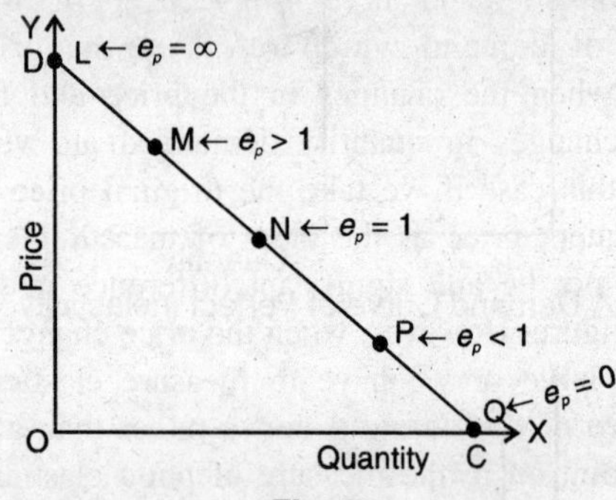

Fig. 7

Let point N be in the middle of the demand curve. So elasticity of demand at point

$$N = \frac{\text{CN (Lower Segment)}}{\text{ND (Upper Segment)}} = \text{Unity}$$

Elasticity of demand at point

$$M = \frac{CM}{MD} = \text{Greater than unity}$$

Elasticity of demand at point

$$L = \frac{CL}{O} = \infty \text{ (infinity)}$$

Elasticity of demand at point

$$P = \frac{CP}{PD} = \text{Less than Unity}$$

Elasticity of demand at point

$$Q = \frac{O}{CD} = 0 \text{ (Zero)}$$

From above it is clear that elasticity at different points on a given demand curve is different. At the mid-point in the demand curve the elasticity of demand is **Unity.** Moving up the demand curve from the mid-point, elasticity becomes greater. When the demand curve touches the Y-axis, elasticity is **infinity. Ipso facto,** any point below the mid-point towards the X-axis will show elastic demand. Elasticity becomes **zero** when the demand curve touches the X-axis.

ARC Elasticity of Demand

We have studied above the measurement of elasticity at a point on a demand curve or the concept of point elasticity of demand which refers to the price elasticity when the changes in the price and the resultant changes in quantity demanded are very small. In this case if we take the original price or the subsequent price as the basis of measurement, there will not be any significant difference in the elasticity figure. However, when the price change is somewhat large or we have to measure elasticity over an **arc of the demand curve** rather than at a specific point on it, the measure of point elasticity namely, $\frac{\Delta q}{\Delta p} \times \frac{p}{q}$, does not provide us the true and correct result of price elasticity of demand. Further, in such cases, the measure of price elasticity would depend upon whether we choose original price and quantity or the subsequent price and quantity demanded as the basis for measurement of price elasticity and there will be significant difference in the two measures of elasticity, obtained from using two basis. Consider the following example of changes in price and consequent changes in quantity demanded.

Price (Rs.)	*Quantity Demanded (units)*
15 (p_1)	100 (q_1)
10 (p_2)	200 (q_2)

If we take Rs. 15 and quantity demanded at it (100 units) as basis of measuring price elasticity with the point elasticity formula, we get the following figure for elasticity :

$$e_P = \frac{\Delta q}{\Delta p} \times \frac{p}{q}$$

$$= \frac{100}{5} \times \frac{15}{100} = 3$$

If we take Rs. 10 and quantity demanded at it (200 units) as the basis of measuring price elasticity with the point elasticity formula, we get the following figure for elasticity :

$$e_P = \frac{\Delta q}{\Delta p} \times \frac{p}{q}$$

$$= \frac{100}{5} \times \frac{10}{200} = 1$$

We thus see that when there is a somewhat large change in price, point elasticity formula will yield two significantly different elasticity measures (as 3 and 1 in our above example) depending upon whether we use the original price and quantity demanded or the subsequent price and quantity demanded as the basis for measurement.

In terms of demand curve, when we have to measure the price elasticity over an **arc of the demand curve** such as between points A and on the demand curve DD in Figure 10 the point elasticity formula will not yield the true and correct measure of price elasticity. For measuring price elasticity in such cases when the changes in price are some what large or the price elasticity over an arc of the demand curve (that is, between the two points on a demand curve which lie close together) is to be measured, the concept of arc elasticity has been evolved. In measurement of arc elasticity, we use the **average** of the two price figures (original and subsequent) and **average** of the two price figures (original and subsequent) and **average** of the two quantity figures (original and subsequent). Thus the formula for measuring **arc price elasticity** of demand is :

$$e_P = \frac{\Delta q}{\frac{(q_1+q_2)}{2}} \div \frac{\Delta p}{\frac{(p_1+p_2)}{2}}$$

$$= \frac{\Delta q}{\left(\frac{q_1+q_2}{2}\right)} \times \frac{\left(\frac{p_1+p_2}{2}\right)}{\Delta p}$$

$$= \frac{\Delta q}{\Delta p} \times \frac{(p_1+p_2)}{(q_1+q_2)}$$

In our above numerical example where when the price of a good falls from Rs. 15 to Rs. 10 per unit, the quantity demanded increases from 100 to 200 units the arc elasticity is :

$$e_P = \frac{\Delta q}{\Delta p} \times \frac{(p_1+p_2)}{(q_1+q_2)}$$

$$= \frac{100}{5} \times \frac{15+10}{100+200}$$

$$= \frac{100}{5} \times \frac{25}{300}$$

$$= 1.66$$

Cross Elasticity of Demand

The change in the demand for one good in response to the change in price of the other good represents the cross elasticity of demand of one good for the other. In other words, the cross elasticity of demand is the relation between percentage change in the quantity demanded of a good to the percentage in the price of a related good.

When the quantity demanded of good x rises as a result of the fall in the price of good y, the coefficient of cross elasticity of demand of x for y will be equal to the relative change in the quantity demanded for good x in response to a given relative change in the price of good y. Therefore,

Coefficients of cross elasticity of demand of x for y

$$= \frac{\text{Percentage change in the quantity demanded of } x}{\text{Percentage change in the price of } y}$$

$$\text{or, } e_c = \frac{\Delta q_x / q_x}{\Delta p_y / p_y}$$

$$= \frac{\Delta q_x}{q_x} \div \frac{\Delta p_y}{p_y}$$

$$= \frac{\Delta q_x}{q_x} \times \frac{p_y}{\Delta p_y}$$

$$= \frac{\Delta q_x}{\Delta p_y} \times \frac{p_y}{q_x}$$

where

e_c stands for cross elasticity of demand of X and Y

q_x stands for the original in quantity demanded of good X

p_y stands for the original price of good Y

Δp_y stands for a small change in the price of Y

There are two types of related goods :

(*i*) Substitutes

(*ii*) Complementaries

Cross Elasticity of Substitutes

In case of substitutes, the cross elasticity is **positive** and large. The higher the coefficient e_c, the better substitutes the good are. If the price of butter rises, it will lead to increase in the demand for Jam, similarly a fall in the price of butter will cause a decrease in the demand for Jam.

If a change in the price of good x leads to more than proportionate change in the demand for good y, the cross elasticity is high ($e_c > 1$). In such case goods are **close substitutes.**

If cross elasticity is less than unity ($e_c < 1$), it means that goods x and y are **poor substitutes** for each other.

In case of the two goods are **perfect substitutes,** the cross elasticity of demand will be infinite ($e_c = \infty$). Hence the cross elasticity of demand for substitutes varies between zero and infinity.

Cross Elasticity of Complementary Goods

If two goods are complementary (jointly demanded), rise in the price of one leads to a fall in the demand for the other. Rise in the prices of cars will bring a fall in their demand together with the demand for petrol. Similarly, a fall in the prices of cars will raise the demand for petrol. Since the price and demand vary in the opposite direction, the cross elasticity of demand in **negative.**

Income Elasticity

The responsiveness of demand to changes in income is termed **income elasticity of demand.** It shows how the quantity demanded will change when the income of the purchaser changes, the price of the commodity remaining the same, it may be defined thus : The Income Elasticity of demand for a good is the ratio of the percentage change in the amount spent on the commodity to a percentage change in the consumer's income price of commodity remaining constant. Thus,

Income Elasticity

$$= \frac{\text{Percentage change in quantity demanded}}{\text{Percentage change in income}}$$

Let y stand for an initial income, Δy for a small change in income, q for the initial quantity purchased, Δq for a change in quantity purchased as a result of a change in income and e_i for income elasticity of demand.

$$\text{Then } e_i = \frac{\Delta q / q}{\Delta y / y} = \frac{\Delta q}{\Delta y} \times \frac{y}{q}$$

We can also express the income elasticity in terms of changes in expenditure made on the good rather than the change in quantity purchased of the good as a result of a change in income. It should be noted that expenditure is equal to the quantity purchased of the good multiplied by the price of the good. If q is the quantity purchased of the good and p the price of the good, then expenditure made on the good is equal to qp.

As defined above, $e_i = \frac{\Delta q}{q} \times \frac{y}{\Delta y}$

Multiplying the numerator and denominator by p, we get $e_i = \frac{\Delta q . p}{q . p} \times \frac{y}{\Delta y}$

Now, as explained above, qp is the expenditure made on the good and Δqp is the change in expenditure made as a result of change in income. Let X-stand for the expenditure made on the good. Then the above equation will income

$$e_i = \frac{\Delta x}{x} \times \frac{y}{\Delta y}$$

$$\text{or} \quad e_i = \frac{y . \Delta x}{x . \Delta y}$$

Thus, Income elasticity

$$= \frac{\text{income} \times \text{Change in expenditure}}{\text{expenditure} \times \text{Change in income}}$$

For most goods, increase in income lead to increases in demand, and income elasticity will be **positive.** For inferior goods, where a rise in income leads consumers to demand less of the commodity, income elasticity will be negative.

Income Elasticity and Proportion of Income Spent

There is a useful relationship between income elasticity for a good and proportion of income spent on it. The relationship between the two is described in the following three propositions :

1. If proportion of income spent on the good remains the same as income increases, then income elasticity for the good is equal to one ($e_i = 1$).
2. If proportion of income spent on the good increase as income increases, then the income elasticity for the good is greater than one ($e_i > 1$).
3. If proportion of income spent on the good decreases as income rises, then income elasticity for the good is less than one ($e_i < 1$).

Income Elasticity : Measures and Meaning

Numerical Value of Income Elasticity	Verbal description
• Negative	Demand for the commodity falls as income rises
• Zero	Demand for the commodity does not change as income changes
• Greater than Zero but less than one	Demand for the commodity rises less than in proportion to the rise in income
• Unity	Demand for the commodity rises in the same proportion as the rise in income
• Greater than Unity	Demand for the commodity rises more than in proportion to the rise in income

Factors Affecting Price Elasticity of Demand

Elasticity of demand for any good is determined or influenced by a number of factors which are discussed as under.

1. **Nature of the Commodity :** The elasticity of demand for any commodity depends upon the category to which it belongs, *i.e.*, whether it is a necessity, comforts or luxury. The demand for necessaries of life or conventional necessaries is generally **less elastic.** The demand for necessaries of efficiency and for comforts is **moderately elastic** because with the rise or fall in their prices, the demand for them decreases or increases moderately. On the other hand, the demand for **luxuries** is **more elastic** because with a small change in their prices there is a large change in their demand.
2. **Existence of Substitutes :** For commodities having substitutes, the demand is elastic, *e.g.*, tea and coffee. If the price of any one of them falls, it will be purchased in larger quantities. If the price rise, demand for it will contract, and its substitutes will be purchased instead. There is, therefore, greater extension or contraction of demand for such commodities when their prices change. Demand for them is elastic.
3. **Several Uses :** The demand for a commodity having several uses is **more elastic.** With a fall in price such a commodity tends to be put to less urgent uses. Thus its demand extends, and **vice-versa.** If a commodity has only one use, a change in price of the commodity will in fluence its one use only. Even if its price falls considerably, it cannot be put to any other use. Hence the demand is in elastic. But it is possible to use it for a number of purposes, the demand will be obviously elastic.
4. **Deferred Consumption :** Commodities whose consumption can be deferred have an elastic demand. This is the case with durable consumer goods, like cloth, bicycle, fan, etc. If the price of any of these articles rises, people will postpone their consumption. As a result their demand will decrease, and **vice-versa.**
5. **Habits :** People who are habituated to the consumption of a particular commodity, like coffee, tea or cigarettee of a particular brand, the demand for it will be **inelastic.**
6. **Income Groups :** The elasticity of demand also depends on the income group to which a person belongs. Persons who belong to the higher income group, their demand for commodity is **less elastic.** On the other hand, the demand of persons in lower income groups is generally **elastic.**
7. **Proportion of Income Spent :** If the consumer spends a small proportion of his income on a commodity at a time, the demand for that commodity is less elastic, but commodities which entail a large proportion of the income of the consumer, the demand for them is more elastic.
8. **Level of Prices :** The level of prices also influences the elasticity of demand for

commodities. When the price level is high, the demand for commodities is **elastic,** and when the price level is low, the demand is less elastic.

9. Time Factor : Time factor plays on important role in influencing the elasticity of demand for commodities. The shorter the time in which the consumer buys a commodity, the lesser will be the elasticity of demand for that product. On the other hand, the longer the time which the consumer takes in buying a commodity, the higher will be the elasticity of demand for that product.

Conclusion : From the above, it will be clear that there is no hard and fast rule to determine whether the demand for any commodity is elastic or inelastic. This will, in fact, depend on several factors connected with that commodity and with the consumer. However, broadly speaking, we can say that the elasticity of demand for any commodity in relation to a certain class of consumers will depend on the availability of its substitutes or the nature of the commodity whether it is a necessary or a luxury.

Elasticity of Supply

Elasticity of supply refers to the sensitiveness or **responsiveness** of the supply to changes in price. In other words, the elasticity of supply is defined as the percentage change in quantity supplied divided by the percentage change in price, and it is a measure of the degree to which the quantity supplied responds to price changes. Thus,

$$\text{Elasticity of Supply} = \frac{\text{Percentage change in quantity supplied}}{\text{Percentage change in price}}$$

Figure 8 illustrator three cases of supply elasticity. The case of **zero supply elasticity** is one in which the quantity supplied does not change as price changes. This would be the case, for example, if suppliers persisted in producing a given quantity, q_1 in Figure 8 *(i)*, and dumping it on the marker for whatever it would bring.

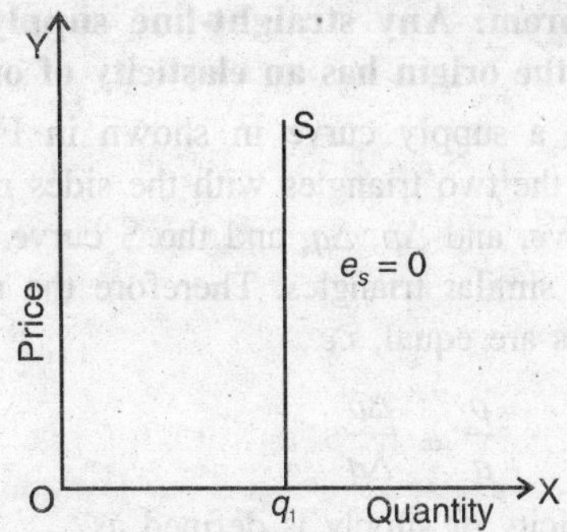

Fig. 8*(i)* *Supply Curve of Zero elasticity*

Infinite supply elasticity is illustrated in Figure 8*(ii)*. The supply elasticity is infinite at the price p_1, because nothing at all is supplied at lower price, but a small increase in price to p_1 causes supply to rise from zero to an indefinitely large amount, indicating that producers would supply any amount demanded at that price.

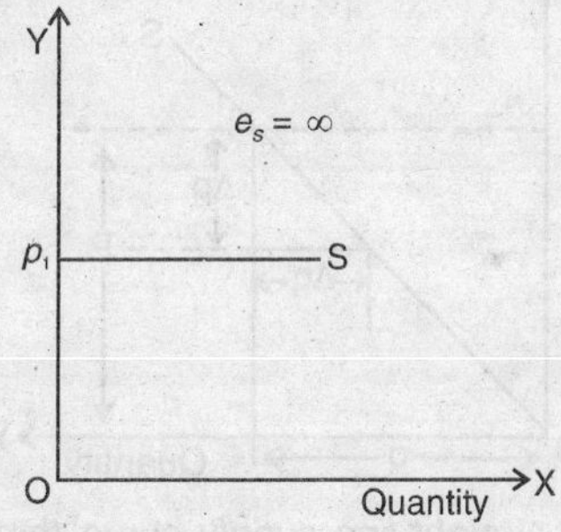

Fig. 8*(ii)* *Supply curve in infinite elasticity*

The case of **unit elasticity of supply** is illustrated in Figure 8*(iii)*. Any straight-line supply curve drawn through the origin has, infact, an elasticity of unity.

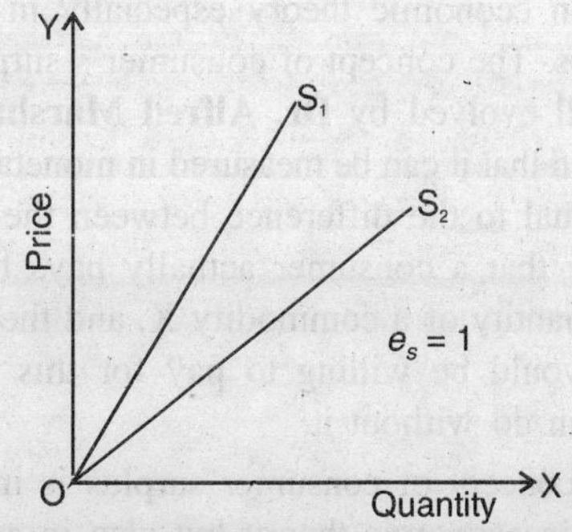

Fig. 8*(iii)* *Supply curve in unit elasticity*

Theorem: Any straight-line supply curve through the origin has an elasticity of one.

Such a supply curve in shown in Figure 9. Consider the two triangles with the sides p, q, and the S curve, and Δp, Δq, and the S curve. Clearly these are similar triangles. Therefore the ratios of their sides are equal, *i.e.*,

$$\frac{p}{q} = \frac{\Delta p}{\Delta q} \qquad ...(1)$$

Elasticity of supply is defined as

$$e_s = \frac{\Delta q}{\Delta p}.\frac{p}{q} \qquad ...(2)$$

which, by substitution from (1), gives

$$e_s = \frac{q}{p}.\frac{p}{q} = 1$$

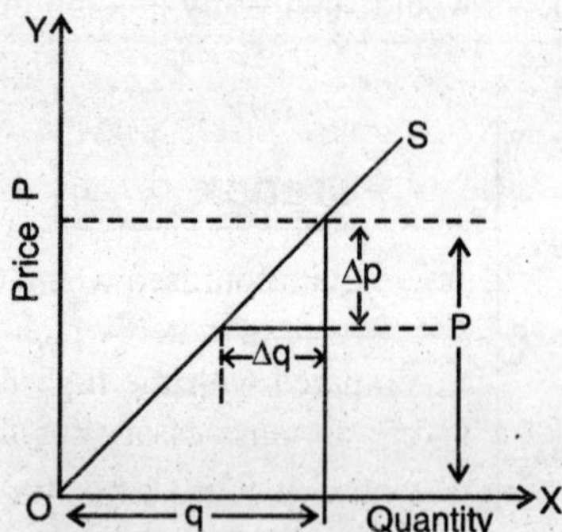

Fig. 9: *A straight-line supply curve through the origin has an elasticity of one.*

Consumer's Surplus

Concept of consumer's surplus is a very important concept in economic theory especially in welfare economics. The concept of consumer's surplus was first of all evolved by **Dr. Alfred Marshall,** who maintained that it can be measured in monetary units, and is equal to the difference between the amount of money that a consumer actually pays to buy a certain quantity of a commodity X, and the amount that he would be willing to pay for this quantity rather than do without it.

The concept of consumer surplus is important not only in economic theory but also in economic policies, such as taxation by the Government and price policy pursued by the monopolistic seller of a product. The essence of the concept of consumer's surplus is that a consumer derives extra satisfaction from the purchases he daily makes over the price he actually pays for them. **Marshall** defines the consumer's surplus in the following words :

"Excess of the price which a consumer would be willing to pay, rather than go without a thing over that which he actually does pay, is the economic measure of this surplus satisfaction ... it may be called consumer's surplus."

The amount of money which a person is prepared to pay for a good indicates the amount of utility he derives from that good, the greater the amount of money he is willing to pay, the greater the satisfaction or utility he will obtain from it. Therefore, the marginal utility of a unit of a good determines the price a consumer will be prepared to pay for that unit. The total utility which a person will get from a good will be given by sum of marginal utilities (ΣMU) of the units of the good purchased and the total price which he will actually pay is equal to the price per unit multiplied by the number of units purchased. Thus,

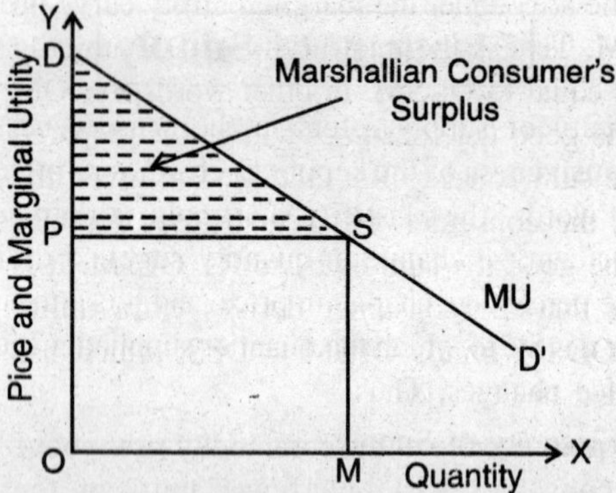

Fig. 10: *Marshall's Measure of Consumer's Surplus*

Consumer's Surplus = What a consumer is prepared to pay minus what he actually pays.

= Σ MU – (Price × Number of units purchased)

The measurement of consumer's surplus is illustrated in Fig. 10 in which along the X-axis the amount of the commodity has been measured and on the Y-axis the marginal utility and the price of the commodity are measured. MU is the marginal utility curve which is sloping downward, indicating that as the consumer buys more units of the commodity, marginal utility of it falls. As said above, marginal utility shows the price which a person will be willing to pay for the different units rather than go without them.

If OP is the price that prevails in the market, then the consumer will be in equilibrium when he buys OM units of the commodity, since at OM units, marginal utility is equal to the given price OP. **The Mth unit of the commodity does not yield any consumer's surplus to the consumer. Since this is the last unit purchased and for this price paid is equal to the marginal utility which indicates the price he will be prepared to pay rather than go without it.** But for the intra marginal units *i.e.,* units before Mth marginal utility is greater than the price and therefore, these units yield consumer's surplus to the consumer. The total utility of a certain quantity of a commodity to consumer can be known by summing up the marginal utilities of the various units purchased.

In Figure 10, the total utility derived by the consumer from OM units of the commodity will be equal to the area under the marginal utility curve up to point M. That is the total utility of DM units in Fig. 10 is equal to ODSM. In other words, for OM units of the good the consumer will be the prepared to pay the sum equal to Rs. ODSM. But given the price OP, the consumer will actually pay for OM units of the good the sum equal to Rs. OPSM. It is thus clear that the consumer derives extra utility equal to ODSM minus OPSM = DPS, which has been shaded in Fig. 10.

If the market price of the commodity rises above OP, the consumer will buy fewer units of the commodity than OM. As a result, consumer's surplus obtained by him from his purchase will decline. On the other hand, if the price falls below OP, the consumer will be in equilibrium when he is purchasing more units of the commodity than OM. As a result of this, the consumer's surplus will increase. Thus, given the marginal utility curve of the consumer, the higher the price, the smaller the consumer's surplus and the lower the price, the greater the consumer's surplus.

It is worth noting here that in our analysis of consumer's surplus, we have assumed that perfect competition prevails in the market so that the consumer faces a given price, whatever the amount of the commodity he purchases. But if the seller of a commodity discriminates the prices and charges different prices for the different units of the good, some units at a higher price and some at a lower price, then in this case consumer's surplus will be smaller. Thus, when the seller makes price discrimination and sells different units of a good at different prices, the consumer will obtain smaller amount of consumer's surplus than under perfect competition. If the seller indulges in **perfect price discrimination,** that is, if he changes price for each unit of the commodity equal to what any consumer will be prepared to pay for it, then in that case no consumer's surplus will accrue to the consumer.

A Note on the Diamond-Water Paradox

Classical economists were quite confused when they were asked about the low price of water, which was so necessary for life, compared with the high price of diamonds, which were so unnecessary for life.

As Figure 11 indicates, it is possible for the marginal utility of diamonds to be relatively high since diamonds are quite scarce, while the marginal utility of water is relatively low since water is quite plentiful, if we view quantities D_1 and W_1, respectively.

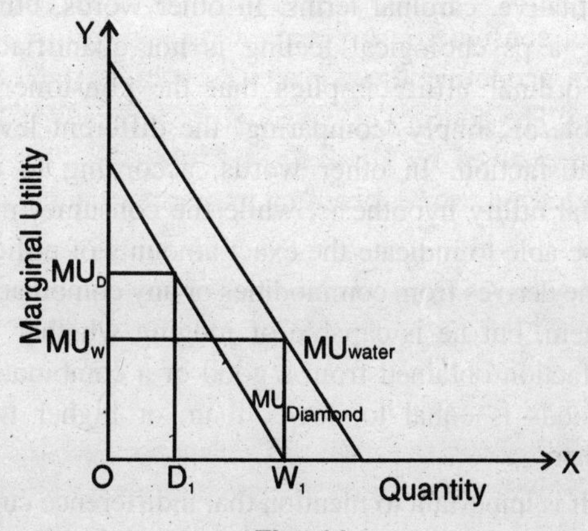

Fig. 11

As a result our marginal utility theory tells us that the price of diamonds will be quite high, while the price of water will be quite low. Nevertheless, the total utility of water can be much greater than the total utility of diamonds. The total utility of water is the area under the marginal utility curve for water upto the level of consumption W_1. That is to say, total utility is the marginal utility of the first unit plus the marginal utility of the second unit, and so on. Since the total utility of diamonds is the area under the marginal utility curve for diamonds up to consumption level D_1, it nicely follows that the total utility derived from water can be greater than the total utility derived from diamonds.

We may conclude that the more there is of a commodity, the lower is the relative desirability of the last unit despite the fact that total utility increases. Thus, a great quantity of water has a low price.

The Indifference Curve Theory

The indifference curve is a geometrical device that has been used to replace the neo-classical cardinal utility concept. **Hicks** presented its comprehensive version in his **value and capital** in 1939 and its major revision in his A Revision of Demand Theory in 1956. The fundamental approach of indifference curve analysis is that it has abandoned the concept of cardinal utility and instead has adopted the concept of **ordinal utility.** According to the supporters of the indifference curves theory, utility is a psychic entity and it cannot therefore be measured in quantitative, cardinal terms. In other words, utility being a psychological feeling is not quantifiable. The ordinal utility implies that the consumer is capable of simply 'comparing' the different levels of satisfaction. In other words, according to the ordinal utility hypothesis, while the consumer may not be able to indicate the exact amounts of utilities that he derives from commodities or any combination of them, but he is capable of judging whether the satisfaction obtained from a good or a combination of goods is equal to, lower than, or higher than another.

It is important to mention that indifference curve analysis of demand is based upon the **weak-ordering** form of preference hypothesis. The weak ordering implies that there is possibility of the consumer being indifferent between two combinations. Thus, the weak ordering recognizes the relation of preference as well as of indifference. The consumer may prefer A to B or B to A or he may be indifferent between A and B. On the contrary, **strong ordering** implies that there can be only the relation of preference, A is preferred to B, or B is preferred to A, the possibility of consumer's indifference between A and B ruled out. Thus the strong-ordering admits only the relation of preference.

Indifference Curves

An indifference curve is the locus of points-particular combinations or bundles of goods-which yields the same utility (level of satisfaction) to the consumer, so that he is indifferent as to the particular combination he consumes. In other words, all combinations of the goods lying on a consumer's indifference curve are equally desirable to or equally preferred by him. To understand indifference curves, it is better to start with indifference schedules.

TABLE 1.2:
Indifference Schedule

Combination	*Good x*	*Good y*
1	1	18
2	2	13
3	3	9
4	4	6
5	5	4
6	6	3

The indifference schedule shows the various combinations of the two commodities such that the consumer is indifferent to those combinations. In table 1.2 indifference schedules is given. In this schedule the amount of goods x and y in each combination are so arranged that the consumer is indifferent among the combinations. In the schedule, the consumer has to start with 1 unit of x and 18 units of y. Now, the consumer is asked to tell how much of good y he will be willing to give up for the gain of additional unit of x so that his level of satisfaction remains the same. If the gain of one unit of x compensates him fully for the loss of 5 units of y, then the next combination of 2 units of x and 13 units of y $(2x + 13y)$ will give him as much satisfaction as the initial combination $(1x + 12y)$. Similarly, by asking the consumer further how much of y he will be prepared to forego for successive increments in his stock of x so that his level of satisfaction remains unaltered, we get combinations $3x + 9y$, $4x + 6y$, $5x + 4x$ and $6x + 3y$, each of which provides the same satisfaction as combination $1x + 18y$ or $2x + 13y$.

Now, we can convert the indifference schedule into indifference curve by plotting the various combinations on a graph paper. In Figure 12 an indifference curve IC is drawn by plotting the various combination in the indifference schedule. Like in an indifference schedule, combinations lying on an indifference curve will be equally desirable to the consumer, that is, will give him the same satisfaction. The smoothness and continuity of an indifference curve means that goods in question are assumed to be **perfectly divisible.**

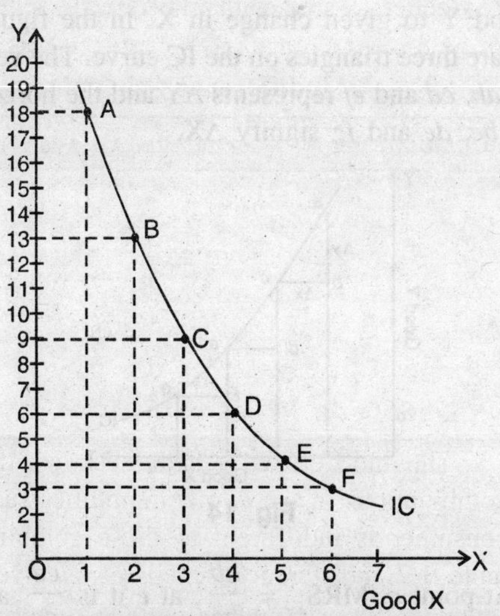

Fig. 12

An indifference map shows all the indifference curves which rank the preferences of the consumer combinations of goods situated on an indifference curve yield the same utility, Combinations of goods lying on a higher indifference curve yield higher level of satisfaction and are preferred. Combinations of goods on a lower indifference curve yield a lower utility. In Figure 13 an indifference map of a consumer is shown which consists of five indifference curves.

The consumer regards all combinations on the indifference curve I as giving him equal satisfaction. Similarly all the combinations lying on indifference curve II provide the same satisfaction but the level of satisfaction on indifference curve II will be greater than the level of satisfaction on indifference curve I. Likewise, all the higher indifference curves, II, III, IV and V represent progressively higher and higher levels of satisfaction. It is important to remember that while the consumer will prefer any combination on a higher indifference curve to any combination on a lower indifference curve, but by **how much he prefers** one combination to another cannot be said.

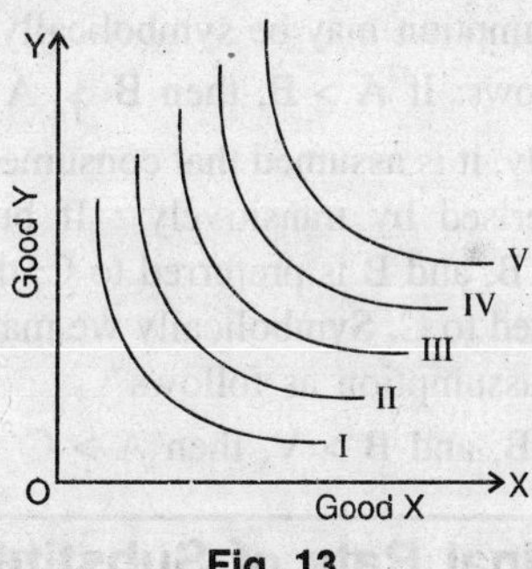

Fig. 13

An indifference map of a consumer represents his tastes for the two goods and his preferences as between different combinations of them. In other words, an indifference map portrays consumer's scale of preferences.

Assumptions

The indifference curve analysis retains some of the assumptions of the cardinal theory, rejects others and formulates its own. The assumptions of the ordinal theory are the following :

1. **Rationality :** The consumer is assumed to be rational-he aims at the maximisation of his utility, given his income and market prices. It is assumed he has full knowledge of all relevant information.

2. **Utility is Ordinal :** It is taken as axiomatically true that the consumer can rank his preferences according to the satisfaction of each combinations. He need not know precisely the amount of satisfaction.
3. **Diminishing Marginal Rate of Substitution :** The indifference-curve theory is based on the axiom of diminishing marginal rate of substitution.
4. The total utility of the consumer depends on the quantities of the commodities consumed.

$$U = f(q_1, q_2, \dots q_n)$$

5. **Consistency and Transitivity of Choice :** It is assumed that the consumer is consistent in his choice, that is, if in one period he chooses bundle A over B, he will not choose B over A in another period if both bundles are available to him. The consistency assumption may be symbolically written as follows: If A > B, then B $\ngtr$ A

Similarly, it is assumed that consumer's choices are characterised by transitively : If bundle A is preferred to B, and B is preferred to C, then bundle A, is preferred to C. Symbolically we may write the transitivity assumption as follows :

If A > B, and B > V, then A > C

Marginal Rate of Substitution

The concept of marginal rate of substitution is an important tool of indifference curve analysis of demand. Marginal rate of substitution of x for y (MRS_{xy}) represents the amount of y which the consumer has to give up for the gain of one additional unit of x so that his level of satisfaction remains the same.

TABLE 1.3

Combination	*Good x*	*Good y*	*MRS_{xy}*
A	1	12	—
B	2	8	4 : 1
C	3	5	3 : 1
D	4	3	2 : 1
E	5	2	1 : 1

In table 1.3, when the consumer moves from combination A to combination B on his indifference schedule he forgoes 4 units of y for the additional one unit gain in *x*. Hence, the marginal rate of substitution of *x* for *y* is 4. Likewise, when the consumer moves from B to C, and C to D, and then from D to E in his indifference schedule, the marginal rate of substitution of *x* for *y* is 3, 2, and 1 respectively. As the consumer proceeds to have additional units of *x*, he is willing to give away less and less units of *y* so that the MRS_{xy} falls from 4 : 1 to 1 : 1 in the Eth combination.

The negative of the slope of an indifference curve at any one point is called the marginal rate of substitution of the two commodities (MRS_{xy}). In other words, the MRS_{xy} is in fact the slope of the curve at a point on the indifference curve. Thus

$$\left[\begin{array}{c}\text{Slopeof} \\ \text{indifference} \\ \text{curve}\end{array}\right] = -\frac{\Delta Y}{\Delta X} = MRS_{xy}$$

It means that the MRS_{xy} is the ratio of change in good Y to given change in X. In the figure 14 there are three triangles on the IC curve. The vertical sides *ab*, *cd* and *ef* represents ΔY and the horizontal sides *bc*, *de* and *fg* signify ΔX.

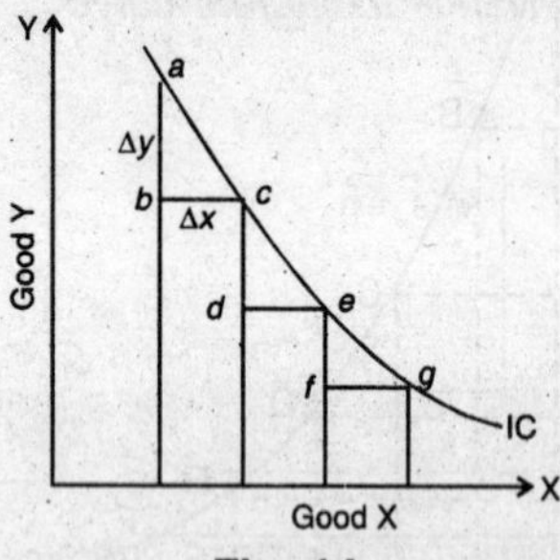

Fig. 14

At point *c*, $MRS_{xy} = \frac{ab}{bc}$, at *e* it is $\frac{cd}{de}$ and at point *g*, MRS_{xy} is equal to $\frac{ef}{fg}$. This also shows that as the consumer moves downwards along the curve, he possesses additional units of *x*, and gives up lesser and lesser units of *y*, *i.e.*, the MRS_{xy} diminishes.

Note

- If the MRS_{xy} is diminishing, the indifference curve must be **convex** to the origin.
- If MRS_{xy} is constant, the indifference curve will be **straight line** sloping downwards to the right.
- If MRS_{xy} is increasing, the indifference curve will be **concave** to the origin.
- In the case of perfect complementaries the MRS_{xy} is zero and the indifference curve will be L shaped.

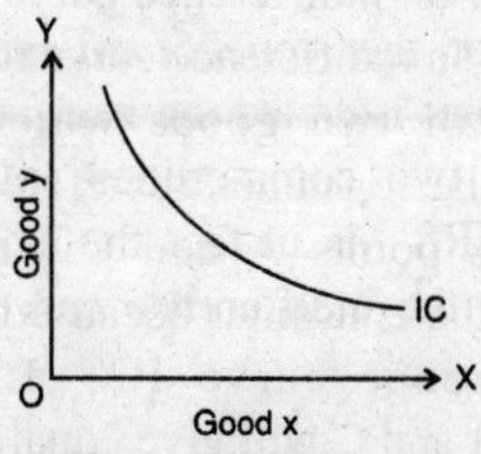

Fig. *Convex indifference curve*

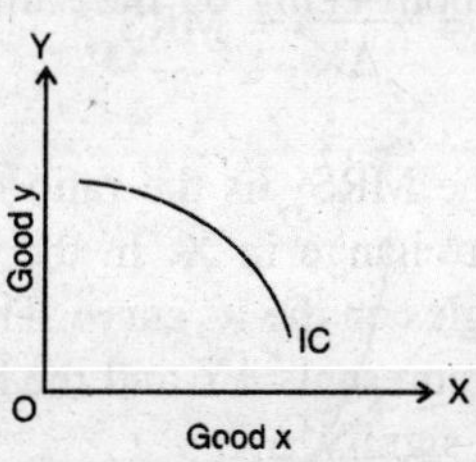

Fig. *Convance indifferent curve*

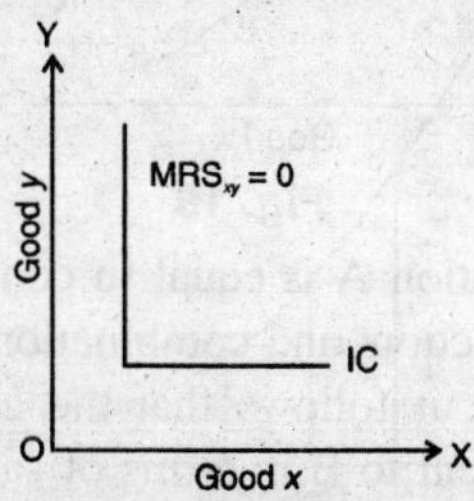

Fig. *L-shaped indifference curve*

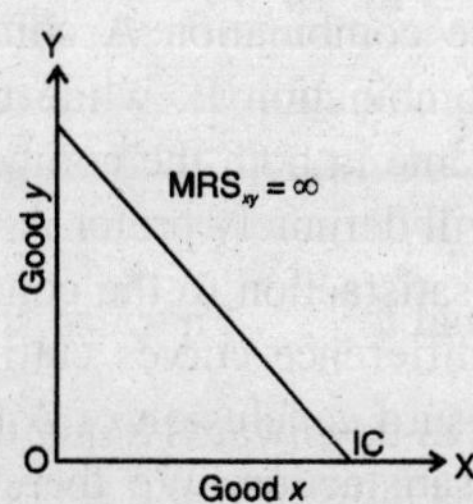

Fig. *Straight line indifference curve*

The Relationship between Marginal Rate of substitution and Marginal Utilities

The slope of a indifference curve at any point is measured by the slope of the tangent at that point. The equation of a tangent is given by the total derivative or total differential, which shows the total change of the function as all its determinants change.

The total utility function in the case of two commodities X and Y is

$$U = f(X, Y)$$

The equation of an indifference curve is

$$U = f(x, y) = K$$

where K is constant.

The total differential of the utility function is

$$\Delta V = \frac{\Delta U}{\Delta Y}\Delta Y + \frac{\Delta U}{\Delta X}\Delta X$$

$$= (MU_y)\ \Delta Y + (MU_x)\ \Delta X$$

It shows that total change in utility as the quantities of both commodities change. The total change in U caused by changes in Y and X is (approximately) equal to the change in Y multiplied by its marginal utility, plus the change in X multiplied by its marginal utility.

Along any particular indifference curve the total differential is by definition equal to zero. Thus for any indifference curve

$$\Delta U = (MU_y)\ \Delta Y + (MU_x)\Delta X$$

$$= 0$$

Rearranging we obtain

$$\text{either} \quad -\frac{\Delta Y}{\Delta X} = \frac{MU_x}{MU_y} = MRS_{x,y}$$

$$\text{or} \quad \frac{\Delta X}{\Delta Y} = \frac{MU_y}{MU_x} = MRS_{y,x}$$

Thus the marginal rate of substitution between two goods is equal to the ratio between the marginal utilities of two goods.

Properties of Indifference Curves

From the assumptions described above the following properties of indifference curves can be deduced.

Indifference Curves slope downward to the right

This property implies that an indifference curve has a negative slope. This means that when the amount of one good in the combination is increased, the amount of the other good is reduced.

Indifference Curves are Convex to the Origin

Another important property of indifference curves is that they are usually convex to the origin. This property of indifference curves based on the marginal rate of substitution of X for Y (MRS_{xy}) diminishes as more and more of X is substituted for Y. Only a convex indifference curve can mean a diminishing marginal rate of substitution of X for Y. If the indifference curve is concave to the origin, it will imply that the marginal rate of substitution of X for Y increases as more and more of X is substituted of Y, as shown in Figure 17.

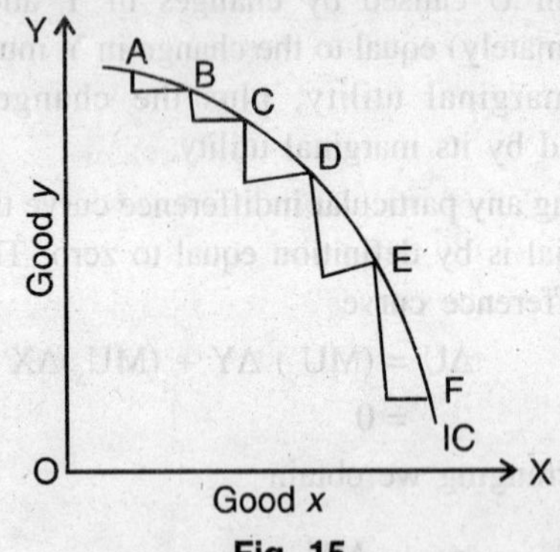

Fig. 15

It will be clear from this fig. that as more and more of x is acquired, for each extra unit of x the consumer is willing to part with more and more of y, that is , MRS_{xy} increases as more and more of x is substituted for y.

The degree of convexity of an indifference curve depends upon the rate of fall in the marginal rate of substitution of x for y.

Indifference Curves cannot Intersect each other

Third important property of indifference curves is that they cannot intersect each other. In other words, only one indifference curve will pass through a point in the indifference map. This property can be easily proved by first making the two indifference curves cut each other and then showing the absurdity or self-contradictory result it leads to. In Figure 16 two indifference curves are shown cutting each other at point C. Now take point A on indifference curve IC_2 and point B on indifference curve IC_1 vertically below A. Since an indifference curve represents those combinations of two goods which give equal satisfaction to the consumer, therefore combinations represented by points A and C will give equal satisfaction to the consumer because both lie on the same indifference curve IC_2. Likewise, the combinations B and C will give equal satisfaction to the consumer, both being on the same indifference curve IC_1.

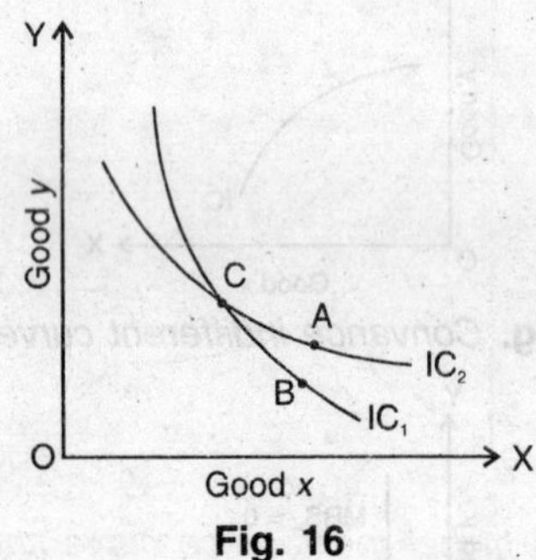

Fig. 16

If combination A is equal to combination C in terms of satisfaction, and combination B is equal to combination C, it follows that the combination A will be equivalent to B in terms of satisfaction. But a glance at Fig. 16 will show that this is absurd conclusion since combination A contains more of good Y then combination B, while the amount of good X is the same in both the combinations. Thus the consumer will definitely prefer A to B, that is A will give more satisfaction to the consumer than B. But the two indifference curves cutting each other lead us to an absurd conclusion of A being equal to B in terms of satisfaction. We therefore conclude that indifference curves cannot cut each other.

Indifference Curves are not necessarily parallel to each other

Though they are falling, negatively inclined to the right, yet the rate of fall will not be the same for all indifference curves. In other words, the diminishing marginal rate of substitution between the two goods is essentially not the same in the case of all indifference schedules. The two curves IC_1 and IC_2 shown in Figure 17 are not parallel to each other.

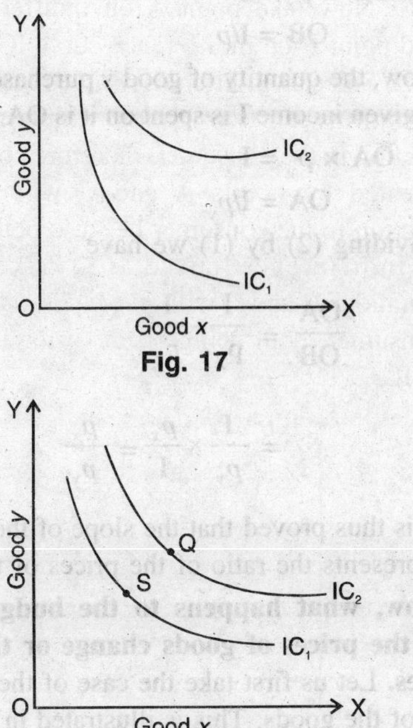

Fig. 17

Fig. 18: *A higher indifference curve shows higher level of satisfaction*

A Higher Indifference Curve represents Higher Level of Satisfaction than the Lower Indifference Curve

Another property of indifference curve is that a higher indifference curve will represent a higher level of satisfaction than a lower indifference curve. In other words, the combinations which lie on a higher indifference which lie on a lower indifference curve. Consider indifference curves IC_2 and IC_1 in Figure 18. IC_2 is a higher indifference curve than IC_1. Combination Q has been taken on a higher indifference curve IC_2 and combination S on a lower indifference curve IC_1.

Combination Q on the higher indifference curve IC_2 will give the consumer more satisfaction than combination S on the lower indifference curve IC_1 because the combination Q contains more of both goods X and Y than the combination S. Hence the consumer must prefer Q to S. And by transitivity, he will prefer any other combination on IC_2 to any combination on IC_1. We, therefore, conclude that a higher indifference curve represents the higher level of satisfaction and combinations on it will be preferred to the combinations on a lower indifference curve.

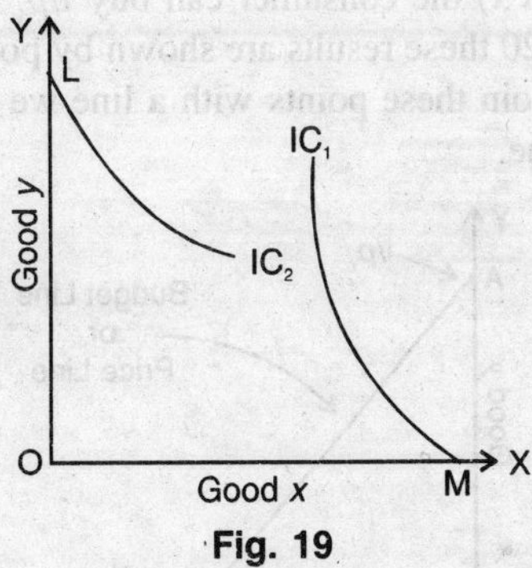

Fig. 19

6. An Indifference Curve cannot Touch either Axis

If it touch *x*-axis as IC_1 in figure 19 at M, the consumer will be having OM quantity of good *x* and none of *y*. Similarly, If an indifference curve IC_2 touches the *y*-axis at L the consumer will have only OL of *y* good and no amount of *x*.

Such curves are in contradiction to the assumption that the consumer buys two goods in combinations.

Price Line or Budget Line

Understanding of the concept of **price line** or **budget line** is essential for understanding the theory of consumer's equilibrium. The consumer has a given income which sets limits to his maximising behaviour. Income acts as a constraint in the attempt for maximising utility. The income constraints, in the case of two commodities, may be written

$$I = p_x q_x + p_y q_y \qquad ...(1)$$

We may present the income constraint graphically by the budget line, whose equation is derived from expression (1), by solving for q_y :

$$q_y = \frac{1}{p_y}\text{I} - \frac{p_x}{p_y}q_x$$

Assigning successive values to q_x (given the income, I and the commodity prices, p_x and p_y), we may find the corresponding values of q_y. Thus if $q_x = 0$ (that is, if the consumer spends all his income on y) the consumer can buy I/p_y units of Y. Similarly, if $q_y = 0$ (that is, if the consumer spends all his income an *x*) the consumer can buy I/p_x units of *x*. In figure 20 these results are shown by points A and B. If we join these points with a line we obtain the budget line.

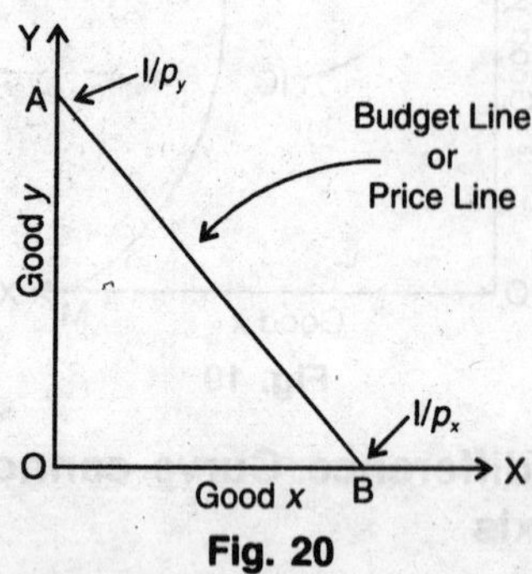

Fig. 20

Consumer can but any combination that lies on the budget line AB with his given money income and given prices of the goods. It should be carefully noted that any combination of good which lies above and outside the given budget line, AB, will be beyond the reach of the consumer. But any combination lying within the price line or budget line, AB, will be well within the reach of the consumer, but if he buys any such combination he will not be spending all his income.

Thus, with the assumption that whole of the given income is spent on the given goods and at given prices of them, the consumer has to choose among from all those combinations which line on the price line or budget line.

Slope of the Budget Line

The slope of the budget line is equal to the ratio of the prices of two goods. This can be proved with the aid of Fig. 20. Suppose the given income of the consumer is I, the given prices of goods *x* and *y* are p_x and p_y respectively. The slope of the price line AB is $\frac{OA}{OB}$. We intend to prove that the slope $\frac{OA}{OB}$ is equal to the ratio of the price of goods *x* and *y*.

The quantity of good *x* purchased if whole of the given income I is spent on it is OB. Therefore

$$OB \times p_x = I$$

$$OB = I/p_x \quad ...(1)$$

Now, the quantity of good *y* purchased if whole of the given income I is spent on it is OA. Therefore,

$$OA \times p_y = I$$

$$OA = I/p_y \quad ...(2)$$

Dividing (2) by (1) we have :

$$\frac{OA}{OB} = \frac{I}{p_y} \div \frac{I}{p_x}$$

$$= \frac{I}{p_y} \times \frac{p_x}{I} = \frac{p_x}{p_y}$$

It is thus proved that the slope of the price line AB represents the ratio of the prices of two goods.

Now, what happens to the budget line. If either the prices of goods change or the income changes. Let us first take the case of the change in prices of the goods. This is illustrated in Figure 21. Suppose the budget line in the beginning is PL, given certain prices of the good *x* and *y* and a certain income. Suppose the price of *x* falls, the price of *y* and income remaining unchanged. Now with a lower price of *x* the consumer will be able to purchase more quantity of *x* than before with his given income. Let at the lower price of *x*, the given income purchases OL' of X which of greater than OL. Since the price of Y remains the same, there can be no change in the quantity purchased of good Y with the same given income and as a result there will be no shift in the point P.

Thus with the fall in the price of good *x*, the consumer's income and the price of Y remaining constant, the budget line will take the new position PL'.

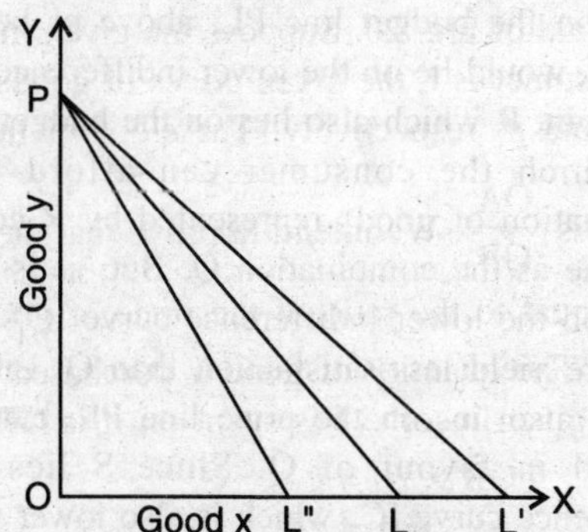

Fig. 21: *Changes in budget line as a result of changes in price of good x*

Now, what will happen to the budget line as the price of good *x* rises, the price of good Y and income remaining unaltered. With higher price of good *x*, the consumer can purchase smaller quantity of X, say OL", than before. Thus with the rise in price of X the budget line will assume the new position PL".

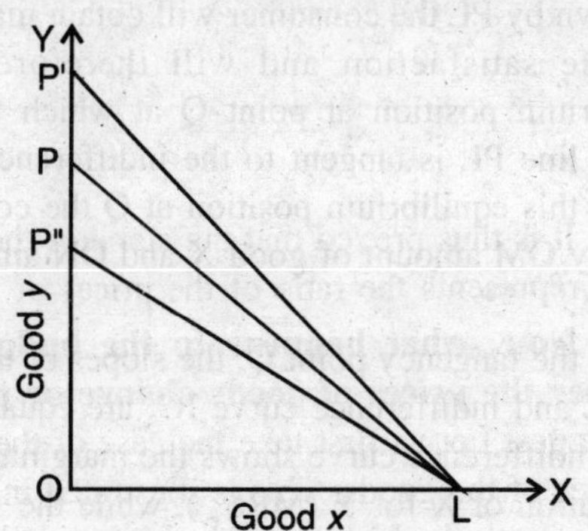

Fig. 22: *Changes in the budget line as a result of changes in price of good Y*

Figure 22 shows the changes in the budget line when the price of good Y falls or rises, with the price of X and income remaining the same.

Now, what happens to the budget line if the income changes, while the prices of goods remain the same. The effect of changes in income on the budget line is shown in Figure 23. Let PL be the initial price line, given certain prices of goods and income. If the consumer's income increases while the prices of both goods X and Y remain unaltered, the price line shifts upward (Say, to P'L') and is parallel to the original price line PL. On the other hand, if the income of the consumer decreases, the prices of both goods X and Y remaining unchanged, the budget line shifts downward (Say, to P"L") but remains parallel to the original price line PL.

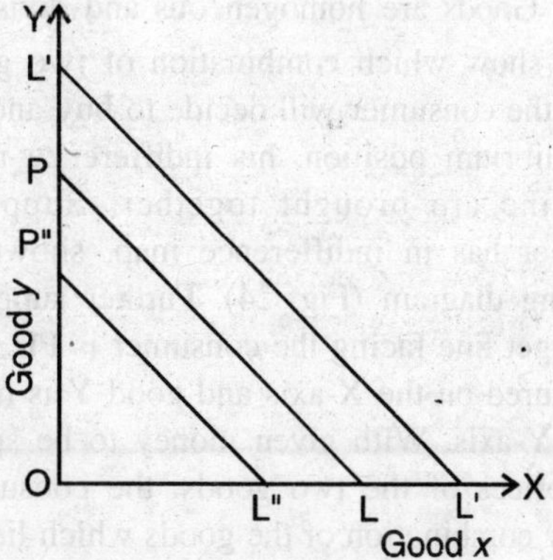

Fig. 23 : *Changes in budget line as a result of changes in income*

It is clear from above that the price line or budget line will change if either the prices of goods change or the income of the consumer changes.

Thus the two determinants of the price line or budget line are :

1. The prices of goods.
2. The consumer's income to be spent on the goods.

Consumer's Equilibrium

A consumer is in equilibrium when given his tastes, and prices of the two goods, he spends a given money income on the purchase of two goods in such a way as to get the maximum satisfaction. In the indifference curve technique the consumer's equilibrium is discussed in respect of the purchases of two goods by the consumer.

The indifference curve analysis of consumer's equilibrium is based on the following assumptions :

1. The consumer has a given indifference map exhibiting his scale of preferences for various combinations of two goods, X and Y.
2. He has a fixed amount of money to spend on the two goods. He has to spend whole of his given money on the two goods.

3. Prices of the goods are given and constant for him. He cannot influence the prices of the goods by buying more or less of them.
4. Goods are homogeneous and divisible.

To show which combination of two goods, X and Y, the consumer will decide to buy and will be in equilibrium position, his indifference map and price line are brought together. Suppose our consumer has in indifference map, shown in the following diagram (Fig. 24). Further suppose that the budget line facing the consumer is PL. Good X is measured on the X-axis and good Y is measured on the Y-axis. With given money to be spent and given prices of the two goods, the consumer can buy any combination of the goods which lies on the price line PL. In order to maximise his satisfaction the consumer will try to reach the highest indifference curve which he could with a given expenditure of money and given prices of the two goods. Budget constraint forces the consumer to remain on the given budget line, that is, to choose any combinations from among only those which lie on the given budget line.

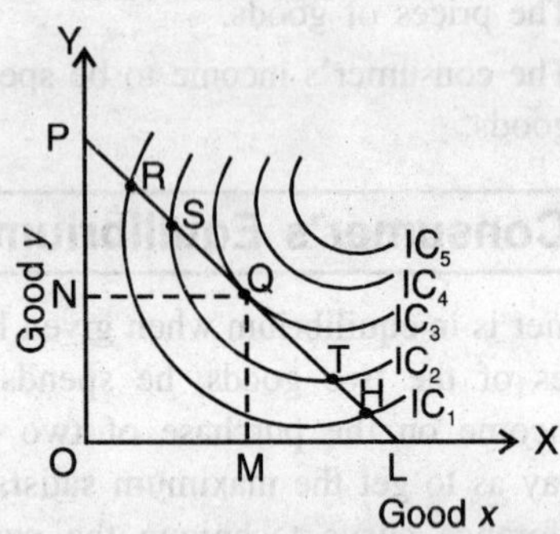

Fig. 24: *Consumer's Equilibrium*

According to the figure 24, the consumer will choose that combination on the price line PL which lies on the highest possible indifference curve. The highest indifference curve to which the consumer can reach is the indifference curve to which the price line PL is tangent. Any other possible combination of the two goods either would lie on a lower indifference curve and thus yield less satisfaction or would be unattainable. In Fig. 24, budget line PL is tangent to indifference curve IC_3 at point Q. Since indifference curves are convex to the origin, all other points on the budget line PL, above or below the point Q, would lie on the lower indifference curves. Take point R which also lies on the budget line PL and which the consumer can afford to buy. Combination of goods represented by R costs him the same as the combination Q. But, as is evident, R lies on the lower indifference curve IC_1 and will therefore yield less satisfaction than Q. Like wise, point S also lies on the price line PL, but will be rejected in favour of Q. Since S lies on the indifference curve IC_2 which is also lower than IC_3 on which Q lies. Similarly, Q will be preferred to all other points on the price line PL which lies below Q, such as T and H. It is thus clear that of all possible combinations lying on PL, combination Q lies on the highest possible indifference curve and yields maximum possible satisfaction.

It is therefore concluded that with the given money expenditure and the given prices of the goods as shown by PL the consumer will obtain maximum possible satisfaction and will therefore be in equilibrium position at point Q at which the rate budget line PL is tangent to the indifference curve IC_3. In this equilibrium position at Q the consumer will buy OM amount of good X and ON amount of good Y.

At the tangency point Q, the slopes of the price line PL and indifference curve IC_3 are equal. Slope of the indifference curve shows the marginal rate of substitution of X for Y (MRS_{xy}), while the slope of the price line indicates the ratio between the price of two goods (p_x/p_y). Thus at the equilibrium point Q,

$$MRS_{xy} = \frac{MU_x}{MU_y} = \frac{P_x}{P_y}$$

This is a necessary but not sufficient condition for equilibrium. The **second condition** is that the indifference curves be convex to the origin, or to put it in another way, the MRS_{xy} must be falling at the point of equilibrium. It will be noticed form Figure 24 that the indifference curve IC_3 is convex to the origin at Q. Thus at point Q both conditions of equilibrium are satisfied. Point Q is the optimum or best choice for the consumer and he will therefore be in stable equilibrium at Q.

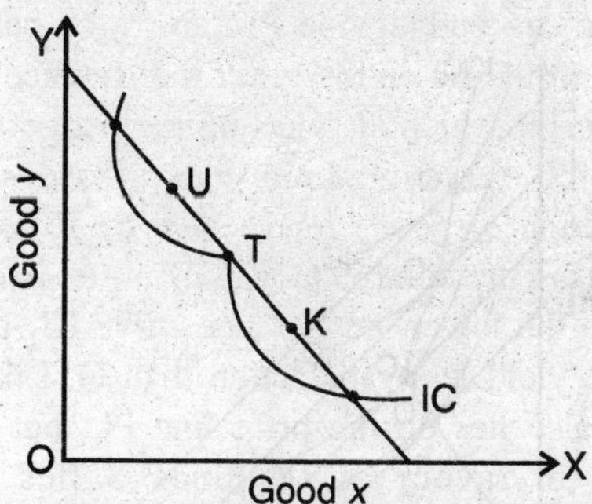

Fig. 25 : *Second order condition for consumer's equilibrium*

But it may happen that while price line is tangent to an indifference curve at a point but the indifference curve may be concave at that point. Take, for instance, Figure 25 where indifference curve IC is concave to the origin around the point T. Price line PL is tangent to the indifference curve IC at point T and MRS_{xy} is equal to the price ratio (p_x/p_y). But T cannot be a position of stable equilibrium because satisfaction would not be maximum there, Indifference curve IC being concave at the tangency point T, there are some points on the given price line PL such as U and K, which will be on indifference curve higher than IC. Thus the consumer by moving along the given price line PL can go to points such as U and K and obtain greater satisfaction than at T. We therefore conclude that for the consumer to be in equilibrium, two conditions are required :

1. A given price line must be tangent to an indifference curve, or marginal rate of substitution of X for Y (MRS_{xy}) must be equal to the price ratio between the two goods (p_x/p_y).

$$MRS_{xy} = \frac{P_x}{P_y} = \frac{MU_x}{MU_y}$$

or. $$\frac{MU_x}{MU_y} = \frac{P_x}{P_y}$$

or, $$\frac{MU_x}{P_x} = \frac{MU_y}{P_y}$$

2. Indifference curve must be convex to the origin at the point of tangency. This condition is fulfilled by the axiom of diminishing MRS_{xy}, which states that the slope of the indifference curve decreases as we move along the curve from the left downwards to the right.

Income Effect

Income effect is the effect on the quantity demanded exclusively as a result of change in money income, all prices remaining constant. It has been shown above how a consumer reaches his equilibrium position with a fixed income and given market prices of the two commodities.

But the question arises what will happen to the consumer's equilibrium and the amounts of the two commodities bought if his income were to change while prices of the commodities remain the same. Obviously, as a result of a change in income, his satisfaction will either increase or diminish, for he has now a larger or smaller income to spend. The result of this type of change is described in technical language as **income effect.**

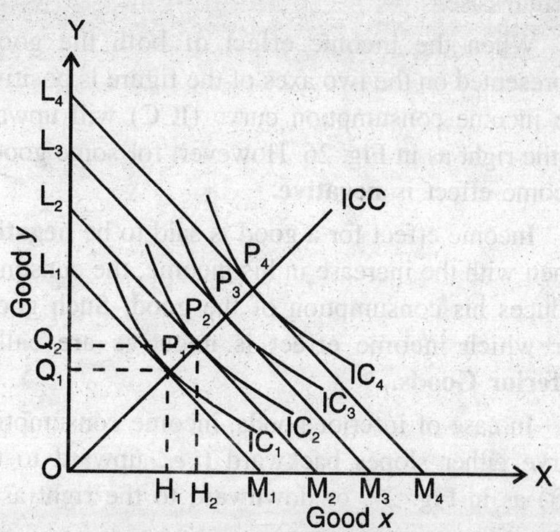

Fig. 26 : *Income Effect*

The income effect has been explained with the help of Figure 26. With Price-line L_1M_1, the consumer is in equilibrium at point P_1. Now suppose the income of the consumer increases so that his new price line is L_2M_2. As a result of this increase in income, the consumer will move to a new equilibrium position, at the point P_2, on a higher indifference curve IC_2 and will be buying OH_2 of commodity X and OQ_2 of commodity Y. Thus, the consumer will get on to a higher level of satisfaction as a result of an increase in his income.

If his income increase still further, so that the new price line becomes L_3M_3, he will be in equilibrium at the point P_3 on an indifference curve IC_3, and so on for further increases in income.

Thus, we get various points of equilibrium such as P_1, P_2, P_3, for different levels of income, prices of the commodities remaining the same. If the points P_1, P_2, P_3, P_4 etc, are joined together by a line passing from the origin, we get, what is called **Income Consumption Curve (ICC).**

Income consumption curve is thus the locus of equilibrium points at various levels of consumer's income. Income consumption curve traces out the income effect on the quantity consumed of the goods.

Income effect can either be **positive** or **negative.** Income effect for good is said to be **positive** when with the increase in income of the consumer, his consumption of the good also increases. This is the normal case.

When the income effect of both the goods represented on the two axes of the figure is positive, the income consumption curve (ICC) will upward to the right as in Fig. 26. However, for some goods, income effect is **negative.**

Income effect for a good is said to be **negative** when with the increase in his income, the consumer reduces his consumption of the good. Such goods for which income effect is negative are called **Inferior Goods.**

In case of inferior goods, income consumption curve either slopes backward (*i.e.,* upward to the left) as in Fig. 27, or downward to the right as in Fig. 28.

It would be noticed from the two figures that income effect becomes negative only after a point. It signifies that only at higher ranges of income, some goods become inferior goods and upto a point changes in their consumption behave like those of normal goods.

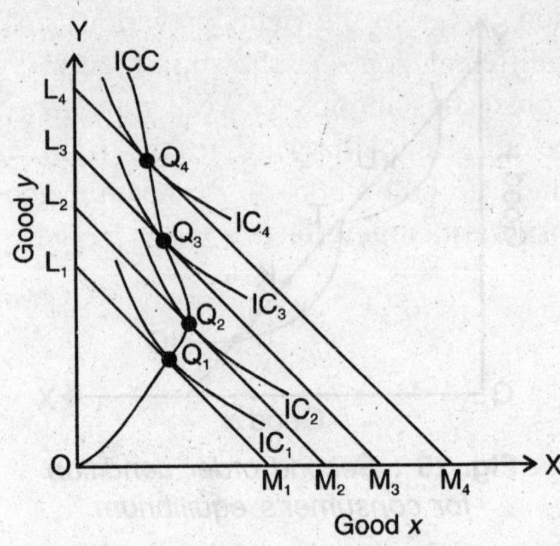

Fig. 27: *ICC in case of Good X being inferior good*

In Figure 29, Income consumption curve (ICC) slopes backward (upward to the left) *i.e.,* bends towards the *y*-axis. This shows good *x* to be an inferior good, since beyond point Q_2, income effect is negative for good X and as a result its quantity demanded falls as income increases.

In Figure 30, ICC-curve slopes downward to the right beyond point Q_2 *i.e.,* bends towards *x*-axis. This signifies that good Y is inferior good because as beyond point Q_2, income effect is negative for good Y and as a result its quantity demanded falls as income increases.

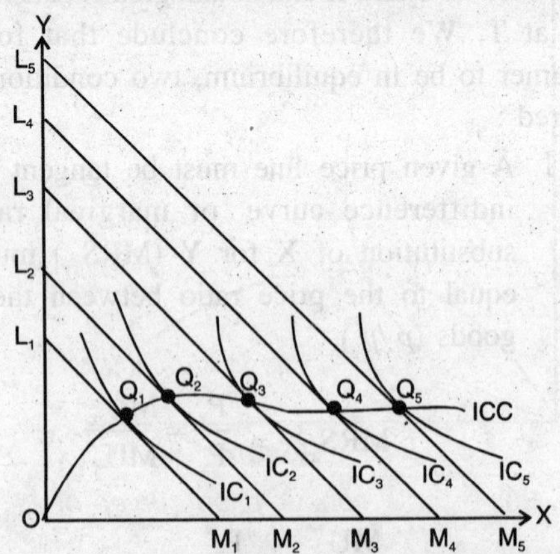

Fig. 28: *Income consumption curve in case of Good Y being Inferior Good*

If the income effect is positive for both the goods X and Y, the ICC will slope upward to the right as in Figure 26. But upward-sloping income consumption curves to the right for various goods may be of different slopes as shown in Figure 29 in which income consumption curves, with varying slopes, are all sloping upward to the right and therefore indicate both goods to be **normal goods having positive income effect.**

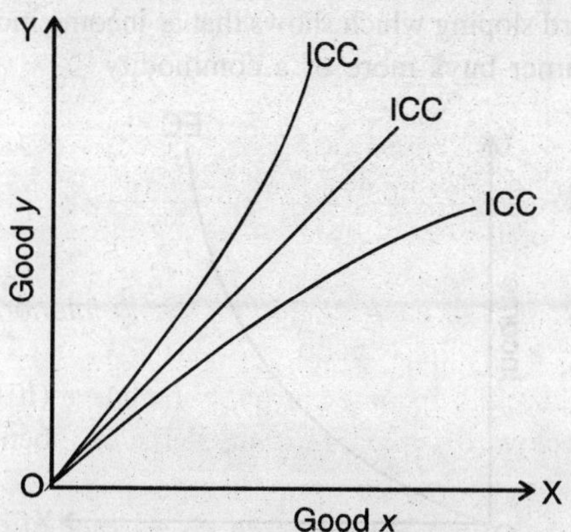

Fig. 29 : *Income consumption curves of Normal Goods*

If the income effect is negative, income consump-tion curve will slope backward to the left as ICC′ in Figure 30. If good X happens to be inferior good, it will slope downward to the right as ICC" in figure 30 if good Y happens to be the inferior good.

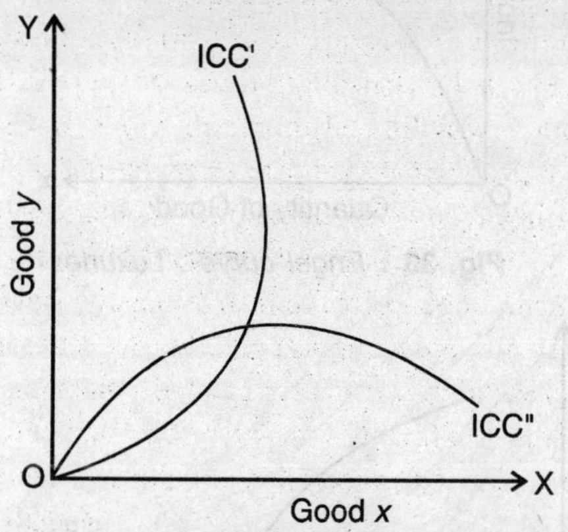

Fig. 30: *Income consumption curves of Inferior Goods*

***Inferior Goods :** Those goods of which the quantity that the consumer would buy less, as his income rises, are called inferior goods. **Inferior goods may be defined as goods for which income effect is negative.**

Substitution Effect

We have discussed above the effect on consumer's equilibrium of a change in consumer's income, relative prices of commodities remaining the same. Now let us see the effect of a change in relative prices, consumer's income remaining the same. This leads us to the study to what is known as the **Substitution Effect.**

Substitution effect means the change in the purchases of a good as a consequence of a change in relative prices alone, real income remaining constant. When the price of a good changes, the real income or purchasing power of the consumer also changes. To keep the real income of the consumer constant so that the effect due to a change in the relative price alone may be known, price change is compensated by a simultaneous change in income. Now, two slightly different concepts of substitution effect have been developed, one by Hicks and Allen and the other by Slutsky. These two concepts of substitution effect have been named after their authors. The two concepts differ in regard to the magnitude of the change in money income which should be effected so as to neutralize the change in real income of the consumer which results from a change in the price.

In **Hicks-Allen Substitution effect** price change is accompanied by so much change in money income that the consumer is neither better or nor worse off than before. In other words, money income of the consumer is changed by an amount which keeps the consumer on the same indifference curve on which he was before the change in the price. Thus **Hick-Allen substitution effect takes place on the same indifference curve.** The amount by which the money income of the consumer is changed so that the consumer is neither better off nor worse off than before is called **Compensating Variation in Income.**

Hicks-Allen substitution effect is illustrated in Figure 31. With a given money income and given prices of the two goods are represented by the price line PL, the consumer is in equilibrium at point Q on the indifference curve IC and is purchasing OM of the good X.

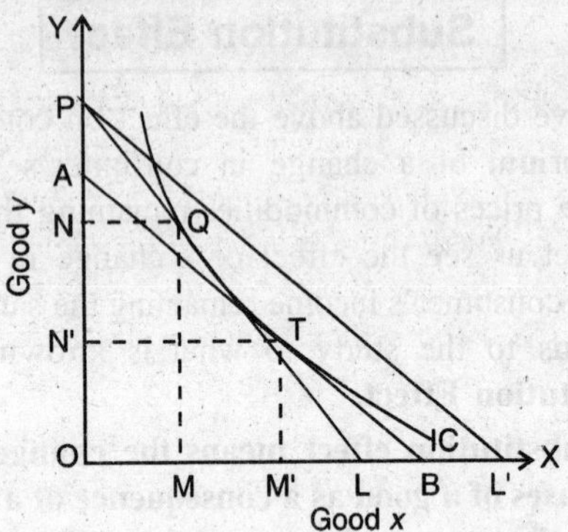

Fig. 31: *Hicks Substitution Effect*

Suppose that the price of good X falls (price of Y remaining unchanged) so that the price line now shifts to PL'. With this fall in price of X, the consumer's real income would increase. In order to find out the substitution effect, this gain in real income should be wiped out by reducing the money income of the consumer by so much amount that forces him to remain on the same indifference curve IC. On which he was before the change in price of the good X. When some money income is taken away from the consumer to cancel out the gain in real income, then the price line which shifted to position PL' will now shift downward but will be parallel to PL'. In Fig. 31, a price line AB parallel to PL' has been drawn as such a distance from PL' that it touches the indifference curve. It means that reduction of consumer's income by the amount PA (in terms of Y) or L'B (in terms of X) had been made so as to keep him on the same indifference curve. PA or L'B is therefore compe sating variation in income.

It will be seen from Figure 31 that with price line AB consumer is in equilibrium at point T and is now buying OM' of X and ON' of Y. This increase in the purchases of good X by MM' and the decrease in the purchases of good Y by NN' is due to the change only in the relative prices of good X and Y. Therefore, movement from Q and T represents the substitution effect. It is thus clear that as a result of substitution effect the consumer remains on the same indifference curve, he is however in equilibrium at a different point from that at which he was before the change in price of X.

Engel Curve

Engel curve shows the quantities of a good which the consumer will purchase at various income level, given his tastes, preferences and the price of the good in question. Engel curve of **normal goods** is upward sloping which shows that as income increases consumer buys more of a commodity.

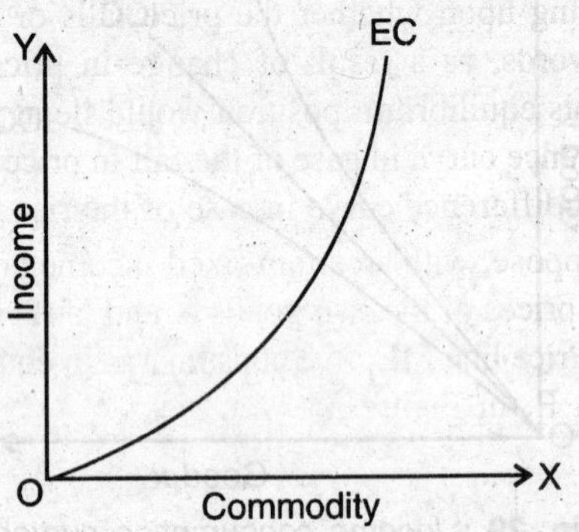

Fig. 32 : *Engel curve : Necessities*

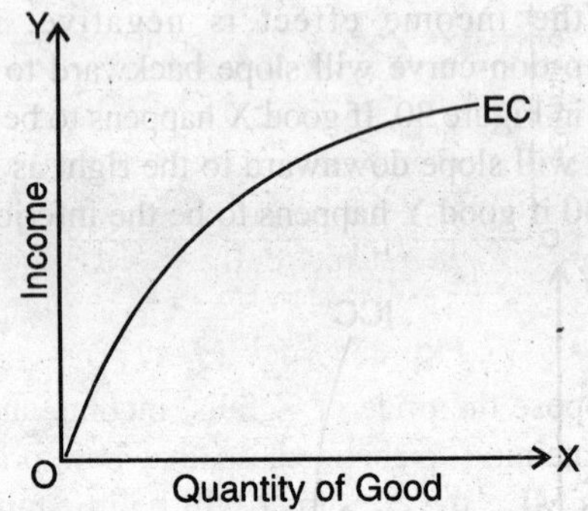

Fig. 33 : *Engel curve : Luxuries*

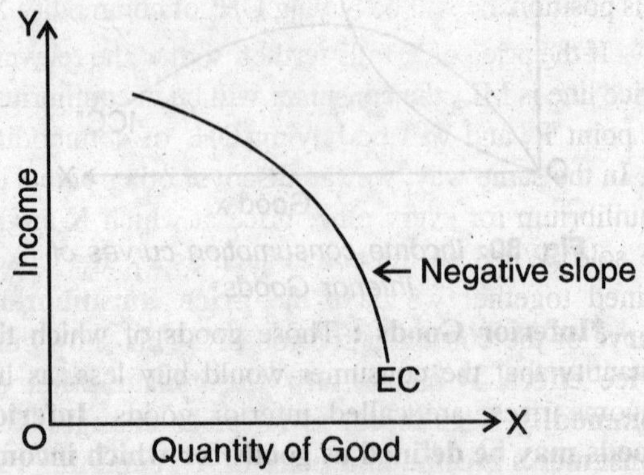

Fig. 34 : *Engel curve: Inferior goods*

Price Effect

We will now explain how the consumer reacts to changes in the price of a good, his money income, tastes and price of the other goods remaining the same.

When the price of a good changes, the consumer would be either better off or worse off them before, depending upon whether the price falls or rises. In other words, as a result of change in price of the good, his equilibrium position would lie at a higher indifference curve in case of the fall in price and at a lower indifference curve in case of the rise in price.

Suppose, with a certain fixed income and given market prices of the two goods X and Y represented by the Price line ML_1, the consumer is in equilibrium at point P_1 in Figure 35.

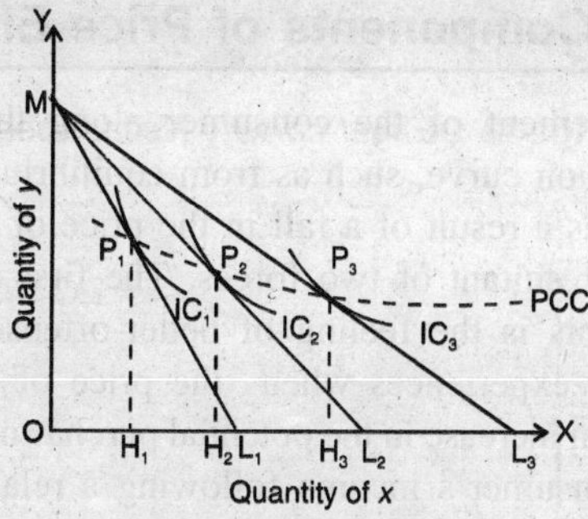

Fig. 35: *Price Effect*

Suppose the price of X falls, income and price of Y remaining unchanged, so that new price line becomes ML_2, the consumer will be in equilibrium at point P_2 on the higher indifference curve IC_2. In this position, he will be buying OH_2 of commodity X.

If the price of X falls further, so that the relevant price line is ML_3 the consumer will be in equilibrium at point P_3 and will be buying OH_3 of commodity X. In the same way, we can discover other points of equilibrium for every other price at which X-might be sold. When all the points such as P_1, P_2, P_3 are joined together we have the **price consumption curve** of the consumer for good X. This shows the **price effect. It shows how the consumption of commodity X changes, as its price changes, the consumer's income and price of Y remaining the same.**

In Fig. 35 price consumption curve (PCC) is sloping downward. Downward-sloping price consumption curve for good X means that as the price of good X falls, the consumer purchases a larger quantity of good X and smaller quantity of good Y. This is quite evident from Fig. 35. We obtain downward sloping price consumption curve for good X when demand for **it is elastic** (*i.e.,* price elasticity is greater than one).

Price consumption curve can have other shapes also. In Fig. 36 upward-sloping price consumption curve is shown. Upward-sloping price consumption curve X means that when the price of good X falls, the quantity demanded of both goods X and Y rises. **We obtain the upward sloping price consumption curve for good X when the demand for good is less elastic (*i.e.,* price elasticity is less them one).**

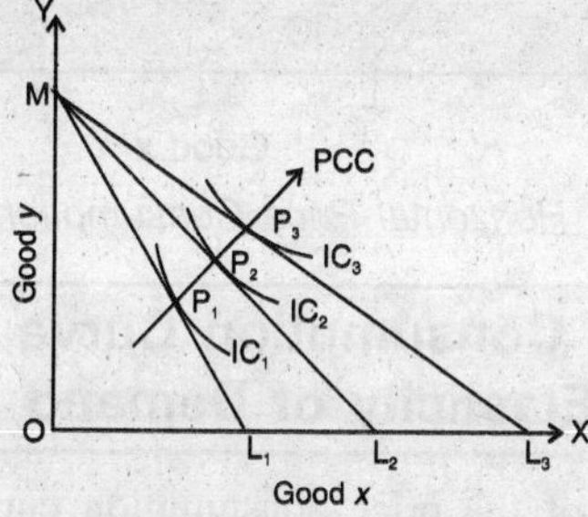

Fig. 36 : *Upward Sloping Consumption Curve*

Price consumption curve can also have a **backward sloping shape,** which is depicted in Fig. 37. Backward sloping price consumption curve for good X indicates that when price of X falls, smaller quantity of it is demanded or purchased. This is the case of **Giffen Goods.**

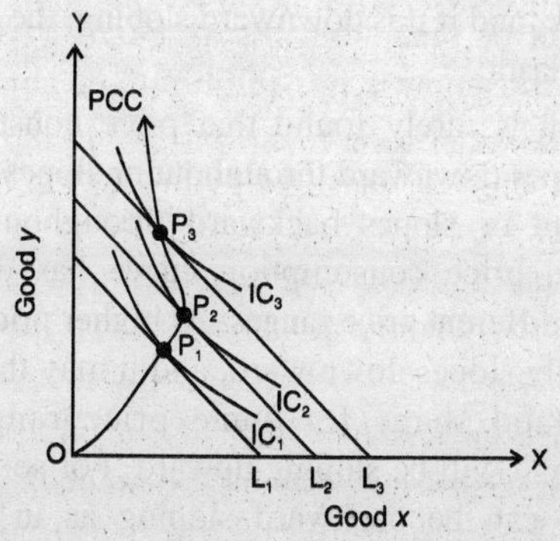

Fig. 37 : *Backward Sloping Price Consumption Curves*

Price consumption curve for a good can take horizontal shape too. It means that when the price of the good X declines, its quantity purchased rises proportionally but quantity purchased of Y remains the same. Horizontal price consumption curve is shown in Fig. 38. **We obtain horizontal price consumption curve of good X when the price elasticity of demand for good X is equal to unity.**

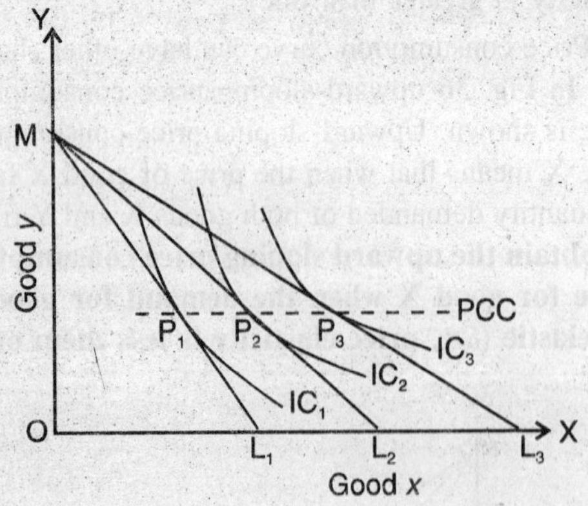

Fig. 38 : *Horizontal Price Consumption Curve*

Price Consumption Curve and Elasticity of Demand

The shape of the price consumption curve shows the degree of elasticity of demand, *i.e.,* the elasticity is unitary, greater than one or less than one. When the price consumption is horizontal, *i.e.,* parallel to X-axis (*i.e.,* has zero slope), the elasticity of demand for good X is unitary, *i.e.,* the total outlay on X remains the same even though price of X rises. If PCC is upward sloping, the demand for the good X is inelastic, and if it is downward sloping, the demand will be elastic.

But it is rarely found that price consumption curve slopes downward throughout or slopes upward throughout or slopes backward throughout. More generally, price consumption curve has different slopes at different price ranges. At higher price levels it generally slopes down ward, and it may then have a horizontal shape for some price ranges but ultimately it will be sloping upward. For some price ranges it can be backward sloping as in case of **Giffen goods.**

A price consumption curve which has different shapes or slopes at different price ranges is drawn in figure 39. Such type of price consumption curve means that price elasticity of demand is different at different price ranges.

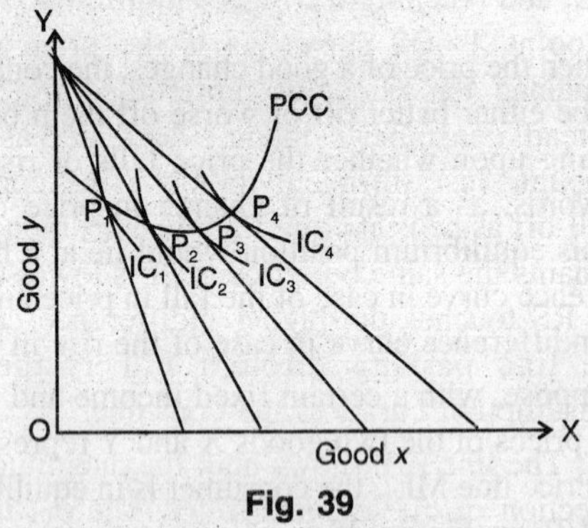

Fig. 39

Two Components of Price Effect

The movement of the consumer along the price consumption curve, such as from equilibrium point P_1 to P_2 as a result of a fall in the price of X, is in reality a resultant of two forces. The first of these components is the feeling of better-offense that a consumer experiences when the price of X falls. There is an increase in the potential purchasing power of the consumer's income following a relative fall in the price of X. It is **Income Effect.** This income effect is the first component of the price effect. The consumer is operating along the income consumption curve.

There is also the second component of the price effect viz., the **Substitution Effect.** Now that X is cheaper than before while the price of Y has remained unchanged, there will naturally be a tendency on the part of the consumer to buy more of the cheaper good and less of the relatively dearer one.

In other words, he will substitute cheaper good for the dearer one. This second components is called the **Substitution Effect** and can be viewed as operating along the price consumption curve. (Fig. 40)

These two components of the movement from P_1 to P_2 are shown in Figure 40. Initially, with the price line ML_1, the consumer is in equilibrium at point P_1. With a fall in price of X, so that the new relevant price line ML_2, he moves to a new equilibrium position P_2 on a higher indifference curve IC_2. RS is a hypothetical price line drawn parallel to ML_1 and touching the higher indifference curve IC_2 at point T. RS shows as if the price of X had remained the same (as represented by ML_1), but instead consumer's income had increased by an amount. Just sufficient to make the consumer as well-off as he is at point P_2, when his money income remains the same but price of X is lower than at P_1. As RS touches the higher indifference curve at T, the line passing through P_1T is the income consumption curve of the consumer.

The line P_1T shows both the magnitude and the direction of the **income effect.** The portion TP_2 of the higher indifference curve IC_2 shows the direction and magnitude of the **substitution effect.** The substitution effect means that the cheaper good X is substituted for the dearer good Y.

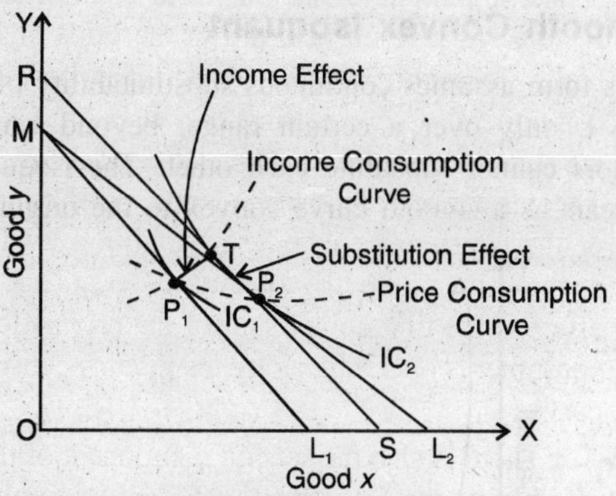

Fig. 40 : *Price Effect = Income Effect + Substitution Effect*

Giffen Good

For a good to be a Giffen good, the following three conditions are necessary :

1. The good must inferior good with a large negative **income effect.**
2. The substitution effect must be small, and
3. The proportion of income spent upon the inferior good must be very large.

Some Facts

(*a*) The quantity demanded of a good varies inversely with price when the income effect is positive or nil.

(*b*) The quantity demanded of a good varies invesely with price when the income effect is negative but is weaker than the substitution effect.

(*c*) The quantity demanded of a good varies directly with price when the income effect for the good is negative and this negative income effect of a change in price is larger than the substitution effect.

PRODUCER BEHAVIOUR & SUPPLY

Theory of Production and Costs

Production Function

The production function expresses a functional relationship between quantities of inputs and outputs. It shows how and to what extent output changes with variations in inputs during a specified period of time. Algebraically, it may be expressed in the form of an equation as

$$Y = f(L, K, R, S)$$

where

Y = output
L = labour input
K = capital input
R = raw materials
S = land input

Equal-Product Curves or Isoquants

Equal-Product curves are similar to the indifference curves of the theory of consumer's behaviour. An equal-product curve represents all those input combinations which are capable of producing the same level of output. These equal-product curves are also known as isoquants and iso-product curves. Since an equal-product curve represents those combinations of inputs which will be capable of producing an equal quantity of output, the producer would be indifferent between them as such. Therefore, another name which often given to the equal product curves is **Production indifference curve.**

The production isoquant may assume various shapes depending on the degree of substitutability of factors.

Linear Isoquant

This type assumes perfect substitutability of factors of production. A given commodity may be produced by using only capital, or only labour, or by an infinite combination of K and L.

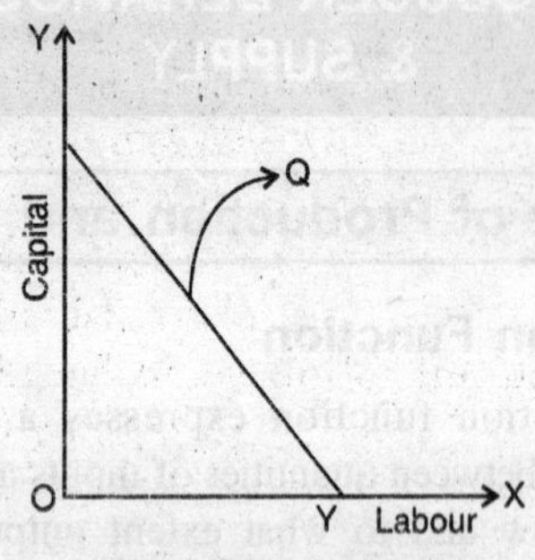

Fig. *Linear isoquant*

Input-Output Isoquant

This assumes strict complementarily (that is, zero substitutability) of the factors of production. There is only one method of production for any one commodity. The isoquant takes the shape of a **right angle.** This type of isoquant is also called **"Leontief isoquant"** after Leontief who invented the input-output analysis.

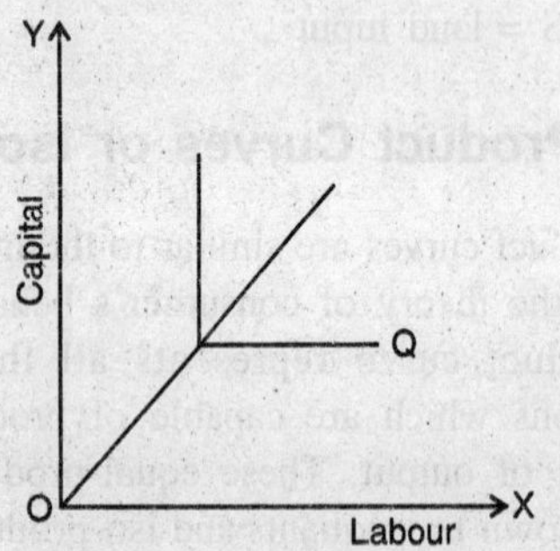

Fig. : *Input-Output isoquant*

Kinked Isoquant

This assumes limited substitutability of K and L. There are only a few processes for producing any one commodity. Substitutability of the factors is possible only at the kinks. This form is also called **'activity analysis-isoquant'** or **'linear-programming isoquant',** because it is basically used in linear programming.

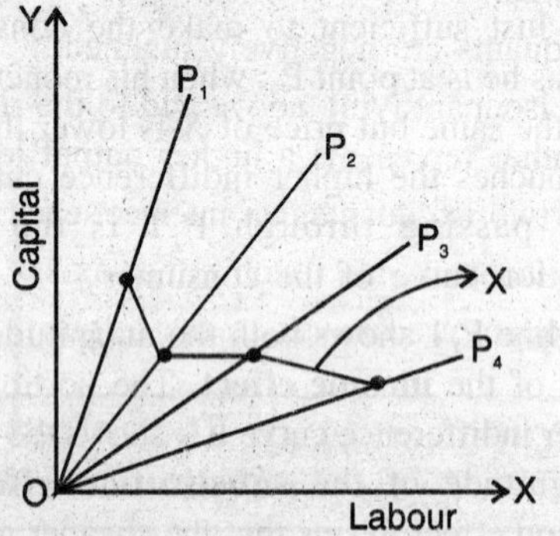

Fig. : *Linear Programming Isoquant*

Smooth Convex Isoquant

This form assumes continuous substitutability of K and L only over a certain range, beyond which factors cannot substitute each other. The isoquant appears as a smooth curve convex to the origin.

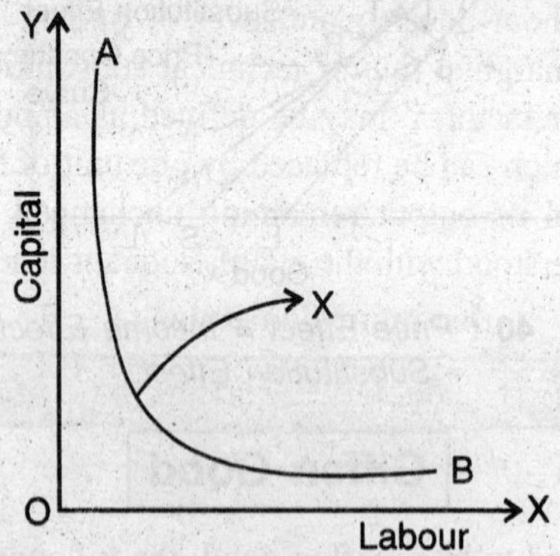

Fig. : *Convex Isoquant*

It should be noted that the kinked isoquants are more realistic. Engineers, managers and production executives consider the production processes as discrete rather than in a continuous array. However, traditional economic theory has mostly adopted the continuous isoquants, because they are mathematically simpler to handle by the simple rules of calculus.

The production function describes not only a single isoquant, but the whole array of isoquant each of which shows a different level of output.

Properties of Isoquants

The following are the important properties of equal product curves.

1. Isoquants are negatively inclined.
2. An isoquant lying above and to the right of another represents a higher output level.
3. No two iso-quants can intersect each other.
4. No isoquant can touch either axis.
5. Isoquant are convex to the origin.

Marginal Rate of Technical Substitution

The principle of marginal rate of technical substitution (MRTS) is based on the production function where two inputs can be substituted in variable proportions in such a way as to produce constant level of output.

Marginal rate of technical substitution indicates the rate at which factors can be substituted at the margin without altering the level of output. More precisely, marginal rate of technical substitution of factor X for factor Y may be defined as amount of factor Y which can be replaced by one unit of factor X, the level of output remaining unchanged. This can be understood with the aid of isoquant schedule.

Isoquant Schedule

Combinations	*Factor X*	*Factor Y*	*$MRTS_{xy}$*
A	1	12	-
B	2	8	4
C	3	5	3
D	4	3	2
E	5	2	1

Each of the input combinations A, B, C, D and E yields the same level of output. Moving down the table from combination A to combination B, 4 units of Y are replaced by 1 units of X in the production process without any change in the level of output. Therefore, the marginal rate of technical substitution is 4 at this stage.

Switching from input combination B to input combination C involves the replacement of 3 units of factor Y by an additional unit of factor X, output remaining the same.

Thus $MRTS_{xy}$ is now 3.

The marginal rate of technical substitution at a point on the equal product curve can be known from the slope of the equal product curve at that point. Consider a small movement down the equal product curve P from G to H in figure 1 where a small amount of factor Y, say *dy* is replaced by an amount of factor X, say *dx* without any loss of output.

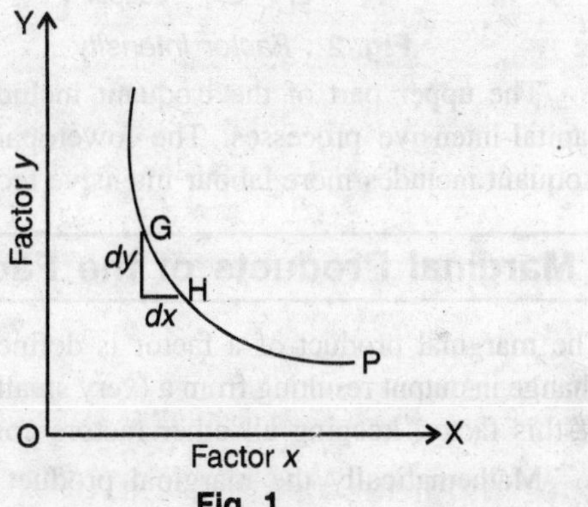

Fig. 1

The slope of the isoproduct curve P at point G is therefore equal to $\frac{dY}{dX}$.

Thus, marginal rate of technical substitution

$$MRTS_{xy} = -\frac{dY}{dX}$$

An important point to be noted about the marginal rate of technical substitution is that it is equal to the ratio of the marginal products of two factors.

Factor Intensity

The factor intensity of any production process is measured by the slope of the line through the origin representing the particular process.

Thus the factor intensity is the capital-labour ratio. In figure 2 process P_1 is more capital intensive than process P_2. Clearly

$$\frac{K_1}{L_1} > \frac{K_2}{L_2}$$

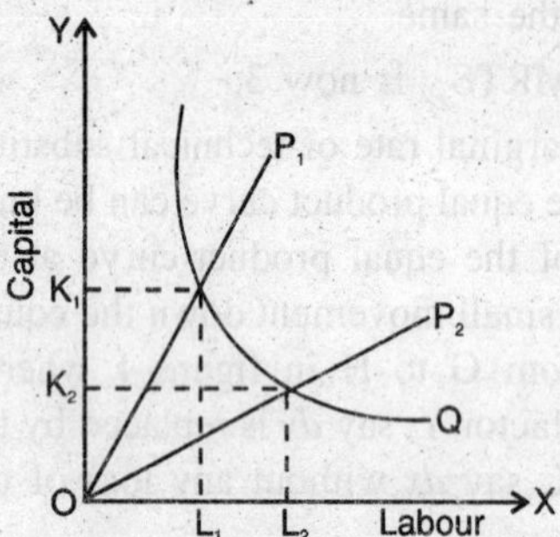

Fig. 2 : *Factor Intensity*

The upper part of the isoquant includes more capital-intensive processes. The lower part of the isoquant includes more labour intensive techniques.

Marginal Products of the Factors

The marginal product of a factor is defined as the change in output resulting from a (very small) change of this factor, keeping all other factors constant.

Mathematically the marginal product of each factor is the partial derivative of the production function with respect to this factor. Thus

$$MP_L = \frac{dQ}{dL}$$

$$\text{and } MP_K = \frac{dQ}{dK}$$

where

MP_L = marginal product of labour
MP_K = marginal product of capital

Graphically the marginal product is shown by the slope of the total product curve.

In principle the marginal product of a factor may assume any value, positive, zero or negative. However, basic production theory concentrates only on the efficient part of the production function, that, on the range of output over which the marginal products of the factors are positive. No rational firm would employ labour beyond OB, or capital beyond OD, since an increase in the factors beyond these levels would results in the reduction of the total output of the firm. Ranges of output over which the marginal products of the factors would be negative inmply irrational behaviour of the firm, and are not considered by the theory of production.

Further more, the basic theory of production usually concentrates on the range of output over which the marginal products of factors, although positive, decrease, that is, over the range of diminishing (but non-negative) productivity of the factors of production : the ranges of output considered by the traditional theory are AB in figure 3 and CD in figure 4.

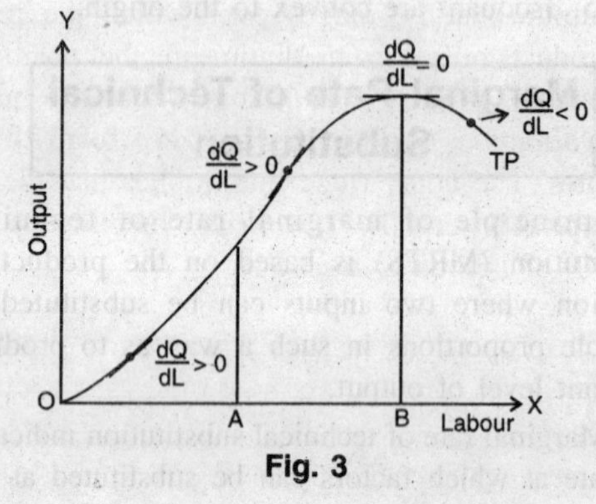

Fig. 3

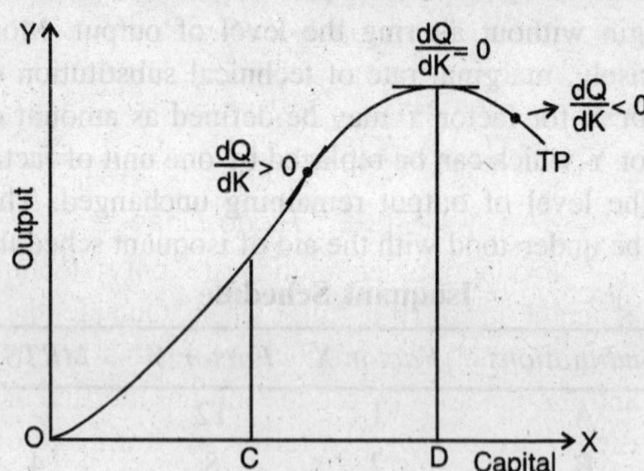

Fig. 4 : *Marginal Product of Capital*

Alternatively we may say that the theory of production concentrates on levels of employment of the factors over which their marginal product are positive but decrease. Thus

$$MP_L > 0 \text{ but } \frac{d(MP_L)}{dL} < 0$$

and $MP_K > 0$ but $\frac{d(MP_K)}{dK} < 0$

These conditions imply that **the traditional theory of production concentrates on the range of isoquants over which their slope is negative and convex to the origin.**

Ridge Lines

In figure 5 the production function is depicted in the form of a set of isoquants. By construction the higher to the right an isoquants, the higher the level of output it depicts. Clearly isoquants cannot intersect, by their construction. We said that traditional economic theory concentrates on efficient ranges of output, that is, ranges over which the marginal products of factors are diminishing but positive. **The locus of points of isoquants where the marginal products of the factors are zero form the ridge lines.** The upper ridge line implies that the MP **of capital is zero.** The lower ridge line implies that the MP **of labour is zero.**

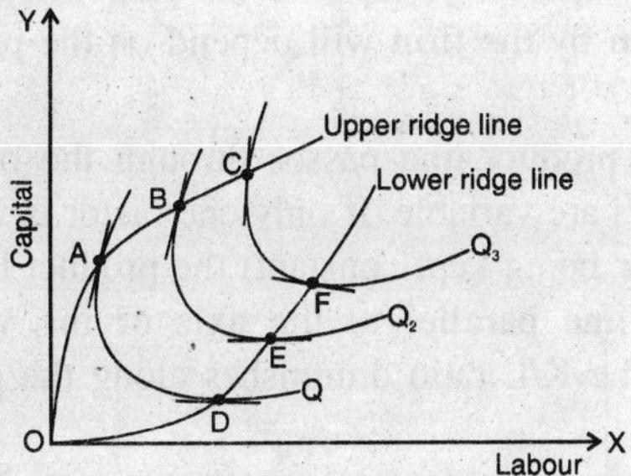

Fig. 5 : *Ridge Lines*

Production techniques are only (technically) efficient inside the ridge lines. Outside the ridge lines the marginal products of factors are negative and the methods of production are inefficient, since they require more quality of both factors for producing a given level of output. Such inefficient methods are not considered by the theory of production, since they are imply irrational behaviour of the firm.

The condition of positive but declining marginal products of the factors defines the range of efficient production (the range of isoquants over which they are convex to the origin).

Laws of Production

The laws of production describe the technically possible ways of increasing the level of production. Output may increase in various ways.

Output can be increased by changing all factors or production. Clearly this is possible only in the long-run. Thus **the laws of returns to scale** refer to the long-run analysis of production.

In the short run output may be increased by using more of the variable factor, while capital (and possibly other factors as well) are kept constant. The marginal product of the variable factor will decline eventually as more and more quantities of this factor are combined with the other constant factors. The expansion of output with one factor constant is described by the **law of diminishing returns** of the variable factor, which is often referred to as the **law of variable proportions.**

Laws of Returns to Scale : Long-Run Analysis of Production

In the long run expansion of output may be achieved by varying all factors. In the long run all factors are variable. The laws of returns to scale refer to the effects of scale relationships.

In the long run output may be increased by changing **all factors by the same proportion,** or by different proportions. Traditional theory of production concentrates on the first case, that is, the study of output as all inputs change by the **same proportion. The term 'return to scale' refers to the changes in output as all factors change by the same proportion.**

Suppose we start from an initial level of inputs and output

$$X_0 = f(L, K)$$

and we increase all the factors by the same proportion *m.* We will clearly obtain a new level of output X^*, higher than the original level X_0,

$$X^* = f(mL, mK)$$

*If X^* increases by the same proportion *m* as the inputs, we say that there are **constant returns to scale.**

*If X^* increases less than proportionally with the increase in the factors, we have **decreasing returns to scale.**

*If X^* increases more than proportionally with the increase in the factors, we have **increasing returns to scale.**

Returns to Scale and Homogeneity of the Production Function

Suppose we increase both factors of the function

$$X_0 = f(L, K)$$

by the same proportion *m,* and we observe the resulting new level of output X^*

$$X^* = f(mL, mK)$$

If *m* can be factored out, then the new level of output X^* can be expressed as a function of *m* (to any power *a*) and the initial level of output

$$X^* = m^a f(L, K)$$

or $$X^* = m^a X_0$$

and the production function is called **homogeneous.** If *m* cannot be factored out, the production function is non-homogeneous. The power *a* of *m* is called the **degree of homogeneity** of the function and is a measure of the returns to scale :

*If $a = 1$, we have constant returns to scale. Thus production function is something called **linear homogeneous.**

*If $a <$ a, we have decreasing returns to scale.

*If $a > 1$, we have increasing returns to scale.

Returns to scale are measured mathematically by the coefficients of the production function. For example, in a **Cobb-Douglas function**

$$X = b_0 L^{b_2} K^{b_2}$$

the returns to scale are measured by the Sum $(b_1 + b_2) = a.$

Proof: Let L and K increase by *m.* The new level of output is

$$X^* = b_0 (mL)^{b_1} (mK)^{b_2}$$

$$= (b_0 L^{b_1} K^{b_2}) m^{b_1 + b_2}$$

or $$X^* = m^{b_1 + b_2} X.$$

Thus $a = (b_1 + b_2)$

Linear Homogeneous Production Function

Production function can take several forms but a particular form of production function enjoys wide popularity among the economists.

This is a linear homogeneous production, that is, production function which is homogeneous of the first degree. Homogeneous production function of the first degree implies that if all the factors of production are increased in some proportion, output also increases in the same proportion.

Hence linear homogeneous production function represents the case of **constant returns to scale.**

Product Lines

A product line shows that movement from one isoquant to another as we change both factors or a single factor. A product line is drawn independently of the prices of factors of production. The product line describes the technically possible alternative paths of expanding output. What path will actually be chosen by the firm will depend on the prices of factors.

The product line passes through the origin if all factors are variable. If only one factor is variable (the other being kept constant) the product line is a straight line parallel to the axis of the variable factor. The K/L ratio diminishes along the product line.

Among all possible product lines of particular interest are the so-called **isoclines. An isocline is the locus of points of different isoquants at which the MRS of factors is constant.**

If the production function is homogeneous the isoclines are straight lines through the origin. Along any one isocline the K/L ratio is constant. Of course the K/L ratio (and the MRS) is different for different isoclines.

If the production function is non-homogeneous the isoclines will not be straight lines, but their shape will be twiddly.

The K/L ratio changes along each isocline. (Fig. 6).

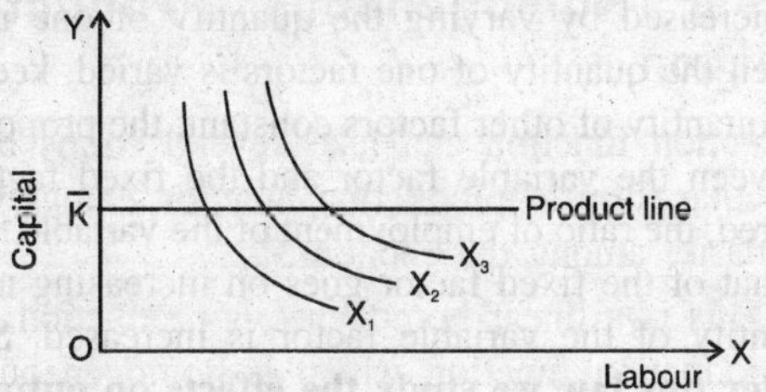

Fig. : *Product line for* $\overline{K}$ *given*

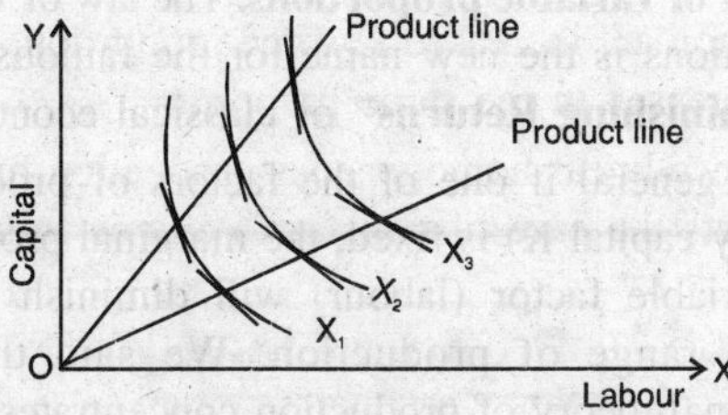

Fig. : *Homogeneous Production Function*

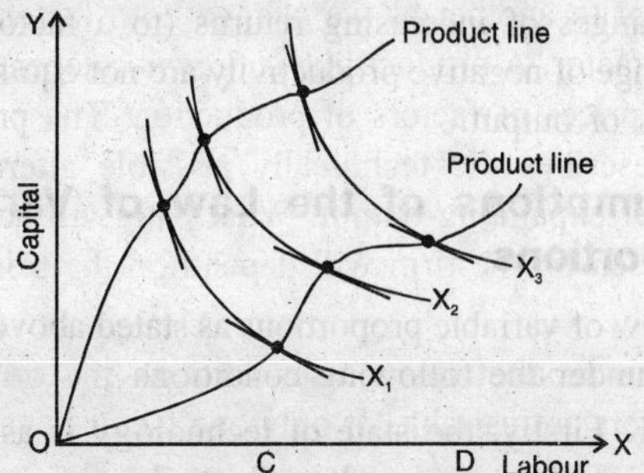

Fig. 6 : *Non-Homogeneous Production Function*

Graphical Presentation of the Returns to Scale for a Homogeneous Production Function

The returns to scale may be shown graphically by the distance (on an isocline) between successive 'multiple-level-of-output' isoquants, that is, isoquants that show levels of output which are multiples of some base level of output *e.g.*, X, 2X, 2X etc.

Constant Returns to Scale

Along any isocline the distance between successive multiple isoquants is constant. Doubling the factor inputs achieves double the level of the initial output, trebling inputs achieves treble output, and so on (Fig. 7).

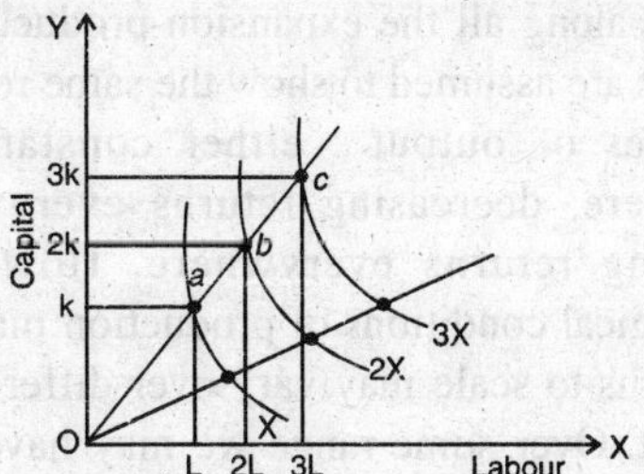

Fig. 7 : *Constant Returns to Scale : oa = ab = bc*

Decreasing Returns to Scale

The distance between consecutive multiple isoquants increases. By doubling the inputs output increases by less than twice its original level. In figure 8 the point *a'*, defined by 2K and 2L, lies on an isoquant below the one showing 2X.

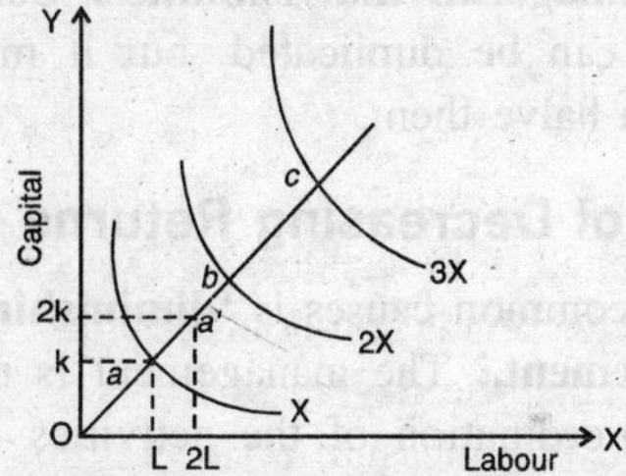

Fig. 8: *Decreasing Returns to Scale : oa < ab < bc*

Increasing Returns to Scale

The distance between consecutive multiple-isoquants decreases. By doubling the inputs, output is more than doubled. In figure 9 doubling K and L leads to point *b′* which lies on an isoquant above the one denoting 2X.

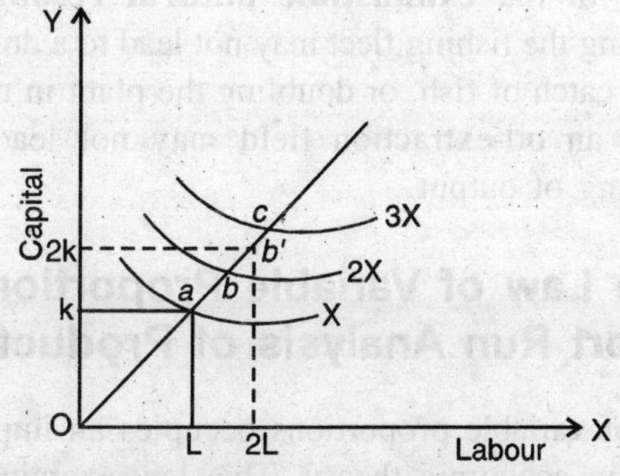

Fig. 9: *Increasing Returns to Scale : oa > ab> bc*

Returns to scale are usually assumed to be the same everywhere on the production surface, that is, the same along all the expansion-product lines. All processes are assumed to show the same returns over all ranges of output : either constant returns everywhere, decreasing returns everywhere, or increasing returns everywhere. However, the technological conditions of production may be such that returns to scale may vary over different ranges of output. Over some range we may have constant returns to scale, while over another range we may have increasing or decreasing returns to scale. Production functions with varying returns to scale are difficult to handle and economists usually ignore for the analysis of production.

Causes of Increasing Returns to Scale

The increasing returns to scale are due to **technical and/or managerial indivisibilities.** Usually most processes can be duplicated, but it may not be possible to halve them.

Causes of Decreasing Returns to Scale

The most common causes is **'diminishing returns to management.'** The management is responsible for the co-ordination of the activities of various sections of the firm. Even when authority is delegated to individual managers (production manager, sales manager, etc.) the final decision have to be taken from the final 'centre of top management.' As the output grows, top management becomes efficient overburdened and hence less difficult in its role as co-ordinator and ultimate decision-maker.

Another cause for decreasing returns may be found in the **exhaustible natural resources :** doubling the fishing fleet may not lead to a doubling of the catch of fish, or doubling the plant in mining or on an oil-extraction field may not lead to a doubling of output.

The Law of Variable Proportions : Short Run Analysis of Production

Law of variable proportions occupies an important place in economic theory. This law examines the production function with one factor variable, keeping the quantities of other factors fixed. In other words, it refers to the input-output relation when the output is increased by varying the quantity of one input. When the quantity of one factors is varied, keeping the quantity of other factors constant, the proportion between the variable factor and the fixed factor is altered, the ratio of employment of the variable factor to that of the fixed factor goes on increasing as the quantity of the variable factor is increased. **Since under this law we study the effects on output of variation in factor proportions, this is known as the law of variable proportions.** The law of variable proportions is the new name for the famous **"Law of Diminishing Returns"** of classical economics.

In general if one of the factors of production (usually capital K) is fixed, the marginal product of the variable factor (labour) will diminish after a certain range of production. We said that the traditional theory of production concentrates on the ranges of the factors are positive but diminishing. The ranges of increasing returns (to a factor) and the range of negative productivity are not equilibrium ranges of output.

Assumptions of the Law of Variable Proportions

The law of variable proportions as stated above holds good under the following conditions :

1. Firstly, the state of technology is assumed to be given and unchanged.
2. Secondly, there must be some inputs whose quantity is kept fixed. It is only in this way that we can alter the factor proportions and know its effects on output. This law does not apply in case all factors are proportionately varied.
3. Thirdly, the law is based upon the possibility of varying the proportions in which the various factors can be combined to produce a product. The law does not apply to those cases where the factors must be used in fixed proportions to yield a product. When the various factors are required to be used in rigidly fixed proportions, then the increase in one factor would not lead to any increase in output, that is the marginal product of the factor will then be zero and not diminishing.

Three Stages of the Law of Variable Proportions

The behaviour of output when the varying quantity of one factor is combined with a fixed quantity of the other can be divided into three distinct stages.

In order to understand these three stages it is better to graphically illustrate the production function with one factor variable. This is done in Fig. 10. In this figure, on the X-axis is measured the quantity of the variable factor and on the Y-axis are measured the total product, average product and the marginal product. The total product curve TP goes on increasing to a point and after that it starts declining. Average and marginal product curves also rise and then decline, marginal product curve starts declining earlier than the average product curve. The behaviour of these total, average and marginal products of the variable factor consequent on the increase in its amount is generally divided into three stages which are explained below.

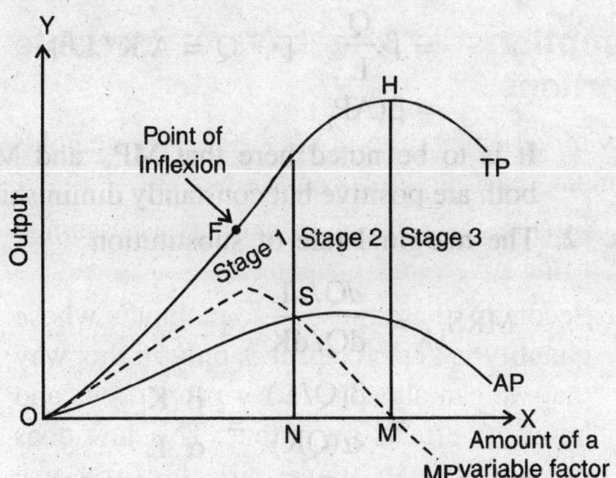

Fig. 10: *Three Stages of the Law of Variable Proportions*

Stage 1

In this stage, total product to a point increases at an increasing rate. In figure 10 from the origin to the point F, slope of the total product curve TP is increasing, that is upto the point F, the total product increases at an increasing rate (the total product curve TP is concave upwards upto the point F), which means that the marginal product MP rises. From the point F onwards during the stage 1, the total product curve goes on rising but its slope is declining which means that from point F onwards the total product increases at a diminishing rate (total product curve is concave downwards), *i.e.*, marginal product falls but is positive. The point F where the total product stops increasing at an increasing rate and starts increasing at the diminishing rate is called the **point of inflexion.** Corresponding vertically to this point of inflexion marginal product is maximum, after which it slopes downwards.

The Stage 1 ends where the average product curve reaches its highest point. During this stage, when marginal product of the variable factor is falling, it still exceeds its average product and so continues to cause the AP-curve to rise. Thus, during the stage 1, whereas MP-curve rises in a part and then falls, the AP-curve rises throughout. In this stage, the quantity of the fixed factor is too much relative to the quantity of the variable factor so that if some of the fixed factor is withdrawn, the total product would increase. Thus, **in the first stage marginal product of the fixed factor is negative.** Stage 1 is known as **the stage of increasing returns** because average product of the variable factor increases throughout this stage.

Stage 2

This stage is also known as the stage of diminishing returns. In stage 2, the total product continues to increase at diminishing rate until it reaches its maximum point H, where the second stage ends. In this stage both the marginal product and average product of the variable factor are diminishing but are positive. At the end of the second stage, that is, at point M marginal product of the variable factor is zero (corresponding to the highest point H of the total product curve TP). Stage 2 is very crucial and important because the firm will seek to produce in its range. This stage is known as the stage of diminishing returns as both the average and marginal products of the variable factors continuously fall during this stage.

Stage 3

In this stage total product declines and therefore the total product curve TP slopes downward. As a result, marginal product of the variable factor is negative and MP-curve goes below the X-axis. In this stage, variable factor is too much relative to the fixed factor. This stage is called the **stage of negative returns,** because the marginal product of the variable factor is negative during this stage.

It may be noted that stage 1 and stage 3 are **completely symmetrical.** In stage 1 the fixed factor is too much relative to the variable factor. Therefore, in stage 1, marginal product of the fixed factor is negative. On the other hand, in stage 3 variable factor is too much relative to the fixed factor. Therefore in, stage 3, the marginal product of the variable factor is negative.

It is this clear from above that the rational producer will never be found producing in stage 1 and stage 3. Stages 1 and 3 represents non-economic region in production function. A rational producer will always seek to produce in stage 2 where both the marginal product and average product of the variable factor are diminishing. At which particular point in this stage, the producer will decide to produce depends upon the prices of factors. The stage 2 represents the range of rational production decisions.

Cobb-Douglas Production Function

The Cobb-Douglas production function is based on the empirical study of the American manufacturing industry made be Paul H. Douglas and C.W. Cobb. It is a linear homogeneous production function which takes into account only two inputs labour and capital for the entire output of the manufacturing industry. The Cobb-Douglas production function is

$$Q = A.K^{\alpha}.L^{\beta}$$

where Q = output

K = capital

L = labour

A, α, β = Positive constants

Properties

The Cobb-Douglas production function has some interesting mathematical properties which make them very useful for managerial decision-making. The important properties are the following :

1. The marginal product of capital and labour depends only on the quantities of capital and labour used in the production process. The equation for the marginal product of capital is given by

$$MP_K = \frac{dQ}{dK} = \alpha A.K^{\alpha-1}.L^{\beta}$$

$$= \alpha(A.K^{\alpha}.L^{\beta})K^{-1}$$

$$= \alpha.\frac{Q}{K} \quad [\because Q = A.K^{\alpha}.L^{\beta}]$$

$$= \alpha(AP_K)$$

where

AP_K = the average product of capital

Similarly, the equation for the marginal product of labour is given by

$$MP_L = \frac{dQ}{dL} = \beta A.K^{\alpha}.L^{\beta-1}$$

$$= \beta(A.K^{\alpha}.L^{\beta})L^{-1}$$

$$= \beta.\frac{Q}{L} \quad [\because Q = A.K^{\alpha}.L^{\beta}]$$

$$= \beta(AP_L)$$

It is to be noted here that MP_K and MP_L both are positive but constantly diminishing.

2. The marginal rate of substitution

$$MRS_{LK} = \frac{dQ/dL}{dQ/dK}$$

$$= \frac{\beta(Q/L)}{\alpha(QK)} = \frac{\beta}{\alpha}.\frac{K}{L}$$

3. Thirdly α and β the exponents of K and L respectively, show the output elasticities of labour (E_L) and capital (E_K).

For $Q = A.K^{\alpha}.L^{\beta}$, the percentage rise in Q for 1% rise in L will be

$$\frac{\%\Delta Q}{\%\Delta L} = \frac{\Delta Q/Q}{\Delta L/L} = \frac{\Delta Q}{\Delta L} \times \frac{L}{Q}$$

In terms of partial derivatives, we can write

$$E_L = \frac{dQ}{dL} \times \frac{L}{Q}$$

$$= \left(\beta \times \frac{Q}{L}\right) \times \frac{L}{Q} = \beta.$$

Similarly,

$$E_K = \frac{dQ}{dK} \times \frac{K}{Q}$$

$$= \left(\alpha \times \frac{Q}{K}\right) \times \frac{K}{Q} = \alpha.$$

Hence if β = 0.5 then 1% rise in the amount of labour used (keeping capital constant) will raise output by 0.5%.

4. The Cobb-Douglas production function can be extended easily to more than two inputs *e.g.,* capital and labour, natural resources, non-production labour, etc.
5. The elasticity of substitution

$$\alpha = \frac{d(K/L)/(K/L)}{d(MRS)/(MRS)}$$

substitute the MRS and obtain

$$\alpha = \frac{d(K/L)/(K/L)}{d\left(\frac{\beta}{\alpha}.\frac{K}{L}\right) \Big/ \left(\frac{\beta}{\alpha}.\frac{K}{L}\right)}$$

$$= \frac{d(K/L)/(\beta/\alpha)}{\left(\frac{\beta}{\alpha}\right) d(K/L)}$$

= 1 = **Hence such a production function the elasticity of factor substitution is equal to one.**

given that β/α is constant and does not affect the derivative.

6. **Factor Intensity:** In a Cobb-Douglas function factor intensity is measured by the ratio β/α. The higher this ratio the more labour intensive the technique. Similarly the lower the ratio β/α the more capital intensive the technique.
7. The sum of the two exponents (α and β) shows returns to scale. In the Cobb-Douglas case the returns to scale cane be predicted as follows.

   (*a*) When (α + β) = 1 the production function exhibits constant returns to scale,

   (*b*) When (α + β) > 1 it exhibits increasing returns to scale, and

   (*c*) When (α + β) < 1 it exhibits decreasing returns to scale.

This property may now be explained and illustrated.

Let us take the Cobb-Douglas function *i.e.,*

$$Q_1 = A.K^{\alpha}.L^{\beta}$$

and multiple each input by the factor *m*. So we get

$$Q_2 = A.(mK)^{\alpha}.(mL)^{\beta}$$
$$= A.m^{\alpha}.K^{\alpha}.m^{\beta}.L^{\beta}$$
$$= A.K^{\alpha}.L^{\beta}.m^{(\alpha+\beta)} = Q_1.\ m^{(\alpha+\beta)}$$

8. The Cobb-Douglas production function has an additional property. It is a homothetic production function. A homothetic production function has **straight line expansion path.**

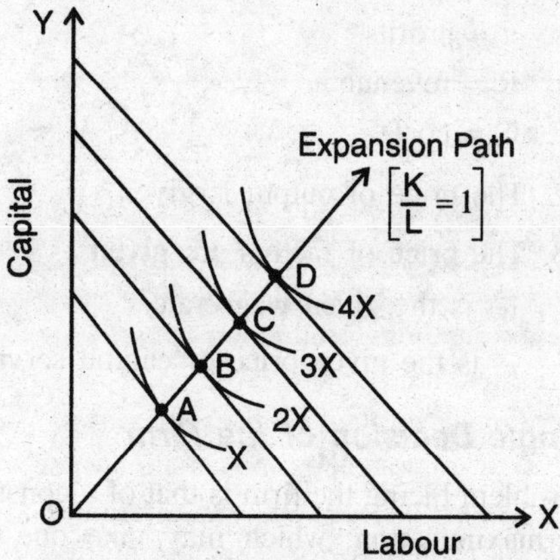

Fig. : *The Expansion Path for the Cobb Douglas Function*

Equilibrium of the Firm : Choice of Optimal Combination of Factors of Production

In this section we shall show the use of the production function in the choice of the optimal combination of factors by the firm. In part A we will examine two cases in which the firm is faced with a single decision, namely maximising output for a given cost, and minimising cost subject to a given output. Both, these decisions comprise cases of constrained profit maximisation in a single period.

In part B we will consider the case of unconstrained profit maximisation, by the expansion of output over time.

In all the above cases it is assumed that the firm can choose the optimal combination of factors, that it can employ any amount of any factor in order to maximise its profits. This assumption is valid if the firm is new, or if the firm is in the long-run. However, an existing firm may be coerced, due to pressure of demand, to expand its output in the short-run, when at least one factor, usually capital, is constant.

In all cases we make the following assumptions:

1. The goal of the firm is profit maximisation-that is, the maximisation of the difference

   $\pi = R - C$

   where

   π = profits

   R = revenue

   C = cost

2. The price of output is given, $\overline{P_X}$.
3. The price of factors are **given :**

   $\overline{w}$ is the given wage rate.

   $\overline{r}$ is the given price of capital services.

A. Single Decision of the Firm

The problem facing the firm is that of a constrained profit maximisation, which may take one of the following forms :

(*a*) **Maximise Profit π, subject to a Cost Constraint.** In this case total cost and price are given $(\overline{c}, \overline{w}, \overline{r}, \overline{p}_x)$ and the problem may be stated as follows

$$\text{Maximum } (\pi) = R - \overline{C}$$

or $\quad \pi = \overline{Px}.X - \overline{C}$

Clearly maximisation of π is achieved in this case if X (output) is maximised, since $\overline{C}$ and $\overline{Px}$ are given constants by assumption.

(*b*) **Maximise Profit π, for a given level of Output.** For example, a contractor wants to build a bridge (X is given) with the maximum profit. In this case we have

$$\text{Maximum (p)} = R - C$$

or $\quad p = \overline{Px}.\overline{X} - C$

Clearly maximisation of π is achieved in this case if C is minimised, given that X and $\overline{Px}$ are given constants by assumption.

For a graphical presentation of the equilibrium of the firm (its profit maximising position) we will use the **isoquant map** (figure 11) and the **isocost-line** (figure 12).

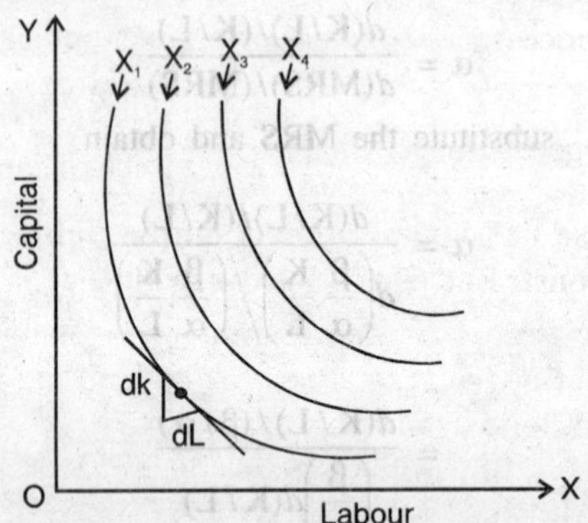

Fig. 11 : *Isoquant Map*

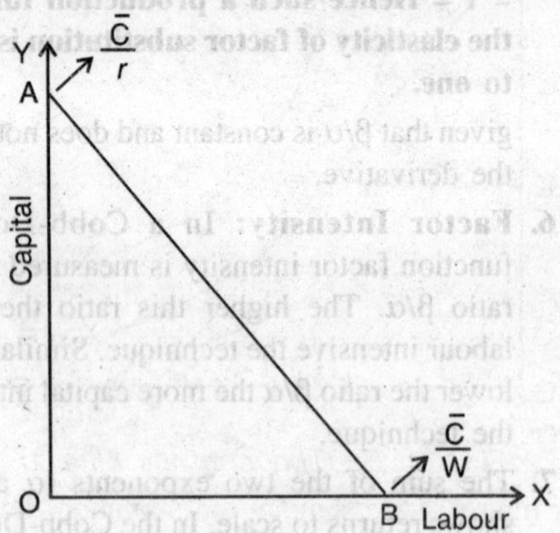

Fig. 12: *Isocost Line*

The Slope of an isoquant is

$$-\frac{dK}{dL} = MRS_{LK} = \frac{MP_L}{MP_K} = \frac{dX/dL}{dX/dK}$$

The isocost line is defined by the cost equation

$$C = (r)\ (K) + (w)\ (L)$$

where

C = cost

w = wage rate

r = price of capital services

K = quantity of capital

L = quantity of labour

The isocost line is the locus of all combinations of factors the firm can purchase with a given monetary cost outlay. There is a close analogy between the consumer's price line and firm's isocost line.

The slope of the isocost line is equal to the ratio of the prices of the factors of production. Thus,.

$$\text{Slope of isocost line} = \frac{w}{r} = \frac{\text{Price of Labour}}{\text{Price of capital}}$$

Case 1 : Maximisation of output Subject to a Cost Constraint (financial constraint)

The firm is in equilibrium when it maximizes its output given its total cost outlay and the prices of the factors, w and r.

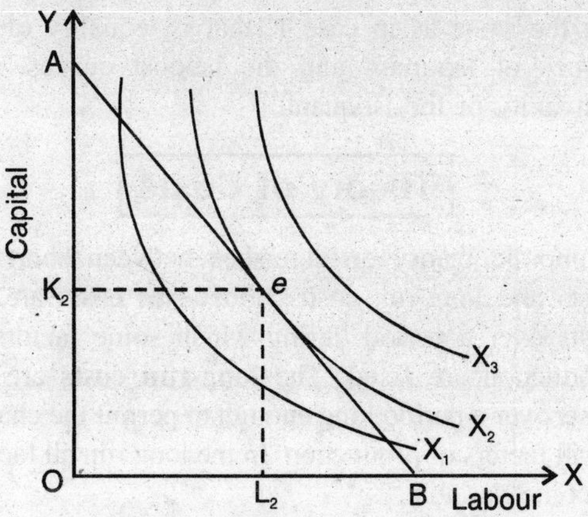

Fig. 13: *Equilibrium of the Firm*

In figure 13 we see that the maximum level of output the firm can produce, given the cost constraint, is X_2 defined by the tangency of the isocost line, and the highest isoquant. The optimal combination of factors of production is K_2 and L_2, for price w and r. Higher levels of output (to the right of e) are desirable but not attainable due to the cost constraint. Other points on AB or below it lie on a lower isoquant than X_2. Hence X_2 is the maximum output possible under the above assumptions (of given cost outlay, given production function, and given factor prices). At the point of tangency (e) the slope of the isocost line (w/r) is equal to the slope of the isoquant (MP_L/MP_K). This constitutes the first condition for equilibrium. The second condition is that the isoquant be convex to the origin. **In summary : the conditions for equilibrium of the firm are :**

(*a*) Slope of Isoquant = Slope of Isocost line

$$\text{or} \quad \frac{w}{r} = \frac{MP_L}{MP_K}$$

$$\frac{w}{r} = \frac{dX/dL}{dX/dK}$$

$$\frac{w}{r} = MRS_{LK}$$

(*b*) The isoquants must be convex to the origin. If the isoquant is concave the point of tangency of the isocost and the isoquant curves does not define an equilibrium position (figure 14).

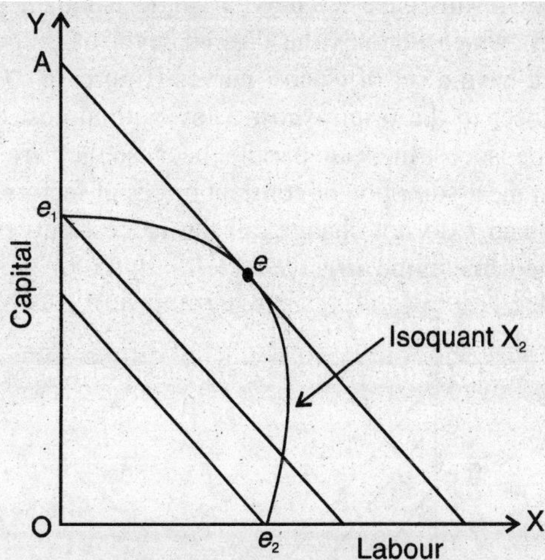

Fig. 14 : *Concave Isoquant*

Output X_2 (depicted by the concave isoquant) can be produced with lower cost at e_2 which lies on a lower isocost curve than e **With a concave isoquant we have *a* 'corner solution'.**

Case 2 : Minimisation of Cost for a given Level of Output

The conditions for equilibrium of the firm are formally the same as in case 1. That is, there must be tangency of the (given) isoquant and the lowest possible isocost curve, and the isoquant must be convex. However, the problem is conceptually different in case of cost minimisation. The entrepreneur wants to produce a given output (for example, a bridge, a building, or $\overline{X}$ tons of a commodity) with the minimum cost outlay.

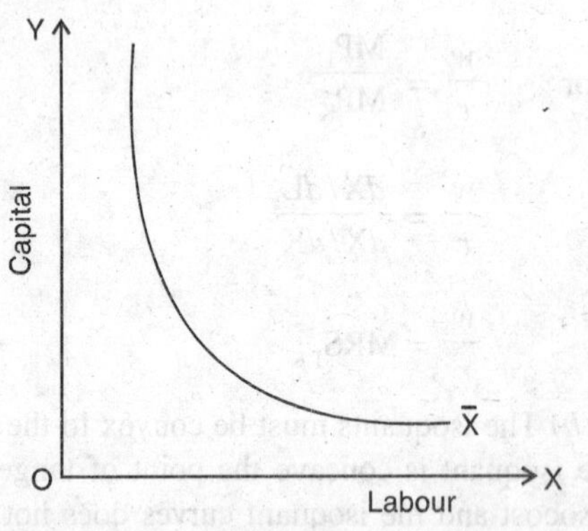

Fig. 15

In this case we have a single isoquant (figure 15) which denotes the desired level of output, but we have a set of isocost curves (figure 16). Curves closer to the origin show a lower total cost outlay. The isocost lines are parallel because they are drawn on the assumption of constant prices of factors. Since w and r do not change, all the isocost curves have the same slope w/r.

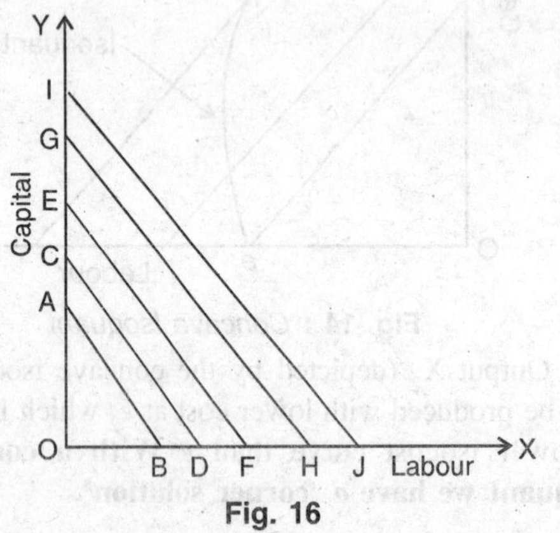

Fig. 16

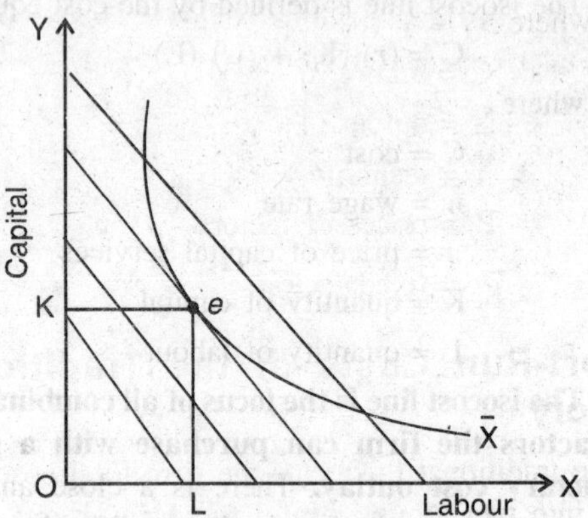

Fig. 17: *Least-Cost Combination*

The firm minimises its costs by employing the combination of K and L determined by the point of tangency of the $\overline{X}$ isoquant with the lowest isocost line (figure 17). Points below e are desirable because they show lower cost but are not attainable for output $\overline{X}$. Points above e show higher costs. Hence point e is the **least-cost point,** the point denoting the **least-cost combination** of the factors K and L for producing $\overline{X}$.

Clearly the conditions for equilibrium (least cost) are the same as in case 1, that is, equality of the slopes of isoquant and the isocost curves, and convexity of the isoquant.

Theory of Costs

Economic theory distinguishes between short-run costs and long-run costs. **Short-run costs** are the costs over a period during which some factors of production are fixed. The **long-run costs** are the costs over a period long enough to permit the change of all factors of production. In the long run all factors become variable.

Both in the short-run and in the long-run, total cost is a multivariable function, that is, total cost is determined by many factors. Symbolically we may write the long-run cost function as

$$C = f(X, T, P_f)$$

and the short-run cost function as

$$C = f(X, T, P_f, \overline{K})$$

where

C = total cost

X = output

T = tcchnology

P_f = prices of factors

$\overline{K}$ = fixed factors

Short-Run Costs of the Traditional Theory

In the traditional theory of the firm total costs are split into two groups : **total fixed costs and total variable costs.**

TC = TFC + TVC

where

TC = total cost

TFC = total fixed cost

TVC = total variable cost

The **fixed costs include :**

(*a*) salaries of administrative staff

(*b*) depreciation of machinery

(*c*) expenses for building depreciation and repairs

(*d*) expenses for land maintenance

The **variable costs include :**

(*a*) the raw materials

(*b*) the cost of direct labour

(*c*) the running expenses of fixed capital, such as fuel, ordinary repairs and routine maintenance.

The total fixed cost is graphically denoted by a straight line parallel to the output axis (figure 18).

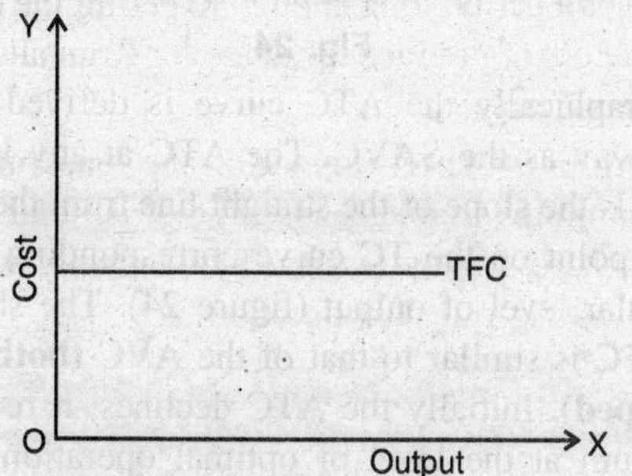

Fig. 18 : *Total Fixed Cost Curve*

The total variable cost in the traditional theory of the firm has broadly an inverse-S shape (figure 19) which reflects the **law of variable proportions.** According to this law, at the initial stages of production with a given plant, as more of the variable factor is employed, its productivity increases and the average variable cost falls.

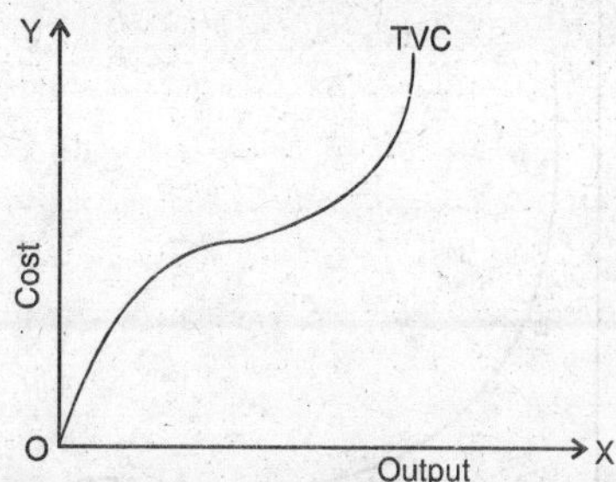

Fig. 19 : *Total Variable Cost Curve*

This continues unit the optimal combination of the fixed and variable factors is reached. Beyond this point as increased qualities of the variable factors are combined with the fixed factor the productivity of the variable factor declines (and the AVC rises). By adding the TFC and TVC we obtain the TC of the firm (figure 20). From the total-cost curves we obtain **average-cost curves.** The average fixed cost is found by dividing TFC by the level of output. Thus

$$AFC = \frac{TFC}{X}$$

Fig. 20 : *TC, TVC and TFC*

Graphically the AFC is a **rectangular hyperbola,** showing at all its points the same magnitude, that is, the level of TFC (figure 21). The average variable cost is similarly obtained by dividing the TVC with the corresponding level of output :

$$AVC = \frac{TVC}{X}$$

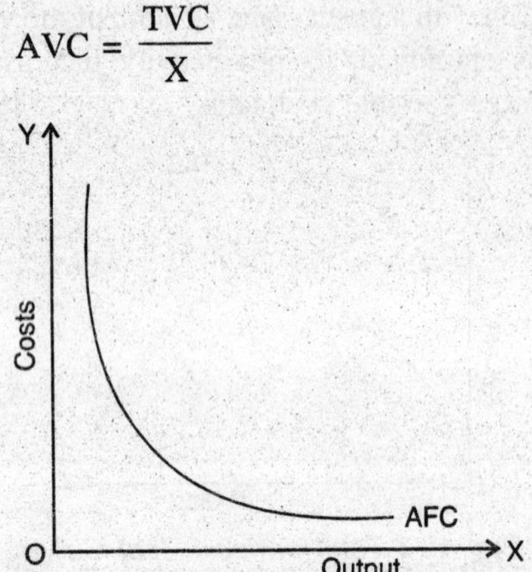

Fig. 21: *Average Fixed Cost Curve*

Graphically the AVC at each level of output is derived from the slopes of a line drawn form the origin to the point on the TVC curve corresponding to the particular level of output. For example, in figure 22 the AVC at X_1 is the slopes of the ray O*a*, the AVC at X_2 is the slope of the ray O*b*, and so on. It is clear from figure 22 that the slope of a ray through the origin declines continuously until the ray becomes tangent to the TVC curve at C. To the right of this point the slope of rays through the origin starts increasing. Thus the SAVC curve falls initially as the productivity of the variable factor increases, reaches a minimum when the plant is operated optimally and rises beyond that point (figure 23).

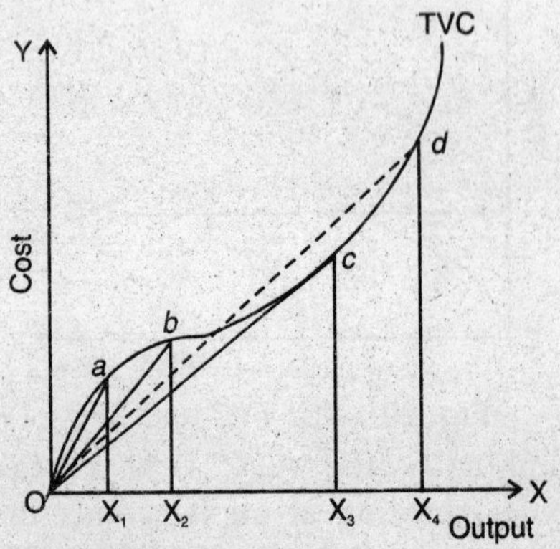

Fig. 22

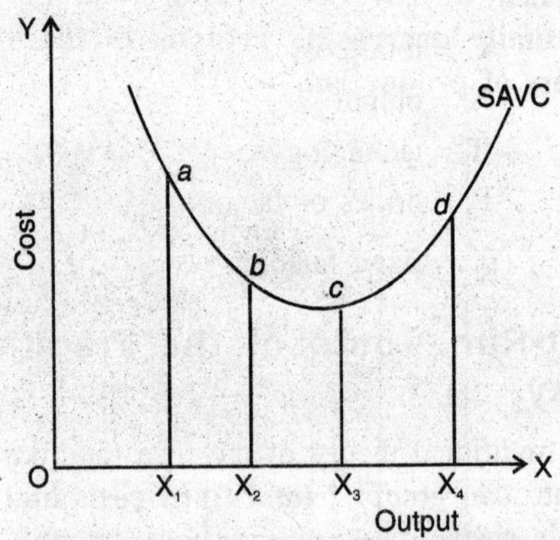

Fig. 23 : *Average Variable Cost*

The ATC is obtained by dividing the TC by the corresponding level of output.

$$ATC = \frac{TC}{X}$$

$$= \frac{TFC+TVC}{X} = AFC + AVC$$

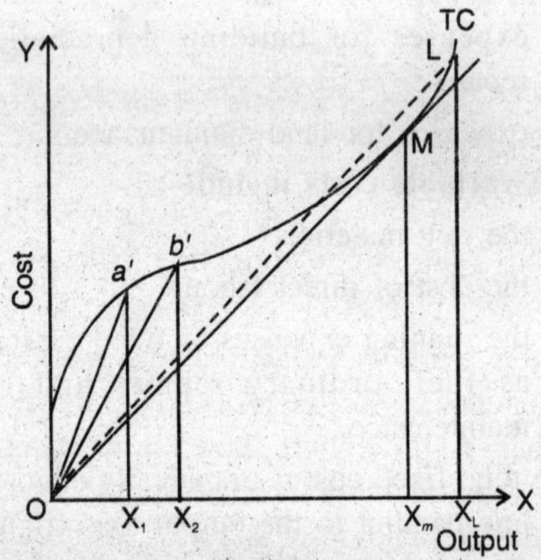

Fig. 24

Graphically the ATC curve is derived in the same way as the SAVC. The ATC at any level of output is the slope of the straight line from the origin to the point on the TC curve corresponding to that particular level of output (figure 24). The shape of the ATC is similar to that of the AVC **(both being U-shaped).** Initially the ATC declines, it reaches a minimum at the level of optimal operation of the plant (X_m) and subsequently rises again (figure 25). The **U-shape** of both the AVC and the ATC reflects the **law of variable proportions** or **law of eventually decreasing returns to the variable factors of production.**

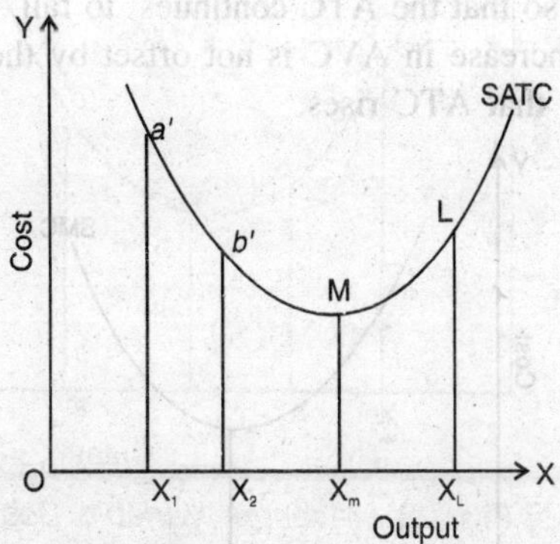

Fig. 25: *Average Total Cost*

Marginal Cost

The marginal cost if defined as the change in TC which results from a unit change in output. In other words, marginal cost is the addition to the total cost of producing n units instead of $(n - 1)$ units where n is say any given number. In symbols :

$$MC_n = TC_n - TC_{n-1}$$

Mathematically the marginal cost is the first derivative of the TC function. Denoting total cost by TC and output by X we have

$$MC = \frac{dTC}{dX}$$

It is worth pointing out that marginal cost is independent of the fixed cost. Since fixed costs do not change with output, there are no marginal fixed costs when output is increased in the short run. It is only the variable costs that vary with output in the short run. Therefore the marginal costs are infact due to the changes in variable costs, and whatever the amount of fixed cost, the marginal cost if unaffected by it.

The independence of the marginal cost from the fixed cost can be proved algebraically as follows:

$$\begin{aligned} MC_n &= TC_n - TC_{n-1} \\ &= (TVC_n + TFC) - (TVC_{n-1} + TFC) \\ &= TVC_n + TFC - TVC_{n-1} - TFC \\ &= TVC_n - TVC_{n-1} \end{aligned}$$

Hence, **marginal cost is the addition to the total variable costs when output is increased from $n - 1$ units to n units of output.** It follows therefore that the marginal cost is independent of the amount of the fixed costs.

It should be noted that marginal cost of production is intimately related to the marginal product of the variable factor.

As noted above,

$$MC = \frac{dTC}{dX}$$

$$\text{or} \quad MC = \frac{d(TVC)}{dX}$$

Since price of the variable factor, *i.e.,* w is assumed to be constant, the change in total variable cost can occur due to the change in the amount of the variable factor.

$$\text{Therefore,} \quad MC = \frac{wdL}{dX} = w.\frac{dL}{dX} \quad ...(1)$$

From above discussion we know that marginal product of the variable factor is the change in total product as a result of the unit change in the variable factor. Thus

$$MP_L = \frac{dX}{dL} \quad \text{or} \quad \frac{1}{MP_L} = \frac{dL}{dX}$$

Substituting $\frac{dL}{dX}$ for $\frac{1}{MP_L}$ in equation (1), we get

$$MC = w.\frac{1}{MP_L}$$

$$\text{or} \quad MC = \frac{w}{MP_L} \quad ...(2)$$

Thus, marginal cost of production is equal to the reciprocal of the marginal product of the variable factor multiplied by the price of variable factor. Therefore, marginal cost varies inversely with the marginal product of the variable factor.

Graphically the MC is the slope of the TC curve (which of course is the same at any point as the slope of the TVC). The slope of a curve at any one of its points is the slope of the tangent at that point. With an inverse-S shape of the TC (and TVC) the MC curve will be U-shaped. In figure 26 we observe that the slope of the tangent to the total-cost curve declines gradually, until it becomes parallel to the X-axis (with its slope being equal to zero at this point), and then starts rising. Accordingly we picture the MC curve in figure 27 as **U-shaped.**

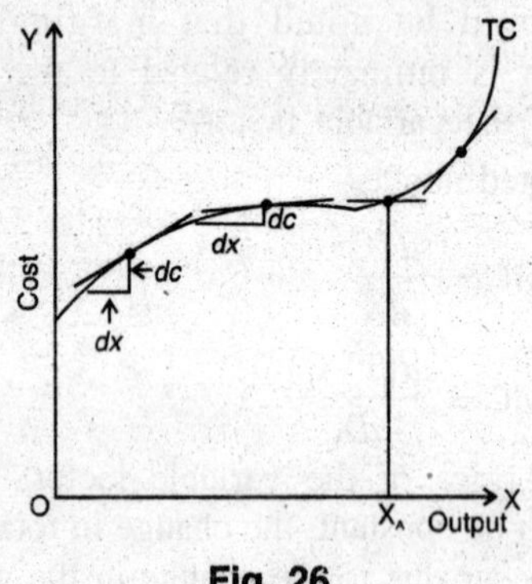

Fig. 26

In Summary : the traditional theory of costs postulates that in the short run the cost curves (AVC, ATC and MC) are **U-shaped,** reflecting the **law of variable proportions.** In the short run with a fixed plant there is a phase of increasing productivity (falling unit costs) and a phase of decreasing productivity (increasing unit costs) of the variable factor. Between these two phases of plant operation there is a single point at which unit costs are at a minimum. When this point on the SATC is reached the plant is utilised optimally, that is, with the optimal combination of fixed and variable factors.

The Relationship Between ATC and AVC

The AVC is a part of the ATC, given ATC = AFC + AVC. Both AVC and ATC are U-shaped, reflecting the law of variable proportions. However, the minimum point of the ATC occurs to the right of the minimum point of the AVC (figure 28). This is due to the fact that ATC includes AFC, and the latter falls continuously with increase in output. After the AVC has reached its lowest point and starts rising, its rise is over a certain range offset by the fall in the AFC, so that the ATC continues to fall (over that range) despite the increase in AVC. However, the rise in AVC eventually becomes greater than the fall in the AFC so that the ATC starts increasing. The AVC approaches the ATC asymptotically as X (output) increases.

In figure 28 the minimum AVC is reached at X, while the ATC is at its minimum at X_2. Between X_1 and X_2 the fall in AFC more than offsets the rise in AVC so that the ATC continues to fall. Beyond X_2 the increase in AVC is not offset by the fall in AFC, so that ATC rises.

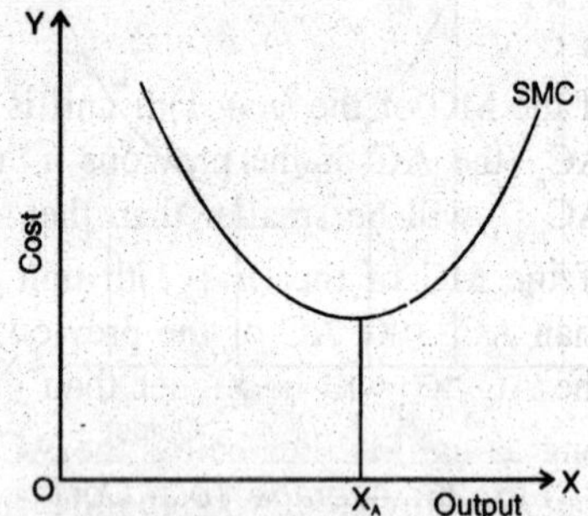

Fig. 27 : *Marginal Cost*

The Relationship between MC and ATC

The MC-curve cuts the ATC-curve and the AVC-curve at their lowest points. We will establish this relation only for the ATC and MC, but the relation between MC and AVC can be established on the same lines of reasoning.

We said that the MC is the change in the TC for producing an extra unit of output. Assume that we start from a level of n units of output. If we increase the output by one unit the MC is the change in total cost resulting from the production of the (n + 1)th unit. The AC at each level of output is found by dividing TC by X (output). Thus the AC at the level of X_n is

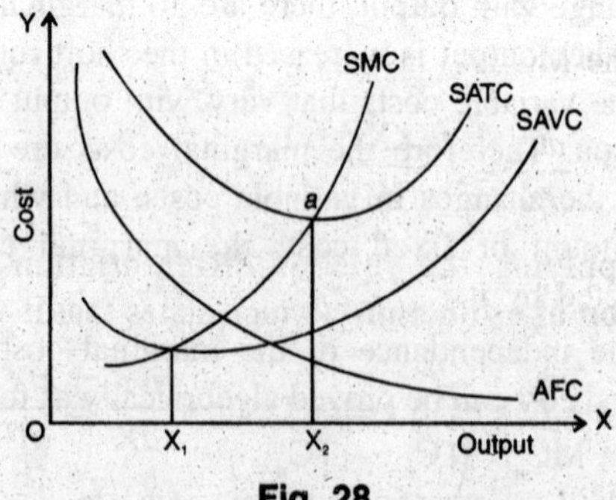

Fig. 28

$$AC_n = \frac{TC_n}{X_n}$$

and the AC at the level X_{n+1} is

$$AC_{n+1} = \frac{TC_{n+1}}{X_{n+1}}$$

Clearly

$$TC_{n+1} = TC_n + MC$$

Thus :

(*a*) If the MC of the (*n* + 1)th unit is less than AC_n (the AC of the previous *n* units) the AC_{n+1} will be smaller than the AC_n.

(*b*) If the MC of the (*n* + 1)th unit is higher than AC_n (the AC of the previous *n* units) the AC_{n+1} will be higher than the AC_n.

So long as the MC lies below the AC-curve, it pulls the latter downwards, when the MC rises above the AC, it pulls the latter upwards. In figure 28 to the left of *a* the MC lies below the AC curve, and hence the latter falls downwards. To the right of *a* the MC-curve lie above the AC curve, so that AC rises. It follows that at point *a,* where the intersection of the MC and AC occurs, the AC has reached its minimum level.

The relationship between the MC and AC curves becomes clearer with the use of simple calculus. Given C = ZX

where

C = total cost

Z = average cost

X = output

Clearly

$$Z = f(X)$$

The MC is

$$\frac{dC}{dX} = \frac{d(ZX)}{d(X)}$$

Applying the rule of differentiation of **'a function of a function'** (which states that if $y = uv$, where $u = f_1(X)$ and $v = f_2(X)$, then $\frac{dY}{dX} = \frac{dY}{dU}.\frac{dU}{dX}$), we obtain

$$MC = \frac{dC}{dX} = Z\frac{dX}{dX} + X\frac{dZ}{dX}$$

or MC = AC + (X). (Slope of AC)

Given that AC > 0 and X > 0, the following results emerge :

(*a*) If slope of AC < 0, then MC < AC.

(*b*) If slope of AC > 0, then MC > AC.

(*c*) If slope of AC = 0, then MC = AC.

The slope of the AC becomes zero at the minimum point of this curve (given that on the theoretical grounds the AC curve is U-shaped). Hence MC = AC at the minimum point of the average cost curve.

Long-Run Costs of the Traditional Theory : The 'Envelope' Curve

In the long run all factors are assumed to become variable. We said that the long-run cost curve is a **planning curve,** in the sense that it is a guide to the entrepreneur in his decision to plan the future expansion of his output.

The long run average-cost is derived from short-run cost curves. Each point on the LAC corresponds to a point on a shout-run cost curve, which is tangent to the LAC at that point.

Long-run average cost curve depicts the least possible average cost for producing all possible levels of output. In order to understand how the long-run average cost curve is derived, consider the three short-run average cost curves as shown in figure 29. These short-run average cost curves are also called **plant curves,** since in the short-run plant is fixed and each of the short-run average cost curve corresponds to a particular plants. In the short run, the firm can be operating on any short-run average cost curve, given the size of plant. Suppose that only these three are technically possible sizes of plants and that no other size of the plant can be built. Given the size of the plant or short run average cost curve the firm will increase or decrease its output by varying the amount of the variable inputs. But in the long-run, the firm can choose among the three possible sizes of plant as depicted by short-run average cost curves SAC_1, SAC_2 and SAC_3. In the long run the firm will examine that with which size of plant or on which short-run average cost curve it should operate to produce a given levels of output at the minimum possible cost.

It will be seen from figure 29 that upto OB amount of output, the firm will operate on the short-run average cost curve SAC_1, though it could also produce with short-run average cost curve SAC_2, because upto OB amount of output, production on SAC_1 curve entails lower cost than on SAC_2. If the firm plans to produce an output which is larger than OB (but less than OD), then it will not be economical to produce on SAC_1. It will be seen from figure 102 that the outputs larger than OB (but less than OD), can be produced at a lower cost per unit on SAC_2 than on SAC_1.

Thus, the output OC is produced on SAC_2 costs CK per unit which is lower than CJ which is the cost incurred when produced on SAC_1. Therefore, if the firm plants to produce between outputs OB and OD, it will employ the plant corresponding to short-run average cost curve SAC_2. If the firm has to produce an output which exceeds OD, then the cost per unit will be lower on SAC_3 than on SAC_2. Therefore, for outputs larger than OD, the firm will employ plant corresponding to the short run average cost curve SAC_3.

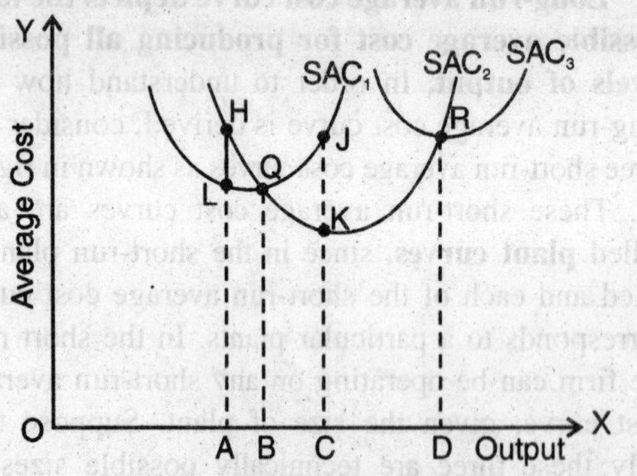

Fig. 29 Plant Curves

It is thus clear that in the long run the firm has a choice in the employment of a plant, and it will employ that plant which yields possible minimum unit cost for producing a given output. The long run average cost curve depicts the least possible average cost for producing various levels of output when all factors including the size of the plant have been adjusted.

Now if we relax the assumption of the existence of only three plants and assume that the available technology includes many plant sizes, each suitable for a certain level of output, the point of intersection of consecutive plants (which are the crucial points for the decision of whether to switch to a larger plant) are more numerous. In the limits, If we assume that there is a very large number (infinite number) of plants, we obtain a continuous curve, which is the planning LAC-curve of the firm. Each point of this curve shows the minimum (optimal) cost for producing the corresponding level of output.

The LAC-curve is the locus of points denoting the least cost of producing the corresponding output. It is a planning curve because on the basis of this curve the firm decides what plant to set up in order to produce optimally (at minimum cost) the expected level of output. The firm chooses the short-run plant which allows it to produce the anticipated (in the long-run) output at the least possible cost. In the traditional theory of the firm the LAC-curve is U-shaped and it is often called the **'envelope curve'** because it **'envelopes'** the SRC-curve (figure 30).

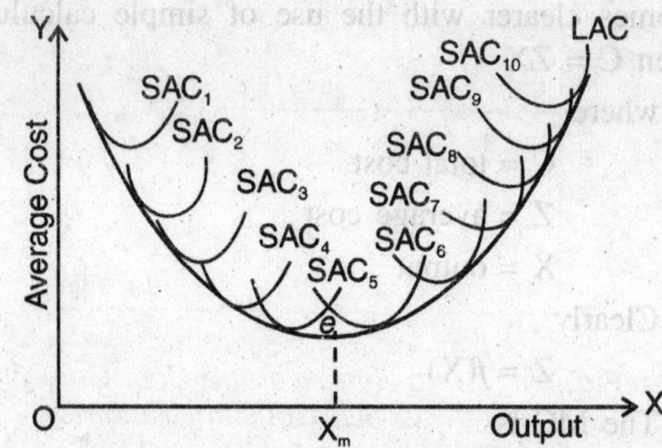

Fig. 30 : *Long Average Cost Curve*

An important fact about the long-run average cost curve is worth mentioning. It is that the long-run average curve LAC is not tangent to the minimum point of the short-run average cost curves. When the long-run average cost curve is declining, that is, for output less than OX_m, it is tangent to the falling portions of the short-run average cost curves.

On the other hand, when the long-run average cost curve is rising, it will be tangent to the rising portions of the short-run average cost curves.

Long-Run Average Cost Curve in Constant Cost Case

If the production function is linear and homogeneous (that is, homogeneous of the first degree) and also the prices of inputs remain constant, then the long-run average cost will remain constant at all levels of output. Linear homogeneous production function implies **constant returns to scale** which means that when all inputs are increased in a certain proportion, the output increases in the same proportion.

Therefore, with the given prices of inputs, when returns to scale are constant, the cost per unit of output remains the same. In this case, the long run average cost curve will be a horizontal straight cost curve will be a horizontal straight line as depicted in figure 31.

In such a case, **the optimum size of the firm in indeterminate,** since all levels of output can be produced at the same long-run average cost which represents the same minimum short-run average costs throughout.

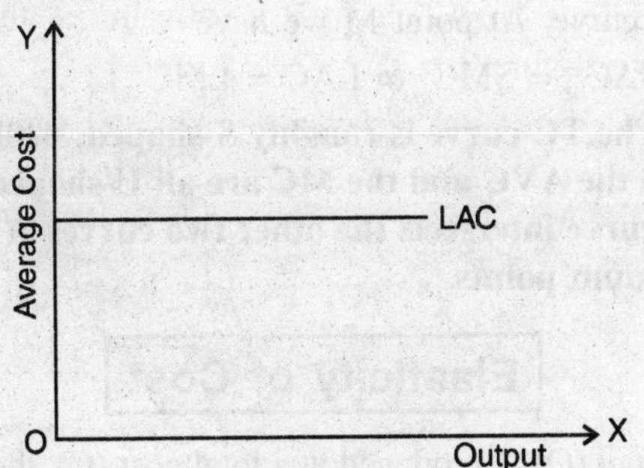

Fig. 31 : *Long-Run Average Cost Curve : Constant Costs, Constant Returns*

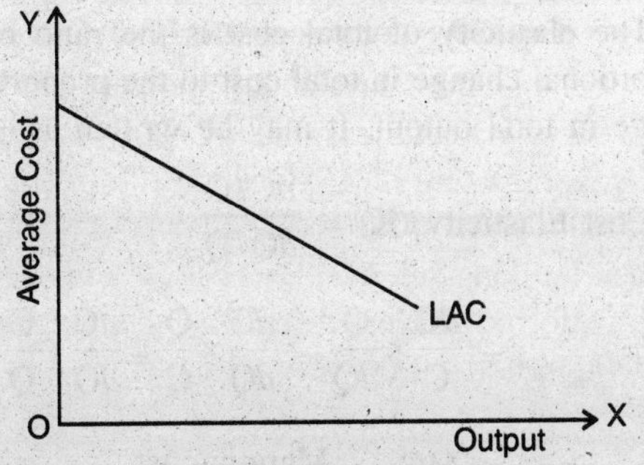

Fig. 32: *Long-Run Average Cost Curve : Decreasing Costs, Increasing Returns*

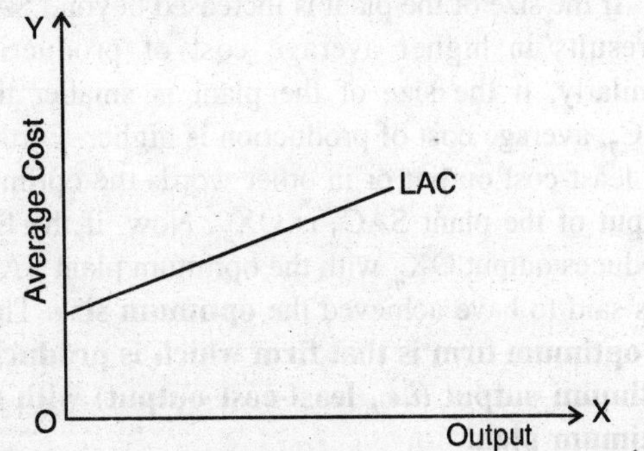

Fig. 33 : *Long-Run Average Cost Curve : Rising Costs, Decreasing Returns*

Optimum Plant, Optimum Output and Optimum Firm

It is clear from figure 30 that in the continuous long-run average cost curve both for outputs less than OX_m and more than OX_m no plant is used at its point of minimum cost. It is only the plant, the minimum point of whose short-run average cost curve coincides with the minimum point of the long-run average cost-curve, which is operated at the point of its minimum average cost of production. In figure 30 for producing output OX_m, the plant of SAC_7 is used at its minimum cost of production $X_m e$. In other words, plant of SAC_7 is being utilized to produce its optimum output, that is to say, it is being used at its capacity.

It should be noted that in figure 30 the plant of SAC_7 is optimum plant, since its minimum cost of production is the lowest of the minimum costs of all other plants.

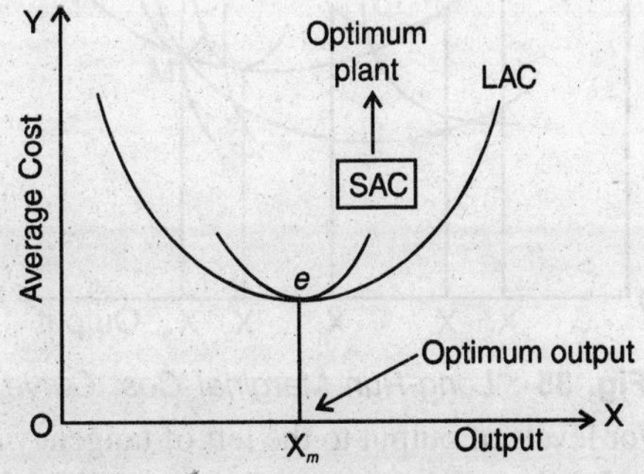

Fig. 34 : *Optimum Plant, Optimum Output And Optimum Firm*

If the size of the plant is increased beyond SAC_7 it results in higher average cost of production. Similarly, if the size of the plant is smaller than SAC_7, average cost of production is higher. Further, the least-cost output or in other words the optimum output of the plant SAC_7 is OX_m. Now, if the firm produces output OX_m with the optimum plant SAC_7, it is said to have achieved the **optimum size.** Thus, **an optimum firm is that firm which is producing optimum output *(i.e.,* least-cost output) with the optimum plant.**

In our figure 30 the firm is of optimum size if it employs plant SAC_7 and uses it to produce OX_m. But the point of minimum cost of the optimum plant (SAC_7) coincides with the minimum point of the long run average cost curve. Therefore, the optimum firm can also be defined as one which produces at the minimum point of the long-run average cost curve (LAC).

Long-Run Marginal Cost Curve

The long-run marginal cost is derived from the SRMC curves, but does not **'envelope'** them. The LRMC is formed from points of intersection of the SRMC curves with vertical lines drawn from the points of tangency of the corresponding SAC-curves and the LRA cost curve (figure 35). The LMC must be equal to the SMC for the output at which the corresponding SAC is tangent to the LAC.

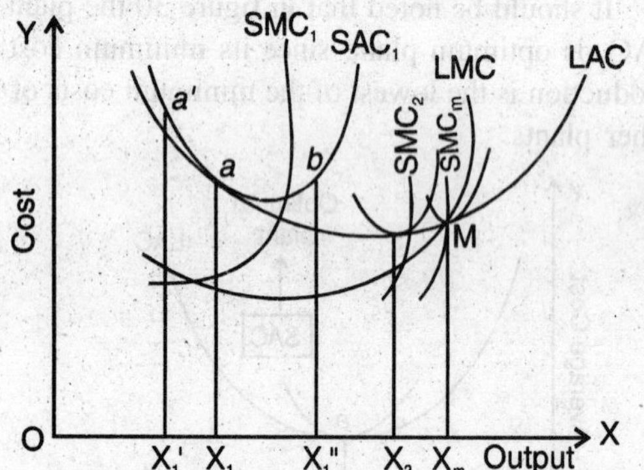

Fig. 35 : *Long-Run Marginal Cost Curve*

For levels of output to the left of tangency *a* the SAC > LAC. At the point of tangency SAC = LAC. As we move from point *a'* to *a,* we actually move form a position of inequality of SARC and LRAC to a position of equality. Hence the change in total cost (*i.e.,* the MC) must be smaller for the short-run curve than for the long-run curve. Thus LMC > SMC to the left of *a.* For an increase in output beyond X_1 (*e.g.,* "X_1") the SAC > LAC. That is, we move from the position *a* of equality of the two costs to the position *b* where SAC is greater than LAC. Hence the addition to total cost (= MC) must be larger for the short-run curve than for the long-run curve. Thus LMC < SMC to the right of *a.*

Since to the lest of *a,* LMC > SMC, and to the right of *a,* LMC < SMC, it follows that at *a,* LMC = SMC. If we draw a vertical line from *a* to the X-axis the point at which it interests the SMC (point A for SAC_1) is a point of the LMC.

If we repeat this procedure for all points of tangency of SRAC and LAC curves to the left of the minimum point of the LAC, we obtain points of the section of the LMC which lies below the LAC. At the minimum point M the LMC intersects the LAC. To the right of M the LMC lies above the LAC curve. At point M we have

$$SAC_m = SMC_m = LAC = LMC$$

The TC curve is roughly S-shaped, while the ATC, the AVC and the MC are all U-shaped, the MC curve intersects the other two curves at their minimum points.

Elasticity of Cost

If output (Q) is produced at a total cost (C), the cost function is

$$C = f(Q).$$

The elasticity of total cost is the ratio of the proportional change in total cost to the proportional change in total output. It may be written as

$$\text{Cost Elasticity (K)} = \frac{dC/C}{dQ/Q}$$

$$= \frac{dC}{C} \times \frac{Q}{dQ} = \frac{dC}{dQ} \times \frac{Q}{C} = \frac{dC}{dQ} \div \frac{C}{Q}$$

$$= \frac{MC}{AC} = \frac{\text{Marginacost}}{\text{Averagecost}}$$

Thus, cost elasticity (K) is equal to the ratio of marginal cost (dC/dQ) to average cost (C/Q). It follows from this that

(*a*) If MC > AC, then K > 1

(*b*) If MC = AC, then K = 1 and

(*c*) If MC < AC, then K < 1.

The Concept of Revenue

The term 'revenue' refers to the receipts obtained by a firm from the sale of certain quantities of a commo-dity at various prices. The revenue concept relates to total revenue, average revenue and marginal revenue.

Total Revenue : Total revenue refers to the total amount of money that the firm receives from the sale of its products. Thus, the total revenue is obviously equal to the quantity sold multiplied by the selling price of the commodity, *i.e.,*

$$TR = P.Q.$$

where

TR = total revenue

P = price per unit

Q = quantity

Average Revenue : Average revenue can be obtained by dividing by the total revenue by the number of units sold. Thus,

$$\text{average revenue} = \frac{\text{total revenue}}{\text{total output sold}}$$

$$\text{or,} \quad AR = \frac{TR}{Q} = \frac{P.Q}{Q} = P$$

Thus, average revenue is the price of commodity. It follows from this that the curve which relates average revenue to output is identical with the demand curve that relates price to output.

Marginal Revenue : Marginal revenue is the net revenue earned by selling on additional unit of the product. In other words, marginal revenue is the addition made to the total revenue by selling one more unit of the good. Putting it in algebraic expression marginal revenue is the addition made to total revenue by selling *n* units of a product instead of ($n - 1$) where *n* is any given number. Therefore,

Marginal Revenue = difference in total revenue in increasing sales from ($n - 1$) units to *n* units

$$MR_n = TR_n - TR_{n-1}$$

If TR stands for total revenue and Q stands for output, then marginal revenue (MR) can be expressed as follows :

$$MR = \frac{d(TR)}{dQ}$$

$\frac{d(TR)}{dQ}$ indicates the slope of the total revenue curve. Thus if the total revenue curve is given to us, we can find out marginal revenue at various levels of output by measuring the slopes at the corresponding points on the total revenue curve.

Average Revenue, Marginal Revenue and Elasticity of Demand

There is a very useful relationship between elasticity of demand, average revenue and marginal revenue at any level of output. We have stressed above that the average revenue curve of a firm is really the same thing as the demand curve of consumer's for the firm's product. Therefore, elasticity of demand at any point on a consumer's demand curve is the same thing as the elasticity of demand on the given point on the firm's average revenue curve.

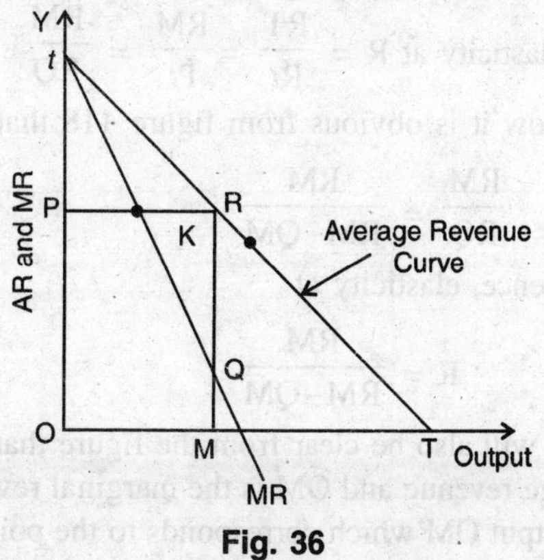

Fig. 36

We know that elasticity of demand at point R on the average revenue curve *t*T in figure 36 is $\frac{RT}{Rt}$. With this measure of point elasticity of demand we can study the relationship between average revenue, marginal revenue and price elasticity at any level of output.

In figure 36, AR and MR are respectively average and marginal revenue curves. Elasticity of demand at point R on the average revenue curve :

$$= \frac{RT}{Tt}$$

Now in triangles PtR and MRT

$\angle t$PR = $\angle$ RMT (right angles)

$\angle t$RP = $\angle$ RTM (corresponding angles)

and $\angle$ PtR = $\angle$ MRT

Therefore, triangles PtR and MRT are equiangular.

$$\text{Hence, } \frac{RT}{Rt} = \frac{RM}{Pt} \quad \text{...(1)}$$

In the triangles PtK and KRQ

PK = RK

$\angle$ PKt = $\angle$ RKQ (vertically opposite)

$\angle t$PK = $\angle$ KRQ (right angles)

Therefore, triangles PtK and KRQ are congruent (*i.e.*, equal in all respects).

Hence

Pt = RQ ...(2)

From (1) and (2), we get

$$\text{Elasticity at R} = \frac{RT}{Rt} = \frac{RM}{Pt} = \frac{RM}{RQ}$$

Now it is obvious from figure 118 that

$$\frac{RM}{RQ} = \frac{RM}{RM-QM}$$

Hence, elasticity at

$$R = \frac{RM}{RM-QM}$$

It will also be clear from the figure that RM is average revenue and QM is the marginal revenue at the output OM which corresponds to the point R on the average revenue curve. Therefore,

Elasticity at

$$R = \frac{\text{Average Revenue}}{\text{Average Revenue} - \text{Marginal Revenue}}$$

If, A stands for average revenue

M stands for marginal revenue

e stands for point elasticity on the average revenue curve.

then

$$e = \frac{A}{A-M}$$

It follows from this that

$$e.A - e.M = A$$

$$e.A - A = e.M$$

$$A(e-1) = e.M$$

$$A = \frac{e.M}{e-1}$$

Hence,

$$A = M\left(\frac{e}{e-1}\right)$$

And also,

$$M = A\left(\frac{e-1}{e}\right)$$

If the demand elasticity is equal to one then

$$MR = AR\left(\frac{e-1}{e}\right) = AR\left(\frac{1-1}{1}\right)$$

$$= AR \times 0 = 0$$

If $e > 1$, Say 2, then

$$MR = AR\left(\frac{2-1}{2}\right)$$

$$MR = \frac{1}{2}.AR$$

$$MR = AR - \frac{AR}{2}$$

MR = Positive

If $e < 1$, Say 1/2, then

$$MR = AR\left(\frac{1/2-1}{1/2}\right)$$

MR = AR – 2AR

MR = Negative

Hence, by applying the formula for various elasticities of demand at different points (or at different levels of output) on the average revenue curve it will be found that marginal revenue is always positive at any point or output where the elasticity of the average revenue curve is greater than one and marginal revenue is always negative where the elasticity of the average revenue curve is less than one.

In case the elasticity of the AR curve is unity throughout its length like a rectangular hyperbola, the MR curve will coincide with the X-axis, shown as a dotted line in figure 37.

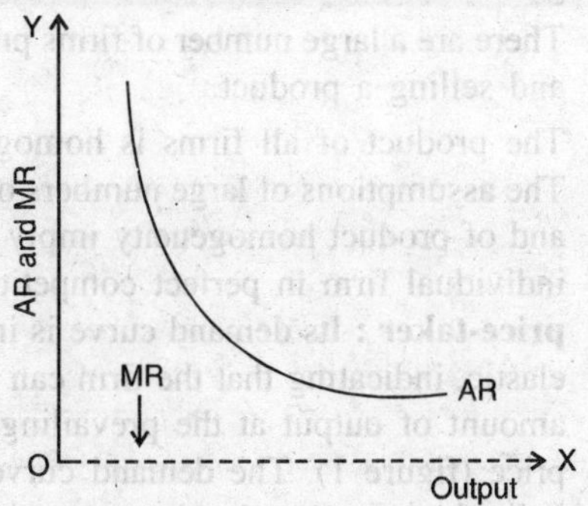

Fig. 37 : *Rectangular Hyperbola AR Curve*

Three Types of Revenue (AR, MR, TR) and Elasticity (e)

We are now in a position to describe the relationship between three types of revenue, namely, AR, MR and TR on the one side and elasticity on the other. From the formula

$$MR = AR\left(\frac{e-1}{e}\right)$$

We can know what would be the marginal revenue, if elasticity and AR are given to us. When the elasticity is equal to one, it follows from the above formula that marginal revenue will be equal to zero.

Thus,

$$MR = AR\left(\frac{e-1}{e}\right)$$

$$MR = AR\left(\frac{1-1}{1}\right)$$

$$MR = AR \times 0$$

$$MR = 0$$

Likewise, it can be proved that,

If $e > 1$, MR is positive, and

If $e < 1$, MR is negative.

In a straight-line demand curve we known that the elasticity at the middle point is equal to one. It follows that marginal revenue corresponding to the middle point of the demand curve (or AR curve) will be equal to zero. Consider figure 38. C is the middle point of the average revenue or demand curve AR. At point C elasticity is equal to one. Corresponding to C on the AR curve, marginal revenue will be zero. Thus MR curve is shown cutting the X-axis at point N which corresponds to point C on the AR curve. At a greater quantity than ON elasticity of the AR curve is less than one and the marginal revenue is negative. Marginal revenue being negative beyond ON means that total revenue will diminish if a quantity greater than ON is sold. Total revenue will be increasing upto ON output, since upto this marginal revenue remains positive. If follows therefore that **total revenue will be maximum where elasticity is equal to one.** This TR curve in this figure is shown to be at its highest level corresponding to the point C on AR curve or ON output where marginal revenue is zero and elasticity is equal to one.

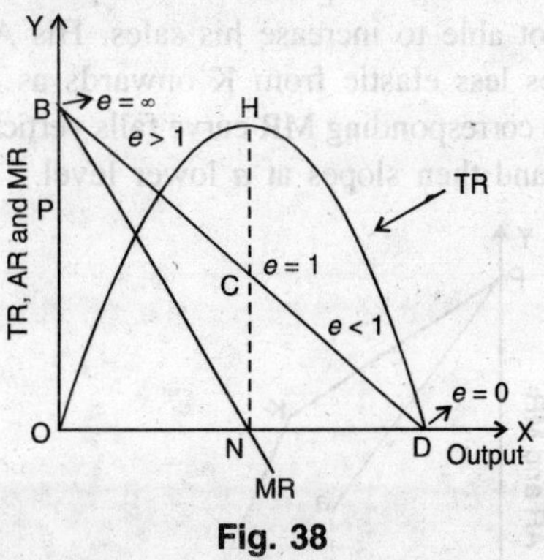

Fig. 38

Kinked Demand Curve and their Corresponding MR Curves

Under Oligopoly, the average and marginal revenue curves do not have a smooth downward slope. They possess Kinks. Since the number of sellers under Oligopoly is small, the effect of a price cut or price increase on the part of one seller will be followed by some changes in the behaviour of other firms. If a seller raises the price of his product, the other sellers will not follow him in order to earn larger profits at the old price. So the price-raising seller will experience a fall in the demand for his product. His average revenue curve in figure 39 becomes elastic after K and its corresponding MR curve rises discontinuously from *a* to *b* and then continues its course at the new higher level.

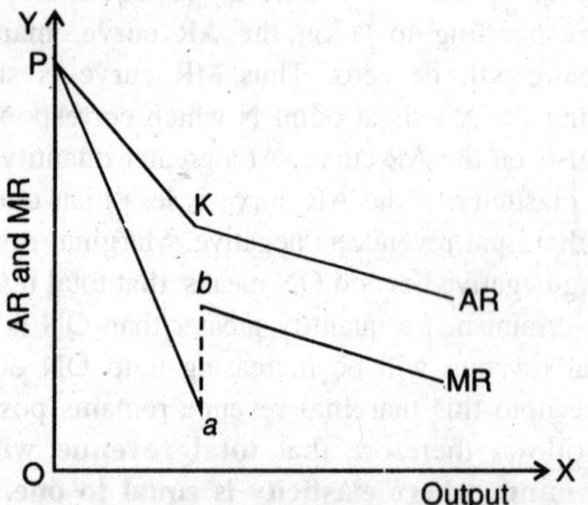

Fig. 39: *Kinked AR Curve*

On the other hand, if the Oligopolistic seller reduces the price of his product, his rivals also follow him in reducing the prices of their product so that he is not able to increase his sales. His AR curve becomes less elastic from K onwards as in figure 40. The corresponding MR curve falls vertically from *a* to *b* and then slopes at *a* lower level.

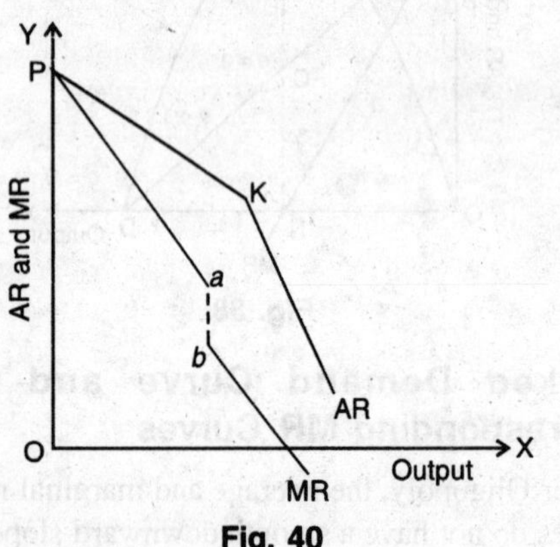

Fig. 40

FORMS OF MARKET AND PRICE DETERMINATION

Perfect Competition

Perfect competition is a market structure characterised by a complete absence of rivalry among the individual firms. In other words, perfect competition implies no rivalry among firms.

Assumptions

The model of perfect competition is based on the following assumptions.

1. There are a large number of firms producing and selling a product.
2. The product of all firms is homogeneous. The assumptions of large numbers of sellers and of product homogeneity imply that the individual firm in perfect competition is a **price-taker :** Its demand curve is infinitely elastic, indicating that the firm can sell any amount of output at the prevailing market price (figure 1). The demand curve of the individual firm is also its average revenue curve and its marginal revenue curve.
3. Both the sellers and buyers have perfect information about the prevailing price in the market.
4. Entry into and exit from the industry is free for the firms.
5. No government regulation.
6. Perfect mobility of factors of production.

Equilibrium of the Firm in the Short Run: By Curves of Total Revenue and Total Cost

The firm is in equilibrium when it maximises its profits (π), defined as the difference between the total cost and total revenue.

$$\pi = TR - TC$$

Given that the normal rate of profit is included in the cost items of the firm, π is the profit above the normal rate of return on capital and the remuneration for the risk-bearing function of the entrepreneur.

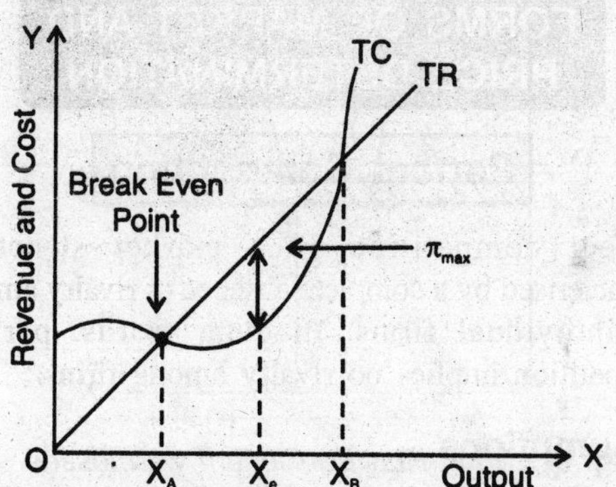

Fig. 1 : *Profit-Maximising Output : Equilibrium of the Firm*

The firm is in equilibrium when it produces the output that maximises that difference between total receipt and total costs. The equilibrium of the firm may be shown graphically in two ways. Either by using the TR and TC curves, or the MR and MC curves.

In figure 1 we show the total revenue and total cost curves of a firm in a perfectly competitive market. The total revenue curve is a straight line through the origin, showing that the price is constant at all levels of output. The firm is a **price-taker** and can sell any amount of output at the going market price, with its TR increasing proportionately with its sales. The slope of the TR curve is the marginal revenue. It is constant and equal to the prevailing market price, since all units are sold at the same price. Thus in pure competition MR = AR = P.

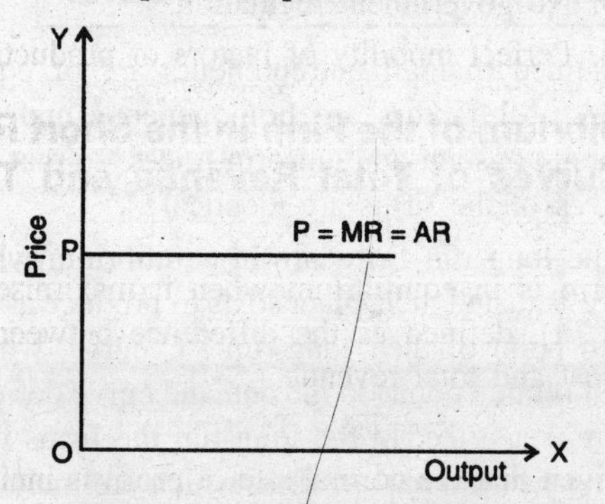

Fig. 2 : *Perfect Competition'*

The shape of the total-cost curve reflects the U shape of the average-cost curve, that is, the law of variable proportions. The firm maximises its profit at the output, X_e, where the distance between the TR and TC curves is the greatest. At lower and higher levels of output total profits is not maximised : at levels smaller than X_A and larger than X_B the firm has losses.

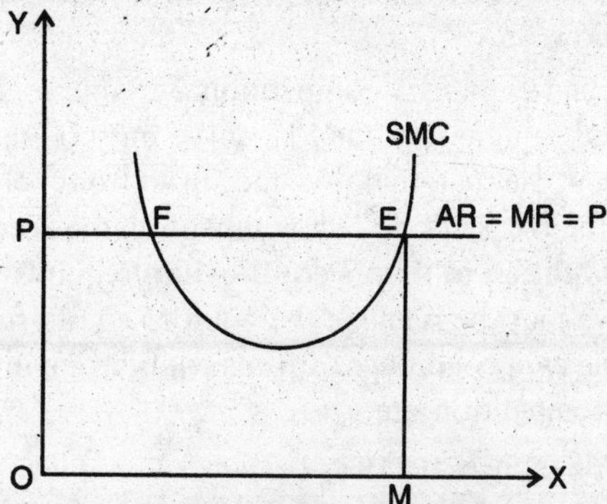

Fig. 3 : *Firm's Equilibrium Under Perfect Competition*

Equilibrium of the Firm : By Curves of Marginal Revenue and Marginal Cost (Identical Cost Conditions)

Identical cost conditions imply that all firms are facing same cost conditions, that is, their average and marginal cost curves are of the same level and shapes.

In figure 3 we show the average and marginal-cost curves of the firm together with its demand curve.

In order to decide about its equilibrium output, the firm will compare marginal cost with marginal revenue. It will be in equilibrium at the level of output at which marginal cost equals marginal revenue and marginal cost curve is curing marginal revenue curve from below. At this level it will be maximising its profits. Consider figure 3 in which price OP is prevailing in the market. PL would then be the demand curve or the average and marginal revenue curve of the firm. It will be seen from figure 3 that MC curve cuts average and marginal revenue curve at two different points, F and E. F can not be the position of equilibrium, since at F second order condition of firm's equilibrium, namely, that the marginal cost curve must cut marginal revenue curve from below at the point of equilibrium, is not satisfied. The firm will be increasing its profits by increasing production beyond F because marginal revenue is greater than marginal cost. The firm will be in equilibrium at point E or output OM since at E marginal cost equals marginal revenue as well as marginal cost curve is cutting marginal revenue curve from below.

As under perfect competition MR curve is a horizontal straight line, the MC curve must be rising so as to cut the marginal revenue curve from below. Therefore, in case of perfect competition the **second order condition of firm's equilibrium** requires that MC curve must be rising at the point of equilibrium. Hence the twin conditions of firms equilibrium under perfect competition are :

1. MC = MR = Price
2. (Slope of MC) > (Slope of MR)

But the fulfilment of the above two conditions does not guarantee that the profits will be earned by the firm. Whether the firm makes excess profits or losses depends on the level of the ATC at the short-run equilibrium. If the ATC is below the price at equilibrium (figure 4) the firm earns excess profits (equal to the area PABE). If, however, the ATC is above the price (figure 5) the firm makes a loss (equal to the area FPEC).

In the latter case **the firm will continue to produce only if it covers its variable costs.** Otherwise, it will close down, since by discontinuing its operations the firm is better off : it minimises its losses.

The point at which the firm covers its variable costs is called **'the closing-down point.'**

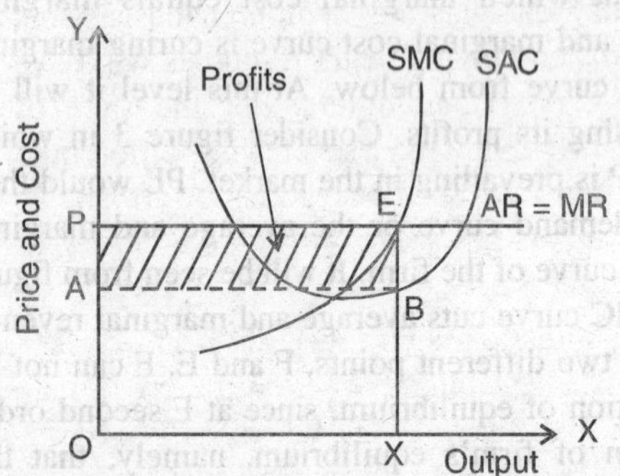

Fig. 4 : *Short-Run Equilibrium with Profit*

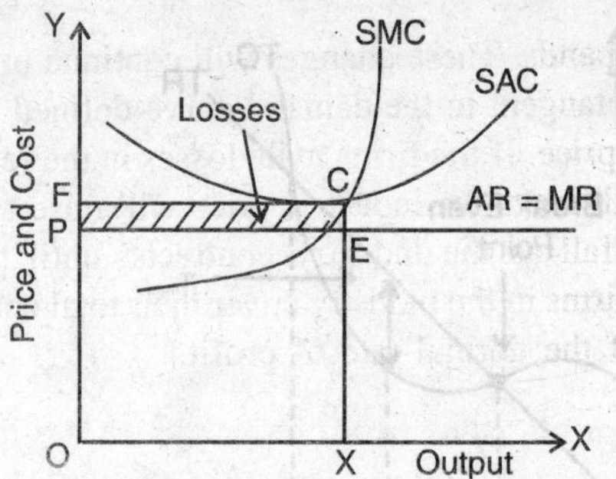

Fig. 5 : *Short-Run Equilibrium with losses*

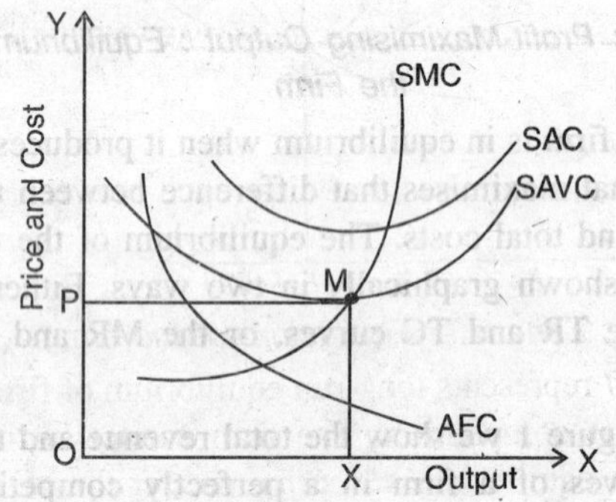

Fig. 6 : *Shut-Down Point for the Perfectly Competitive Firm*

In figure 6 the closing-down point of the firm is denoted by point M. If price falls below P the firm does not cover its **variable costs** and is better off its closes down.

Long-Run Equilibrium of the Firm (Identical Costs)

It is assumed that all entrepreneurs are of equal efficiency. All factors are homogeneous and are available at constant and uniform prices, so that the cost curves of the firms are identical.

In the long run firms are in equilibrium when they have adjusted their plant so as to produce at the minimum point of their long-run AC curve, which is tangent (at this point) to the demand curve defined by the market price. In the long-run the firms will be earning just **normal profits,** which are included in the LAC. If they are making excess profits new firms will be attracted in the industry, this will lead to a fall in price and an upward shift of the cost curves due to increase of the prices of factors as the industry expands. These changes will continue until the LAC is tangent to the demand curve defined by the market price. If the firms male losses in the long run they will leave the industry, price will raise and costs may fall as the industry contracts, until the remaining firms in the industry cover their total costs inclusive of the normal rate of profit.

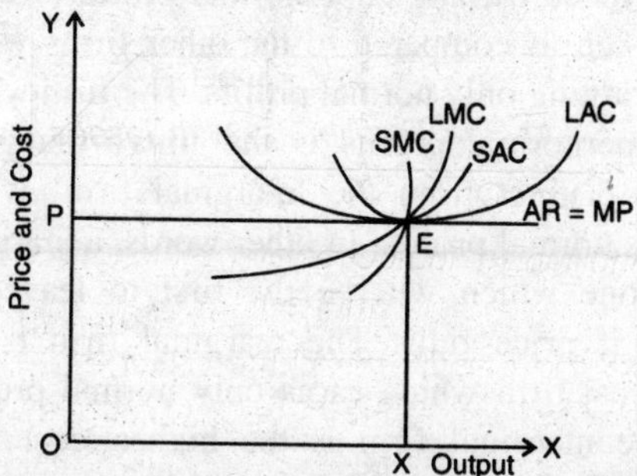

Fig. 7 : *Long-Run Equilibrium of the firm*

Figure 7 represents long-run equilibrium of firm under perfect competition. The firm cannot be in the long-run equilibrium at a price greater than OP in figure 7. Since if price is greater than OP, then the price line (demand curve) would lie somewhere above the minimum point of the average cost curve so that marginal cost and price will be equal where the firm is earning abnormal profits. Since there will be tendency for new firms to enter and compete away these abnormal profits the form cannot be in equilibrium at any price higher than OP. Likewise, the firm cannot be in long-run equilibrium at a price lower than OP in figure 7 under perfect competition.

If price is lower than OP, the demand curve will lie below the average cost curve so that the marginal cost and price will be equal at the point where the firm is making losses. Therefore, there will be tendency for some of the firms in the industry to go out with the result that price will rise and the firms left in the field make normal profits. We therefore conclude that firm can be in long-run equilibrium under perfect competition only when price is at such a level that the horizontal demand curve is tangent to the AC curve, so the price equals average cost and firm makes only normal profits. Therefore, the condition for long-run equilibrium of firm can be written as :

SMC = SAC = LMC = LAC = MR = Price

It should be noted that a horizontal demand line can be tangent to a U-shaped average cost curve only at the latter's minimum point. Since at the minimum point of the average cost curve the marginal cost and average cost are equal, price in long-run equilibrium is equal to both MC and AC. In other words, double condition of long-run equilibrium is fulfilled at the minimum point of the average cost curve.

It is clear from above that **long-run equilibrium of the firm under perfect competition is established at the minimum point of the long-run average cost curve.** Operating at the minimum point of the long-run average cost curve signifies that the firm is of **optimum size,** that is, it is producing output at the **lowest possible cost.** The fact that the firm, working under conditions of perfect competition, tends to be of optimum size in the long run is beneficial from the social point of view in two ways. **Firstly,** working at optimum size implies that the resources of the society are being utilized in the most efficient way. **Secondly,** it signifies that the consumers are getting the goods at the lowest possible price.

Short-Run Equilibrium of the Firm: Differential Cost Conditions

If entrepreneurs differ in efficiency the cost curves of the firms vary from each other. Firms with more efficient entrepreneurs will be able to produce at lower costs than the others. Thus different firms selling the same product at one price will be producing different quantities at different costs. More efficient firms employing better resources will have lower cost curves than others. For the sake of convenience we divide the firms having differential cost conditions into three categories A, B and C whose cost curves are shown in figure 8. Figure 8 represents differential cost conditions.

If price in market is OP, then the firm of every category will adjust output where price OP equals its marginal cost. Firm A will be in equilibrium at E and will be producing OM output, firm B will be in equilibrium at L and will be producing ON, form C will be in equilibrium at K and will be producing

OT. While for all the firms, price equals their marginal cost at equilibrium output, but firm A in equilibrium is making super-normal profits, B is earning only normal profits and C is making losses. This is so because cost conditions are different for the three firms.

Thus, under conditions of different costs and in short-run equilibrium, some firms in the industry may be earning super-normal profits. Some may be making only normal profits, and some others may be incurring losses. **In such a situation the industry cannot be in full equilibrium.**

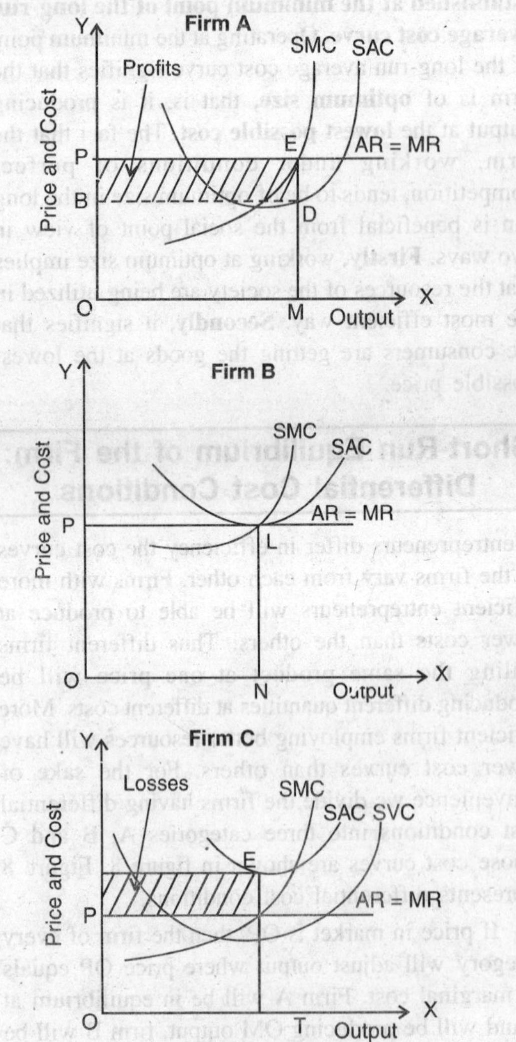

Fig. 8

Long-Run Equilibrium of Firms : Differential Cost Conditions

In case the entrepreneurs are of different efficiency, the cost curves of the firms will also differ. A firm with a superior entrepreneur than the others will be able to produce the same output at lower costs. Such a firm will be earning supernormal profits even in the long-run as compared to the other firms which may be earning only normal profits. The firm which earns supernormal profits is the **'intra-marginal firm'** as distinct from the 'marginal firm' which just earns normal profits. In other words, a marginal firm is one which will be the first to leave the industry if price falls. The marginal firm is the highest-cost firm which earns only normal profits. Since the marginal firm is the highest-cost firm making only normal profits, it will be first to quit the industry if the price falls as with the fall in price its profits sink below normal.

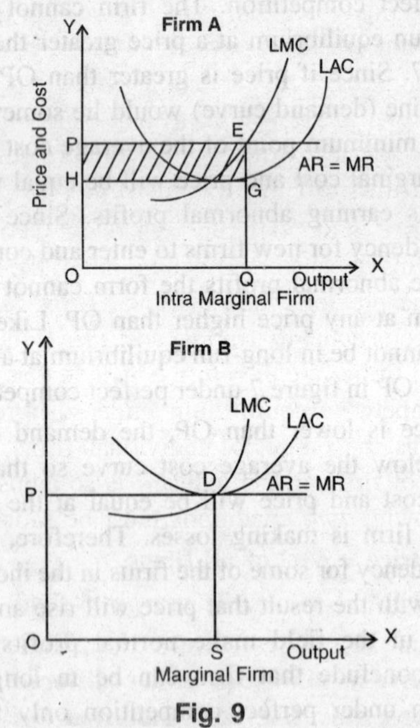

Fig. 9

Figure 9 represents long-run equilibrium of firms, which are of three categories in respect of cost conditions. The price prevailing in the long-run is OP which equals marginal cost of firm A at output OQ and marginal cost of firm B at output OS. For

A Classification of Market Forms

Forms of Market Structure	*Number of Firms*	*Price Elasticity of Demand for an individual firms*	*Degree of Control over price*
(a) **Perfect Competition**	A large number of firms	Infinite	None
(b) **Imperfect Competition**	A large number of firms	Large	Some
(i) **Monopolistic Competition**	—	Large	Some
(ii) **Pure Oligopoly** (Oligopoly without Product Differentiation)	Few firms	Small	Some
(iii) **Differentiated Oligopoly** (Oligopoly with product differentiation)	Few firms	Small	Some
(c) **Monopoly**	One	Very Small	Considerable

firms of category B price is equal to average cost, therefore they make only normal profits. Thus, firms of category B are marginal firms which will go out of the industry if the price falls below the present price OP. But price OP is greater than average cost at equilibrium output of intra-marginal firm A and therefore this firm make super-normal profits. The price being equal to average cost of the marginal firm guarantees that the marginal firm will be making only normal profits and therefore there will be no tendency for new firms to enter or for some of the existing firms to leave the industry.

If price in the long run falls below OP in figure 9, the firms of category B will go out of the industry and some previous intra-marginal firms for which new price is equal to average cost firm will become marginal firms. We therefore conclude that in long-run competitive equilibrium under different cost conditions the output of individual firms and the number of firms in the industry is so adjusted that the following two conditions must be satisfied.

1. **Price = MC of all firms,**
2. **Price = AC of the marginal firm.**

From above it follows that **in long-run competitive equilibrium under differential cost conditions only the marginal firm will be of optimum size,** because the equilibrium of only marginal firm will be established at the minimum point of the average cost curve. The intra-marginal firms will be of more than optimum size, as is clear from figure 9.

Thus in the long-run where cost curves are not identical some firms may be earning supernormal profits. The industry will be in full equilibrium only by accident.

The Supply Curve of the Firm and the Industry

The supply curve of the firm may be derived by the points of intersection of its MC curve with successive demand curves. Assume that the market price increases gradually. This causes an upward shift of the demand curve of the firm. Given the positive slope of the MC curve, each higher demand curve cuts the (given) MC curve to a point which lies to the right of the previous intersection. This implies that the quantity supplied by the firm increases as price rises. The firm, given its cost structure, will not supply any quantity if the price falls below P, because at a lower price the firm does not cover its variable cots (figure 10).

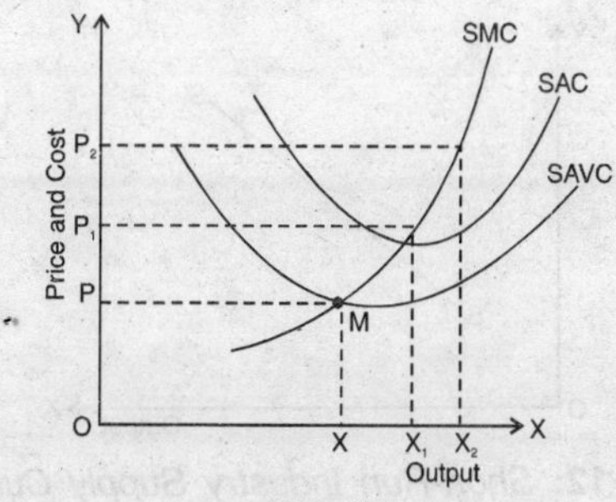

Fig. 10

If we plot the successive points of intersection of MC and the demand curves on a separate graph we observe that the supply curve of the individual firm is identical to its MC curve to the right of the closing-down point (above AVC) M. Below P the quantity supplied by the firm is zero. As price rises above P the quantity supplied increases. The supply curve of the firm is shown in figure 11.

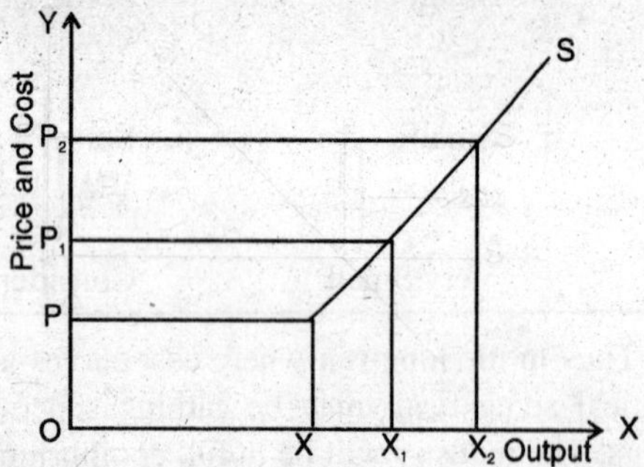

Fig. 11 : *Short-Run Supply Curve of a Firm*

The Industry-supply curve is the **horizontal summation** of the supply curves of the individual firms. It is assumed that the factor prices and the technology are given and that the number of firms is very large. Under these conditions the total quantity supplied in the market at each price is the sum of the quantities supplied by all firms at that price. In figure 12 we show the industry supply as a straight line with a positive slope. It should, however, be noted that the particular shape of the market-supply curve depends on the technology and on factors prices, as well as the size distribution of the firms in the industry. All firms are not usually of the same size. The particular size of each firm in perfect competition depends on the entrepreneurial efficiency of the businessman, which is traditionally considered as a random attribute.

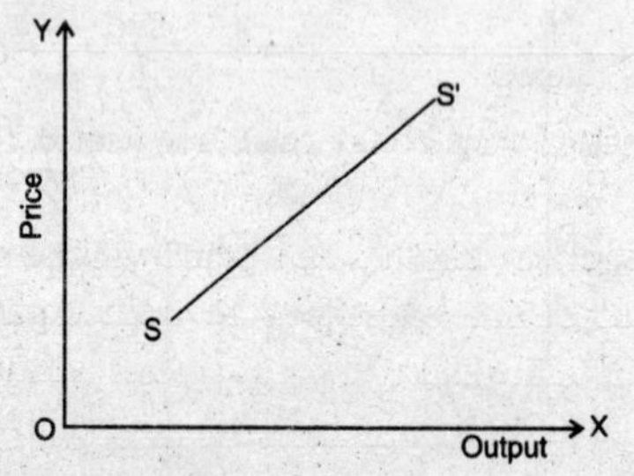

Fig. 12: *Short-Run Industry Supply Curve*

Short-Run Equilibrium of the Industry

Given the market demand and the market supply the industry is in equilibrium at that price at which the quantity demanded is equal to the quantity supplied. In figure 13 the industry is in equilibrium at price P, at which the quantity demanded and supplied is Q. However, this will be a short-run equilibrium, if at the prevailing price firms are making excess profits or losses.

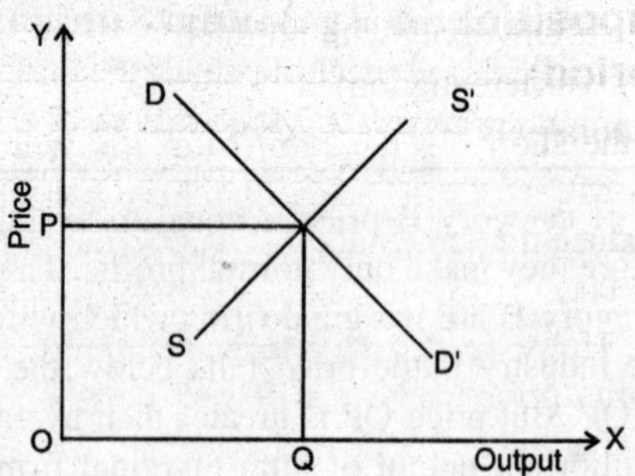

Fig. 13 : *Short-Run Industry Equilibrium*

In the long-run, firms that make losses and cannot read just their plant will close down. Those that make excess profits will expand their capacity, while excess profits will also attract new firms into the industry. Entry exit and readjustment of the remaining firms in the industry will lead to a long run equilibrium in which forms will just be earning normal profits and there will be no entry or exit from the industry.

Optimal Resource Allocation

In perfect competition the market mechanism leads to an optimal allocation of resources. The optimality is shown by the following conditions which prevail in the long-run equilibrium of the industry :

(*a*) The output is produced at the minimum feasible cost.

(*b*) Consumers pay the minimum possible price which just covers the marginal cost of the product,, that is, **price = opportunity cost.**

(*c*) Plants are used at full capacity in the long run, so that there is no waste of resources.

(*d*) Firms only earn normal profits.

In the long run these conditions prevail in all markets, so that resources are optimally allocated in the economy as a whole.

Effect of Imposition of A Tax (Perfect Competition)

We will examine the effects of the imposition by the government of a lump-sum tax, a profits tax, and a specific tax, that is, a tax per unit of output.

Imposition of a Lump-Sum Tax (Per Period)

In the short run the **lump-sum tax** will not affect the MC cost curve and the firm will continue to produce the same output as before the imposition of the tax.

However, if the firm was earning just normal profits prior to the tax, it will not be covering its ATC at the going market price and will close down in the long-run. Thus in the long run the market-supply curve will shift to the left as firms leave the industry, the output will be lower and the price higher as compared with the pre-tax equilibrium.

Imposition of Profits Tax

This tax takes the form of a percentage on the net profit of the firm. The effects of a profits tax are the same with those of a lump-sum tax. The profits tax, while reducing the profits, will not affect its MC. Hence in the short-run the equilibrium of the firm and the industry will not change.

However, in the long-run, exit of firms will be inevitable if in the pre-tax period firms were earning just normal profits. In the long run the supply in the market would shift to the left and a new equilibrium would be reached with a higher price, a lower quantity produced and a smaller number of firms.

Imposition of a Specific Sales Tax

This takes the form of a given amount of money (*e.g.*, Rs. 2) pre unit of output produced. Such a tax clearly affects the MC of the firm. The MC curve, which is also the supply curve of the firm, will shift upwards to the left, and the amount produced at the going price will be reduced.

The market-supply curve will shift upwards to the left and price will rise. The important question here is by how much will the price increase : Will the increase in P be smaller, equal, or greater than the specific tax? This is an important question because it relates to who is going to bear the specific sales tax : the consumer-buyer, the firm, or both?

The answer to this question is that the burden of the specific tax that will be borne by the consumer (buyer) depends on the price elasticity of supply, given the market demand. In general, the most elastic the market supply the higher the proportion of the tax that the consumer will bear and the less the burden of the firm from the specific tax.

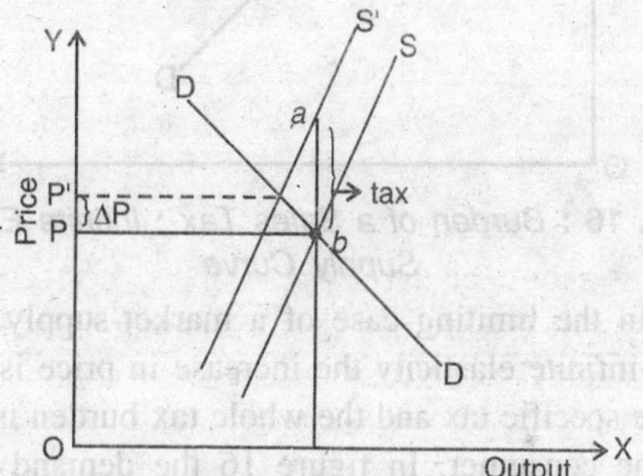

Fig. 14 : *Burden of a Sales Tax : Less Elastic Supply Curve*

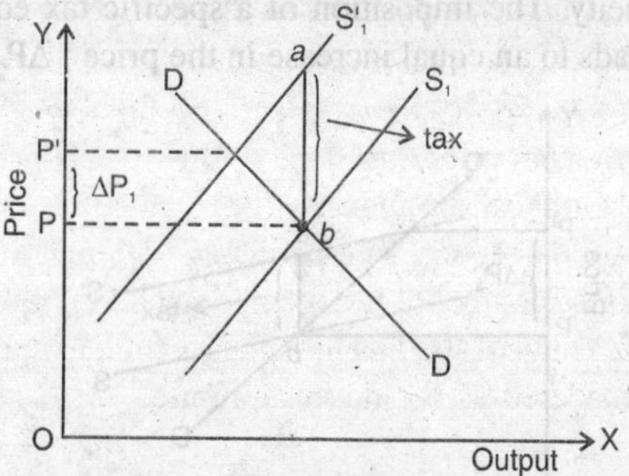

Fig. 15 : *Burden of a Sales Tax : More Elastic Supply Curve*

So long as the market supply has a positive slope the specific tax will be paid partly by the buyer and partly by the firm. The burden to the firm will be smaller the greater the elasticity of supply. In other words, the firm will be able to pass on to the consumer more of the specific tax, the more elastic the market supply. This is illustrated in figure 14 and 15. The demand curve is identical in both figures and the initial (pre-tax) price is the same, but the supply curve in figure 15 is more elastic. Imposition of a specific tax equal to *ab* raises the price by ΔP in figure 14 and by ΔP_1 in figure 15. Clearly $\Delta P_1 > \Delta P$, that is, the tax burden to the consumer is greater in the case of a more elastic supply curve (given the market demand).

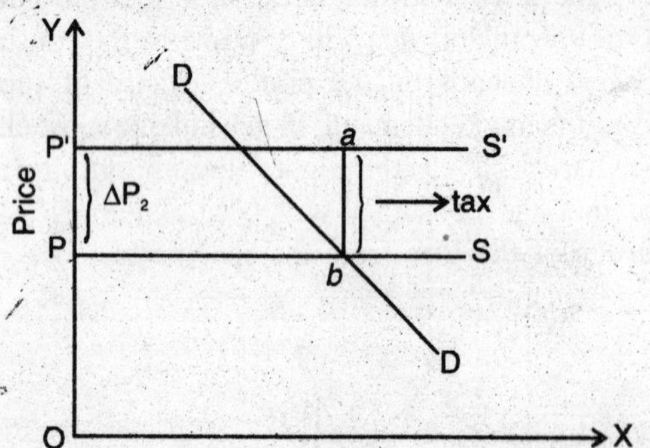

Fig. 16 : *Burden of a Sales Tax : Infinite Elastic Supply Curve*

In the limiting case of a market-supply curve with infinite elasticity the increase in price is equal to the specific tax and the whole tax burden is force by the consumer. In figure 16 the demand is the same as in figure 14 and 15, but the supply curve is parallel to the horizontal axis, showing infinite price elasticity, The imposition of a specific tax equal to *ab* leads to an equal increase in the price : $\Delta P_2 = ab$.

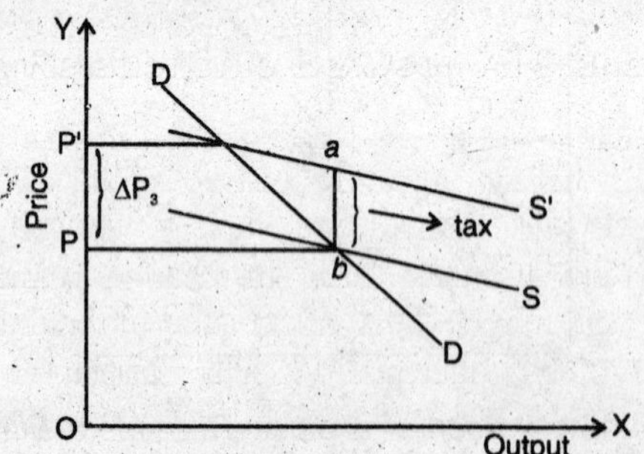

Fig. 17 : *Burden of a Sales Tax : Supply is Negatively Sloping*

If the supply curve has a negative slope (figure 17) the imposition of a specific tax results in an increase in the price which is greater than the tax. In figure 17 the demand is identical as in the above-examined cases but the supply curve is negatively sloping (with its slope smaller than the slope of the DD curve). Under these conditions a specific tax of *ab* leads to an increase in the market price equal to ΔP_3, which is obviously larger than the unit tax.

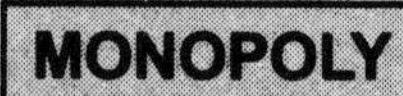

Definition

Monopoly is a market structure in which there is a single seller, there are no close substitutes for the commodity it produces and there are barriers to entry. Two points are worth noting in this definition. *Firstly*, there must be a single producer or seller of a product if there is to be monopoly. A *second condition* which is essential for a firm to be called monopolist is that no *close substitutes* for the product of that firm should be available.

We can express the second condtion of monopoly in terms of *cross elasticity of demand* also. Cross elsticity of demand shows a change in the demand for a good as a result of change in the price of another good. Therefore, if there is to be monopoly *the cross elasticity of demand between the product of the monopolist and the product of any other producer must be very small.*

The above two conditions ensure that the monopolist can set the price of his product and can pursue an independent price policy. Power to influence price is very essence of monopoly. From this it must not be gathered that the monopolist is so powerful that he can dictate the price as wel as the amount sold. Monopolist can do one of these things only; either he can fix the price leaving the amount sold to the consumers, or he can fix the quantity he wants to produce and sell and leave the price to be determined by the demand of the consumers.

Average and Marginal Revenue for a Monopolist

In perfect competition the price is unaffected by variations in the Firm's output, and if follows that the addition to revenue resulting from increasing the level of sales by one more unit is the market price of that unit. Thus the marginal and average revenue curves coincide in the same horizontal straight line. In the case of monopoly, however, the average revenue curve, which is the same as the market demand curve, is *downward sloping*. Furthermore, the marginal revenue curve does not coincide with the demand curve : since the side of an extra unit forces down the price at which all units already being sold can now be sold, the sale of an extra unit results in a net addition to revenue of an amount less that its own selling price.

It is easy to prove algebraically that, if the demand curve slopes downwards, marginal revenue is always less than price. Let subscripts n and $(n + 1)$ indicate the revenue associated with the sale of nth and the $(n + 1)$th unit. So that, e.g., TR_n is the total revenue associated with the sale of n units period.

$$MR_{n+1} = TR_{n+1} - TR_n$$
$$= (n + 1)\,P_{n+1} - n.P_n$$
$$= n.P_{n+1} + P_{n+1} - n.P_n$$
$$= n\,(P_{n+1} + P_n) + P_{n+1}.$$

Since the demand curve slopes downwards P_{n+1} (the price ruling when $n + 1$ units are sold) will be less than P_n (the price ruling when n units are sold). Thus the MR of the $(n + 1)$th unit is less than P_{n+1}.

Demand and Revenue

Since there is a single Firm in the industry, the Firm's demand curve is the industry demand curve. The demand equation (linear demand function), *ceteris paribus*, is

$$X = b_0 - b_1.P$$

The clause cetris paribus implies that all the other factors (such as income, tastes, other prices which affect demand are assumed constant. Changes in these factors will shift the demand curve (Figure 18).

The slope of the demand curve (DD') is

$$\frac{dX}{dP} = \frac{d\,(b_0 - b_1.P)}{dX} = -\,b_1$$

The price elasticity of demand is

$$e_P = \frac{dX}{dP}.\frac{P}{X} = -b_1.\frac{P}{X}$$

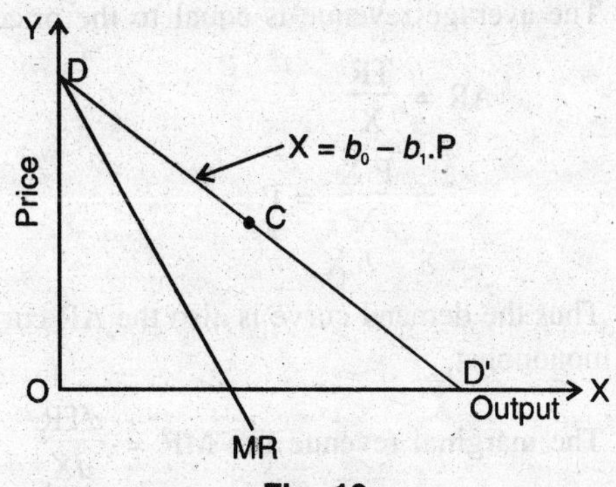

Fig. 18

That is, elasticity changes at any one point of the demand curve.

(a) At point D the elasticity approaches infinity.

$$e_P = -b_1.\frac{P}{X} \rightarrow \infty$$

(b) At point D' on the demand curve DD', the elasticity is zero.

$$e_P = -b_1.\frac{P}{X}$$

$$= -b_1.\frac{0}{X} = 0$$

(c) At the mid point C the price elasticity is unity.

$$e_P = -\,1$$

The total revenue of the monopolist is

$$TR = P.X$$

Solving the demand equation for P we find

$$P = \frac{b_0}{b_1} - \frac{1}{b_1}.X$$

Setting $\left(\frac{b_0}{b_1}\right) = a$ and $\left(\frac{1}{b_1}\right) = b$ we may rewrite the price equation as

$$P = a - b.X$$

Substituting into the revenue equation we find

$$TR = P.X$$
$$TR = (a - b.X)\,X$$
$$TR = a.X - b.X^2$$

The average revenue is equal to the price :

$$AR = \frac{TR}{X}$$

$$= \frac{P.X}{X} = P$$

$$= a - b.X$$

Thus the demand curve is also the AR curve of the monopolist.

The marginal revenue is : $MR = \frac{dTR}{dX}$

$$= \frac{d(a.X - b.X^2)}{dX}$$

$$= a - 2b.X$$

That is, the MR is a straight line with the same intercept as the demand curve, but twice as steep.

The general relation between P and MR is found as follows. Given

$$TR = P.X$$

$$MR = \frac{dTR}{dX}$$

$$MR = \frac{d(P.X)}{dX}$$

$$MR = P.\frac{dX}{dX} + X.\frac{dP}{dX}$$

$$\therefore \quad MR = P + X.\frac{dP}{dX}$$

The marginal revenue is at all levels of output smaller than P, given that

$$P = MR - X.\frac{dP}{dX}$$

and the term $\left(X.\frac{dP}{dX}\right)$ is positive (sicne the slope of the demand curve, $\frac{dP}{dX} > 0$.

Hence P > MR

Costs

In the traditional theory of monopoly the shapes of the cost curves are the same as in the theory of perfect competition. The AVC, MC and ATC are U-shaped, while the AFC is a *rectangular hyperbola*. However, the particular shape of the cost curves does not make any difference to the determination of the equilibrium of the Firm, provided that the slope of the MC is greater than the slope of the MR curve.

One point should be stressed here. *The MC curve is not the supply curve of the monopolist, as is the case in perfect competition.*

In monopoly there is no unique relationship betwen price and the quantity supplied.

Equilibrium of the Monopolist

A. Short-Run Equilibrium

The monopolist maximises his short-run profits if the following two conditions are fulfilled :

1. MC = MR
2. The slope of MC is greater than the slope of the MR at the point of the intersection.

In Figure 19 the equilibrium of the monopolist is defined by point E, at which the MC intersects the MR curve from below. Thus both condtions for equilibrium are fulfilled. Price is P and the quantity is X.

The monopolist realises excess profits equal to the shaded area APCB. Note that the price is higher than the MR.

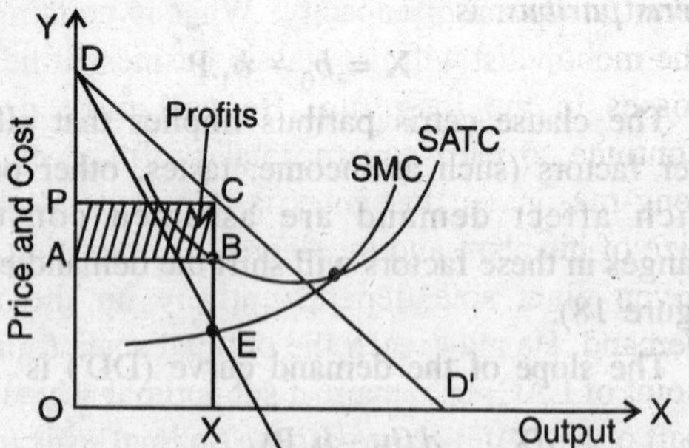

Fig. 19 : *Short-Run Equilibrium Under Monopoly*

It is generaly thought that monopolists always earn profits and therefore in layman's mind profits are generally associated with monopoly. But this is a wrong notion.

In the short-run, monopolist can make losses also. If demand is inadequate, the complete absence of competition is of little benefit to the seller. In the short-run, monopolist will continue working so long as price is above the average variable cost. If the price falls below average variable cost, the monopolist would shut down even in the short-run.

In perfect competition the Firm is a price-taker, so that its only decision is output determination. The monopolist is faced by two decisions : setting his price and his output. However, given the downward-sloping demand curve, the two decisions are interdependent. The monopolist will either set his price and sell the amount that the market will take at it, or he will produce the output defined by the intersection of MC and MR, which will be sold at the corresponding price, P. *The monopolist cannot decide independently both the quantity and the price at which he wants to sell it.* The crucial condition for the maximisation of the monopolist's profit is the equality of his MC and MR, provided that the MC cuts the MR from below.

B. Long-Run Equilibrium

In the long-run the monopolist has the time to expand his plant, or to use his existing plant at any level which will maximise his profit. With entry blocked, however, it is not necessary for the monopolist to reach an optimal scale (that is, to build up his plant until he reaches the minimum point of LAC). Neither is there any guarantee that he will use his existing plant at optimum capacity. What is certain is that the monopolist will not stay in business if he makes losses in the long run. He will most probably continue to earn supernormal profits even in the long-run, given that entry is barred. However, the size of his plant and the degree of utilisation of any given plant size depend entirely on the market demand. He may reach the optimal scale (minimum point of LAC) or remain at suboptimal scale (falling part of his LAC) or surpass the optimal scale (expand beyond the minimum LAC) depending on the market conditions. In Figure 20 we depict the case in which the market size does not permit the monopolist to expand to the minimum point of LAC. In this case not only is his plant of suboptimal size but also the existing plant is under utilized. This is because to the left of the minimum point of the LAC the SAC is tangent to the LAC at its falling part, and also because the short-run MC must be equal to the LMC. This occurs at E, while the minimum LAC is at *b* and the optimal use of the existing plant is at *a*. Since it is utilised at the level E', there is excess capacity.

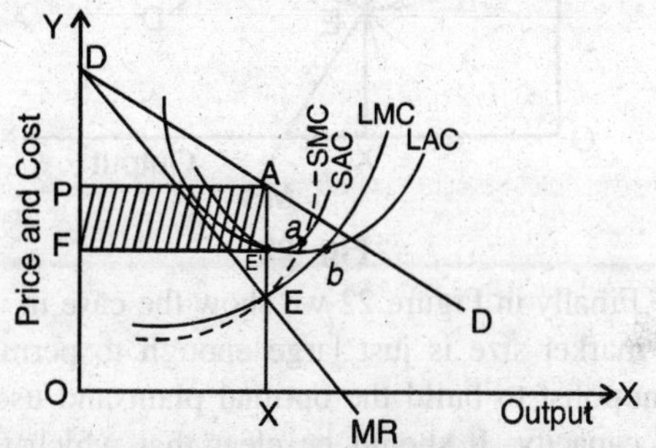

Fig. 20 : *Monopolist with Suboptimal Plant and Excess Capacity*

In Figure 21 we depict the case where the size of the market is so large that the monopolist, in order to maximise his output, must build a plant larger than the optimal and overutilise it. This is because to the right of the minimum point of the LAC the SAC and the LAC are tangent at a point of their positive slope, and also because the SMC must be equal to the LAC. Thus the plant that maximes the monopolist's profits leads to higher costs for two reasons : Firstly because it is larger than the optimal size, and secondly because it is overutilised.

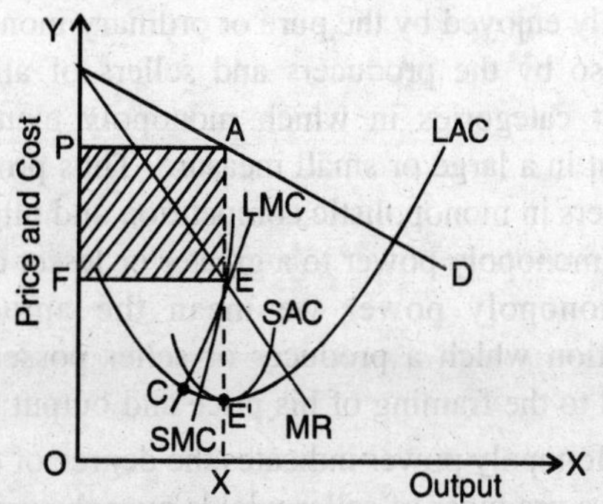

Fig. 21 : *Monopolist Operating in a Large Market: His Plant is Larger than the Optimal (C) and it is being overutilised.*

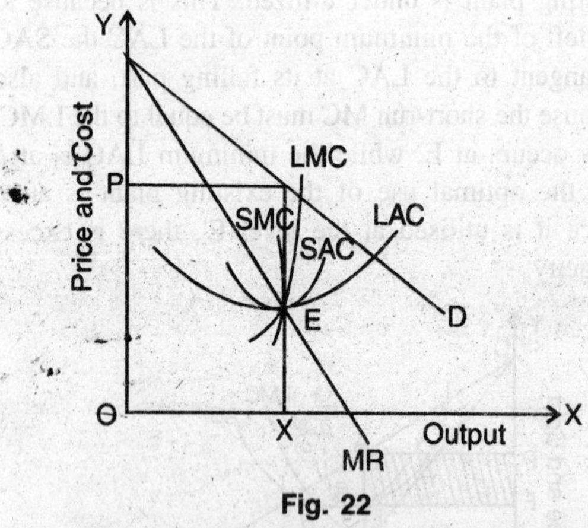

Fig. 22

Finally in Figure 22 we show the case in which the market size is just large enough to permit the monopolist to build the optimal plant and use it at full capacity. It should be clear that which of the above situations will emerge in any particular case depends on the size of the market (given the technology of the monopolist). There is no certainty that in the long-run the monopolist will reach the optimal scale, as is the case in a perfect competitive market. In monopoly there are no market forces similar to those in perfect competition which lead the firms to operate at optimum plant size in the long run.

Measurement of the Degree of Monopoly Power

Monopoly is a matter of degree. Monopoly power is not only enjoyed by the pure or ordinary monopolist but also by the producers and sellers of all those market categories in which monopoly element is present in a large or small measure. Thus producers or sellers in monopolistic competition and oligopoly enjoy monopoly power to a greater or lesser degree. By monopoly power we mean the amount of discretion which a producer or seller possesses in regard to the framing of his price and output policy.

Monopoly power indicates the degree of control which a producer of seller wields over the price and output to his product. Various measures of monopoly power have been suggested by different economists, we shall discuss some of them below.

Lerner's Measure

One of the earliest methods' to measure monopoly power is expressed by Prof. A.P. Lerner in terms of the bargaining strength. **The difference between price and marginal cost is the measure of the degree of monopoly power.** A seller's monopoly power depends upon his ability to sell his product at a price much above his marginal cost. The larger the gap between price and marginal cost, the greater is the monopoly power. Hence

$$\text{Degree of monopoly power} = \frac{P-MC}{P}$$

where P = price

MC = marginal cost

When competition is pure or perfect, price (P) is equal to marginal cost and therefore Lerner's index of monopoly power is equal to zero indicating no monopoly power at all, for when price is equal to marginal cost, (P – MC) will be equal to zero and the above formula will yield the value of index as zero.

Thus under pure or perfect competition, Lerner's index of monopoly power

$$\frac{(P-MC)}{P} = \frac{0}{P} = 0.$$

On the other hand, when the monopolised product entails no cost of production, that is, when the product is a free good whose supply is controlled by one person, the marginal cost will be equal to zero and Lerner's index of monopoly power $\left(\frac{P-MC}{P}\right)$ would be equal to one or unity. Thus when MC is equal to zero.

$$\text{Degree of monopoly} = \frac{P-MC}{P} = \frac{P-O}{P} = 1$$

It is thus clear that Lerner's index of **monopoly power can vary from zero to unity.** Within this range, the greater the value of the index $\left(\frac{P-MC}{P}\right)$, the greater the degree of monopoly power possessed by the seller.

Now it has been that **Lerner's index of monopoly power is nothing else but the inverse of the price elasticity of demand.** We can prove this as follows :

Lerner's degree of monopoly power

$$= \frac{P-MC}{P}$$

For profit maximisation, MC = MR, and this formula becomes

$$= \frac{P-MR}{P} \qquad ...(1)$$

We know that $MR = P\left(\frac{e-1}{e}\right)$, where e is price elasticity of demand at the equilibrium output. Thus putting $P\left(\frac{e-1}{e}\right)$ in the place of MR in (1) above we get,

Lerner's degree of monopoly power

$$= \frac{P-P\left(\frac{e-1}{e}\right)}{P} = \frac{P-P\left(1-\frac{1}{e}\right)}{P}$$

$$= \frac{P\left[1-\left(1-\frac{1}{e}\right)\right]}{P} = 1-1+\frac{1}{e} = \frac{1}{e}$$

= inverse of the elasticity of demand

It therefore follows that Lerner's index of monopoly power is equal to the inverse of price elasticity of demand. This degree of monopoly power can be judged by merely knowing the elasticity of demand at the equilibrium output.

The degree of monopoly varies inversely with the elasticity of the demand for the good.

Price Discrimination

Price discrimination refers to the practice of a seller of selling the same good at different prices to different buyers.

When is Price Discrimination Possible?

The necessary conditions, which must be fulfilled for the implementation of price discrimination are thc following :

1. The market must be divided into sub-markets with different price elasticities.
2. There must be effective separation of the sub-markets, so that no reselling can take place from a low-price market to a high-price market.

Oligopoly

We have studied price and output determination under three market forms, namely, perfect competition, monopoly, and monopolistic competition. However, in the real world economies we find that many of the markets or industries are oligopolistic. Oligopoly is an important form of imperfect competition. **Oligopoly is said to prevail when there are few firms or sellers in the market producing or selling a product.** In other words, when there are two or more than two, but not many, producers or sellers of a product, oligopoly is said to exist. Oligopoly is also often referred to as **"Competition among the Few."** The simplest case of oligopoly is duopoly which prevails when there are only two producers or sellers of a product.

When products of few sellers are homogeneous, we talk of **Oligopoly without Product Differentiation or Pure Oligopoly.** On the other hand, when products of the few sellers or firms instead of being homogeneous, are differentiated but close substitutes of each other, Oligopoly with Product Differentiation or Differentiated Oligopoly is said to prevail.capacity, as is the case under perfect competition.

Kinky Demand Curve

The Kinked demand curve hypothesis was put forward by **Paul M. Sweezy.** In explaining price and output especially under oligopoly with product differentiation economists often use the kinked demand curve hypothesis. This is because when under oligopoly products are differentiated, it is unlikely that when a firm raises its price, all customers would leave it because some customers are intimately attached to it due to product differentiation. As a result, demand curve facing a firm under differentiated oligopoly is not perfectly elastic.

The demand curve facing an oligopolist, according to the kinked demand curve hypothesis, has a **'Kink'** at the level of the prevailing price. The kink is formed at the prevailing price level because the segment of the demand curve above the prevailing price level is highly elastic and the segment of the demand curve below the prevailing price level is inelastic. A kinked demand curve D with a kink at point P has been shown in figure 23. The prevailing price level is MP and the firm is producing and selling the output OM.

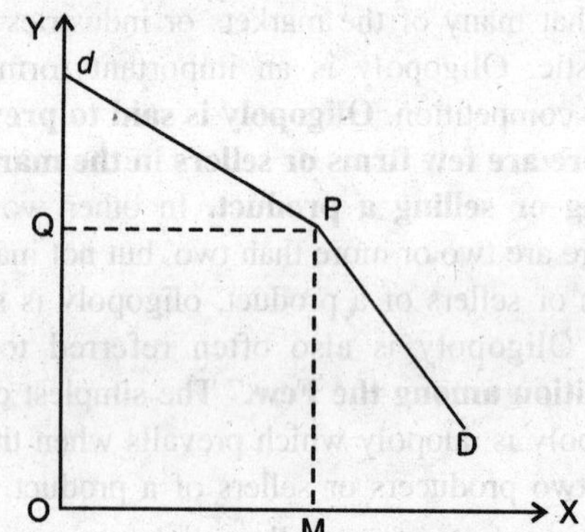

Fig. 23 : *Kinked Demand Curve Under Oligopoly.*

Now the upper segment *d*P of the demand curve dD is relatively elastic and the lower segment PD is relatively inelastic. This difference in elasticities is due to the particular competitive reaction pattern assumed by kinky oligopoly demand curve hypothesis.

The competitive reaction pattern assumed by the kinky oligopoly demand curve theory is as follows:

Each oligopolist believes that if he lowers the price below the prevailing level his competitors will follow him and will accordingly lower their prices, whereas if he raises the price above the prevailing level his competitors will not follow his increase in price.

The 'Adding-Up' Problem: 'Product Exhaustion' Theorems

As soon as it was propounded that the factors of production are paid equal to their marginal products, a perplexing problem cropped up over which there was a serious debate among the famous economists at that time. The perplexing problem which was posed was that if all factors were paid rewards equal to their marginal products, would the total product be just exactly exhausted?

In other words, If each factor is rewarded equal to its marginal product, the total product should be disposed of without any surplus or deficit. The problem of proving that the total product will be just exhausted if all factors are paid rewards equal to their marginal products has been called **"Adding-up-Problem"** or **Product Exhaustion Problem.**

The Theory of Rent

Rent as an economic surplus, as used by modern economists means the earning of a factor of production in excess of the minimum amount necessary to keep it in its present use. It is not a differential surplus, the difference between the superior and the inferior grades of lands as **Ricardo** meant by rent. Moreover, it accrues not to land alone, but to all other factor services.

Ricardian Theory of Rent

David Ricardo was a brilliant 19th century economist of England who propounded a systematic theory of rent which is in many ways the basis of the modern concept of rent.

Ricardo defined rent as follows: **"Rent is that portion of the produce of earth which is paid to the land lord for the use of the original and indestructible powers of the soil."** It should be noticed that land rent, according to Ricardian definition, is a payment for the use of only land and is different from contractual rent which includes.

- According to Ricardo, marginal land earns no rent.

- In Ricardian Theory, rent is not price determining. In fact, in this theory rent is price determined, that is, it is price which determines rent. To quote Ricardo, **"Corn is not high because a rent is paid, but a rent is paid because corn is high."**

Modern Theory of Rent

Modern theory of rent does not confine itself to the determination of the reward of only land as a factor of production. Rent according to the modern sense can arise in respect of any factor of product ion. It is a surplus payment in excess of transfer earnings of that factor. **Transfer earnings means the amount of money which any particular unit of a factor could earn in its next best alternative use.** In other words, economic rent in such a case is the difference between the present earnings and transfer earnings. **In Joan Robinson's words,** "The essence of the conception of rent is the conception of a surplus earned by a particular part of a factor of production over and above the minimum earnings necessary to induce it to its work."

How Economic Rent Arises

Now the question is how economic rent arises. Economic rent in the sense of surplus over transfer earnings will arise when the supply of the factor units is less **than perfectly elastic or not perfectly elastic.** From the point of view of elasticity of supply, there are three possibilities:

(*a*) When the supply is perfectly elastic

(*b*) When it is less than perfectly elastic, and

(*c*) When it is inelastic.

(a) When the supply of factor units is perfectly elastic

In this case, there will be no surplus or economic rent and the actual earnings and transfer earnings will be equal. When the supply of a factor is perfectly elastic, it means that at a given price, or remuneration, the entrepreneur can engage or employ any number of the factor units. It is obvious that, when the factor units are available at a minimum price or transfer earnings, their equilibrium price will be equal to that minimum price at which the present earnings are equal to the transfer earnings. Thus, no factor unit in such a situation will be able to earn more than its transfer earnings. That is, there will be no rent or surplus earnings.

This is shown in figure 24 given below. In this figure, the supply curve of the factor of production SS is perfectly elastic and is, therefore, shown as a horizontal straight line. This means that all factor units are available at the given price OS or in other words, the transfer earnings of each factor unit are also equal to OS. DD is the demand curve. The two curves intersect at P. OM is the quantity of the factor used. The price determined is OS. The total earnings are OSPM. But since transfer earnings are equal to the actual earnings, they are also equal to OSPM. There is no surplus and hence no rent.

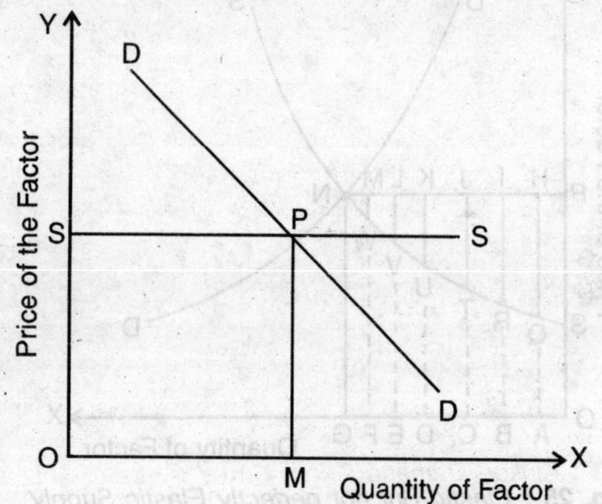

Fig. 24 : *Perfectly Elastic Supply*

If this firm does not pay the price OS, the factor units will be shifted to some other use and earn there as much, because present earnings are equal to transfer earnings.

Thus, it is clear that if the supply of factor units is perfectly elastic for a particular use or industry, then no factor unit can earn surplus or economic rent.

(b) Less than Perfectly Elastic Supply

Now let us take a case when the supply is less than perfectly elastic, i.e., it is some what, elastic. This means that the transfer earnings of all the factor units are not equal. As, in some industry or use, the price of the factor increases, more and more of the factor units will offer their services to this industry in use. Suppose that in a particular industry or use, a factor unit can earn Rs. 200 p.m. It is obvious that only such units of the factor will offer their services to this industry whose price in other alternative occupations is less than Rs. 200 or in other words the transfer earnings are less than the present earnings.

In this manner, as the price paid for a factor in a particular industry or occupation increases, the supply of the factor will increase if the transfer earnings are less. It is clear that the supply of a factor of production depends on its transfer earnings. This is shown in the figure 25.

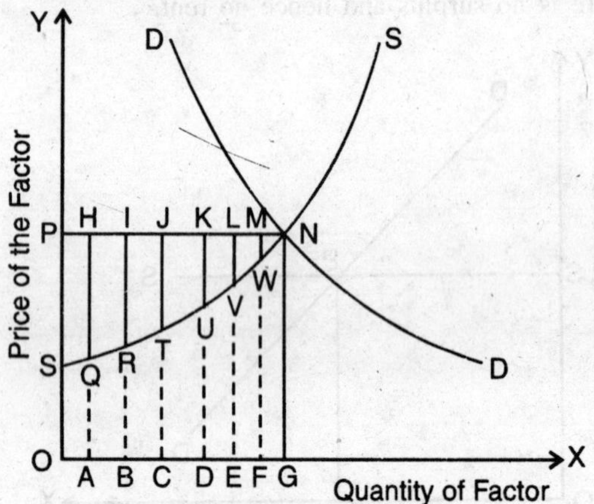

Fig. 25 : *Elastic But not perfectly Elastic Supply*

SS is the supply curve sloping upwards to the right. It is somewhat elastic but not perfectly elastic as in the case (a). The supply curve SS indicates what quantity of the factor will be available at various prices. In other words, it shows the transfer earnings of different factor units. Thus, the transfer earnings of A unit of the factor, is AQ whereas the price is OP.

Therefore, surplus or rent, is HQ. In the same manner, the other units earn surplus or rent. It is assumed that all factor units are equally useful for this industry. Hence, the price of all factor units in the industry will be the same. The supply curve cuts DD demand curve at N. In this case, OG is the quantity of the factor used. The rent or price per unit is OP (= GN). But the transfer earnings of each factor unit are less than the price OP. All units except the last G unit are earning more than their transfer earnings.

That is they are earning economic rent. Economic rent or surplus will be different for different units because the transfer earnings are different, although the price is the same.

The total earnings are OGNP. But the transfer earnings are OGNS. Hence

Economic Rent = OGNP − OGNS = PNS

(c) Absolutely Inelastic Supply

Now we come to a case when the supply of a factor is absolutely inelastic. The obvious example of this case is the supply of land for the community as a whole. We know that land for the community is fixed and it cannot be increased or decreased whatever the price offered. High price will not increase it or low price will not decrease it. That is why it is said that land has no supply price.

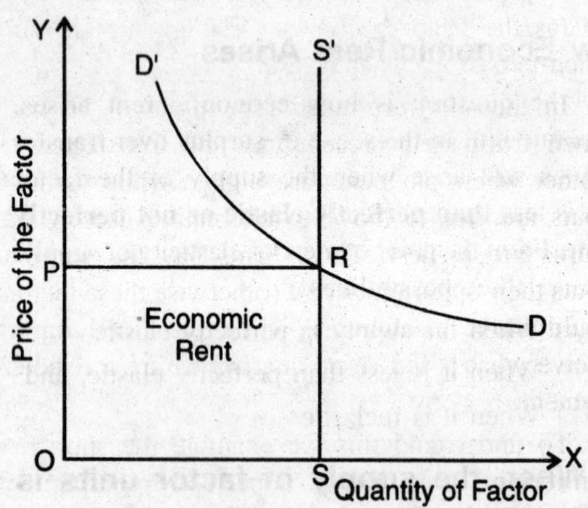

Fig. 26 : *Absolutely Inelastic Supply*

In the figure 26, the supply curve SS shows an absolutely inelastic supply which represents the supply of land for the community as a whole. Since the supply is fixed, the supply curve SS' is a vertical straight line. This means that from the point of view of the community as a whole, the transfer earnings are zero, since the land cannot be transferred to any other place.

In this figure DD' is the demand curve for the whole land. The supply curve SS' and the demand curve DD' intersect at R. In equilibrium the price of land or rent is determined at OP and the total earnings of land are equal to OPRS area. Since in this situation the transfer earnings of land are zero, the entire earnings of land, i.e., OPRS is rent.

Thus, it is clear that is case the supply of a factor is absolutely inelastic, its earnings are rent.

Conclusion. We may conclude that rent arises when the supply of a factor is less than perfectly elastic.

Quasi-Rent

The doctrine of quasi-rent was introduced in to economic literature by **Marshall** who extended Ricardo's theory of land-rent to other factors fixed in supply during the short-run.

In short run some factors are fixed, while in the long-run they become variable. The payment to an input which is in fixed supply in the short run is called **quasi-rent,** because it disappears in the long-run (as the factor becomes variable), unlike rents which persist in the long-run.

In the short-run fixed inputs cannot be with drawn from their present use and transferred to another where payments are higher, while variable inputs are free to move to alternative uses where returns are highest. Thus, firms pay the variable inputs their opportunity cost (otherwise these factors would move elsewhere), while the fixed inputs receive what is left over; quasi-rents are a residual payment.

To understand this we examine the short-run equilibrium of a firm in a perfectly competitive market (figure 27). Assume the price is P. The firm maximises its profit, producing OX units of output, from which it receives a total revenue (TR) equal to the area OPEX.

The firm pays OXBA = TVC to the variable factors. (it cannot pay less and keep them in its employment). The fixed factors earn the residual ABEP, which is the quasi-rent. Thus

Quasi-Rent = TR – TVC

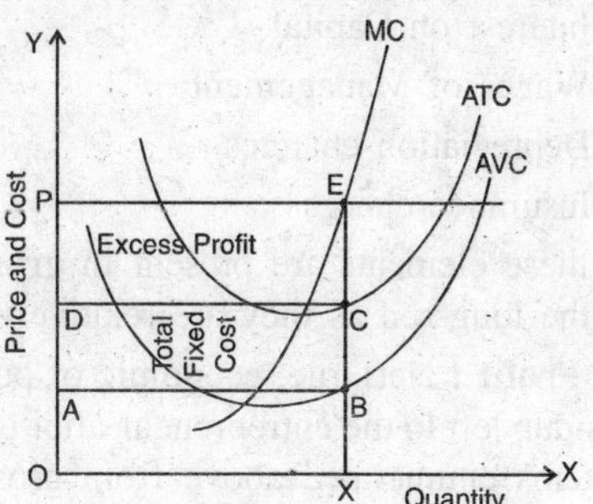

Fig. 27 : *Quasi Rent*

The quasi-rent can be divided into two parts, the total fixed cost (area ABCD in figure 27) and excess (or pure) profit (DCEP). The TFC is the opportunity cost of the fixed factors, that is, the return that would have been earned if the fixed factors were utilised in their best alternative employment (e.g. by another firm in the same industry which pays higher returns on the fixed factors). The excess profit is the difference between the quasi-rent and the TFC:

Quasi-Rent = TFC + Excess Profit

or

Excess Profit = Quasi-Rent – TFC

In the long run the quasi-rent becomes zero and the firm is in equilibrium, earning just normal profits. **In summary.** The price of a factor, whose supply is fixed in the long-run, is called **rent.** The price of a factor, which is in fixed supply only in the short-run, is called **quasi-rent**. Rent persists in the long-run, whereas quasi-rent disappears in the long-run as the factor becomes variable.

Profits

In ordinary parlance, profit is the surplus of income over expenses of production according to a businessman. It is the amount left with him after he has made payments for all factor services used by him in the process of production. But he may not have been careful in calculating all such expenses of production in the economic sense. Therefore, economists regard businessman's profit as gross profit as distinct from pure or net profit because it includes the following constituents.

1. Rent on Land

2. Interest on Capital
3. Wages of Management
4. Depreciation changes
5. Insurance charges

All these elements are present in **gross profit** even in the long-run as they are relatively stable.

Net Profit : Net, true, economic or pure profit is the residue left to the entrepreneur after deducting all the items enumerated above from gross profit. Net profit, however, includes the following elements within it.

1. Reward for Uncertainty Bearing
2. Reward for coordination
3. Rent of Ability
4. Reward of Innovation
5. Monopoly Gains
6. Windfalls

We may conclude that an economist's profit is quite distinct from a businessman's profit. The former is concerned with net profit which is arrived at by deducting from the businessman's gross profit, the remuneration for the latter's own land, labour and capital.

Some Important Points

- **Prof. J.B. Clark** propounded his dynamic theory of profit in 1900. According to him profits are a dynamic surplus.
- The Rent Theory of Profit was propounded by the American economist, **F.A. Walker.**
- The risk theory of profit is associated with H.B. Hawley who regards risk-taking as the main function of the entrepreneur. Profit is the residual income which the entrepreneur receives because he assumes risks.
- **Prof. Frank H. Knight** regards profit as the reward of bearing non-insurable uncertainties.
- The Innovation Theory of Profit is associated with **Joseph A. Schumpeter.** According to Schumpeter, the principal function of the entrepreneur is to make innovations and profits are a reward for performing this important function.

NATIONAL INCOME AND RELATED AGGRETATES

Concept and Measurement

Economic well-being of society is obviously influenced by the volume of total output as well as by composition of the output and relative size of the shares received by various groups.

The portion of economic theory which deals with the determination of total output is known as *National Income Analysis* or the process of National Income Accounting.

National income is an uncertain term which is used interchangeably with national dividend, national output and national expenditure. On this basis, national income has been defined in a number of ways. In common parfance, national income means the total value of goods and services produced annually in a country. In other words, the total amount of income accruing to a country from economic activities in a year's time, is known as national income. It includes payments made to all resources in the form of wages, interest, rent and profits.

Definitions of National Income

The definitions of national income can be grouped into two classes. One, the *traditional definitions* advanced by Marshall, Pigou and Fisher; and two, modern definitions. According to Marshall, "*The labour and capital of a country acting on its natural resources produce annually a certain net aggregate of commodities, material and immaterial imcluding services of all kinds. This is the true net annual income or revenue of the country or national dividend.*" In this definition, the word'net' refers to deductions from the gross national income in respect of depreciation and weaving out of machines. And to this must be added income from abroad.

National income, according to *Pigou, "is that part of the objective income of the community including, of course, income derived from abroad, which can be measured in money."*

Fisher odopted *'Consumption'* as the criterion of national income whereas Marshall and Pigou regarded it to be production. According to Fisher, ''The national dividend or income consists solely of services as received by ultimate comsumers, whether from their material or human environments. Thus, a piano, or an overcoat made for me this year is not a part of this year's income, but an addition to the capital. Only the services rendered to me during this year by these things are income.'' fisher's definition is considered to be better them that of Marshall or Pigou, because Fisher's definition provides an adequate concept of economic welfare which is dependent on consumption and consumption represents our standard of living.

From the modern point of view, *Simon Kuznets* has defined national income as ''the net output of cmmodities and services flowing during the year from the country's productive system in the hands of the ultimate consumers.''

Concepts of National Income

There are various concepts of national income which we shall study one by one.

1. Gross National product (GNP)

Gross National product is defined as the total market value of all final goods and services produced in a year. Two things must be noted in regard to gross national product. *First,* it measures the market value of annual output. In other words, GNP is a *monetary measure.*

Secondly, for calculating gross national product accurately, all goods and services produced in any given year must be counted once, and not more than once. Most of the goods go through a series of production stages before reaching a market. As a result, parts or components of mony goods are bought and sold many times. Hence to avoid counting several times the parts of goods that are sold and resold, gross national product only includes the market value of final goods and ignores transactions involving intermediate goods.

The ''gross national product at market prices'' may be obtained by adding up :

A. What private persons spend on consumption, or what is called *personal consumption* expenditure.

B. What private businessmen spend on replacement, renewal and new investment. This is called *gross domestic private investment.*

C. What the rest of the world spends on the output of the national economy over and above what this economy spends on the output of the rest of the world, *i.e.*, export-import or net foreign investment; and

D. What the government spends on the purchase of goods and services, *i.e.*, *government purchases.*

2. GNP at Factor Cost

GNP at factor cost is the sum of the money value of the income produced by and accruing to the various factors of production in one year in a country.

GNP at market prices, always includes indirect taxes levied by the government on goods which raise their prices. But GNP at factor cost is the income which the factors of production receive in return for their services alone. It is the cost of production. Thus GNP at market prices is always higher than GNP at factor cost. Therefore, in order to arrive at GNP at factor cost, we deduct indirect taxes from GNP at market prices. Again, it of ten happens that the cost of production of a commadity to the producer is higher than the price of a similar commodity in the market. In order to protect such producers, the government helps them by granting monetary help in the form of subsidy equal to the difference between the market price and the cost of production of the commodity. Thus in order to arrive at GNP at factor cost, subsidies are added to GNP at market prices.

GNP at Factor Cost = GNP at Market Prices – Indirect Taxes + Subsidies,

3. Gross Domestic Product (GDP)

GDP = GNP – Net Foreign Investment

Net Foreign Investment = Export – Import (X – M)

$\therefore$ GDP = GNP – (X– M)

4. Net National Product (NNP)

GNP includes the value of total output of consumption goods and investment goods. But the process of production uses up a certain amount of fixed capital. Some fixed equipment wears out, its other components are damaged or destroyed, and still other some rendered obsolete through technological changes. All this process is termed depreciation or capital consumption allowance. In order to arrive at NNP, we deduct depreciation from GNP. The word 'net' refers to the exclusion of that part of total output which represents depreciation.

NNP = GNP – Depreciation

5. NNP at Market Prices

Net National Product at Market prices is the net value of final goods and services evaluated at market prices in the course of one year in a country. If we deduct depreciation from GNP at market prices, we get NNP at market prices. Thus NNP at Market Prices = GNP at Market Prices – Depreciation.

6. NNP at Factor Cost

Net National Product at factor cost is the net output evaluated at factor prices. It includes income earned by factors of production through participation in the production process such as wages and salaries, rates, profits, etc. It is also called *National Income.* This measure differs from NNP at market prices in that indirect taxes are deducted and subsidies are added to NNP at market prices in order to arrive at NNP at factor cost. Thus

NNP ar factor cost = NNP at Market Prices – Indirect Taxes + Subsidies.

= GNP at Market Prices – Depreciation – Indirect Taxes + Subsidies.

= National Income

7. NDP at Factor Cost

Net Domestic Product at factor cost is arrived by making adjustments for net indirect taxes *i.e.* indirect taxes and subsidies in the Net Domestic Product at market prices. The market prices contain an element of indirect taxes which though paid out by the buyers in the form of Product Prices, do not accrue to the production units.

Hence to find out factor incomes, we deduct the indirect taxes from the Net Domestic Product at market prices. Like wise, we add subsidies to the Net Domestic Product at market prices because these subsidies form the factor incomes though they are not a part of the market prices. Thus,

Net Domestic Product at Factor Cost = Net Domestic Product at Market Prices – Indirect Taxes + Subsidies.

8. Private Income

Private income is income obtained by private individuals from any source, productive or other wise, and the retained income of corporations. It can be arrived at from NNP at factor cost by marking certain additions and deductions. The additions include transfer payments such as pensions, unemployment allowances, sickness and other social security benefits, gifts and remittances from abroad, windfall gains and from lotteries or from horse racing , and interest on public debt. The deductions include income from government departments as well as surpluses from public under takings and employee's contribution to social security schemes like provident funds, life insurance, etc. Thus,

Private Income = National Income + Transfer payments + Interest on Public Debt – Social Security. Profits and Surpluses of Public under takings.

9. Personal Income

Personal income is the total income received by the individuals of a country from all sources before direct taxes in one year. Personal income is never equal to the national income, because the former includes the transfer payments where as they are not included in national income.

Personal income is derived from national income by deducting undistributed corporate profits, profit taxes, and employee's contributions to social security schemes. But business and government transfer payments, and transfer payments from abroad in the form of gifts and remittances, wind fall gains and interest on public dept which are a source of income for in dividuals are added to national income. Thus,

Personal Income = National income – Undistributed Corporate profits – Profit Taxes – Social Security Contributions + Transfer Payments + Interest on Public Debt.

Personal income differs from private income in that it is less than the latter because it excludes undistributed corporate profits. Thus,

Personal Income = Private Income – Undistributed Corporate Profits – Profit Taxes

10. Disposable Income

The concept of disposable income tells us the amount of money available to individuals and house holds in a year for the purposes of spending. After a good part of personal income is paid to government in the form of personal taxes like income tax, personal property tax etc, what remains of personal income is called disposable income. Thus,

Disposable Income = Personal Income – Direct Taxes. Disposable Income can either be consumed or saved. Therefore,

Disposable Income = Consumption + Saving.

11. Real Income

Real income is national income expressed in terms of a general level of prices of a particular year taken as base. National income is the value of goods and services prduced as expressed in terms of money at current prices. But it does not indicate the real state of the economy. It is possible that the net national product of goods and services this year might have been less than that of last year, but owing to an increase in prices, the NNP might be higher this year. On the contrary, it is also possible that NNP might have increased but the price level might have fallen, as a result of which national income would appear to be less than that of the last year. In both the situations, the national income does not depict the real state of the country. To rectify such a mistake, the concept of real income has been propounded.

In order to find out the real income of a country, a particular year is taken as base year when the general price level is neither too high nor too low and the price level for that year is assumed to be 100. New the general level of the prices of the given year for which the national income (real) is to be determined is assessed in accordance with the prices of the base year. For this purpose the following formula is employed

$$\text{Real National Income} = \text{National Income for the current year} \times \frac{100}{\text{Current year Index}}$$

Suppose 1970 is the base year and the national income for 1980 is Rs. 20000 crores and the index number for this year is 250. Hence,

Real National Income for 1966

$$= 20000 \times \frac{100}{250}$$

= Rs. 80000 crores.

This is also known as National Income at constant prices.

12. Per Capita Income

The average income of the people of a country in a particular year is called Per Capital Income for that year. This concept also refers to the measurement of income at current prices and at constant prices. For instance, in order to find out the per capital income for 2001, at current prices, the national income of a country is divided by the population of the country in that year

Per Capita Income for 2001

$$= \frac{\text{National income for 2001}}{\text{population in 2001}}$$

Similarly, for the purpose of arriving at the Real Per Capita Income, the following formula is employed.

Real Per Capita Income for 2001

$$= \frac{\text{Real National Income for 2001}}{\text{Population in 2001}}$$

This concept enables us to know the average income and the standard of living of the people. But it is not very reliable, because in every country due to unequal distribution of national income a major portion of it goes to the richer sections of the society and thus income received by the common man is lower than the per capita income.

Methods of Measuring National Income

There are four methods of measuring national income. which method is to be employed depends on the availability of data in country and the purpose in hand.

1. Product Method

Accordig to this method, the total value of final goods and services produced in a country during a year is calculated at market prices.

To final out the GNP, the data of all productive activities, such as agricultural products, wood received from forests, mineral received from mines, commodities produced by industries, the contributions to production made by transport, communications, insurance companies, lawyers, doctors, teachers etc. are collected and assessed at market prices. Only the final goods and services are included and the intermediary goods and services are left out.

2. Income Method

According to this method, the net income payments received by all citizens of a country in a particular year are added up, *i.e.* net incomes that accrue to all factors of production by way of net rents, net wages, net interest and net profits are all added together but incomes received in the form of transfer paymets are not included in it.

The data pertaining to income are obtained from different sources, for instance, from income tax department in respect of high income groups and in case of workers from their wages will.

3. Expenditure Method

According to this method, the total expenditure incurred by the society in a particular year is added together and includes personal consumption expenditure, net domestic investment, government expenditure on goods and services and net foreign investment.

This concept is based on the assumption that national income equals national expenditure.

4. Value Added Method

Another method of measuring national income is the value added by industries. The difference between the value of material outputs and inputs at each stage of production is the value added. If all such differences are added up for all industries in the economy, we arrive at the gross domestic product.

Difficulties In The Measurement of National Income

To calculate the national income of a country is a complicated problem and is beset with the following difficulties :

1. National income is always measured in money, but there are a number of goods and services which are difficult to be assessed in terms of money, *e.g.,* painting as a hobby by an individual, the bringing up of children by the mother. Similarly, when the owner of a firm gets married to his lady secretary, her services, though a part of national income are not included in it. By excluding all such services from it, the national income will work out to be less than what it actually is.
2. The greatest difficulty in calculating the national income is of double counting, which arises from the failure to distinguish properly between a final and an intermediate product. There always exists the fear of goods or a service being included more than once. If it so happens, the national income would work out to be many time the actual. Flour used by a bakery is an intermediate product and that by a house hold the final product. To solve this difficulty, only the final goods and services are taken in to account and that is not so easy a task.
3. Income earned through illegal activities such as gembling or illicit extraction of wine etc. is not included in national income. Such goods and services do have value and meet the needs of the consumers. But by leaving

them out the national income works out to less than the actual.

4. Then there arises the difficulty of including transfer payments in the national income. Individuals get pension, unemployment allowance and interest on public loans, but whether these should be included in national income is a difficult problem. On the one hand, these earnings are a part of individual income and on the other they are government expenditure. To avoid this difficulty these are deducted from national income.
5. The question of calculation of depreciation on capital consumption presents another formidable difficulty. If there were no changes in the form or quality of capital, there would not be much of a problem; but in fact both the amount and the composition of our capital are changing all the time. There are not accepted standard rates of depreciation applicable to the various categories of macines. Unless from the gross national income correct deductions are made for depreciation, the estimate of net national income is bound to go wrong.
6. All inventory changes whether negative or positive are included in the GNP. The procedure is to take positive or negative changes in physical units of inventories and multiply than by current prices. Then this figure is added to total current production of the firm. But the problem is that firms record inventories at their original costs rather than at replacement costs, When prices rise there are gains in the book value of inventories. Contrariwise, there are losses when prices fall. So the book value of inventories overstates or understates the actual inventories. Thus for correct imputation of GNP, inventory evaluation is required. But inventory valuation is a very difficult and cumbersome procedure.
7. In calculating national income, a good number of public services are also taken which cannot be estimated correctly. How should the police and military services be estimated ? In the days of war, the forces are active, but during peace they rest in cantonments. Similarly, to estimate the contribution made to national income by profits earned on irrigation and power projects in terms of money is also a difficult problem.
8. Another major problem arises with regard to the treatment of income arising out of activities of the foreign firms in a country. Should their income firm a part of the national income of the country in which they are located or should it belong to the national income of the country owning the firm? On this point, the IMF viewpoint is that production and income arising from an enterprise should be ascribed to the territory in which production takes place. However, profits earned by foreign branches and subsidiaries are credited to the parent country.

Problems of Measurement In A Developing Economy

In a developing economy, complete and reliable information relating to the various methods of estimating nationl income are not available due to the following problems :

1. Non-monetised sector
2. Lack of occuptional specialisation
3. Non-market Transactions
4. Illiteracy
5. Non availability of Data

Inflation and Deflation

By inflation, in ordinary language, we mean a general rise in prices. However, when discussing inflation, we are thinking of a persistent rise in prices rather than a once–for–all rise in prices (which may be, for example, brought about by a bad weather leading to destruction of crops).

Inflationary Gap

Inflationary gap arises when consumption and investment spending together is greater than the full employment GNP level. This means that people are demanding more goods and services than can be produced. In other wores, the amount by which the actual aggregate demand exceeds the level of national income corresponding to full employment is known as **inflationary gap** because this excess in aggregate demand causes inflation or rise in prices in the country. Diagramatically, the inflationary gap EE' is shown in figure 1. Y_f is the full employment level of income which is arrived at by the equality of aggregate consumption and investment expenditure line C + I + G and the 45° line representing aggregate supply of goods at point E.

At the full employment level, there is excess demand because consumers, firms and government expenditure more than the available output at current prices by EE' amount. This increased demand or expenditure shifts the C + I + G curve upward to C + I + G′ position. This intersects the 45° line at E_1 so that the total expenditure is E_1 Y_1 while the available output is EY_f. Thus E_1A = EE' is the inflationary gap.

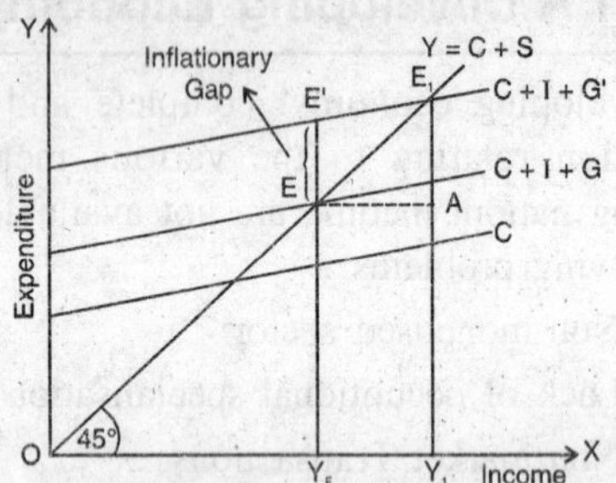

Fig. 1 : *Inflationary Gap*

The inflationary gap can be wiped out by increase in saving so that aggregate demand is reduced. Another soluation is to raise the value of available output to match the disposable income. But output cannot be increased during the short run. Private investment cannot be reduced while the government expenditure is autonomous. So both cannot be reduced during the short run. Thus the only alternatives left to the government are to increase taxation and induce saving.

Deflationary Gap

Deflationary gap represents the difference between the acutal aggregate demand and the aggregate demand which is required to establish the equilibrium at full employment level of income. The concept of deflationary gap is illustrated in figure 2 in which along the x–axis national income is measured and long the y–axis expenditure is measured.

Suppose national income at the equilibrium level of full employment is equal to OY_f. Now the equilibrium level of income and employment would be established at OY_f when aggregate demand (C + I +G) is equal to Y_fE (which is equal to national income OY_f). But in the real world if aggregate demand is less than the full employment level of income OY_f or it is less than Y_FE then the problem of deficiency of aggregate demand will arise.

Therefore, EH in figure 2 represents deflationary gap. It should be carefully understood that due to deflationary gap E, the level of national income and employment will decline. The decline in national income and employment will not only be equal to the deflationary gap EH but it will be much greater than this.

The decline in national income is determined by the value of the multiplier. In figure 2 when aggregate demand is Y_F H i.e, deflationary gap is equal to EH, then the aggregate demand curve is C + I + G' which cuts the 45° line at point Q as a result of which equilibrium is established at OY_1 level of national income. It will be seen from figure 2 that OY_1 is less than full employment level of income OY_f.

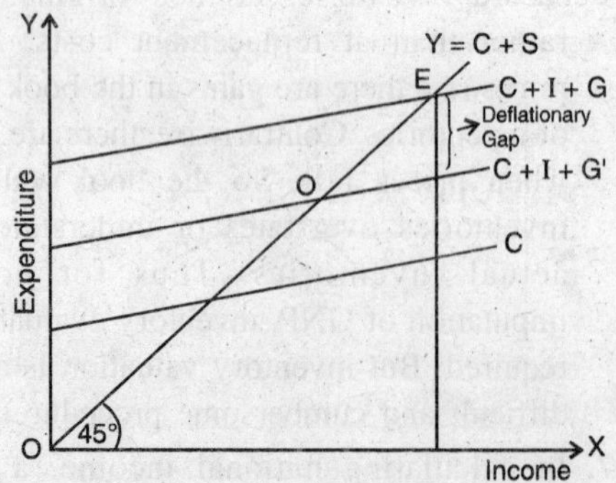

Fig. 2 : *Deflationary Gap*

Demand–Push Inflation

Basically, inflation represents a stuation where by the pressure of aggregate demand for goods and services exceeds the available supply of output. In such a situation, the rise in price level is the natural consequence. Now this excess of aggregate demand over supply may be the result of more than one force at work. As we know, aggregate demand is the sum of consumer's spending on goods and services, government spending on goods and services and net investment being contemplated by the entrepreneurs. Inflation is thus caused when aggregate demand for all purposes–consumption, investment and government expenditure, exceeds the supply of goods at current prices. Thus is demand pull inflation. Demand–pull inflation can be illustrated with aggregate demand and aggregate supply curves. Consider figure 3 in which aggregate demand and suply are measured along the x–axis and general price level along the Y–axis. Curve AS represents the aggregate supply which rises upward in the beginning but when at full employment level aggregate supply OY_f is reached, aggregate supply curve AS takes a vetical shape. This is because after the level of full employment, supply of output cannot be increase. When aggregate demand curve is AD_1, the equilibrium is at the full employment level where price level OP_1 is determined.

Now, if the aggregate demand increases to AD_2 and aggregate supply cannot be raised, the price level will rise to OP_2 due to the excess of demand. If the aggregate demand further increases to AD_3, the price level rises to OP_3 under the pressure of more demand.

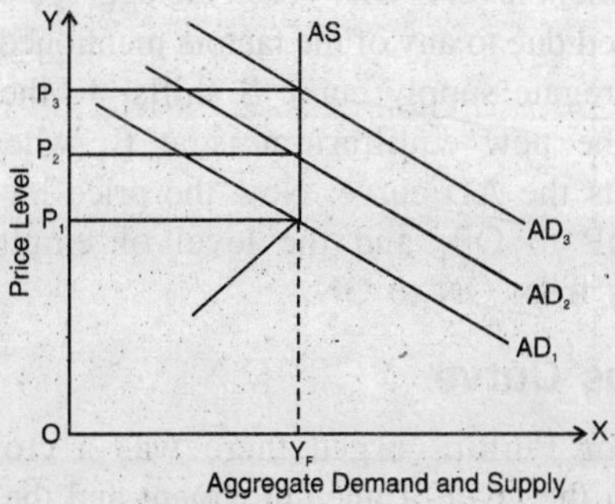

Fig. 3 : *Demand-Pull Inflation*

Cost–Push Inflation

We can visualise a situtation where, even though there is no increase in aggregate demands, prices may still rise. This may happen if costs, particularly the wage costs, go on rising. Now as the level of employment rises, the demand for workers also rises so that the bargaining position of the workers becomes stronger. To exploit this situation, they may ask for an increase in wage rates which are not justifiable on grounds either of a prior rise of productivity or of cost of living.

The employers in a situation of high demand and employment are more agreeable to concede these wage claims, because they hope to pass on these rises in costs to the consumers in the shape of rise in prices. If this happens, we have another inflationary factor at work and the inflation thus caused is called the **wage–induced** or **cost–push inflation.**

Besides the increase in wages of lablur without any increase in its productivity, there is another factor responsible for cost–push inflation. This is the increase in the profit margin by the firms, working under monopolistic or oligopolistic conditions and as a result charging higher prices from the consumers. In the former case when the cause of cost–push–inflation is the rise in wages, it is called **wage–push inflation** and in the latter case when the cause of cost–push inflation is the rise in profit margins, it is called **profit–push–inflation.**

The cost–push–inflation can also be illustrated with the aggregate demand and supply curves. In figure AD is the aggregate demand curve and AS_1 and AS_3 curves are aggregate supply curves.

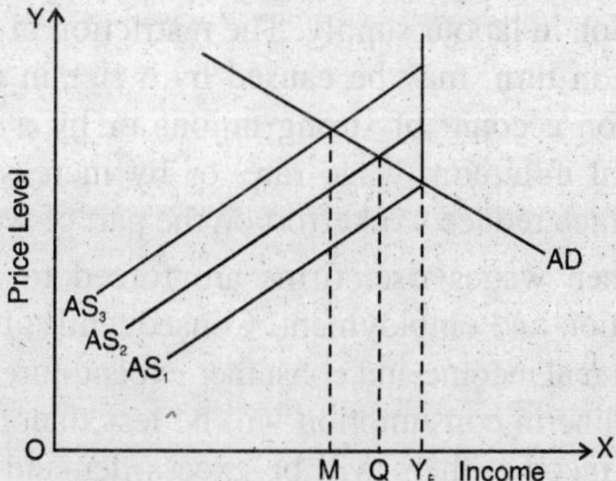

Fig. 4 : *Cost-Push Inflation*

Since aggregate supply curves become vertical at full emloyment level their vertical portions coincide. Now, when wages increase, and as a result cost of production increases, the aggregate supply curve would shift upward. As will be seen in figure 4, when there is an upward shift in the aggregate supply curve form AS_1, to AS_2 due to the rise in wages, price level rises from OP_1 to OP_2. It should be noted that price level OP_1 corresponds to the full employment, since aggregate demand curve AD intersects original aggregate supply curve AS at full employment level OY_f. If the wages further rise and the aggregate supply curve shifts upwards to AS_3, the equilibrium price level rises to OP_3.

We have thus seen above that cause of inflation may be that aggregate demand has become excessive in relation to supply of output (demand–pull–inflation) or it may be that costs have risen because of the increase in wages of labour or profit margins of the producers (cost–pust–inflation).

Stagflation

The word "Stagflation" is the combination of stag plus flation, taking 'stag' from stagnation and 'flation' from inflation. Thus it is a paradoxical situation where the economy experiences stagnation or unemployment alongwith a high rate of inflation. It is, therefore, also called **inflationary recession**. In other words, the stagflation refers to a situation when a high rate of inflation occurs simultancously with a high rate of unemployment.

One of the principal causes of stagflation has been restriction in the aggregate supply. When aggregate supply is reduced, there is a fall in output and employment, and the price level rises. A reduction in aggregate supply may be due to a restriction in labour supply. The restriction in labour supply, in turn, may be caused by a rise in money wages on account of strong unions or by a rise in the legal minimum wage rate, or by increased tax rates which reduce workeffort on the part of workers.

When wages rise, firms are forced to reduce production and employment. Consequently, there is a fall in real income and consumer expenditure. Since the decline in consumption will be less than the fall in real income, there will be excess demand in the commodity market which will push up the price level.

The rise in the price level, in turn, reduces output and employment in the following three ways:

(*a*) It reduces the real quantity of money, raises interest rates and brings a fall in investment expenditure.

(*b*) The rise in the price level reduces the real value of cash balances with the government and the private sector via the pigou effect which reduces their consumption expenditure.

(*c*) The rise in prices of domestic goods makes exports dearer to foreighers and makes exports goods relatively more attractive to domestic output and employment.

Restriction on aggregate supply may also be caused by external factors such as rise in the world prices of foods grains and crude aid prices. In all these cases, the domestic price level is raised by outside forces. When international prices of food grains and crude oil rise, they lead to the outflow of purchasing power away from domestic consumers. They accentuate inflation, raise wages and prices. As a result, the real quantity of money declines, interest rates rise and investment declines, via the pigou effect, and making exports dearer and imports attractive, domestic output and employment decline. They lead to **Stagflation**.

The phenomenon of stagflation is illustrated in figure 5, where employment is measured on the horizontal axis and the price level on the vertical axis.

The initial equilibrium is at E where aggregate demand curve AD intersects the aggregate supply curve AS and the price level is OP and the employment level is ON. When the aggregate supply is reduced due to any of the factors mentioned above, the aggregate supply curve S shifts to the left at AS_1. The new equilibrium is at E_1 where AS_1 intersects the AD curve. Now the price level rises from OP to OP_1 and the level of employment declines from ON to ON_1.

Phillips Curve

Professor Phillips urged there was a close link between the level of unemployment and the rate of wage increase. Phillips curve expresses an inverse relationship between the rate of unemployment and the rate of increase in money wages.

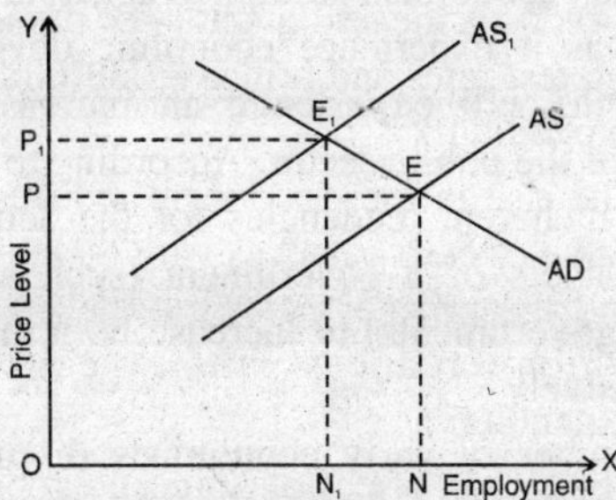

Fig. 5 : *Stagflation*

Prof. Phillips studied the relationship between unemployment and changes in money wages in the U.K. over the period 1862–1957. As a result of this study, he seems to have discovered a stable and inverse relationship over the whole period between the rate of wage increase and the per cent of unemployment. The Phillips curve depicts the **trade off** betweeen umemployment and money wages. It relates percentage change in money wages on the vertical axis with percentage of labour force unemployment on the horizontal axis.

Suppose that ON rate of unemployment (3%) is associated with OM growth rate of money wages (2%). Suppose also that the rate of labour productivity is 2 per cent, that is, equal to OM. Since the growth rate of money wages equals the rate of labour productivity, the price level remains constant. If now aggregate demand is increased, this lowers the unemployment rate to OT (2%) and raises the wages rate to OS (4%) per year. If lower productivity continues to grow at 2% per annum, the price level will also rise at the rate of 2 per cent per annum at OS in the figure.

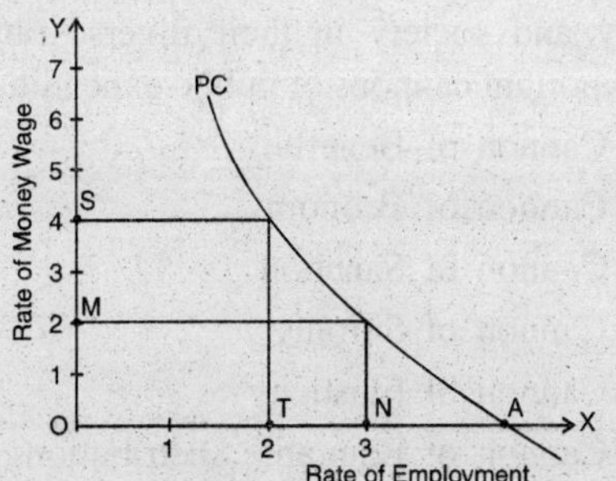

Fig. 6 : *Phillips Curve*

Thus a money wage rate increase which in excess of labour productivity leads to inflation. To keep wage increase to the level of labour productivity (OM) in order to avoid inflation, ON rate of unemployment will have to be tolerated.

Samuelson and Solow extended the Phillip's analysis to the **trade off** between the level of unemployment and the rate of change in the level of prices. Thus, **the Phillips curve suggests that unemployment can always be reduced by having more inflation and that the inflation rate can also be reduced by having more unemployment.**

Its Criticism

Economists have criticised the phillips curve. They argue that the phillips curve relates to the short run and it does not remain stable. It shifts with changes in expectations of inflation. *In the long run, there is no trade off between inflation and employment.* These views have been expounded by *friedman and phelps* in what has come to be known as the ''accelerationist'' hypothesis.

According to friedman, the long run phillips curve is vertical.

Tobin's View : James Tobin in his presidential address before the American Economic Association in 1971 proposed a compromise between the negatively sloping and vertical phillips curve. Tobin believes that them is a phillips curve within limits, but as the economy expands and employment grows, the curve becomes even more fragile and vanishes until it becomes vertical at some critically low rate of unemployment. Thus Tobin's Phillips curve is kinked-shaped, a part like a normal phillips curve and the rest vertical, as shown in figure 7.

In the figure U*c* is the critical rate of unemployment at which the phillips curve becomes vertical where there is no trade off between unemployment and in flation. According to Tobin, the vertical portion of the curve is not due to increase in the demand for more wages but emerges from imperfections of the labour market. At the U*c* level, it is not possible to provide more employment because the job seekers have wrong skills or wrong age or sex or are in the wrong place.

Regarding the normal portion of the phillips curve which is negatively sloping, wages are sticky downward because labourers resist decline in their relative wages.

Solow's View : Like Tobin *Robert Solow* does not believe that the phillips curve is vertical at all rate of inflation. According to him, the curve is vertical at positive rates of inflation and is horizontal at negative rates of inflation.

MONEY AND BANKING

Public Expenditure

Public Expenditure is the expenditure incurred by public authorities-central, state and local governments-either for the satisfaction of collective needs of the citizens or for promoting their economic and social welfare. The volume of public expenditure has been increasing in almost all countries of the world, because of the continuous expansion in the activities of state and other public bodies on several fronts.

A theory of public expenditure in the nineteenth century was not very necessary because the scope of the functions of government was restricted. In the twentieth century the development of the functions of the state in social matters, *e.g.*, in education, public health and in commercial and industrial undertakings, such as railways, irrigation and similar projects have increased public expenditure in a large degree.

Reasons For the Growth of Public Expenditure

1. Increase in the Activities of the state
2. Industrial Development
3. Social Security Measure
4. Nationalisation of Industries and Trade
5. Development of Agriculture
6. Rising Trend of Prices
7. Problems of Defence
8. Urbanisation
9. Economic Development

Wagner's Views on Public Expenditure

The German economist, Adolph Wagner, argued that a nation, as it experience economic development and growth, will experience an increase in the activities of the public sector. According to Wagner there are in herent tendencies for the activities of different layers of a government (such as central and state governments) to increase both intensively and extensively.

A number of early economists discussed the relationship between the level of development and public expenditure. However, Wagner was the first to butteress such remark with an extensive theoretical foundation.

To justify his generalisation that the share of public consumption expenditure would increase, Wagner divided public expenditure into two categories, expenditures for internal and external security and expenditures for "cultural and welfare" which should include education, health, transportation, banking and the like expenditures for external security would increase in a growing economy as the nature of the use of force by the state changes from simple aggression to prevention of attack and as armies use more capital equipment. For internal security Wagner Foresaw greater expenditure because of greater friction between economic units and people as urbanisation progressed.

Canons of Public Expenditure

Like cannons of taxation, people have pro-pounded canons of public expenditure also which should govern the public expenditure decision. some of these canons are in the nature of administrative safeguards while others are expected to be of help to the economy and society in their diverse objectives. Some important cannons of public expenditure are—

1. Cannon of Benefit
2. Cannon of Economy
3. Cannon of Sanction
4. Cannon of Surplus
5. Cannon of Elasticity
6. Cannon of Equitable Distribution
7. Cannon of Productivity

Wiseman-Peacock Hypothesis

The another thesis of the growth of public expenditure was put forth by **Wiseman and Peapock** in their study of public expenditure in UK for the period 1890-1955. The main thesis of the authors is that public expenditure does not increase in a smooth and continuous manner, but in Jerks or steplike fashion. At times some social or other disturbance takes place which at once shows the need for increased public expenditure which the existing public revenue cannot meet. While earlier, due to an insufficient pressure for public expenditure, the revenue constraint was dominating and restraining an expansion in public expenditure, now under changed requirements such a restraint gives way. The public expenditure increases and makes the inadequacy of the present revenue quite clear to every one. The movement from the older level of expenditure and taxation to a new and higher level is the 'displacement effect.' The inadequacy of the revenue as compared with the 'required' public expenditure creates an 'inspection effect.' The government and the people review the revenue position and the need to find a solution of the important problems that have come up and agree to the required adjustments to finance the increased expenditure. They attain a new level of 'tax tolerance.' They are now ready to tolerate a greater burden of taxation and as a result the general level of expenditure and revenue goes up. In this way, the public expenditure and revenue get stabilized at a new level till another disturbance occurs to cause a 'displacement effect.' Since each major disturbance leads to the government assuming a larger proportion of the total national economic activity, the net result is the 'concentration effect.' The concentration effect also refers to the apparent tendency for central government economic activity to grow faster than that of the state and local level governments. British data are consistent with this finding, but its application to other countries needs verification.

The Public Budget

A budget is the statement of the financial plan of a government. It indicates the revenue and expenditure of the last completed financial year, the probable revenue and expenditure estimates for the current year, *i.e.*, not completed and the estimates of the anticipated revenue and proposed expenditure for the next financial year.

In the constitution of India, a budget has been referred to as the annual financial statement of the estimated receipts and expenditure of the government of India or of a state government, in respect of a financial year. **Article 112** of the constitution of India states that "an annual financial statement" will be placed before both Lok Sabha, and Rajya Sabha, while Article 202 of the constitution states that a similar financial statement for each state will be placed before the Legislature of that state.

Revenue and Capital Budgets

In many countries, the budget is divided into revenue and capital accounts. Revenue account covers those items which are of recurring nature; while capital account covers those items which are in the nature of the acquiring and disposing of capital assets.

In India, the constitution demands that the budget must distinguish expenditure on Revenue Accounts from other expenditure. Accordingly, the budget is necessarily presented into two parts, namely, **Revenue Budget** and **Capital Budget**. Revenue Budget consists of the revenue receipts — both tax revenue and non-tax revenue — and the expenditure met out of revenue receipts. The non-tax-revenue receipts include revenue from currency, coinage and mint, interest receipts, dividends, profits revenue from general services (such as police, jails, public works etc.), revenue from social and community services (such as education, health, housing, broadcasting and so on), and revenue from economic services (such as agriculture and allied services, industry and mines, transport and communications, etc.)

Capital Account receipts, on the other hand, include market loans, borrowings from the RBI, etc., through the sale of Treasury Bills, loans from foreign governments and institutions, and repayment of loans by state governments and others to the central government. Capital disbursements would include expenditure on acquisition of various physical assets like land, buildings, machinery and equipment, investments in shares and debentures and loans to state governments and other bodies.

Zero-Base Budgeting

Zero-base budgeting (ZBB) is an innovative technique to guard against wastage in public expenditure. The technique works not through auditing which is a post — operative check, but through an examination of the very rational of an expenditure item under consideration. In a more practical way, ZBB means the evaluation and prioritisation of all programmes at different levels of efforts. To be more simple, each department is required to justify its budget requests from the bottom up, evaluating alternative programme packages and ranking programmes so as to select the best alternative and allocate resources accordingly. Thus, no consideration is given to the post or existing at present, any programme may be included or excluded. The Budget is considered as a whole and a fresh, *i.e.*, from zero-Base.

In the sphere of public budgeting, ZBB was first tried by **Mr. Jimmy Carter** in1973 when he was the Governer of Georgia, with proper remoulding. Later on its was adopted by a number of states in the U.S.A.

Performance Budgeting

Performance Budgetting is generally understood as a system of presentation of public expenditure in terms of functions, programmes, performance units, viz., activities, projects, etc., reflecting primarily the government out-put and its cost.

The U.S. Bureau of the Budget defines a performance budget in these words, "As performance budget in one which presents the purpose and objectives for which funds are required, the cost of the programmes proposed for achieving those objective and quantitative data measuring the accomplishment and work performed under each programme."

Under Performance Budgeting System the over all budget is divided into functions based on the major purpose of government and then sub divided into programme and activities, funds are granted for doing a specific quantity of work. Performance budgeting implies that the budget statement should indicate the actual achievement expected by a Ministry over a period of time from certain amount of expenditure.

Thus, the process of performance budgeting is not merely a technique, it constitutes a new approach to budget formation and execution. Since the cost and benefits indicated side by side, this technique helps in the decision-making regarding allocations of funds.

Types of Deficits

1. **Revenue Deficits.** Revenue Deficit = Revenue Expenditure-Revenue Receipts

   Current revenue expenditure of the central government is composed of plan and non-plan expanditure, and current-revenue receipts include net tax revenue and non-tax revenue of the central government.

2. **Budget Deficit.** Budget Deficit = Total Expenditure-Total Receipts

   The total expenditure of the central governments always exceeded its total revenue which is known as budget deficit or overall budgetary deficit.

3. **Fiscal Deficit.** In simple terms, fiscal deficit is budgetary deficit plus market borrowings and other liabilities of the government of India.

   ∴ Fiscal Deficit = Revenue receipts (Net tax revenue + Non-tax revenue) + Capital receipts (only recoveries of loans and other receipts)– Total expenditure (Plan and non-plan)

4. **Primary Deficit.** The excess of fiscal deficit over payments of interest is called primary deficit.

5. **Monetised Deficit.** The increase in net RBI credit for central government is called monetised deficit. It includes:

   A. Net increase in holdings of treasury bills of RBI.

   B. Contribution of RBI in market borrowings of the govt.

Public Revenue

Like any other economic unit, a government also needs funds to finance its activities. Such funds are raised from various sources. It is difficult to give a complete list of all the sources of public revenue, but the important and common sources of public revenue would include taxes, income from currency, market borrowings, sale of public assets, income from public undertakings, fees, fines, gifts and donations, etc.

What is a Tax?

A tax is a compulsory levy and those who are taxed have to pay the sums irrespective of any corresponding return of services or goods by the government. In other words, a tax-payer does not receive a definite and direct quid pro quo from the government. Note the word *direct* here. It is not a price paid by the tax-payer for any definite service rendered or a commodity supplied by the government. The tax-payers do get many benefits from the government but no tax-payer has a right to any benefit from the public expenditure on the ground that he is paying a tax.

The Base of Tax

The base of a tax is the legal description of the object with reference to which the tax applies. For example, the base of an excise duty is the production or packing or processing of a specific goods; the base of an income tax is the income of the assessee defined and estimated in terms of certain rules laid down for this purpose. Note that the base of each tax has to be defined legally and it is to be quantified for the purpose of determining the tax liability of an individual tax-payer. Each tax-payer is considered a legal entity for this purpose. It should be noted that a tax base may have a time dimension also. For example, income-tax is usually on an annual basis and the law has to decide whether income would be taxed on the basis of accrual or receipt. The authorities, while determining a tax base, are expected to give due consideration to various questions like those of cost of collection, administration and effects of that tax. With the passage of time, a tax base under consideration may grow or may shrink. For example, as production of excisable goods increases, the base of excise duties would be termed to have grown. Also, by low, new items may be brought under particular taxation, or the relevant provisions, definitions and rules etc. may be changed to extend the coverage or base of a tax. Thus, if new items are brought under excise duties, we shall say that the coverage of excise taxation has been extended and the base of excise taxation has been widened.

Buoyancy and Elasticity of a Tax

These terms denote the factors responsible for an increase in the yield of a tax over time. If a tax revenue increases with the growth of its base, but without an extension of the tax coverage or an upward revision of the tax rates, then the tax is said to be buoyant. It has an inherent tendency to yield more tax revenue with the growth of the base. Thus, for example, with given rates of income-tax and the definition of taxable income, if yield from income-tax increases as national income increases, it would be termed a buoyent tax. Similarly, excise duties are levied on production of specified goods. If new items are not brought under these duties and the rates of existing duties remain unchanged, but the revenue from excise duties increases with an increase in the production of excisable items, we have a case of buoyancy of excise duties. Numerically, the buoyancy of a tax is measured as a ratio of the proportionate increase in tax revenue to a proportionate increase in the tax base.

The yield of a tax may also go up on account of extension of its coverage or a revision of its rates. Such a characteristic of a tax is referred to as its elasticity. In other words, elasticity of a tax refers to its responsiveness to steps taken up authorities in increasing its yeild through an extension of its coverage or revision of its rates. Numerically, the elasticity of a tax would be measured by as a ratio of the proportionate change in its yield to the proportionate change in its yield to the proportionate change in its coverage or rates.

Principles of Taxation

A good tax system is one which is designed on the basis of an appropriate set of principles, such as equality and certainty. Adam Smith was probably the first economist, who stated the general principle of taxation or rules of taxation (which he called the canons of taxation).

The four canons of taxation as prescribed by **Adam Smith** are the following:

1. Canon of Equality
2. Cannon of Certainty
3. Cannon of Convenience
4. Cannon of Economy

   Some writers, like Bastable, have added a few more canons of taxation to Adam Smith's four.

5. Canon of Productivity
6. Canon of Elasticity
7. Canon of Diversity
8. Canon of Simplicity
9. Canon of Co-ordination

Different Approaches to the Division of Tax Burden

Financial Approach

There are various theories with regard to the distribution of burden of taxation among the people. One of them is often called the financial theory, which embodied in principle attributed to collect, Pluck the goose with as little squealing as possible. It aims at obtaining maximum amount of revenue rather than on proper distribution of burden of taxation. The greatest danger of this theory is that the burden of taxation may fall mainly on weak and voiceless people rather than on rich and vocal.

Cost-of-Service Approach

This is one of the oldest principles advocated for the distribution of the tax burden. According to this thoery, the basis of taxation should be the cost incurred by government on different services for the benefit of the individual tax-payers. Each tax-payer has to pay the tax equal to the cost of service to him. It means, the higher the cost, the higher should be the tax rate and *vice versa*. The government acts like a producer of a commodity, who charges the price from his customers equal to the amount of cost of production of the commodity.

However, this principle cannot be accepted as the basis of taxation because of several reasons. In the first place, it is very difficult to estimate the cost of service to every individuals, *e.g.*, the government can estimate total expenditure on the defence of the country, but it is difficult to estimate the expenditure incurred by the government on the defence for a particular individual. Secondly the basis of cost of service principle is not fair in a welfare state. If cost is taken as the basis of taxation, the government may not perform various functions which may be very much desirable for the welfare of the country as a whole, *e.g.*, relief in times of drought, flood and earthquake, free education and free medical facilities, etc. Hence, the cost of service principles cannot be accepted as the basis of taxation. Moreover, this principle is not in accordance with the character of a tax. A tax is a compulsory payment and there is no quid-pro-quo in return of the payment of a tax. But according to this theory, the payment of a tax is, in return of the cost of service.

The Benefits-Received Theory

According to this theory, the burden of taxation should be divided among the people in proporiton to the benefits received from the state. The persons receiving equal benefits from the state should pay equal amount as taxes and those who received greater benefits should pay more as taxes than those getting less benefit. The benefit principle is very much similar to the cost of service principle, the former looks at the problem from the side of demand while the latter looks at it from the side of supply.

Ability-to-Pay Approach

This approach considers the tax liability in its true form-a compulsory payment to the state without *quid pro quo*. It does not assume any commercial or semi-commercial relationshjip between the state and the citizens. According to this approach, a citizen is to pay taxes because he can, and his relative share in the total tax burden is to be determined by his relative paying capacity.

Incidence of Taxes

The burden of a tax does not always lie on the person from whom it is collected. In many cases it is borne by other people also. Thus, the person who initially pays the tax may not be actually bearing its money burden as such. Hence, it is necessary to know who bears the immediate burden of a tax and who bears the ultimate burden of the tax. The problem of determining the ultimate burden of a tax is the problem of determining the incidence of the tax.

Impact of a tax is its first point of contact with the tax-payers. It is upon those who bear the first responsibility of paying it to the authorities, that is those who have the statutory responsibility of paying it to the government. Incidence of a tax, on the other hand, is defined as its final resting place. To put it differently, the incidence of a tax is upon those economic units which finally bear the money burden of it and which are not able to pass it on to others. Incidence lies upon that final source from which the tax money comes.

Effects of a Tax

When a tax is imposed and collected, it involves certain responses from the tax-payers, and the economy. Such responses can be of great variety and can profoundly influence the working of the economy in terms of production, growth, saving, investment, choice of techniques of productions, regional in balances, in equalities of income and wealth, and so on. These responses and their results are collectively called the **effects of that tax**. The effects of a tax, therefore, stand apart, both conceptually, and analytically, from both the impact and the incidence of the tax. While the impact of a tax is its first point of contact with the tax-payers and while incidence is its final resting place, its effects will be the resultant responses and changes in the economy. These effects can be the result of the fact of tax imposition itself and they could also follow from the process of shifting its incidence.

Demand and Supply Theory of Tax Shifting

This is the most acceptable approach in explaining the incidence of a tax. Tax incidence can be shifted only through sale/purchase transactions and only through a revision of the prices. A price revision is possible and is determined by the relative values of demand and supply elasticities. A tax can, therefore, be shifted only through a shift in the demand and/or supply curves and the sharing of the incidence will be determined by the demand and supply elasticities. The general rule is that irrespec-tives of whether the statutory liability of a tax (the impact of the tax) rests upon the buyer or the seller, the share of the tax borne by the seller will be the larger according as the elasticity of demand is larger; and the share of the tax borne by the buyer will be the larger according as the elasticity of supply is larger. Actually, the tax burden will be shared between the buyer and the seller in the ratio of the elasticities of supply and demand.

Let us illustrate this statement by first taking the case of a single commodity which has been subjected to a specific (per unit) tax. Let us assume that the impact of the tax is upon the sellers. Let the original demand and supply curves for the commodity by DD' and SS'. With the imposition of a tax SS_1 per unit upon the commodity, the supply curve shifts to S_1S_1' and the price of the commodity rise from PM to P'M'. However, out of this P'M', the sellers get only Am', the balance being collected by the government by way of tax. In other words, the incidence upon the sellers is equal to BA per unit. On the other hand, the buyers are paying now P'M' instead of PM, an increase of P'B per unit which is the incidence upon them.

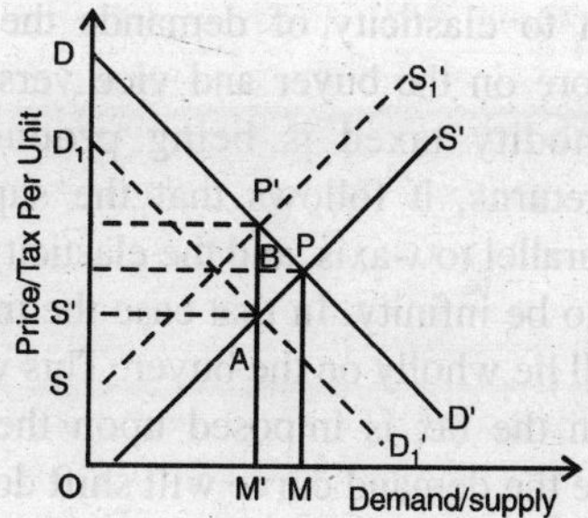

It can be shown that this division of the tax P'A between the two shares P'B and BA is in the ratio of the elasticity of supply to the elasticity of demand. The elasticity of demand is given by proportionate change in demand divided by the proportionate change in the price to the buyers. That is to say, the elasticity of demand E_α is given by

$$E_d = \frac{\frac{MM'}{OM}}{\frac{P'B}{PM}}$$

Similarly, the elasticity of supply is given by the proportionate change in supply divided by the proportionate change in price to the sellers. That is to say the elasticity of supply, E_s is given by

$$E_s = \frac{\frac{MM'}{OM}}{\frac{BA}{PM}}$$

Therefore,

$$\frac{E_s}{E_\alpha} = \left(\frac{MM'}{OM} \Big/ \frac{BA}{PM}\right) \Big/ \left(\frac{MM'}{OM} \Big/ \frac{P'B}{PM}\right)$$

$$= \frac{P'B}{BA}$$

$$= \frac{\text{Incidence on Buyers}}{\text{Incidence on Sellers}}$$

If the tax is imposed upon the buyer, the demand curve would shift left and down wards to D_1D_1. The buyers would then pay a price of AM[1] to the sellers and a tax P'A per unit to the authorities. The resultant incidence on the two parties will ramain unchanged. The formula

$$\frac{\text{Buyers's Share of Incidence}}{\text{Sellers's Share of Incidence}} = \frac{E_s}{E_d}$$

Shows that as the elasticity of supply increases in relation to elasticity of demands the incidence will be more on the buyer and vice versa. Thus, if the commodity taxed is being produced under constant returns, it follows that the supply curve will run parallel to *x*-axis, and the elasticity of supply will tend to be infinity. In that case the incidence of the tax will lie wholly on the buyer. This will happen even when the tax is imposed upon the buyer (in which case the demand curve will shift downwards). Figure A illustrates this phenomenon and it is seen that here the points A and B coincide, so that P'B = P'A.

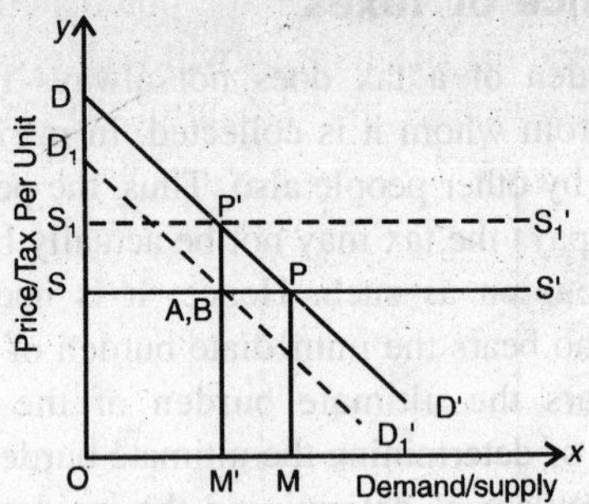

Fig. A

The tax will be fully borne by the buyers if the demand elasticity is zero (in the ratio E_s / E_d, the denominator becomes zero, see Fig. B). Here the demand curve will run parallel to *y*-axis and an upward shift in the supply curve will automatically mean an equivalent increase in the price being paid by the buyer. If the tax is ad valorem, say *t* per cent, the price will increase by exactly *t* per cent because the quantity demanded and supplied remains unchanged.

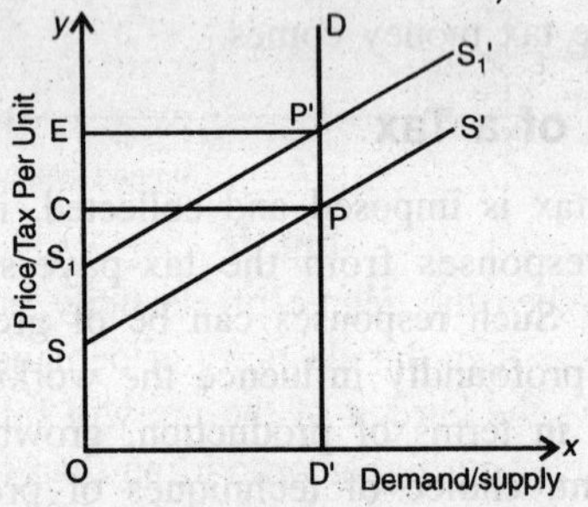

Fig. B

It can be shown in the same way that if the elasticity of supply is zero, or if the elasticity of demand is perfect, the sellers will bear the full incidence of the tax (see figs. C and D).

Conclusion

1. If the elasticity of supply is equal to the elasticity of demand, *i.e.*, $e_s = e_d$; the burden of the tax is equally divided between buyers and sellers, and the price of the commodity will rise by half the amount of tax.

2. When the degree of elasticity of supply is greater than the elasticity of dem and, *i.e.*, $e_s > e_d$, the burden of tax will fall upon the buyers in higher proportion than the sellers, and the rise in price will be more than fifty per cent of the amount of the tax per unit.

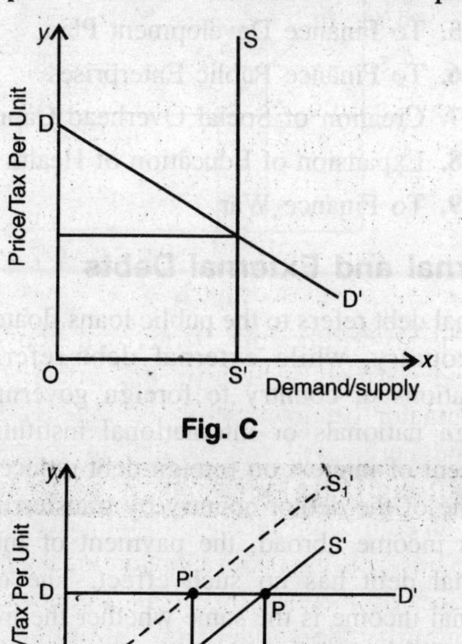

Fig. C

Fig. D

3. When the degree of elasticity of supply is less than the elasticity of demand, *i.e.*, $e_s < e_d$, the burden of the tax will fall upon the seller in higher proportion than the buyers, and the rise in price will be less than fifty per cent of the tax per unit.
4. If the demand for a commodity is perfectly elastic and its supply is inelastic, the entire burden of the tax will be upon the seller.
5. If the demand for commodity is perfectly in elastic and its supply is elastic, the entire burden of the tax will be upon the buyer.
6. If the supply of a commodity is perfectly elastic and the demand is relatively in elastic the entire burden of the tax will be upon the buyer.
7. If the supply of a commodity is perfectly inelastic and the demand is elastic, the entire burden will be upon the seller.

The Theory of Social and Private Goods

Private Goods have been defined as "Private goods yield utility (satisfaction) only to the person consuming the good, it is denied to others, only the person who drinks a cup of coffee, for example, benefits from the consumption of that cup of coffee. And the coffee consumed by one person cannot be consumed by any one else. The space in which a person parks his car given satisfaction only to the person whose car is parked there at that time. And during that time, the space is denied to other. Thus, private goods are said to be rival in consumption.

Again, a private goods is priced in the market and only those may be allowed the use of it who pay its stipulated price. Thus, those who do not agree to pay its market price, or those who cannot pay for it, are excluded from the use of this good. It means the principle of **exclusion** is applicable in case of private goods. The good becomes divisible so far at its use is concerned. Suppose an individual does not voluntarily agree to pay the market price for milk, the market would refuse to supply him the required quantity. Thus the ability to price a goods, the divisibility of a good and the exclusion principle, all go together in case of private goods.

A pure public goods is defined as a goods that one person's consumption of the goods does not reduce the amount available to other; that is, the consumption of a public goods is non-rival. That is they are goods where A's partaking of consumption benefits does not reduce the benefits derived by all othes. The same benefits are available to all and without mutual interference. So the total supply available to the community can be made available to each person in community. For example, a television signal that is available to one person can be made available to all persons in the area within the range of the signal. And one viewer's use of the signal does not reduce the amount of entertainment for others. A dam that controls flooding, benefits everyone in the flood region, and the benefit enjoyed by one property owner does not reduce the benefit available to others. It means a pure public goods is **indivisible**.

Merit Goods

Some goods are considered 'meritorious' while other are held undesirable. For instance, low cost housing is subsidised because decent housing is held to be desirable, while some taxes are imposed on liquor because drinking is held undesirable. Note, however, that the consumption choices which are supported or penalised may involve goods which are private (rival in consumption) as well as goods which are social (non rival). thus, goods for which it is thought that consumption should be encouraged are called merit goods; goods having the opposite characteristic may be called non merit goods or demerit goods. They (merit goods) become public goods if considered so meritorious that their satisfaction is provided for through the public budget, over and above what is provided for through the market and paid for by private buyers.

Difference Between Public Goods and Merit Goods

The Public goods satisfy the conditions of non-excludability, indivisibility and non-rival nature of consumption of goods while these are not the necessary conditions for merit goods, *i.e.*, they may apply or may not apply.

Public Debt

Public debt arises due to borrowing by the government. The government may borrow from banks, business organisations, business houses and individuals. The borrowings of the government may be within the country or from outside the country or both. The public debt is generally in the form of bonds (or treasury bills. if the loans are required for a short period), which carries with them the promises of the government to pay interests, to the holders of these bonds at stipulated rate of interest at regular intervals, or lump sum at the end, in addition to the principal which has to be repaid at the stated time.

Objectives of Public Debt

1. To Cover Budget Deficits
2. Rapid Expansion in the States Functions
3. In Times of Depression
4. To Curb Inflation
5. To Finance Development Plan
6. To Finance Public Enterprises
7. Creation of Social Overhead Capital
8. Expansion of Education of Health Services
9. To Finance War

Internal and External Debts

Internal debt refers to the public loans floated within the country, while external debt refers to the obligations of country to foreign governments or foreign nationals or international institution. The payment of interest on foreign debt reduces the net income of the debtor country by transferring a part of its income abroad, the payment of interest on internal debt has no such effect. The country's national income is the same whether the interest on internal debt is left with the tax-payers or is taken from them as taxes and paid out as interest on internal loan.

Factors on which the Effects of Public Debt Depend

The effects of public debt depend upon such factors as the sources of borrowing, the purpose for which borrowing is done, the terms and conditions under which the debt is floated, the volume of the existing public debt, the interest rates, the types of loan employed and the general economic condition of the community.

Effects of the Public Debt Upon the Economy

1. Effects on Consumption
2. Effects on Production
3. Effects on Distribution
4. Effects on Private Sector
5. Effects on the cost of Production
6. Effects of Public Debt on Investment

7. Effects of Public Debt on Working of the Money Market
8. Effects of Public Debt on Resource Allocation and National Income

Public Debt Management

The objective of the management of public debt refers to the aim that the method of borrowing funds and the repayment of loans by the government should not have any adverse effect upon the economic situation of the country.

Moreover, the methods of borrowing funds and repayment of loans should help to maintain economic stability, *i.e.*, It should reduce inflationary or deflationary effects upon the economy, and should make available the needed funds to the government.

Therefore, all those methods which are adopted by the government to achieve these obejectives, through the process of borrowing funds and repayment of loans, come under public debt management.

Principles of Public Debt Management

1. The Interest Cost of Servicing Public Debts must be Minimised
2. Satisfaction of the Needs of Investors
3. Public Debt Policy must be co-ordinated with Fiscal and Monetary Policy

Redemption of Public Debt

Redemption means repayment of a loans. All government loans, excepting permanent investment in self supporting industries, should be repaid promptly.

Advantages of Debt Redemption

1. It saves the government from bankruptcy.
2. It discourages extravagant expenditure of the government.
3. It maintains the confidence of the lenders.
4. It would be easy for the government to float loan in future.
5. It reduces the cost of debt management.

Fiscal Policy

Fiscal Policy relates to the governmental decision-making with respect to (1) taxation (2) government spending (3) government borrowing and (4) the management of the government debt.

Classical Concept of Fiscal Policy

Classical economists believed in the policy of *laissez faire*. They believed that supply creates its own demand and, therefore, general over production or involuntary unemployment is well nigh impossible. They believed that a free operation of market forces would achieve full employment and ensure an optimum allocation of resources in an economy. Thus, according to classical economists, full employment is supposed to reach automatically and there is no necessity of any interference.

Modern Concept of Fiscal Policy

The classical concept of fiscal policy has not been accepted by the modern economists like Keynes and Lerner. They believed that the government has to pay a positive role so as to regulate and control the economy by means of taxes and expenditure, which they called as the principle of functional finance.

Modern economists rejected the concept of classical economists, that supply creates it own demand and, therefore, there is no possibility of unemployment, and the equilibrium in the economy is automatically achieved due to the market forces. Contrary to this, Keynes believed that in an advanced economy, the propensity to consume tends to diminish as income increases, in other words, propensity to save increases with the increase in income. Hence, a larger proportion of the additional incomes is saved and not spent. The tendency of less consumption and larger savings results in lowering the demand for goods and services produced at that time; hence dis-equilibrium occurs in the economy. Thus, to maintain income and employment at the present level, it is necessary to offset the effects of decrease in demand for output due to decrease in consumption by a corresponding increase in public expenditure. Hence, if unemployment is to be avoided, the gap between the income and expenditure must be filled either by government expenditure or by increasing the propensity to consume. For instance, during the period of depression, the effective demand is not enough to absorb the available supply of goods and services, resulting in umemployment and under-employment. Therefore, according to modern economists, to maintain full employment and income, it is the duty of the government to increase public expenditure directly by under taking public works programmes on large scale and thereby inducing people to spend more.

Thus, modern fiscal policy is the policy of government under which the government uses its expenditure and revenue programmes to produce desirable of the increase in aggregate production and employment.

In other words, the modern fiscal policy is a technique to attain and maintain full employment by manipulating public expenditure and revenue in such a way so as to keep an equilibrium between effective demand and supply of goods and services at that time. Thus, modern fiscal policy is nothing but the application of the principle of functional finance.

Functional Finance

The concept of functional finance was first stated by Keynes and was developed by **Prof. AP. Lerner. Prof. Lerner** believed that Fiscal measures should be judged only by their effects. The way is which the fiscal measures work in the economy is called as functional finance by Prof. Lerner.

The central idea is that the government's Fiscal policy involves government spending, and taxing, spending and borrowing of loans, issue of new money and wirhdrawl of money from circulation should all be viewed with the consideration of their impact upon the national economy as a whole and not to any established doctrine of finance, just as the doctrine of sound finance was established by classical economists.

Hence, Judging a Fiscal policy by its effects or the way in which it functions in an economy is called as functional finance.

Balanced Budget

The budget is the most important instrument of fiscal policy, since the necessary finance is obtained and the public expenditure is made through budget. A government budget is said to be balanced when its tax revenues and expenditures are equal. When the budget is not balanced, there is either a deficit or surplus budget and it is said to be an unbalanced budget in either case. The value of multiplier is more than 1 in case of unbalanced budget, it is1 in case of balanced budget and less than 1 in case of surplus budget.

Balance of Payments

Meaning and Components

The balance of payments of a country is a statistical record kept in the form of a balance sheet comprising of all her foreign economic transactions during any given period of time. It presents a summary account of all international transactions of a country during a certain given period of time.

Since the balance of payments is a systematic record of a country's total money receipts from and payments to abroad, the difference between receipts and payments is the surplus or deficit. A country's total money receipts are the receipts or payments that accrue to its residents while the total payments refer to the payments made by the residents of a country. Dividing resident's total receipts, R, and their total payments, P, into their domestic and foreign components and if the domestic receipts and domestic payments are identical, then the international balance of payments, B, of a country can be expressed as

$$B = R - P$$
$$= (R_d + R_f) - (P_d + P_f)$$
$$= R_f - P_f \quad (\text{since } R_d = P_d)$$

For an open economy, the total receipts may differ from the total payments and their difference represents the difference between foreign receipts (R_f) and foreign payments (P_f). The positive difference is termed as a surplus while the negative difference is termed as a deficit in the balance of payments of a country.

The balance of payments of a country is not a balance-sheet showing a country's foreign assets and liabilities at any given point of time. It shows for any given period of time the flow of a nation's total receipts from abroad and its total payments made to abroad. Following the conventional rules of double entry accounting, a nation's total payments and total receipts for any given period of time must be in balance. Further more, one nation's receipts are payments for others while the receipts of other nations are payments for the nation.

Usually, a country's balance of payments distinguishes between items on the current and capital accounts. In the current account are included all kinds of exports and imports of goods and services, interest and dividend payments, private gifts and so on. The capital account, sub-divided into short term capital transfers, lists the imports and exports of all kinds of debt instruments and corporate stocks as well as imports and exports of monetary gold. The following table explains the different items included under various subheads in the balance of payments of a country.

Components of Balance of Payments

Receipts (Credits)	*Payments (Debits)*
1. Exports of goods	1. Imports of goods
2. Exports of services	2. Imports of services
3. Unrequited receipts (gifts, indemnities, etc., from foreigners)	3. Unrequited payments (gifts, indemnities, etc. to foreigners)
4. Capital receipts (borrowings from, capital repayments by, or sale of assets to, foreigners)	4. Capital payments (lending to, capital repayments to, or purchase of assets from, foreigners)

Balance of Payments and Balance of Trade

The concepts of balance of trade and balance of payments are often misunderstood. Economists frequently say that while the balance of payments includes the balance of trade, the balance of trade does not include the balance of payments. A country exports and imports many **visible** goods and **invisible** services. **Invisible services** include tourism, shipping and other transport services, banking and insurance services for whose exports and imports payments are made and received by the country in international trade. A country's balance of trade refers to the value of imports and exports of commodities only. The balance of payments is, however, more comprehensive including as it does the total debits and credits relating to all the items on account of which a country makes payments to and receives payments from rest of the world. In short, the balance of trade is only a part of the balance of payments.

Equilibrium and Disequilibrium

The balance of payments of a country is said to be in equilibrium when the demand for foreign exchange is exactly equivalent to the supply of it. The balance of payments is in disequilibrium when there is either a surplus or deficit in the balance of payments. When there is a deficit in the balance of payments, the demand for foreign exchange exceeds the supply for it.

Correction of Disequilibrium

A country may not be bothered about a surplus in the balance of payments; but every country strives to remove, or at least to reduce a balance of payments deficit. A number of measures are available for correcting the balance of payments disequilibrium. We outline below the important measures for correcting the dis-equilibrium caused by a deficit in the balance of payments.

A. Monetary measures

B. Trade measures

C. Miscellaneous

A. Monetary Measures

The important monetary measures are outlined below:

Monetary Contraction

The level of aggregate domestic demand, the domestic price level and the demand for imports and exports may be influenced by a contraction or expansion in money supply and correct the balance of payments disequilibrium. The measure required is a contraction in money supply.

A contraction in money supply is likely to reduce the purchasing power and there by the aggregate demand. It is also likely to bring about a fall in domestic prices. The fall in the domestic aggregate demand and domestic prices reduce the demand for imports. The fall in domestic prices is likely to increase exports. Thus, the fall in imports and the rise in exports would help to correct the disequilibrium.

Devaluation

Devaluation means a reduction in the official rate at which one currency is exchanged for another currency.

A country with a fundamental disequili-brium in the balance of payments may devalue its currency in order to stimulate its exports and discourage imports to correct the disequilibrium.

The balance of payments deficit of a country will be eliminated as a consequence of devaluation, *i.e.*, the position of the country's balance of payments will improve if the price elasticities of demand for the currency devaluing country's imports and exports are high and at any rate in order to effect improvement in the country's balance of payments the combined absolute value of the two demand elasticities must be greater than one, *i.e.*,

$$e_x + e_m > 1$$

Where the terms e_x and e_m respectively represent the price elasticity of demand for exports, and imports, of the currency devaluing country.

Exchange Control

Exchange control is a popular method employed to influence the balance of payments position of a country. Under exchange control, the government or central bank assumes complete control of the foreign exchange reserves and earnings of the country. The recipients of foreign exchange such as exporters, are required to surrender foreign exchange to the government/central bank in exchange for domestic currency. By the virtue of its control over the use of foreign exchange the government can control the imports.

B. Trade Measures

Trade measures include export promotion measures and import control measures.

Exports may be encouraged by reducing or abolishing export duties, providing an export subsidy and encouraging export production and export marketing by offering monetary, fiscal, physical and institutional incentives and facilities.

Imports may be controlled by imposing or enhancing import duties, restricting imports through import quotas and licensing and even by prohibiting altogether the import of certain non-essential items.

C. Miscellaneous Measures

Apart from the measures mentioned above, there are a number of other measures that can help to make the Balance of Payments position more favourable, such as obtaining foreign loans, encouraging foreign investment in the home country, development of tourism to attract foreign tourists, providing incentives to enhance inward remittances, developing import substituting industries, etc.

The Import Function

Imports are an increasing function of income. This functional relationship can be expressed in the following way

$$M = M(y)$$

A country's average propensity to import is defined as the total imports divided by the total national income, *i.e.*

$$API = \frac{M}{Y}$$

The marginal propensity to import measures how much of a change in the national income is spent on imports.

Using algebraic terms it is defined as $\frac{\Delta M}{\Delta Y}$.

The Foreign Trade Multiplier

In equilibrium

$$Y = C + I + X - M \quad ...(1)$$

Where Y = national income

C = consumption

I = investment

X = exports

M = imports

We can rewrite equation (1) as

$$\Delta Y = \Delta C + \Delta I + \Delta X - \Delta M$$

$$\Rightarrow \quad \Delta Y = c\Delta Y + \Delta I + \Delta X - m\Delta Y$$

$$\Rightarrow \Delta Y[1 - c + m] = \Delta I + \Delta X$$

$$\Rightarrow \quad \Delta y = \frac{1}{1 - c + m}(\Delta I + \Delta X) \quad ...(2)$$

Where c = MPC

m = MPI

From equation 2 we see that the effect of a change in exports on the national income equals the change in exports multiplied by the expression $1/(1 - c + m)$, which is the foreign trade multiplier.

Devaluation

By devaluation of a country's currency unit is meant the decrease in the external value of a unit of that currency expressed in terms of gold, SDR or foreign currency by government edict. A country may reduce the foreign exchange value of her currency unit for more than one reason, *e.g.*, to create surplus in her balance of payments by means of dumping her goods abroad, or to remove deficit in her external balance of payments. In short, devaluation means an act of officially reducing the external value of the currency unit of the country and appreciation to the extent of devaluation in the external value of the currency unit of the country in whose relationship the country has devalued her currency.

Methods of Removing Balance of Payments Deficit

The conditions under which devaluation would cause an improvement in the balance of payments position of the currency devaluing country have been discussed by Lerner, Robinson, Meade and others. The extent to which deficit of the external balance of payments of the currency devaluing country can be corrected through devaluation depends upon the price elasticities of demand and the price elasticities of supply of her exports and imports.

Considering first the price elasticity of demand for the exports of the country, if the price elasticity of demand for the exports of the currency-devaluing country is less than unity in absolute value, devaluation will not reduce deficit of the balance of payments of the country; rather the balance of payments deficit of the country would increase as a consequence of devaluation.

If the price elasticity of demand for the exports of the country is less than unity, a given percentage fall in the rate of exchange, say of 20 percent, will cause less than 20 per cent (say only 10 per cent) increase in the total quantity of exports of the country.

This is the positive quantity effect of devaluation. But while the total quantity of exports increases by 10 per cent the total foreign exchange earnings or total value of exports of the country will be less than the pre-devaluation total value of exports because while the total quantity of exports has increased by 10 per cent, the foreign currency price per unit of export goods has fallen by 20 per cent.

The negative price factor more than offsets the positive quantity factor reflected in the increase of the total quantity of exports, making the net effect on the total foreign exchange earnings of the country through exports negative.

It has been illustrated in figure 1 where the two countries taken are India and America with India devaluing her currency rupee in order to correct her external balance of payments deficit.

In this figure, the demand and supply of India's exports have been shown on the *x*-axis and price expressed in the US dollars has been shown on the Y-axis. D_xD_x is inelastic demand curve for India's exports while AS_x is perfectly elastic supply curve of Indian exports.

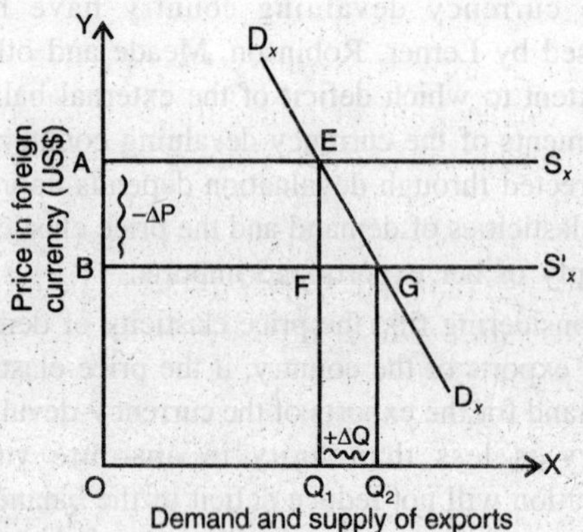

Fig. 1

Before devaluation of the Indian rupee, the dollar price of export was OA, the total quantity exported was OQ_1 and the total foreign exchange (dollars) earned by the country through the exports was $OQ_1 \times OA$ (= rectangle AOQ_1E).

Consequent on devaluation of the rupee, the dollar (foreign currency) price of Indian exports falls by AB from OA to OB showing that the dollar price in percentage terms has fallen by the full extent of devaluation. Consequently, the supply curve of India's exports As_x shifts downward to the position of BS'_x while the total quantity of exports increases by Q_1Q_2 ($=\Delta Q$) from OQ_1 to OQ_2. The new total foreign exchange revenue (total dollar earnings) is $OQ_2 \times OB$ (= rectangle BOQ_2G).

The net change in the total foreign exchange earnings of the country due to devaluation will be positive (increase) or negative (decrease) according as ABFE is smaller or greater than rectangle Q_1Q_2 GF. In this case, the demand for India's exports being inelastic, rectangle ABFE > rectangle Q_1Q_2 GF. Consequently devaluation increases rather than decrease the deficit of India's balance of payments. It, therefore, follows that although currency devaluation will always lead to an increase in the total quantity of exports of the currency-devaluing country (unless the price elasticity of demand for her exports is zero), it does not, however, necessarily follow from this that it will always also lead to an increase in the total foreign exchange earnings of the country from exports.

Figure 2 shows the position of total export earnings in terms of rupees (domestic currency). It is obvious that the total rupee-earnings will always increase as result of devaluation even when the foreign demand for country's exports is inelastic. In this case, instead of the country's perfectly elastic supply curve shifting downward the demand curve shifts upward from D_xD_x to $D'_xD'_x$, showing higher demand for exports at each different rupee-price since the same rupee-price now means lower dollar-price for the Americans inducing them to buy Q_1Q_2 amount more.

However, although the total rupee earnings from exports increase by EQ_1Q_2F amount but it does not necessarily follow from this that the total dollar-earnings also increase.

Coming to imports, devaluation will help in reducing the deficit of external balance of payments only if the price elasticity of domestic demand for imports is greater than unity ($e_m > 1$) because in that situation a given percentage increase in the price of imports measured in terms of the domestic currency would cause more than proportionate fall in the quantity of imports as shown in figure 3 when the demand for and supply of imports have been shown on the X-axis and the price of imports expressed in domestic currency has been shown on the Y-axis. D_mD_m is the demand curve for imports while AS_m is the perfectly elastic supply curve for imports.

Before devaluation, the rupee-price of imports was OA and the total imports were OQ_1 giving the total rupee value of imports represented by rectangle OQ_1EA (= OA × OQ_1). As a consequence of devaluation, although the price of imports in foreign currency (dollars) remains unchanged, since the supply curve for imports is expressed in terms of the domestic currency, it shifts upward by the full amount of the difference between the pre-devaluation and post-devaluation rupee-price.

The new supply curve is now BS'_m. Consequently, the total amount of imports decreases by Q_1Q_2 from OQ_1 to OQ_2. However, after devaluation India pays higher price OB for her imports. The total rupee-cost of imports is now OQ_2GB. The improvement in the balance of payments resulting from decrease in total imports consequent on devaluation of the rupee would depend on the relative sizes of rectangle Q_2Q_1EF and ABGF. If the elasticity of demand for imports is greater than unity, then rectangle Q_2Q_1EF will be larger than rectangle ABGF. Consequently, the balance of payments position of the country, in so far as imports are concerned, will improve due to devaluation.

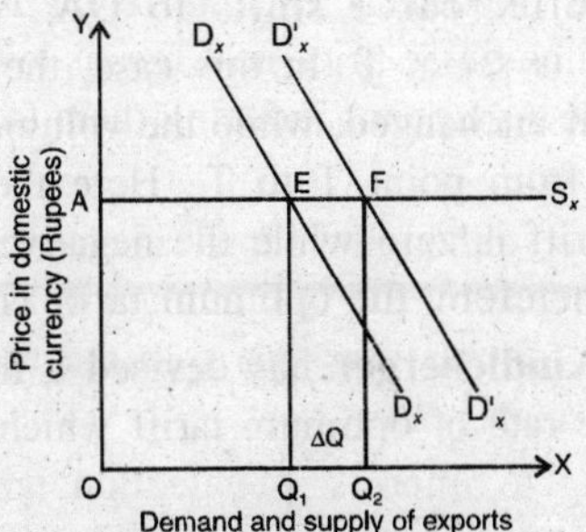

Fig. 2

Figure 4 shows the effect of devaluation on the total imports and total foreign exchange bill which must fall unless the demand for imports is perfectly inelastic. However, although the total dollar payments obligation is reduced from OQ_1EA to OQ_2FA but it does not necessarily follow from this that the total rupee-payments burden of the country will also fall.

It will fall only if the demand for imports is elastic, *i.e.*, if the elasticity of demand for imports is greater than unity. There will be no change in the total-rupee payments burden if the elasticity of demand for imports is unity and the burden will increase in the event of the elasticity of demand for imports being less than unity.

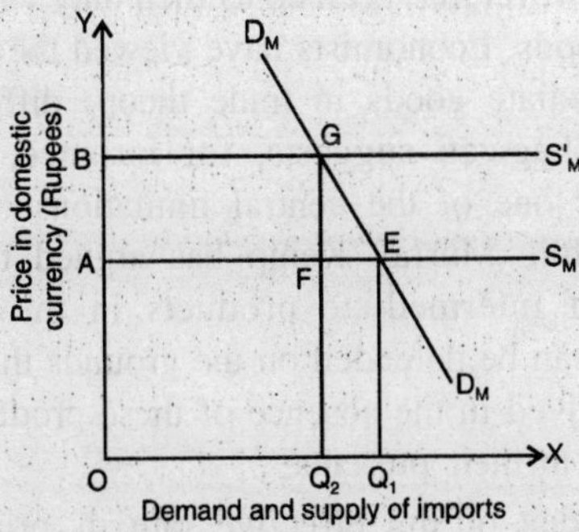

Fig. 3

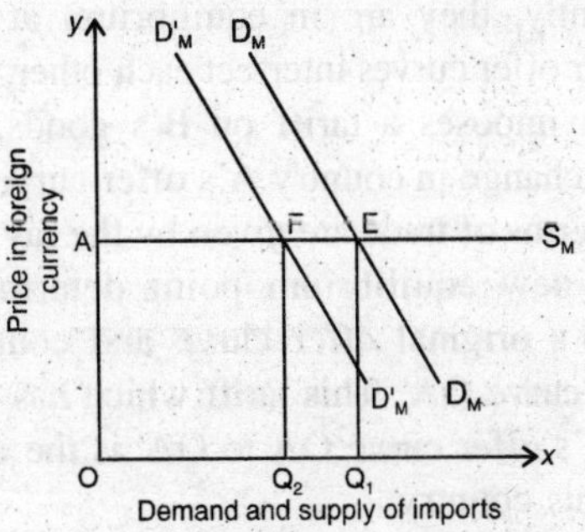

Fig. 4

It can be proved by means of a formula that under conditions of perfectly elastic supply of imports and exports, if a country devalues her currency in order to remove her external balance of payments deficit, the sum of the price elasticities of demand for the currency devaluing country's exports and imports should be greater than unity in absolute value, *i.e.*, $e_x + e_m > 1$.

This is the well-known **Marshall-Lerner Condition.** If $e_x + e_m = 1$, no improvement in the balance of payments deficit of the country will result from devaluation. If $e_x + e_m < 1$, devaluation will increase rather than decrease the balance of payments deficit of the country.

Miscellaneous

The Optimum Tariff

Usually, the imposition of a tariff improves the terms of trade of the imposing country, reduces the volume of trade, and may improve the country's welfare. The improvement in the terms of trade is the positive effect of a tariff and the reduction in the volume of trade is the negative effect of a tariff. It is only when the positive effect of a tariff is larger than its negative effect that there is improvement in the welfare of a country. The tariff that maximises a country's welfare, is called the **optimum tariff**.

The optimum tariff is explained with the help of figure A where OA is the offer curve of country A and OB is the offer curve of country B. C_a is the community indifference curve of country A. Under free trade the terms of trade between the two countries are given by the ray OT from the origin.

Consequently, they are in equilibrium at point T where their offer curves intersect each other. Suppose country A imposes a tariff on B's goods. This is shown by change in country A's offer curve to OA′. The new terms of trade are given by the ray OT' and T' is the new equilibrium point determined by country B's original offer curve and country A's new offer curve OA'. This tariff which has changed country A's offer curve OA to OA' is the optimum tariff of this country.

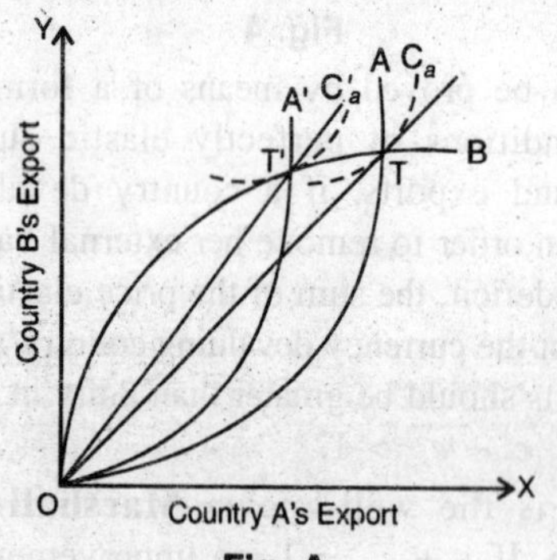

Fig. A

Fig. B

The point T' where country A's community indifference curve C'_a is tangent to country B's offer curve, is the point where the tariff is the optimum. The welfare of the people in country A is greater at point T' than at point T. This is because at T' they are at the C'*a* indifference curve which is above the C*a* indifference curve. Thus this is the optimum tariff.

The tariff imposing country can gain from the optimum tariff only if the offer curve of the other trading country is less than perfectly elastic. If the offer curve of the other country is infinitely elastic, levying a tariff will not increase the welfare of the tariff-imposing country. This is illustrated in figure B where the offer curve of country B is shown as the straight line curve OB and OA is the offer curve of country A. Under free trade, the terms of trade are given by OT and the equilibrium is established at point T where the two offer curves intersect each other. When country A imposes a tariff, its offer curve shifts to OA'. The new equilibrium is set at T. In this case, the terms of trade remain unchanged, while the volume of trade is reduced from point T to T'. Here the positive effect of tariff is zero while the negative effect is stronger. Therefore, the optimum tariff is zero.

Prof. Kindleberger has devised a formula to measure the rate of optimum tariff which is

$$T = \frac{1}{e-1}$$

where T = optimum tariff rate

e = point elasticity of the offer curve of the other country.

By applying this formula to the above case of a straight line offer curve having infinite elasticity, the optimum tariff is $1/(\infty - 1) = 0$. Thus the higher the elasticity of the offer curve of other country, the lower the level of the optimum tariff of a country and vice versa.

Effective Rates of Protection

Expirical estimates have shown that a large share and perhaps most of international trade consists of trade in intermediate goods which are used as inputs in the production of other goods. Most of trade theory, however, has been concerned only with trade in final goods. Economists have viewed the neglect of intermediate goods in trade theory differently. Jagdish Bhagwati suggests, for instance, that it constitutes one of the central limitations of trade theory, while Murray Kemp has argued that the neglect of intermediate products in the earlier literature can be defended on the grounds that most results derived in the absence of these products are also valid in their presence.

The idea of the effective rate of protection (E.R.P.) is that when inputs are taken into account the nominal tariff of a good may differ from the rate of protection given to the value added in the production of the good. According to the proponents of the theory, it is the protection to the value added that is of importance, not the nominal tariff on the final good.

Assume that the final tariff on a good is 10 percent and that inputs (raw material, intermediate goods, etc.) used in the production of the good amount to 50 per cent of the value of production and that these inputs are imported without duty. The effective rate of protection accorded to value added is then 20 per cent, not 10 per cent as the manifest duty implies.

The formula for the Effective Rate of Protection

$$r = \frac{v' - v}{v}$$

where r = rate of effective protection

v' = value added per unit of output with protection

v = value added per unit of output without protection

Trade Creation and Trade Diversion

The pioneering study of the theory of customs unions was made by **Jacob Viner**. In the beginning, customs unions had been viewed favourably. The reasoning was as follows: free trade maximizes welfare; customs unions are a move toward free trade; therefore, they will increase welfare even though they might not maximize it.

Viner showed this conclusion to be incorrect. He introduced, instead, the key concepts of **trade creation** and **trade diversion**. They might best be illustrated by table-1. The table measures the production cost of a commodity in three countries.

Table-1 : Production cost of commodity X in three countries

	Country		
	A	*B*	*C*
Production cost	50	40	30

Let us disregard transportation cost, etc., so that production cost completely determines the supply price of the good and tariffs are the only source of diversion between price and cost. If country A has a tariff of 100 percent on X, there will be no imports of the good, but domestic producers will dominate the home market. If A had levied a lower tariff, say 50 per cent, and it was non-discriminatory, it would have imported the good from the lower cost source, country C, and the price in A's home market would be 45.

Let us now assume that A and B form a customs union. A will then, instead, import X from B and the price in A's market will be 40. Imports will be switched from the low-cost supplier, C, to the high-cost supplier B. This is an example of **trade diversion.** Trade diversion takes place when imports from a more efficiently producing country are switched to a less efficiently producing country because of the customs union. Trade diversion will lead to a lowering of welfare, as it entails a less efficient allocation of resources.

We must mention here that this analysis assumes that the countries involved are fully employed both before and after the formation of the customs union. In this sense the analysis is of a neoclassical type. This being the case, it is natural to let the analysis primarily be concerned with the effects on the allocation of resources and the welfare implications of these effects.

This kind of analysis gives rise to three possibilities. **First,** neither of the two countries forming the union produces the good in question. The customs union would then be of no significance, as both countries would import the good from a third country just as they did before forming the union. **Second,** one of the countries forming the union produces the good inefficiently. The union partner would then import from the cheaper source and there will be a case of trade diversion. **Third,** both countries forming the customs union produce the good, in which case one of the countries would be more efficient than the other. The market in both countries will then be secured for the more efficient industry and there will be **trade creation.**

Spot and Forward Foreign Exchange Rates

There are the spot rate of exchange and the forward rate of exchange ruling in the foreign exchange markets. The spot rate of exchange is the rate or price expressed in terms of the home currency which is payable for spot delivery of a specified type of foreign exchange. The forward rate of exchange is the rate or price at which a transaction will be consummated at some specified time in future.

Arbitrage

An arbitrageur is a dealer or trader who by taking advantage of "inconsistencies" in the buying and selling prices quotes in different parts of the foreign exchange market makes profit. Unlike the risky activities of a speculator, the activities of an arbitrageur are free from exchange risk because he never takes an uncovered position in the foreign currency. The arbitrageur may trade either in spot or in forward foreign exchange or he may even simultaneously trade in both the spot and forward foreign exchange.

Theories of Foreign Exchange Rate

1. **The Mint Par Parity Theory :** This theory is associated with the working of the international gold standard. Under this system, the currency in use was made of gold or was convertible into gold at a fixed rate. The value of the currency unit was defined in terms of certain weight of gold, that is, so many grains of gold to the rupee, the dollar, the pound, etc. The central bank of the country was always ready to buy and sell gold at the specified price. The rate at which the standard money of the country was convertible into gold was called the mint price of gold. If the official British price of gold was 6 per ounce and of the US price of gold 35 per ounce, they were the mint prices of gold in the respective countries. The exchange rate between the dollar and the pound would be fixed at $\frac{36}{£6}$ = \$6. This rate was called the mint parity or mint par of exchange because it was based on the mint price of gold. Thus under the gold standard, the normal or basic rate of exchange was equal to the ratio of their mint par values (R = \$/£).
2. **The Purchasing Power Parity Theory :** The purchasing power parity theory was developed by **Gustav Cassel** in 1920 to determine the exchange rate between countries on the basis of inconvertible paper currencies. The theory states that equilibrium exchange rate between two inconvertible paper currencies is determined by the equality of their purchasing power. In other words, the rate of exchange between two countries is determined by their relatives price levels.

Cassel's purchasing power parity theory became very popular among economists during 1914-1924 and was widely accepted as a realistic explanation of the determination of foreign exchange rate under inconvertible paper currencies. But it has been severely criticised for its weak theoretical base.

International Economics

International trade deals with business transactions that take place between citizens of different nations and with considerations of commercial diplomacy that spring from such business transactions. Consequently, international trade may be defined as the exchange of goods and services among the citizens of independent or sovereign states or countries. It consists of the exchange by each country of its low-priced goods and services for those goods and services which can be secured at lower prices from abroad than the prices at home.

A. Absolute Cost Advantage Theory of Adam Smith

In Smith's model of international trade, every one will be better off without making any one worse off. As such each country will gain by trading. Taking the case of two individual producers, a tailor and a shoe-maker, tailor does not make his own shoes; he exchanges a suit with shoes. Thereby both the shoe-maker and the tailor gain. In the same manner, Smith argued, a whole country can gain by trading with other countries.

If it takes 10 labour units to manufacture 1 unit of good A in country I but 20 labour units in country II, and if it takes 20 units of labour to manufacture 1 unit of good B in country I but only 10 labour units in country II, then both countries can gain by trading.

If the two countries exchanged the 2 goods at a ratio of 1 to 1, so that 1 unit of good A is exchanged for 1 unit of good B, country I could get 1 unit of good B by sacrificing only 10 units of labour, whereas it would have to give up 20 units of labour if it produced the good itself. Likewise, country II would have to sacrifice only 10 units of labour to get 1 unit of good A, whereas it would have to give up 20 units of labour if it produced it itself. The implication of this is clearly that both countries could have more of both goods, with a given effort, by trading.

This was a simple and powerful illustration of the benefits of trade, and on it Adam Smith rested his plea for non-interference for free trade as the best policy for trade between nations. Smith's argument seems convincing, but it is not very deep. It was left to Torrens and Ricardo to produce the stronger and more subtle argument for the benefits of trade contained in the theory of comparative advantage.

B. David Ricardo and the Theory of Comparative Cost Advantage

While it is true that a large part of world trade rests upon absolute differences in costs, such differences in costs cannot explain trade that takes place between two such countries one of which can produce both commodities at a cheaper cost than the other country but she can produce one commodity more cheaply. To express the same idea differently : Why does trade take place when one country produces both goods at an absolutely lower unit cost than the other but her cost is comparatively lower in the production of one good, *i.e.*, the country commands comparative cost advantage in the production of only one good although she possess absolute cost advantage in the production of both the goods? It was David Ricardo who first explained the basis of trade under such situations. According to Ricardo, "Each country will specialise in the production of those commodities in which it has greater comparative advantage or least comparative disadvantage. Thus a country will export those commodities in which its comparative advantage is the greatest, and import those commodities in which its comparative disadvantage is the least."

Assumptions of the Theory

The Ricardian theory is based on the following assumptions :

1. Labour is the only factor of production.
2. All labour units are homogeneous.
3. Labour is perfectly mobile within the country but is perfectly immobile between different countries.
4. Production of two goods takes place under constant cost conditions so that the unit cost ratios of the two goods are constant.
5. Trade takes place between only two countries and in two commodities produced by labour alone. In other words, Ricardian theory is a 2 × 2 × 1 trade model.
6. Prices of the two commodities are determined by labour cost, *i.e.*, the number of labour units employed to produce each.
7. Technological knowledge is unchanged.
8. There is free trade between the two countries, there being no trade barriers or restrictions in the movement of commodities.
9. No transport costs are involved in carrying trade between the two countries.
10. All factors of production are fully employed in both the countries.

Given these asssumptions, Ricardo enunciated the "principle of comparative costs," also called the "principle of comparative cost advantage" by taking the example of two countries England and Portugal and of two commodities wine and cloth. In his celebrated example, Portugal produces both wine and cloth at an absolutely lower cost than does England, *i.e.*, she possesses absolute advantage over England in the production of the both goods. Her comparative advantage is, however, greater in the production of wine than in the production of cloth. Conversely, England is inefficient in the production of both wine and cloth as her absolute real cost of production of both wine and cloth is higher compared with that of Portugal.

However, her inefficiency is less marked in the production of cloth than in the production of wine. Under such a situation, it would be mutually advantageous for both the countries if Portugal concentrated only on the production of wine and exchanged her surplus wine against England's surplus cloth and England concentrated only on the manufacture of cloth exchanging her surplus production of cloth for the Portuguese wine. We may now reproduce Ricardo's celebrated example of Portugal and England by means of the following table:

	Per Unit Cost (in labour hours) of	
Country	*Wine*	*Cloth*
Portugal	80	90
England	120	100

According to the above cost data, one unit of wine costs 80 labour hours and one unit of cloth costs 90 hours of labour in Portugal. The corresponding cost of producing 1 unit of wine and 1 unit of cloth in England is 120 and 100 hours of labour. It is, therefore, obvious that Portugal commands absolute superiority over England in the production of both the goods.

This absolute superiority of Portugal is, however, more marked (greater) in the production of wine than in the production of cloth. She has, therefore, a comparative cost advantage in the production of wine because here her cost ratio difference (or productivity) is relatively higher than it is in the case of cloth, *i.e.*, 80/120 < 90/100 < 1. It means that Portuguese labour's productivity in wine is 1.5 times (120/80) that of the productivity of English labour while her labour's productivity in cloth is only 1.1 times (100/90) that of the English labour. Since both 1.5 and 1.1 are greater than 1, it follows that Portugal's labour is more efficient or productive than England's labour in both the branches of production. It is, however, equally true that, since 1.5 is greater than 1.1, Portuguese labour is relatively more efficient or productive in wine than in cloth. In other wods, Portugal possesses a comparative advantage over England in the production of wine relative to the production of cloth. Conversely, England suffers from a greater disadvantage in wine than in cloth.

But how can it be said that in the situation envisaged by Ricardo both countries will gain from trade? Returning to Ricardo's example, in the absence of trade 1 unit of wine will exchange for 0.88 unit of cloth in Portugal while in England 1 unit of wine will exchange for 1.2 units of cloth. If trade between the two countries begins, it is to the advantage of Portugal to export wine to England where 1 unit of it is exchanged for 1.2 units of cloth. Assuming perfect interindustry labour mobility within the country, Portugal will produce wine instead of cloth. Conversely, it will be to the advantage of England to specialise in the manufacture of cloth because she can obtain wine at a cheaper cost from Portugal by exchanging cloth against wine. There exists sufficient inducement for both the countries to engage in trade. Portugal would gain by trading off her surplus wine against English cloth so long as she can get more than 0.88 unit of cloth for 1 unit of wine while England would gain so long as she is asked to give less than 1.2 units of cloth for 1 unit of wine. Consequently, any exchange ratio between 0.88 and 1.2 units of cloth for 1 unit of wine will be acceptable to both the countries making trade possible between them. The theory of comparative cost advantage leads to the conclusion that each country will specialise in the production of that good in which it enjoys comparative cost advantages as by doing so it will be able to obtain a greater total product-mix from its given endowment of factors of production. Ricardo did not, however, explain where the actual exchange ratio between 0.88

and 1.2 units of cloth for 1 unit of wine will be fixed. In fact, there are possible a vast myriad of exchange ratios between the range of 0.88 and 1.2.

Its Criticism

The principle of comparative advantage has been criticised on the following grounds.

1. Unrealistic Assumption of Labour Theory of Value
2. Static Assumption of Fixed Proportions
3. Unrealistic Assumption of Constant Costs
4. Two-country Two-commodity Model is Unrealistic
5. Unrealistic Assumption of Free Trade
6. Neglects the Role of Technology
7. Unrealistic Assumption of Full Employment
8. Consider only Supply Side of International Trade

C. Modern Theory : Heckscher-Ohlin Theory

Bertin Ohlin in his famous book "Interregional and International Trade" criticised the classical theory of international trade and formulated the General Equilibrium or Factor Endowment Theory of International Trade. It is also known as the *Modern Theory of International Trade* or the Heckshar-Ohlin Theorem. In fact, it was Eli Hecksher, Ohlin's teacher, who first propounded the idea in 1919 that trade results from differences in factor endowments in different countries, and Ohlin carried it forward to build the modern theory of international trade.

Assumptions of the Theory

1. It is a 2 × 2 × 2 model, *i.e.*, there are two countries (A and B), two commodities (X and Y) and two factors of production (capital and labour).
2. There is perfect competition in commodity as well as factor markets.
3. There is full employment of resources.
4. There are quantitative differences in factor endowments in different regions, but qualitatively they are homogeneous.
5. The production function of the two commodities have different factor intensities, *i.e.*, labour-intensive and capital-intensive.
6. The production functions are different for different commodities, but are the same for each good in both countries. It means that the production function of commodity X is different from commodity Y. But the technique used to produce commodity X in both countries is the same, and the technique used to produce commodity Y in both countries is the same.
7. There is perfect mobility of factors within each region but internationally they are immobile.
8. There are no transport costs.
9. There is free trade between the two countries.
10. There are constant returns to scale in the production of each commodity in each region.
11. There is no change in technological knowledge.

Given these assumptions, Ohlin contends that the immediate cause of international trade is the difference in relative commodity prices caused by differences in relative demand and supply of factors (factor prices) as a result of differences in factor endowments between two countries. Fundamentally the relative scarcity of factors-the shortage of supply in relation to demand-is essential for trade between two regions. Commodities which use large quantities of scarce factors are imported because their prices are high, while those using abundant factors are exported because their prices are low.

Factor Abundance in Terms of Factor Prices

Ohlin explains richness in factor endowment in terms of factor prices. According to his definition, country A is abundant in capital if $\left(\frac{P_C}{P_L}\right)_A < \left(\frac{P_C}{P_L}\right)_B$, where P_C and P_L refer to prices of capital and labour and the subscripts A and B denote the two countries. In other words, if capital is relatively cheap in country A, the country is abundant in capital, and if labour is cheap in country B, the country is abundant in labour. Thus country A will export the capital-intensive good and country B will export the labour-intensive good.

Factor Abundance in Physical Terms

Another way to explain the Ohlin theorem is in physical terms of factor abundance. If country A is relatively capital-abundant and country B is relatively labour abundant, then measured in physical amounts $\left(\frac{C_A}{L_A}\right) > \frac{C_B}{L_B}$, where C_A and L_A are the total amounts of capital and labour respectively in country A and C_B and L_B are the total amounts of capital and labour respectively in country B.

Its Superiority Over the Classical Theory

Ohlin's theory is an improvement over the classical theory of international trade in many respects.

1. Ohlin's theory is superior to the classical theory in that it regards international trade as a special case of interregional or inter-local trade as distinct from the classical theory which considers international trade totally different from domestic trade.
2. The Ohlin model takes two factors-labour and capital-as against the one factor (labour) classical model, and is thus superior to the latter.
3. Again, the Ohlin theory is superior to the Ricardian theory in that it regards differences in factor supplies as basic for determining the pattern of international trade while the latter theory takes no notice of it.
4. The Ohlin model is more realistic because it is based on the relative prices of factors which in turn influence the relative prices of goods, while the Ricardian theory considers the relative prices of goods only.

Its Criticism

Ohlin's theory has been criticised on the following grounds.

1. Two-by-two-by-two Model is Unrealistic.
2. Static Theory
3. Factors not Homogeneous
4. Production Techniques not Homogeneous
5. Leontief Paradox has Falsified the Theory

Leontief Paradox

The most interesting empirical test of the Heckscher-Ohlin theorem that has been made so far is the study undertaken by Wassily Leontief in the early 1950s. Leontief tests his hypothesis with the help of an input-output table for the United States for 1947. He attempted to verify the empirical validity of the Heckscher-Ohlin theorem that a capital abundant country would export relatively capital intensive goods and in turn import more labour intensive goods.

In context of U.S.A. economy, the Heckscher-Ohlin model tells that this country specialised in export of those good which use more capital than labour and import relatively labour intensive goods. But by Leontief's practical test, it was found that U.S.A. exported more of labour intensive goods and imported more of capital intensive goods, a situation that was in direct contrast to its relative factor endowment position.

As such Leontief's result came as a great surprise to many economists of the world. Some economists criticised Leontief's findings on the ground that 1947 was not the right year for testing the theory as during this year the economy was beset with the post war disorganisation of production.

In defence to criticisms Leontief stated that America's participation in international division of labour was based on its specialisation in labour intensive rather than capital intensive lines of production. In other words the country resorts to foreign trade in order to economise its capital and dispose of its surplus labour, rather than the reverse. It was also argued that the U.S. export industries employed more skilled labour and are thus human capital intensive rather than physical capital intensive. Abundance of human capital in the U.S. economy explains its exports of labour intensive goods.

Haberler's Theory of Opportunity Cost

The Opportunity Cost Theory, propounded by *Prof. Gottfried Haberler* in 1883, has been applied to the theory of international trade as a substitute for the doctrine of comparative cost expressed in terms of labour cost or real cost.

Haberler's theory explains that if a country can produce either commodity X or Y, the opportunity cost of commodity X is the amount of the other commodity Y that must be given up in order to get one additional unit of commodity X.

To explain this theory let us take examples of two countries say England and Russia. Suppose with the given resources England can produce 30 kgs. of wheat and no cloth or 90 metres of cloth and no wheat.

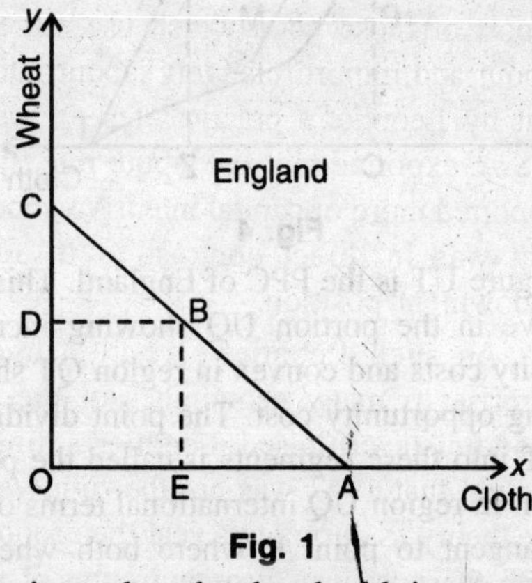

Fig. 1

Russia on the other hand with its resources can produce 60 kgs. of wheat and no cloth or 90 metres of cloth and no wheat. The opportunity cost of wheat is the production of cloth foregone, *i.e.*, it is the amount of one commodity given up to get the other commodity. Thus in England opportunity cost is

$$30W = 90C$$

$$\Rightarrow \quad 1W = 3C$$

and in Russia opportunity cost is

$$60W = 90C$$

$$\Rightarrow \quad 1W = 1.5C$$

The production possibilities of wheat and cloth in England and Russia and their opportunity cost can be shown in the following figures.

Since, with all its resources England can produce either OC of wheat or OA of cloth, the line CA is the production possibility curve in figure 1. The point B on production possibility line CA, shows that England can produce OD of wheat and OE of cloth. Hence CD of wheat is the opportunity cost of OE of cloth in England, in the same way as OC of wheat is the opportunity cost of OA of cloth. Since the production possibility curve AC is a straight line. It bears a constant slope. It shows the constant opportunity cost of wheat in terms of cloth and cloth in terms of wheat.

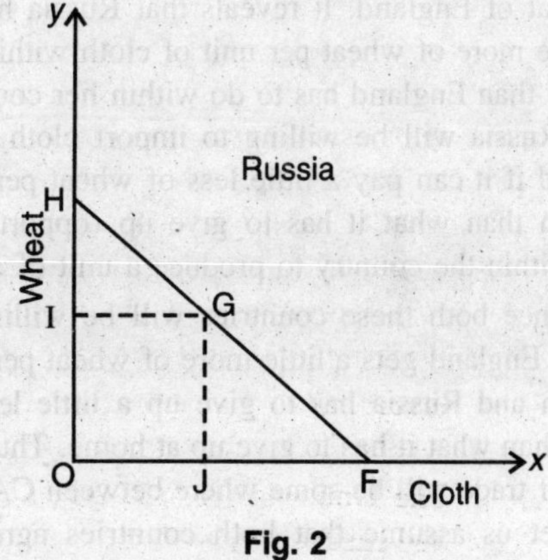

Fig. 2

In the same way FH is the production possibility curve of Russia. At point G Russia can produce OI of wheat and OJ of cloth.

Hence IH of wheat is the opportunity cost of OJ of cloth in the same way as OH of wheat is the opportunity cost of OF of cloth.

Trade under Constant Opportunity Costs

Whatever we have explained earlier, was the individual opportunity costs of nations before trade. Now suppose trade begins what will be the gain to England and Russia from this trade. This we can explain by superimposing the production possibility curve of England on that of Russia in order to know England's gain from trade and the reverse for Russia's gain from trade.

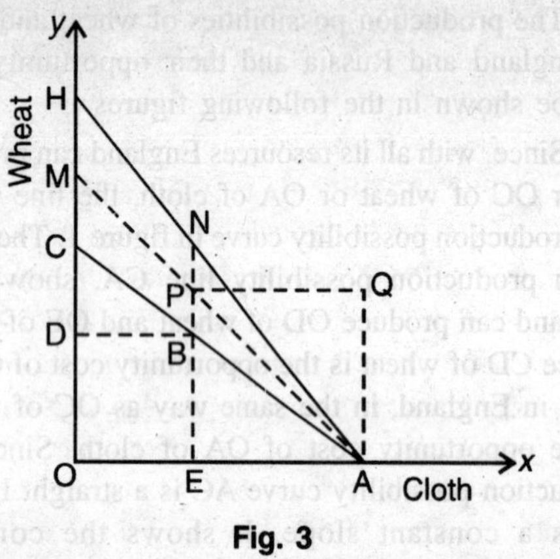

Fig. 3

From the above figure it is clear that the production possibility curve of Russia (AH) is higher than that of England. It reveals that Russia has to sacrifice more of wheat per unit of cloth within the country than England has to do within her country. Thus, Russia will be willing to import cloth from England if it can pay a little less of wheat per unit of cloth than what it has to give up (opportunity cost) within the country to produce a unit of cloth.

Hence both these countries will be willing to trade if England gets a little more of wheat per unit of cloth and Russia has to give up a little less of wheat than what it has to give up at home. Thus the terms of trade will be some where between CA and HA. Let us assume that both countries agree to exchange wheat for cloth at a ratio shown by the line AM which we may call the terms of trade line. Now England will specialise in production of cloth and Russia will specialise in production of wheat. Now England will produce OA of cloth from which OE amount will be kept for domestic consumption and will export EA of cloth for PB amount of wheat which it imports from Russia. Thus England gets an additional amount of wheat PB through specialisation and trade. Hence after trade PQ=EA are England's export and PE = QA are its imports. In the similar process Russia too gains from specialisation and trade through its exports of wheat sacrificing the units of production of cloth.

Trade Under Increasing and Decreasing Opportunity Cost Conditions

The implicit assumption behind the straight line production possibility curve is that all the factors used in production process and equally efficient both in production of wheat and cloth. But the fact is that all factors are not equally efficient in production of both these goods. So the slope of the production possibility curve cannot be a straight line. It is also not possible that both the commodities may be produced either under decreasing opportunity costs or under increasing opportunity costs. Rather the situation may be where wheat is being produced under decreasing opportunity costs and cloth under increasing opportunity costs. This can be shown with the following figure.

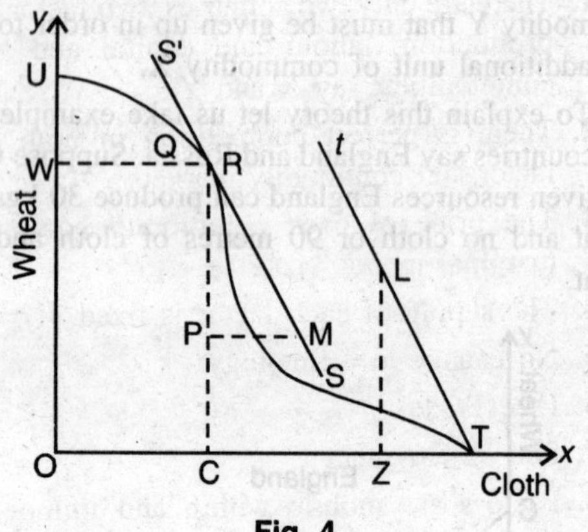

Fig. 4

In figure UT is the PPC of England. This curve is concave in the portion UQ showing increasing opportunity costs and convex in region QT showing decreasing opportunity cost. The point dividing the curve UT into these segments is called the point of inflection. In region UQ international terms of trade line is tangent to point R where both wheat and cloth are being produced under increasing opportunity cost. Russia is producing OC of cloth and OW of wheat. Its consumption point is at M whereby it imports PM of cloth and exports PR of wheat. Since point M is outside the production possibility curve, the country is better off trading with the other country. When the production of cloth starts under decreasing opportunity costs due to internal economics and the PPC becomes convex in the region QT of the UT curve. Consequently as more and more of cloth is produced costs of production diminishes. Now the country (England) reaches point T when it completely specialises in production of cloth.

Assuming that the international terms of trade remain the same as before we draw Tt parallel to SS' so that the new consumption point is T. The country will now export ZT of cloth and import LZ of wheat. The country gains more from trade at L than point M. This is possible so long as the terms of trade line Tt is to the right of SS'.

Assumptions

Haberler makes the following assumptions for his theory.

1. There are only two countries, two factors of production, labour and capital and two commodities, say X and Y.
2. There is perfect competition in both the factor and commodity markets.
3. The price of each commodity equals it marginal money costs.
4. The supply of each factor is fixed.
5. No change in technology.
6. Free Trade
7. Full employment
8. Factors are mobile within and immobile between the countries.

Terms of Trade

The terms of trade is one of the measurements of the gains from international trade to a particular country.

In international economics, the phrase terms of trade refers to the ratio index of export prices to import prices. In other words, it is the rate at which a country's exports are exchanged for imports. John Stuart Mill, one of the great classical economists has shown that the terms of trade between two commodities depend upon the strength of the world supply and demand for each of the two commodities. In other words, the terms of trade are determined by reciprocal demand.

Different Concepts of Terms of Trade

Several concept of terms of trade, such as the net barter, gross barter, income, single factoral, and double factoral terms of trade have been given by different writers.

These several concepts have been put by **Meier** under the following three broad groups.

1. Those terms of trade that relate to the real ratio of international exchange between the commodities. In this group we have the
   A. Net barter terms of trade
   B. Gross barter terms of trade
   C. Income terms of trade
2. Those terms of trade that relate to their interchange between the productive resources. In this group we have the
   A. Single factoral terms of trade
   B. Double factoral terms of trade
3. Those terms of trade that interpret the gains from trade in terms of the utility analysis. In this group we have the
   A. Real cost terms of trade
   B. Utility terms of trade

Net Barter or Commodity Terms of Trade

While discussing the terms of trade, **Frank William Taussing** introduced the concept of the net barter or commodity terms of trade.

His net barter terms of trade, popularly called 'the commodity terms of trade,' is the ratio between import prices and export-prices and can be written as

$$T_C = \frac{P_x}{P_m}$$

Where

T_c = net barter terms of trade

P_x = price of export commodity

P_m = price of import commodity

When this concept of net barter terms of trade is applied to more than one export and import commodity we use the export price and the import price indices instead of using the prices of particular export and import goods. Consequently, a change in the net barter terms of trade would be written as

$$T_c = \frac{P_{x_1}/P_{x_0}}{P_{M_1}/P_{M_0}}$$

$$= \frac{P_{x_1}}{P_{M_1}} \cdot \frac{P_{M_0}}{P_{x_0}}$$

Where

T_C = net barter terms of trade

P_{x_1} = price index of exports for any given year

P_{M_1} = price index of imports for any given year

P_{x_0} = price index of exports for base year

P_{M_0} = price index of imports for base year

As the price index of imports and exports for the base year will always be equal to 100, the term P_{M_0} / P_{x_0} in the formula will be equal to 100/100 = 1. Consequently, the net barter terms of trade will, therefore, move in accordance with the movement of any given year's price indices of imports and exports.

Let us suppose that the price index of imports and exports in India in the base year 1960 is 100 and in 1988 the price indices of imports and exports are 120 and 160 respectively. Consequently, the net barter terms of trade will be

$$T_C = \frac{160}{120} \cdot \frac{100}{100}$$

$$= 1.33$$

This means that in 1988 the net barter terms of trade show an improvement of 33 percent over the base year.

Gross Barter Terms of Trade

Introduced by **Taussing**, the gross barter terms of trade is the ratio of the total physical quantity of imports to the total physical quantity of exports of a country, greater this ratio the more favourable being the gross barter terms of trade. Taussing introduced this concept to correct the commodity or net barter terms of trade for unilateral transactions, or unrequited exports or imports such as tributes, gifts, immigrant's remittance etc.

The gross barter terms of trade can be expressed as:

$$T_G = \frac{Q_M}{Q_x}$$

where

T_G = gross barter terms of trade

Q_M = total quantity of imports

Q_x = total quantity of exports

For comparing changes in the gross barter terms of trade between two time periods we use the index numbers of the quantities of exports and imports in the two time periods instead of the quantities alone. The ratio is expressed as

$$T_G = \frac{Q_{M_1}}{Q_{x_1}} \cdot \frac{Q_{x_0}}{Q_{M_0}}$$

where the terms Q_x and Q_M stand for the index of quantity of exports and imports of the country and the subscripts 0 to 1 stand for the base year and the given year respectively.

Income Terms of Trade

Dorrance and Staehle refined the concept of the commodity terms of trade and developed a new concept known as the 'income terms of trade.' The income terms of trade is the ratio of the value of exports divided by the price index of imports and can be written as

$$T_I = \frac{P_x Q_M}{P_M}$$

where T_I = income terms of trade

P_x = price of exports

P_M = price of imports

Q_M = quantity of exports

It is obvious from the formula that given the import prices, if the export prices rise and the volume of country's exports fall equally, the net barter terms of trade will improve while the income terms of trade will show no change.

Unilateral or Single Factoral Terms of Trade

With changing factor productivity, the concept of the net barter terms of trade is distinctly misleading as a measure of the gains for a country from trade without keeping in view the improvement in factor productivity which results from trading. The concepts which used the commodity technical coefficient index were developed by **Jacob Viner**. The concepts developed by him are known as the 'single factoral' terms of trade.

The single factoral terms of trade is the ratio of the export price index and the import price index adjusted for changes in the productivity of a country's factors of production engaged in the production of export commodities.

If the commodity terms of trade index is multiplied by the reciprocal of the export commodity technical coefficients index, the resultant index is known as the 'single factoral terms of trade' which can be expressed as

$$T_S = \frac{P_x}{P_M}.Z_x$$

where T_S = single factoral terms of trade

$\frac{P_x}{P_M}$ = net barter terms of trade

Z_x = index of factor productivity in exports

Bilateral or Double Factoral Terms of Trade

The concept of the double factoral terms of trade takes account of the productivity of factors of production entering into the production of country's exports as well as of the productivity of foreign factors of production producing country's imports. The concept of double factoral terms of trade can be expressed as

$$T_D = \frac{P_x}{P_M}.\frac{Z_x}{Z_M}$$

where T_D = double factoral terms of trade

Z_M = index of factor productivity in imports

Z_x = index of factor productivity in exports

P_x = price index of exports

P_M = price index of imports

Real Cost Terms of Trade

The real cost terms of trade are obtained by multiplying the single factoral terms of trade with the index of the amount of disutility per unit of the productive resources employed in producing the exports. The real cost terms of trade can be symbolically expressed as

$$T_R = T_S.R_x$$

$$= \frac{P_x}{P_M}.Z_x.R_x$$

where T_R denotes the real cost terms of trade and R_x stands for the index of the amount of disutility suffered per unit of productive resources employed in producing exports. The terms R_x, P_M and Z_x have the same meaning as they have in the formula of the single factoral terms of trade.

Utility Terms of Trade

The utility terms of trade are obtained by multiplying the real cost terms of trade with the index of the relative desirability or utility of imports as compared to the goods that could have been produced for home consumption with those factors of production which are now used in the production of export goods (U_M). The utility terms of trade may be written as

$$T_U = T_R.U_M$$

$$= \frac{P_x}{P_M}.Z_x.R_x.U_x$$

Factors Affecting the Terms of Trade

The major factors which affect the terms of the trade of a country are:

1. Economic growth
2. Shifts in the demand for exports and/or import
3. Tariff
4. Devaluation
5. Availability of Substitutes.

INDIAN ECONOMY

NATIONAL INCOME

- According to the National Income Committee (1949), "A national income estimate measures the volume of commodities and service turned out during a given period counted without duplication". Thus, national income measures the net value of goods and services produced in a country during a year and it also includes net earned foreign income. In other words, a total of national income measures the flow of goods and services in an economy.
- National income is a flow concept not a stock concept.
- In India, National income estimates are related with the financial year (April 1 to 31st March).
- The various concepts of national income are as follows:
  - (*i*) **GNP (Gross National Product):** GNP refers to the money value of total output or production of final goods and services produced by the nationals of a country during a given period of time, generally a year.
  - (*ii*) **NNP (Net National Product):** NNP is obtained by subtracting depreciation value from GNP. NNP can be calculated in two ways: (*a*) at market prices of goods and services and (*b*) at factor cost.
  - (*iii*) **National Income:** When NNP is obtained at factor cost, it is known as National Income. National Income is calculated by subtracting net indirect taxes from NNP at market prices. The obtained value is known as NNP at factor cost or National income.
  - (*iv*) **Personal Income:** Personal income is that income which is actually obtained by nationals. Personal income is obtained by subtracting corporate taxes and payments made for social securities provisions from national income and adding to it government transfer payments, business transfer payments and net interest paid by the government.

Methods of Measuring National Income

- According to Simon Kuznets, national income of a country is calculated by following mentioned three methods:
  - (*i*) **Product Method:** S. Kuznets gave a new name to this method, *i.e.*, product service method. In this method, net value of final goods and services produced in a country during a year is obtained and the total obtained value is called total final product.
  - (*ii*) **Income Method:** In this method, a total of net incomes earned by working people in different sectors and commercial enterprises is obtained.
  - (*iii*) **Consumption Method:** It is also called expenditure method. Income is either spent on consumption or saved. Hence, national income is the addition of total consumption and total savings.
- In India, a combination of production method and income method is used for measuring estimating national income.
- For measuring national income in India, in 1868, the first attempt was made by *Dada Bhai Nauroji.* He, in his book, *"Poverty and Un-British Rule in India"*, estimated Indian per capita annual income at a level of ₹ 20.
- After independence, the Government of India appointed the National Income Committee in August, 1949, under the Chairmanship of Prof. P.C. Mahalanobies, to compile authoritative estimates of national income.
- Estimation and publishing of National Income data by CSO (Central Statistical Organization) is done every year.

- National income includes the contribution of three sectors—primary sector, secondary sector, Tertiary sector.
- Under Primary Sector—Agriculture, Forest, Fisheries and allied sector are included.
- Under Secondary Sector—Manufacturing, Construction, Electricity, Gas and Water Supply are included.
- Under Teritiary Sector—Trade, Transport, Communication, Banking, Insurance, Real Estate, Community and Personal Services are included.
- The contribution of primary sector in GDP was 55.4% in 1950-1951. But now the share of primary sector in national income has come down.
- In 2023-2024, the contribution of primary sector in GDP was 17.66%.
- The contribution of secondary sector has shown a steady increase from 15% in 1950-51 to 27.63% in 2023-24.
- The contribution of tertiary sector indicated a sharp improvement from 29.6% in 1950-51 to about 54.71% in 2023-24.
- At present estimation of national income is based on the base year of 2011-2012.
- The structural change in the composition of national income by industrial origin is the consequence of the process of economic growth initiated during the plans. Since the growth process involved a rapid expansion of manufacturing in the organised sector, the share of manufacturing was bound to indicate a relatively sharp increase. However, agriculture did not indicate a fast rate of growth.

Annual Average of Growth Rate in Various Plans

Five Year Plan	*NNI at Constant Price*	*Per Capita NNI*
First Plan (1951-56)	4.6	2.7
Second Plan (1956-61)	4.1	2.1
Third Plan (1961-66)	3.3	1.0
Three Annual Plans (1966-69)	3.5	1.3
Fourth Plan (1969-74)	3.0	0.7
Fifth Plan (1974-79)	5.0	2.7
Annual Plan (1979-80)	−5.9	−8.2
Sixth Plan (1980-85)	5.3	3.1
Seventh Plan (1985-90)	5.8	3.6
Two Annual Plan (1990-92)	2.8	0.8
Eighth Plan (1992-97)	6.5	4.4
Ninth Plan (1997-2002)	5.4	3.4
Tenth Plan (2002-07)	7.6	5.9
Eleventh Plan (2007-12)	7.5	6.0
Twelfth Plan (2012-17)	—	—

Source: CSO

POPULATION

- Every year 11th July is celebrated as the World Population Day.
- The first census of India was done in 1872 during the reign of Viceroy Lord Mayo. But a series of census (After every ten years) was adopted in 1881 during the reign of Viceroy Lord Ripon.
- 2011 census is the 15th census of India, and the 7th census of free India.
- The entire census of 2011 exercise has been completed by March 15, 2011.
- The term density of population implies the average number of persons living per sq. km. It is denoted in the following way:

The density of population

$$= \frac{\text{Total population of a certain place}}{\text{Total area of the certain place}}$$

- No. of females in comparison to per 1000 males is known as sex ratio. It is denoted in the following way:

$$\text{Sex Ratio} = \frac{\text{No. of Females}}{\text{No. of Males}} \times 1000$$

- No. of females in age group between 0-6 year, in comparison of per 1000 males of same age group is known as child sex ratio. It is denoted in the following way:
  Child Sex Ratio (0-6 year)

$$= \frac{\text{No. of Females Children (0-6)}}{\text{No. of Males Children (0-6)}} \times 1000$$

- Birth Rate (or crude Birth Rate) is number of the birth per thousand of the population during a period, usually a year. Only live births are included in the calculation of birth rate.
- Death rate signifies the number of deaths in a year per thousand of the population. It is mostly known as crude death rate. Life expectancy is important determinant of death rate. A country having high life expectancy will have a high crude death rate.
- The term fertility refers to the actual bearing of children or 'occurrence of births'. Fertility rate measures the average number of the live births per 1000 women. This rate is one of the most important and useful aids to population projection. It helps in assessing population trends in the economy.
- Percentage of literates between the age of 7 and above of total population is called 'Literacy Rate'.
- The people between the age of 7 and above, who can understand, write and read any language are known as 'literate'.
- An urban area having population of 1,00,000 or above persons is known as a city.
- In the 2011 census, an urban area was defined as follows:
  - (a) All places with a municipality, corporation, cantonment board or notified towns area committee, etc.
  - (b) All other places which satisfied the following criteria:
    - (i) A minimum population of 5,000;
    - (ii) At least 75 per cent of male main working population engaged in non-agricultural pursuits; and
    - (iii) A density of population of at least 400 persons per sq. km (1,000 persons per sq. mile).
- From the 1920s onwards, the rate of growth of population picked up. The year 1921 is termed as year of 'great divide'.
- High birth rate supplemented with improved health and medical facilities (which makes death rate fall) pushes the economy towards the state of "population explosion". India faces the same situation at present.
- An increasing difference between birth rate and death rate has created a scene of population explosion in India. This problem in India is not the result of declining death rate alone, which is actually an indicator of social development. But a simultaneous effort for reducing birth rate should have been made, where we have totally failed.
- The framework of the new population policy, 2000 was derived from recommendations of M.S. Swaminathan Committee. Three main objectives of this policy are:
  - (i) The immediate objective of this policy is to address the unmet needs of contraception, health infrastructure, health personnel and to provide integrated service delivery for basic reproductive and child healthcare.
  - (ii) The medium term objective is to bring the total fertility rates to replacement level by 2010.
  - (iii) The long-term objective is to achieve a stable population by 2045.
- The National Commission on Population (NCP) was constituted in May 2000 to review, monitor and give direction for the implementation of the National Population Policy (NPP), 2000.
- The National Commission of Population was reconstituted on 11th April, 2005 with 40 members under the chairmanship of the Prime Minister. Minister of Health and Family Welfare and the Deputy Chairman of the Planning Commission are Vice Chairmen of the Commission. The present membership also includes the Chief Ministers of the states of Uttar Pradesh, Madhya Pradesh, Rajasthan, Bihar, Jharkhand, Kerala and Tamil Nadu.

- According to the census 2011, total population of India is 1,21,08,54,977. Census 2011 makes India the second most populated country in the world.
- The growth rate of the population between 2001 and 2011 is 17.7 per cent. Meghalaya recorded the highest growth rate of 27.9 per cent while Nagaland the lowest –0.6 per cent.
- There were 623.27 million males and 587.58 million females according to Census 2011, making a ratio of 943 males per 1000 females. Kerala is the only state where females outnumber males. The sex-ratio these was 1084 females per 1000 males.
- According to census 2011, five most populous states (in descending order) are: Uttar Pradesh (19.9 crore), Maharashtra (11.2 crore), Bihar (10.4 crore), W. Bengal (9.12 crore) and Andhra Pradesh (8.4 crore).
- According to census 2011, three least populous states (in ascending order) are: Sikkim (6.10 lakh), Mizoram (10.9 lakh) and Arunachal Pradesh (13.8 lakh).
- According to census 2011, three most populous Union Territories (in descending order) are: Delhi, Puducherry and Chandigarh.
- According to census 2011, three least populous Union Territories (in ascending order) are: Lakshadweep, Daman and Diu, Dadra and Nagar Haveli.
- **Population Density:** In 2011, 382 persons were living in per square km area. Bihar was most densely populated state with a population density of 1,106 followed by West Bengal (1,028). Among the Union Territories, Delhi had the density of 11,320 and Chandigarh of 9,258. In Arunachal Pradesh, only 17 people were living in per sq. km area while in Mizoram 52.
- According to census-2011, 73.0 per cent of the country's population are literate. The male literacy rate (80.9%) is far more than the female literacy rate (64.6%). Kerala retains the top spot with 94.0 per cent literacy rate. Bihar is at the bottom with a literacy rate of 61.8 per cent.
- According to census 2011, five states with least sex ratio (in ascending order) are: Haryana (879), Jammu & Kashmir (889), Sikkim (890), Punjab (895), and Uttar Pradesh (912).
- According to census 2011, five states with most decadal growth rate (in descending order) are: Meghalaya (27.9%), Arunachal Pradesh (26%), Bihar (25.4), Jammu & Kashmir (23.6%), and Mizoram (23.5%).

Occupational Pattern 2011 (per cent)

Category	*Total Population*	*Rural Population*	*Urban Population*
Main Worker			
Cultivators	26.44	37.74	2.66
Agricultural Labourers	23.77	32.94	4.46
Household Industry Workers	3.4	2.95	4.36
Other Workers	46.38	26.37	88.52
Marginal Workers			
Cultivators	19.15	21.62	3.77
Agricultural Labourers	48.75	54.48	12.93
Household Industry Workers	5.03	4.58	7.91
Other Work	27.06	19.33	75.38

India's Population At A Glance : 2011 (Final Data)

S.I. No.	State/UTs	Population	Sex Ratio	Density	Literacy Rate	(%) Decadel Growth Rate (2001-2011)
1.	Jammu & Kashmir	1,25,41,302	889	124	67.2	23.6
2.	Himachal Pradesh	68,64,602	972	123	82.8	12.9
3.	Punjab	2,77,43,338	895	551	75.8	13.9
4.	Chandigarh	10,55,450	818	9258	86.0	17.2
5.	Uttarakhand	1,00,86,292	963	189	78.8	18.8
6.	Haryana	2,53,51,462	879	573	75.6	19.9
7.	Delhi	1,67,87,941	868	11320	85.2	21.2
8.	Rajasthan	6,85,48,437	928	200	66.1	21.3
9.	Uttar Pradesh	19,98,12,341	912	829	66.7	20.2
10.	Bihar	10,40,99,452	918	1106	61.8	25.4
11.	Sikkim	6,10,577	890	86	81.4	12.9
12.	Arunachal Pradesh	13,83,727	938	17	65.4	26.0
13.	Nagaland	19,78,502	931	119	79.6	–0.6
14.	Manipur	28,55,794	985	128	79.2	24.50
15.	Mizoram	10,97,206	976	52	91.3	23.5
16.	Tripura	36,73,917	960	350	87.2	14.8
17.	Meghalaya	29,66,889	989	132	74.4	27.9
18.	Assam	3,12,05,576	958	398	72.2	17.1
19.	Pachim Banga	9,12,76,115	950	1028	76.3	13.8
20.	Jharkhand	3,29,88,134	949	414	66.4	22.4
21.	Odisha	4,19,74,218	979	270	72.9	14.0
22.	Chhattisgarh	2,55,45,198	991	189	70.3	22.6
23.	Madhya Pradesh	7,26,26,809	931	236	69.3	20.3
24.	Gujarat	6,04,39,692	919	308	78.0	19.3
25.	Daman & Diu	2,43,247	618	2191	87.1	53.8
26.	Dadra & Nagar Haveli	3,43,709	774	700	76.2	55.9
27.	Maharashtra	11,23,74,333	929	365	82.3	16.0
28.	Andhra Pradesh	4,93,86,799	993	308	67.0	11.0
29.	Karnataka	6,10,95,297	973	319	75.4	15.6
30.	Goa	14,58,545	973	394	88.7	8.2
31.	Lakshadweep	64,473	947	2149	91.8	6.3
32.	Kerala	3,34,06,061	1084	860	94.0	4.9
33.	Tamil Nadu	7,21,47,030	996	555	80.1	15.6
34.	Puducherry	12,47,953	1037	2546	85.8	28.1
35.	Andaman & Nicobar Island	3,80,581	876	46	86.6	6.9
36.	Telangana	3,51,93,978	988	307	66.4	13.58
	India	**1,21,08,54,977**	**943**	**382**	**73.0**	**17.7**

Census-2011: Rural and Urban Population

S. No.	State/UTs	Rural Population	Urban Population	Percentage of Rural Population	Percentage of Urban Population
1.	J&K	91,08,060	34,33,242	72.6	27.4
2.	Himachal Pradesh	61,76,050	6,88,552	90.0	10.0
3.	Punjab	1,73,44,192	1,03,99,146	62.5	37.5
4.	Chandigarh	28,991	10,26,459	2.7	97.3
5.	Uttarakhand	70,36,954	30,49,338	69.8	30.2
6.	Haryana	1,65,09,359	88,42,103	65.1	34.9
7.	Delhi	4,19,042	1,63,68,899	2.5	97.5
8.	Rajasthan	5,15,00,352	1,70,48,085	75.1	24.9
9.	Uttar Pradesh	15,53,17,278	4,44,95,063	77.7	22.3
10.	Bihar	9,23,41,436	1,17,58,016	88.7	11.3
11.	Sikkim	4,56,999	1,53,578	74.8	25.2
12.	Arunachal Pradesh	10,66,358	3,17,369	77.1	22.9
13.	Nagaland	14,07,536	5,70,966	71.1	28.9
14.	Manipur	20,21,640	8,34,154	70.8	29.2
15.	Mizoram	5,25,435	5,71,771	47.9	52.1
16.	Tripura	27,12,464	9,61,453	73.8	26.2
17.	Meghalaya	23,71,439	5,95,450	79.9	20.1
18.	Assam	2,68,07,034	43,98,542	85.9	14.1
19.	West Bengal	6,21,83,113	2,90,93,002	68.1	31.9
20.	Jharkhand	2,50,55,073	79,33,061	76.0	24.0
21.	Odisha	3,49,70,562	70,03,656	83.3	16.7
22.	Chhattisgarh	1,96,07,961	59,37,237	76.8	23.2
23.	Madhya Pradesh	5,25,57,404	2,00,69,405	72.4	27.6
24.	Gujarat	3,46,94,609	2,57,45,083	57.4	42.6
25.	Daman & Diu	60,396	1,82,851	24.8	75.2
26.	Dadra & N. Haveli	1,83,114	1,60,595	53.3	46.7
27.	Maharashtra	6,15,56,074	5,08,18,259	54.8	45.2
28.	Andhra Pradesh	3,99,70,761	1,46,10,410	66.6	33.4
29.	Karnataka	3,74,69,335	2,36,25,962	61.3	38.7
30.	Goa	5,51,731	9,06,814	37.8	62.2
31.	Lakshadweep	14,141	50,332	21.9	78.1
32.	Kerala	1,74,71,135	1,59,34,926	52.3	47.7
33.	Tamil Nadu	3,72,29,590	3,49,17,440	51.6	48.4
34.	Puducherry	3,95,200	8,52,753	31.7	68.3
35.	Andman & Nicobar Islands	2,37,093	1,43,488	62.3	37.7
36.	Telangana	2,15,85,313	1,36,08,665	61.33	38.64
	India	**83,37,48,852**	**37,71,06,125**	**68.9**	**31.1**

POVERTY

- Poverty can be defined as a social phenomenon in which a section of society is unable to fulfil even the basic necessities of life.
- The term 'poverty' has been defined in different societies in a different ways but all of them are conditioned by the vision of minimum or good life living in society.
- The concept of poverty in the U.S.A. would be significantly different from that in India because the average person is able to afford a much higher level of living in the United States.
- There is an effort in all definitions of poverty to approach the average level of living in a society and as such these definitions reflect the existence of inequalities in a society and the extent to which different societies are prepared to tolerate them.
- In India, the generally accepted definition of poverty emphasises minimum level of living rather than a reasonable level of living.
- Several economists and crganisations have given different estimates of poverty. Most of them estimated poverty line on the basis of an average number of persons below the calories intake of 2250 per capita per day, according to the report of 'Task Force on Minimum Needs and Effective Consumption Demand'.
- An expert group of planning commission, defined poverty line on a nutritional norm of per capita daily intake of 2400 calories in rural areas and 2100 calories for urban areas. A person who fails to obtain this minimum level of calories is treated as being below the poverty line.
- There are two types of common standards in economic literature for the measurement of poverty:
    1. **Absolute Poverty:** In the absolute standard, minimum physical quantities of cereals, pulses, milk, butter, etc. are determined for a subsistence level and then the price quotations converted into monetary terms the physical quantities. Aggregating all of the quantities included, a figure expressing per capita consumer expenditure is determined. The population whose level of income or expenditure below the figure, is considered to be below the poverty line.
    2. **Relative Standard:** According to the relative standard, income distribution of the population in different fractile groups is estimated and a comparison of the levels of living of the top 5 to 10 per cent with the bottom 5 to 10 per cent of the population reflects the relative standards of poverty.
- The defect of the relative standard approach is that it indicates the relative position of different segments of the population in the income hierarchy. Even in affluent societies, such pockets of poverty exist. But for underdeveloped countries, it is the existence of mass poverty that is the cause for concern.
- The NITI Aayog, the nodal agency for estimating the number and proportion of people living below the poverty line at national and state levels, separately for rural and urban areas, makes poverty estimates based on a large sample survey of household consumption expenditure carried out by the National Sample Survey Office (NSSO) approximately every five years.
- For estimation and review of poverty, the Planning Commission constituted an expert group under the chairmanship of Prof. Suresh D. Tendulkar in December 2005, which submitted its report in December 2009.
- The recomputed poverty estimates for the years 1993-94 and 2004-05 as recommended by the Tendulkar Committee have been accepted by the Planning Commission.
- As per the Tendulkar Committee Report, the national poverty line at 2004-05 prices was a monthly per capita consumption expenditure of ₹ 446.68 in rural and ₹ 578.80 in urban areas in 2004-05.

Poverty Line

Committee	Year	Per capita Expenditure per day (₹)		Per capita Average Montly Expenditure (₹)		All India Poverty Line (Average Monthly Expenditure per Family of 5)	
		Rural	*Urban*	*Rural*	*Urban*	*Rural*	*Urban*
Rangarajan	2011-12	32.4	46.9	972	1407	4760	7035
	2009-10	26.7	39.9	801	1198	4005	5990
Tendulkar	2011-12	27.2	33.3	816	1000	4080	5000
	2009-10	22.4	28.7	673	860	3365	4300

Various Employment Generations Programmes

S. N.	Programme	Year of beginning	Objective
1.	Community Development Programme (CDP)	1952	Overall development of rural areas with people's participation.
2.	Green Revolution	1966-67	To increase the foodgrains, specially wheat production.
3.	Drought-Prone Area Programme (DPAP)	1973	To try an expedient for protection from drought by achieving environmental balance and by developing the ground water.
4.	Command Area Development Programme (CADP)	1974-75	To ensure better and rapid utilisation of irrigation capacities of medium and large projects.
5.	Twenty Point Programme (TPP)	1975	Poverty eradication and raising the standard of living.
6.	Antyodaya Yojana	1977-78	To make the poorest families of the village economically independent (only in Rajasthan State).
7.	Training Rural Youth for Self-Employment (TRYSEM)	Aug., 15, 1979	Programme of training rural youth for self-employment.
8.	Integrated Rural Development Programme (IRDP)	Oct., 2, 1980	All-round development of the rural poor through a programme of asset endowment for self-employment.
9.	National Rural Employment Programme (NREP)	1980	To provide profitable employment opportunities to the rural poor.
10.	Development of Women and Children in Rural Areas (DWCRA)	Sept. 1982	To provide suitable opportunities of self-employment to the women belonging to the rural families who are living below the poverty line.
11.	Comprehensive Crop Insurance Scheme	April 1, 1985	For insurance of agricultural crops.

S. N.	Programme	Year of beginning	Objective
12.	Council for Advancement of People's Action and Rural Technology (CAPART)	Sept. 1, 1986	To provide assistance for rural prosperity.
13.	Jawahar Rozgar Yojana	April 1989	For providing employment to rural unemployed.
14.	Nehru Rozgar Yojana	Oct. 1989	For providing employment to urban unemployed.
15.	Supply of Improved Toolkits to Rural Artisans	July 1992	To supply modern toolkits to the rural craftsmen except the weavers, tailors, embroiders and tobacco labourers who are living below the poverty line.
16.	Employment Assurance Scheme (EAS)	Oct., 2, 1993	To provide employment of at least 100 days in a year in villages.
17.	District Rural Development Agency (DRDA)	1993	To provide financial assistance for rural development.
18.	Mahila Samridhi Yojana	2 Oct., 1993	To encourage the rural women to deposit in Post-office Saving Account.
19.	Ganga Kalyan Yojana	1997-98	To provide financial assistance to farmers for exploring and developing ground and surface water resources.
20.	Kasturba Gandhi Education Scheme	Aug., 15, 1997	To establish girls schools in districts having low female literacy rate.
21.	Swarna Jayanti Shahari Rozgar Yojana (SJSRY)	Dec., 1997	To provide gainful employment to urban un-employed and under-employed poor through self-employment or wage-employment.
22.	Bhagya Shree Bal Kalyan Policy	Oct., 19, 1998	To uplift the girls conditions.
23.	Rajrajeshwari Mahila Kalyan Yojana	Oct., 19, 1998	To provide insurance protection to women.
24.	Swarna Jayanti Gram Swarozgar Yojana	April 1999	For eliminating Rural poverty and unemploy-ment and promoting self-employment.
25.	Jan Shree Bima Yojana	Aug., 10, 2000	Providing Insurance Security to people living below poverty line.
26.	Antyodaya Anna Yojana	Dec., 25, 2000	To provide food security to poor.
27.	Ashraya Bima Yojana	June 2001	To provide compensation to labourers who have lost their employment.
28.	Pradhan Mantri Gram Sadak Yojana (PMGSY)	Dec., 25, 2000	To line all villages with Pacca Road.

S. N.	Programme	Year of beginning	Objective
29.	Mahatma Gandhi National Rural Employment Guarantee Act (MNREGA)	Feb., 2, 2006	To provide at least 100 days wage-employment in rural areas.
30.	Pradhan Mantri Kaushal Vikas Yojana	March 2015	To Provide skill training to youth.
31.	Pradhan Mantri Jeevan Jyoti Bima Yojana	2015-16	Renewable one year life cover of ₹ 2 lakh to all savings bank account holders in the age group of 18-50 years covering death due to any reason for a premium of ₹ 330 per annum per sub-scriber.
32.	Pradhan Mantri Suraksha Bima Yojana	2015-16	Renewable one year accidental death cum disability to all savings bank account holders in the age group of 18-70 years for a premium of ₹ 12 per annum per subscriber.
33.	Atal Pension Yojana	2015-16	Pension to the labourers of unorganized sector
34.	Deen Dayal Upadhyay Grameen Kaushlya Yojana	Sep. 24, 2015	Skill development of rural youth.
35.	Atal Innovation Mission	2015-16	Atal Innovation Mission and Self Employement and Talent Utilisation.
36.	Swachh Bharat Mission	Oct. 2, 2014	Providing access to clean toilet to all rural households and initiating solid and liquid waste management activities in all gram panchayats.
37.	Pandit Deen Dayal Upadhyay Shramev Jayate Scheme	Oct. 16, 2014	To improve employability, skill development and other conveniences for labour.
38.	Shyama Prasad Mukherjee Rurban Mission	Sept. 16, 2015	Setting up 300 village clusters by 2019-20 across the country with all possible urban amenities.
39.	HriDay	2015-16	Heritage City Development and Augmentation Yojana to preserve and rejuvenate the rich cultural heritage of the country through the identified 12 cities.
40.	PRASAD	2015-16	National Mission on Pilgrimage Rejuvenation and Spiritual Augmentation Drive (PRASAD).
41.	'Housing for all by 2022'	June 18, 2015	Providing affordable housing in Urban Areas.
42.	Pradhan Mantri Awas Yojana	June 25, 2015	Providing housing facilities in rural areas.
43.	Startup India, Standup India	16 Jan., 2016	To provide Support to all start-up businesses in all aspects of doing business in India.
44.	Pradhan Mantri Ujjwala Yojana	May 1, 2016	Launched to Provide free LPG connection to women from below poverty line families.

S. N.	Programme	Year of beginning	Objective
45.	Urja Ganga Yojana (UGY)	Oct. 24, 2016	To provide the accessibility of approx, 5 Lakh LPG gas cylinders within next 5 years.
46.	Pradhan Mantri Surakshit Matritva Abhiyan	June 9, 2016	To improve the quality and coverage of Antenatal care with Diagnostics and counselling Services as part of Reproductive Maternal Neonatal Child and Adolescent Health.
47.	Pradhan Mantri Vittiya Saksharta Abhiyan (PMVSA)	Dec. 1, 2016	To go for cashless transaction and payment modes like using credit or debit cards or the payment wallets to reduce the malpractice in the country.
48.	Digi Dhan Vyapar Yojana (DDVY)	Dec. 15, 2016	To increase the "Cashless Transactions".
49.	Pradhan Mantri Garib Kalyan Yojana (PMGKY)	Dec. 2016	To improve the financial position of the poor people.
50.	Atal Amrit Abhiyan (AAA)	Dec. 25, 2016	To provide health insurance against 437 illnesses including 5 critical diseases.
51.	Pradhan Mantri Sahaj Bijli Har Ghar Yojana "Saubhagya"	Sep. 25, 2017	The objective of the 'Saubhagya' is to Provide energy access to all by last mile connectivity and electricity connections to all remaining un-electrified households in rural as well as urban areas to achieve universal household electrification in the country.
52.	New India Literacy Programme	Feb., 2022	New scheme of Adult Education for FY 2022-27.
53.	PM Vishwakarma Scheme	17 September, 2023	The scheme aims to help craftsmen and artisans of 18 traditional trades.
54.	Prime Minister's Internship Scheme	2024-25	To provide internship opportunities to one crore youth in top 500 companies in five years.
55.	Prime Minister Dhan-Dhaanya Krishi Yojana	Feb. 2025	The programme aims to enhance agricultural productivity.

AGRICULTURE

- Agriculture is an important sector of the economy. Though the share of agriculture in national income has come down since the inception of planning era in the economy but still it has substantial share in GDP.
- About 54.6% of total work force in India is engaged in agriculture and allied activities.
- Gross Capital Formation (GCF) in Agriculture and Allied sector relative to GVA in this sector has been snowing a fluctuating trent from 18.3 per cent in 2011-12 to 18.4 per cent in 2022-23.
- Agriculture provides raw materials to various industries and other agro-based industries. Cotton and Jute textile industries, Sugar, Vanaspati industry etc. are directly dependent on agriculture.
- India's foreign trade is deeply associated with Agriculture Sector. Value of agriculture exports to total exports of the country was 13.8 per cent in 2013. But the share of agriculture has come down in foreign trade at present. Share of agriculture in foreign trade was 11.8 per cent in 2022-23.

Land Reform Programmes

- Land reform programme in India include:
  - (*i*) Elimination of intermediaries.
  - (*ii*) Tenancy Reform.
  - (*iii*) Determination of ceiling of holding per family and to distribute surplus land among landless people.
  - (*iv*) Consolidation of holdings.
- The legislation for abolition of intermediaries was aimed at providing land to the tiller.
- Measures of tenancy reform pertain to—
  - (*i*) Regulation of rent
  - (*ii*) Security of tenure
  - (*iii*) Confirment of ownership on tenants.
- Land ceiling laws were first enacted in the 50s and 60s. It was further revised in 1972. Family ceiling were lowered to 5 hectares for irrigated land with two crops, 7.5 hectares for irrigated land with one crops and 12 hectares for other lands.

Irrigation

- India, currently, has an overall irrigation potential in the country of about 140 million hectares, out of which only about 109 million hectare have been created, and about 80 million hectare utilised. Gross irrigated area, as a per cent of Gross cropped area has increased from 34 per cent in 1990-91 to 51 per cent in 2014-15.
- The planning commission has introduced a new classification of irrigation schemes:
  1. **Major Irrigation Schemes**—Those with culturable command areas (CCA) more than 10,000 hectares.
  2. **Medium Irrigation Schemes**—Those with culturable command areas (CCA) between 2,000 to 10,000 hectares.
  3. **Minor Irrigation Scheme**—Those with culturable command area (CCA) upto 2,000 hectares.
- **Micro Irrigation:** A centrally sponsored scheme on Micro Irrigation (MI) was launched in Tenth Plan for promoting water use efficiency by adopting drip and sprinkler irrigation. All states and Union Territories and all horticulture as well as agricultural crops are covered under the scheme. The National Committee on Plasticulture Applications in horticulture (NCPAH) provides the required technical guidance in association with Precision Farming Development Centers (PDFCs) at 22 locations. The PRI's are involved in selecting the beneficiaries. Since its inception, about 10 lakh hactares has been covered under drip and sprinkler irrigation.
- **Sprinkler/Drip Irrigation:** Under Sprinkler/ Drip Irrigation System water is sprinkled evenly on total agriculture ground through a pipe network cropped area. Empircal studies show that this system of drip irrigation saves 30% to 40% water as compared to irrigation with traditional method, *i.e.*, surface irrigation. This new system of irrigation also ensures 20-25% more productivity per hectare.
- **Source of Irrigation:** There are three main sources of irrigation in India:

  Canals: Canals water apporoximately 26% of irrigation in India. This include large areas in Punjab, Haryana, Uttar Pradesh, Bihar and some parts of the Southern States.

  Well & Tubewells: Wells and Tubewell irrigate around 64% of the irrigated land in India. Wells and Tubewells are now spread over large area of Punjab, Uttar Pradesh, Bihar, Rajasthan, Tamil Nadu and Haryana.

  Tanks: Tank irrigation is resorted to mostly in Tamil Nadu, Andhra Pradesh, and some parts of West Bengal and Bihar. Tanks irragate arround 8% of the irrigated land.
- In agriculture, new technology was tried in 1960-61 as a pilot project in seven districts and was called Intensive Agricultural District Programme (IADP). Later, the high-yielding varieties programme (HYVP) was also added and the strategy was extended to cover the entire country. This strategy has been called by various names—modern agricultural technology, seed-fertilizer-water technology or simply Green revolution.

Achievements of the New Agricultural Strategy

(*i*) Increase in the production of cereals.

(*ii*) Increase in the production of commercial crops.

(*iii*) Significant changes in the crop pattern.

(*iv*) Boost to agricultural production and employment.

Agricultural Prices

- **Minimum Support Prices (MSP):** Keeping in view the interests of the farmers as also the need of self reliance, Govt. has been announcing minimum support price. The main objectives of announcing MSP are:
  1. To prevent fall in price in the situation of over production.
  2. To protect the interest of farmers by ensuring them a minimum price for their crops in the situation of a price fall in the market.
- **Procurement Prices:** The price at which government buys surplus from the farming coming in the market. The minimum support price and the procurement price may be the same.
- **Issue Prices:** The prices at which fair price shops sell cereals like wheat rice etc.

New Agricultural Policy (2000)

Union Government has announced new Agricultural Policy in the parliament on July 28, 2000.

This policy has been planned under the povisions of WTO so as to face the challenges of agriculture sector.

This policy gives emphasis on promoting agricultural exports after fulfilling domestic demand.

The sailent features of this policy are:

- To achieve 4% growth rate per annum for the next two decades.
- To do Land reforms to provide land to poor farmers.
- Consolidation of holding in all states of the nation.
- Promoting private investment in agriculture.
- To provide insurance umbrella for crops to farmers.
- To promote biotechnology.
- Promoting research for developing new varieties and ensuring protection to the developed varieties.
- New Agriculture policy has been described as 'Rainbow Revolution' which includes the following revolutions:

(*i*) Green	–	(Food Grain Production)
(*ii*) White	–	(Milk)
(*iii*) Yellow	–	(Oil Seeds)
(*iv*) Blue	–	(Fisheries)
(*v*) Red	–	(Meat/Tomato)
(*vi*) Golden	–	(Fruits-Apple)
(*vii*) Grey	–	(Fertiliser)
(*viii*) Black/Brown	–	(Non-conventional Energy Sources)
(*ix*) Silver	–	(Eggs)
(*x*) Round	–	(Potato)

Major Crops and Their Seasons

The Indian crops can be devided into two major groups:

1. **Kharif Crops:** This crop is sown in the month of July and harvested in October every year. Kharif crop includes—Rice (Paddy), Jowar, Bajra, Maize, Cotton, Sugarcane, Seasamum, Soyabean, and Groundnut etc.
2. **Rabi Crop:** This crop is sown in October end and harvested in March/April every year. Rabi crop includes—Wheat, Jowar, Barley, Gram, Tur, Rapseed, and Mustard etc.
3. **Zayad Crop:** In some parts of the country a crop, known as Zayad crop is sown during March to June every year. Zayad crops include—Melon, Watermelon, Vegetables, Cucumber, Moong, and Urad etc.

Commercial Crops

Commercial crops are those crops which are produced for trade purpose and earning money and not for self-consumption by the farmers. These commercial crops include:

(*i*) **Oilseeds crops:** Groundnut, Mustard, Sesamum, Rapeseed, Linseed, Castor, Sunflower, Nigenseed and Soyabean etc.

(*ii*) **Sugar Crops:** Sugarcane and Beat.

(*iii*) **Fibre Crops:** Jute, Mesta, Sunhemp and Cotton.

(*iv*) **Narcotic Crop:** Tobacco.

(*v*) **Beverage Crops:** Tea, Coffee.

National Mission on Edible Oils–Oil Palm

The Union Cabinet on August 18, 2021 gave its approval to launch a new Mission on Oil palm to be known as the National Mission on Edible Oils–Oil Palm (NMEO-OP) as a new Centrally Sponsored Scheme with a special focus on the North-East region and the Andaman and Nicobar Islands. Due to the heavy dependence on imports for edible oils, it is important to make efforts for increasing the domestic production of edible oils in which increasing area and productivity of oil palm plays an important part. Key features of the NMEO-OP are the following: • A financial outlay of the NMEO-OP is ₹ 11,040 crore, out of which ₹ 8,844 crore is the Government of India share and ₹ 2,196 crore is State share and this includes the viability gap funding also. • Under the scheme, it is proposed to cover an additional area of 6.5 lakh hectare for oil palm till the year 2025-26 and thereby reaching the target of 10 lakh hectare ultimately. • The production of Crude Palm Oil (CPO) is expected to go upto 11.20 lakh tonnes by 2025-26 and upto 28 lakh tonnes by 2029-30.

National Mission for Sustainable Agriculture

(NMSA) as a programmatic intervention made operational from the year 2014-15 aims at making agriculture more productive, sustainable and remunerative and climate resilient by promoting location specific integrated / composite farming systems; soil and moisture conservation measures; comprehensive soil health management; efficient water management practices and mainstreaming rainfed technologies.

Various Crops and their producing states

Crops/Groups of Crops	Producing State (In Descending Order)
I. Foodgrains	
Rice	Telangana, Uttar Pradesh, West Bengal
Wheat	Uttar Pradesh, Madhya Pradesh, Punjab
Maize	Karnataka, Bihar, Madhya Pradesh
Total Coarse Cereals	Karnataka, Rajasthan Madhya Pradesh
Gram	Maharashtra, Madhya Pradesh, Rajasthan
Tur	Maharashtra, Karnataka, Uttar Pradesh
Total Pulses	Madhya Pradesh, Maharashtra, Rajasthan
Total Food-grains	Uttar Pradesh, Madhya Pradesh, Punjab
II. Oilseeds	
Groundnut	Gujarat, Rajasthan, Madhya Pradesh
Rapeseed & Mustard	Rajasthan, Uttar Pradesh, Madhya Pradesh
Soyabean	Madhya Pradesh, Maharashtra, Rajasthan
Sunflower	Karnataka, Haryana, Odisha
Total Oilseeds	Rajasthan, Madhya Pradesh, Gujarat
III. Other Cash Crops	
Sugarcane	Uttar Pradesh, Maharashtra, Karnataka
Cotton	Gujarat, Maharashtra, Telangana
Jute & Mesta	West Bengal, Assam, Bihar

Source: Economic Survey 2023-24

Paramparagat Krishi Vikas Yojana

The Parampragat Krishi Vikas Yojana (PKVY) is the first comprehensive scheme launched in 2015-16 by the Central Government as a centrally sponsored programme for promotion of organic farming in the country. This was done taking into account agro-climatic conditions, natural resources and technology for ensuring more inclusive and integrated development of agriculture and allied sectors. A dedicated online web portal– www.jaivikkheti.in/ has been created to encourage, sale of organic products directly by farmers to consumers farming by directly connecting the consumers.

Various Brands have been developed by the State for marketing of Organic Produce under the PKVY Scheme. Government has initiated Large Area Certification (LAC) programme since 2020-21 to certify large traditional/default organic areas such as hills, islands, tribal or desert belt with no past history of GMO and agro chemical uses.

Major Schemes/Programmes in the Agriculture Sector

Agriculture Research and Education

Agriculture is the primary source of livelihood for more than 50 per cent of India's population. The present government's target is to achieve the ambitious goal of doubling farm income by 2022. Towards this target, the government has increased investment in agricultural infrastructure such as irrigation facilities, warehousing and cold storage. Towards these basic goals, DARE coordinates and promotes agricultural research and education in the country through its autonomous bodies, viz. Indian Council of Agricultural Research (ICAR), Central Agricultural University (CAU), Imphal, Dr. Rajendra Prasad Central Agricultural University (DRPCAU), Pusa, Bihar, and Rani Lakshmi Bai Central Agricultural University (RLBCAU), Jhansi, UP. ICAR with 113 institutes spread across the country, is one of the largest national agricultural research systems in the world. The Department of Agricultural Research and Education (DARE) was established in the Ministry of Agriculture in December,1973. It provides the necessary government linkages for ICAR, the premier research organisation for co-ordinating, guiding and managing research and education in agriculture including horticulture, fisheries and animal sciences in the entire country.

Commission for Agricultural Costs and Prices

Commission for Agricultural Costs and Prices (CACP), set up with a view to evolve a balanced and integrated price structure, is mandated to advice on the price policy (MSP) of 23 crops. These include seven cereal crops (paddy, wheat, jowar, bajra, maize, ragi and barley); five pulse crops (gram, tur, moong, urad and lentil); seven oilseeds (groundnut, sunflower seed, soybean, rapeseed mustard, safflower, nigerseed and sesamum); copra (dried coconut); cotton; raw jute and sugarcane. CACP submits its recommendations in the form of Price Policy Reports every year, separately for five groups of commodities namely kharif crops, rabi crops, sugarcane, raw jute and copra.

Determinants of MSP

Cost of Production (CoP) is one of the important factors in the determination of MSP of mandated crops. Besides cost, the Commission considers other important factors such as demand and supply, price trend in the domestic and international markets, inter-crop price parity, terms of trade between agricultural and non-agricultural sectors and the likely impact of MSP on consumers, in addition to ensuring rational utilisation of natural resources like land and water. Thus, pricing policy is rooted not in 'cost plus' approach, though cost is an important determinant of MSP.

Rashtriya Krishi Vikas Yojana (RKVY)

The RKVY was launched in 2007-08 with an outlay of of ₹25,000 crore for the 11th five year plan. The RKVY aims at achieving the 4% annual growth in the agriculture sector during the 11th five year plan period by ensuring a holistic development of agriculture and allied sectors. The funds under the RKVY is provided to the states as 100 per cent grant by the Central Government. The main objective of the schemes were:

- To incentivise the states to increase public investment to achieve 4% growth in agriculture and allied sector during 11th plan.
- To provide flexibility and autonomy to the states in planning and exceuting agriculture and allied sector schemes.
- To ensure the preparation of plans for the district and the states based on agro-climatic conditions, availability of technology and natural resources.
- To ensure that the local needs/crops priorities are better reflected.
- To achieve the goal of reducing the yield gaps in important crops, through focused interventions.
- To maximize returns to farmers.

Indian Council of Agricultural Research

The Indian Council of Agricultural Research (ICAR), under Department of Agricultural Research and Education, Government of India, established in 1929, has recently entered the centenary decade of its existence. During the last nine decades, this premier organisation has immensely contributed to Indian agriculture. The Council has always been ahead of its times in visualising the future agricultural scenario and accordingly developing appropriate futuristic technology solutions for farmers. ICAR is developing competent human resources and trained manpower and is reaching out to farmers to train them and demonstrate various technologies on their fields to ensure its adoption. The Council has been coordinating with various stakeholders to mitigate the challenges confronted by Indian agriculture.

National Mission for Sustainable Agriculture (NMSA)

NMSA as a programmatic intervention made operational from the year 2014-15 aims at making agriculture more productive, sustainable and remunerative and climate resilient by promoting location specific integrated/composite farming systems; soil and moisture conservation measures; comprehensive soil health management; efficient water management practices and mainstreaming rainfed technologies.

Pradhan Mantri Krishi Sinchai Yojana (PMKSY)

The major objective of PMKSY is to: achieve convergence of investments in irrigation at the field level; expand cultivable area under assured irrigation, improve on-farm water use efficiency to reduce wastage of water; enhance the adoption of precision irrigation and other water saving technologies (Per drop, More crop); and promote sustainable water conservation practices, etc. Cabinet decision was taken in July 2016 for implementation of PMKSY in a mission mode. The mission is administered by Ministry of Water Resources, River Development and Ganga Rejuvenation with the 'Per Drop More Crop' component being administered by Department of Agriculture and Farmers Welfare (earlier Department of Agriculture, Cooperation and Farmers Welfare).

Mission for Integrated Development of Horticulture

The Mission for Integrated Development of Horticulture (MIDH), was launched during the Twelfth Plan with effect from 2014-15, for the holistic development of the horticulture sector covering fruits, vegetables, mushrooms, spices, flowers, aromatic plants, coconut, cashew, cocoa and bamboo. The MIDH subsumes the National Horticulture Mission (NHM), the Horticulture Mission for North East & Himalayan States (HMNEH), the National Bamboo Mission (NBM), the National Horticulture Board (NHB), the Coconut Development Board (CDB) and the Central Institute for Horticulture (CIH), Nagaland.

The Government of India (GOI) contributes 85 per cent of the total outlay for developmental programmes in all the states.

Soil and Water Productivity

The National Bureau of Soil Survey and Land Use Planning (NBSS & LUP) developed NBSS BHOOMI Geo-portal to access various thematic information on major physiographic regions, sub-physiographic regions, agro-ecological regions (1992), agro-ecological regions (2015) and agro-ecological sub-regions of the country. Area/region specific efficient and remunerative crops and cropping sequences were delineated based on soils, landforms, rainfall, temperature, length of growing period and irrigability.

The NBSS & LUP developed an android-based mobile application on CIS platform to facilitate web-based decision support system (DSS) for land use planning and dissemination of soil health cards information at village and farm level for Gujarat. App will display details of soil map unit information and suggested land use plan for that survey number.

Pradhan Mantri Fasal Bima Yojana

After detailed discussions with various stakeholders including state governments, representatives of farmer organisations, Government of India had formulated the new crop insurance scheme, viz., Pradhan Mantri Fasal Bima Yojana (PMFBY), which is being implemented in various states/union territories of the country from Kharif 2016. The scheme is being implemented through 18 General Insurance Companies including all the 5 Government Sector Companies. Under PMFBY, a uniform maximum premium of only 2 per cent of the sum insured is paid by farmers for all Kharif crops and 1.5 per cent for all Rabi crops.

In case of annual commercial and horticultural crops, the maximum premium to be paid by farmers is up to 5 per cent. The premium rates to be paid by farmers are very low and the balance of actuarial premium is being borne by the Government, to be shared equally by the state and central government (except in North Eastern States where the subsidy sharing pattern between central and state government is 90 : 10) to provide fully insured amount to the farmers against crop loss on account of natural calamities.

Crop Improvement

Major emphasis was given to develop new varieties/hybrids tolerant to various biotic and abiotic stresses with enhanced quality. About 209 varieties were developed—117 high-yielding varieties/hybrids of cereals comprising 65 of rice, 14 of wheat, 24 of maize, 5 of finger millet, 3 of pearl millet, one each of sorghum, barley, foxtail millet, kodo millet, little millet and proso millet—and released for cultivation in different agro-ecological regions of the country. About 28 high-yielding varieties of oil seeds, 32 of pulses, 24 of commercial crops (cotton, sugarcane and jute) and eight of forage crops were released for cultivation in different agro-ecologies.

Agricultural Credit

The Government has taken many policy initiatives for strengthening of farm credit delivery system for providing credit at affordable rate of interest to support the resource requirements of the agricultural sector. Some sources of agricultural credit are as follows:

- Agricultural credit is disbursed through a Multi Agency network comprising of Commercial Banks (CBs), Regional Rural Bank (RRBs) and Cooperative with theri vast network covering almost all the villages in the country and outreach extending to the remotest part of the country. In addition, on the lines of the Business Correspondent and Business Facilitator model, Banks are using the services of NGOs, SHGs, Joint Liability Groups (JLGs), Micro Finance Institutions and other civil society organisation as intermediates in providing financial and banking services in the rural areas.
- Kisan Credit Card (KCC) scheme was introduced in August, 1998 with major share of crop loans being routed through it. Banks were advised that the credit card should normally be valid for 3 years subject to an annual review.

- The scheme was revised in October 2004. The revised scheme aims at providing adequate and timely credit for the comprehensive credit requirements of farmers under single window, with flexible and simplified procedure, adopting whole farm approach including the short term credit needs, term loan and a reasonable component for consumption needs, through Kisan Credit Card.
- Over the past decade (2014-15 to 2023-24), agricultural credit disbursement has witnessed an average annual growth rate of more than 13%. In the financial year 2023-24, agricultural credit disbursement reached ₹ 25.48 lakh crore.

Agricultural Insurance

There are various major crop insurance schemes under implementation in the country.

Some Insurance schemes are as follows:

1. **National Agricultural Insurance Scheme (NAIS):** With a view to provide insurance coverage and financial support to the farmers in the event of failure of any of the notified crop in the notified areas as a result of natural calamities, pest and diseases; to encourage the farmers to adopt progressive farming practices, high value inputs and higher technology in agriculture and to stabilise farm incomes, particularly in disaster years, NAIS is being implemented in the country from Rabi 1999-2000 season.
2. **Modified NAIS (MNAIS):** With the aim of further improving crop insurance scheme, the MNAIS is under implementation on pilot basis in 50 districts in the country from the Rabi 2010-11 season.

The Salient features of MNAIS are as under:

- only upfront premium is shared by the Central and State Governments on 50 : 50 basis and all chains liability would be on the insurance companies.
- Actuarial premium with subsidy in premium ranging 40% to 75% to all farmers.
- Unit area of insurance reduced to village/village panchayat level for major crops.
- Indemnity for prevented sowing/planting risk and for post harvest losses due to cyclone.
- One account payment up to 25% advance of likely claims as immediate relief.
- Minimum indemnity level of 70% instead of 60%.
- Scheme is available to all the farmers—loanee and non-loanee—irrespective of their size of holding.
- Loanee farmers are covered on compulsory basis in a notified area for notified crops whereas for non-loanee farmers scheme is voluntary.
- Uniform seasonality disciplines both for loanee and non-loanee farmers.
- Participation of private sector insurers for creation of competitive environment for crop insurance.

3. **Weather Based Crop Insurance Scheme (WBCIS):** The WBCIS is being implemented as a central-sector scheme from Kharif 2007 season. The scheme is intended to provide insurance protection to farmers against adverse weather incidence, such as deficit and excess rainfall, high or low temperature and humidity that are deemed to adversely impact crop production. The WBCIS is based on actuarial rates of premium but to make the scheme attractive, premium actually charged from farmers has been restricted to be on a par with NAIS.
4. **Coconut Palm Insurance Scheme (CPIS):** The Department of Agriculture and Cooperation is implementing CPIs on pilot basis during years 2009-10 and 2010-11 in the selected areas of Andhra Pradesh, Goa, Karnataka, Kerala, Maharashtra, Odisha, Tamilnadu and West

Bengal. The scheme is being administered by the Coconut Development Board (CDB) through AIC. The scheme propose to cover entire palms in the region selected for implementation, according to eligibility criteria. The Sum Insured (SI) is based on average input cost of the plantation and the age of the specific plant.

Agricultural Marketing

Organised marketing of agricultural commodities has been promoted of regulated markets. Most of the state governments and Union Territories have enacted legislations (APMC Act) to provide for regulation of agricultural produce market. According to the provision of the APMC Acts of the state every APMC is authorised to collect market fees from the buyers/traders in the prescribed manner on the sale of notified agricultural produce.

The Government of India has circulated model legislation titled "The State Agricultural Produce Marketing (Development and Regulation) Act 2003 to bring about reform in agricultural marketing. Contract farming, direct marketing and public-private partnership in management and development of agricultural markets are the major instruments of change among others.

Infrastructure Requirement

Investment requirement for the development of marketing, storage and cold storage infrastructure in the country has been estimated to be huge and with a view to induce investment in the development of marketing infrastructure as envisaged above, the Ministry has implemented the following plan schemes:

(*i*) **Grameen Bhandaran Yojana:** The Government of India, Ministry of Agriculture has launched 'Grameen Bhandaran Yojana' w.e.f. 1st April, 2011. The main objectives of the scheme include creation of scientific storage capacity with allied facilities in rural areas to meet out various requirements of farmers for storing farm produce, processed farm produce, agricultural inputs, etc, and prevention of distress sale by creating the facility of pledge loan and marketing credit.

(*ii*) **Marketing Research and Information Network:** The Ministry of Agriculture has launched an ICT based Central Sector Scheme of Marketing Research and Information Network in March 2000 to provide electronic connectivity to important wholesale agricultural markets in the country for collection and dissemination of wholesale prices and other market related information to the farmers and other users through AGMARKNET portal (www.agmarknet.nic.in). As on date, 3026 markets have been linked with AGMARKNET portal from all over the country. These markets are reporting daily prices and arrival in respect of more than 300 commodities and 2000 varieties from more than 1800 market covering all major agricultural and horticultural produce.

(*iii*) **Development/Strengthening of Agricultural Marketing Infrastructure, Grading and Standardization:** The Ministry of Agriculture is implementing another Central Sector Scheme for 'Development Strengthening of Agricultural Marketing Infrastructure, Grading and Standardisation' under which, investment subsidy is provided @ 25 per cent on the capital cost of the marketing infrastructure development subject to a maximum of ₹ 60 lakh for each project in case of North-Eastern States, Jammu and Kashmir, Uttarakhand, Himachal Pradesh, hilly area and to SC/ST and their cooperatives.

(*iv*) **Terminal Market Complex:** The Department has taken the initiative to promote modern terminal markets for fruits, vegetables and other perishables in important urban centres of the country. These markets would provide state of art infrastructure facilities for electronic auction, cold chain and logistics and operate through primary collection centres conveniently locate in producing areas to allow easy access to farmers.

Food Management

Food Management in India has three basic objectives:

- Procurement of foodgrains from farmers at remunerative prices.
- Distribution of foodgrains to the consumers particularly, the vulnerable sections of the society at affordable prices.
- Maintenance of food buffers for food security and price stability. The instruments for food management are—the Minimum Support Price (MSP) and Central Issue Price (CIP).
- Food Stock are maintained by the Central Government for three purposes:
  - (*i*) Meeting the prescribed minimum buffer stock norms for food security.
  - (*ii*) For monthly release of foodgrains for supply through Public Distribution System (PDS).
  - (*iii*) For market intervention to augment supply so as to help moderate the open market prices.

Miscellaneous

- ***Krishi Shramik Suraksha Yojana:*** The multi-benefit scheme for the agricultural workers, commenced on 1 July, 2001 provides life insurance protection, perodical lumpsum survival benefit and pension to those who were between the age of 18-50 years.
- ***Farm Income Insurance Scheme (FIIS):*** Prime Minister inaugurated this scheme in January 2002. Main features of this scheme are:
  - (*i*) Farmers will be protected by ensuring minimum guarnteed income.
  - (*ii*) If the actual income of the farmers falls short of the guaranteed income (product of average yield and MSP) of the farmers they would be eligible for compensation to the extent of indemnity from the Agriculture Insurance company of India Ltd (AICI).
  - (*iii*) Area approach as in National Agricultural Insurance scheme (NAIS) would be used for actual yield and price measurement of the insured crop.
  - (*iv*) Initially the scheme would cover paddy and wheat only.
  - (*v*) The scheme would be available for all the states compulsory for farmers availing crop loans.
  - (*vi*) NAIS will be withdrawn for the crops covered under FIIS but would continue to be applicable for other crops.
- ***Command Area Development & Water Management Programme (CADWMP):*** The centrally-sponsored Command Area Development (CAD) programme was launched in 1974-75, with the main objectives of improving the utilisation of created irrigation potential and optimising agriculture production and productivity from irrigated lands on sustainable basis, by integrating all functions related with irrigated agriculture through a multi-disciplinary team under an area Development Authority. The CAD Programme was initiated with 60 major and medium irrigation projects. The CAD Programme has been restructured and renamed as Command Area Development and Water Management Programme (CADWMP) w.e.f. 1st April, 2004.

INDUSTRY

- After independence, the first industrial policy was declared on April 6, 1948 by then Union Industry Minister Mr. Shyama Prasad Mukherjee.
- Under this first industrial policy established a base for Mixed and Controlled Economy in India and clearly divided the industrial sector into private and public sectors.
- Second Industrial Policy Resolution declared on April 30, 1956 with the basic objective of establishing 'Socialistic Pattern of Society' in the country.
- To control and regulate the process of industrial development in the country, an Act was passed by the parliament in October 1951. Known as

the Industries (Development and Regulation) Act, 1951, the Act came into force on May 8, 1952. Though it aimed at both, development and regulation of private sector, its main task over the year has been to concentrate more on the 'regulation aspect'.

- Because of the criticisms indicating the failure of the industrial licensing policy in achieving its objectives, the Government of India announced a number of liberalisation measures in the industrial Licensing Policy announced in 1970, 1973 and 1978. In 1980, the government came forward with an Industrial Policy statement which served as a guideline to various liberalisation measures undertaken all through the 1980s.
- In line with the liberalisation measures announced during the 1980s, the government announced a New Industrial Policy on July 24, 1991. This new policy de-regulates the industrial economy in a substantial manner. The major objectives of the new policy are "to build on the gains already made, correct the distortions or weaknesses that might have crept in, maintain a sustained growth in productivity and gainful employment, and attain international competitiveness." In pursuit of these objectives, the government announced a series of initiatives in respect of the policies relating to the following areas:

  1. **Abolition of Industrial Licencing:** Industrial licensing policy in India has been governed by the Industries (Development and Regulation) Act, 1951. Industrial licensing policy and procedures have been liberalised considerably from time to time. Yet, the industrial licensing policy has all along been resented to by the entrepreneurs as it led to unnecessary governmental interference, delays in investment decisions and bureaucratic red-tapism, corruption etc. Not only this, the industrial licensing policy was also unable to achieve the objectives laid down for it by the government. On account of these considerations, and in order to liberalise the economy and to enable the entrepreneurs to make investment decisions on the basis of their own commercial judgement, the 1991 industrial policy abolished industrial licensing for all but 18. The 18 industries for which licensing was kept necessary, with the passage of time, most of these industries have also been delicensed. As of now, licensing is compulsory for only 5 industries. These are:

     (*a*) Distillation and brewing of alcoholic drinks.

     (*b*) Cigar, Cigarettes and other substitutes of prepared tobacco.

     (*c*) Electronic, Aerospace and all types of defence equipment.

     (*d*) Industrial Explosive including match boxes.

     (*e*) Hazardous chemicals.

  2. **Public Sector's Role Diluted:** The 1956 Resolution had reserved 17 industries for the public sector. The 1991 industrial policy reduced this number to 8. The policy has been liberalised progressively and presently only 3 industries are reserved for the public sector. These are: .

     (*a*) atomic energy,

     (*b*) the substances specified in the schedule to the notification of the Government of India in the Department of Atomic Energy dated the 15 March, 1995 and

     (*c*) railway transport.

- The new Index of industrial production (IIP) series with 2011-12 as base years was released in 12 May, 2017, replacing the earlier IIP series with base year 1993-94.
- The new IIP series not only has a more recent base, it has larger and more representative product basket and weights that appropriately reflect the relative importance of the sectors, products and product group.
- The government released the National Manufacturing policy (NMP) on 4 November 2011 for bringing about a quantitative and qualitative change with objectives to

(*i*) increase manufacturing sector growth to 12-14 per cent over the medium term;

(*ii*) enable manufacturing to contribute at least 25 per cent of GDP by 2022;

(*iii*) create 100 million additional jobs in the manufacturing sector by 2022;

(*iv*) create appropriate skill sets among the rural migrant and urban poor for their easy absorption in manufacturing;

(*v*) increase domesting value addition and technological depth in manufacturing; and

(*vi*) enhance global competitiveness of Indian manufacturing.

- With a view to delegating enhanced financial and operational powers to CPSEs (Central Public Sector Enterprises), the government introduced the Navratna Scheme in July 1997.
- In December 2009, the Government introduced the Maharatna Scheme enhancing financial delegation to CPSEs.
- In December 2004, the government established a Board for Reconstruction of Public Sector Enterprises (BRPSE) to advice on revival/restructuring of sick and loss-making CPSEs.
- Some of the recent reforms are: reducing the list of industries that can be considered defence industries requiring industrial licence; and amendments in FDI policy which include allowing FDI in defence up to 49 per cent, in railway infrastructure up to 100 per cent and in the insurance and pension sector up to 49 per cent.
- The government has launched several programmes/initiatives such as ease of doing business, Make in India, Invest India, and e-biz Mission Mode Project under the National e-Governance Plan.
- With the objective of making India a global hub of manufacturing, design and innovation, the Make in India initiative, which is based on four pillars — new processes, new infrastructure, new sectors and new mindset — has been taken by the government. The initiative is set to boost entrepreneurship, not only in manufacturing but in relevant infrastructure and service sectors as well.
- The 1991 industrial policy brought the public sector units at par with the private sector units. As a result, the public sector units were also brought within the jurisdiction of Board of Industrial and Financial Reconstruction (BIFR). Thus BIFR was given the responsibility to decide whether a sick public sector unit can be effectively restructured or whether it has to be closed down.
- One of the major initiatives towards the public sector as outlined in the new industrial policy of July 1991 was to bring all public sector enterprises under the system of Memorandum of Understanding (MoU). The system of MoU envisages an arm's length relationship between the PSU and the administrative ministries. It gives clear targets to PSUs and ensures operational autonomy to them for achieving those targets. The MoU system was started in 1987-88.
- The first unit in the public sector, now known as the Visvesvaraya Iron and Steel Works Ltd., started functioning at Bhadravati in 1923.
- During the second five year plan (1956-61) a major task in industry was building up of three steel plants in the public sector—Rourkela Steel Plant in Odisha (then Orissa), Bhilai Steel Plant in Chhattisgarh (then Madhya Pradesh) and Durgapur Steel Plant in West Bengal. The three steel plants came into operation in stage between 1959 and 1962.
- Bokaro steel plant was established in third five year plan.
- Increased production capacity of iron and steel was planned by establishing new steel plants at Salem (Tamil Nadu), Vijai Nagar (Karnataka) and Vishakhapatanam (Andhra Pradesh), during the fourth-five year plan.
- In 1974, the Steel Authority of India Limited (SAIL) was created and was made responsible for the development of steel industry.
- SAIL is also responsible for management of Bhilai, Durgapur, Rourkela, Bokaro and Burnpur steel plants. Besides SAIL has been given responsibility of managing Alloy Steel Plant, Durgapur and Salem Steel Plant.

- On July 14, 1976, the Government took over the ownership of IISCO plant and as a result IISCO also came under the control of SAIL.
- The National Steel Policy (NSP) 2005 has already been approved by Government. The long-term goal of NSP is to ensure that India has a modern and efficient steel industry, capable of standing up to international competition and catering to the growing domestic demand for steel.
- Globally, India is the largest producer and second largest exporter of jute goods. West Bengal, Bihar, Uttar Pradesh, Andhra Pradesh, Assam and Chhattisgarh are main jute producing states.
- The government has formulated first ever National Jute policy in 2005 with an objective of increasing production, improving quality, ensuring remunerative prices to the jute farmers and per hectare yield.
- Sugar industry occupies an important place among agriculture based industries. This industry took a shape of a large industry in the beginning of 20th century. Sugar industry is the second largest industry after cotton textile industry among agriculture based industries of the country.
- India is the second largest producer of cement in the world after China. The cement industry was delicensed in 1991.
- The small and medium sector has been defined as micro, small and medium enterprises with effect from October 2, 2006 (the Act defined the medium enterprises for the first time). Further, separate investment limits have been prescribed for manufacturing and service enterprises.

Revised MSME Classification (Union Budget 2025-26)

Composite Criteria : Investment and Annual Turnover			
Classification	**Micro**	**Small**	**Medium**
Manufacturing & Services	Investment in plants and machinery less than ₹ 2.5 crore and Turn-over less than ₹ 10 crore.	Investment in plants and machinery greater than ₹ 2.5 crore & less than ₹ 25 crore and Turn-over greater than ₹ 10 crore & less than ₹ 100 crore.	Investment in plants and machinery greater than ₹ 25 crore & less than ₹ 125 crore and Turn-over greater than ₹ 100 crore & less than ₹ 500 crore.

- **Micro, Small and Medium Enterprises (MSME):** The MSME sector continues to be a cornerstone of India's economic growth, contributing signifianctly to employment, manufacturing, and exports. In recent years, the sector has displayed remarkable resilience, with its share in the country's Gross Value Added (GVA) increasing from 27.3% in 2020-21 to 29.6% in 2021-22 and 30.1% in 2022-23.
- A Cottage Industries Board was set up in 1947 itself. This was split into the following three board during the First Five Year Plan—All India Handloom Board, All India Handicrafts Board, and All India Khadi and Village Industries Board. In addition, three more boards were set up. These were the small scale Industries Board, Coir Board and Central Silk Board. Thus at the end of First Five Year Plan, there were a total of six boards covering the entire field of small-scale and cottage industries.
- Small Industries Development Organisation (SIDO) was set up in 1954. It functions as an apex body in the formulation of policies and co-ordination of institutional activities for sustained and organised growth of small-scale industries. It has a large network of small industries services institutes, branch institutes, toolrooms etc. SIDO has now been renamed as

the Micro, Small and Medium Enterprises Development Organisation.

- National Small Industries Corporation Ltd. (NSIC) was set up in 1955 to provide machinery to small-scale units an hire-purchase basis and to assist these units in procuring orders from government departments and offices.
- The programme of District Industries Centre (DICs) was introduced in May 1979. The idea was to establish on agency in each district called the District Industries Centre to provide and arrange a package of assistance and facilities for credit guidance, raw materials, training, marketing etc. including the necessary help to unemployed educated young entrepreneurs in general and custom services.
- Several Schemes were introduced to provide financial assistance to small scale industries. These include—
  - (*i*) **SIDF :** The Small Industries Development Fund (SIDF) was set up in 1986. It provides refinance assistance for development, expansion, diversification and rehabilitation of small scale, cottage and village industries and tiny sector in rural areas.
  - (*ii*) **NEF :** National Equity Fund (NEF) was set up in 1987. It provides equity type support to small entrepreneurs for setting up new projects in tiny/small scale sector and also assistance for rehabilitation of viable sick units in the small-scale sector.
  - (*iii*) **SWS :** Single Window Scheme (SWS) was set up in 1988. It provides working capital loans alongwith term loans for fixed capital to new tiny and small scale units.
- Small Industries Development Bank of India (SIDBI) was set up in 1990. It is a Separate Apex Bank, to provide financial assistance to the small-scale industries.
- Due to the policy of de-reservation, the number of items reserved for the SSI Sector (Small Scale Industry Sector) came down from 836 in July 1969 to 114 in March 2007. At present, only 20 items are reserved for the small-scale sector.
- Since the adoption of the economic reforms programme in 1991, the argument is that the MRTP Act has lost its relevance in the new liberalised and global competitive scenario. In view of this, the government appointed an expert committee headed by SVS Raghavan to examine the whole issue. The Raghavan Committee submitted its Report to the government on May 22, 2000 wherein it proposed the adoption of a new competition law and doing away with the MRTP Act, 1969.
- Accordingly, the government decided to enact a law on competition. Competition Bill, 2001 was introduced in parliament and passed in December 2002. The Act is called Competition Act, 2002. The Act was amended in September 2007.
- The definition of a sick industrial company was changed by the companies (Second Amendment) Act, 2002. According to this Act, "sick industrial company" means an industrial company which has—
  - (*i*) the accumulated losses in any financial year which are equal to 50 per cent or more of its average network during four years immediately preceding such financial year; or
  - (*ii*) failed to repay its debt within any three consecutive quarters on demand made in writing for its repayment by a creditor or creditors of such company.
- By a notification issued on March 20, 1985, the government converted the IRCI (which was a company registered under the companies Act, 1956) into a statutory corporation and it was given the name Industrial Reconstruction Bank of India (IRBI). The authorised capital and paid-up capital of IRBI are ₹ 200 crore and ₹ 50 crore respectively.
- IRBI was reconstituted into a full-fledged all purpose development financial institution with effect from March 27, 1997 and its new name is Industrial Investment Bank of India Ltd. (IIBIL). The head office of IIBIL is situated at Kolkata.

LABOUR

- Labour policy in India has evolved in response to sepcific needs of the situation to suit the requirements of a planned economic development and social justice and has a two fold objective—(*i*) Maintaining Industrial peace and (*ii*) promoting the welfare of labour.
- The Factories Act, 1948 is the principal legislation for regulating various aspects relating to safety, health and welfare of workers employed in factories. This Act is a Central Enactment, which aims at protecting workers employed in factories from industrial and occupational hazards.
- The Factories Act, 1948 prescribes a 48 hours week for adult workers and forbids employment of children below the age of 14 years in any factory.
- The Minimum Wages Act, 1948 was enacted primarily to safeguard the interests of the workers engaged in an unorganised sector who are vulnerable to exploitation due to illiteracy and lack of bargaining power. The Act binds the employers to pay the minimum wages to the workers as fixed under the statute and workers get protected against exploitation.
- Under the provisions of the Minimum Wages Act, 1948 both the Central and State Governments are appropriate Governments to fix, review, revise and enforce the minimum rates of wages for workers employed in the scheduled emplo-yments under their respective jurisdictions. All the provisions of the Act equally apply to both male and female.
- The Payment of Wages Act, 1936, which is labour-friendly legislation, ensures primarly timely payment of wages and that no unauthorized deductions are made from the wages of the workers.
- The Central Government, on the basis of figures of the Consumer Expenditure Survey published by National Sample Survey Organization, has enhanced the wage ceiling from ₹ 10,000 to ₹ 24,000 per month from September 2018.
- The payment of Bonus Act, 1965 provides for payment of bonus to employees of the factories and other establishments employing 20 or more persons. The minimum bonus of 8.33% is payable by every industry and establishment under the section 10 of the Act. The maximum bonus including productivity linked bonus that can be paid in any accounting year shall not exceed 20% of the salary/wage of an employee under the Sections 11 and 31A of the Act.
- The Working Journalist and other Newspaper Employees (conditions of service) and Miscellaneous Provisions Act, 1955 regulates conditions of service of working journalists and other persons employed in newspaper establishments. The Act provides for setting up of Wage Board for fixation and revision of rates of wages in respect of working journalists and non-journalists newspaper/news agency employees.
- Child Labour (Prohibition & Regulation) Act, 1986, employment of children below the age of 14 years are prohibited in notified hazardous occupations and processes. The Act also regulates employment of children in non-hazardous occupations and processes. There are at present 16 hazardous occupations and 65 processes, where employment of children is prohibited.
- The issue of 'Bonded Labour came in force first in national politics, when it was included in the old 20-point programme in 1975. To implement this Bonded Labour System (Abolition) ordinance was promulgated. This was later replaced by the Bonded Labour System (Abolition) Act, 1976. The district and sub-district magistrates have been entrusted with certain duties and responsibilities towards implementation of statutory provisions.
- The Social Security Act, 2008, provides the social security of unorganised sector workers. The 'unorganised sector' means an enterprise owned by individuals or self-employed workers.

and engaged in the production or sale of goods or providing service of any kind whatsoever, and where the enterprise employs workers, the number of such workers is less than ten.

- V.V. Giri National Labour Institute is a premier institution involved with research, training, education, publication, and consultancy on labour and related issues. The institute, established in 1974, at Noida (Uttar Pradesh), is an autonomous body of the Ministry of Labour and Employment, Government of India. The Institute engages in research pertaining to labour and training of labour, administrators concerned with labour. Seminar, workshops and lectures are organised on specific issues from time to time.
- The Central Board for Workers Education (CBWE) was established in 1958 by the Ministry of Labour & Employment, Government of India to implement the workers education scheme at national, regional and unit/village levels for the workers from organized, unorganized and rural sectors. The Board has its headquarters at Nagpur with a network of 50 Regional and Subregional Directorates spread throughout the country. The six Zonal Directorates at Delhi, Guwahati, Kolkata, Chennai, Mumbai and Bhopal monitor the activities of the Regional Directorates within respective zone. The Board has an apex training institute at Mumbai called IIWE.

Worker's Safety Act

- The Factories Act, 1948 is the principal legislation for regulating various aspects relating to safety, health and welfare of workers employed in factories. This Act is a Central Enactment, which aims at protecting workers employed in factories from industrial and occupational hazards. The factories employing one thousand workers or more and five hundred workers or more, are required to employ safety officer/s and welfare officer/s respectively.
- Provisions relating to safety, health and welfare of workers employed in docks are contained in the Dock Workers (Safty, Health and Welfare) Act, 1986 and rules and regulations framed there under. The Act came into force on 15th April, 1987.
- Provisions for safety, health and welfare of workers employed in mines are contained in the Mines Act, 1952 and rules and regulations framed there under. These provisions are enforced by the Ministry of Labour and Employment through the Directorate General of Mines Safety. The Directorate General, has its headquarters at Dhanbad.
- The National Safety Council was set up in 1966 to promote safety consciousness among workers to prevent accidents, minimize dangers and mitigate human suffering, arrange programmes, lectures and conferences on safety, conduct educational compaign to increase consciousness among employers and workers and collect educational and information datas, etc.

Industrial Relations

- The Industrial Disputes Act, 1947 provides the machinery and procedure for the investigation and settlement of industrial disputes. The Act has been amended vide the Industrial Disputes (Amendment) Act, 2010 and enforced w.e.f. 15th September, 2010.
- The Trade Unions Act, 1926 provides for registration of trade unions of employers and workers, and in certain respects, it defined the law relating to registered trade union. It confers legal and corporate status on registered trade unions. The Trade Unions Act, 1926 is administered by the concerned State Governments. The act has been amended and enforced from 9th January, 2002.
- The Plantations Labour Act, 1951 provides for welfare of plantation labourers and regulates their conditions of work. The Plantations Labour Act, 1951 has been amended and the Plantation Labour (Amendement) Act, 2010 has been enforced w.e.f. 7th June, 2010.
- The 'Rashtriya Swasthya Bima Yojana' for BPL families (a unit of five) in Unorganised Sector

was launched on 1st October, 2007 and became operational w.e.f. 1st April, 2008. Under the scheme, smart card based cashless health insurance cover of ₹ 30,000 per annum on a family is provided. The premium is shared on 75:25 basis by centre and state Government. In case of states of North East region and Jammu & Kashmir, the premium is shared in the ratio of 90:10.

Social Security

- A beginning in social security in India was made in 1923 when Workmen's Compensation Act was passed. The Act is very wide in coverage and covers many diverse industries including mines, factories, transport, plantations, construction activities, electricity generation etc.
- The Workmen's Compensation Act, 1923, does not apply to those industries or factories where Employee's State Insurance Act, 1948, is in operation.
- The Workmen's Compensation Act was amended in 2000. Under this amendment, the workmen or their family members will get the compensation money at the enhanced rate if they die or get disabled. As a result of the death in the working capacity, the compensation money will be minimum 1,20,000. The maximum limit can be ₹ 9.14 lakhs. In the case of disability, the minimum limit is increased from 90,000 to 1,40,000 rupees. The maximum limit in this case, can go upto 10.97 lakh rupees.
- The Maternity Benefit Act, 1961, regulates the employment of women in certain establishments for certain period before and after child birth (six week before and six weeks after confinement) and provides for maternity and other benefits.
- The Materity Benefit Act, 1961 applies to mines, factories, circus, industry, plantations, shops and establishments employing 10 or more persons except the employees who are covered under the ESI Act, 1948. There is no wage limit coverage under the Act.
- The most important step in the field of social security was taken in 1948 when the Employee's State Insurance (ESI) Act was passed. The Act is applicable to non-seasonal factories using power and employing 10 or more persons and non-power using factories employing 20 or more persons. The Employees' State Insurance Corporation (ESIC) raised the monthly wage limit to ₹ 21,000 from the existing ₹ 15,000 for coverage with effect from 1st January, 2017.
- The Employees Provident Funds and Miscellaneous Provision Act, 1952 seeks to provide the financial social security to the employees in the form of provident fund, pension and deposit-linked insurance. It extends to the whole of India including Jammu and Kashmir and Ladakh. It applies to every establishment specified in the schedule and in which 20 or more persons are employed. The object of this Act is to make:
  - (*i*) Some provisions for the future of the industrial workers after the retirement.
  - (*ii*) to provide for the dependants in the case of the employee's death, and
  - (*iii*) to cultivate the spirit of saving among the employees.
- Other important social security schemes are:
  - (*a*) The payment of Gratuity Act, 1972.
  - (*b*) Employee's Deposit Linked Insurance Scheme, 1976.
  - (*c*) Employee's Pension Scheme, 1995.

Trade Union

- Trade unions are voluntary organisations of workers formed to protect the interest of workers through collective action.
- In India, the first trade union was formed in 1918.
- There are number of trade unions in India, which are associated with main political parties. Some important trade unions are as follows:
  - (*i*) Bharatiya Mazdoor Sangh (BMS), associated with the Bharatiya Janta Party.

(*ii*) Indian National Trade Union Congress (INTUC), associated with the Congress Party.

(*iii*) All-India Trade Union Congress (AITUC), associated with the Communist Party of India.

(*iv*) Centre of Indian Trade Unions (CITU), associated with the CPI (M).

- The First National Labour Commission was formed on December 24, 1966.
- The Second National Labour Commission was formed on October 15, 1999 under the Chairmanship of Ravindra Verma.
- Trade Union (Amendment) Act, 2001 was introduced with the following objectives:

(*i*) To control multiplicity of trade unions.

(*ii*) Establishing industrial democracy.

(*iii*) Encourage well managed expansion of trade unions.

- The amended Act was introduced after incorporating the recommendations of Ramanujan Committee. The Act has following important provisions:

(*i*) Minimum 10% of the total labour force or 100 labourers in an organization (whichever is less) must be required to form trade union.

(*ii*) No. of members should not be less than of in any condition.

(*iii*) At least 5 members or one-third (whichever is less) should be the employees of the concern.

(*iv*) Annual contribution for trade union should not be less than ₹ 12.00

ECONOMIC PLANNING

- Economic Planning refers to any directing or planning of economic activity outside the mechanisms of the market. Planning is an economic mechanism for resources allocation and decision-making held in contrast with the market mechanism. Economic Planning can be applied to production, investment, distribution or all three of these functions.
- In the year 1934, Sir M. Visheshvraya wrote a book named 'Planned Economy for India', which was the first attempt in this direction.
- In 1938, the Indian National Congress, under the leadership of Pt. Jawaharlal Nehru, made a National Planning Committee.
- In 1944, eight industrialists of Bombay (Now Mumbai) presented a well-organised plan called 'The Bombay Plan'.
- Inspired by the economic views of Mahatma Gandhi, Shri Sriman Narayan Constructed a plan in 1944 which is known as 'Gandhian Plan'.
- Mr. M.N. Rao, chairman of post-war Reconstruction Committee of Indian Trade Union, introduced a 'People's Plan' in April 1945.
- In January 1950, Shri Jaiprakash Narayan published a plan called 'Sarvodaya Plan'.
- The Planning Commission was constituted on 15th March, 1950, by the Government of India.

Niti Aayog

- The National Institution for Transforming India (NITI Aayog) came into existence in 2015 replacing the Planning Commission which was established in 1950. The NITI Aayog is the successor to the Planning Commission. The new institution was envisaged to be a catalyst to the developmental process, nurturing an overall enabling environment—through a holistic approach to development—going beyond the limited sphere of the public sector and Government of India. This is built on the foundation of: an empowered role of states as equal partners in national development; operationalising the principle of cooperative federalism; a knowledge hub of internal as well as external resources; serving as repository of good governance best practices, and a think tank offering domain knowledge as well as strategic expertise to all levels of government;

a collaborative platform facilitating implementation; by monitoring progress, plugging gaps and bringing together the various ministries at the centre and in states, in the joint pursuit of developmental goals.

Composition

- The composition of the NITI Aayog is as follows:

  Prime Minister of India is the Chairperson. The Governing Council comprises the Chief Ministers of all the states, Chief Ministers of union territories with legislatures, viz., Delhi and Puducherry and Lt. Governors of other union territories. Experts, specialists and practitioners with relevant domain knowledge as special invitees are nominated by the Prime Minister. The full-time organisational framework consists of, in addition to the Prime Minister as Chairperson, a Vice-Chairperson that is appointed by the Prime Minister. Full-time and part-time members are maximum of 2, from leading universities, research organisations and other relevant institutions in an ex-officio capacity. Part-time members are on a rotational basis. Ex-officio members are maximum of 4 members of the Union Council of Ministers who are nominated by the Prime Minister. Chief Executive Officer is appointed by the Prime Minister for a fixed tenure, in the rank of Secretary to the Government of India/Secretariat, as deemed necessary.

First Five Year Plan (1951-1956)

- The First Five Year Plan began on April 1, 1951 and ended on March 31, 1956.
- The plan was based on the model of Harrod-Domer.
- The plan has given highest priority to agriculture, irrigation and power projects.
- The achievements of this plan were more than its targets. The annual compound growth rate of national income was 3.6% (target 2.1%) during the planning period.
- The per capita income growth rate was 1.8% and ICOR was 2.95 during this plan.

Second Five Year Plan (1956-1961)

- Based on the model prepared by Prof. P.C. Mahalnobis, the Second Five Year Plan was started on April 1, 1956 and ended on March 31, 1961.
- The fundamental objective of this plan was to initiate and accelerate the process of industrialisation so that the development of Indian economy takes a firm base.
- The Industrial policy, 1956 (During Second Five Year Plan), was based on the objective of establishing the socialistic pattern of society.
- Large industries including steel plants (Durgapur, Bhilai and Rourkela) were set up. The Locomotive factory at Chittaranjan and Coach factory at Perambur were other major projects of this period.

Third Five Year Plan (1961-1966)

- This plan started on April 1, 1961 and ended on March 31, 1966.
- The basic aim of this plan was to push the economy upto the take-off stage development.
- This plan set as its goal the establishment of a self-reliant and self-generating economy.
- In this plan top priority was given to agriculture but it also laid adequate emphasis on the development of basic industries, which were vitally necessary for rapid economic development of the country.

Annual Plans (1966-1969)

- The Fourth Plan was scheduled to begin from April 1, 1966, but due to the unfortunate failure of third plan, the production in various sector of the economy became stagnant.
- In 1966, the Government of India declared the devaluation of rupee, with a view to increase the exports of the country. However, favourable results couldnot be obtained.
- Under these circumstances the fourth plan was postponed for sometime and Three Annual Plans were implemented during this period.
- Some of the economists called this period, *i.e.* from 1966 to 1969 as 'Plan Holiday' because no regular planning was done during this period.

Fourth Five Year Plan (1969-1974)

- The Fourth Plan started on April 1, 1969 and ended on March 31, 1974.
- Growth with stability and progress towards self-reliance were the prime objective of the plan.
- The plan aimed at 5.5 per cent average rate of growth in the national income.

Fifth Five Year Plan (1974-1979)

- The Fifth Five Year Plan began on April 1, 1974 which was scheduled to end on March 31, 1979.
- The final draft of the Fifth Plan was prepared and launched by D.P. Dhar proposed to achieve the two main objectives—removal of poverty and attainment of self-reliance.
- The plan objective, 'removal of poverty is also known as the slogan 'Garibi Hatao'.
- This plan also gave high priority to bring inflation under control and to achieve stability in economic situation.

Sixth Five Year Plan (1980-1985)

- The Janta Government ended the Fifth Five Year Plan, one year to its term, *i.e.,* only within four years span (1974-78) and introduced a new plan since April 1, 1978. This plan was named as the "Rolling Plan".
- In 1980, the Sixth Plan (Rolling Plan) prepared by Janta Government was abandoned by the Congress Government and a new Sixth Plan was introduced for the period 1980-85.
- The focus of Janta Government's Sixth Plan (Rolling Plan) was enlargement of the employment potential in agriculture and allied activities, whereas the focus of Congress Sixth Plan was to solve the problem of poverty by creating conditions of an expanding economy.

Seventh Five Year Plan (1985-1990)

- The 7th plan began on April 1, 1985 and ended on March 31, 1990.
- This plan emphasised policies and programmes which aimed at rapid growth in foodgrains production, increased employment opportunities and productivity within the framework of basic tenents of planning, *i.e.*, growth, modernisation, self-reliance and social justice.

Eighth Five Year Plan (1992-1997)

- The 8th Five Year Plan which was supposed to start from April 1, 1990 could not be started on scheduled time because of some political changes at the Centre during 1990-92.
- NDC ratified the format of the Plan in one of its meeting held on May 23, 1992. This Plan began on April 1, 1992 which ended on March 31, 1997.
- The Plan has initiated the process of fiscal reforms as also of economic reforms with a view to provide a new dynamism to economy.
- Fundamental objective of this Plan was human development.
- Pradhanmantri Rojgar Yojana (1993) was started during this Plan.

Ninth Five Year Plan (1997-2002)

- The 9th Plan began on April 1, 1997 and ended on March 31, 2007.
- 'Growth with Equity and Distributive Justice' was determined as the main focus of the Ninth Plan. In order to achieve this focus, four fields were identified which are as follows:

  (*i*) Quality of life

  (*ii*) Employment promotion

  (*iii*) Regional imbalance

  (*iv*) Self-dependence

Tenth Five Year Plan (2002-2007)

- The 10th Plan began on April 1, 2002 and ended on March 31, 2007.
- The Plan has not been able to achieve its target of 8 per cent growth of GDP, but has taken the economy to a higher trajectory of growth rate at 7.8 per cent as against 5.5 per cent in the 9th Plan.
- Gross domestic savings averaged 28.2 per cent in 10th Plan as against 23.1 per cent in the 9th plan.
- The economy has been able to reduce its ICOR from a level of 4.3 during the 9th Plan to a level of 4.2 during the 10th Plan.

- Our foreign exchange reserve reached a level of US $ 185 billion in February 2007. This is another indication of the strength of the economy.

Eleventh Five Year Plan (2007-12)

- The 11th Plan began on April 1, 2007 and ended on March 31, 2012.
- The 11th Plan visualises "Faster and more inclusive growth" as its objective.
- 11th Plan has fixed a target of pushing up overall GDP growth to an average rate of 9.0 per cent.

Twelfth Five Year Plan (2012-17)

- The 12th Plan began on April 1, 2012 and will end on March 31, 2017.
- Real GDP Growth Rate of 8.0 per cent.
- Agriculture Growth Rate of 4.0 per cent.
- Manufacturing Growth Rate of 7.1 per cent.
- Industrial Sector Growth Rate of 7.6 per cent.
- Service Sector Growth Rate of 9.0 per cent.
- Generate 50 million new work opportunities.
- Eliminate gender and social gap in school enrolment.
- Reduce Total Fertility Rate to 2.1 by the end of Twelfth Five Year Plan.

15-Year Vision Plan

- With the end of the Twelfth Plan in March 2017 the era of five year plans came to an end. NITI Aayog has come forward with a draft 15-year vision plan to catapult the country's economy to more than three times as compared to the present day. The new plan is set to replace the centralised five-year plans the country has been following for decades. The new plan is accompanied by shorter sub-plans—a seven-year strategy for 2017-24, and a three-year 'Action Agenda' from 2017-18 to 2019-20. No less than 300 specific action points covering a wide range of sectors have been drawn up as part of the 15-year vision. The 15-year vision document has a seven-year strategy document for 2017-24 as the 'National Development Agenda'. Separately, a three-year 'Action Agenda' from 2017-18 to 2019-20 is also under works to assess funding requirements. The three-year agenda is further divided into seven parts, with a number of specific action points for each part to boost economic growth. India's urban population is expected to increase by 22 crores by 2031. The plan is likely to lay emphasis on urban development, taking a note from China's elaborate long-term development agenda.

MONEY AND BANKING

- A money market is not a market for money but it is the market for lending and borrowing of short term funds. It is the market where the short-terms surplus investible funds for bank and other financial institutions are demanded by borrowers comprising of individuals, companies and the Government.
- Capital market is the market for long-term funds. It refers to all the facilities and the institutional arrangements for borrowing and lending term funds (medium-term and long-term funds). It does not deal in capital for purposes of investment.
- In monetary economics, control of money supply usually refers to control of the supply of currency and deposit money.
- The RBI now calculates on four concepts of money supply in India. These are known as money stock measures or measures of monetary aggregate. The four concepts of money supply are:

M_1 = Currency with the public, i.e. coins and currency notes + demand deposits of the public; also known as narrow money.

M_2 = M_1 + Post office saving deposits

M_3 = M_1 + Time deposits of the public with banks; also known as broad money

M_4 = M_3 + Total post office deposits

- The monetary policy referes to a regulatory policy whereby the central bank (RBI) maintains its control over the supply of monetary for the realisation of general economic goals.

- Among the functions of RBI, one main function is to control and regulate the credit in the country. In India, this function is performed by the Reserve Bank of India (RBI). The measures of credit control can be divided into two types:
  (*i*) Quantitative Credit Control
  (*ii*) Selective Credit Control
- The main objective of quantitative credit control is to establish control over the total quantity of credit in the country. For quantitative credit control, the central bank (RBI) takes the help of bank rate, open market operations, SLR and CRR, whereas publicity, rationing of credit, regulation of consumer credit, moral suasion, variation in margin requirements are the selective credit (qualitative) control methods.
- Reserve Bank of India (RBI) is the central bank of the country.
- Reserve Bank of India was established on April 1, 1935 under Reserve Bank of India Act, 1934 with a authorised capital of ₹ 5 crore.
- The Reserve Bank of India was nationalised on January 1, 1949.
- The general administration and direction of RBI is managed by a Central Board of Directors consisting of 20 members which includes 1 Governor and 4 Deputy Governors.
- The head office of the Reserve Bank of India is in Mumbai.
- SBI functions as an agent of RBI, where there are not any branches of RBI.
- Functions of Reserve Bank of India:
  ❖ Issue of Notes.
  ❖ Bankers to the Government.
  ❖ Banker's Bank.
  ❖ Controller of Credit.
  ❖ Custodian of Foreign Reserves.
  ❖ Other Functions (function of clearing house arranging credit for agriculture, collecting and publishing the economic data, buying and selling of government securities and trade bills etc.)
- **Bank Rate:** Bank Rate is the rate of discount at which the central bank of the country discounts first class bills. It is the rate of interest at which the central bank lends money to the lower banking institutions. Bank rate is a direct quantitative method of credit control in the economy.
- **Cash Reserve Ratio (CRR):** Commercial banks are required to keep a certain amount of cash reserves at the central bank. This percentage amount is called CRR. It influences the commercial bank's volume of credit because variation in CRR affects the liquidity position of the banks and hence their ability to lend.
- **Prime Lending Rate (PLR):** Prime Lending Rate (PLR) is that rate of interest at which bank gives loan to its most reliable customer. This reliability means 'zero risk'. Thus, PLR provides the role of a basic interest rate at which loan is provided to other customers.
- **Repo Rate:** Repo (Repurchase option) rate is a instrument under the Liquidity Adjustment Facility (LAF) at which RBI lends to commercial banks. In case of inflationary tendencies RBI perceived need to inject liquidity into the system, RBI can reduce the Repo rate which will lead to release of money into the market.
- **Reverse Repo Rate:** Reverse Repo Rate is the rate at which RBI borrows from commercial banks. In case of inflationary tendencies, RBI can hike the Reverse Repo rate to absorb the excess liquidity in the market. It is also a Liquidity Adjustment facility instrument.
- **Statutory Liquidity Ratio (SLR):** Commercial banks are also required to keep (in additon to CRR) a certain percentage of their net demand and time liabilities (NDTL) as liquid assets in the shape of cash, gold or approved securities. As most of the SLR money is kept in treasury bills, government had, in the past, been using SLR as a means to mobilise low cost resources. In 2024 it was 18 per cent whereas upper limitation of SLR is as usual (40%).
- The Reserve Bank Act, 1934 and the Banking Regulation Act, 1949 have given the RBI wide powers of supervision and control over commercial and co-operative banks, relating to licensing and establishments, branch expansion, liquidity of their assets, management and method of working, amalgmation, reconstruction and liquidation.

- On the recommendation of the Rural Credit Survey Committee the Imperial Bank of India was converted into the State Bank of India on July 1, 1955.
- On 1st April, 2017, State Bank of India, which is India's largest Bank merged with five of its Associate Banks (State Bank of Bikaner & Jaipur, State Bank of Hyderabad, State Bank of Mysore, State Bank of Patiala and State Bank of Travancore) and Bharatiya Mahil Bank with itself. This is the first ever large scale consolidation in the Indian Banking Industry.
- **Nationalisation of Banks:** 14 major Banks with deposits of ₹ 50 crore or more were nationalised on July 19, 1969. They were (1) Central Bank of India; (2) Bank of India; (3) Punjab National Bank; (4) Bank of Baroda; (5) United Commercial Bank; (6) Canara Bank; (7) United Bank of India; (8) Dena Bank; (9) Syndicate Bank; (10) Union Bank of India; (11) Allahabad Bank; (12) Indian Bank; (13) Bank of Maharashtra, and (14) Indian Overseas Bank. In another bout the following scheduled commercial banks were nationalised on April 15, 1980: (1) Andhra Bank; (2) Corporation Bank; (3) New Bank of India; (4) Oriental Bank of Commerce; (5) Punjab and Sind Bank; and (6) Vijaya Bank. Of these, the New Bank of India was merged with the Punjab National Bank in September 1993 and Vijya Bank and Dena Bank with Bank of Baroda in April 2019. In 2020 Oriental Bank of Commerce and United Bank of India were merged into Punjab National Bank, Syndicate Bank was merged in Canara Bank, Andhra Bank and Corporation Bank were merged into Union Bank of India, and Allahabad Bank was merged in Indian Bank.

Types of Banks

On the basis of functions, the banking institutions in India may be divided into the following types:

Central Bank

A bank which is entrusted with the functions of guiding and regulating the banking system of a country is known as its Central bank. Such a bank does not deal with the general public. The Reserve Bank of India is the central bank of our country.

Commercial Banks

Commercial Banks are banking institutions that accept deposits and grant short-term loans and advances to their customers. In addition to giving short-term loans, commercial banks also give medium-term and long-term loan to business enterprises.

Development Banks

Business often requires medium and long-term capital for purchase of machinery and equipment, for using latest technology, or for expansion and moder-nization. Such financial assistance is provided by Development Banks. Industrial Finance Corporation of India (IFCI) and State Financial Corporations (SFCs) are examples of development banks in India.

Co-operative Banks

Co-operative banks in India also perform fundamental banking activities but they are different from commercial banks. Commercial banks have been constituted by an Act passed by parliament while co-operative banks have been constituted by different States under various Acts related to co-operative societies of various states. Co-operative bank organisation in India has three tier set up: 1. State Co-operative Bank is the apex co-operative institution in the state. 2. Central or District Co-operative Bank works at district level. 3. Primary Credit societies which works at the lowest or village level.

Classification of Commercial Banks

The commercial banking institutions of the country can be divided into two groups:

A. **Scheduled Banks:** Those banks are scheduled banks which have been included in the Schedule (Second) of Reserve Bank Act, 1934. The banks included in this scheduled list should fulfil two conditions:

1. The paid up capital and collected funds of bank should not be less than ₹ 5 lakh.
2. Any activity of the bank should not adversely affect the interest of depositors.

Every scheduled bank enjoys following facilities:

1. Such bank becomes eligible for obtaining debts/loans on bank rate from RBI.
2. Such bank automatically acquires the membership of clearing house.
3. Such banks also get the facility of rediscount of first class exchange bills from RBI.

B. Non-scheduled Banks: Those banks which are not included in the list of scheduled banks are called non-scheduled banks. These non-scheduled banks are not eligible for having loans from RBI for meeting their day-to-day general activities but under emergency conditions these banks can be granted loans by RBI.

Functions of Commercial Banks

The functions of commercial banks are of **two** types.

(A) Primary functions; and

(B) Secondary functions.

Primary Functions

There are two primary functions of a commercial bank. These are:

(*a*) ***Accepting deposits:*** The most important activity of a commercial bank is to mobilise deposits from the public. People who have surplus income and savings find it convenient to deposit the amounts with banks. Depending upon the nature of deposits, funds deposited with bank also earn interest.

(*b*) ***Grant loans and advances:*** The second important function of a commercial bank is to grant loans and advances. Such loans and advances are given to members of the public and to the business community at a higher rate of interest than allowed by banks on various deposit accounts.

Secondary Functions

In addition to the primary functions of accepting deposits and lending money, banks perform a number of other functions, which are called secondary functions.

These are as follows:

(a) Issuing letters of credit, travellers cheque, etc.

(b) Undertaking safe custody of valuables, important document and securities by providing safe deposit vaults or lockers.

(c) Providing customers with facilities of foreign exchange dealings.

(d) Transferring money from one account to another; and from one branch to another branch of the bank through cheque, pay order, demand draft.

(e) Standing guarantee on behalf of its customers, for making payment for purchase of goods, machinery, vehicles etc.

(f) Collecting and supplying business information.

(g) Providing reports on the credit-worthiness of customers.

(i) Providing consumer finance for individuals by way of loans on easy terms for purchase of consumer durables like televisions, refrigerators, etc.

(j) Educational loans to students at reasonable rate of interest for higher studies, especially for professional courses.

Non-Banking Financial Companies (NBFCs)

Introduction

Non-banking financial companies (NBFCs) are fast emerging as an important segment of Indian financial system.

It is an heterogeneous group of institutions (other than commercial and co-operative banks) performing financial intermediation in a variety of ways, like accepting deposits, making loans and advances, leasing, hire purchase, etc.

Differences Between Banks & NBFCs

NBFCs are doing functions akin to that of banks, however there are a few differences:

(*i*) An NBFC cannot accept demand deposits (demand deposits are funds deposited at a depository institution that are payable on demand—immediately or within a very short period—like your current or savings accounts.)

(*ii*) It is not a part of the payment and settlement system and as such cannot issue cheque books to its customers; and

(*iii*) Deposit insurance facility of DICGC is not available for NBFC depositors unlike in case of banks.

Types of NBFCs

The types of NBFCs registered with the RBI are:

1. **Equipment leasing companies:** It is any financial institution whose principal business is that of leasing equipments or financing of such an activity.
2. **Hire-purchase companies:** It is any financial intermediary whose principal business relates to hire purchase transactions or financing of such transactions.
3. **Loan companies:** It means any financial institution whose principal business is that of providing finance, whether by making loans or advances or otherwise for any activity other than its own (excluding any equipment leasing or hire-purchase finance activity).
4. **Investment companies:** It is any financial intermediary whose principal business is that of buying and selling of securities.

Salient Features of RBI Amendment Act, 1997 Regarding NBFSc

RBI has taken a series of measures to enhance the regulatory and supervisory standards of the NBFCs and to bring them at par with commercial banks over a period of time. These include:

1. Secure a certificate of registration from RBI, the net owned funds (NoF) should be ₹ 2 crores (initially) only ₹ 25 lakhs).
2. There is a quantum of public deposits which can be received by an NBFC, depending upon whether it is a loan and investment company or whether it is a leasing and hire-purchase company, and so on—fixed between 1.5 times to 4 times NoF.
3. NBFCs have to invest at least 5 per cent of their assets in unencumbered approved securities.
4. Every NBFC has to create a reserve fund and transfer at least 20 per cent of its net profit every year to the reserve fund.
5. Prudential norms are fixed for those NBFCs which are raising public deposits. For instance, such NBFCs should maintain Capital to Risks Asset Ratio (CRAR) comprising TIER I and II Capital:

   12% for leasing hire-purchase finance companies.

   15% for loan and investment companies, and

   12% for RNBCs (Residuary Non-Banking Companies).

   Certain norms were prescribed for all NBFCs whether they hold or receive public deposits or not.
6. Under RBI regulations, RNBCs are required to invest not less than 80 per cent of aggregate liabilities with the depositors in Government securities, Government-guaranteed bonds, debentures, etc. RBI has reviewed these regulations.
7. All registered NBFCs should submit half yearly returns to RBI at the end of March and September every year. As non-submission of periodic returns to RBI was a common feature, RBI has now decided to impose penalties besides cancellation of certificates of registration and permission to receive deposits from the public.

The RBI is now entrusted with the following powers:

(a) specify from time to time a minimum percentage of investment for NBFCs in unencumbered "approved" securities;

(b) determine their policies and give directions to any or all NBFCs on capital adequacy, provisioning and other prudential norms, as also on the deployment of funds (similar to those applicable to banks).

(c) direct them on balance sheet, profit and loss accounts and disclosure of liabilities,

(d) levy fines and penalty on an NBFC for contravention and default, as also cancel its registration,

(e) prohibit an NBFC from accepting deposits and alienate its assets; and

(f) file a winding up petition for continued violation of the provisions of the Act and / or failure to comply with any direction or orders of the RBI.

- Liquidity Adjustment Facility (LAF) is started by RBI in June 2000.
- Liquidity Adjustment Facility (LAF) refers to RBI's policy of Using Repos and Reverse Repos to adjust liquidity on a day to day basis.
- Regional Rural Banks (RRBs) were established since 1975 under the provisions of the RRB Act 1976 with a view to developing the rural economy as well as to creating an alternative channel to 'Co-operatives'.
- With a view to consolidating and strengthening RRBs, the Government of India initiated in September 2005, the process of amalgamation of RRBs in a phased manner.
- RBI introduced a Banking ombudsman scheme in the country on June 14, 1995, for giving a solution for customer's complaints.
- The IDBI which was established as Development Finance Institution under IDBI Act, 1964 has been converted as a banking company (on October 11, 2004)
- Small Industries Development Bank of India (SIDBI) was established as wholly-owned subsidiary of IDBI under the Small Industries Development Bank of India Act, 1989 as the principal financial institution for promotion, financing and development of industries in the Small Scale Sector. Its headquarter is situated at Lucknow.
- ICICI was established in 1955 as public limited company under Indian Companies Act for developing medium and small industries of private sector.
- With effect from May 3, 2002, erstwhile ICICI limited and two of its wholly-owned subsidiaries were merged with ICICI Bank. The appointed date for merger was March 30, 2002.
- In 1987, a National Equity Fund Scheme was started for providing equity assistance to Tiny Small Scale units having capital investment of less than ₹ 10 lakh and working in areas having population less than 5 lakh (15 lakh for hill areas and north-east areas). SIDBI and Central Government contribute 50:50 share in this scheme of SIDBI.
- IRBI was established on March 20, 1985 under Indian Industrial Reconstruction Bank Act, 1984 as a Result of reconstituting Indian Industrial Reconstruction Corporation Ltd. The basic aim of establishing IRBI was to revive sick and closed industrial units and to act as a prime loan and reconstruction agency.
- But now under the new arrangements, IRBI is functioning with the new name IIBIL (Industrial Investment Bank of India Ltd.). IIBIL's head office is situated at Kolkata.
- State Governments have established State Industrial Development Corporations (SIDCs) under their sole ownerships. The objectives of SIDCs include:

  (*i*) To develop industrial areas

  (*ii*) To esnure market facilities

  (*iii*) To establish new development centres.
- EXIM bank in India was established on January 1, 1982 for financing, facilitaing and promoting foreign trade in India. Besides, EXIM Bank also discharge duties of coordinating the activities of various financial invititutions, providing finances for export-imports of goods and services.

  Besides India, this bank also manages finances to third world countries for export-import of goods and services.

Establishment Years of Major Financial Institutions in India

Institution	Year
❑ Imperial Bank of India	1921
❑ Reserve Bank of India (Nationalisation of RBI took place on January 1, 1949)	April 1, 1935
❑ Industrial Finance Corporation of India (IFCI)	1948
❑ State Bank of India (SBI)	July 1, 1955
❑ Unit Trust of India (UTI)	Feb. 1, 1964
❑ IDBI	July 1964
❑ NABARD	July 12, 1982
❑ IRBI (Now it has been renamed as IIBIL since March 6, 1997)	March 20, 1985
❑ SIDBI	1990
❑ EXIM Bank	January 1, 1982
❑ National Housing Bank (NHB)	July 1988
❑ Life Insurance Corporation (LIC)	September 1956
❑ General Insurance Corporation (GIC)	November 1972
❑ Regional Rural Banks (RRBs)	Oct. 2, 1975
❑ Risk Capital and Technology Finance Corporation Ltd.	March 1975
❑ Technology Development & Information Co. of India Ltd.	1989
❑ Infrastructure Leasing & Financial Services Ltd.	1988
❑ Housing Development Finance Corporation Ltd. (HDFC)	1977

- National Housing Bank (NHB) was established in July 1988 as wholly owned subsidiary of RBI. A major activity of NHB includes extending financial assistance to eligible institutions in the housing sector by way of refinance and direct finance.
- National Bank for Agriculture and Rural Development (NABARD) is the apex banking institution providing finance for agriculture and rural development. It was established on July 12, 1982 with the paid-up capital of ₹ 100 crore having 50:50 contribution of Indian Government and RBI. NABARD's head office is situated at Mumbai.
- IDFC (Infrastructure Development Finance Company) was proposed to be established on January 31, 1997, Under Companies Act, 1956, for financing infrastructure sector for the country. The mission of IDFC is to:
  - (*i*) Lead private capital to commercially viable intrastructural projects in India.
  - (*ii*) Provide a strong policy advisory role to government to meet this objective.
  - (*iii*) Develop and strengthen the connectivity of infrastructure projects to markets and institutions.
- Agriculture and Rural Development Banks basically known as Land Mortgage Banks/Land Development Banks have now been redesignated as Agricultural and Rural Development. These banks provide long term credit to agriculture and rural sector. A two-tier structure is in operation:
  - ⇒ State Co-operative and Rural Development Banks (SCARDBs).
  - ⇒ Primary Co-operative Agriculture and Rural Development Banks (PCARDBs).
- Under an Act passed by the parliament, on September 1, 1956 Life Insurance Corporation (LIC) of India was established with the capital of ₹ 5 crore given by the Government of India. LIC head office is situated at Mumbai.

- General Insurance Company (GIC) was established in November, 1972.
- The insurance sector was opened for private participation with the enactment of Insurance Regulatory and Development Authority Act (IRDA Act), 1999.
- On the recommendation of Malhotra committee, government has permitted privatization of Insurance sector. The committee was constituted in April 1993.
- The Wholesale Price Index (WPI) is the price of a representative basket of wholesale goods. It also influences stock and fixed price markets. The WPI is published by the Economic Adviser in the Ministry of Commerce and Industry. The Wholesale Price Index focuses on the price of goods traded between corporations, rather than goods bought by consumers, which is measured by the Consumer Price Index.
- The wholesale price index (WPI) is based on the wholesale price of a few relevant commodities of over 240 commodities available. The commodities chosen for the calculation are based on their importance in the region and the point of time the WPI is employed. For example in India about 435 items were used for calculating the WPI in base year 1993-94 while the advanced base year 2004-05 uses 676 items. Currently the base year has been revised from 2004-05 to 2011-12 by the Office of Economic Advisor (OEA), Department of Industrial Policy and Promotion, Ministry of Commerce and Industry.

Non-Performing Assets (NPA)

In simple words the assets of the Banks which don't perform (means don't bring any return) are called Non- Performing Assets. In more general sense they are 'bad loans'. Any asset, including a based asset, becomes non-performing when it ceases to generate income for the bank.

However, there is a prescribed definition by the RBI which defines the NPAs as—

- Terms loans on which interest and/or instalment of principal remain overdue for a particular quarter for a period of more than 90 days from the end of that particular quarter.
- The Bills those remain overdue for a period of more than 90 days from the end of a quarter.
- Any amount to be received remains overdue for a period of more than 90 days.
- The Cash Credit Account remains out of order for a period of more than 90 days. Out of order means over the sanctioned limit.

Printing of Securities and Minting in India

- ***India Security Press (Nasik Road) :*** Postal Material, Postal Stamps, Non-postal Stamps, Judicial and Non-judicial Stamps, Cheques, Bonds, NSCs, Kisan Vikas Patras, Securities of State Governments, Public Sector Enterprise and Financial Corporations.
- ***Security Printing Press (Hyderabad) :*** Established in 1982 for meeting the demand for postal material by Southern States. It also fulfils the demand for Union Excise Duty Stamps of the Country.
- ***Currency Notes Press (Nasik Road):*** Since 1991, this press prints currency notes of ₹ 10, ₹ 50, ₹ 100, ₹ 200 and ₹ 500.
- ***Bank Notes Press (Dewas):*** Currency notes of ₹ 20, ₹ 50, ₹ 100, ₹ 200 and ₹ 500 are printed here.
- ***Modernised Currency Notes Press:*** Two new modernised currency notes press are established at Mysore (Karnataka) and Salboni (West Bengal).
- ***Security Paper Hoshangabad*** (Established in 1967-68) makes production of Bank and Currency notes paper.
- ***Coins are minted at four places:*** Mumbai, Kolkata, Hyderabad and Noida.
- ***Bhartiya Reserve Bank Note Mudran Private Limited Mysore:*** Currency notes of ₹ 200 and ₹ 500 are printed here.
- Capital Market may be defined as a market dealing in medium and long-term funds. It is an institutional arrangement for borrowing medium

and long term funds and which provides facilities for marketing and trading of securities.

- Capital Market Constitutes all long term borrowings from banks and financial institutions, borrowings from foreign markets and raising of capital by issue various securities such as share debentures, bonds etc.
- For trading of securities there are two different segments in capital market. They are:

  1. Primary Market, 2. Secondary Market.

Primary Market

- The primary market deals with new/fresh issue of securities and is, therefore known as new issue market.
- The new issue market primarily consists of the arrangements, which facilitates the procurement of long-term finance by the companies in the form of shares, debentures and bonds. The companies usually issue those securities at the initial stages of their formation and so also later on for expansion and/or modernization of their activities.
- However, the selling of securities is not an easy task, as the companies have to fulfil various legal requirements and decide upon the appropriate timing and the method of issue.
- The new issues seek assistance of various inter-median'es such as merchant bankers, underwriters, stock brokers etc. All these intermediaries form an integral part of the primary market.

Secondary Market

- The secondary market is an association or organisation or a body of individuals established for the purpose of assisting, regulating and controlling the business of buying selling and dealing in securities.
- It may noted that it is called a secondary market because only the securities already issued can be traded on the floor of the stock exchange.
- Secondary market is open only to its members, most of whom are brokers acting as agents of the buyers and sellers of securities.
- The main functions of this market lie in providing liquidity to securities and safety in dealing. It is because of the availability of such facilities that people are ready to invest in securities.
- Discount Bill Market is one that deals in short-term loans. Treasury Bills and Commercial Bills of Exchange also fall in this category.
- Dividend is the amount which the company distributes to shareholders when the profits of the company are calculated by the board of directors.
- The debenture is a written acknowledgement of money borrowed. It specifies the terms and conditions, such as rate of interest, time of repayment, security offered, etc. These are offered to the public to subscribe in the same manner as is done in the case of shares.
- Share is the smallest unit into which the total capital of the company is divided. For example, when a company decides to raise ₹ 50 crores of capital from the public by issuing shares, then it can divide its capital into units of a definite value, say ₹ 10/or ₹ 100/- each, these individual units are called as its share. In order to tap the savings of different types of people, a company can issue two type of Shares—(*a*) Equity Shares, and (*b*) Preference Shares.

  (*a*) ***Equity Shares:*** Equity shares are shares, which do not enjoy any preferential right in the matter of claim of dividend or repayment of capital. The equity shareholders get dividend only after making the payment of dividends on preference shares. There is no fixed rate of dividend for equity shareholders.

  (*b*) ***Preference Shares:*** Preference Shares are those shares, which carry preferential rights in respect of dividend and return of capital. Before any dividend is paid to the equity shares, the dividend at a fixed rate must be paid on the preference shares. However, this dividend is payable only if there are profits.
- Financial institutions which are engaged in borrowing and lending money are called

financial intermediaries. It also includes commercial banks. Financial intermediary is a middle man between manufacturer and whole-seller and retailer and between a retailer and consumer.

- Business in the country's oldest stock exchange, namely the Bombay Stock Exchange (BSE) dating back to 1875, which is also one of the oldest stock exchanges in the world, continued to operate.
- The National Stock Exchange (NSE), which emerged in the mid-1990 and catalysed improvements in trading system to provide the necessary depth and choice to investors, made sustained progress.
- On June 15, 1998 National Stock Exchange has launched two new Reference Rates for the loans of Inter-Bank Call Money Market. These rates are MIBOR (Mumbai Inter Bank Offer Rate) and MIBID (Mumbai Inter-Bank Bide Rate)
- MIBOR will be the indicator of Lending Rate for loans while MIBID will be the lending rate for receipts.

Securities and Exchange Board of India (SEBI)

- Securities and Exchange Board of India (SEBI) is an independent statutory regulatory authority.
- SEBI was initially constituted on April 12, 1988 as a non-statutory body through a resolution of the Government for dealing with all matters relating to development and regulation of securities market and investor protection and to advise the Government of all these matters.
- SEBI was given statutory status and powers through an ordinance promulgated on January 30, 1992.
- SEBI is managed by six members—one chairman (nominated by Central Government), two members (officers of Central Ministries), one member (from RBI) and remaining two members are nominated by Central Government.
- The office of SEBI is situated at Mumbai with its regional office at Kolkata, Delhi and Chennai.

Functions of SEBI

- To safeguard the interests of investors and to regulate capital market with suitable measures.
- To regulate the business of stock exchanges and other securities market.
- To regulate the working of Stock Brokers. Sub-brokers, Share Transfer Agents, Trustees, Merchant Bankers, Underwriters, Portfolio Managers etc. and also to make their registration.
- To register and regulate collective investment plans of mutual funds.
- To encourage self-regulatory organisations.
- To eliminate malpractices of security markets.
- To train the persons associated with security markets and also to encourage investors' education.
- To check insider trading of securities.
- To supervise the working of various organisations trading in security market and also to ensure systematic dealings.
- To promote research and investigations for ensuring the attainment of above objectives.

Rural Infrastructure Development Fund

All domestic scheduled commercial banks are required to lend 40% of their net credit to priority sector with sub-target of 18% for lending to 18% for lending to agriculture. Banks having shortfall in lending to priority/agriculture sector are required to contribute to Rural Infrastructure Development Fund (RIDF) which was established on April 1, 1995 to assist State Governments/State owned Corporations in quick completion of ongoing projects relating to medium and minor irrigation, soil conservation watershed management, and other forms of rural infrastructure. Now the scope of RIDF has been enlarged by including development projects implemented by Gram Panchayats, Self-help groups and NGOs. The Fund is maintained by the National Bank for Agriculture and Rural Development (NABARD). Domestic commerical banks contribute to the Fund to the extent of their shortfall in stipulated priority sector lending to agriculture. The main objective of the Fund is to provide loans to State Governments and State-owned corporations to enables them to complete ongoing rural infrastructure projects.

Concept of Depository System

Depository system is that system in which ownership of security is changed by an electronic account entry and physical transaction of securities does not take place. The main functions of depository are as follows:

- To accept deposits for ensuring safe custody of securities.
- To make computerised account entry for ensuring evidence of ownership transfer.
- To keep record of mortgaged securities.
- Different countries possess generally two types of depositories:
  (*a*) Securities immobilisation system of depositories.
  (*b*) Securities dematerialisation system of depositories.

Main Share Price Index in Famous Share Market of the World

BSE (Mumbai)	SENSEX
NSE (Mumbai)	S & P CNX Nifty
New York	DOW JONES
Tokyo	NIKKEI
Frankfurt (Germany)	MID DAX
Hong Kong	HANG SENG
Singapore	SIMEX STRAITS TIMES

PUBLIC FINANCE

- Direct Taxes are—Income Tax, Corporation Tax, Wealth Tax, Estate Duty, Gift Tax, Expenditure Tax and Interest Tax.
- Indirect Taxes are—Custom Duties, Union Excise Duties, Sale/Purchase Tax, Advertisements Tax, Goods and Services Tax (GST).
- India possesses a federal structure in which a clear distinction is made between the Union and the State functions and sources of revenue.
- Our constitution provides residual powers of the centre. Article 264 and 293 explain the financial relations between the Union and State Government.

A. The List I of Seventh Schedule of Indian Constitution enlists the Union taxes which are as follows:

- Taxes on income other than agriculture income
- Corporation tax
- Custom duties
- Excise duties except on alcoholic liquors and narcotics not contained in medical or toilet preparation
- Estate and succession duties other than on agricultural land
- Taxes on the capital value of assets except agricultural land of individuals and companies
- Rates of stamp duties on financial documents
- Taxes other than stamp duties on transactions in stock exchanges and future markets
- Taxes on sales or purchases of newspapers and on advertisements therein
- Taxes on railway freight and fares
- Terminal taxes on goods or passengers carried by railways, sea or air
- Taxes on the sale or purchase of goods in the course of inter state trade

B. List II of Seventh Schedule enlists the taxes which are within the jurisdiction of the states:

- Land revenue
- Taxes on the sale and purchase of goods, except newspapers
- Taxes on agricultural income
- Taxes on land buildings
- Succession and estate duties on agricultural land
- Excise on alcoholic liquors and narcotics
- Taxes on the entry of goods into a local area
- Taxes on the consumption and sale of electricity
- Taxes on mineral rights (subject to any limitations imposed by the Parliament)
- Taxes on vehicles, animals and boats
- Stamp duties except those on financial documents

- Taxes on luxuries including entertainments, betting and gambling
- Tolls
- Taxes on professions, trades, callings and employment
- Capitation taxation
- Taxes on advertisements other than those contained in newspapers

C. Apart from taxes levied and collected by the states, the constitution has provided for the revenues for certain taxes on the union list to be alloted, partly or wholly to the states. These provisions fall into various categories:

- Duties which are levied by the Union Government but are collected and appropriated by the States. These include stamp duties, excise duties on medical preparations containing alcohol or narcotics.
- Taxes which are levied and collected by the union, but the entire proceeds of which are assigned to the states, in proportion determined by the Parliament.

  These taxes include:

  (*i*) Succession and Estate duty
  (*ii*) Taxes on railway freight and fares
  (*iii*) Terminal taxes on goods and passengers
  (*iv*) Taxes on transactions in stock exchanges and future markets
  (*v*) Taxes on sale and purchase of newspapers and advertisements therein
- Central taxes on income and union excise duties are levied and collected by the union but are shared by it with the states in a prescribed manner.
- Proceeds of additional excise duty on mill made textiles, sugar and tobacco which are levied by the union since 1957 in replacement of state sales taxes on these commodities, are wholly distributed among the states in a manner as to guarantee their former incomes from the displaced sales taxes.

D. Taxes levied and distributed between the Union and the States—As per the provisions of the Article (1), all taxes and duties referred to in the Union List, except the duties and taxes referred to in Articles 268 and 269, respectively, surcharge on taxes and duties referred to in Article 271 and any cess levied for specific purposes under any law made by Parliament shall be levied and collected by the Government of India and shall be distributed between the Union and the States in the manner provided in clause (2).

(2) Such percentage, as may be prescribed of the net proceeds of any such tax or duty in any financial year shall not form part of the Consolidated Fund of India, but shall be assigned to the States within which that tax or duty is leviable in that year, and shall be distributed among those States in such manner and from such time as may be prescribed in the manner provided in clause (3).

(3) In this Article, 'prescribed' means—(*i*) until a Finance Commission has been constituted, prescribed by the President by order, and (*ii*) after a Finance Commission has been constituted, prescribed by the President by order after considering the recommendations of the Finance Commission.

- Like all other countries, tendency of income tax is progressive in India.
- The Laffer Effect which implies that a reduction in the rate of taxation leads to more than proportionate increase in tax yield.
- Minimum Alternative Tax—MAT has been levying on companies.
- Estate Duty was first introduced in India in 1953. It was levied on total property passing on the death of a person. The whole property of the deceased constituted the estate and was considered liable to pay estate duty. Hence, the central government decided to abolish it with effect from April 1, 1985.
- An Annual Tax on wealth was first introduced in May 1957 on the recommendations of Kaldor. It is levied on the excess of net wealth over exemption of individuals, joint Hindu families and companies.
- Excise duties on commodities other than alcoholic liquors and narcotics are levied by the central government.

- Service tax was introduced in 1994-95 in a small way to operationalise the principle of neutrality of the tax system to different forms of production and in recognition of the fact that value additions whether in manufacturing or service should form the basis of taxation.
- VAT (Value Added Tax) seeks to tax the value added at every stage of manufacturing and sale, with a provision of refunding the amount of VAT already paid at earlier stages to avoid double taxation. In other words, the tax already paid can be claimed at the next stage of value addition.
- Following the June 18, 2004 decision of the Empowered Committee of State Finance Ministers to implement state-level VAT from April 1, 2005, all states/UTs had introduced VAT to replace the sales tax by December 31, 2005. Haryana was the first state to introduce VAT in 2003.
- CENVAT, was introduced at first in budget of 2000-01.
- Performance Budgetting is generally understood as a system of presentation of public expenditure in terms of functions, programmes, performance units, viz; activities, projects, etc., reflecting primarily the government output and its cost. At first it adopted by USA federal government in 1951.
- Zero-base budgeting (ZBB) is an innovative technique to guard against wastage in public expenditure. The technique works not through auditing which is a post-operative check, but through an examination of the very rational of an expenditure item under consideration.
- After 17 arduous years of negotiations by successive governments at the Centre and in the States, the Narendra Modi government has finally introduced a uniform Goods and Services Tax (GST) regime that converts the country into a single market. The biggest tax reform in Independent India, the Goods and Services Tax (GST), finally rolled out at the midnight hour on June 30, 2017, with President Pranab Mukherjee and Prime Minister Narendra Modi pressing a button to mark the occasion in the historic central hall of Parliament. Calling the GST "a good and simple tax", Modi said the country was moving towards a modern taxation system, much simpler and more transparent than the existing one. "From Gandhinagar to Itanagar, from Leh to Lakshadweep, the dream of one nation, one tax will come true," he added. The GST replaces 17 central and state taxes, including services tax, value-added tax, octroi, duties and other charges, except Customs levy, across the country. The tax will create a common market in the $2-trillion economy with 1.3 billion people. It is expected to curb "tax terrorism and inspector raj". All goods and services have been slotted under six tax slabs: 0 per cent, 3 per cent (for bullion), 5 per cent, 12 per cent, 18 per cent, and 28 per cent. There is also cess, over and above the highest rate, for demerit goods.
- Finance Commission is constituted to define financial relations between the Centre and the States. Under the provision of Article 280(1) of the constitution, the President appoints a Finance Commission for the specific purpose of devolution of non-plan revenue resources.

Various Types of Deficits of the Central Government

- Budget may take a shape of deficit when the public revenue falls short to public expenditure. Budget deficit is the difference between the estimated public expenditure and public revenue. The government meets this deficit by way of printing new currency or by borrowing. Some types of deficits are as follows:
- **Revenue Deficits:** Revenue Deficit = Revenue Expenditure-Revenue Receipts
  Current revenue expenditure of the central government is composed of plan and non-plan expenditure, and current-revenue receipts include net tax revenue and non-tax revenue of the central government.
- **Budget Deficit:** Budget Deficit = Total Expenditure—Total Receipts
  The total expenditure of the central governments always exceeded its total revenue which is known as budget deficit or overall budgetary deficit.

Multiple Choice Questions

1. The law of Demand refers to:
   A. Price-supply relationship
   B. Price-cost relationship
   C. Price-demand relationship
   D. Price-income relationship

2. In a typical demand schedule, quantity demanded:
   A. Varies directly with price
   B. Varies proportionately with price
   C. Varies inversely with price
   D. Is independent of price

3. Normally when price per unit of a goods falls, its:
   A. Quantity demanded increases
   B. Quantity demanded decreases
   C. Quantity demanded remains constant
   D. None of these happens

4. A fall in the price of a commodity leads to:
   A. A shift in demand
   B. A fall in demand
   C. A rise in consumers real income
   D. A fall in the consumers real income

5. Demand schedule is shown as:
   A. A result of increase in the size of the family
   B. A result of change in state
   C. A function of price alone
   D. None of these

6. Market demand for any goods is a function of the:
   A. Price per unit of the goods
   B. Price per unit of other goods
   C. Income of consumers
   D. All of the above

7. The demand curve for a commodity is generally drawn on the assumption that:
   A. The commodity has no substitutes
   B. Tastes, income and all other prices remain constant
   C. The average house hold consists of two persons
   D. Purchases of the commodity are made by a free market.

8. A typical demand curve cannot be:
   A. Convex to the origin
   B. A straight line parallel to y-axis
   C. A straight line parallel to x-axis
   D. Rising upwards to the right

9. When the law of demand operates the demand curve:
   A. Slopes downward from left to right
   B. Slopes upward from left to right
   C. Slopes upward from right to left
   D. Parallel to horizontal axis

10. For most consumers apples and oranges are substitutes goods. Therefore we would expect a rise in the price of apples to lead to:
    A. A right ward shift in the demand curve of oranges
    B. A left ward shift in the supply curve of apples
    C. A downward change in the demand curve of oranges
    D. A fall in the price of oranges

11. 'Ceteris paribus' clause in the Law of Demand does not mean:
    A. The price of the commodity does not change
    B. The price of its substitutes does not change
    C. The income of the consumer does not change
    D. The price of complementary goods does not change

12. Which of the following could provide an example of exceptional demand curves?
    I. Demand for "Giffen goods"
    I. Demand based on fears of a future rise in prices
    III. Demand for second-hand clothes
    IV. Demand for daily newspapers
    A. I only
    B. I and II
    C. II and III
    D. I, II, III and IV

13. Which one of the following is true increase of normal goods?
A. When Price increases, demand decreases
B. When Price increases, demand also increases
C. When Price remains constant, demand falls down
D. When Price falls down, demand remains constant

14. An exceptional demand curve is one that slopes:
A. Upwards to the right
B. Down wards to the right
C. Upwards to the left
D. Horizontally

15. When there is decrease in demand the demand curve:
A. Moves downwards towards the axis
B. Moves upwards away from the axis
C. Remains unchanged
D. None of the above

16. Two goods have to be consumed simultaneously are:
A. Identical B. Complementary
C. Substitutes D. None of these

17. Which of the following pairs of commodities is an example of substitutes?
A. Coffee and milk
B. Diamond and Cow
C. Pen and ink
D. Mustard oil and coconut oil

18. Bread and butter, lamb and mint sauce, illustrate the type of inter related demand known as:
A. Rival demand
B. Composite demand
C. Competitive demand
D. Joint demand

19. A commodity, the price of which has fallen but is expected to fall further, will present a demand curve:
A. Regressive at the lower end
B. Regressive at the upper end
C. Kinked in the middle
D. Downward sloping to right

20. When an individual's income falls (while everything else remains the same), his demand for an inferior goods:
A. Increases
B. Decreases
C. Remains unchanged
D. We cannot say without additional information

21. If two goods are complements, this means that a rise in the price of one commodity will induce:
A. An upward shift in demand for the other commodity
B. A rise in the price of the other commodity
C. A downward shift in demand for the other commodity
D. No shift in demand for the other commodity

22. An income-demand curve for a "Luxury commodity" slopes:
A. Upwards to the right from the origin
B. Vertically
C. Upwards from left to right only beyond a certain level of consumer's income
D. Horizontally

23. An income demand curve for inferior commodity always slopes:
A. Upwards to the right
B. Backwards to the left
C. Downwards to the right
D. Horizontally

24. 'Change in quantity demanded' refers to:
A. Upward shift of the demand curve
B. Downward shift of the demand curve
C. Movement on the same demand curve
D. None of these

25. When the price of a substitute of commodity X falls, the demand for X:
A. Rises
B. Falls
C. Remains unchanged
D. Any of the above

26. An increase in demand can result from:
A. A decline in market price
B. An increase in income
C. A reduction in the price of substitutes
D. An increase in the price of complements

27. If the price of coffee suddenly shoots up, ceteris paribus, the demand for Tea is expected to:
A. Move rightward along the original demand curve
B. Increase
C. Remain unaffected
D. Decrease

28. In the case of Giffen goods like bajra, a fall in its price tends to:
A. Make the demand remain constant
B. Reduce the demand
C. Increase the demand
D. Change demand in an abnormal way

29. Cross demand is the change in the quantity demanded to a given commodity in response to the:
A. Change in the utility of another commodity
B. Change in the price of another commodity
C. Change in the nature of another commodity
D. Change in the size of another commodity

30. To calculate the elasticity of demand which of the following formula is used:
A. $\dfrac{\text{Percentage change in demand}}{\text{Original demand}}$
B. $\dfrac{\text{Proportionate change in demand}}{\text{Proportionate change in price}}$
C. $\dfrac{\text{Change in demand}}{\text{Change in price}} \div \dfrac{\text{original demand}}{\text{original price}}$
D. $\dfrac{\text{Change in demand}}{\text{Change in price}}$

31. When the demand curve is a rectangular hyperbola, it represents:
A. Unitary elastic demand
B. Perfectly elastic demand
C. Perfectly inelastic demand
D. Relatively elastic demand

32. If total consumer expenditure on a goods falls as its price falls this indicates that:
A. $e_P < 1$ B. $e_P > 1$
C. $e_P = 1$ D. $e_P = \infty$

33. Market demand is:
A. The sum of all individual demands
B. Demand at prevailing average prices
C. Ability to pay the price asked
D. Demand in a perfectly free market

34. Extension and contraction of demand are results of:
A. Change in consumer's income
B. Change in consumer's tastes
C. Change in price
D. None of these

35. 'Extension of demand' means:
A. More quantity demanded at a lower price
B. More quantity demanded at a higher price
C. More quantity demanded at the same price
D. None of these

36. A negative income elasticity of demand for a commodity indicates that as income falls the amount of the commodity purchased:
A. Rises
B. Falls
C. Remains unchanged
D. Any of the above

37. Giffen goods are those goods:
A. For which demand increases as price increases
B. Which have a high income elasticity of demand
C. Which are in very short supply
D. None of these

38. In measuring price-elasticity:
A. Price is a dependent variable and quantity is an independent variable
B. Price is a independent variable and quantity is a dependent variable
C. Price and quantity both are independent variables
D. Price and quantity both are dependent variables

39. The demand for pepper is likely to have a low price elasticity because it:
1. Involves only a small proportion of consumers expenditure
2. It is single-use goods
3. Has no close substitutes
4. Can readily be foregone

A. 1 and 2 only B. 1 and 3 only
C. 2 and 3 only D. 2 and 4 only

40. Consider a demand curve which takes the form of a straight line cutting both axis. Elasticity at the mid-point of the line would be:

A. 0 B. 1.0
C. 1.5 D. 2.0

41. When with a change in price the total outlay on a commodity remains constant, it is a case of:

A. Perfect elasticity B. Perfect inelasticity
C. Unit elasticity D. Zero elasticity

42. Income-Elasticity of demand will be zero when a given change in income brings about:

A. A less than proportionate change in quantity demanded
B. A more than proportionate change in quantity demanded
C. The same proportionate change in demand
D. No change in demand

43. Cross elasticity of complementary goods is:

A. Negative B. Zero
C. High D. Infinite

44. One common definition of luxury goods is goods with an income elasticity:

A. Greater than one
B. Equal to one
C. Less than one but more than zero
D. None of these

45. Match the following:

1. For a given 10 per cent change in price, demand changes by zero per eent — (*i*) $e > 1$
2. For a given 10 per cent change in price, demand changes by 5 per cent — (*ii*) $e = 1$
3. For a given 10 per cent change in price, demand changes by 10 per cent — (*iii*) $e < 1$
4. For a given 10 per cent change in price, demand changes by 20 per cent — (*iv*) $e = 0$

	1	2	3	4
A.	(*iii*)	(*i*)	(*ii*)	(*iv*)
B.	(*iv*)	(*iii*)	(*ii*)	(*i*)
C.	(*i*)	(*ii*)	(*iii*)	(*iv*)
D.	(*ii*)	(*iii*)	(*i*)	(*iv*)

46. A straight line, downward-sloping demand curve implies that, as price falls, the elasticity of demand:

A. Increases
B. Decreases
C. Remains the same
D. is zero

47. In the longer period permitting adjustment, demand is likely to be:

A. Inelastic B. Elastic
C. Unit elastic D. Cannot be known

48. Elasticity of demand is equal to unity while marginal revenue is:

A. Positive B. Zero
C. Negative D. Indeterminate

49. A demand curve which takes the form of a horizontal line parallel to the quantity axis illustrates elasticity which is:

A. Zero B. Infinite
C. > 1 D. < 1

50. Which of the following does not have a uniform elasticity of demand at all points:

A. A downward sloping demand curve
B. A vertical demand curve
C. A rectangular hyperbola demand curve
D. A horizontal demand curve

51. If the percentage increase in the quantity of a commodity demanded is smaller than the percentage fall in its price, the coefficient of price elasticity of demand is:

A. Greater than 1 B. Equal to 1
C. Less than 1 D. Zero

52. Match the following:

1. Responsiveness of demand to change in price — (*i*) Income elasticity of demand
2. Responsiveness of demand to change in tastes — (*ii*) Price elasticity of demand
3. Responsiveness of demand to change in income — (*iii*) Cross elasticity of demand
4. Responsiveness of demand to change in price of related goods. — (*iv*) Taste elasticity of demand

	1	2	3	4
A.	(*i*)	(*ii*)	(*iii*)	(*iv*)
B.	(*iv*)	(*iii*)	(*i*)	(*ii*)
C.	(*iii*)	(*iv*)	(*ii*)	(*i*)
D.	(*ii*)	(*iv*)	(*i*)	(*iii*)

53. A monopolist charging high price operates on:
A. The elastic part of a demand curve
B. The inelastic part of a demand curve
C. The constant elastic part of a demand curve
D. Ignores elasticity of demand altogether

54. Elasticity of demand in the following figure at point Q_1 is:

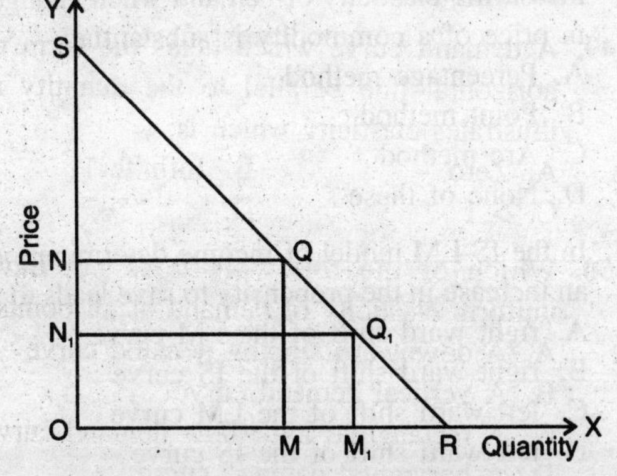

A. $\frac{RQ_1}{SQ_1}$ B. $\frac{Q_1N_1}{OS}$

C. $\frac{Q_1F}{RQ_1}$ D. $\frac{RQ}{RQ_1}$

55. Arc elasticity gives a better measure of point elasticity of a curvilinear demand curve as:
A. The size of the arc becomes smaller
B. The curvature of the demand curve over the arc becomes less
C. Both of the above
D. Neither of the above

56. Ceteris paribus, a change in the price of a commodity causes the quantity purchased of its complements to move:
A. In the same direction
B. In the opposite direction
C. In an insignificant manner
D. Cannot be known

57. If there were no changes in the quantity of food sold, even when its price falls, we would know that:
A. Demand was entirely inelastic
B. Demand was entirely elastic
C. Demand was more elastic than one
D. Demand was unit elastic

58. When the income elasticity of demand is greater than unity, the commodity is:
A. A necessity
B. A luxury
C. An inferior good
D. A non-related good

59. Which of the following statement is correct:
A. When the slope of the demand curve is zero, demand is infinitely elastic and when the slope is infinite, elasticity is zero
B. When the slope of the demand curve is zero, elasticity is also zero and when the slope is infinite, elasticity is also infinite
C. When the slope of the demand curve is zero, elasticity is unity and also when the slope is infinite, elasticity is unity
D. None of these

60. If two commodities are substitutes a change in the price of one, ceteris paribus, causes a change in the quantity purchased of the other:
A. In the same direction
B. In the opposite direction
C. In an insignificant manner
D. Cannot be known

61. Income elasticity of demand is expressed as:
A. $\frac{\text{Percentage change in quantity demanded}}{\text{Percentage change in income}}$
B. $\frac{\text{Percentage change in income}}{\text{Change in quantity demanded}}$
C. Change in quantity demanded $\times \frac{\text{Change in marginal income}}{100}$
D. $\frac{\text{Change in income}}{100 \times \text{change in quantity demanded}}$

62. In the case of an inferior commodity, the income elasticity of demand is:
A. Positive B. Unitary
C. Negative D. Infinity

63. Income elasticity of demand will be zero when a given change in income brings about:
A. A less than proportionate change in quantity demanded
B. A more than proportionate change in quantity demanded
C. The same proportionate change in demand
D. No change in demand

64. The degree of price elasticity of demand used for goods is influenced by whether:
1. It has close substitutes
2. Its output is easily altered
3. It account for a small input
4. It is a durable use or single use goods
A. 1, 3 and 4 only B. 1 and 2 only
C. 2 and 3 only D. 2, 3 and 4 only

65. Pick out the correct formula for arc elasticity:
A. $\frac{\Delta q}{\Delta P} \cdot \frac{P_1 + P_2}{q_1 + q_2}$ B. $\frac{\Delta P}{\Delta q} \cdot \frac{P_1 + P_2}{q_1 + q_2}$
C. $\frac{\Delta P}{\Delta q} \cdot \frac{100}{q_1 + P_1}$ D. $\frac{\Delta q \times 100}{P}$

66. A country is advised to devalue (reduce external value of) its currency only when its exports face:
A. Inelastic demand in foreign markets
B. Elastic demand in foreign markets
C. Unit elastic demand in foreign markets
D. None of these

67. Consider the following demand schedule:

Price per unit (₹)	*Quantity demanded* (000)
6	3
5	9
4	15
3	20

When price falls from ₹ 5 to ₹ 4, elasticity of demand can be expressed numerically as:
A. 1.0 B. 2.5
C. 3.3 D. 3.75

68. Two commodities are considered to be perfect substitutes for each other if the elasticity of substitution is:
A. Positive B. Negative
C. Zero D. Infinite

69. If a straight line demand curve is tangent to a curvilinear demand curve, the elasticity of the two demand curves at the points of tangency is:
A. The same
B. Different
C. Can be the same or different
D. Depends on the location of the point of tangency

70. Which of the following is the method of measuring elasticity of demand when changes in price of a commodity is substantial:
A. Percentage method
B. Point method
C. Arc method
D. None of these

71. In the IS-LM model of income determination, an increase in the propensity to save leads to a:
A. right ward shift of the LM curve
B. right ward shift of the IS curve
C. left ward shift of the LM curve
D. left ward shift of the IS curve

72. Under the Keynesian system, a full in money wage rate will lead to a/am:
A. increase in employment
B. fall in the price level
C. fall in the interest rate
D. fall in the quantity of money

73. If there is to be large oscillation in the path of income through the interaction of multiplier and accelerator then the:
A. value of marginal propensity to save must be less than the value of accelerator
B. value of marginal propensity to save must be greater than the value of accelerator
C. value of accelerator must be greater than one
D. Sum of the value of marginal propensity to save and accelerator must be greater than one

74. Neutrality of money implies that a given increase in the money supply will:
A. increase all prices in the same proportion
B. increase all prices in different proportions
C. decrease all prices in the same proportion
D. not change prices at all.

75. The theory that the transactions demand for money also depends on the rate of interests, was put forward by:
A. Keynes and Pigou
B. Bumal and Tobin
C. Hicks and Solow
D. Samuelson and Meada

76. The quantity theory of money implies that an increase in the price level will be associated with:
A. an increase in output
B. an increase in money supply
C. a decrease in money supply
D. both (A) and (B)

77. High powered money is:
A. Bank's reserves at the Central Bank
B. all loans and advances of banks
C. money held by banks
D. currency held by public and reserves with the Central Bank

78. Which one of the following pair is NOT correctly matched?
A. Inflationary Gap : Keynes
B. Cash Balance Approach : Pigou
C. Accelerator-Multiplier : Hicks Analysis
D. Equation of Exchange : Marshall

79. Given the total investment expenditure, an increase in the propensity to save will lead to a:
A. rise in income
B. rise in the rate of interest
C. fall in savings
D. fall in income

80. Liquidity preference curve slopes downward to right because:
A. as rate of interest rises, the opportunity cost of holding money falls.
B. as rate of interest rises, the opportunity cost of holding money rises.
C. as rate of interest falls, the opportunity cost of holding money does not change.
D. when the rate of interest is low, the central banks reduces the supply of money.

81. Quantity theory of money should be regarded as a theory of demand for money. This view has been given by:
A. D.H. Robertson
B. J.M. Keynes
C. A.C. Pigou
D. M. Friedman

82. Inflation is unjust and deflation is inexpedient. Of the two, deflation is worse. Who made this statement:
A. J.M. Keynes B. G. Crowther
C. A. Marshall D. A.H. Hansen

83. The quantity theory of money was first propounded by:
A. D. Ricardo B. Davanzatti
C. D. Hume D. J. Mill

84. Money is an asset. Its demand is determined along with the demand for all the other assets. This view has been held by:
A. A. Marshal B. J. Tobin
C. M. Friedman D. H. Johnson

85. Who among the following Economists, was the first to mention effective demand as a determinant of the level of economic activity:
A. D. Ricardo B. T.R. Malthus
C. A. Marshall D. J.M. Keynes

86. In classical theory of employment what ensures the perfect clearing of the labour market:
A. flexibility of interest rate
B. flexibility of wage rate
C. flexibility of prices of the commodity
D. classical assumptim of perfect competition in the product market

87. When a linear consumption function undergoes a parallel shift downwards, the investment multiplier:
A. falls B. rises
C. doubles D. does not change

88. A direct increase in initial employment leads to a multiple increase in total employment. This relationship was propounded by:
A. J.M. Keynes B. R.F. Kahn
C. A.C. Pigou D. J. Robertson

89. Who among the following Economists introduced the concept of permanent income as a determination of consumption function:
A. M. Friedman
B. J.M. Keynes
C. J.S. Duesenberry
D. N. Kaldor

90. An increase in money supply leads to:
A. rightward shift of IS curve
B. leftward shift of IS curve
C. leftward shift of LM curve
D. rightward shift of LM curve

91. Consider the following statements in relation to Accelerator and choose the correct answer from the code given below:
1. It depends on the rate of growth of demand.
2. It works when there is no idle capacity in the economy.
3. It increases with increase in the rate of depreciation.
4. It depends on the level of demand.

Code:
A. 1 and 2 are correct.
B. 2 and 3 are correct.
C. 3 and 4 are correct.
D. 2, 3 and 4 are corect.

92. According to the IS-LM model, given by Hicks-Hansen there is simultaneous equilibrium between:
A. income level and rate of interest
B. income level and consumption
C. inflation and unemployment
D. demand and supply of money

93. Before full employment, if price level falls, aggregate demand will increase which will lead to rise in employment and income. This relationship between price level and aggregate demand has been called:
A. real balance effect
B. income effect
C. price effect
D. employment effect

94. Keynes was most concerned with:
A. demand-pull inflation
B. cost-push inflation
C. structural inflation
D. stagflation

95. The speculative demand for money depends only on the expected prices of bonds. This view has been held by:
A. J.M. Keynes
B. K. Wickscell
C. D.H. Robertson
D. M. Friedman

96. Money multiplier is the ratio between:
A. quantity of total money and money national income
B. quantity of primany money and quantity of secondary money
C. quanity of primary money and quantity of total money
D. quantity of money and aggregate investment

97. According to the quantity theory of money, the price level rises if:
A. there is a decrease in money supply
B. the velocity of circulation of money rises
C. the aggregate volume of transactions increases
D. the real demand for money rises

98. An increase in fiscal spending leads to:
A. a shift of the Phillips curve to the right
B. a shift of the Phillips curve to the left
C. movement along the Phillips curve such that unemployment rises and inflation falls
D. movement along the Phillips curve such that unemployment falls and inflation rises

99. 'The propensity to consume of an individual with respect to his disposable income and wealth depends on his age.' The statement refers to the:
A. relative income hypothesis
B. permanent income hypothesis
C. life-cycle hypothesis
D. absolute income hypothesis

100. When income falls, what happens to the liquidity preference curve?
A. It does not shift
B. It shifts to the left
C. It shifts to the right
D. It becomes parallel to the vertical axis

101. Stagflation refers to situation which is characterised by:
A. deflation and rising unemployment
B. inflation and rising employment
C. inflation and rising unemployment
D. stagnant employment and deflation

102. The elasticity in respect of speculative demand for money under the liquidity trap condition is:
A. zero B. one
C. greater than one D. infinite

103. Which one of the following factors affects velocity of circulation?
A. Time unit of income receipts
B. Frequency of transaction
C. Liquidity preference
D. All of the above

104. To which one of the following, does the liquidity trap correspond?
A. Consumption function
B. Production function
C. Money demand function
D. Labour demand function

105. The speculative demand for money, according to Keynes, is a function of:
A. Rate of interest
B. Level of income
C. Level of savings
D. Level of output

106. Gresham's law explains that:
A. two grams of silver is equal to half gram gold for conversion
B. good money chases bad money out
C. velocity of circulation of money fluctuates rapidly
D. bad money drives good money out of circulation

107. Match List-I (Economists) with List-II (Concepts) and select the correct answer using the codes given below the lists:

List-I	*List-II*
(*a*) Keynes	1. Money illusion
(*b*) Modigliani	2. IS-curve
(*c*) Hicks	3. Life cycle hypothesis
(*d*) Pigou	4. Liquidity trap

Codes:

	(*a*)	(*b*)	(*c*)	(*d*)
A.	4	1	2	3
B.	2	3	4	1
C.	4	3	2	1
D.	2	1	4	3

108. Supply of money remaining the same, when there is an increase in demand for money, there will be:
A. a fall in the level of prices
B. an increase in the rate of interest
C. a decreacse in the rate of interest
D. an increase in the level of income and employment

109. Fisher's equation of exchange establishes:
A. direct relationship between money and prices
B. inverse relationship between money and prices
C. direct and proportionate relationship between money and prices
D. inverse and porportinate relationship between money and prices

110. Given the total investment expenditure an increase in the propensity to save will lead to a:

A. fall in the rate of interest
B. fall in income
C. rise in the rate of interest
D. rise in income

111. According to Keynes, marginal propensity to consume:

A. can never exceed unity
B. may exceed unity when dissaving occurs
C. can never exceed the average propensity to consume
D. is the reciprocal of the marginal propensity to save

112. Super multiplier refers to:

A. interaction of the Multiplier and the Accelerator
B. reciprocal of the marginal propensity to consume
C. capital output ratio
D. budget multiplier

113. Consider the following:

1. Money supply M_1.
2. Saving deposits with Post Office saving banks.
3. Net time deposits of banks.
4. Total deposits of the Post Office saving banks excluding NSC.

The measure of money supply M_3 would include:

A. 1, 2 and 3 B. 1 and 3
C. 1 and 4 D. 3 and 4

114. If cash reserve ratio is 40% and the commercial banks get a fresh cash of ₹ 15 crores as a result of government spending then the increase in loans advanced by the commercial banks will be:

A. ₹ 37.5 crores B. ₹ 40 crores
C. ₹ 60 crores D. ₹ 30.5 crores

115. Liquidity preference refers to:

A. the extent to which investors prefer to keep their assets in money
B. RBI's share holdings in other financial institutions
C. community's preference for gold
D. community's effective demand for capital goods

116. Excess of ex-ante savings over ex-ante investment means that:

A. income will fall
B. income will rise
C. income will remain the same
D. price will rise and inventories will accumulate

117. Suppose, MPC falls. The IS curve shifts to the left. Then what happens ceteris paribus?

A. The level of equilibrium becomes lower
B. The level of equilibrium becomes higher
C. There is no change in equilibrium
D. Only the rate of interest becomes lower

118. The IS-LM model has been formulated by:

A. J.R. Hicks B. F. Modigliane
C. P.A. Samuelson D. J.M. Keynes

119. Which one of the following is represented by M_3?

A. M_1 + post office savings bank deposits
B. Currency with the public + demand deposits
C. M_1 + time deposits with bank
D. None of these

120. When a linear consumption function undergoes a parallel shift down wards, the investment multiplier will:

A. fall B. rise marginally
C. remain as before D. become double

121. If the consumption function passes through the origin, then APC = MPC it must be:

A. linear without any intercept
B. non-linear without any intercept
C. linear with a negative intercept on the income axis
D. linear with a positive intercept on the consumption axis

122. Portfolio theory of the demand for money assumes that the individual:

A. disregards risk B. is risk neutral
C. is risk lover D. is risk averse

123. If the rate of interest increases, people holdig bonds will:
A. experience a capital gain on the bonds
B. experience a capital loss on the bonds
C. not be able to find a buyer should they decide to sale
D. experience neither capital gains nor a capital loss

124. When the demand for money is infinitely interest elastic, the effectiveness of an expansionary monetary policy is:
A. the highest B. mode rate
C. very low D. nil

125. Which of the following is a transfer payment?
A. Payment made to housewife
B. Pocket allowance to children
C. Maintenance allowance to old parents
D. All of the above

126. The difference between gross domestic product and net domestic product equals:
A. Transfer payments
B. Depreciation cost
C. Indirect taxes
D. Subsidies

127. The best method of computing national income is:
A. Product Method
B. Income Method
C. Expenditure Method
D. Combination of income and production method

128. Which of the following will directly increase the GNP?
A. A rise in the market price
B. A surplus in budget
C. An increase in investment
D. A deficit in budget

129. "National dividend is that part of objective income of the community, including of course the income derived from abroad which can be measured in money"
This is the remark of:
A. Marshall B. J.R. Hicks
C. David Ricardo D. A.C. Pigou

130. While calculating personal income, we have to deduct the following from private income:
A. Saving of private corporate sector and corporation tax
B. Consumption of fixed capital
C. Direct taxes paid by households
D. All of the above

131. The National income is equal to:
A. GNP – Subsidies – Taxes
B. NNP – Indirect Taxes + Subsidies
C. NNP – Direct Taxes + Subsidies
D. GNP – Subsidies + Taxes

132. The total income earned in any given year by the owners of productive resources is measured by:
A. Personal income
B. Disposable Income
C. Gross national product
D. National income

133. In calculating a country's GNP at market prices one of the following is not included:
A. Wages and salaries before tax
B. Indirect taxes
C. Bonds to the employees
D. Depreciation allowances

134. An example of double counting in national income would be:
A. Wages of bus and train drivers
B. Cotton output and cotton cloth output
C. Electricity output and water output
D. Tax receipts and earnings of inland revenue officials

135. Double counting must be avoided when calculating national income. This means that there must be a deduction of the value of:
A. Food subsidies
B. Personal consumption of alcoholic drinks
C. Transfer payments
D. Net interest from abroad

136. Which of the following is counted in determining GNP?
A. A do it yourself roof repair job
B. A housewife's work at home

C. An operation performed in a hospital
D. Vegetables grown by a farmer for his own use

137. The difference between Gross National Product and Gross Domestic Product is equal to:
A. Gross Domestic investment
B. Net Foreign Investment
C. Net imports
D. Net factor income from abroad

138. Net domestic product at factor cost equals net domestic product at market prices:
A. Plus subsidies – indirect taxes
B. Minus subsidies + indirect taxes
C. Minus subsidies
D. Plus indirect taxes

139. National product is not affected by which of the following?
A. Sale of a second hand automobile by A to B
B. Sale of a new car by an automobile dealer
C. Sale of a new car by an automobile company
D. Sale of a new car on hire purchase

140. "Disposable income" does not include:
A. Business transfer payments
B. Social security benefits
C. Corporate dividends
D. Personal income taxes

141. Depreciation means:
A. Destruction of a plant in a fire accident
B. Loss of equipment over time due to wear and tear
C. Closure of the plant due to raw material problem
D. Closure of the plant due to lockout

142. Which of the following is not a method of estimating GNP?
A. The value added approach
B. Product approach
C. Income approach
D. The financial approach

143. Depreciation is the loss of value of:
A. Capital assets B. Stocks
C. Intermediate goods D. Final goods

144. Net exports are negative when:
A. Net investment is positive
B. Exports are exceeded by imports
C. Exports exceed private transfer to foreigners
D. Imports are exceeded by exports

145. Which one of the following measures does not include final goods and services?
A. GNP
B. NNP
C. Disposable income
D. National income

146. When less output is consumed than produced during a given income period, national wealth:
A. Increases
B. Remains unchanged as there is no relationship
C. Decreases
D. May increase or decrease

147. Social accounting system in India is classified into which one of the following sets of sectors?
A. Enterprise, households and government
B. Assets, liabilities and debt position
C. Public sector, private sector and joint sector
D. Income, production and expenditure

148. The GNP gap is the gap between:
A. GNP and NNP
B. GNP and depreciation
C. GNP and GDP
D. Potential and actual GNP

149. Value added means value of:
A. output at market prices
B. goods and services less depreciation
C. goods and services less cost of intermediate goods and services
D. output at factor cost

150. GNP exceeds NNP by:
A. the amount of total taxes
B. government expenditure
C. transfer payments
D. the difference between gross investment and net investment

151. In which plan phase of industrialisation was initiated?
A. Fourth B. Third
C. Second D. First

152. Which is the first Export Processing Zone declared as Free Trade Zone in India?
A. Santacruz B. Kandla
C. Falta D. Noida

153. Which institution is known as 'soft loan window' of World Bank?
A. IFC
B. IDA
C. IMF
D. Indian Development Forum

154. 'Backwash Effect' was firstly introduced by:
A. Gunnar Myrdal B. Peter Suderland
C. Arthur Dunkel D. Kindelberger

155. Finance Commission is appointed by the President under Article:
A. 256 of constitution
B. 280 of constitution
C. 293 of constitution
D. 356 of constitution

156. 'SAPTA' is related to:
A. Education B. Trade
C. Security D. Environment

157. Scheduled bank is that bank which is:
A. Nationalised
B. Not–nationalised
C. Based at foreign country
D. Included in the second schedule of R.B.F

158. Which one of the following committees was set up to review the concept of poverty line?
A. S. Chakravarty Committee
B. K.N. Wanchoo Committee
C. D.T. Lakdawala Committee
D. R.C. Dutt Committee

159. Which one of the folloiwng is not the canon of taxation as stated by Adam Smith?
A. Canon of productivity
B. Canon of convenience
C. Canon of certainty
D. None of these

160. Which place India holds in milk production?
A. Fourth B. Third
C. Second D. First

161. Who is the chairman of Island Development Authority?
A. President B. Prime Minister
C. Home Minister D. Planning Minister

162. The book 'Politics with Charkha' is written by:
A. Ashok Mehta B. J.B. Kriplani
C. K.G. Mashruwala D. Morarji Desai

163. CAPART is related with:
A. Assisting and evaluating rural welfare programmes
B. Computer hardware
C. Consultant service of export promotion
D. Controlling pollution in big industries

164. Which of the following does not grant any tax rebate?
A. National Saving Certificate
B. Indira Vikas Patra
C. National Saving Scheme
D. Public Provident Fund

165. SEBI was established in:
A. 1993 B. 1992
C. 1988 D. 1990

166. The "Ad hoc Treasury Bill System" of meeting budget deficit in India was replaced by 'Ways and means Advances System' which has come into force on:
A. March 31, 1997 B. April 1, 1996
C. April 1, 1997 D. None of these

167. Pradhan Mantri Gram Sadak Yojana (PMGSY) was launched in:
A. 2000 B. 1999
C. 2001 D. 2004

168. The Headquarter of CAPART is situated at:
A. Mumbai B. Kolkata
C. New Delhi D. Bangalore

169. The main security guard of International Trade is:
A. IMF B. World Bank
C. WTO D. IFC

170. Cheque which is crossed can be encashed only:
A. Through SBI
B. Through the payee
C. Through any bank
D. None of these

171. 'Closed Economy' is that economy in which:
A. Only export takes place
B. Money supply is fully controlled
C. Deficit financing takes place
D. Neither export nor import takes place

172. Which one of the following method is not used by N.S.S.O. for the measurement of unemployment in India?
A. Current Monthly Status
B. Current Weekly Status
C. Current Daily Status
D. Usual Principal Status

173. National Rural Development Institute is situated at:
A. Shimla B. Hyderabad
C. Patna D. New Delhi

174. The Headquarter of World Bank is situated at:
A. Manila B. Washington D.C.
C. New York D. Geneva

175. Which state has a lower literacy rate than country's literacy rate according to 2011 census?
A. Maharashtra B. Gujarat
C. Odisha D. West Bengal

176. Which pair is not correct?
A. EXIM Bank—Financing for export-import
B. RBI—Banker's bank
C. IDBI—Industrial finance
D. FCI—Financial assistance to commercial institutions

177. Which of the rate is not determined by RBI?
A. Bank Rate B. CRR
C. SLR D. PLR

178. The main foodgrains of India is:
A. Rice B. Wheat
C. Sugarcane D. Maize

179. Which of the following days has been announced as 'Antyodaya Day'?
A. August 25 B. September
C. September 25 D. October 1

180. 'Food for work programme' was renamed as:
A. RLEGP B. IRDP
C. NREP D. MNP

181. Agriculture Price Commission and Food Corporation of India were established in:
A. 1960 B. 1965
C. 1966 D. 1969

182. Employees State Insurance Scheme in India was introduced in:
A. 1947 B. 1952
C. 1955 D. 1972

183. The goods can be taxed heavily to earn additional revenue if they are:
A. Highly elastic B. Unit elastic
C. Perfectly elastic D. Inelastic

184. Scheduled Bank is that bank which is:
A. Nationalised
B. Not nationalised
C. Based at foreign country
D. Included in the second schedule of RBI

185. India's National Hydroelectric Power corporation is establishing 'Tamarthi Power Project' in:
A. Bangiadesh
B. Bhutan
C. Myanmar
D. Nepal

186. 'Hydro carbon Vision-2025' is associated with:
A. Storage of petroleum products
B. Euro-I & Euro II
C. Green house effect
D. None of these

187. GST has been implemented from:
A. January 1, 2017
B. January 1, 2018
C. April 1, 2018
D. July 1, 2017

188. What is 'NIKKEI'?
A. Share Price Index of Tokyo Share Market
B. Name of Japanese Central Bank
C. Japanese name of Country's Planning Commission
D. Foreign Exchange Market of Japan

189. The field given to Rangarajan Committee was:
A. Modernisation of Cloth Industry
B. To probe Share scam
C. To probe Sugar scam
D. To suggest measures for controlling BOP deficit

190. VAT is imposed:
A. Directly on consumer
B. On final stage of production
C. On first stage of production
D. On all stages between production and final sale

191. The Headquarter of 'Economic and Social Commission for Asia and Pacific' is at:
A. Singapore B. Bangkok
C. Manila D. Hong Kong

192. Which is the most liquid measure of money supply?
A. M_1 B. M_2
C. M_3 D. M_4

193. NITI Aayog was constituted in:
A. 1948 B. 1949
C. 2015 D. 1951

194. Gresham's Law is related to:
A. Consumption and Demand
B. Supply and Demand
C. Circulation of Money
D. Deficit Financing

195. TRYSEM was:
A. a modern technique of agriculture production
B. a code used in space science
C. a programme to train rural youth for self employment
D. none of these

196. Kelkar committee report is related on:
A. Tax Reforms
B. Financial Sector Reforms
C. Trade Reforms
D. Administrative Reforms

197. The process of budget making after re-evaluating every item of expenditure in every financial year is known as:
A. Performance Budgeting
B. Deficit Budgeting
C. Zero Based Budgeting
D. Fresh Budgeting

198. In which production India has attained self-sufficiency?
A. Fertilizers B. Foodgrains
C. Edible oil D. Petroleum

199. If the capital stock is always stable, its depreciation will be:
A. High B. Low
C. Zero D. Infinite

200. When development in economy takes place the share of tertiary sector in National Income?
A. Declines
B. Increases
C. Remains constant
D. First rises and then falls

ANSWERS

1	2	3	4	5	6	7	8	9	10
C	C	A	B	C	D	B	D	A	A
11	**12**	**13**	**14**	**15**	**16**	**17**	**18**	**19**	**20**
A	B	A	A	A	B	D	D	A	A
21	**22**	**23**	**24**	**25**	**26**	**27**	**28**	**29**	**30**
A	C	B	C	B	B	B	B	B	B

31	32	33	34	35	36	37	38	39	40
A	A	A	C	A	A	A	B	C	B
41	**42**	**43**	**44**	**45**	**46**	**47**	**48**	**49**	**50**
C	D	A	A	B	B	B	B	B	A
51	**52**	**53**	**54**	**55**	**56**	**57**	**58**	**59**	**60**
C	D	A	A	C	B	A	B	A	A
61	**62**	**63**	**64**	**65**	**66**	**67**	**68**	**69**	**70**
A	C	D	D	A	B	C	D	A	A
71	**72**	**73**	**74**	**75**	**76**	**77**	**78**	**79**	**80**
D	C	A	D	B	B	D	D	D	B
81	**82**	**83**	**84**	**85**	**86**	**87**	**88**	**89**	**90**
D	A	B	C	B	B	D	B	A	D
91	**92**	**93**	**94**	**95**	**96**	**97**	**98**	**99**	**100**
D	A	A	A	A	B	B	D	C	C
101	**102**	**103**	**104**	**105**	**106**	**107**	**108**	**109**	**110**
C	D	D	C	A	D	C	B	C	B
111	**112**	**113**	**114**	**115**	**116**	**117**	**118**	**119**	**120**
A	A	B	A	A	A	A	A	C	C
121	**122**	**123**	**124**	**125**	**126**	**127**	**128**	**129**	**130**
A	C	B	D	D	B	D	C	D	A
131	**132**	**133**	**134**	**135**	**136**	**137**	**138**	**139**	**140**
B	D	D	B	C	C	D	A	A	D
141	**142**	**143**	**144**	**145**	**146**	**147**	**148**	**149**	**150**
B	D	A	D	C	A	D	D	C	D
151	**152**	**153**	**154**	**155**	**156**	**157**	**158**	**159**	**160**
C	A	B	A	B	B	D	C	A	D
161	**162**	**163**	**164**	**165**	**166**	**167**	**168**	**169**	**170**
B	B	A	B	C	C	A	C	C	C
171	**172**	**173**	**174**	**175**	**176**	**177**	**178**	**179**	**180**
D	D	B	B	C	D	D	A	C	C
181	**182**	**183**	**184**	**185**	**186**	**187**	**188**	**189**	**190**
B	B	D	D	B	A	D	A	D	D
191	**192**	**193**	**194**	**195**	**196**	**197**	**198**	**199**	**200**
B	A	C	C	C	A	C	B	C	B

●●●

CIVICS

Indian Constitution

Every Independent, sovereign country has its own Constitution and so does India. The Constituent Assembly of India, set up in 1946, consisted of the representatives from the provinces and the princely states. 296 members from provinces were elected by the legislative assemblies while 93 representatives of states were elected in accordance with the system settled by negotiations. Till independence, it worked within the framework of the Cabinet Mission Plan but after 15th August, 1947, its position changed.

The inaugural meeting of the Constituent Assembly was held on 9th December, 1946. It was presided over by Dr. Sachchidananda Sinha who was the oldest member of the assembly. On 11th December, 1946, Dr. Rajendra Prasad was elected president of the Constituent Assembly and all further deliberations of the assembly were conducted under his chairmanship.

Various committees and sub-committees were setup to examine the different aspects of the Constitution. The drafting committee was under the chairmanship of Dr. B.R. Ambedkar and produced the draft constitution with 315 articles and 8 schedules. The draft constitution was considered by the Constituent Assembly and when it took final shape, it had 395 articles and 8 schedules. The time taken to complete the task was 2 years, 11 months and 18 days from the first meeting of the Constituent Assembly. The draft was finally adopted on 26th November, 1949. The Constitution was put into operation on 26th January, 1950.

The framing of the Constitution of India has been influenced by social, economic, political and historical factors. The social evils like caste system, social inequalities and communalism were sought to be eradicated by the provisions of the Constitution. Extreme poverty and economic disparity were reflected in many provisions of the Constitution, *e.g.*, directive principles. The partition of the country, long spell of colonialism, wide geography, the problems of princely states and desire to preserve the country's unity and sovereignty prompted the Constitution makers to make strong Centre.

The Indian Constitution has its roots in several Acts introduced by British rulers. The Government of India Act, 1858, the Indian Council Act, 1892, the Indian Councils Act, 1909 (Morley-Minto reforms) and the Government of India Act, 1919 (Montague-Chelmsford reforms) provided the basis of popular representation, division of work between Centre and States and strong Centre. The Government of India Act, 1935 is more often reflected in the Constitution as it contained several provisions of the British parliamentary procedures.

The Indian Constitution, besides reflecting the system of its British rulers, also contains several features borrowed from American, Canadian, South African and Irish Constitutions. The framers made suitable changes according to prevailing conditions in India. Whereas the parliamentary system of Government comes from the British Constitution, Fundamental rights, Citizenship and Independence of Judiciary comes from the American Constitution. The federal system bears the impact of the Canadian and Australian Constitutions. The Constitution of Rajya Sabha bears resemblance to the upper house of South Africa. The emergency provisions comes from Germany while Directive Principles Concept has been borrowed from Ireland.

Preamble

"We, THE PEOPLE OF INDIA, having solemnly resolved to constitute India into a SOVEREIGN, SOCIALIST, SECULAR, DEMOCRATIC REPUBLIC, and to secure to all its citizens: JUSTICE, social, economic and political; LIBERTY of thought, expression, belief, faith and worship; EQUALITY of status and opportunity; and to promote among them all FRATERNITY assuring the dignity of the individual and the unity and INTEGRITY of the nation; IN OUR CONSTITUENT ASSEMBLY this twenty-sixth day of November, 1949, do HEREBY ADOPT, ENACT AND GIVE TO OURSELVES THIS CONSTITUTION."

The preamble of the Constitution is the basic philosophy of the Constitution on which it is based. It is the Key of the Constitution. Though it has a limited role legally, whenever there is an ambiguity, the courts refer to the Preamble to get insight into various clauses of the Constitution. The words SECULAR and SOCIALIST were not there in the original Constitution but were incorporated subsequently in 1976 after the 42nd constitutional amendment.

The preamble clearly outlines the essential features of our Constitution:

1. The final power lies in the hands of the people.
2. India is a sovereign, socialist, secular, democratic republic.
3. Efforts will be made to give social, economic and political justice.
4. Every citizen of India will have liberty of thought, expression, belief, faith and worship.
5. There will be equality of status and opportunity.
6. The feeling of fraternity among the people will be encouraged.
7. The Unity and Integrity of the nation is of paramount importance.

Salient Features of the Indian Constitution

1. The Indian Constitution is a written and detailed one. The framers, considering the political inexperience of the countrymen and complicated situation, deemed it fit to explain the provisions and not leave anything to chance.
2. India is a Sovereign, Socialist, Secular, Democratic republic. The real power vests with the people. They elect their representatives who, in turn, take decisions on their behalf. The country does not encourage any religion and does not interfere in religious affairs. The country is trying to bridge differences between people, varying in social or economic grounds. The country does not have a monarch. We have a President, who is the head of the nation.
3. Indian Constitution has provided a Federal Government. Our Constitution is written and rigid. There is a clear division of powers between the Centre and States. The Supreme Court has been established to give judgements in case of differences between the Centre and States.
4. Indian Constitution has a unitary bias. The Centre has been made powerful than States with more powers in the executive, legislative and financial fields. The entity of States can be dissolved but the Centre will always exist.
5. Parliamentary form of Government has been provided. The head of the nation is President and he is indirectly elected. To advise the President, a Council of Ministers exists. The Council is responsible to the Parliament. The members of Parliament are elected by adult universal suffrage.
6. India has been made a secular country, with no interference in religious affairs.
7. Unlike America, India has single citizenship. People, living in any State, will be citizens of India only.

8. The Indian Constitution has a combination of flexibility and rigidity. Some provisions can be altered by a simple majority in the parliament while a few need ratification by States. Already, over 100 amendments in the Constitution have been made.
9. The Indian Constitution provided for seven fundamental rights, which are essential for all-round development of an individual. These are written and can get remedy from the courts, in case of violation. After 44th amendment, one fundamental right—Right to Property has been deleted.
10. The Indian Constitution envisages fundamental duties for all citizens. All these duties make people aware of their responsibilities towards the nation.
11. The Directive Principles of State Policy are the guidelines and objectives which every state and Central government should aspire. These principles cannot be enforced legally but have the moral backing of people.
12. Independent judiciary is an important achievement of the Constitution. The judiciary has been kept away from executive control. Moreover, rule of law has been applied. The criminal law is same all over the country but personal laws, as per religion and caste, have been allowed.
13. Judicial review has been allowed. So, the legislature and the executive are kept in check. Any transgression on the basic feature of the Constitution is declared null and void by the courts.

Territory of the Union

India is a Union of States and Union Territories. Parliament has the power to create any State, increase the area of any State, reduce it, change the name or boundaries of any State. However, the President's prior approval is required before the introduction of a bill in the Parliament. The President can consult the concerned State but the view of the latter are not binding.

Citizenship

The Constitution provides for a single citizenship. Following categories of persons became citizens of India at the commencement of the Constitution:

1. Persons born and domiciled in India.
2. Persons domiciled in India and either of whose parents was born in India.
3. Persons domiciled in India and residing in India ordinarily for a period of at least five years.
4. Certain categories of people, who had migrated from Pakistan to India.
5. Indians residing abroad but who make an application to acquire Indian citizenship.

The Parliament passed Citizenship Act in 1955, providing for following methods for acquiring Indian citizenship:

1. Citizenship by birth
2. Citizenship by descent
3. Citizenship by registration
4. Citizenship by naturalisation
5. Citizenship by incorporation of territory

The Central Government has the discretion to waive off any or all the conditions of citizenship if it thinks that the applicant has rendered distinguished service to the cause of science, art, philosophy, literature, world peace or human progress in general.

Indian citizenship can be lost by:

(a) renunciation;
(b) termination — it takes place if a citizen of India voluntary acquires the citizenship of another country; and
(c) deprivation — if the Government terminates the citizenship.

Some of the Fundamental Rights belong only to the citizens. They only can contest for the public offices in the country like President, Prime Minister, Chief Minister etc. Indian citizens also get the right to vote.

Fundamental Rights

In a democratic set-up, people are given several rights. Some of them are essential for the all-round development of human beings. These fundamental rights are basic in the governance of the State. These rights

1. are given to everyone, without any discrimination. It is felt that in their absence, a person will not be able to develop his physical, spiritual and moral capabilities;
2. are provided in the basic law or Constitution of the country. The government cannot alter them according to its wishes;
3. cannot be ignored or suppressed. The country's executive and legislature have to respect them;
4. are justiciable. In case of violation of Fundamental Rights, citizens can approach the court for remedy.

The Fundamental Rights in India have some special features:

1. They are discussed in detail, with all associated limitation enumerated.
2. Fundamental Rights are both in the form of positive and negative. The negative Rights prohibit the State from doing several things while positive Rights allows people to do many things. The negative Rights are absolute while positive Rights are limited. Only those positive Rights, that are specified in the Constitution, are Fundamental Rights.
3. Fundamental Rights put limitations on different authorities — Central Government, State Governments and Local bodies.
4. Fundamental Rights are not absolute. The Parliament can put up restrictions, in the interest of the nation. They can suspend or even amend these Rights.
5. Some Fundamental Rights, like freedom of expression are available to Indian citizens only, while some like equality before law are available to foreigners also.
6. There is no natural or unenumerated rights in India. Whatever has been specified in the Constitution, the courts can only protect those interests.

Various Fundamental Rights

Right to Equality

Articles 14, 15, 16, 17 and 18 ensure that every citizen and foreign national within the country, is treated equally before law. Article 14 says that the State shall not deny to any person equality before the law or the equal protection of the law within the territory of India. The right lays down the foundation of Rule of Law in India. Article 15 says that they shall not discriminate against any citizen on grounds only of religion, race, caste, sex, place of birth or any of them. No one can be denied access to public places on either of the above ground. However, there are two exceptions to the above Right. The Government can make special arrangements for children and women.

The Government has been allowed to give special consideration to Scheduled Castes, Scheduled Tribes and others socially and educationally backward. Article 16 deals with equality of opportunity in matters of public employment. It says there shall be equality of opportunity for all citizens in matters relating to employment or appointment to any office under the State. No citizen shall, on grounds of any religion, race, caste, sex, descent, place of birth, residence, or any of them, be ineligible for, or discriminated against, in respect, of any employment or office under the State. Article 17 deals with abolition of untouchability and makes an act of untouchability cognizable offence. Article 18 deals with abolition of titles. The exceptions are titles regarding special qualification, education or given by armed forces.

Right to Freedom

These rights guaranteed under Article 19 to 22 of the Constitution, are available only to the Indian citizens. Article 19 provide six freedoms — Freedom of speech and expression; Freedom to assemble peacefully and without arms; Freedom to form associations or union; Freedom to move freely; Freedom to reside and settle; and Freedom to practise any profession or to carry on any occupation, trade or volume.

Right Against Exploitation

Article 23 of the Constitution prohibits traffic in human beings and different forms of forced labour. Article 24 prohibits the employment of children under the age of 14 in any factory or in any other hazardous work.

Right to Freedom of Religion

India is a secular country and every religion and community is equal in the eyes of the State. Article 25 of the Constitution provides freedom of conscience and free profession and propagation of religion. However, everyone must respect public order, health and morality. Article 26 provides that every religion or its section, subject to public order, morality and health, has the right to maintain its own institutions for religious and charitable purposes, to manage its own affairs in matters of religion and to own, acquire and administer moveable and immovable property in accordance with law. Article 27 prohibits levying of any tax on the proceeds which are meant to be spent for the maintenance or promotion of any religious activity. Article 28 states that no religious instruction can be given in any educational institution which is wholly maintained out of State funds. Person attending an educational institution recognised and aided by the State cannot be compelled to take part in any religious instruction or worship conducted by it.

Cultural and Educational Rights

These rights, under Article 29 and 30, provide every opportunity to the minority communities to protect and enrich their language, script, and culture. No one can be denied admission to an educational institution that is run by the State or funded by the State. Every minority group can establish, administer or develop an educational institution to protect their language, script or culture and the Government will not discriminate in any manner in giving aid on the ground that it is managed by a religious or linguistic minority.

Right to Constitutional Remedies

Article 32 is the most important Article, as far as Fundamental Rights are concerned because it ensures their compliance. Every citizen has the right to move the Supreme Court for the enforcement of his constitutionally guarded rights.

The Supreme Court or High Courts can issue writs of Habeas Corpus, Mandamus, Prohibition, Quo Warranto and Certiorari for the compliance of Fundamental Rights.

Fundamental Duties

For the first time, ten Fundamental Duties have been enumerated in the Constitution with the 42nd Amendment Act of 1976. These have been provided in Part (IV) A, Article 51A, and are as under :

It shall be duty of every citizen of India—

(*a*) To abide by the Constitution and respect its ideals, institutions, the National flag and the National anthem;

(*b*) To cherish and follow the noble ideas which inspired our national struggle for freedom;

(*c*) To uphold and protect the sovereignty, unity and integrity of India;

(*d*) To defend the country and render national service when called upon to do so;

(*e*) To promote harmony and the spirit of common brotherhood amongst all the people of India transcending religious, linguistic and regional or sectional diversities; to renounce practices derogatory to the dignity of women;

(*f*) To value and preserve the rich heritage of our composite culture;

(*g*) To protect and improve the natural environment including forests, lakes, rivers and wildlife, and to have compassion for living creatures;

(*h*) To develop the scientific temper, humanism and spirit of inquiry and reform;

(*i*) To safeguard public property and abjure violence; and

(*j*) To strive towards excellence in all spheres of individual and collective activity so that the nation constantly rises to higher levels of endeavour and achievement.

(*k*) Who is a parent or guardian to provide opportunities for education to his child or, as the case may be, ward between the age of six and fourteen years.

The last Fundamental Duty [Article 51A (k) was added through the 86th Constitutional Amendment Act, 2002.

Directive Principles of State Policy

Article 36 to 51 incorporate the Directive Principles of State policy. They are in the form of instructions to the Central and State Governments which they must take into consideration while making policies and programmes.

The compliance with these principles can help the Government give several social and economic rights to the citizens. The framers of the Constitution tried to incorporate social, liberal and Gandhian ideas through these directive principles. They thought that these ideals cannot be incorporated as rights or made compulsory but over a period of time, these should be complied with.

They can lead to the formation of a welfare State, give direction to the developmental policies, preserve unity and promote efforts to promote international security and peace. These principles, covering wide area, are not justiciable but have the backing of the popular will. While Fundamental Rights concern citizens, the Directive Principles can be implemented by States. In case of conflict between the two, the Fundamental Rights contained in Articles 14 and 19 cannot stand in the way of implementation of any of Directive Principle. So, if any law is made to implement Directive Principles, it cannot be declared null and void on the ground that it conflicted with Fundamental Rights. Any country, especially a democratic one, cannot ignore these principles as they outline the salient features of good governance.

The Directive Principles can be categorised as:

(A) Economic Principles

1. Equal pay for men and women
2. Provisions for adequate means of livelihood for all citizens
3. Endeavour to secure just and human conditions of work, a living wage, a decent standard of living
4. Establish economic democracy and justice by securing certain economic rights
5. Promotion of cottage industries
6. Organisation of agricultural and animal husbandry on scientific lines and try to discourage killing of milch animals
7. Secure equitable distribution of the material sources of the community and prevention of concentration of wealth and means of production
8. Strive to promote the welfare of the people by securing a social order permeated by social, political and economic justice to minimise inequa-lity of income, status, facilities and opportunities, amongst individuals and groups
9. Endeavour to raise the level of nutrition and standard of living and to improve public health
10. Protection of workers and children from exploitation
11. Strive to get wages for the workers so that besides meeting bare essential needs, they can improve standard of life and utilize their spare time.

(B) Social and Education Related Principles

1. Provide free and compulsory education to all children upto the age of 14 years
2. Provide special arrangements for the upliftment and development of untouchables and backward castes and ensure that no social injustice or exploitation is being done.
3. Strive to improve the life style and moral standards of its citizens and prohibit consumption of liquor and intoxicating drugs
4. Try to secure a uniform civil code for citizens
5. Protect and preserve places of historic or artistic interest.

(C) Principles Concerning Governance

1. Try to organise village Panchayats as units of self-government
2. Attempt to separate the judiciary from the executive.

(D) Principles Concerning International Peace and Security

1. Endeavour to promote international peace and amity
2. Foster respect for international law and international treaty obligations
3. Encourage the settlement of international disputes through arbitration
4. Encourage just and mutually respectable relations between the nations

Indian Federal Structure

Indian Constitution provides amalgamation of federal as well as unitary structures. The Constitution makers in the wake of partition, problems of princely States, India's long history of disunity and increasing tendencies of centralisation world over, decided to confer more powers to the Centre. Following provisions clearly show that the centre is more powerful:

- The President appoints Governors in States who act as eyes and ears of the Centre. The Governor can send some bills to the President for his assent. He can send reports, recommending removal of the State Government. In case of imposition of emergency, the Governor rules the State as the representative of the President.
- Parliament can make legislations on the subjects even if they belong to State list. Even otherwise, the Centre has more important and powerful subjects.
- Parliament has powers to make new States and make alternatives in the boundaries of existing States.
- Articles 352, 356 and 360 are the emergency provisions which dissolve the federal characteristics and give Centre more powers.

But under the normal circumstances, the federal characteristics are important.

- Country has been divided into States and Union Territories.
- There is a division of work between the Centre and the States.
- The Constitution is written and supreme. Its provisions cannot be altered easily.
- The courts derive their authority from the Constitution. They have powers to arbitrate in disputes between the Centre and the States.

Legislative Relations between the Centre and the States

Various subjects of administration and welfare have been put under three lists in the constitution Union list, State list and Concurrent list. There are 100 subjects under the Union List on which the Central Government can make laws. Important ones are — Defence, Foreign Affairs, War, Treaty, Atomic Energy, Railways, Airlines, Post and Telecommunication, Broadcasting, Foreign Trade, Notes and Currency, Foreign Debt, Insurance, Patent, Copyright, Custom, Excise Duty etc.

There are 61 subjects under the States List on which various State Governments can make laws. Important ones are—Law and Order, Police, Prisons, Local Administration, Health, Agriculture, Irrigation, Entertainment, Industrial Development, etc.

52 subjects come under the Concurrent List on which both the Centre as well as States can make laws. Important ones are — Industries, Preventive Detention, Education, Forests, Marriage, Planning, Divorce, Electricity, Price Control, Newspapers, Transfer of Property, Trade Unions, Press.

It is obvious that the Centre has been given more powers in the distribution of subjects. Only the Centre can make laws on the subjects in the Union List. In the State List, under the special circumstances, the Central Government can also legislate. These circumstances can be either of the given below:

- If Rajya Sabha passes, by two-third majority, a proposal that the subject has become nationally important.

- If emergency is imposed in the country.
- If two or more State Assemblies pass a resolution asking Centre to make laws on one or more subjects given in the State List.
- If President's Rule is imposed in a State, then laws for that particular State can be made by Parliament.
- If Central Government has entered into an international agreement or treaty, and it is necessary to make laws to implement them even though the subject belongs to the State List.
- In the Concurrent List, both the Centre and States can legislate but the former is more powerful.
- If there is a contradiction between the laws passed by the Centre and the States, the latter's laws will be declared null and void if they trespass the former's laws.
- In case of national emergency or constitutional crisis in a State, the subjects are transferred to the Parliament.
- The Governor has the discretionary powers to send the bills on the subjects in Concurrent List for the President's approval. The President can accept the bill or return it with suggestions.

The subjects not listed in either of the three lists — residuary subjects — go to the Centre. The Parliament alone, can make legislations on the matters in the Union List.

Administrative Relations between the Centre and the States

The Central Government has been given powers to control the State Governments:

- The President appoints the Governor, who in turn, keeps check on the State Government. He, can use his discretionary powers on some occasions.
- State Governments and their officials are given administration of some Union List subjects by the President. They are also given powers to carry out duties, in this connection.
- The Union Government can issue directions to the State Governments so that the administrative powers of the two do not conflict.
- The Union Government can direct the State Government to develop communication media so that these can be used for military purposes.
- The State Governments are bound to follow the Centre's directions. If they fail to do so, it will be treated as breakdown of constitutional machinery.
- The Central Government can legislate on the matters concerning rivers flowing through more than one State.
- If there is a constitutional crisis, the Governor can recommend imposition of President's Rule.
- In case of national emergency, the President can order the State Governments.
- President has powers to constitute Inter-State Council, which will tackle differences among States and recommend cordial relations, cooperation and harmony.

Financial Relations between the Centre and the States

In the field of finance also, the Centre has been made more resourceful. The sources which generate large revenues, are with the Centre while the social welfare programmes, which need large outlays, are with State Governments. The States are looking towards the Centre for assistance and aid.

The Central Government imposes following taxes — Income tax except income from agriculture, Custom Duty, Import Duty, Excise Duty, Corporation Tax, Gift Tax, Stamp Duty, Tax on the sale-purchase of newspapers, Tax on advertisements published in newspapers, Tax on the passengers and goods being carried by train, ships and aeroplanes, Property tax, Service tax. The Central Government also gets revenue through commercial operations of railways, post and telegraph, telecom services, ships, factories, industries, banks and insurance services.

The State Government's main sources of income are — Revenue, Tax on Agricultural Income, Inheritance Tax on Agricultural land, House Tax, Sales Tax on goods except newspapers, Tax on Advertisements, Road Tax, Octroi, Passenger Tax, Entertainment Tax, Professional Tax, Tax on Registration of Documents. The State Governments also get Income from their undertakings and industries.

The Centre shares some of its revenue with the States. Some taxes like tax on cheques, Affidavits, Letters of Credit, Insurance Policies, Stamps on Receipts are imposed by the Centre but collected by States and kept by them. Some taxes are imposed and collected by the Centre but revenue is given to respective States. The revenue of some other taxes like Income Tax and Excise Duty, is shared with States on a formula, decided by the Finance Commission. The State Governments can borrow but only within the country. The Centre gives grant-in-aid to the States. All these means enable transfer of money but make States dependent on the Centre.

Finance Commission

The Constitution provides for the appointment of a Finance Commission every five years by the President to recommend measures relating to the distribution of financial resources between Union and States. The Chairman of the Commission has to be a person having experience in public affairs and the other four members have to be appointed from amongst the following:

(a) A High Court judge or one qualified to be appointed as such; or

(b) A person having special knowledge of finance and accounts of the Government; or

(c) A person having wide experience in financial matters and administration; or

(d) A person having special knowledge of economics.

The Commission is asked to make recommendations as to:

(a) the distribution between the Union and the States of the net proceeds of taxes which are to be or may be divided between them and the allocation between the State of the respective shares of such proceeds;

(b) the principles which should govern the grant-in-aid to the revenues of the States out of the Consolidated Fund of India;

(c) Any other matter referred to the Commission by the President in the interests of sound finance.

The Finance Commission is not a permanent body. It is dissolved after it has submitted its recommendations.

President

According to the Constitution, the powers of the executive lie with the President who uses them directly or through subordinate officials. He uses his powers as per the advise given by the Council of Ministers. The President of India is indirectly elected and anyone with following qualifications is eligible to be a candidate for the post:

- Citizen of India.
- Completed 35 years of age.
- Eligible to be elected as Member of Parliament.
- Does not hold any office of profit under the Government of India or any State Government or any local or other authority subject to the control of any Government.

Nomination and ratification of the proposal of the candidature is done by at least fifty electorates.

The President is elected by the members of an electoral college consisting of the elected members of both the Houses of Parliament and Legislative Assemblies of the States. Both the Parliament and Legislative Assemblies of the States have equal number of votes.

The value of votes of each MLA in the election depends on the population of the State and number of elected MLAs in the State. Similarly, the value of each MP's vote depends on the total number of MPs and total number of votes of MLAs of all the States. The single transferable voting system is adopted so that the President-elect has more than fifty per cent support of the voters. The voters give their first, second, third and so on, preferences which are then redistributed unless the final selection is done. The voting at such election is by secret ballot and any dispute regarding the election, can only be sorted out by the Supreme Court.

The tenure of the President's term is five years. If no one is elected at the end of the term, the incumbent stays on till the election of the successor. If the President dies during the tenure or resigns or is not well or is impeached, the Vice-President takes over for the interim period till the election is held. If the Vice-President cannot take over for any reason, the Chief Justice of the Supreme Court or otherwise, the senior most judge of the Supreme Court fills the gap. The elections have to be held within six months.

The President can be re-elected any number of time. He can be removed from the office, before completion of the term for violation of the Constitution, by impeachment. Any house of the Parliament can initiate the impeachment process. At least one-fourth members of the house initiating the process must sign the proposal. Fourteen days notice about the proposal is given to the President. The President has the right to defend himself and prove innocence, either by appearing personally or sending a representative to the Parliament. If a house approves the proposal by two-thirds majority, it is sent to the second house.

If that house also accepts the proposal to impeach by two-thirds majority, the President stands impeached and relieved from the office since that day. There is no provision of appeal against the impeachment in any court.

The President, upon election, cannot be a member of the Parliament or any Legislative Assembly. He cannot hold any other office of profit. He is entitled, without payment of rent, to the use of his official residence and is entitled to such emoluments, allowances and privileges. The emoluments and allowances of the President cannot be diminished during his office. Upon retirement, he gets pension, other allowances and free medical facilities.

Executive Powers of the President

The President is the Chief Executive head of the nation and the administration of the Union is carried out in his name. All the decisions of the Government are considered decisions of the President. All treaties and agreements are entered into by the Union Government in the name of the President. The President appoints the leader of the majority party in Lok Sabha as the Prime Minister and appoints a Council of Ministers on the advise of the Prime Minister. He distributes work among them and can dismiss any one of them on the Prime Minister's recommendation.

The President is the supreme commander of the armed forces.. He appoints officers of the armed forces. The President appoints Governors, Judges of High Court and the Supreme Court, Attorney General, Comptroller and Auditor-General and Ambassadors and Consulate-Generals abroad, Election Commissioners and various other officers. The President is informed regularly of the Cabinet decisions and he can return these decisions for cabinet's reconsideration. He confers awards and decorations of civil and military nature. He is empowered to establish diplomatic relations with other countries. The President has special responsibility for the administration of border areas and Union Territories.

Legislative Powers of the President

Though the President is not a member of Parliament, but he is its integral part. He can call, adjourn or prorogue the session of Parliament. He has powers to dissolve the Lok Sabha. He can address either one or both the houses in joint sitting. He can send message also to the Parliament. He addresses the first sitting of the new Parliament and first sitting of the new year. He can call for the joint sitting of Parliament for certain purposes. He nominates 12 members to Rajya Sabha who are eminent in the fields of art, literature or science. All bills passed by Parliament are sent to him for his assent. He may give his assent to a bill or may send the bill back to Parliament for reconsideration or may veto a bill. If a bill, sent for reconsideration, is again passed by Parliament, the President is bound to give his assent. However, there is no time limit for giving the assent.

No money bill can be introduced in Parliament without the President's prior consent. He causes the budget to be laid in the house. He, however, cannot veto a money bill. Similarly, the bills with provisions to alter boundaries or status of States, need the President's prior approval. Some bills, passed by legislative assemblies are sent to the President for his assent. The Constitutional Amendment bills come into force only after the President's signatures. When the Parliament is not in session, the President can issue ordinance on subjects which are urgent. The Ordinance remains valid for at the most six weeks after the convening of Parliament session. The Parliament can meanwhile, take a decision on the subject.

Judicial Powers of the President

The President appoints the judges of High Courts and the Supreme Court but has no right to remove them from their position. He has power to grant pardon, reprieve, amnesty or commutation to a guilty person.

The President is not answerable to any Court of Law for the exercise of powers and duties of his office. No criminal proceeding can be brought against him during his term of office.

Emergency Powers of the President

The President can declare emergency in three situations:

(a) ***National Emergency:*** If the President is satisfied that the security of the nation or any part thereof is threatened by war or external aggression or internal disturbances, he can issue a proclamation of emergency. The Union Cabinet must give its recommendation in writing, then only the President can issue proclamation. Parliament has to approve the President's order within a month by two-thirds majority, to continue it after a month otherwise the order lapses. If the Lok Sabha has been dissolved or its term expires within these two months, Rajya Sabha can approve the proclamation. The national emergency can be continued indefinitely if Parliament approves it every six months by two-thirds majority.

To avoid misuse of national emergency provisions, certain safeguards have been provided. Armed rebellion is the only condition for internal disturbance. The Union Cabinet has to give its recommendation in writing for the proclamation within a month and after every six months to continue it. Two-thirds majority in Parliament is required for approving the proclamation. If Lok Sabha passes a resolution by a simple majority to end the emergency, the President has to call off the emergency. One-tenth of Lok Sabha MPs can call for the Parliament session to discuss the issue of continuation of emergency. The Fundamental Rights can be superceded only in case of external aggression or war and not in case of internal armed rebellion. The Personal liberty, as given in the Constitution, cannot be taken away during the emergency.

The national emergency gives the nation a unitary character. Parliament gets total right to make laws on State List subjects. If any State legislature had made a law in contradiction with Parliament's law, the former is declared null and void. The President can order an end to freedoms, given as Fundamental Rights. The citizens cannot move the court for the redressal regarding their right's violation. The State executives have to follow Union executive's orders and directions. The provisions of distribution of revenue between the Centre and the States can be stopped by the President, give more finances to the Centre.

The Parliament can extend the tenure of Lok Sabha by a year. The Lok Sabha's tenure ends six months after the expiry of emergency.

(b) ***Constitutional Emergency:*** If the President is satisfied that Governance of a State cannot be carried on in accordance with the provisions of the Constitution, emergency can be proclaimed in the State. The Governor of the State can send a report of the breakdown of Constitutional machinery or otherwise the President himself can get the information from other sources. The Constitutional emergency can be continued for one year after Parliament passes resolutions two times after every six months interval. The emergency has to be approved by Parliament, within two months of proclamation. However, the Constitutional emergency can be extended beyond one year of *(1)* that time, that is a national emergency in the country, state or its part. *(2)* Election Commission certifies that free and fair polls are not possible. This way, Constitutional emergency can be extended upto three years. Beyond that, amendment to Constitution is required.

This type of emergency is popularly called President's Rule imposition. All the executive, legislature and other powers barring the judiciary of the States comes under the President's jurisdiction. The Governor rules the State on the behalf of the President. The Parliament make laws and rules for the State on subjects given in the State List. The Council of Ministers in the State is removed from the office and the legislature is either suspended or dissolved.

(c) ***Financial Emergency:*** The President can issue a proclamation of financial emergency if he is satisfied that the financial credit of India is threatened. The proclamation can last for two months without Parliament's approval. After coming into effect, the President will have to issue a second order to cancel the proclamation. There is no maximum time limit for this emergency.

The Central Government gets the power to direct State Governments to follow certain policies on financial matters and the latter are duty bound to follow that. The Central Government can order reduction in the salaries of judges, civil servants and other employees of State and Central Governments. No money bill in any State legislature can be introduced without prior approval of the President. He can make changes in the distribution of financial resources between the Union and States.

President's Position

The President is the head of the nation. The Government's actions are taken on his behalf. He represents the whole country. But his powers are limited in the sense that he acts on the advice of the Union Cabinet. The President can, however, guide the executive and restrain them from following a wrong path. He can return, veto or delay a legislation. His discretionary powers are limited but at the time of lack of clear majority in the Parliament or division in the ruling party, he plays an important role.

Vice-President

The Vice-President has been provided in the Constitution to act as the President during the interim period, if required. Anyone, with the following qualifications can become Vice-President.

- Should be a citizen of India.
- Should be 35 years of age.
- Should be eligible to be election as a member of Rajya Sabha.

The Vice-President is not a member of either House of Parliament or a House of the Legislature of any State. If he is a member, then after the elections, he is deemed to have vacated his seat in the house on the date on which he enters upon his office as Vice-President.

The Vice-President is elected by an electoral college, consisting of the Members of both Houses of Parliament (elected and nominated) in accordance with the system of proportional representation by means of a single transferable vote. The voting at such election is by secret ballot. The election process for Vice-President can be challenged only in the Supreme Court.

The Vice-President holds office for a term of five years from the date on which he enters the office. He will continue to occupy the office even after five years if no successor has been elected. He can resign before the completion of the term. He can be removed from the office by a resolution, before the completion of five years term. A 14 days notice has to be given before introducing the resolution. If the resolution is passed by a majority of the total members of the Rajya Sabha and agreed by the Lok Sabha, the Vice-President stands removed from the office.

Powers of Vice-President

Though the Vice-President is not a member of Rajya Sabha, he is its Ex-officio Chairman. He manages the affairs of the house. However, if the Vice-President is acting as the President, he ceases to be Chairman of Rajya Sabha and is not entitled to the salary of its office.

The major function of the Vice-President is to act as President or to discharge his functions during vacancy or absence of the President. In the event of the occurrence of vacancy in the office of the President by reasons of death, resignation or removal, the Vice-President can act as President until the date on which a new President is elected to fill such vacancy. When the President is unable to discharge the functions of his office, either because of illness or absence or any other reason, the Vice-President fills in the gap.

Prime Minister

The Prime Minister heads the Council of Ministers which advises the President on all important legislative, executive and administrative matters. He is the first among the equals and is the most powerful person in the country. He is appointed by the President. The leader of the majority group of parties or party is invited to form the Government. But if there is no clear majority, the President can use discretion as the Constitution is silent on the matter. Legally, he stays in office during the pleasure of the President but actually, he remains in office so long as he enjoys the support and confidence of the majority of members of the Lok Sabha.

Anyone, who is eligible to become a member of the either house of the Parliament, can become the Prime Minister. At the time of swearing-in, he need not be a member of the Parliament but must get himself elected within six months of swearing-in. So far, most of the Prime Ministers have been members of Lok Sabha, the exceptions being Indira Gandhi in 1966, H.D. Deve Gowda in 1996, I.K. Gujral in 1997 and Dr. Manmohan Singh in 2004 and 2009.

Functions and Powers

The Prime Minister appoints ministers and allocates work among them. The Council of Ministers has three levels — Cabinet, State and Deputy. The Cabinet level ministers are the senior most, hold independent charges and take part in the Cabinet meeting, where important policy and other decisions are taken. The State level ministers can be given independent charge or work with a cabinet level ministers. The deputy ministers always assist their senior ministers. The Prime Minister has the prerogative to choose his team, either from the supporting group or outside. Distinguished persons can also be invited to join the ministry. The Prime Minister can change the portfolios of the ministers, can ask for anyone's resignation or recommend to the President to dismiss a minister.

All the ministers take the Prime Minister into confidence before taking an important decision. The Prime Minister's viewpoint cannot be overlooked. The Prime Minister chairs the Cabinet meetings where important political, economic, defence and external affairs policy decisions are taken. The Prime Minister coordinates the working of various ministries, ensuring that there is no conflict in the overall working of the Government. The Prime Minister recommends the names for the posts where the appointments are made by the President.

The Prime Minister leads the Government in the Lok Sabha. He is responsible for the functioning of the Government and announces the major policy decisions. The Prime Minister is the link between the President and the Council of Ministers as he communicates and conveys the latter's decisions to the former.

During emergency, the Prime Minister exercises the powers that have been vested with the President. So, the Prime Minister is the most powerful person in the country.

Council of Ministers

According to the Constitution, the President can act only on the advice of the Council of Ministers whose head is the Prime Minister. The Council of Ministers — Cabinet, State and Deputy Ministers — are appointed on the advice of the Prime Minister. The Council of Ministers is responsible to the Lok Sabha for its survival. The ministers are individually as well as collectively responsible which means that if a resolution or bill moved by a minister is lost in the Lok Sabha, all the ministers have to resign. The opposition can bring in no-confidence motion against the Council to remove them and if outvoted, the Government falls. The Council has to resign if the budget is rejected, a resolution recommending reduction in minister's salaries is passed or a resolution condemning the Government's policy is passed.

The Council of Ministers makes policy decisions, administers the country, decides on the economic and financial matters, introduces legislations in the Parliament, recommends appointments to higher posts, decides on foreign policy matters, decides on the imposition of emergency and can recommend dissolution of Lok Sabha.

Parliament

The Indian Parliament is one of the most powerful legislature in the world. It has two houses.

Lok Sabha

The lower house of the Parliament is called Lok Sabha or House of the People. The maximum strength of the House envisaged by the Constitution is now 550. By the 104th amendment, 2019 of the Constitution the provision of nomination of 2 members of Anglo-Indian community have been abolished. The Lok Sabha at present consists of 543 members. The number remains the same until the year 2026. The break up of state-wise Lok Sabha seats is as follows:

States/Union Territories	Seats
Andhra Pradesh	25
Arunachal Pradesh	2
Assam	14
Bihar	40
Chhattisgarh	11
Goa	2
Gujarat	26
Haryana	10
Himachal Pradesh	4
Jharkhand	14
Karnataka	28
Kerala	20
Madhya Pradesh	29
Maharashtra	48
Manipur	2
Meghalaya	2
Mizoram	1
Nagaland	1
Odisha	21
Punjab	13
Rajasthan	25
Sikkim	1
Tamil Nadu	39
Telangana	17
Tripura	2
West Bengal	42
Uttarakhand	5
Uttar Pradesh	80
Jammu & Kashmir	5
Andaman and Nicobar	1
Chandigarh	1
Delhi	7
Dadra & Nagar Haveli and Daman and Diu	2
Lakshdweep	1
Puducherry	1
Ladakh	1

To be a member of the Lok Sabha, a person

(*a*) should be a citizen of India.

(*b*) should have completed 25 years of age.

(*c*) should not be holding any office of profit under the Union or the State or the local authority and should not have been disqualified under any law from contesting the elections.

A person can retain membership of only one seat even if elected from multiple places. If the person does not participate in the session's meeting for 60 consecutive days without any permission, he can be disqualified. There is reservation of seats for the Scheduled Castes and Scheduled Tribes. The term of the Lok Sabha, under normal circumstances is five years but can be extended by one year at a time during emergency. It can be dissolved earlier also.

Speaker of the Lok Sabha

The members of the Lok Sabha elect the Speaker. A voting may be held and the person receiving the highest number of votes, is declared elected. He is entitled to free residential accommodation and pay and allowances as decided by the Parliament. The Speaker can resign from the post or can be removed by passing a no-confidence vote. The Speaker is given an advance notice of 14 days before the start of discussion of no-confidence vote against him. The Speaker can personally present his point of view before the house. If the resolution is accepted by a simple majority, the Speaker is deemed to have been removed from the post. The sitting of the house during the proceedings is presided over by the Deputy Speaker. Under normal circumstances, the Speaker continues to remain in the office even if the Lok Sabha is dissolved. He continues to retain the post till the election of the new Speaker.

Though the Speaker continues to remain a member of a political party, yet he is supposed to be impartial in carrying out his duties. He presides over the house meetings and enforces order and discipline. His orders have to be accepted by one and all. He takes decisions on the bringing in of resolutions and motions in the house. All the bills are introduced with his assent. He allocates time to various members on a particular issue. He can issue warnings to errant members and can even order them to leave the house or can even ask the house marshals to take a member out. He decides on what goes into the house records and can expunge unparliamentary language. He appoints the chairmen and members of the select committees. He can regulate the presence of people in the spectators gallery. The Speaker can adjourn the house. He decides whether the bill is a money bill or a non-money bill. After a bill is passed by Lok Sabha, the Speaker sends it to the Rajya Sabha or the President, after signing on it. The Speaker protects the special privileges provided to the members. He decides about the quorum in the house. At least ten per cent of the members must be present in the house otherwise the house has to be adjourned. He can call for voting in the house on a bill, and if there is a tie, with both sides getting equal number of votes, the Speaker can use his casting vote to decide the fate of the bill. The Speaker also presides over the joint sitting of both the houses.

After the General elections, the President appoints a Protem Speaker who performs the duties of the Speaker of the Lok Sabha until a newly elected legislature elects a new one. The newly elected members are sworn-in by the Protem Speaker. As per the practice in India, the senior most MP is made the Protem Speaker.

Deputy-Speaker of the Lok Sabha

The Deputy Speaker of the Lok Sabha is also elected by the members of this house. He assists the Speaker in his duties and in the absence of the Speaker, presides over the meetings of the house. The post of Deputy-Speaker is very often, offered to the opposition party.

Leader of the Opposition

A resolution was passed by the Parliament in 1977 whereby the leader of the opposition is given the status and facilities equivalent to the rank of cabinet ministers. The opposition party with the largest number of MPs and whose number is at least one-tenth of the total house, will have its leader elected as the leader of the opposition.

Sittings of Lok Sabha

Article 85(1) of the Constitution says that the President will call for sittings of each house regularly, at a place and time deemed fit by him, provided there is no gap of six months between the last sitting of a session and the first sitting of the forthcoming session.

Rajya Sabha

The upper house of the Parliament is the Council of States or the Rajya Sabha. It is a permanent house. The members of the house are senior reputed persons.

The maximum strength of the house is 250, out of which 238 members are elected from state assemblies and union territories. Twelve members, who have made special contributions in the fields of art, literature, science and public service, are nominated by the President. The Rajya Sabha at present consists of 245 members.

The members from the States and Union Territories are elected by the elected members of respective assemblies. The election is on the basis of proportional representation system with a single transferable vote. The States have been given seats on the basis of their population. To qualify for the membership of Rajya Sabha, one has to: (1) be a citizen of India; (2) be at least 30 years of age; (3) fulfill the qualifications of becoming a member of Parliament; and (4) be a voter in any Lok Sabha constituency of the State.

Rajya Sabha is a permanent house. All its members do not retire at the same time. Each member is elected for 6 years and after every two years, one-third of the members retire.

The Vice-President is the ex-officio Chairman of Rajya Sabha but he is not its member. The Chairman has similar duties as the Speaker of the Lok Sabha. A Deputy Chairman is elected by the Rajya Sabha members to assist the Chairman.

Powers of Parliament

The Parliament can make laws on the subjects given in the Union List and in the Concurrent List. If Rajya Sabha passes a resolution by two-thirds majority or there is a national emergency in the country or an international treaty has to be implemented the Parliament can make laws on the subjects listed the State List also. If the two houses do not agree on a bill, the President can call for a joint sitting and the decision on the basis of majority opinion is taken.

No taxes can be levied and no expenditure can be incurred without the consent of the Parliament. In financial matters, Lok Sabha enjoys a superior position. A money bill can be introduced only in Lok Sabha. After its approval, Rajya Sabha is asked to approve it within 14 days. Rajya Sabha cannot reject the bill. It can only return it with suggestions. The bill is deemed to have been accepted by Rajya Sabha after 14 days. Lok Sabha is free to take a decision on the suggestions of Rajya Sabha.

The Parliament has control over the executive. Lok Sabha has the power to remove the executive from the office by passing a no-confidence vote. However, both the houses can question the ministers, criticise them, pass resolutions and participate in discussions involving policy matters. The Parliament decides about pay and allowances of the executive.

The Parliament has Constitutional powers. A bill providing for amendment of Constitution can be introduced in either house and both houses have to pass the bill separately. Some constitutional amendment bills have to be ratified by State legislatives also. However, the Parliament cannot alter the basic features of the Constitution.

The Parliament can initiate impeachment of the President, Vice-President, and judges of the Supreme Court and High Courts.

Both the houses of Parliament elect the Vice-President. They, along with State and Union Territory Assemblies, elect the President.

Any type of emergency cannot be continued without Parliament's approval. Both the houses have to ratify the proclamation. They can initiate proceedings to revoke the proclamation.

Rajya Sabha can also recommend constituting of an All-India Service.

Among the two houses, Lok Sabha is perceived to be powerful. In the case of money bills, Rajya Sabha does not have much say. It has no control over the budget. It cannot prevent non-money bills from being passed if Lok Sabha is determined to pass it. The Council of Ministers are responsible only to the Lok Sabha and usually most of the ministers are from the Lower House. The Rajya Sabha, however, has its importance as it is a permanent house and members take part in election and impeachment of President and Vice-President, Constitutional amendment and impeachment of Supreme Court judges. New All India Services creation and extension of Parliament's legislative competence on a State subject can be extended only by its resolution. Moreover, during dissolved Lok Sabha periods, Rajya Sabha plays a crucial role.

Privileges of Parliament Members

To ensure free and fair working of the Parliament, members of both the houses have been given certain privileges. They have been given total freedom to express themselves in the house, under the rules and guidelines of the house. They cannot be questioned in any court for their utterances in Parliament. They cannot be arrested except in serious criminal or anti-national activities, during the session of the house. If the arrest is unavoidable, immediate information has to be given to the presiding officer of the concerned house. The members can publish their speeches made in the house.

Disqualification of Members

No person can be a member of both Houses of Parliament. Neither can one be a member of either House of Parliament and any State Legislature. The person has the choice to retain any seat if elected to more than one house. A member can resign or can even be disqualified from the membership of house. One can be disqualified if-

- he holds any office of profit under the Government of India or any State Government; or
- he is of unsound mind and has been declared so by a competent court; or
- he is an undischarged insolvent; or
- he has lost citizenship of India; or
- he has been disqualified by or under any law made by Parliament; or
- he has been absent from the house for more than sixty days.

A person is not deemed to hold an office of profit if he is minister either for the Union or for States.

Quorum

Either House of Parliament can hold meeting only if a minimum number of members are present. This number is called Quorum. One-tenth of the total number of members of the House constitute the Quorum. If at anytime during a meeting of a house there is a no quorum, the presiding officer has to either adjourn the house or suspend the meeting till there is a quorum.

Committee System in the Parliament

The Parliament is a big body where the actions of the members are decided more or less by party affiliation. Moreover, a large number of responsibilities have been bestowed upon the Parliament for which the time is limited. All the issues cannot be discussed threadbare, dispassionately and objectively in the Parliament. So, committees are set up, involving Parliamentarians, to cope with the legislative work. These committees can even consult experts and question officials and concerned persons. The committees are of two types — Ad-hoc or Standing. The ad-hoc committees are set up for special assignments and are wound up when the work is over. Any bill, when introduced in the Parliament, can be sent to a select committee of a house or joint committees, set up combined by both houses. The joint committees have also been set up to undertake parliamentary investigations. The prominent standing committees are:

1. **Public Accounts Committee:** It, comprising 15 Lok Sabha and 7 Rajya Sabha MPs, ascertains that the expenditure does not exceeds the grants and money has been spent for the same purpose for which it was sanctioned.

2. **Estimates Committee:** The 30 Lok Sabha members of this committee, examine the estimates of various ministries and departments and suggests alternative policies to the Government to ensure efficiency and economy in administration.
3. **Committee on Public Undertakings:** It, consisting of 15 Lok Sabha and 7 Rajya Sabha MPs, looks into the working of public undertakings, particularly their accounts, reports, efficiency and autonomy.
4. **Business Advisory Committee:** Such a committee of each house decides time and durations for legislative and other works.
5. **Committee on Private Members Bills:** It examines bills submitted to it by individual members and classifies them according to its importance.
6. **Committee on Petitions:** It examines the petitions made by the MPs and suggests remedial measures.
7. **Privileges Committee:** It safeguards the privileges of the members.
8. **Committee on Government Assurances:** It ensures that the assurances and promises made by the Government are fulfilled.
9. **Rules Committee:** It determines the procedure and the conduct of business in the house.
10. **Committee on Subordinate Legislations:** It examines the rules and regulations by various departments for which the powers of making laws has been delegated by the Parliament.

Legislative Procedures in the Parliament

Different procedures are adopted for the ordinary non-money bills and money bills. An ordinary bill can be introduced in either house of the Parliament. At the first reading, the title of the bill is read and aims of the bills are explained. At the second reading stage, general principles of the bill are discussed. At the committee stage, it is decided whether the bill has to be sent to a committee or the discussion will take place in the Parliament. Different provisions of the bill are thoroughly examined and changes suggested. At the report stage, the bill is discussed clause by clause and each clause is voted. Amendments can be moved. In the third and final reading, general discussion and voting is held. If the bill is passed by a house, it is sent to the second house where it goes through all the stages as in the first house. If the bill is approved by the second house, it is sent to the President for his signatures. However, if the two houses disagree the President calls a joint sitting and the majority view prevails. After the President's approval, the bill has to be notified for implementation.

The procedure adopted in money bill is a little different. These can be laid only in Lok Sabha and that too after the President's prior approval. After Lok Sabha's approval, bills are sent to Rajya Sabha which can

- accept the bill in toto, or
- reject the bill within 14 days, or
- return with some amendments, or
- does not approve within 14 days.

Lok Sabha can discuss the amendments suggested by Rajya Sabha but is not bound to accept them. In other three circumstances, money bill is sent to the President. There is no provision of a joint sitting in case of money bill. The money bills involve expenditure or revenue generation.

Motions in the Parliament

A. **Adjournment Motion:** A motion for adjournment is meant to draw the attention of the house to a matter of urgent public importance. Such a motion is intended to focus the attention of the house to a specific act or Commission or Omission of the Government. The motion compels the Government to act quickly in an appropriate manner, otherwise it runs the risk of losing the Confidence of the House. Adjournment motions are unusual features and restored to sparingly.

B. No Confidence or Censure Motion: A censure motion is an expression of lack of confidence in the ministry. Resort to a no-confidence motion is not made under normal circumstances. Only if the opposition feels it has a reasonable chance of defeating the Government, they press for it. Sometimes, this motion is moved to stress a very important point or score a political victory. Sometimes, no voting is done and the motion is allowed to fall through voice vote only. The motion is an important political weapon in the hand of the opposition and can lead to fall of the Government.

C. Call Attention Motion: Any member, with the permission of the chair, can move the motion for discussion on a matter of general public interest. The motion must be supported by at least ten per cent of the members. If allowed by the Speaker, discussion is held for a fixed period. The adoption of motion is no reflection on the Government as they themselves bring it to initiate the discussion.

D. Closure Motion: When the time set for a particular measure is over, although the discussion is incomplete a vote may be taken on the motion before the house after adopting the closure motion. Any member can move it and if adopted, discussion is stopped immediately and vote is taken. This process is also called "Guillotine".

Financial Procedure

Parliament has the unquestioned and unique right not only to ensure that public funds are raised only with its consent but also to exercise total control over the way in which the country's revenues are spent by the Government. The main principles governing the financial provisions of the Constitution are as follows:

(*a*) There can be no expenditure without the authority of Parliament.

(*b*) There can be no levy of tax without a law authorising it.

(*c*) All revenues received by the Union Government should form the 'Consolidated Fund of India' — the Government shall withdraw money for its expenditure from this fund alone.

(*d*) A reserve fund called 'Contingency Fund of India' is placed at the disposal of Government to meet unforeseen requirements.

(*e*) The Lok Sabha has supremacy over the Rajya Sabha in all financial matters.

(*f*) The President even cannot withhold his assent from a Money Bill passed by Parliament.

(*g*) Income and property of the Union is exempted to a certain extent from taxation by the State Governments.

(*h*) At the beginning of every financial year, the President causes to be laid before both the houses a statement of the estimated receipts and expenditure of the Government in respect of the forthcoming year. This financial statement is called the Budget.

(*i*) Among the expenditures planned, no voting takes place on certain items as their payments are guaranteed by the Constitution. These are salaries and allowances of the President, Presiding Officers of the Houses of Parliament, Judges of Supreme Court and High Courts and Comptroller and Auditor General of India and debt charges of India.

(*j*) With regard to items other than the non-votable ones, the Government submits estimates in the form of demands for grants. These are discussed and the Lok Sabha even has the powers to vote on it. After the approval of both houses of Parliament, the papers are sent for President's signatures. All the expenditures are incurred in the name of President.

State Executive

The Governor

A Governor in the State is analogous to the President in the Centre. He is the constitutional head and carries out his duties, in consultation with the Council of Ministers.

The Governor is appointed by the President on the advice of the Prime Minister for a five year term. He holds office during the pleasure of the President. His tenure can be extended by the President and he continues to be in the office till the appointment of his replacement. He can resign before the completion of his tenure. Usually, each State has a Governor but a Governor can be given additional charge of other States. By convention, Governor is usually a non-resident of the State where he is appointed. The State Government may be consulted in the appointment of a Governor.

Any person, who is a citizen of India, has completed 35 years of age and does not hold any office of profit in the State or Central Government, can become Governor of a State.

Powers and Position of the Governor

The executive powers of the State are vested in the Governor. He exercises the power directly or through officers subordinate to him. He is the executive head of the State and all actions are taken in his name. He is advised by the Council of Ministers which in turn is appointed by the Governor. The leader of the majority party in the assembly is appointed Chief Minister. Other ministers are appointed on the advise of the Chief Minister. The work is also allocated among the ministers by the Governor as per Chief Minister's recommendations. The Governor can advise or warn the ministers. He is regularly informed of the decisions taken by the Council of Ministers. The Governor appoints the Advocate General, members of State Public Service Commission and judges at the district level.

The Governor summons and prorogues legislative assemblies and councils. He has the power to dissolve the assembly. He can send messages or address both the houses of legislature. He can nominate a few members to the legislative council among the persons who are eminent in the field of science, art, literature or social service. A bill does not become law even if passed by both the houses, if it is not signed by the Governor. A bill can be accepted, rejected, sent back with recommendations or kept for the President's consideration by the Governor. If the bills, rejected or sent with recommendations, are again passed by the legislature, the Governor has to sign on them. He cannot reject the money bills. When the legislature is not in session and a law is to be made on a subject on which the State legislature has the authority to legislate, the Governor can promulgate an ordinance. The ordinance remains into force for six weeks after the convening of legislative session. If legislature accepts them, it becomes law, otherwise it becomes defunct.

As far as the financial powers are concerned, the Governor advises the Government to lay the annual statement of accounts and proposals for the next year in the assembly. Only after the assembly's approval the Government can impose taxes or incur expenditure. A supplementary budget may also be laid before the assembly for additional requirements. All the money bills are brought in the house only with the Governor's prior permission.

The Governor appoints the judges at the district level. He is consulted by the President in the appointment of Chief Justice of the State High Court. The Governor has the powers to reduce or suspend sentences or pardon anyone, who has been charged with violating a law made by the State legislature.

Though the Governor is just like a rubber stamp, in the normal circumstances, acting on the basis of State Government's recommendations, he has been vested with discretionary powers to deal with extraordinary situations. That way, he acts as a watchdog of the Central Government. He can send any bill for the President's recommendation besides sending a bill for reconsideration of the State legislature. If the administration of a Union Territory is given to the Governor as an additional charge, he need not consult the State Government.

The Governor has the special responsibilities to look after the welfare of tribal people and people living in Special Area as listed in the Constitution. The most important discretionary power of the Governor is the freedom to recommend dismissal of a Government and imposition of President's rule in the State. If the Governor feels that the administration of the State cannot be run according to the Constitution, he can recommend for the President's rule.

The discretionary powers make the Governor's post a unique and powerful one. He is not a member of the State legislature, neither elected by them nor having a stake in the State's policies. Since, he is nominated by the President and stays till the President's pleasure, he is more loyal to the Central Government. Since he is not involved in the State policies, he can give impartial advice to the State Government. At the time of President's rule, the State is administered by the Governor, on the President's behalf.

However, the Governor's position has become quite controversial recently. The State Governments have been complaining that persons are imposed as Governors. They say that some Governors have been biased, played politics and sided with the ruling party at the Centre. There have been instances when the Governor has given a report proclaiming breakdown of constitutional machinery, on political grounds. The good Centre-State relation demand an impartial Governor who has loyalty towards the Constitution only. Sarkaria Commission had recommended that politicians should not be posted as Governors and State Governments should be consulted before the appointment.

Council of Ministers

As in the Centre, there is a Council of Ministers at the State level. It is appointed by the Governor but is responsible to Vidhan Sabha, the lower house of State legislature. The leader of the majority party/group is appointed Chief Minister and other ministers are appointed on his recommendation. The Chief Minister allocates work among the ministers. He can recommend their dismissal, or can bring about changes in the portfolios of the ministers. All the ministers are individually as well as collectively responsible to Vidhan Sabha.

The Chief Minister is first among the equals. Besides appointing his other ministers and allocating work to them, he takes all the major policy decisions. He presides over the Cabinet meetings and all the ministers consult him on important matters. The Chief Minister suggests names for the posts for which the Governor makes appointments in the State. He is the Chief spokesman of the Government and is the communication link between the Government and the Governor.

State Legislature

For every State there is a legislature comprising the Governor and two houses. However, some legislatures do not have the upper house –– the legislative council. As of March 2025, Six States have a Legislative Council. They are Andhra Pradesh, Bihar, Karnataka, Maharashtra, Telangana and Uttar Pradesh. The legislative assemblies have the right to pass a resolution to abolish or create the legislative council.

It must be passed by a majority of the total membership of the assembly and a two-third majority of the members of the assembly present and voting. The resolution is then sent to the Parliament which makes law, creating or abolishing the Council.

The legislative council cannot have less than forty members and not more than one-third of the strength of the assembly. One-third of the council members are elected by an electoral college, consisting of members of municipalities, district boards and other local bodies. One-third of the council members are elected by assembly members. One-twelfth members are elected by graduates of the State who have been qualified for at least three years. One-twelfth of the members are elected by persons who have been for at least three years engaged in teaching in educational institutions, not lower in standard than that of a secondary school, in the State. The remaining number is filled through Governor's nomination.

The legislative council elections are held on the basis of proportional representation with a single transferable votes. The candidates have to be above 30 years of age, voter in any assembly constituency of the State and is not an employee of the Government. It is a permanent house, with one-third members retiring every two years. The legislative council of a State is not subject to dissolution.

The legislative assembly is the lower house and in each State, its members are directly elected by the residents of the State. Legislative Assembly (Vidhan Sabha) of a state consists of not more than 500 and not less than 60 members (Legislative Assembly of Sikkim has 32 members vide Article 371F of the Constitution) chosen by direct election from territorial constituencies in the state.

The candidate for assembly seats have to be 25 years of age, citizens of India, not disqualified by any court, have his name in the voter list and does not hold any office of profit in the Government. If a member of assembly abstains for 60 days without informing the house, he stands disqualified. If a person is elected from two assembly seats or from one assembly seat and a parliamentary seat, he can retain only one seat.

The tenure of the assembly is five years, but it can be dissolved earlier also. The Governor summons the house regularly, but not more than six months gap can be there between the last meeting of a session and the first meeting of the forthcoming session. Each assembly has a speaker and a deputy speaker who preside over the meetings. One-tenth of the total members or ten members form the quorum, without which the meeting cannot begin.

The State legislatures can make laws on subjects given in the State or Concurrent List. However, some laws have to be approved by the President while some need prior approval of the President, even before introduction in the legislature. During emergency all subjects, and, in case of Rajya Sabha passing a resolution, a particular subject comes under the Parliament's jurisdiction. The legislature passes all financial bills, without which the State Government cannot spend a single paisa. The legislature controls the executive, through no-Confidence motion, adjournment motion, rejecting the budget, proposing changes in the budget or asking questions. Among the two houses, the lower house or legislative assembly is mere powerful as it can even recommend abolition of the upper house. The State Government is also responsible to the assembly and in the field of legislations, its role is paramount.

Judicial System in India

The judicial system in India is unitary, with the Supreme Court at the apex and High Courts at the State level. Below, come, district level courts and other functionaries. At the lower level, there are separate courts to deal with criminal and civil cases. Supreme Court and High Courts, however, can deal with all cases.

The Supreme Court has 33 judges and a Chief Justice. *Ad hoc* judges may be appointed to the Supreme Court, after the President's prior approval. The President appoints the judges and the Chief Justice. Usually, the seniormost judge is appointed as the Chief Justice. Other judges are appointed, in consultation with the Chief Justice. To qualify for a Supreme Court judge's post, one has to be a citizen of India. He should have been working for at least five years regularly in one or more high courts of the country or should have been working as an advocate in a High Court for not less than ten years or should be a distinguished jurist, in the opinion of the President.

The Supreme Court judges remain in office till they attain 65 years of age. However, they can resign before the completion of the term or can be impeached and removed. To make judiciary independent from the control of the executive, the process of removing judges has been made difficult. Moreover, their salary and allowances are paid from the consolidated funds and no discussion is held in the Parliament on the conduct of the judiciary. The service conditions of the judges, cannot be changed to their disadvantage. In case of financial emergency, salaries of judges can be reduced.

A Supreme Court judge can be impeached for unconstitutional conduct or proven misbehaviour or incapacity. If both the houses of Parliament, in the same session, pass an address with majority of total membership of each house and that majority must not be less than two-third majority of the members present and voting, the President passes an order removing the judges. When the address is under consideration, the judge can present himself and defend. Since the procedure is so difficult, no judge in India has so far been impeached.

A Supreme Court judge, after retirement, resignation or removal, cannot plead or act in any court or before any authority within the territory of India.

The Supreme Court has only one seat, and that is in Delhi. It has no other branch. But a sitting can be held elsewhere, if the President approves. The Supreme Court has original and appellate jurisdiction.

Original Jurisdiction

The Supreme Court has original jurisdiction in any dispute between: *(a)* the Government of India and one or more States; or *(b)* the Government of India and any State or States on one side and one or more than one State on the other; or *(c)* between two or more States. The Supreme Court has exclusive jurisdiction in regard to questions as to constitutional validity of Central laws.

Appellate Jurisdiction

An appeal against the High Court decision can be made in the Supreme Court. These cases can be constitutional, civil, criminal or special appeals. However, Supreme Court cannot be approached against the decision of military courts.

If the High Court certifies that the case involves a substantial question of law or needs interpretation of Constitution, the case can be taken to the Supreme Court.

In the civil cases, appeal against the High Court decisions can be made if the High Court certifies that the case involves a substantial question of law and need to be decided by the Supreme Court.

An appeal in the criminal case lies to the Supreme Court if the High Court certifies it, fit for appeal. In cases, where the High Court has reversed the acquittal order of a lower court and sentenced the accused to death; or where the High Court, having withdrawn, for trial, a case from a lower court before it, has tried the accused and sentenced him to death, the Supreme Court can be approached even if the High Court does not certify.

In cases, civil or criminal, where no appeal can lie to the Supreme Court, the court may in its discretion grant special leave of appeal from any judgement, decree, sentence or order in any case made by any court or tribunal within India. This is a very wide discretion given to the Supreme Court concerning appellate cases and through this, it can ensure that no injustice is done.

Advisory Jurisdiction

The President can refer any matter of law or fact of public importance to the consideration of Supreme Court to seek its advice where it is expedient to do so. However, under Article 143 the advice is not binding upon the President. If, the advice is sought under Article 131, Supreme Court is bound to give its opinion.

Guardian of Fundamental Rights

Article 32 of the Constitution empowers Supreme Court to issue writs of various kinds for the enforcement of Fundamental Rights. This special responsibility conferred on Supreme Court makes it guardian of Fundamental Rights. Supreme Court can issue writs — *Habeas Corpus, Mandamus, Prohibition, Quo-Warranto* and *Certiorari* to protect Fundamental Rights.

Supreme Court can undertake review of its own decisions and correct the mistakes or change the decisions.

Supreme Court acts as a guardian of the Constitution. It has the powers of judicial review whereby it can review any law made by the Parliament or any State legislature to check that these laws do not contravene the Constitution. If they do so, Supreme Court can declare them null and void.

Supreme Court also acts as a court of record. Its decisions are published and are referred to in future cases. It also has the power to punish persons who are guilty of its contempt.

High Courts in the States

The Constitution provides for a High Court for every State. However, the Parliament can provide for one High Court for two or more States. The Parliament can provide for a separate High Court for a Union Territory or include a Union Territory in the jurisdiction of a High Court of a State.

Each High Court has a Chief Justice and several judges whose number is decided by the President. The State Governor is consulted in their appointment. In the appointment of other judges, Chief Justice of the High Court is also consulted. The judges hold office upto the age of 62. The salaries and allowances of the judges once fixed cannot be changed to their disadvantage except in financial emergency. Their salaries are charged to the consolidated fund of India.

The Government can appoint additional and acting judges, if required. The President has the powers to transfer a judge from one High Court to the other. This provision in the Constitution was made to ensure impartiality and unbiasedness by the judges. However, these transfers cannot be used as punishments. Effective consultation with the Chief Justice of Supreme Court is essential before ordering the transfer.

The qualifications required for judges of a High Court are: *(1)* He must be a citizen of India; *(2)* He must have held a judicial office in India, or must have practised as an advocate of a High Court for at least 10 years. A High Court judge can resign before the retirement age of 62 years or can be promoted to Supreme Court. He can also be removed from his office by the President on an address presented to him by the Parliament after having passed it in each house by a majority of its total membership as well as by two-thirds of those present and voting. The only ground on which such an address can be passed by the Parliament is either proven misbehaviour or incapacity.

Jurisdiction

Ordinarily, the jurisdiction of a High Court of a State or of a Union Territory is coterminus with the territorial limits of that State or Union Territory. However, the Parliament has powers to extend the jurisdiction of one High Court to an adjoining State or Union Territory. Usually, High Courts are courts of appeal and their area of original jurisdiction is limited. In the presidency towns of Kolkata, Mumbai and Chennai, High Courts had some original jurisdiction, *e.g.*, they could hear the cases, involving Christians and Parsis. After the independence also, these High Courts have retained these powers. Cases, involving marriage laws, divorce, inheritance or contempt of High Court can be directly taken to the High Court.

Otherwise, High Courts have wide powers in appeal cases. In the criminal cases, an appeal against the Session Court judgement can be made in a High Court. In civil cases, an appeal can go to the High Court if the amount involved in the case exceeds the limits. In the economic offences, appeals against tribunal can be made in the High Courts. High Courts have power to issue writs, for the enforcement of fundamental rights and other purposes. High Courts have the power to transfer cases either to themselves or from one court to another. If a case involves interpretation of Constitution, High Court can transfer the case to itself. High Court acts as a court of record. Its decisions are published and can be referred to. It can sentence anyone for the contempt of Court.

High Courts have superintendence over all courts and tribunals throughout the territories in relation to which it exercises jurisdiction except military courts. This is a wide power because it includes all courts or tribunals whether an appeal against its decision lies to the High Court or not. High Courts can intervene and revise the decisions where it feels gross injustice or non-exercise or abuse of jurisdiction. High Courts have administrative control over the subordinate judiciary in the State which includes district judges, judges of city civil courts as well as Metropolitan magistrates and members of the judicial service of the State. This control is exercised in the manner of appointments, posting, promotion and administrative controls. They can make and issue general rules and prescribe forms for regulating the practice and proceedings of lower courts. They can transfer case from the court to the other.

Independence of Judiciary

The Supreme Court and High Courts are the pillars of our democratic set up. It is very essential that they work without any fear or favour. Therefore, their postings are done by the President and is for a fixed tenure. They cannot be easily removed from their posts. Their salaries and allowances cannot be ordinarily reduced and is debited to the consolidated fund of India for which there is no voting. Any law, limiting the powers of High Court, can be referred to the President by the Governor for his advice. Supreme Court judges cannot practice after retirement while High Court judges cannot practice in the Courts where they have worked.

Procedure for Constitutional Amendment

Indian freedom fighters, while framing the Constitution, realised that the basic document of the nation must reflect the spirit and character of the country. It must change with the changing time and should be able to cope up with changing environment. But they did not relish the Constitution to be a loosely bound set of rules which could be broken very easily. To amalgam the freedom to change with the rigidity of sticking to basic guidelines, they provided different procedures for Constitutional amendment. Today, we have made more than 100 amendments yet the basic features are still intact.

Some provisions of the Constitution can be changed by the simple majority of the Parliament. These include creation of new states, change of name of states and change in the state boundaries. But a legislation to this effect can only be introduced with the President's approval and the President can consult the concerned states. The creation or abolition of legislative council in a state can be done by passing a legislation in the Parliament by a simple majority. Parliament is empowered to pass an amendment bill, regarding administration of union territories. All these amendments, which are approved by Parliament's simple majority, are usually not listed in the Constitutional amendment.

The Constitutional amendment bills related to the method of election of the President, the Vice-President's election, representation of states in the Parliament, jurisdiction of the Supreme Court and High Courts, distribution of executive and legislative powers between the Union and states, method of the constitutional amendment and change in the list given in the seventh schedule, have to be amended in a special way. The bills pertaining to them have to be passed by two-third majority by each house of the Parliament and subsequently approved by the legislatures of not less than half of the states' legislatures.

All other provisions of the Constitution except those mentioned above can be amended if a bill to that effect is passed by each house of the Parliament by two-third majority of the members present and voting which should not be less than the majority of all the members of the house. If such a bill is not passed by either house the bill falls as there is no provision of joint sitting to pass the constitutional amendment bill.

The Constitutional amendment bills, after being passed by the Parliament and state legislatures, if necessary, are presented to the President for his assent. The President has no choice but to give assent to the Constitutional amendment bill.

Amendments to Constitution

1. **The constitution (First Amendment) Act, 1950:** This amendment aimed to impose restrictions on the right to freedom of expression and the right to practise or to carry out any trade or business contained in Article 19. These restrictions were concerned with public order, friendly relationships with foreign States or incitement to an offence in relation to the right of freedom of speech. This amendment also empowered the State to prescribe professional or technical qualifications or conduct of any trade, business, industry or service by the State in relation to the right to carry on any trade or business. The State was also allowed to impose restrictions on the rights of the citizens to carry

on any trade, business, industry or service. Two new Articles (31A and 31B) and the Ninth Schedule were added in this amendment.

2. **The Constitution (Second Amendment) Act, 1952:** This amendment aimed at the readjustment of the scale and representation for election to the Lok Sabha.
3. **The Constitution (Third Amendment) Act, 1954:** Substituted Entry 33 of List III (*i.e.*, the concurrent List) of the Seventh Schedule to make it correspond to Article 369.
4. **The Constitution (Fourth Amendment) Act, 1955:** Under this amendment, Article 31(2) of the constitution was amended to restate the power of the State of compulsory acquisition and requisition of private property. Article 31A was also amended in order to abolish *Zamindaris,* effect planning of urban and rural areas and assume complete control over the mineral and oil resources of the country. Six Acts were included in the Ninth Schedule. Article 305 was amended to save some laws which gave monopolies to the State.
5. **The Constitution (Fifth Amendment) Act, 1955:** It changed Article 3 so that the President was empowered to specify a time limit for state legislatures to convey their views on central laws which made impact upon areas and boundaries of the states.
6. **The Constitution (Sixth Amendment) Act, 1956:** This amendment altered Article 269 and Article 286 which were related to sales taxes and purchase taxes during the interstate trading activities. An entry (92A) was added to the Union List.
7. **The Constitution (Seventh Amendment) Act, 1956:** Under this amendment, the existing states were changed to have a two-fold classification of States and UTs. Further, the House of the People was formed and readjustment was accepted after every census. It also provided the provisions for establishment of new High Courts and High Court Judges etc.
8. **The Constitution (Eighth Amendment) Act, 1960:** Article 334 was amended with a view to extend the period of reservation of seats of SCs, STs and the reservation of Anglo-Indians by nomination in the Parliament and in the State Legislatures for 10 years.
9. **The Constitution (Ninth Amendment) Act, 1960:** This amendment was done in order to transfer some territories to Pakistan as this was not possible under Article 3.
10. **The Constitution (Tenth Amendment) Act, 1961:** It changed the Article 240 and the First Schedule to include Dadra and Nagar Haveli as a UT.
11. **The Constitution (Eleventh Amendment) Act, 1961:** It aimed at amending Article 66 and Article 71 under the aegis of which the election of the President or the Vice-President could not be challenged on the ground of any vacancy in the appropriate electoral college.
12. **The Constitution (Twelfth Amendment) Act, 1962:** Article 240 was amended and as a consequence Goa, Daman and Diu was included in Indian Union as a UT.
13. **The Constitution (Thirteenth Amendment) Act, 1962:** A new Article 371A was added to make provisions for Nagaland in accordance with an agreement between Government of India and Naga People's Convention.
14. **The Constitutional (Fourteen Amendment) Act, 1962:** Pondicherry was included in the First Schedule as a UT. Further legislatures were created by the Parliamentary law for Himachal Pradesh, Manipur, Tripura, Goa, Daman and Diu and Pondicherry.
15. **The Constitution (Fifteenth Amendment) Act, 1963:** It aimed for increasing the retirement age of the High Court Judges and for provision of compensatory allowances to the Judges who were transferred from one High Court to another. Further, it provided for the appointment of retired Judges act as the Judges of High Court. Article 226 was amended to empower the High Court so that it could issue direction, orders or writs to a

government authority. The Act also allowed one of the members of the Service Commissions to exercise the powers of the Chairman if the latter was absent.

16. **The Constitution (Sixteenth Amendment) Act, 1963:** Article 19 was amended by this Act to impose more restrictions on the rights to freedom of speech and expression, to assemble peacefully and to form associations in the interest of national integrity. The oath of affirmation to be subscribed by the candidate for Parliamentary and state legislature elections was modified and it was added that the Candidates would uphold the integrity of the nation.

17. **The Constitution (Seventeenth Amendment) Act, 1964:** Article 31A was amended again to prohibit the acquisition of land under personal a cultivation unless the market value of the land is paid as compensation. The definition of 'estate' in that Article was enlarged. The Ninth Schedule was amended to include 44 more Acts.

18. **The Constitution (Eighteenth Amendment Act), 1966:** Article 3 was amended by this Act to specify that 'State' would include a UT as well. Further, the amendment asserted that the power to form a new state under this article includes a power to form a new state or a UT by uniting a part of a state or a UT to another State or UT.

19. **The Constitution (Nineteenth Amendment) Act, 1966:** Article 324 was amended to effect a change as a result of decision to abolish Election Tribunals and let the election petitions be heard by High Courts.

20. **The Constitution (Twentieth Amendment) Act, 1966:** A new Article 233A was added. The appointments made by the Governor were validated.

21. **The Constitution (Twenty-first Amendment) Act, 1967:** Sindhi language was included in the Eighth Schedule.

22. **The Constitution (Twenty-second Amendment) Act, 1969:** Formation of Meghalaya within the state of Assam was facilitated.

23. **The Constitution (Twenty-third Amendment) Act, 1969:** Article 334 was amended in order to safeguard the reservation of seats of SCs and STs and Anglo-Indians in Parliament and the state legislatures, for a period of another 10 years.

24. **The Constitution (Twenty-fourth Amendment) Act, 1971:** Article 13 and Article 368 were amended to remove doubts regarding the power of Parliament to amend the Constitution including the Fundamental Rights.

25. **The Constitution (Twenty-fifth Amendment) Act, 1971:** It amended Article 31 again in the wake of bank nationalization in the country. The word 'Compensation' was replaced with the word 'amount'.

26. **The Constitution (Twenty-sixth Amendment) Act, 1971:** The privy and privileges of the former rulers of Indian States were abolished.

27. **The Constitution (Twenty-seventh) Amendment Act, 1971:** This amendment was passed to provide for some matters which resulted due to reorganization of north-eastern states. A new Article 239B was inserted which allowed the administrators of some UTs to promulgate the Ordinances.

28. **The Constitution (Twenty-eighth Amendment) Act, 1972:** The special privileges of members of Indian Civil Services in the matters of leave, pension and their rights regarding disciplinary matters were abolished.

29. **The Constitution (Twenty-ninth Amendment) Act, 1972:** The Ninth Schedule was amended to include to acts of Kerala regarding land reforms.

30. **The Constitution (Thirtieth Amendment) Act, 1972:** A valuation test of Rs. 20,000 under article 133 was removed and instead of the same, an appeal to the Supreme Court in civil proceedings was allowed to be provided only on a certificate issued by a High Court (that the matter deserves the scrutiny of the Supreme Court).

31. **The Constitution (Thirty-first Amendment) Act, 1973:** The upper limit of representation of states was raised from 500 to 525. The upper limit for representation of the UTs was reduced from 25 to 20.
32. **The Constitution (Thirty-second Amendment) Act, 1973:** Constitutional authority was granted for granting equal opportunities to different areas of Andhra Pradesh. An Administrative Tribunal was also allowed to be constituted which had the Jurisdiction to deal with the grievances relating to public services. The parliament was also empowered to legislate for establishment of a central university in the State.
33. **The Constitution (Thirty-third Amendment) Act, 1974:** Articles 101 and 190 were amended to streamline the procedure for resignation of MPs and State legislatures.
34. **The Constitution (Thirty-fourth Amendment) Act, 1974:** Twenty more land tenure and land reforms laws enacted by various state legislatures were included in the Ninth Schedule under this amendment.
35. **The Constitution (Thirty-fifth Amendment) Act, 1974:** A new Article 2A was added and Sikkim was declared an associate of the Indian Union. Article 80 and Article 81 were amended and a new Schedule (Tenth Schedule) was added which laid down terms for association of the Sikkim with the Union.
36. **The Constitution (Thirty-sixth Amendment) Act, 1975:** Sikkim was made a full-fledged state of Indian Union and it was included in the First Schedule. Sikkim was allotted one seat in the council of States and one seat in the House of the People. Article 2A and the Tenth Schedule (inserted under Thirty-fifth Amendment) were deleted. Article 80 and Article 81 were suitably amended due to these changes.
37. **The Constitution (Thirty-seventh Amendment) Act, 1975:** The UT of Arunachal Pradesh was provided with a legislative assembly. Article 240 was amended under which it was provided that the power of the President to make regulations for the UT of Arunachal Pradesh may be exercised only when the assembly is either dissolved or its functions remain suspended.
38. **The Constitution (Thirty-eighth Amendment) Act, 1975:** This act led to the amendment of Article 123, Article 213 and Article 352 which stated that the satisfaction of President or of Governor contained in these Articles would be called in question in any court of law.
39. **The Constitution (Thirty-ninth Amendment) Act, 1975:** According to this amendment, the disputes relating to the election of President, Vice-President, PM and Speaker are to be determine by such authority as may be determined by Parliamentary law. Some central enactments were also included in the Ninth Schedule.
40. **The Constitution (Fortieth Amendment) Act, 1976:** This amendment gave all the powers to the Union with respect to all mines, minerals and items of value lying in the ocean within the territorial waters or on the continental shelf or within the exclusive economic zone of India. The Act also stated that the limits of territories waters, continental shelf, exclusive economic zone and the maritime zones of India shall be as specified from time to time or under any law made by Parliament. Further, some Acts were added to the Ninth Schedule.
41. **The Constitution (Forty-first Amendment) Act, 1976:** Article 316 was amended to raise the retirement age of the members of Public Service Commissions and Joint Public Service Commissions from 60 years to 62 years.
42. **The Constitution (Forty-second Amendment) Act, 1976:** This amendment was done in accordance with the recommendations of Swaran Singh Committee and included a number of amendments. These amendments included the clear delineation of socialistic ideals, secularism and national integrity.

Further, Directive Principles were made more comprehensive and were given precedence over the Fundamental Rights. A new chapter on Fundamental Duties of the citizens was added. Special provisions were made for dealing with anti-national activities. For declaring any law to be constitutionally invalid, the requirements of a minimum number of Judges were also laid down. Further, Administrative and other Tribunals were constituted for preserving the jurisdiction of Supreme Court Under Article 136. Amendments were also made for reducing arrears in High Courts, for securing speedy disposal of service matters, for revenue issues and other vital issues related to socio-economic development (Tribunals were created for ensuring these developments in the country). Article 226 was modified.

43. **The Constitution (Forty-third Amendment) Act, 1977:** It provided for the restoration of the Jurisdiction of the Supreme Court and High Courts, curtailed by the enactment of the Constitution (Forty-second Amendment) Act, 1976. Therefore, Article 32A, Article 131A, Article 144A, Article 226A and Article 228A were deleted by this amendment. It also deleted Article 31D which gave special powers to Parliament to enact some laws in connection with anti-national activities.

44. **The Constitution (Forty-fourth Amendment) Act, 1978:** The right to property was deleted as Fundamental Right and was made a legal right. Article 352 was amended to provide "armed rebellion" as one of the circumstance for declaration of emergency. The right to personal liberty (as contained in Articles 21 and Article 22) was strengthened by the provision that a law for preventive detention cannot authorize the detention for a period longer than two months unless an Advisory Board has reported that there is a sufficient cause for such a detention. Further, the amendment confirmed that the Chairman of the Advisory Board shall be a serving Judge of the appropriate High Court and that the Board shall be constituted in accordance with the recommendations of the Chief Justice of that High Court. Through this amendment, Article 132 and Article 134 were amended and a new Article 134A was inserted. Some amendments were made for removing or correcting the distortions which had crept into the constitution due to amendments effected during internal emergency.

45. **The Constitution (Forty-fifth Amendment) Act, 1980:** This amendment was due to safeguard the interests of SCs, STs and Anglo-Indians in Parliament and the State Assemblies for another 10 years.

46. **The Constitution (Forty-sixth Amendment) Act, 1982:** Article 269 was amended so that the tax levied on the consignment of goods during the inter-state trade or commerce could be assigned to the states. Further, amendment was done to enable the Parliament to formulate the principle for determining when a consignment of goods takes place in the course of inter-state trade or commerce. A new entry 92B was added in the Union List which ensured the levy of tax on the consignment of goods where such a consignment took place in the course of inter-state trade or commerce. Further, Clause (3) of Article 286 was amended for specifying conditions of levy rates, taxes on goods transfer involved in the execution of a works contract, delivery of goods on hire-purchase or payment system through instalment etc.

    Further, Article 366 was amended and a definition of "tax on the sale or purchase of goods" to include the transfer for consideration of controlled commodities, transfer of property in goods involved in the execution of a works contract, delivery of goods on hire-purchase or any system of payment by instalments etc.

47. **The Constitution (Forty-seventh Amendment) Act, 1984:** Some land reforms Acts were included in the Ninth Schedule.

48. **The Constitution (Forty-eighth Amendment) Act, 1984:** Article 356 was amended keeping in mind the situation in Punjab.

49. **The Constitution (Forty-ninth Amendment) Act, 1984:** The amendment gave a constitutional security to the autonomous District Council functioning in the State.

50. **The Constitution (Fiftieth Amendment) Act, 1984:** By Article 33, Parliament can enact laws for determining to what extent any of the rights conferred by Part III of the Constitution shall (In their application to members of Armed forces or the Forces charged with the maintenance of public order), be restricted or abrogated so that they could discharge their duties.

51. **The Constitution (Fifty-first Amendment) Act, 1984:** Article 330 has been amended and seats for the STs in Meghalaya, Nagaland, Arunachal Pradesh and Mizoram have been ensured. Further, Article 332 has been amended to provide similar reservation in the Legislative Assemblies of Nagaland and Meghalaya for reservation of the seats of tribals.

52. **The Constitution (Fifty-second Amendment) Act, 1985:** This amendment states that a MP or a State Legislature, who defects or is expelled from the party which set him up as a candidate (or an independent member of the house), joins a political party after the expiry of SIX months from the date on which he takes seat in the House, shall be disqualified to remain a member of the House.

53. **The Constitution (Fifty-third Amendment) Act, 1986:** The Memorandum of Settlement of Mizoram was given effect (this memorandum was signed on June 30, 1986). For this purpose, a new Article 371G was inserted *Inter alia* preventing application of any Act of Parliament in Mizoram with respect of religions or social practices of Mizos, their civil and criminal practices and laws regarding land transfers (unless a resolution was passed in the Legislative Assembly to this effect). The new Article make the minimum number of members of Legislative Assembly as 40.

54. **The Constitution (Fifty-fourth Amendment) Act, 1986:** The salary of Chief Justice of India was increased to Rs. 10,000 per month. Similarly, the salaries of Judges of Supreme Court, Chief Justice of High Court, Judges of High Court were increased to Rs. 9,000 per month, Rs. 9,000 per month and Rs. 8,000 per month respectively. This Act also amended Part D of the Second Schedule and made enabling provisions in Articles 125 and Article 221 for changes in the salaries of Judges in future through a law of Parliament.

55. **The Constitution (Fifty-fifth Amendment) Act, 1986:** The proposal to give statehood to Arunachal Pradesh was given effect. A new Article 371H was added that the governor shall discharge his functions in consultation with the Council of Ministers. Further, the Act amended the minimum seats of the Assembly to be thirty in number.

56. **The Constitution (Fifty-sixth Amendment) Act, 1987:** The UT of Goa Converted into Goa state through this amendment whereas Daman and Diu were organized under a new UT. The number of members of Goa Legislative Assembly was fixed at 40 and two members of the UT of Daman and Diu were excluded from this Assembly.

57. **The Constitution (Fifty-seventh Amendment) Act, 1987:** It was amended to provide reservation of seats in the House of the People for STs in the States of Nagaland, Meghalaya, Mizoram and Arunachal Pradesh. Article 330 and Article 332 were amended for reservation of seats for STs in Legislative Assemblies of Nagaland and Meghalaya.

58. **The Constitution (Fifty-eighth Amendment) Act, 1987:** The Constitution was amended to empower the President to publish the translation of Constitution of India in Hindi with modifications which may be necessary (including the translation of the Amendments).

59. **The Constitution (Fifty-ninth Amendment) Act, 1988:** It amends Article 365 (5) of the Constitution so as to facilitate the extension of a Presidential Proclamation issued under Clause (1) of Article 356 beyond a period of

one year (if necessary upto a period of three years), as permissible under Clause (4) of Article 356 with respect to Punjab.

60. The Constitution (Sixtieth Amendment) Act, 1988: This Act amends clause (2) of Article 276 to increase the ceiling of taxes on professions, trades, callings and employment from Rs. 250 pm to Rs. 2,500 pm.

61. The Constitution (Sixty-first Amendment) Act, 1989: It reduces the voting age from 21 years to 18 years and amends Article 326 to this effect.

62. The Constitution (Sixty-Second Amendment) Act, 1989: Article 334 continues the reservation of Seats for SCs, STs and anglo-Indian Community by nomination in the Lok Sabha and in the Legislative Assemblies for a further period of 10 years.

63. The Constitution (Sixty-third Amendment) Act, 1989: The Clause (5) of Article 356 and Article 359 A of the constitution were omitted which were enacted earlier in March, 1988 through Fifty-ninth Amendment. The proclamation of emergency in Punjab was thus no longer deemed necessary.

64. The Constitution (Sixty-fourth Amendment) Act, 1990: It amends Clause (4) and Clause (5) of Article 356 for facilitating the extension of the proclamation issued under the Clause (1) of Article 356 on May 11, 1987, upto a period of three years and six months in relation to the state of Punjab.

65. The Constitution (Sixty-fifth Amendment) Act, 1990: Article 338 provides for a special officer for SCs and STs to investigate into the matters related to safeguards provided for them. This officer reports to the President. This Article has been amended for the Constitution of a National Commission for SCs and STs comprising a chairperson, Vice Chair person and five other members to be appointed by the President. The Article delineates the powers of the Commission and states that its reports should be presented to the Parliament and to the Legislatures of the states.

66. The Constitution (Sixty-sixth Amendment) Act, 1990: This Act protects 55 State Acts relating to land reforms and ceiling an agricultural land holdings enacted by states of Andhra Pradesh, Bihar, Gujarat, Himachal Pradesh, Karnataka, Kerala, Madhya Pradesh, Maharashtra, Orissa, Rajasthan, Tamil Nadu, Uttar Pradesh, West Bengal and the administration of Pondicherry (UT), from challenge in courts, by including them in the Ninth Schedule.

67. The Constitution (Sixty-seventh Amendment) Act, 1990: The three year period in the case of proclamation issued on May 11, 1987, with respect to the State of Punjab was extended to three years and Six months by the Constitution (Sixty-fourth Amendment) Act, 1990. This Act also amends Clause (4) of Article 356 so as to extend the period upto a period of four years.

68. The Constitution (Sixty-eighth Amendment) Act, 1991: The three year period in the case of proclamation issued on May 17, 1987, with respect to the State of Punjab was further increase upto a total period of five years and Clause (4) of Article 356 was modified to this effect.

69. The Constitution (Sixty-ninth Amendment) Act, 1991: A committee was set up which gave the recommendations that Delhi should be retained as a UT and may be provided with a Legislative Assembly and a Council of Ministers. The committee also recommended that Delhi should be accorded the Status of UT. Sixty-ninth amendment was passed to give effect to these aforementioned recommendations.

70. The Constitution (Seventieth Amendment) Act, 1992: An explanation was inserted in Article 54 to provide that reference to 'State' in Article 54 and Article 55 would include the National Capital Territory of Delhi and Pondicherry (UT) for constituting the electoral college for the election of the President.

The provisions of Article 239A would allow the members of Legislative Assembly of Pondicherry to cast their votes in the process for election of the President. Similarly Article 239AA provides similar powers to the Legislatures of Delhi.

71. **The Constitution (Seventy-first Amendment) Act, 1992:** Konkani, Manipuri and Nepali languages were added in the Eighth Schedule.

72. **The Constitution (Seventy-second Amendment) Act, 1992:** A Memorandum of Settlement was signed by the Government of India with Tripura National Volunteers on August 12, 1988 for restoring peace in Tripura. In order to implement this Memorandum, Article 332 was amended and temporary provision for the determination of the number of seats for STs in the State Assembly of Tripura until the readjustment of the Seats is made in 2000 AD under Article 170.

73. **The Constitution (Seventy-third Amendment) Act, 1993:** Article 40 is related to the organization of Panchayats. A new Part IX relating to the Panchayats has been inserted in the Constitution to provide for, among other things, *Gram Sabha* in a village or in a group of villages, constitution of Panchayats at village and other levels direct elections to all the seats in Panchayats at the village and the intermediate level; reservation of seats of SCs and STs in proportion to their population for the membership of Panchayats and offices of Chair persons in Panchayats at each level; reservation of not less than one-third of seats for women; fixing tenure of five years for Panchayats and holding elections within a period of six months in the event of suppression of any Panchayat.

74. **The Constitution (Seventy-fourth Amendment) Act, 1993:** A new Part IX - A relating to Municipalities has been incorporated to provide for, among other things, constitution of Nagar Panchayats, Municipal Councils and Municipal Corporations.

75. **The Constitution (Seventy-fifth Amendment) Act, 1994:** This Act amends Article 323 B in Part XIV-A of the Constitution to give timely relief to the rent litigants by providing for setting up of state-level Rent Tribunals in order to reduce the tiers of appeals and to exclude the Jurisdiction of all courts, except that of Supreme Court, under Article 136 of the Constitution.

76. **The Constitution (Seventy-sixth Amendment) Act, 1994:** The Tamil Nadu government enacted a legislation known as Tamil Nadu Backward Classes, Scheduled Castes and Scheduled Tribes Bill, 1993 and send it to Government of India for consideration of the President in terms of Article 31-C of the Constitution. The President gave his assent to the Bill. As a corollary to this decision, it was necessary that the Tamil Nadu Act 45 of 1994 was brought within the purview of Ninth Schedule so that it could be protected under Article 31B of the Constitution. This Act amends the Constitution to amend the aforementioned objectives.

77. **The Constitution (Seventy-seventh Amendment) Act, 1995:** For protecting the interests of SCs and STs, the government decided to continue the existing policy of reservation in promotion for the SCs and STs. Article 16 was therefore, amended by inserting a new clause (MA) in the said Article to provide for reservation for promotion for the SCs and STs. This act seeks to achieve the aforementioned objective.

78. **The Constitution (Seventy-eighth Amendment) Act, 1995:** The inclusion of land reform laws in the Ninth Schedule was effected so that they were not challenged before the courts. Further, since the amendment to Acts which are already placed in the Ninth Schedule are not automatically immunized from legal challenge, a number of amending Acts along with a few principal Acts have been included in the Ninth Schedule so as to ensure that implementation of these Acts is not adversely affected by litigation.

79. The Constitution (Seventy-ninth Amendment) Act, 1999: Extends the reservations for SC/ST in the House of people and in the Legislative Assemblies of the states as also nomination of 2 Anglo-Indians to Lok Sabha up to 2010.

80. The Constitution (Eightieth Amendment) Act, 2000: Relates to the tenth finance commission, an alternative scheme for sharing taxes between the union and the states.

81. The Constitution (Eighty-first Amend-ment) Act, 2000: It provides that the unfilled vacancies of a year reserved for SC/ST kept for being filled up in a year as per Article 16, shall be considered separately for filling vacancies in the succeeding year and the previous list will not be considered for filling the 50% quota of the respective year.

82. The Constitution (Eighty-second Amendment) Act, 2000: Provides that states can make any provisions in favour of the members of the Scheduled Castes and Scheduled Tribes for relaxation in qualifying marks in any examination or lowering the standards of evaluation for reservation in matters of promotion to any class of services in connection with affairs of the union or of a state.

83. The Constitution (Eighty-third Amendment) Act, 2000: The Act emended Article 243M of the Constitution to provide that no reservation in Panchayats need be made in favour of the Scheduled Castes in Arunachal Pradesh wholly inhabited by tribal population.

84. The Constitution (Eighty-fourth Amendment) Act, 2001: The Act amended Article 82 and 170(3) to read just the territorial constituencies in the States, without altering the number of seats allotted to each State in House of People and Assemblies, including the SC and ST constituencies 1991.

85. The Constitution (Eighty-fifth Amendment) Act, 2001: Provides consequential seniority in the case of promotion by virtue of rule of reservation for the government servants belonging to the Scheduled Castes and Scheduled Tribes.

86. The Constitution (Eighty-sixth Amendment) Act, 2002: It provides for (i) insertion of a new article 21A that the State shall provide free and compulsory education to all children of the age of six to fourteen years in such manner as the State may, by law determine.

87. The Constitution (Eighty-seventh Amendment) Act, 2003: In Article 81 of the Constitution, in clause (3), in the proviso, in clause (*ii*), for the figures '1991', the figures '2001' shall be substituted. In Article 170 of the Constitution, in the third proviso, in clause (*ii*), for the figures '1991', the figures '2001' shall be substituted.

88. The Constitution (Eighty-eight Amendment) Act, 2003: Relates to the taxes on services levied by the union government.

89. The Constitution (Eighty-ninth Amendment) Act, 2003: It provides for the amendment of Article 338 and insertion of a new article 338A which provides that there shall be a National commission for ST.

90. The Constitution (Ninety Amendment) Act, 2003: In Article 332 of the Constitution, in clause (6), the following proviso shall be inserted, namely: "Provided that for elections to the Legislative Assembly of the State of Assam, the representation of the Scheduled Tribes and non-Scheduled Tribes in the Constituencies included in the Bodoland Territorial Areas District, so notified, and existing prior to the constitution of the Bodoland Territorial Areas District, shall be maintained".

91. The Constitution (Ninety-first Amendment) Act, 2003: The numbers of council of ministers is limited by this amendment act. The number shall not exceed fifteen per cent.

92. The Constitution (Ninety-second Amendment) Act, 2003: Provided for the Amendment of Eighth Schedule by adding four new regional languages (Bodo, Maithili, Santhali and Dogri), thus extending the list to 22 languages.

93. The Constitution (Ninety-third Amendment) Act, 2006: Relates to reservation of Scheduled

Castes, Scheduled Tribes and other socially and educationally backward classes in higher and professional education.

94. **The Constitution (Ninety-fourth Amendment) Act, 2006:** To provide for a Minister of Tribal Welfare in newly created Jharkhand and Chhattisgarh.

95. **The Constitution (Ninety-fifth Amendment) Act, 2010:** In Article 334, Extended the reservation of the Seats for SCs and STs in the Lok Sabha and State Assemblies from Sixty years to Seventy years.

96. **The Constitution (Ninety-sixth Amendment) Act, 2011:** Substituted 'Odia' for 'Oriya'.

97. **The Constitution (Ninety-seventh Amendment) Act, 2011:** provided for the Co-operative Societies in Part IX B of the Constitution of India.

98. **The Constitution (Ninety-eighth Amendment) Act, 2012:** Provides for special provisions for the Hyderabad-Karnataka region of the State of Karnataka.

99. **The Constitution (Ninety-nine Amendment) Act, 2015:** It provides for formation of a National Judicial Appointment Commission.

100. **The Constitution (Hundred Amendment) Act, 2015:** It provides for amending First Schedule, that deals with acquisition of certain territories of Bangladesh following agreement between India and Bangladesh.

101. **The Constitution (Hundred-first Amendment) Act, 2017:** The Constitutional 101st Amendment Act, 2016, contains the provisions necessary for the implementation of GST Regime. The amendment Act contains 20 amendments. The important changes made in constitution (new articles/amended articles) via this law are Article 246 (A), Article 269A, and Article 279-A.

102. **The Constitution (One Hundred and Second Amendment) Act, 2018:** The Act provided constitutional status to be the National Commission for Backward Classes (NCBC).

103. **The Constitution (One Hundred and Third Amendment) Act, 2019:** The Act introduced ten per cent reservation for economically weaker sections (EWS) from the upper castes of the society in central government jobs as well as admission in central government-run and private educational institutions.

104. **The Constitution (One Hundred and Fourth Amendment) Act, 2019:** This Act ceased the reservation of seats for Anglo-Indians in the Lok Sabha and State Legislative assemblies and extended reservations for SCs and STs for up to ten years.

105. **The Constitution (One Hundred and Fifth Amendment) Act, 2021:** This Act restores the power of State Governments to identify and specify Socially and Economically Backward Classes (SEBCs).

106. **The Constitution (One Hundred and Sixth Amendment) Act, 2023:** The Act provides 33 per cent reservation to women in the Lok Sabha and State Assemblies.

Schedules to the Constitution

Our Constitution originally contained ten schedules which were given towards the end and contained several details, necessary for the proper implementation. Subsequently, two more were added, taking the total to twelve.

- **First Schedule:** It contains list of the States and the Union Territories that comprise the union of India.

States/UTs

1. Andhra Pradesh	12. Manipur	27. Uttarakhand
	13. Meghalaya	28. Jharkhand
2. Arunachal Pradesh	14. Maharashtra	29. Jammu & Kashmir
	15. Mizoram	
3. Assam	16. Nagaland	30. Andaman & Nicobar Islands
4. Bihar	17. Odisha	
5. Goa	18. Punjab	31. Chandigarh
6. Gujarat	19. Rajasthan	32. Dadra and Nagar Haveli and Daman and Diu
7. Haryana	20. Sikkim	
8. Himachal Pradesh	21. Tamil Nadu	
	22. Telangana	
9. Kerala	23. Tripura	33. Delhi
10. Karnataka	24. Uttar Pradesh	34. Lakshdweep
11. Madhya Pradesh	25. West Bengal	35. Puducherry
	26. Chhattisgarh	36. Ladakh

- **Second Schedule:** It prescribes the salaries payable to the President, Governors, Chief Justice of the Supreme Court, other judges, judges of High Courts, the Comptroller and Auditor-General, etc.
- **Third Schedule:** It contains the forms of oaths and attestations which various functionaries have to take before being sworn in.
- **Fourth Schedule:** It lists the allocation of seats in the Rajya Sabha to various states.
- **Fifth Schedule:** It contains provisions as to the administration and control of scheduled areas and scheduled tribes.
- **Sixth Schedule:** It contains provisions as to the administration of tribal areas in Assam, Meghalaya, Tripura, Mizoram and Arunachal Pradesh.
- **Seventh Schedule:** It provides for the distribution of subjects between the Centre and States. The centre has more important subjects and the Union list contains 100 subjects. The State list has less important 61 subjects. The concurrent list has 52 subjects on which the centre as well as states can make law.
- **Eighth Schedule:** It contains the list of national languages. The original list had Assamese, Bengali, Gujarati, Hindi, Kannada, Kashmiri, Malayalam, Marathi, Odia, Punjabi, Sanskrit, Tamil, Telugu and Urdu languages. Sindhi, Manipuri, Nepali, Konkani, Bodo, Maithili, Santhali and Dogri were added subsequently.
- **Ninth Schedule:** This list was not there in the original Constitution and was subsequently added in 1951. It contains acquisition laws under which property can be acquired. These laws, made by the centre or states, cannot be declared invalid on the ground of inconsistency with any of the Fundamental Rights. The courts cannot intervene in these laws.
- **Tenth Schedule:** It was added in 1985. It contains provisions as to disqualification of MPs and MLAs on ground of defection. It recognised the concept of political party.
- **Eleventh Schedule:** It was added by the Constitution (Seventy-third Amendment) Act, 1992. It delineates 29 items over which Panchayats shall have the powers as well as the authority in order to function as the institutions of self-government.
- **Twelfth Schedule:** It was added by the Constitution (Seventy-fourth Amendment) Act, 1992. It delineates 18 items on which the Municipalities shall have powers as well as the authority to function as institutions of self-government.

Election Commission

The Election Commission is a constitutional body which has the responsibility of holding free and fair elections. It also enforces the model code of conduct for the parties and candidates to ensure that the people get a chance to elect their true representative. It allocates symbols to parties and candidates. It recognises parties, whether national, regional or recognised. It ensures that political parties follow the rules. It can order repolling or postponement of elections, depending on the contigencies. In case of dispute between political parties regarding election symbol, the Election Commission can give a decision. The Election Commission consists of the Chief Election Commissioner and such other Election Commissioners whose number may be decided by the President. Their appointment is done by the President, on the advice of the Council of Ministers.

The service conditions and tenure of the Chief Election Commissioner and other Election Commissioners may be decided by the President. Presently, they are appointed for six years. The Chief Election Commissioner cannot be removed from office except in like manner and on like grounds as a judge of the Supreme Court.

The exclusive forum for adjudicating disputes relating to the President and the Vice-President is the Supreme Court, while any dispute relating to the election of the Prime Minister or Speaker of the Lok Sabha can be determined by an election petition before the High Court. There is only one electoral roll for every territorial constituency for election to either the Parliament or state legislatures. No person is ineligible for inclusion in any such roll or grounds only of religion, race, caste, sex or all of them. All citizens, who have completed 18 years of age and are not disqualified, can participate in elections. One can be disqualified under the Constitution or laws made by the Parliament on grounds of non-residence, unsoundness of mind, crime or corrupt or illegal practice.

Comptroller and Auditor General of India

The Comptroller and Auditor General was given a constitutional status, to carry out the duty. His appointment is made by the President. He performs such duties and exercises such powers in relation to the accounts of the Union and of the states and of any other authority or body as may be prescribed by or under any law made by the Parliament.

The reports of the Comptroller and Auditor-General of India relating to the accounts of the Union are submitted to the President who causes them to be laid before the Parliament. The CAG's reports relating to the accounts of a state are submitted to the Governor of the state who causes them to be laid before the state legislature. The CAG report is an important document for the Public Accounts Committee. The CAG not only checks that the amount spent was the amount sanctioned by the Parliament or state legislature but also whether the amount has been judiciously spent.

Attorney-General of India

The President appoints the Attorney-General of India. The person should be qualified to become a Supreme Court judge. The duties of the Attorney-General include giving advice to the Union Government upon legal matters, performing such other duties of a legal character as may be referred or assigned to him by the President. In the performance of his duties, the Attorney-General has a right of audience in all courts in the territory of India. He is neither a member of Cabinet nor of Parliament but he can take part in discussions in Parliament or its Committees. He, however, cannot vote. He holds the post till the pleasure of the President.

Public Service Commissions

There is a Union Public Service Commission to recruit people to serve under the Central Government and a Public Service Commission for each state to recruit people for the State Civil Services. If two or more states agree to have a Common Public Service Commission and a resolution to that effect is passed by both the houses, the Parliament may by law provide for the appointment of a joint State Public Service Commission. The Union Public Service Commission, if requested by the Governor of a state may with the approval of the President, agree to serve all or any of the needs of the state.

The Chairman and other members of Union Public Service Commission or Joint Public Service Commission are appointed by the President. For State Public Service Commission, appointment are made by the Governors. Usually, senior and eminent persons are made members of such Commissions. The appointment is usually for a six-year term or until they attain the age of 65 years in Union Public Service Commission or 62 years in case of State or Joint Commission. The members of the Commissions can retire before the end of the tenure. To ensure the integrity and independence of the Commission, the Constitution debars the members or the Chairman to seek further employment after retirement, either under the Central Government or any state Government. The Chairman or any member of a Public Service Commission can only be removed from his office by order of the President on the ground of misbehaviour, after the Supreme Court, on reference being made to it by the President, inquires and reports that the concerned person ought to be removed from the post. Till the enquiry report is received, the concerned Chairman or the member may be suspended. The Public Service Commissions conduct examinations for appointments to the Services of the Union and the Services of the State respectively. They may assist in framing and operating schemes for any service for which candidates with special qualifications are required.

The annual report of the Union Public Service Commission is presented to the President, giving details of the work done by the Commission. The President causes the report to be laid in the

Parliament. In respect of the cases, where advice of the Commission was not accepted, the Government attaches an explanation, giving reasons thereof. Similarly, the Governor of the State causes the annual report of the State Public Service Commission to be laid before the legislature.

Civil Services in India

In a democratic set up, the political leaders keep on changing. Moreover, the politicians are not experienced administrators and are not expected to know the nitty-gritty of the problems. The political leaders can only frame the guidelines and give directions in the policy matters. However, to fill in the essential gaps in the policies, frame programmes accordingly and implement the policies, a permanent body is required. The Civil Services in India is an elaborate organisation, providing continuity and bringing in experience. They ensure that the country is well governed and administered. The majority of the Government officials can be classified in three main categories: (1) All India Services, (2) Central Services, and (3) State Services. The Central Services are for performing the functions, given in the Union list. Their recruitment and service condition is controlled by the Central Government. Similarly, the State Services officials perform the functions as given in the State list and are controlled by respective State Government.

All India Services have been provided in the Constitution itself. The officials of these services serve Central as well as State Governments. They are recruited by Union Public Service Commission and are controlled jointly by the Centre and States. Originally, the Constitution provided for two All India Services—Indian Administrative Service and Indian Police Service. However, the Parliament has been empowered to create more such services. Rajya Sabha can pass a resolution by two-third majority to create an All India Service. Following this procedure, a few more All India Services like the Indian Service of Engineers, Indian Medical and Health Service and the Indian Forests Service have been created. In the All India Services, the recruitment is done at the Class-I gazetted level only and there are no subordinate services and lower categories of services in the All India Services.

For the Central Services Class-I gazetted officers the recruitment is done by the Union Public Service Commission, through the Combined Civil Service examination which is same for the All India Services. The Central Services are horizontally as well as vertically classified. The Indian Customs and Excise Service, Indian Revenue Service, Indian Information Service, Indian Railway Traffic Service, Indian Audit and Accounts Service, Indian Civil Accounts Service, Indian Posts and Telecom Accounts Service, and Indian Defence Estate Service are some of the Central Services.

The appointments for Class-II officers are also made by the UPSC. However, the Staff Selection Commission (SSC) makes recruitment to non-technical class III or Group 'C' posts. The Commission also has been entrusted with the responsibility of making recruitment to certain Group 'B' services like Assistants' Grade.

Administration of Union Territories

The administration of the Union Territories lies with the Union Government. According to Article 238 (1). "Save as otherwise provided by the Parliament by law, every Union Territory shall be administered by the President acting, to such an extent as he thinks fit, through an administrator appointed by him with such designation as he may specify. Thus Andaman and Nicobar Islands, Delhi, Puducherry, Jammu and Kashmir and Ladakh have Lieutenant Governors and Chandigarh, Lakshdweep and Dadra Nagar Haveli and Daman and Diu have Administrators.

Under the pattern of Government administered by Administrator/Chief Commissioner, the legislations are made by regulations as there is no provision for a legislative assembly and a Council of Ministers. There are advisory committees attached with the Home Ministry to help the administrators in respect of policy, legislative proposals, budgeting matters, development plans and other matters of importance. There is another advisory committee attached with the administrator of the Union Territory similar in all respects.

The legislature-cum-cabinet pattern prevailing in Puducherry is based on the provisions by the Government of Union Territories Act 1963. There are two sources of power, one coming from the Central Government and the other from the Union Territory Government. The executive head, known as Lieutenant Governor, is appointed by the President. He is aided and advised by the Council of Ministers which is also appointed by the President. The pattern of Government is different from those at the States. The administrator is not a constitutional and formal head but a real head with the power to override the decisions of the ministers.

Delhi which is a Union Territory as well as the national capital has a unique arrangement. The National Capital Territory region has an assembly and an elected government. However, its powers are limited and for every major policy matter, it has to seek the Centre's approval. Besides, there are the Municipal Corporation, Municipal Council and Cantonment Board to look after the local work. The Municipal Corporation and Cantonment Boards are elected bodies while Municipal Council is a nominated body. Besides, there is a Delhi Development Authority, constituted to prepare a master plan for Delhi and secure its development.

Zonal Councils

To promote inter-state cooperation and coordination, advisory bodies, called Zonal Councils, have been set up in the country. The six Zonal Councils, are formed on the basis of the region.

(*a*) Northern zone, comprises the states and UTs of Punjab, Haryana, Rajasthan, Himachal Pradesh and Union Territories of Delhi, Chandigarh, Jammu and Kashmir and Ladakh.

(*b*) Central Zone comprises the states of Uttar Pradesh and Madhya Pradesh.

(*c*) Eastern Zone comprises the states of Bihar, Odisha, Sikkim and West Bengal.

(*d*) Western Zone comprises the states of Gujarat, Maharashtra, Goa and Union Territories of Dadra Nagar Haveli and Daman and Diu.

(*e*) Southern Zone comprises the states of Andhra Pradesh, Karnataka, Kerala and Tamil Nadu and Union Territory of Puducherry.

(*f*) North Eastern Zone comprises the states of Assam, Arunachal Pradesh, Nagaland, Manipur, Tripura, Meghalaya and Mizoram.

Andaman Nicobar Islands and Lakshdweep Islands are not covered in any Zonal Council.

The Union Home Minister is the Chairman of the Zonal Council and Chief Ministers of the States included in the zone act as Vice-Chairman of the Council by rotation, each holding office for a period of one year at a time. The proceedings and recommendations of the council meetings are forwarded to the Central Government and concerned State Governments. A joint meeting of two or more Zonal Councils may decide issues of common interest to states of more than one zone.

The Jammu and Kashmir Reorganisation Act, 2019

The Jammu and Kashmir Reorganisation Bill, 2019 was passed by Parliament on August 6, 2019. The Act provides for reorganisation of the state of Jammu and Kashmir into the Union Territory of Jammu and Kashmir and Union Territory of Ladakh.

- **Reorganisation of Jammu and Kashmir:** The Act reorganises the state of Jammu and Kashmir into: (i) the Union Territory of Jammu and Kashmir with a legislature, and (ii) the Union Territory of Ladakh without a legislature. The Union Territory of Ladakh will comprise Kargil and Leh districts, and the Union Territory of Jammu and Kashmir will comprise the remaining territories of the existing state of Jammu and Kashmir.
- **Lieutenant Governor:** The Union Territory of Jammu and Kashmir will be administered by the President, through an administrator appointed by him known as the Lieutenant Governor. The Union Territory of Ladakh will be administered by the President, through a Lieutenant Governor appointed by him.
- **Legislative Assembly of Jammu and Kashmir:** The Act provides for a Legislative Assembly for the Union Territory of Jammu and Kashmir. The total number of seats in the Assembly will be 107. Of these, 24 seats will remain vacant on account of certain areas of Jammu and Kashmir being under the occupation of Pakistan. Further,

seats will be reserved in the Assembly for Scheduled Castes and Scheduled Tribes in proportion to their population in the Union Territory of Jammu and Kashmir. In addition, the Lieutenant Governor may nominate two members to the Legislative Assembly to give representation to women, if they are not adequately represented.

- The Assembly will have a term of five years, and the Lieutenant Governor must summon the Assembly at least once in six months. The Legislative Assembly may make laws for any part of the Union Territory of Jammu and Kashmir related to: (i) any matters specified in the State List of the Constitution, except "Police" and "Public Order", and (ii) any matter in the Concurrent List applicable to Union Territories. Further, Parliament will have the power to make laws in relation to any matter for the Union Territory of Jammu and Kashmir.
- **Council of Ministers:** The Union Territory of Jammu and Kashmir will have a Council of Ministers of not more than ten per cent of the total number of members in the Assembly. The Council will aide and advise the Lieutenant Governor on matters that the Assembly has powers to make laws. The Chief Minister will communicate all decisions of the Council to the Lieutenant Governor.
- **High Court:** The High Court of Jammu and Kashmir will be the common High Court for the Union Territories of Ladakh, and Jammu and Kashmir. Further, the Union Territory of Jammu and Kashmir will have an Advocate General to provide legal advice to the government of the Union Territory.
- **Legislative Council:** The Legislative Council of the state of Jammu and Kashmir will be abolished. Upon dissolution, all Bills pending in the Council will lapse.
- **Advisory Committees:** The central government will appoint Advisory Committees, for various purposes, including: (i) distribution of assets and liabilities of corporations of the state of Jammu and Kashmir between the two Union Territories, (ii) issues related to the generation and supply of electricity and water, and (iii) issues related to the Jammu and Kashmir State Financial Corporation. These Committees must submit their reports within six months to the Lieutenant Governor of Jammu and Kashmir, who must act on these recommendations within 30 days.

Inter-State Council

The Constitution provides for the setting up of an Inter-state Council by the President, to enquire into and advise upon Inter-state disputes, if he is satisfied that public interest would be served by the establishment of such a Council. The Council does not only have an advisory role but also for the purpose of investigating and discussing subjects in which some or all of the states have a common interest. The Council can play an important role in the federal set up, overcoming differences and disputes between the states and between states and the Centre.

Scheduled Areas

The expression "Scheduled Areas" in the Constitution means such areas as the President may by order declare to be scheduled areas. The President can order that the whole or any scheduled parts of a scheduled area ceases to be a scheduled area or a part of such an area. He can increase the area of any scheduled area in a state after consultation with the Governor of the state. The President can rectify or alter the boundaries of scheduled areas. On any alteration of the boundaries of a state or on the admission into the union or the establishment of a state, the President can declare any territory not previously included in any state to be, or to form part of, a scheduled area. To safeguard the interests of the people staying in scheduled areas, the Governor of the state, can issue a public notification, directing that any particular Act of the Parliament, or the state legislature is not applicable to a scheduled area or any part thereof in the state. He can also make exceptions and modifications to the Acts before making them applicable to the scheduled areas or parts thereof. He can also issue directions to give retrospective effect to the Acts.

The Governor can make regulations for the peace and good governance of any area, or part of the scheduled area. He can prohibit or restrict the transfer of land by or among members of the Scheduled Tribes in such area. He can regulate the allotment of land to members of the Scheduled Tribes in such area. He can regulate the carrying on of the business as money-lender by persons who lend money to members of the Scheduled Tribes in such area. All such regulations, however, are submitted to the President and are applicable only after his assent.

District Administration

District is the most important unit as well as link in the administrative organisation in the country. There are approximately eight hundred districts in the country, carved out on the geographical continuity and administrative convenience basis. They provide link between villages, towns and cities with the State Capital. As an administrative unit, it contains officers of all the Government departments of the state, *e.g.*, District Magistrate, Superintendent of Police, District Health Officer, District Education Officer, Executive Engineer etc. Districts are further subdivided into *tehsils* or sub-divisions and villages. The administration, developmental work and planning in the state is done on the district basis. Local-self governments also have districts at the top of the three level hierarchy.

The administrative control of the district vests with the district officer who is also called Collector or Deputy Commissioner. These officers either belong to IAS or the State Civil Service. They are the kingpin of administration and other officers of various departments. Maintenance of law and order, collection of revenue, general administration, coordination among various departments and representing state Government are important responsibilities of the district officer. During natural calamities, wars, riots, elections, he gets special responsibilities. Though the separation of Executive powers from judiciary, introduction of democratic institutions, appointment of specialists in other departments and introduction of social and economic planning have undermined his position, but still he is the most powerful and important official in the district.

Panchayati Raj

Since time immemorial, Panchayats have existed in India at the village levels. They have looked after the welfare of the villagers, planned the developmental work and even carried out the judicial work. Though our Constitution did not prescribe any particular structure for democratic institutions at lower levels, the directive principles did include this as one of the aim. A three tier set up was formed by the Government, with the Village Panchayats at the lowest level and Zila Parishads at the districts level. However, some states adopted two-tier structure. Moreover, it was observed that the state Governments were reluctant to share power with the lower level democratic institutions. So, these bodies were deprived of financial resources, elections were not held regularly and no attempt was made to facilitate their smooth working.

In order to provide statutory backing to the Panchayati Raj Institutions and given them more powers and responsibilities, a Constitutional Amendment Bill was introduced in the Parliament in 1989. It was adopted in the Lok Sabha but fell through in the Rajya Sabha. In 1992, the bill was introduced again and this time it was approved by both the houses.

The bill stipulates setting up of three level Panchayati Raj institutions in all the states. The elections after five years have been made mandatory. Those institutions have been provided with adequate financial sources and administrative support. Their responsibility has been outlined and local developmental work has been given to them. In addition, these bodies play an important role in the planning process. The bodies are called Gram Panchayat, Panchayat Samiti and Zila Parishad.

A bill to provide statutory backing to these Urban Local Government has also been approved. In the cities and bigger towns, corporations are set up. In smaller towns, Municipal Committees or Councils are set up. In even smaller towns, Town Area Committees and Notified Area Committees are set up.

Multiple Choice Questions

1. The first step taken by the British Government to control and regulate the affairs of the East India Company in India was:
A. Charter Act, 1833
B. Regulating Act, 1773
C. Pitts India Act, 1784
D. Government of India Act, 1858

2. Which one of the following act made the Governor-General of Bengal as the Governor-General of India?
A. Regulating Act, 1773
B. Charter Act, 1853
C. Pitts India Act, 1784
D. Charter Act, 1813

3. In which Act the law member was made a full member of the Governor-General's executive council?
A. Regulating Act, 1773
B. The Amending Act, 1781
C. Pitts India Act, 1784
D. Charter Act, 1853

4. The Act which made the Governor-General as the Viceroy of India:
A. Indian Council Act, 1861
B. Indian Council Act, 1892
C. Government of India Act, 1858
D. Indian Council Act, 1909

5. The Act provide for all administrative subjects were divided into two groups central and provincial is:
A. Indian Council Act, 1909
B. Government of India Act, 1919
C. Montague-Chelmsford Act
D. both B and C

6. The Act discuss about the distribution of power between centre and state is:
A. Government of India act, 1935
B. Charter Act, 1833
C. Indian Council Act, 1909
D. The August Offer, 1940

7. The Act empowers the transfer of power from the British Government to the Indians is referred as to:
A. Cabinet Mission Plan
B. Wavell Plan
C. C. R. Formula
D. Indian Independence Act, 1947

8. The plan granting dominion status in the near future and giving power to Indian to draft their constitution was:
A. Cripps proposal
B. The August offer
C. Wavell plan
D. Cabinet Mission plan

9. The Act abolished the Dyarchy in the provinces and introduced 'Provincial Autonomy' is:
A. Government of India Act, 1935
B. Montague-Chelmsford Act, 1919
C. Indian Council Act, 1909
D. Indian Council Act, 1892

10. The proposal by which the Muslim League would support the Congress demand for complete freedom is known as:
A. Cripps Proposal
B. The August offer, 1940
C. Wavell plan, 1945
D. C.R. Formula, 1944

11. Which one of the following exercised the most profound influence on the Indian Constitution?
A. The Government of India Act, 1935
B. The U.S. Constitution
C. British Constitution
D. The U.N. Charter

12. Which British India Act has separated the representation of Muslim Community?
A. Indian Council Act, 1892
B. Indian Council Act, 1909
C. Govt. of India Act, 1919
D. Govt of India Act, 1935

13. Which Act prescribed a federation, taking the provinces and the Indian states as its units?
A. Govt. of India Act, 1858
B. Govt. of India Act, 1919
C. Govt. of India Act, 1935
D. Indian Independence Act, 1947

14. On which date the first meeting of the Constituent Assembly were held?
A. December 9, 1946 B. 16 August, 1947
C. 26 January, 1946 D. 30 January, 1947

15. On the day of adoption of the Constitution *i.e.,* 26th November, 1949 how many members were present and signed the approved Constitution?
A. 299 B. 329
C. 284 D. 257

16. East India Company acquired control over Bengal in:
A. 1765 B. 1785
C. 1775 D. None of these

17. The Indian Councils Act, 1909 is also known as:
A. Montague-Chelmsford Reform Act
B. Morley-Minto Reform Act
C. Government of India Act
D. None of these

18. Which of the following Acts introduced communal electorates?
A. Morley - Minto Reform Act
B. Montague - Chelmsford Reform Act
C. Regulating Act
D. None of these

19. The Government of India Act 1919 is also known as:
A. Montague - Chelmsford Reform Act
B. Morley - Minto Reform Act
C. Both A and B
D. None of these

20. Which of the following Acts provided a bi-cameral legislature at the centre?
A. Government of India Act, 1935
B. Indian Independence Act, 1947
C. Montague - Chelmsford Reform Act, 1919
D. None of these

21. The term 'Union' was suggested by:
A. Dr. B.R. Ambedkar
B. D.D. Basu
C. Dr. Rajendra Prasad
D. J. L. Nehru

22. The French Settlement of Puducherry (together with Karai Kal, Mahe and Yanam), ceded to India by the French Government in:
A. 1964 B. 1954
C. 1968 D. 1971

23. Which one of following article says that parliament may alter the area, boundaries and name of the existing states and create and abolish existing states?
A. Article 1 B. Article 2
C. Article 3 D. Article 4

24. A bill containing provision under Article 3 can be introduced in:
A. Lok Sabha only after the recommendation of President
B. Rajya Sabha only after the recommendation of President
C. Either house of parliament only on the recommendation of the President
D. None of the above

25. The article of the constitution related to the procedure for amending the boundaries of the states is/are:
A. Article 1, 2 and 3 B. Article 2, 3 and 4
C. Article 3, 4 and 5 D. Article 4, 5 and 6

26. In 1975 Sikkim was admitted to the Indian Union as the:
A. 20th State B. 21st State
C. 22nd State D. 23rd State

27. The Amendment Act related the formation of Sikkim as 22nd state is:
A. 34th Amendment Act
B. 35th Amendment Act
C. 36th Amendment Act
D. 37th Amendment Act

28. The 23rd and 24th state of India are:
A. Mizoram and Arunachal Pradesh
B. Odisha and Bihar
C. Punjab and Haryana
D. Tripura and Meghalaya

29. The Assam Reorganisation Act, 1969, created an autonomous sub-state named:
A. Meghalaya B. Mizoram
C. Manipur D. Tripura

30. The North Eastern Area (Reorganisation) Act, 1971 brought up Mizoram and Arunachal Pradesh to the list of:
A. State
B. Union territories
C. Mizoram as State and Arunachal Pradesh as Union territories
D. Arunachal Pradesh as State and Mizoram as Union territories

31. Arunachal Pradesh a Union Territory was made a state by State of Arunachal Pradesh Act, in:
A. 1987 B. 1986
C. 1982 D. 1981

32. A new state of Chhattisgarh was created by carrying out its territory from that of the territories of Madhya Pradesh by enacting the Madhya Pradesh Reorganisation Act, 2000 w.e.f.:
A. 1.11.2000 B. 9.11.2000
C. 15.11.2000 D. 15.12.2000

33. Match List-I with List-II and select the correct answer from the code given below:

List-I ***(States)***	***List-II*** ***(Formation year)***
(*a*) Himachal Pradesh	1. 2000
(*b*) Goa	2. 1986
(*c*) Arunachal Pradesh	3. 1987
(*d*) Jharkhand	4. 1954

Codes:

	(*a*)	(*b*)	(*c*)	(*d*)
A.	4	3	1	2
B.	4	3	2	1
C.	3	1	2	4
D.	3	2	4	1

34. Which one of the following was the chairman of the drafting committee of the constitution?
A. Rajendra Prasad B. B. R. Ambedkar
C. Sachidanand Sinha D. K. M. Munshi

35. Which one of the following was not a member of drafting committee of the constitution?
A. Mahatma Gandhi
B. K. M. Munshi
C. Dr. D. P. Khaitan
D. T.T. Krishnamachari

36. The preamble in constitution borrowed from:
A. Russian Constitution
B. French Constitution
C. USA Constitution
D. UK Constitution

37. The provision of fundamental duties has source from:
A. UK Constitution
B. USA Constitution
C. Nepali Constitution
D. Russian Constitution

38. The provision of Rule of law, Parliamentary system and Single citizenship borrowed from:
A. UK Constitution
B. Japanese Constitution
C. Irish Constitution
D. USA Constitution

39. USA Constitution provided which of the following provision of the constitution?
A. Preamble
B. Independence of Judiciary
C. Fundamental rights
D. All of the above

40. The provision for Directive Principles of State Policy (DPSP) is derived from:
A. USA Constitution
B. Irish Constitution
C. UK Constitution
D. Australian Constitution

41. The provision for the concurrent lists and trade and commerce is derived from:
A. South African Constitution
B. Australian Constitution
C. German Constitution
D. Irish Constitution

42. South African Constitution provides for which of the following provision:
A. Constitutional Amendment
B. The Union List
C. Emergency Provisions
D. Fundamental Duties

43. Universal Adult Franchise provision defined under:
A. Article 326 B. Article 312
C. Article 12 D. Article 21

44. The word 'secular' was missing from over constitution and it is inserted by the Amendment of the constitution:
A. 21st Amendment B. 22nd Amendment
C. 42nd Amendment D. 44th Amendment

45. Which one of the following Act is referred as 'mini constitution':
A. The Indian Act, 1909
B. The Indian Act, 1919
C. The Government of India Act, 1935
D. The India Independent Act, 1947

46. The Article 36 to 51 of the Indian Constitution has provision for:
A. Citizenship
B. Fundamental Rights
C. Directive Principles of State Policy
D. Fundamental Duties

47. The Article 352 of the Indian Constitution deals with:
A. Financial emergency
B. National emergency
C. State emergency
D. None of the above

48. The provision for Republican System is derived from:
A. USA Constitution
B. Japanese Constitution
C. French Constitution
D. UK Constitution

49. The Drafting Committee of the Constitution including the chairman, comprised of:
A. seven members B. five members
C. nine members D. three members

50. How many committees were set up by the Constituent Assembly for framing the Constitution of India?
A. Thirteen B. Nine
C. Seventeen D. Seven

51. The Constitution of India was enacted by a Constituent Assembly set up:
A. under the Cabinet Mission Plan, 1946
B. under a resolution of the Provisional Government
C. under the Indian Independence Act, 1947
D. by the Indian National Congress

52. The words "Satyameva Jayate," inscribed the National Emblem, are taken from:
A. Jataka B. Mundaka Upnishad
C. Mahabharata D. Puranas

53. Match the following:

List-I	*List-II*
1. Lord Mountbatten	(*a*) Chairman of the Drafting Committee
2. Dr. Rajendra Prasad	(*b*) First Prime Minister of India
3. Dr. B.R. Ambedkar	(*c*) Member of the Constituent Assembly
4. Pandit J.L. Nehru	(*d*) Last British Governor General
5. Dr. K.M. Munshi	(*e*) President of the Constituent Assembly

A. 1-(*e*), 2-(*d*), 3-(*a*), 4-(*c*), 5-(*b*)
B. 1-(*d*), 2-(*a*), 3-(*b*), 4-(*c*), 5-(*e*)
C. 1-(*d*), 2-(*e*), 3-(*a*), 4-(*b*), 5-(*c*)
D. 1-(*e*), 2-(*b*), 3-(*a*), 4-(*d*), 5-(*c*)

54. Who among the following were the members of Drafting Committee of the Constitution?
1. K.M. Munshi
2. Jawaharlal Nehru
3. Alladi Krishnaswami
4. Sardar Patel

Codes:
A. 1, 3 and 4 B. 1 and 4
C. 1, 3 D. 2, 3 and 4

55. Match the following features of the Indian Constitution and their sources from which they have been incorporated.

List-I	*List-II*
(*a*) Bill of Rights and Judicial Review	1. England
(*b*) Parliamentary system of democracy	2. Ireland
(*c*) Directive Principles	3. U.S.A.
(*d*) Residuary powers with Centre	4. Canada

A. (*a*)-4, (*b*)-1, (*c*)-2, (*d*)-3
B. (*a*)-1, (*b*)-2, (*c*)-3, (*d*)-4
C. (*a*)-3, (*b*)-4, (*c*)-2. (*d*)-1
D. (*a*)-3, (*b*)-1, (*c*)-2, (*d*)-4

56. The members of the Constituent Assembly were:
A. directly elected by the people
B. all nominated by the Indian Congress and the Muslim League
C. indirectly elected by the Provincial Assemblies
D. all nominated by the British Government

57. Who was the head of the Drafting Committee of the Constitution?
A. Sachidanand SinhaB. B.N. Rao
C. Jawaharlal Nehru D. B.R. Ambedkar

58. Who is considered to be the architect of the Indian Constitution?
A. B.R. Ambedkar B. Jawaharlal Nehru
C. Rajendra Prasad D. B.N. Rao

59. Who of the following acted as the Constitutional Advisor to Constituent Assembly?
A. B.R. Ambedkar B. Dr. Rajendra Prasad
C. B.N. Rao D. J.L. Nehru

60. The Objective Resolution, which outlined the philosophy of the Indian Constitution, was moved in the Constituent Assembly by:
A. Dr. S. Radhakrishnan
B. Dr. Rajendra Prasad
C. Jawaharlal Nehru
D. B.R. Ambedkar

61. Which of the following rights is/are not available to non-citizen?
A. Article 15
B. Article 16
C. Right to equality of opportunity in public employment
D. All of the above

62. The right available to only Indian Citizen is/are:
A. Article 15 B. Article 16
C. Article 326 D. All of the above

63. The constitution provided Indian citizenship Act in:
A. 1965 B. 1947
C. 1955 D. 1995

64. Which of the following is/are a means of acquisition of citizenship?
A. Citizenship by Birth
B. Citizenship by Descent
C. Citizenship by Registration
D. All of the above

65. Which one of the following is/are of the method(s) through which citizenship loss?
A. Renunciation B. Termination
C. Deprivation D. All of the above

66. The compulsory termination of the citizenship of India obtained by registration or naturalisation is referred as:
A. Renunciation B. Termination
C. Deprivation D. Registration

67. When an Indian citizen voluntarily acquires the citizenship of another country then its citizenship cancelled by the process of:
A. Renunciation B. Termination
C. Deprivation D. Registration

68. Which of the following is/are a method(s) of acquiring citizenship by means of Registration:
A. A person who is of Indian origin and has been residing in India for 5 years immediately before an application registration was made
B. Women married to an Indian citizen
C. Miner children of Indian citizen
D. All of the above

69. The Person of Indian Origin (PIO) of which one of the following countries can apply for the dual citizenship?
A. Australia B. Pakistan
C. Bangladesh D. Sri Lanka

70. In India dual citizenship is applicable for resident of:
A. Bihar B. Uttar Pradesh
C. Meghalaya D. Jammu and Kashmir

71. A British Citizen staying in India cannot claim right to:
A. Freedom of trade and profession
B. Equality before the law
C. Equal protection of life and personal liberty
D. Freedom of religion

72. Who is competent to prescribe conditions for acquisition of citizenship?
A. Election Commission

B. Parliament
C. President
D. Parliament and state legislative jointly

73. What is the minimum duration of stay essential before a person can apply for Indian citizenship?
A. 3 years B. 5 years
C. 7 years D. 10 years

74. The detailed provisions regarding acquisition and termination of Indian citizenship are contained in the Citizenship Act which was passed by:
A. the Indian Parliament in 1955
B. the Indian Parliament in 1950
C. the British Parliament in August 1948
D. the Constituent Assembly in 1949

75. The Constitution of India has provided for:
A. single citizenship
B. multiple citizenship
C. double citizenship
D. none of the above

76. Which of the following is not a condition for becoming a citizen of India?
A. Birth B. Descent
C. Acquiring property D. Naturalisation

77. The Constitution of India has introduced single citizenship on the pattern of:
A. Britain B. Canada
C. Both A and B D. United States

78. The detailed provisions regarding acquisition and termination of Indian citizenship are contained in:
A. the Indian Independence Act, 1947
B. the orders issued by Provisional Government in 1946
C. an act passed by the Indian Parliament in 1955
D. part VII of the constitution

79. When can citizenship not be terminated?
A. When there is Emergency
B. When there is war
C. When there are elections
D. It can be terminated regardless of conditions

80. Indian citizenship is lost when:
A. a person acquires a foreign citizenship
B. the person renounces the citizenship
C. the government deprives a citizenship for some cause
D. in all the above cases

81. Which one of the following has been wrongly listed as a freedom provided to the Indian citizens under Article 19?
A. Freedom of speech and expression
B. Freedom of residence and settlement
C. Freedom of profession
D. Freedom of press

82. The right to freedom guaranteed under Article 19 can be restricted:
A. in the interest of security of state
B. in the interest of friendly relations with a foreign state
C. in the interest of public order, public health and public morality
D. on all the above grounds

83. Which one of the following rights was described by B.R. Ambedkar as 'the heart and soul of the Constitution'?
A. Right of freedom of religion
B. Right of property
C. Right of equality
D. Right to constitutional remedies.

84. The Preventive Detention Act has a restraining effect on:
A. Right of Equality
B. Right to Freedom
C. Right to Religion
D. Right to Constitutional Remedies

85. Reasonable restrictions on the rights of Indian citizens can be imposed by:
A. the President B. the Parliament
C. the Supreme Court D. none of the above

86. Under which Article of the Constitution can an individual move the Supreme Court directly in case of any violation of a Fundamental Right?
A. Article 13 B. Article 14
C. Article 32 D. Article 34

87. Freedom of speech under the Indian constitution is subject to reasonable restriction on the grounds of protection of:
A. sovereignty and integrity of the country
B. the dignity of the office of the Prime Minister
C. both A and B
D. none of the above

88. Cultural and Educational rights include:
A. Right of minorities to establish and administer their educational institutions
B. Right of minorities to promote their language
C. Right against discrimination for admission to educational institutions on the grounds of religion, race or caste
D. All of these

89. The granting of fundamental rights to citizens aims at ensuring:
A. an independent judiciary
B. socialistic government
C. individual liberty
D. none of these

90. Which fundamental right is concerned with abolition of social distinctions?
A. Right to equality
B. Right against exploitation
C. Right to life and liberty
D. Cultural and educational rights

91. The Fundamental Rights have the sanction of:
A. the Supreme Court
B. the Constitution
C. majority opinion
D. the Government

92. How can the Fundamental Rights be suspended?
A. If Parliament passes a law by two-thirds majority
B. If the Supreme Court orders it
C. If the President orders it in the time of National Emergency
D. They can never be suspended

93. Which one of the following writs literally means 'we command'?
A. Habeas Corpus B. Mandamus
C. Quo Warranto D. Certiorari

94. In India, Mandamus will lie against:
A. officers bound to do a public duty
B. Government
C. both officers and the Government
D. none of these

95. The writ of prohibition issued by the Supreme Court or a High Court is issued against:
A. judicial or quasi-judicial authorities
B. administrative and judicial authorities
C. administrative authorities only
D. administrative authorities and government

96. The writ of Mandamus is available for the purpose of:
I. Enforcement of fundamental rights
II. Compelling a court or judicial tribunal to exercise its jurisdiction when it has refused to exercise it
III. Directing a public official or the Government not to enforce a law which is unconstitutional
A. I only B. II and III
C. I and III D. I, II and III

97. The authority to issue writs for the enforcement of Fundamental Rights rests with whom?
A. All the courts in India
B. The Parliament
C. The Supreme Court
D. The President of India

98. How can the Fundamental Rights be protected by a citizen?
A. By approaching the Supreme Court which will issue appropriate writs against the authority
B. Parliament will take note of such violations and tell the courts
C. The Executive will inform the Courts
D. It is automatically protected

99. Can Parliament amend or modify any of the Fundamental Rights given in the Constitution?
A. Parliament can do so only after a referendum
B. Parliament can amend them by special majority
C. Parliament cannot amend any
D. Only the President can issue directions to amend them

100. Right to participate in government and equal opportunity to occupy the highest office by qualification gives the citizens:
A. national liberty B. political liberty
C. natural liberty D. civil liberty

101. Which one of the following Fundamental Rights has been subject of maximum litigation since the inauguration of the Constitution?
A. Right to freedom of speech
B. Right to constitutional remedies
C. Right to property
D. Right against exploitation

102. The Constitution prescribes the:
A. way of detecting the practice of untouchability
B. abolition of untouchability as a Directive Principle of State Policy
C. abolition of untouchability as a Fundamental Right
D. punishment for the practice of untouchability

103. A citizen's freedom of speech and expression may be subjected to reasonable restriction on the grounds of all except:
A. sovereignty of India
B. public order
C. contempt of court
D. unbecoming criticism

104. The Indian Constitution declares that protection of life and liberty:
A. can never be taken away in any condition
B. can be taken away only according to procedure established by law
C. can be taken away during the Emergency through Presidential order
D. none of the above

105. Habeas Corpus means:
A. an order from a court to free a person who had been illegally detained by the police or any other person
B. an order from a superior court calling up the record of a proceeding in an inferior court for review
C. an order from the superior court to an official to show his right to the office
D. an order from a higher court to stop proceedings in a certain case

106. What is a Writ of Quo Warranto?
A. It is a writ from a superior court commanding some officer or particular authority to do a specific act
B. It is an order from a higher court to stop proceedings in a certain case
C. It is an order from the superior court to any official to show his right to the office
D. To produce the body of a person

107. Writ of Mandamus is:
A. an order to produce the body of a person
B. an order from a superior court to any official to show his right to the office.
C. an order from a higher court to stop proceedings in a certain case
D. a writ from a superior court commanding some officer or particular authority to do a specific act

108. Who of the following does not constitute an exception to the provision of Article 14 ('equality before the law')?
A. The President
B. The Governor
C. The Prime Minister
D. The foreign diplomats

109. What does the phrase 'equality before the law' used in Article 14, mean?
A. That all individuals are equal
B. That all laws are the same for everybody
C. That all individuals are equally subjected to the ordinary law of the land
D. That everybody is to be treated equally by law in equal circumstances

110. Which Fundamental Right can be said to be specially applicable to children?
A. Right to education up to 14 years of age
B. Right against employment up to 14 years of the age
C. Right to be educated in the mother-tongue in primary education
D. Right against employment in dangerous occupations

111. Which of the following are a Directive Principle of State Policy?
I. Equal pay for equal work for men and women

II. Equal right to an adequate means of livelihood

III. Abolition of untouchability

IV. Just and human condition of work

Codes:

A. I, II, III, IV B. I, II, IV

C. I, II, III D. Only III

112. A socialistic ideology is reflected in the Directive Principle, which calls for:

A. Securing equitable distribution of material resources of the country to prevent concentration of wealth

B. Promotion of cottage industries

C. Free and compulsory education for children up to 14 years of age

D. All the above

113. Which of the following directives has not been included in the Constitution with regard to conduct of international relations?

A. Work for the maintenance of just and honourable relations between nations

B. Show respect for international law and treaty obligations

C. Encourage settlement of international disputes through arbitration

D. Work for disarmament

114. The Directive Principles were accorded an overriding position over the Fundamental Rights under certain circumstances by:

A. The Constitution

B. The Forty-Second Amendment

C. The Forty-Fourth Amendment

D. The Twenty-Fifth Amendment

115. What is meant by saying that the Directive Principles of State Policy are non-justiciable?

1. In case they are violated the matter cannot be taken to the Court
2. Courts are debarred from consideration of Directive Principles
3. The law of the land does not recognize their existence
4. They are sacrosanct

Codes:

A. 1 & 2 B. 1 only

C. 1, 2 & 3 D. 1, 2, 3, 4

116. What are the Gandhian Principles incorporated in the Indian Constitution?

(*i*) Efforts to be made for the development of weaker or backward sections of the society

(*ii*) Prohibition on the use of intoxicating liquor except for medicinal purposes

(*iii*) Organisation of village panchayats

(*iv*) Establishment of cottage and small scale industries in rural areas

Codes:

A. (*i*), (*ii*), (*iv*) B. (*i*), (*ii*), (*iii*)

C. (*ii*), (*iii*) & (*iv*) D. All four

117. The basic difference between the Fundamental Rights and Directive Principles is:

A. Fundamental Rights are positive while Directive Principles are negative

B. Directive Principles are given precedence over Fundamental Rights by the Courts in all cases

C. Fundamental Rights are justiciable while Directive Principles are not

D. None of the above

118. The Directive Principles are in the nature of:

A. judicial injunctions to the Government to enact certain laws

B. request to the Government to pay attention to certain subjects

C. injunctions to the Government to refrain from doing certain things

D. instructions to the Government to do certain things

119. Which article ensures protection and improvement of environment and safeguarding of forests wild life?

A. Art. 51 A B. Art. 37

C. Art. 44 D. Art. 48 A

120. Which Constitutional Amendment granted a position of primacy to all the Directive Principles over Fundamental Rights?

A. 24th B. 25th

C. 36th D. 42nd

121. One of the following is not a method by which the Parliament expresses lack of confidence in the Council of Ministers:

I. Declaring that the taxes proposed have to be reduced

II. Passing a bill introduced by a private member to which the Council of Ministers is opposed

III. Rejecting a bill introduced by a Minister

Codes:

A. I B. I and III

C. II D. III

122. Which of the following executive functions of the Council of Ministers are correctly given?

1. It formulates the executive policy of the country
2. It co-ordinates the policies, programs and activities of various departments
3. It has an important role in filling up various political, judicial and ambassadorial assignments
4. It has an important role in the election of the President

Codes:

A. 2, 3, 4 B. 1, 2, 3

C. 1, 2, 4 D. 1, 2, 3, 4

123. Which of the following statements are correct regarding the Prime Minister's position?

1. He presides over the meetings of the Cabinet
2. He can remove any minister who refuses to co-operate with him
3. He and his ministers are responsible to the Lok Sabha
4. When the Prime Minister resigns, the senior-most minister in the Council of Ministers is appointed the Prime Minister

Codes:

A. 1, 2, 3 B. 1 & 3

C. 1, 2, 4 D. 1, 2, 3, 4

124. The Vice-President of India can be removed from his office before the expiry of his term:

A. by the Rajya Sabha through a resolution passed by two-thirds majority and agreed to by the Lok Sabha

B. by the President on the recommendation of the Supreme Court of India

C. by the Central Council of Ministers

D. by the President

125. Which of the following steps can be taken by the President during the Financial Emergency?

1. Direct the Union and of State Governments to observe such canons of financial propriety as he deems desirable
2. Suspend the Fundamental Rights of the Indian citizens
3. Order reduction of salaries and allowances of all the Civil Servants
4. Order the reduction of the salaries of the Supreme Court and High Court Judges

Codes:

A. 1, 3, 4 B. 1, 2, 4

C. 2, 3, 4 D. 1, 2, 3

126. Which of the following statements are correct?

1. The President can send messages to the Parliament
2. The President can dissolve the Lok Sabha
3. The President can summon each House of the Parliament
4. The President is not a part of the Parliament

Codes:

A. 1, 3, 4 B. 1, 4

C. 1, 2, 3, 4 D. 1, 2, 3

127. A member of the Parliament or a State legislature can be elected as the President, but:

I. he has to relinquish his seat within six months of his election

II. he has to resign his seat before contesting the election

III. he has to relinquish his seat as soon as he is elected

Codes:

A. II only B. I only

C. III only D. None of above

128. When does the President of India have a choice in the appointment of the Primé Minister?

A. When one party has an absolute majority in the Lok Sabha

B. The President do not have any choice in the appointment of the PM and is bound to follow

C. When no single party has an absolute majority in the Lok Sabha

D. When no recognised party has a majority in the Lok Sabha

129. How long can a Presidential ordinance remain in force?

A. 1 year
B. Two months
C. Till the President revokes it
D. Six months

130. The President can be removed from office:

I. He cannot leave office once elected unless illness or death occurs
II. On resignation before expiry of term of five years
III. On impeachment by Parliament

Codes:

A. II and III B. I, II and III
C. II only D. I, II

131. Generally the first session of the Parliament starts with an address of the President in which:

A. he makes a survey of the achievements of the Government during the previous year
B. he makes suggestions to the Government regarding the policy it should follow in the interest of the Country
C. he outlines the policy and program of the Government during the ensuing year
D. he does none of the above things

132. Which of the following powers of the Prime Minister in relation to the President have been listed correctly?

1. he communicates all the decisions of the Council of Ministers to the President
2. he supplies such information to the President regarding proposals of legislation and administration of the Union as the President may need
3. he signs the bills passed by the two Houses of the Parliament on behalf of the President during his absence
4. he assists the President in making all the appointments

Codes:

A. 1, 2, 3 B. 2, 3, 4
C. 1, 2, 4 D. 1, 2, 3, 4

133. The executive authority of the Union is vested by the Constitution in the:

A. Prime Minister B. President
C. Cabinet D. Union Legislature

134. Which of the following groups take/takes part in the election of the President of India?

I. All Members of Parliament
II. Members of State Legislative Assemblies
III. Elected members of State Legislative Assemblies
IV. Elected members of State Legislative Councils

Codes:

A. I and III B. I and II
C. I, II and III D. III only

135. Disputes regarding the election of the President and Vice-President are settled:

A. In the Supreme Court
B. By the Election Commission
C. By a Parliamentary Committee
D. In the Supreme Court or High Courts

136. The President addresses his resignation letter to the:

A. Chief Justice of India B. Speaker
C. Vice-President D. Prime Minister

137. If a resolution impeaching the President is passed, the President is considered to have been removed:

A. From the date on which the resolution is passed
B. Once the Chief Justice of India takes out an order to the effect
C. As soon as the Gazette of India notifies it
D. Once the new incumbent is elected

138. Which of the following matters requires the previous sanction of the President for introducing legislation on it?

I. A money bill
II. A bill affecting taxation in which States are interested
III. States bills imposing restrictions upon the freedom of trade

Codes:

A. I, II, III B. II, III
C. I, III D. I, II

139. When the Vice-President acts as President he gets as emoluments of the:

A. President
B. Vice-President
C. Chairman of Rajya Sabha
D. President in addition to what he gets as Chairman of Rajya Sabha

140. The President may send the advice received from the Council of Ministers on a matter back to them for reconsideration. This power can be exercised by him ... on the same matter.

A. Once
B. Twice
C. Thrice
D. Any number of times

141. Which one of the following statement is not correct?

A. In Lok Sabha, no-confidence motion has to set out the grounds on which it is based
B. In the case of a no-confidence motion in Lok Sabha, no conditions of admissibility have been laid down in the rules
C. Rajya Sabha is not empowered to entertain a motion of no-confidence
D. None of the above

142. With reference to Indian Parliament which one of the following is not correct?

A. The Appropriation Bill must be passed by both the Houses of Parliament before it can be enacted into law
B. No money shall be with drawn from the consolidated fund of India except under the appropriation made by the Appropriation Act
C. Finance bill is required for proposing new taxes but no another Bill/Act is require for making changes in the rates of taxes which are already under operation
D. No money bill can be introduced except on the recommendation of the President

143. Consider the following statements:

1. The constitution of the USA came into force is year 1820.
2. All Revenue Bills must originate in the House of Representative of the US congress.
3. Barak Obama is the only Black president in the history of USA.

Which of the statement given above is/are correct?

A. 1 only B. 2 only
C. 1 and 2 D. 2 and 3

144. Consider the following statements:

1. The Parliament can not enlarge the jurisdiction of the Supreme Court of India as its jurisdiction is limited to that conferred by the Constitution.
2. The officers and servants of the Supreme Court and High Courts are appointed by the concerned Chief Justice and the administrative expenses are charged on the consolidated fund of India.

Which of the statement given above is/are correct?

A. 1 only B. 2 only
C. Both 1 and 2 D. Neither 1 nor 2

145. Which of the following are the circumstances under which an elected member of Parliament may be disqualified on the ground of defection?

1. If he voluntarily gives up his membership of a political party
2. If he votes or abstains from voting contrary to any direction issued by his political party without prior permission of the political party
3. If he is expelled by the party for anti-party activities
4. If he joins a political party other than the party on whose ticket he contested and got elected

Select the correct answer from the codes given below:

Codes:

A. 1, 2, 3 and 4 B. 1, 2 and 4
C. 1, 3 and 4 D. 2, 3 and 4

146. Seats are allotted the various states in the Lok Sabha on the basis of:

A. their size and resources
B. their population
C. their size, resources and population
D. none of the above

147. The Committee of Indian Parliament which has the largest membership is:

A. Committee on Privileges
B. The Public Accounts Committee
C. The Estimates Committee
D. The Committee on Public Undertakings

148. The Constitution of India provides that a bill passed by the Union Parliament cannot become a law until the President accords his approval to it. Normally, the President accords his approval but he can withhold his assent and can ask the House to reconsider it.
This power is applicable to the:
1. Money Bills
2. Ordinary Bills
3. Financial Bills
Codes:
A. 1 and 2 B. 2 only
C. 2 and 3 D. 1, 2 and 3

149. Expenses incurred out of the Contingency Fund of India are:
A. subsequently recouped by transferring savings from other heads of budget
B. recouped through supplementary, addition or excess grants by Parliament
C. not recouped till the whole fund is exhausted
D. recouped by collecting contributions from various states

150. The Consolidated Fund of India is a fund in which:
A. all taxes collected by the Union as well as State governments are deposited
B. all money received by or on behalf of the Government of India is deposited
C. the Union as well as State Governments make equal contribution to this fund and out of this, all charged expenses are met
D. savings of the Union and State Governments are deposited to meet unforeseen expenses

151. Article 156 of the Constitution of India provides that a Governor shall hold office for a term of 5 years from the date on which he enters upon his office. Which of the following can be deduced from this:
1. No Governor can be removed from office till the completion of his term.
2. No Governor can continue his/her office beyond a period of 5 years.
A. 1 only B. 2 only
C. 1 and 2 D. Neither 1 nor 2

152. Which one of the following is incorrect in repsect of Local Government in India?
A. According to the Indian Constitution, local government is not an independent tier in the federal system
B. 30% of the seats in local bodies are reserved for women
C. Local government finances are to be provided by a commission
D. Elections to local bodies are to be determined by a commission

153. Executive powers of the State Council of Ministers include:
I. formulating the policy of the government
II. responsibility for the smooth administration of the State
III. assisting the Governor in making all important appointments in the State
A. I and II B. I and III
C. III D. All of them

154. The members of the Council of Ministers in a State must:
A. be members of either House of State Legislature
B. be members of the Legislative Assembly
C. be eminent citizens of the State
D. be members of Legislative Council

155. The salary and allowances of the members of the State Council of Ministers are:
A. prescribed in the Constitution
B. fixed by Parliament
C. fixed by the Governor in consultation with the President
D. fixed the State Legislature

156. The strength of the Council of Ministers:
A. is fixed by the Constitution
B. is determined by Parliament
C. is determined by the State Legislature of every State
D. is determined by the Chief Minister

157. Which one of the following is not an executive function of the Council of Ministers of a State?
A. To run the administration of the State in accordance with the provisions of the Constitution

B. to bring about necessary cohesion in the policies of the various ministries
C. To formulate the policy of the State Government and give it practical shape
D. To assist the President in the administration of the State during the President's Rule in the State

158. Which one of the following is not legislative power of the State Council of Ministers?
I. Summoning and proroguing the session of either or both the Houses of the State Legislature
II. Determining the business and timetable of the State Legislature
III. Introducing the important Bills in the State Legislature
A. I B. III
C. II D. I and II

159. The Executive of the State is headed by:
A. The Governor
B. The Chief Minister
C. The State Cabinet
D. The State Legislative Council

160. A Governor can issue an ordinance:
A. whenever he likes
B. whenever the Chief Minister advises him
C. whenever the State Legislature is not in session and the Governor is satisfied that immediate action is needed
D. when the Union Government tells him to do so

161. The ordinances promulgated by the Governor are subject to the approval of the:
A. President B. State Legislature
C. Vice-President D. Prime Minister

162. Under which of the following circumstances can President's rule be imposed in a State?
A. If no stable government can be formed
B. If the Cabinet has lost majority and no other ministry commanding a majority in the Assembly can be formed at once
C. If the State Government does not obey the directives given by the Union Government
D. In all the above cases

163. Which one of the following legislative powers of the Governor has been wrongly listed?
A. He summons or prorogues either House of State Legislature
B. He addresses either or both the Houses at the commencement of the new session after each General Election
C. He dissolves both the Houses in case of difference over the enactment of law
D. He sends messages to the State Legislature on a Bill pending before it

164. When a Governor reserves a Bill passed by the State Legislature:
A. he may be impeached
B. he sends it to the President
C. he may keep the Bill pending indefinitely
D. he may give assent to the Bill later

165. When does the Governor recommend the imposition of the President's rule in a State?
A. On the recommendation of the Centre
B. On the recommendation of the Chief Minister
C. On the recommendation of the Council of Ministers
D. If he is satisfied that the Government of the State cannot be carried on in accordance with the provisions of the Constitution

166. The Governor can reserve:
A. all Bills passed by State Legislature for the assent of the President
B. certain types of Bills passed by State Legislature for the approval of the President
C. no Bill passed by the State Legislature for the approval of the President
D. only Financial Bills for the approval of the President

167. The judicial powers of the Governor do not include the right to:
A. be consulted by the President about appointment of Judges of State High Court
B. grant pardon
C. remit punishment or suspend the sentence
D. pardon death sentence

168. When can the Governor exercise his discretionary powers?
A. In appointment of Chief Minister if not a single party has clear cut majority in the House or there is no recognised leader of the majority party
B. In reservation of a Bill passed by State Legislature for the assent of the President
C. Dismissing a ministry if he is convinced it has lost majority support in the Assembly
D. All the above cases are valid

169. How is a Governor paid if he acts as the Governor of more than one State?
A. His salary is paid by the Central Government
B. His salary is paid by the State where his head-quarters are located
C. His salary is shared by the concerned States in equal proportion
D. He cannot be a Governor of more than one State

170. The ordinance of the Governor:
A. has the same force as the law made by the State Legislature
B. is more extensive than the law made by the State Legislature
C. is much narrower than a law made by the State Legislature
D. has little value

171. In India which of the following voting system present in state legislative election:
A. Hare system
B. Cumulative vote system
C. First-past-the post system
D. Plural vote system

172. Which one of the following states of India does not have a legislative council so far even through the Constitution (seventh Amendment) Act, 1956 provides for it?
A. Maharashtra B. Bihar
C. Uttar Pradesh D. Madhya Pradesh

173. Which one of the following powers of the State Legislature has been incorrectly given?
I. It takes part in the election of the President
II. It plays an important role in amendment of the Constitution
III. It considers the report of the State Public Service Commission.
A. I B. II
C. I and II D. None is incorrect

174. Which of the following States has no Legislative Council?
A. Rajasthan B. Uttar Pradesh
C. Maharashtra D. Bihar

175. What is the maximum period upto which the Legislative Councils can delay the consideration of a Bill that has been already passed once by State Assembly of the State?
A. One month B. Two months
C. Three months D. Six months

176. The phrase 'bicameral legislature' means:
A. a single assembly
B. an elected legislature
C. a legislature consisting of a lower and an upper chamber
D. Parliamentary system of Government

177. The number of schedules in the Constitution is:
A. 12 B. 18
C. 24 D. 30

178. Legislative Assembly of which one of the following States has less than the required minimum of members?
A. Rajasthan B. Manipur
C. Meghalaya D. Sikkim

179. The Legislative Council:
A. has a term of six years
B. has a term of five years
C. is a permanent House
D. has a term of two years

180. The Speaker of the Legislative Assembly can be removed from office before his normal term by:
A. the Chief Minister
B. the Government
C. the Legislative Assembly by passing a resolution by majority of its total membership
D. none of the above

181. The power to enlarge the jurisdiction of the Supreme Court of India with respect to any matter included in the Union List of Legislative Powers vests with:

A. The President of India
B. The Parliament
C. The Chief Justice of India
D. The Prime Minister

182. Which one of the following High courts has the territorial Jurisdiction over Nagaland?

A. Calcutta
B. Andhra Pradesh
C. Gauhati
D. Patna

183. Consider the following statements:

1. Desputes with mobile companies
2. Motor accident cases
3. Disputes such as pension cases

Which of the above are Lok Adalat held?

A. 1 only B. 2 only
C. 1 and 2 D. 1, 2 and 3

184. Consider the following statements:

1. There are 25 High Courts in India.
2. Punjab, Haryana and the UTs of Chandigarh have a common High Court
3. National Capital Territory of Delhi has a high court of its own.

Which of the following given above is/are correct:

A. 1, 2 and 3 B. 2 and 3
C. 1 and 3 D. 1 and 3

185. Which of the following are the state in which the Lok Ayukta Act includes the Chief Minister in its ambit?

A. West Bengal and Kerala
B. Gujarat and Maharashtra
C. MP and Odisha
D. Himachal Pradesh and Andhra Pradesh

186. The power of the Supreme Court of India to decide disputes between the centre and the state falls under its:

A. Advisory jurisdiction
B. Appellate jurisdiction
C. Original jurisdiction
D. Constitutional jurisdiction

187. When the chief justice of a high court acts in an administrative capacity he is subject to:

A. the writ jurisdiction of any of the other judges of the high court
B. special control exercised by the chief Justice of India
C. discretionary powers of the Governor of the state
D. special powers provided to the Chief Minister in this regard

188. Accroding to the constitutions of India the term 'district Judge' shall not include:

A. Chief presidency magistrate
B. Session judges
C. Tribunal judges
D. Chief judge of a small cause court

189. Assertion (A): Wilful disobedience or non-compliance of court orders and use of derogatory language about judicial behaviour amount to contempt of court.

Reason (R): Judicial activism cannot be practised without arming the judiciary with punitive powers to punish contemptuous behaviours.

A. Both (A) and (R) are true and (R) is the correct explanation of (A)
B. Both (A) and (R) are true, but (R) is not the correct explanation of (A)
C. (A) is true, but (R) is false
D. (A) is false, but (R) is true

190. The Supreme Court of India tenders advice to the President on a matter of law or fact:

A. on its own initiative
B. only if he seeks such advice
C. only if the matter violates to the fundamental rights of citizens
D. All of the above

191. Match List-I with List-II and select the correct answer using the codes given below the lists:

List-I *(Local bodies)*	*List-II* *(States as in 1999)*
(*a*) Zila Parishads at the sub divisional level	1. Andhra Pradesh

(*b*) Mandal Praja Parishad	2. Mizoram	
(*c*) Tribal Council	3. Meghalaya	
(*d*) Absence of Village Panchayats	4. Assam	

Codes:

	(*a*)	(*b*)	(*c*)	(*d*)
A.	3	1	4	2
B.	3	1	2	4
C.	4	1	3	2
D.	4	1	2	3

192. In which of the following areas does the State Government not have control over its local bodies?
A. Financial matters
B. Legislative control
C. Citizen's grievances
D. None of these

193. Indian Citizenship cannot be terminated by:
A. Renunciation
B. Deprivation
C. Imprisonment
D. Termination

194. Panchayati Raj is based on the principle of:
A. democratic decentralisation
B. community cooperation and development
C. people's participation in government
D. cultivation of political awareness among the rural masses

195. One of the main advantages of Panchayati Raj is that:
A. it gives a sense of political awareness to the rural masses
B. it gives a parallel government to rural areas
C. it serves the rural people well
D. it increases employment in rural areas

196. In which respect have the Centre-State relations been specifically termed as 'municipal relations'?
A. Centre's control of the State in the legislative sphere
B. Centre's control of the State in financial matters
C. Centre's control of the State in the administrative sector
D. Centre's control of the State in the planning process

197. The Balwant Rai G Mehta team was set up in 1956 by the National Development Council for the purpose of:
A. suggesting measures for democratic decentralization
B. reporting on the working of the village panchayats at that time suggesting measures for better efficiency in the implementation of the Community
C. Development projects investigating the feasibility of setting up the new panchayat machinery
D. None of these

198. Which of the following States has no Panchayat Raj institution at all?
A. Assam
B. Nagaland
C. Tripura
D. Kerala

199. Which among the following are true about the 73rd Constitutional Amendment in the area of Panchayati Raj?
1. Thirty per cent seats in all elected rural local bodies will be reserved for women candidates at all levels.
2. The States will constitute their Finance Commissions to allocate resources to Panchayati Raj institutions.
3. The Panchayati Raj elected functionaries will be disqualified to hold their offices if they have more than two children.
4. The elections will be held in six months time if Panchayati Raj bodies are superceded or dissolved by the State government.

A. 2 and 4
B. 1 and 4
C. 1, 3 and 4
D. 1, 2 and 4

200. First General elections in India were held in:
A. 1952 B. 1948
C. 1950 D. 1949

ANSWERS

1	2	3	4	5	6	7	8	9	10
B	B	D	C	D	A	D	C	A	D
11	12	13	14	15	16	17	18	19	20
A	B	C	A	C	A	B	A	A	C
21	22	23	24	25	26	27	28	29	30
A	B	C	C	B	C	C	A	A	B
31	32	33	34	35	36	37	38	39	40
B	A	B	B	A	C	D	A	D	B
41	42	43	44	45	46	47	48	49	50
B	A	A	C	C	C	B	C	A	A
51	52	53	54	55	56	57	58	59	60
A	B	C	C	D	C	D	A	C	C
61	62	63	64	65	66	67	68	69	70
D	D	C	D	D	C	B	D	A	D
71	72	73	74	75	76	77	78	79	80
A	B	C	A	A	C	C	C	B	D
81	82	83	84	85	86	87	88	89	90
D	D	D	B	B	C	A	D	C	A
91	92	93	94	95	96	97	98	99	100
B	C	B	C	A	D	C	A	B	B
101	102	103	104	105	106	107	108	109	110
C	C	D	B	A	C	D	C	C	D
111	112	113	114	115	116	117	118	119	120
B	A	D	B	A	D	D	D	D	D
121	122	123	124	125	126	127	128	129	130
C	B	A	C	A	D	C	C	C	A
131	132	133	134	135	136	137	138	139	140
C	B	D	D	A	C	A	A	A	A
141	142	143	144	145	146	147	148	149	150
A	A	D	B	B	B	C	C	B	B
151	152	153	154	155	156	157	158	159	160
D	B	D	A	D	A	D	A	A	C
161	162	163	164	165	166	167	168	169	170
D	D	C	B	D	B	D	D	C	A
171	172	173	174	175	176	177	178	179	180
C	D	D	A	A	C	A	D	C	C
181	182	183	184	185	186	187	188	189	190
B	C	D	A	D	C	B	C	A	B
191	192	193	194	195	196	197	198	199	200
D	C	C	A	A	D	C	B	D	A

●●●

2505